This book is dedicated to the Councils
Margie, Howie, Bart, Bruce, Leslie, and Ondina

A HISTORY OF FILMS

A HISTORY OF FILMS

JOHN FELL
San Francisco State University

HOLT, RINEHART AND WINSTON
New York   Chicago   San Francisco   Atlanta
Dallas   Montreal   Toronto

Editor   Roth Wilkofsky
Project Editor   Susan Adams
Picture Research Consultant   Enid Klass
Production Manager   Robert de Villeneuve
Designer (text and cover)   Mary Weindorf
Composition by Ruttle, Shaw, and Wetherill, Inc.
Printing and binding by Von Hoffmann Press, Inc.

Library of Congress Cataloging in Publication Data

Fell, John L
A history of films.

Includes bibliographies and indexes
1. Moving-pictures—History.   I. Title.

PN1993.5.A1F38   791.43′09   78–16203

ISBN 0–03–036316–0

9 0123   032   9 87654321

Preface

The notion of designing a film history that effectively contributes to all our courses is undercut by the state of film study today. Much recent work, especially American film research, unearths and restructures subject matter in terms of directors, and increasingly outré ones at that. But other energies are pressing to bury auteurs underneath culture and ideology.

Since the days when movies went after mass audiences, production has required expensive technology and underwriting; its character is inescapably, cumbersomely inflected by commerce. Or has this made film vitally mythic because it is popular? Film history often discloses caricatures of social attitudes toward women, minority groups, and the conventions on which a culture girds its stability and sustains its optimism. Deeper lie the unadmitted suspicions and anxieties that characterize all audiences, including women and minorities. Formal likenesses among feature films transcend national boundaries; they often span decades. Both the techniques and the esthetics of other arts, in particular prose and theater, have drastically colored mainstream, narrative film.

What, in fact, is the "history" of a commercial art like the movies? It depends on the historian. I can only suggest answers in the following pages; the reader is owed some introductory remarks about the particular notions that underlay the design.

The book carries certain disproportionate emphases. Most obviously, it is weighted toward the narrative film made for large audiences. Nonetheless, I have tried to provide useful sections on documentary, experimentation, and animation. Emphasis also rests on spoken (or intertitled) English-language productions, because the book is intended to serve as a classroom text, and courses appear to concentrate, often unreasonably, on this idiom.

Having decided what to discuss, history asks us to establish a discourse, a way of talking about it. Most films cited in this or any similar book will not be seen in class and probably never by most students. No one remembers unelaborated film titles that float through history texts like cakes of ice in *Way Down East.* Yet to omit these titles turns a film history into a compendium of "significant" landmarks, which come increasingly to resemble park statues, turning green and nesting molting pigeons. Realizing the shortcomings, I have nevertheless tried to provide many, many productions with some kind of minimal description, in hopes that these may lodge more comfortably in a reader's, if not a viewer's, memory.

So far as possible, I speak about films as they seem now. Such a perspective sometimes distorts what may have been historically important, more often unimportant, on first exhibition. For example, *Zéro de conduite* wasn't seen in France for many years, Dimitri Kirsanoff was a very minor, independent filmmaker; but Vigo and *Ménilmontant* assume different roles today; *A Woman of Paris* looks like a lemon.

Without tangling up the exposition, an effort was sometimes made to relate certain films to others, chronology and provenance notwithstanding. More implicit than stated is a presumption that the evolution of popular film pursues a chronology of sensibility. This becomes apparent with filmmakers who have been lucky enough to survive decades. Thus, Carol Reed and David Lean are grouped with early sound directors when, arguably, they should appear later. Discussions of the work of Hitchcock, Ford, et al., are telescoped into mini-essays, instead of scattered throughout. From such a frame of reference, events like World War II do not always assume the dividing-line, chapter-heading function of other film books.

The book has not given its heart to auteurism, genre study, Marxism, art history, social history, the Writers Guild of America, East or West, the Late Late Show, nostalgia presses, or old *Society of Motion Picture Engineers* journals. It tries to adopt useful perspectives where each applies. As a result, it may be reasonably accused of structural ambiguity. Eclecticism is the price we pay for rejecting the *idée fixe.*

Because of the decision to concentrate on film texts, the book sacrifices attention that might otherwise have been directed toward the many social, political, and economic contexts from which films have emerged. I do not mean that these are ignored; neither, for that matter, are discussions of esthetic movements. Some topics (production methods, for example) are shortchanged. Because of a human interest in the costs of filmmaking, I have tried to provide siginificant figures from time to time, as well as to consider some of the realities of film distribution and financing. Given our decisions to include filmographies, to incorporate many illustrations, and to locate each wherever it proved most useful, the design of the book just couldn't tolerate any additional material. I couldn't fit everything in.

I am woefully ignorant of Oriental animation and of much European experimental film dating in the seventies. What I do know, such as the work of Peter Kubelka and Kurt Kren, is of course included, but I apologize for omissions that result from my lacks.

It is impossible not to be judgmental about films, and I have sought to flag my pleasures and pains with short adjectives, rather than guise them in polysyllabic distinctions.

Film titles are customarily presented in a form thought to be most commonly shared in this country. Where translations may be helpful, and I am capable, these are provided in parentheses. Films known by one or more titles are either so indicated by parenthetical remarks or, in the case of two languages, by a slash, e.g., *Justice est faite/Let Justice Be Done* (1950). (It didn't get into the book.)

It is hoped that the filmographies may serve useful purposes, although one must emphasize that most are incomplete because of space limitations. Filmographies spare a lot of prosaic explanation; they encourage perspective; they have a certain reference utility. Of course, they also dramatize notions of authorship.

Popular histories always astound me with the amount an author has learned from no apparent source. I am greatly in debt to thousands of books and try to acknowledge that obligation in bibliographies. Footnotes are limited to direct quotations and parenthetical remarks, most of which suggest other references. While far from complete, the bibliography for each chapter may serve as a useful reference source for students' further research. The bibliographies are as updated as the production schedule of the book allowed.

. . .

Thanks to Denise Rathbun, who got me involved in the project in the first place. Thanks also to Geoffrey Bell and to Jim Kitses for providing photographs that would never otherwise have appeared. The acquisition of pictures was terribly involved and time consuming, and it was carried out by Enid Klass with perseverance, imagination, and grace. Along the line, she was served beyond the call of duty by Michelle Snapes and her staff at the British Film Institute and by Mary Corliss and Carol Carey at the Museum of Modern Art. Jim Kitses and Alan Lovell instructed me with some remarkable ideas about how to write captions. At Holt, Rinehart and Winston, Roth Wilkofsky and Joan Greene were helpful and good humored, Susan Adams proved tactful and exceptionally patient toward my syntactical curiosities, and, without the firm support of Ellen Small, this book would never have reached its final stages of completion in our lifetime. She has my deepest gratitude. Of course, all of the mistakes in the book are my own.

J.L.F.

CONTENTS

A HISTORY OF FILMS

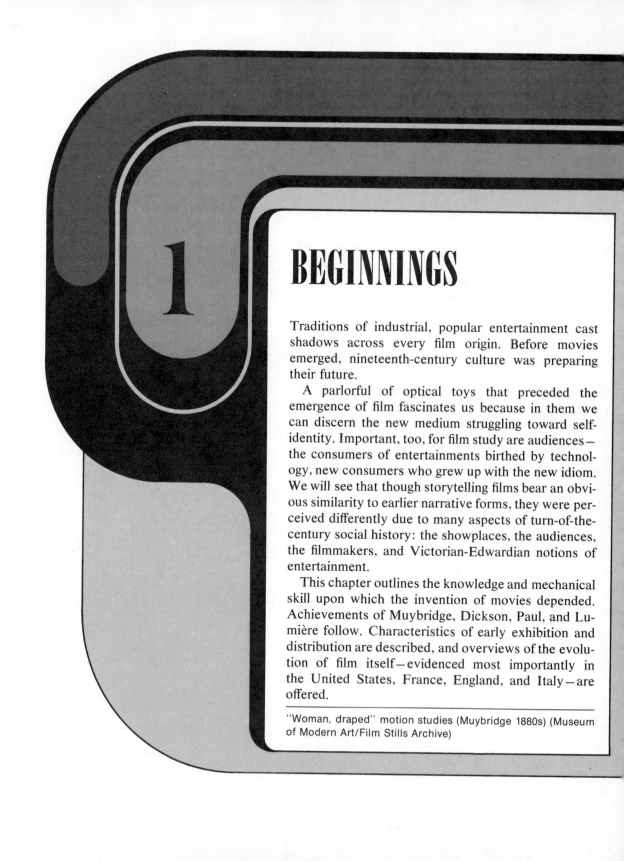

BEGINNINGS

Traditions of industrial, popular entertainment cast shadows across every film origin. Before movies emerged, nineteenth-century culture was preparing their future.

A parlorful of optical toys that preceded the emergence of film fascinates us because in them we can discern the new medium struggling toward self-identity. Important, too, for film study are audiences — the consumers of entertainments birthed by technology, new consumers who grew up with the new idiom. We will see that though storytelling films bear an obvious similarity to earlier narrative forms, they were perceived differently due to many aspects of turn-of-the-century social history: the showplaces, the audiences, the filmmakers, and Victorian-Edwardian notions of entertainment.

This chapter outlines the knowledge and mechanical skill upon which the invention of movies depended. Achievements of Muybridge, Dickson, Paul, and Lumière follow. Characteristics of early exhibition and distribution are described, and overviews of the evolution of film itself — evidenced most importantly in the United States, France, England, and Italy — are offered.

"Woman, draped" motion studies (Muybridge 1880s) (Museum of Modern Art/Film Stills Archive)

PRECEDENTS

In order to view a projected image we need three things: a light source, a lens, and a viewing environment. The sun was the first light source and magnifying glasses have existed for centuries. John Babtista Porta, a zealous Neapolitan who wrote *Natural Magick*, first published in 1589, speaks of a "parabolical section" that would "kindle fire at a mile distant."

More to the point is Porta's description of a use for a " 'Concave-Glass' by whose agency great secrets of nature may appear":

You must shut all the Chamber windows, and it will do well to shut up all holes besides, lest any light breaking in should spoil all. Onely make one hole, that shall be a hand's breadth and length; above this sit a little leaden or brass Table, and glew it, so thick as a paper, open a round hole in the middle of it, as great as your little finger; over against this, let there be white walls of paper, or white clothes, so shall you see all that is done without in the sun, and those that walk in the streets, like to Antipodes, and what is right will be left, and all things changed; and the farther they are off from the hole, the greater they will appear. If you bring your paper or white Table nearer, they will show less and clearer.

Book 17, Of Strange Glasses; Chapter VI, "Other Operations of a Concave-Glass"

Porta was describing the *camera obscura*, a scheme to convert the interior of a darkened room into what has proved to be the design of every still and motion picture camera. As outlined by Leonardo da Vinci, the camera obscura used a small opening in one side of an enclosure so as to project outside scenes onto a flat surface opposite the aperture, upside down.

Properly located, a hole in the ceiling enhanced the study of eclipses. Primitively, we sometimes experience the camera obscura in a theater itself when the room is in semidarkness and figures in the lobby project fuzzily onto the screen through an open exit.

Early in the seventeenth century, an astronomer, Johannes Kepler, combined the camera obscura with the telescope, eventually terming it simply a *camera*. Portable cameras followed, used to study the heavens and as an aid to painters until the invention of photography. The work of Jan Vermeer, for example, sometimes clearly evidences the effects of optical projection.

Athanasius Kircher, a seventeenth-century Jesuit mathematics professor, substituted artificial light (a candle) for sun, moon, and stars, locating a concave mirror behind in order to focus the image. Silhouetted slides, first only letters, cast shadows against a wall; then Kircher introduced a lens. His projection apparatus, dubbed a *magick lantern,* was popularized across Europe and refined in process so that slides, often drawn on glass, could be mounted on horizontal strips or on circular discs to ease their passage. The apparatus itself figured as part of the show, just as early movies in Japan were sometimes projected on stage in order that an audience might watch the equipment at work. Kircher's machinery figured in scientific demonstrations, but itinerant entertainers more often adapted it to spectacle.

Magick (soon magic) lanterns organized information in sequential, static series. The apparent reproduction of movement depended upon another form of illusion. Aristotle first described this effect, noting our impression that a whirling torch becomes a constant, circling flame instead of a succession of discrete images. Nineteenth-century investigators called this effect persistence of vision (also known as retinal persistence), which is decribed as the disposition of any image to remain momentarily on the eye's retina after it is no longer "seen." A Czech inventor, J. E. Purkyne, wrote on the phenomenon in 1818; Peter Mark Roget discussed persistence of vision before the British Royal Society in 1824.

Put to mechanical "use," this quality in our perception facilitated an appearance of movement "between" the two sides of a toy, the *Thaumatrope*, popularized soon after by an English doctor, John Paris. Separate drawings appeared on either side of a disc, spun by strings attached to opposite edges. When the strings were wound tight, then drawn apart, the disc revolved. Each picture replaced its mate so quickly that they blended into a composite: a bird in a cage or a rider on a horse.

A Belgian scientist name Joseph Plateau studied both motion and vision, and his research led to the construction in 1832 of an optical mechanism which he dubbed the *Phénakistoscope* (also called Phénakistiscope). Plateau combined sequential images

Phénakistoscope wheels from the collection of the Smithsonian Institution. These examples use an edge (or near-edge) notched "shutter"; other models located the slits closer to the center of the picture. Phénakistoscope means "deceitful view." A similar device, independently invented in Germany in the same year, was Simon Ritter von Stampfer's Stroboscop or "whirling view." (History of Photography Collection, Smithsonian Institution. Photo No. 71-843) (Museum of Modern Art/Film Stills Archive)

Coleman Sellers, a Philadelphia mechanical engineer, photographed his sons in a series of sequential poses in 1860. Revolved on a paddle wheel, viewed through a peephole, the cumulative effect of the series was one of continuous, cycled movement. Sellers' work and Henry R. Heyl's Phasmatrope, which projected sequentially posed photographs, are reenacted in Geoffrey Bell's film, *First (Motion) Picture Show* (1977). (Geoffrey Bell, Franklin Institute)

with after-image retention to produce a semblance of motion where none existed in fact—the movement was in the eye of the beholder. One drawing was momentarily blacked from sight while being replaced by another image differing only slightly in the depiction of an action sequence. Repeating themselves after a revolution, the Phénakistoscope's revolving discs injected a sense of time and change into the illusion.

In mid-century, Franz Uchatius, an Austrian soldier, combined Plateau's disc with the magic lantern in order to magnify and to project the sensation. Twelve slides were painted on a disc. Each picture had its own projection lens, each lens skewed slightly toward the disc's axis. A light source—now limelight (created by heating lime to incandesence)—was revolved behind the slides. One projected image replaced another in turn on the identical screen location, affording a shared visual experience to what had before been private.

Spearheaded by Nicéphore Niepce and Jacques Mandé Daguerre, photography evolved coincidentally with persistence of vision technology. From this point on, through the period of early movie director-cameramen, even into Hollywood studio years, most motion picture innovators numbered photography and darkroom technique among their skills. At the same time, still photography had its foot-dragging effects on the evolution of cinema. Interiors or exteriors, compositions of the movie camera were long wedded to still photography esthetics, just as they were joined to dramatic staging. As it escaped the proscenium, the development of film technique likewise required a developing awareness of how film space differed from still images. Film had to free itself from the still camera as well as from theater.

Photographs replaced the hand-painted images of lantern slides. Henry R. Heyl, employing what he described as the *Phasmatrope*, effected wet-plate photographs onto glass and projected the images on a screen at the Academy of Music in Philadelphia in

1870. Heyl replaced Uchatius' revolving lime-light with a shutter device situated between light and slide, located at the center of his wheel. The Heyl pictures were sequentially posed still photos which completed a cycle: an acrobat, the movements of a waltz step.

Edward Muybridge—born Edward James Muggeridge and eventually calling himself Eadweard Muybridge—next captured one continuous live movement in a series of still photographs. An eccentric Englishman, Muybridge settled in the San Francisco area about the time of the Civil War. During the 1870s he was commissioned by Leland Stanford, former governor of California who lived in Palo Alto, to assist in a study of horses' gaits. Although a popular story describes Stanford's motive as a $25,000 bet on whether a horse ever had all four feet off the ground (it did), Stanford was more likely concerned with breeding and training race horses on his Peninsula ranch.

After unsuccessful efforts, Muybridge, aided by John Isaacs, finally managed impressive pictures of an animal's gait. First with twelve cameras, later twenty-four, Muybridge photographed movement by tripping the shutters with threads or other activating devices strung along the horse's path. This was accomplished in Summer 1877. Work continued in 1878, and Muybridge commenced a series

of successful lectures, projecting his photographs as silhouettes first by magic lantern, then in 1880 with an adapted *Zoetrope*. The Zoetrope, popular as a toy since 1834, operated on the principles of Plateau's Phénakistoscope. Muybridge prepared a series of his horse photographs on a circular glass. In the manner of Heyl's Phasmatrope, he overlaid a metal plate with lateral slits concentric with the glass slides and moving in the opposite direction. This served as a shutter; so Muybridge combined projection with his photographs to simulate not simply movement, but a curious, new sort of reenactment from the past.

Muybridge's photographs were well publicized by way of journals, books, Leland Stanford's travels, and the photographer's own lecture tours. When the Englishman visited France in 1881, a man who viewed the work with special interest was Etienne Jules Marey, an eminent Parisian physiologist. In consequence, Marey perfected a gun that substituted film for bullets so as to photograph sequentially the movements of birds in flight. By 1888, he had introduced strips of photographic paper into the apparatus. The machine photographed twenty (or sixty) separate pictures per second. Next year, attending the Paris Exposition, Marey was introduced to Thomas Alva Edison.

An action sequence from *Animal Motion,* published by Muybridge in 1888. The new gelatin dry plates gave faster, more dependable emulsion speeds than earlier wet-plate, Palo Alto photos. Muybridge could photograph at one six-thousandth of a second but rarely needed such controls.

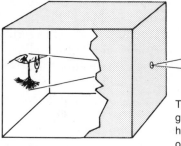

The camera obscura was the prototype of every projecting and photographing apparatus — still or motion picture — ever to follow. Aristotle had first noted a crescent, eclipsing sun inflected through sieve holes onto the ground; the smaller the hole, the sharper the image. Arab scholars preserved Aristotle's design through the Dark Ages.

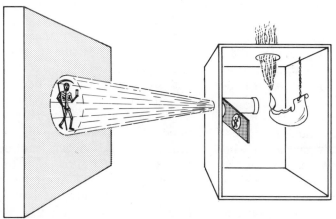

Athanasius Kircher developed a portable camera obscura, then translated the principle to slide projection. The illustration is based on a woodcut in *Ars Magna Lucis et Umbrae* (The Great Art of Light and Shadow) (1649). Note that there is a condensing lens behind the slide but no focusing lens in front in this model.

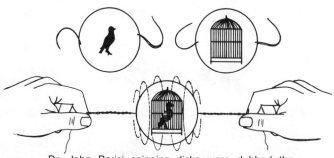

Dr. John Paris' spinning disks were dubbed the Thaumatrope and commercially marketed during the 1820s. This one is accompanied by two captions: "Why is this parrot like a drunken man?" "Because he is often in the cage."

Other magick lanterns with exterior lens systems appeared at the same time as Kircher's models. Some mounted slides on circular plates. Other slides appeared successively on strips, as here. E. G. Robertson's eighteenth-century *Phantasmagoria* illustrated Gothic narratives with rear projection, dramatically enlarging apparitions by pulling his magick lantern sharply back from the screen.

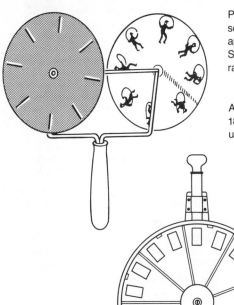

Plateau's Phénakistoscope first combined a shutter with separate images, leaguing movement illusion to the appearance of sequential progression. Stampfer's Stroboskop (left) mounted shutter and pictures on separate disks.

Adapted to a cylindrical modality, the Phénakistoscope reappeared in 1834 as the Daedaleum (after Daedalus who animated artificial figures). In 1867, the design was patented as the Zoetrope.

The Phasmatrope was first employed by Henry Renno Heyl before an audience of 1,500 on February 5, 1870. A succession of eighteen photographs passed before the projection light, each picture successively exposed through a revolving shutter. The tiny glass photographs consisted of six posed waltz positions arranged in three successive cycles.

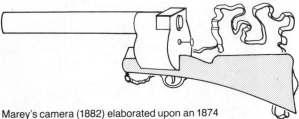

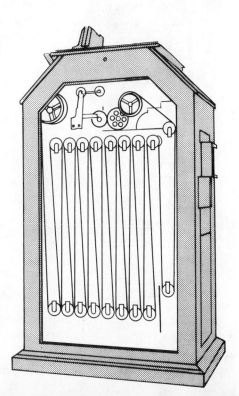

Marey's camera (1882) elaborated upon an 1874 device for photographing astronomical effects. Using dry plates, Marey was able to capture birds in flight with faster exposures: twelve per second. Marey progressed from glass plates to paper rolls of film and eventually to celluloid.

The Kinetoscope transported forty-to-fifty foot films, looped — in the absence of reels — along a spool bank by means of a battery-driven motor. The pictures were provided visibility by an electric light, each image exposed to the eye through a revolving shutter. Edison conserved manpower costs by adapting his machine to nickel-in-the-slot automation.

THE MOTION PICTURE

In fact, Edison had conferred with Muybridge in West Orange, New Jersey in 1888 to discuss an alliance of the phonograph with Muybridge's pictures and projector, but there was no known way to connect sound and picture. That same year, an Edison employee, William Kennedy Laurie Dickson, was commissioned to work on a motion picture camera. Recorded sound had been obtained on cylinders, so Dickson tried to capture visual action on tiny cylinder pictures. He concluded that faithful reproduction required forty images per second. Mounting sound and picture cylinders on a single shaft, Dickson made

and viewed the "pin head photographs" with microscopic lenses. However, because of inferior picture quality, Edison abandoned the cylinder scheme. Celluloid was beginning to replace glass as a photographic base, and the two men devised a new plan. Coated with unexposed raw-film emulsion, a celluloid strip paused momentarily before a camera lens to record its image, then passed on, drawn by a Geneva cross that engaged sprocket holes on the edge of the strip. Dickson perforated the holes with Edison's automatic paper telegraph machine.

The technique worked, but celluloid strips had drawbacks. They were too short (eighteen inches) to accomodate many pictures, besides being thick and heavy. Nonetheless, Dickson

Edison with projector in a pose variously dated 1897 and 1905. On February 17, 1912, he presented a "Talking Picture Play" on the Kinetophone with an Amberola phonograph playing seven-minute cylinders in accompaniment to *Julius Caesar*. When synchronization slipped, a projectionist used fish line to readjust record speeds. (Courtesy of Western Electric)

had a working camera by Autumn 1888. He negotiated with the willing George Eastman, who was experimenting on a more pliable thin cellulose base to be used in roll-film still cameras.[1] In 1889, Dickson used Eastman's new film to produce a fully functioning movie camera, which Edison termed the *kinetograph,* at the same time claiming its invention.[2]

Then Edison appears temporarily to have lost interest in movies, "a silly little device for making pictures that would dance." A reader is left with the impression that the Wizard of Menlo Park continued to think of film as the tiny pictures Dickson had first tried to animate on the surface of a cylinder—this despite Dickson's invention of a projector, companion to the kinetograph, which incorporated Edison's electric light, a shutter, and a film transport mechanism. Ever the businessman, Edison saw little commercial promise in projection, indeed fearing that large-scale exposure to motion pictures by auditorium-sized audiences would quickly slake public interest. Edison preferred the *kinetoscope,* another invention, that ran films on continuous fifty-foot loops through a box, viewed by a single spectator who peeped through an eyehole in the top. Thus Edison perpetuated the optical toy traditions of the Thaumatrope, Phénakistoscope and parlor Zoetrope and momentarily forestalled implications of projection.

At this point, movie origins cloud with claims and counterclaims of inventive priority. The issue is colored, too, by the nationality of any historian one chooses to believe. Our understanding of what follows will be enhanced if we recognize three limitations of the Dickson-Edison apparatus:

The kinetoscope used continuous movement and a flashing light source to perpetuate its illusion, but the camera necessarily required a shutter and intermittent film transport. While passing before the lens to expose each frame (picture) without blurring the exposure, the film had to pause momentarily. Since the remainder of the passage was one of continuous movement, the film was subject to an unending series of stops and starts. If a roll of Eastman's film was much longer than fifty feet, its weight and inertia led the strip to tear as it was pulled from dead stop into the accumulated take-up reel.

Second, Edison had preserved the 40-frames-per-second standard conceived when working with cylinders. So rapid a speed for photography and viewing quickly exhausted the resources of a fifty-foot or shorter reel of film.

Finally, Edison's very diffidence about his invention led to confusion and dispute. He actually had to be convinced to market his kinetoscope, which was sold for $250. Each fifty-foot film cost $10 outright. The first kinetoscope proprietors at 1155 Broadway in New York City charged 25¢ for a customer to view a row of five machines. Edison never even bothered to apply for foreign patent rights for either invention. In terms of lost royalties, this proved lamentably expensive for Edison, but it served to free the field for other inventors and entrepreneurs.

Encouraged by study of the kinetoscope business, two brothers, Grey and Otway Latham, first exploited the machine while they were employed by Edison. Then the Lathams researched the matter of projection and found a solution to the problem of intermittent film transport that limited Edison's invention. The

---

[1] *The Eastman film width of 1 3/8" conforms to the standard of 35mm film today. Dickson's picture dimensions were 1" by 3/4".*

[2] *Dickson's place in film history was obscured for years by the reputation of Thomas Edison, but a strong case for his inventive preeminence is made in Gordon Hendricks,* The Edison Motion Picture Myth. *Dickson recounts his early work in "A Brief History of the Kinetograph, the Kinetoscope, and the Kinete-Phonograph."* Journal of the Society of Motion Picture Engineers *(December 1933). Reprinted in Raymond Fielding,* A Technical History of Motion Pictures and Television.

brothers introduced small film loops immediately above and below the lens aperture in a camera. The Latham Loop cushioned continuous pulling on the film at the point of intermittency. The pressure was blocked by sprocket gears at either extremity of the loops. (Perhaps a loop existed in Marey's apparatus of 1888.) Curiously, the first Latham projector failed to incorporate the loop; it was exhibited as the *pantoptikon* on May 20, 1895.

While the Lathams worked in New York, kinetoscopes enjoyed growing success in England where Robert W. Paul first manufactured new machines independently because the design was unprotected by copyright. He later faced retribution from Edison's agents, however—they cut off supplies of films. As a result, Paul designed a motion picture camera. This not only incorporated his own version of the Latham Loop, but also reduced exposure speed to 20 frames per second. In contrast to Edison's battery drive, the Paul *animatograph* was hand operated and portable enough to be carried in the field. Edison's heavy camera was unwieldy.

At the same time in France, the success of a Parisian kinetoscope parlor impressed Louis Lumière, a manufacturer of photographic materials. He enlisted the aid of his brother Auguste and devised the *cinématographe,* which combined in a single mechanism camera, projector and even developing machine. Portable and hand-cranked like Paul's animatograph, the cinématographe set a standard of 16 frames-per-second; finally even Edison followed suit. The cinématographe was exhibited publicly on March 22, 1895.

In September of the same year, Thomas Armat showed an Atlanta, Georgia audience his own projector at the Cotton States Exposition. Armat's machine improved on all previous models and serves as the basis for today's projectors. Unlike Edison's kinetograph and the Lathams' pantoptikon, the Armat projector ran film intermittently past the lens with an incorporation of his own Latham Loop.

Unlike Lumière's cinématographe, Armat's shutter exposure maximized audience viewing time for each frame, which increased picture brightness substantially.

A last mechanism must be indicated: the mutoscope, product of the K.M.C.D. Syndicate. This organization was an alliance between three businessmen (E. B. Koopman, H. N. Marvin, Herman Casler) and W. K. L. Dickson. Dickson had quarreled with Edison's business manager and joined forces with Marvin, conceiving a film viewing machine to rival the kinetoscope. Rather than employing perforated film, the Dickson version used heavy cardboard cards on which photographs were mounted. The cards were racked on a wheel to be exposed like children's flip books one by one before a single viewer's eyes.

Since Edison refused to provide his own movies for such competition, a new camera also was devised by Dickson. Because the mutoscope's pictures required no continuous placement, spacing between each frame was unimportant. A film roll passed in front of a lens where it was stopped, perforated to facilitate later printing as an ordinary photograph, then pulled forward. Because the photographs had to reflect their light source, they were far larger than the little moving picture camera frames; mutoscope pictures were post card size. K.M.C.D. viewing machines may still be found in penny arcades. The rotary wheel of photographs has proved more durable than motion picture film, even though projected film soon clearly won the day.

EXHIBITION

Limited in length and prone to unpredictable projector performance, the earliest films perpetuated something akin to magic lantern and optical toy entertainment.

Lumière's *L'Arroseur arrosé* in fact and facsimile. Soon after its first showing, the scenario was said to have been copied by nine rivals in the new industry of filmmaking. Lumière's hand-cranked cinématographe used an ether lamp and was highly portable and therefore capable to serve where electricity was unknown. (Museum of Modern Art/Film Stills Archive)

Kinetoscope subjects were also influenced by the circumstances of production. Because of the weight and bulk of the kinetograph and because of its battery drive, exterior use was difficult, although hardly impossible. W. K. L. Dickson and Edison constructed a utilitarian black shack, covered with tarpaulin and mounted on a turntable. The turntable permitted the building, dubbed the Black Maria by workers, to be revolved in order to maximize sunlight. Dickson was charged with all aspects of film production. He preferred to think of his studio as the Kinetographic Theater, posing subjects against a black background, marking off their playing areas with strings that radiated out from the camera.

Performers were picked from music hall and variety acts. The earliest fifty-foot Edison films document turn-of-the-century figures like Buffalo Bill firing a rifle, Annie Oakley demonstrating her own, superior shooting skills, Crissie Sheridan doing the Butterfly Dance, Sandow showing off his muscles, and a simulation of the Sioux Indians' Ghost Dance.

There is also an historical reenactment, the execution of Mary, Queen of Scots, done in August 1895. In this film, Dickson stopped his camera to replace an actress at the block with a dummy, and a lopped-off head serves as finale.

In contrast, the Lumières' camera and system led to quite different results. The brothers exploited their multipurpose invention by dispatching agents throughout the world. These men financed their ventures by mounting itinerant exhibitions. Further, they filmed subjects of interest in the travels and, using the same machine, even developed the work en route. Lumière film repertory grew in the course of each trip. Audiences worldwide made temporary acquaintance with different people, places, fashions and behavior.

The earliest commercial cinématographe run, held at the Grand Café on the Boulevard des Capucines in Paris on December 28, 1895, already indicates the range and character of Lumière's work, evocative of picture postcards and stereoscope "views":

1. *Leaving the Lumière Factory at Lyon*
2. *Tuileries Fountain*
3. *The Train*
4. *The Regiment*
5. *Cavalry Sergeant*
6. *A Game of Cards*
7. *The Weeds*
8. *The Wall*
9. *The Sea*
10. *Quarrel of the Babies*

Despite accumulating public evidence for the commercial superiority of projected film to peep shows, Edison continued to devote his personal attention, if at all, to the latter. As late as 1895, he was working on a *kinetophone,* which combined kinetoscope and phonograph, the viewer listening to an unsynchronized Edison cylinder through ear tubes as he watched a short film. The experience endorses the company's view that film, like recordings, was a documenting tool for performances that originated in another idiom.

Edison's managers of the Kinetoscope Company grew restive and apprehensive after the success of the projection exhibitions presented by Lumière and Paul. Kinetoscope executives responded to a feeler from Thomas Armat, and finally persuaded Edison to manufacture Armat's projector. The machines were made in Orange, New Jersey and marketed, with Armat's agreement, as another Edison invention, which was named the *vitascope.*

The vitascope's first showing was held at Koster and Bial's, a music hall in New York's Herald Square on April 23, 1896. Its reception is documented in a journalist's review:

The exhibition was a success in every way, and the large audience testified its approval of the novelty by the heartiest kind of applause.

The Vitascope is nothing more or less than an enlarged Kinetoscope. Those who are familiar with the workings of the Kinetoscope will understand what the Vitascope is, when it is explained that the pictures are thrown upon a screen, and that the figures move as they do in the Kinetoscope. They appear with all the colors of the original, too, which adds greatly to the effect.

The first picture shown was the Leigh Sisters in their umbrella dance. The effect was the same as if the girls were there on the stage; all of their smiles and kicks and bows were seen. The second picture represented the breaking of waves on the seashore. Wave after wave came tumbling on the sand, and as they struck, broke into tiny floods just like the real thing. Some of the people in the front rows seemed to be afraid they were going to get wet, and looked about to see where they could run to, in case the waves came too close. The third picture showed a burlesque boxing match between Walton and Mayon, the long and short comedians. Then followed in quick succession a scene from *A Milk White Flag* in which a couple of dozen people appeared; a serpentine dance with all the colored calcium effects, and an amusing picture showing an argument between John Bull and Uncle Sam.

The Vitascope is a big success, and Mr. Edison is to be congratulated for his splendid contribution to the people's pleasure.[3]

What the reviewer describes as "all the colors of the original" were in fact hand-tinted efforts. Significantly, the segment that appears to have struck writer and front row audience most forcefully was the one shot out of doors. This was *The Beach at Dover,* actually filmed by Robert Paul and pirated (illegally copied) by Edison from a print of the Englishman's work.

Most of the earliest film exhibitions understandably emphasized the novelty and sometimes the scientific marvel of the motion pic-

[3] New York Dramatic Mirror, *vol. 34, no. 905 (May 2, 1896), p. 19.*

ture. A hall like Koster and Bial's was reputable family entertainment, and other film shows were held at places like Keith's Union Square Theatre and the Olympia Music Hall in New York City, at Marlborough Hall Polytechnic and the Empire Theatre in London, in churches as distant as Australia and Ithaca, New York and on board the R.M.S. *Omrah* in the Mediterranean. Touring exhibitors often worked legitimate theaters every day but Sunday, then rented a hall for the Sabbath in order to circumscribe local blue laws.

One curiosity of film exhibition nearly bore fruit in a collaboration between Robert Paul and H. G. Wells, then popular for his science fiction romance. (Wells' *The Time Machine* was most recently filmed by the English in 1960.) On reading *The Time Machine*, Paul wrote Wells, and the two met. Inspired, Paul invented a unique exhibition theater and applied for a patent in 1895. In his theater, audiences would sit on a rocking platform that suggested movement through space. Bursts of air would simulate propulsion, and viewers would witness hypothetical landscapes, navigable balloons and visual evidence of past and future worlds. These were to be effected by animatograph projection and lantern slides—the machines mounted on tracks to enlarge or diminish the images—with colored slides adding impressions of light and weather change. Unhappily for science romance, Paul's theater never left the drawing board.

Less affluent audiences frequented kinetoscope parlors. Prizefight films demonstrate early efforts by exhibitors to locate and to exploit a specialized market. It was the Latham brothers who secured permission from Edison to produce fight films. In the Black Maria, they staged a battle between Michael Leonard and Jack Cushing, then exhibited the results, round by round, in successive kinetoscopes, each adapted to accomodate greater film length. The success of this venture encouraged the Lathams to pursue film projection. Of course, peepshow and

church audiences might cross over, but audiences were beginning to segregate, distanced by taste. A British film producer and exhibitor, Henry V. Hopwood, noted as early as 1899:

... It is well to bear in mind the story which recently set the lantern world smiling at the perplexity of a minister who found himself taking the chair at a prize fight, and who could find nothing in the program to suit his cloth, with the single exception of "Feeding the Baby."[4]

One of the marvels of the Saint Louis Exposition of 1903 was Hale's Tours and Scenes of the World, the brainchild of George C. Hale, a former fire chief of Kansas City, Missouri. The exhibit was fashioned in the manner of a railroad coach; a conductor collected tickets. Seated inside, spectators felt apparent movement and heard appropriate railway sounds. Then, at the far end of the car, projected film gave the impression of a trip itself as scenery rushed from center screen past the picture edges. This effect was achieved by mounting a movie camera on the front of a moving train, a device that dates at least as early as *The Mount Tamalpais Railway* (1898) executed by the Edison Company. Like pictures from exotic foreign lands, Hale's Tours seemed to provide film audiences a safe, comfortable, adventurous illusion. Hale toured successfully across the United States, earning half a million dollars in two years.[5]

In the storefront theaters, a dozen or so titles comprised fifteen- to twenty-minute shows. Vaudeville and variety house exhibi-

[4] *Henry V. Hopwood*, Living Pictures, Their History, Photo-Production and Practical Working *(London: 1899; reprinted New York, 1970), p. 223.*
[5] *Raymond Fielding, "Hale's Tours: Ultrarealism in the Pre-1910 Motion Picture,"* Cinema Journal, *vol. X, no. 1 (Fall 1970), pp. 34-47.*

tions followed the precedent of Edison's premiere at Koster and Bial's—a short program scheduled among the other acts. Sometimes the film bit replaced one of the little, truncated theatrical melodramas, a vanishing reminder of the last century's live popular theater. Sometimes the films occupied a bottom-of-the-bill slot, but it does not appear that film was characteristically used to clear the house, as historians have claimed in the past.

From the earliest times, music hall film exhibition enjoyed sound effects and musical accompaniment. Synchronization between lightning flashes and thunder machines, for example, was accomplished as in popular theater. Music was used to support a general mood or theme: martial airs with military footage, for instance. The music hall orchestra also blanketed projection noise. In cheaper houses, music was reduced to small instrumental combinations, and ultimately to the single pianist we nostalgically associate with silents. Later, a hallmark of opulent movie palaces, grandiloquent pipe organs replaced pianos and orchestras.

In transition from earlier magic lantern performances, slides were often interposed with short films. Early projection was flickery and ill-focused; slides provided a rest for the eyes. They also gave an operator time to change reels or to repair torn film.

Storefront theater managers had to program films and to intuit the tastes of their particular audiences, not only by gauging spectator reaction at the box office but through eavesdropping on comments at the end of a show. This quality of pragmatism among hustling, success-driven entrepreneurs was retained by many of the same men when they became movie producers.

A constant danger in the houses was fire. Film used a base of highly flammable cellulose nitrate, and stores and halls were often firetraps. Gas-lit projection posed hazards. For a short while, movie theaters escaped controls imposed on "legitimate" stages, but an increasing number of disasters triggered demand for local regulation. At a Charity Bazaar in Paris in 1897, 150 patrons died through projection negligence. A panic ensued in Stafford, England when smoke from a projector frightened spectators. Soon ordinances regulated movie theater standards, controlling the design of projection booths, and establishing policies concerning exits, curtains, smoking, and room capacity.

DISTRIBUTION

Popularity strained relations between exhibitors and filmmakers. On the advice of his manager W. E. Gilmore in late 1897, Edison came to realize that impressive profits were escaping him. Lacking European copyright sanctions, Edison was confined to the United States, where he initiated patent infringement suits against filmmakers (Vitagraph, for example, in 1897 and 1902), importers and producers alike. Some patent fights occurred, too, in France and England, but in the United States they amounted to more than 200 separate actions by 1907.

Court dispute continued for ten years with mixed results. Some companies made settlements with the inventor. Others went out of business, at least temporarily, while many small businessmen persevered, a step ahead of patent attorneys. As Edison failed to satisfy a growing market, his competition tried to meet the market for fifty-foot entertainments. Length increased gradually to a thousand feet, a reel, roughly eleven to sixteen minutes depending on projection speed.

Hampered by time-consuming court actions and unsettled by a major decision Edison won against William N. Selig, film corporations enjoying legitimate or semilegitimate status made a deal with Edison. These firms included Vitagraph, Lubin, Selig, Essanay, Pathé, Lumière, Kalem, George Kleine, and American Mutoscope and Biograph. A transformation of the K.M.C.D. Syndicate, American Muto-scope and Biograph was in a position of some power through having acquired rights to Latham's and Armat's machines.

In 1908, together with Edison, the producers formed what came to be known popularly as the Trust, otherwise as the Motion Picture Patents Company. Operating effectively for the next four to seven years, the Trust took firm control of all the legal aspects of filmmaking and exhibition, licensing cameras and projectors over which it maintained patent controls. Before its power slipped away and dissension intervened, the Trust was largely disposed to maintain 1-reel lengths for films it circulated, altough Vitagraph made a 5-reel *The Life of Moses* in 1910 and *Vanity Fair* (3 reels) in 1911. While no rival to Charleton Heston, Moses parting the Red Sea maintains a curious dignity.

Before 1903, motion pictures were not rented but sold, one print at a time, usually for ten to twelve cents per foot, so that an exhibitor would pay about one hundred dollars for a reel's entertainment. If their theaters were well located in a densely populated location (a metropolitan center, for instance), managers might sustain long runs with one film, but audience interest dissipated faster than the life of a print, so exhibitors soon developed ways to increase the value of their purchases.

One practice was to seek out new audiences by roadshowing: taking films on tour and promoting them at each stop. Exhibitors also adopted the technique of passing films back and forth among themselves. In the Bay Area, two San Francisco brothers, Herbert and Harry J. Miles, institutionalized the exchange service by purchasing films and renting the titles to participating exhibitors at twenty-five percent of cost. In 1904, the French founded a similar system; its success led Pathé, a major film producer, to abandon sales in 1907 and to lease instead. Exchanges encouraged the growth of moving picture theaters by reducing overhead. As theaters increased, so did exchanges, numbering more than a hundred in this country in 1907.

Operating expenses for a motion picture theater varied, of course, depending on location, audience size and the ambitions of the proprietor. A 1913 book of business advice gives some figures for the establishment and maintenance of a store-front city theater, automatic or manual, one using a muslin screen, a piano and 192 kitchen or opera chairs:

The complete change in the store room, ready for chairs, piano, wiring and projecting machine, should not exceed $150; 200 chairs of the kitchen variety at $100; electric lamps and wiring at $100; a projection machine at $165; and a rented piano—the total expense amounting to about $500. With a small additional amount for supplies and initial advertising expense, the manager will be able to open his doors to the public at a total cash expense of not more than $600, and no debts.[6]

A theater such as this would depend upon ticket sales from $100 to $150 per week to assure minimum profit to the manager and a return on his investment. Weekly operating expenses for a evening-only program of 2 reels and a song might run:

Rent and Heat	$10.00
Electricity	5.00
Film	20.00
Song Slides	2.00
Supplies	13.00
Operator	15.00
Cashier	3.00
Doorkeeper	5.00
Pianist	5.00
Singer	5.00
Weekly Expenses	$83.00[7]

[6] *David S. Hulfish,* Motion Picture Work *(Chicago, 1913), p. 180.*
[7] *Ibid., p. 181.*

Song slides, originally provided free, were now rented by New York City music publishers. As in the music halls, the slides served to plug (popularize) new creations of Tin Pan Alley by familiarizing audiences with works in hope that they might buy piano sheet music. Supplies included an assortment of ticket rolls. A wary theater manager was advised to be sure that each ticket was destroyed so that it could not be reused or even resold (at a loss of five cents) by an unscrupulous cashier/doorkeeper (ticket chopper) team. He was also advised to change the ticket color daily. The manager was encouraged to make careful note of successful and unsatisfactory film fare and to try to influence his film exchange in the direction of the most successful titles.

The words "try to influence his film exchange," are carefully chosen to express the true position of the exhibitor, or theater manager, in the matter of obtaining film pictures acceptable to his patrons. The film exchanges as a rule take all the film pictures produced by the particular manufacturers from whom they buy. All of these film reels look alike to the film exchange man, and he would like to send them indiscriminately to his customers, to the exhibitors, or to theater managers. The service the theater manager will get, therefore, will be "hit or miss" of the film exchange stock of reels unless some influence is used by the manager to govern the classes of pictures furnished him.[8]

Theaters blossomed across the country. Harry Davis and John P. Harris were early Pittsburgh businessmen who converted an unused storeroom into an exhibition hall and eventually ran fourteen like spots in the area. Soon dubbed nickel parlors, nickelets or nickelodeons, the businesses appeared not only in the major cities but in small towns across the country. Political decisions sometimes af-

[8] *Ibid., p. 196.*

fected audience size, as with New York City's Board of Aldermen. This body declared that a seating capacity of 299 or fewer constituted a "common show," subject to no more than a $25 tax, while the presence of more patrons indicated a "theater," to be taxed at $500. There were 8–10,000 nickelodeons operating in 1908. It is not true that early exhibition was confined to immigrant metropolitan areas as some historians maintain. Nickelodeons soon enjoyed broad middle-class support.

If his traffic ran high enough, the exhibitor might also maximize gains by increasing theater hours. Since programs consisted of 1 to 2 reels of film with song slides perhaps interspersed, turnover was enormous. William Fox accomplished a daily attendance of 8000 at his New York City theater.

Aware of increasing competition, vaudeville managers sometimes combined live entertainment with film in small town locations that had earlier failed to support a circuit stop. In this environment and period, future exhibition and production figures surfaced: people like Fox; B. F. Keith, who owned the Union Square Theater; Marcus Loew, who began with penny arcades; Harry Cohn, a song-slide vocalist; Adolph Zukor, also out of the penny arcades, and Carl Laemmle, who opened the Whitefront Theater in Chicago in 1906. Louis B. Mayer bought a little theater in Haverhill, Massachusetts in 1907.

PRODUCTION

The Trust gave Edison a royalty on everything it sold, but most production derived from the member companies. Although filmmaking localized along the East Coast or in Chicago, many parts of the United States saw production: Worcester, Massachusetts (Prudential Film Corporation), San Antonio (Méliès' Star Films), Wilkes-Barre (United States Motion Picture Corporation) and Ogden, Utah

Early Selig Polyscope studio, perhaps 1888, with open air sets and overhead gauzing designed to maximize natural light. Selig's arrangement with pulp-publisher Street and Smith guaranteed exclusive rights to new stories for his films. The company produced five-color advertising "one sheets" for each production and sold them to theaters at a dime apiece. In 1914, Selig, Lubin, Essanay, and Vitagraph combined to produce longer films that General Films (the Trust) would not handle. (Museum of Modern Art/ Film Stills Archive)

(Ogden Film Company).[9] As early as 1908, Jacksonville variously hosted Kalem, Lubin, Selig, Thanhauser, Vitagraph, Essanay, Biograph, Gaumont, and Eagle. William Bitzer shot *Auto Races, Ormond, Florida* in 1905.[10] Corporations geared themselves to an expanded market by grinding out acceptable if uncreative products. Sigmund Lubin was a Philadelphia filmmaker whose new studio allowed four films to be undertaken at once. William Selig had a Chicago firm. Little companies, whose relation to the Trust was tenuous or nonexistent, continued to operate in smaller, out-of-the-way locations.

The public taste, quickly reported by watchful theater managers, was increasingly for more sustained narrative in the films.

The public wants a story. We run to comics generally; they seem to take best. So-and-so, however, leans more to melodrama. When we started we used to give just flashes—an engine chasing to a fire, a base runner sliding home, a charge of cavalry. Now, for instance, if we want to work in a horse race, it has to be a scene in the life of the jockey, who is the hero of the piece—we've got to give them a story; they won't take anthing else—a story with plenty of action. You can't show large conversations, you know, on the screen. More story, larger story, better story with action—that is our tendency.[11]

[9] Karr, Kathleen, "Horray for Providence, Wilkes-Barre, Saranac Lake—and Hollywood," in The American Film Heritage—Impressions from the American Film Institute Archives *(Washington, D.C., 1972), p. 104.*

[10] Nelson, Richard Alan. "Florida: The Forgotten Film Capital," Journal of the University Film Association *(Summer 1977)*

[11] Patterson, Joseph Medill, "The Nickelodeons," Saturday Evening Post *(Nov. 23, 1907). Anthologized in Roger Butterfield, ed.,* The Saturday Evening Post Treasury *(New York, 1954).*

How these stories were told is the subject of Chapter 2, but their effect on production figures here. As plot lines developed, still restricted within the regimen of 1 reel, it became evident that on-the-spot improvised methods were inefficient. Worse, they were less successful commercially. Filmmakers began buying story "ideas." At Biograph, H. N. Marvin paid up to fifteen dollars. Narrativity had financial and logistical as well as formal consequences. Stories required performers who might both look and act appropriate to a particular role.

Larger studios worked indoors under glass roofs, on rooftops or, increasingly, inside with artificial light. A shooting location in New Jersey or across-the-Hudson New York might be used to simulate western locale. The West itself appeared first on screens when G. M. Anderson, an actor who emerged in Edison's films and then became the "ay" of Essanay (Spoor and Anderson), made the first of his Bronco Billy cowboy series in Colorado. Later, Anderson proceeded to Niles, California. His western series ran 366 consecutive weeks in many theaters.

Independence

By 1912, independent production units grew increasingly restive under Trust controls.[12] One of the restrictive Trust practices was to prohibit identification by name of favorite actors and actresses. Accurately, the monop-

[12] By 1911, there were 11,500 movie houses that negotiated with one or more of the 150 rental exchanges for all or part of their film programs each week. Figures of the Motion Picture Patents Company dating from December 18, 1911 locate 6,236 of its licenses each of whom paid a weekly fee of two dollars, 5,205 nonlicensees, and an assortment of legitimate theaters that sometimes used films. Ralph Cassedy, "Monopoly in Motion Picture Production and Distribution: 1908-1915," Southern California Law Review, vol. XXXII, no. 4 (1959), p. 374, n. 287.

oly reasoned that notoriety would lead to salary demands, although the Trust failed to realize that the use of actors' names would also help draw a larger audience. Perhaps the first anonymous star was Florence Turner, who became The Vitagraph Girl in 1907 and formed the Turner Film Company in England at Hepworth Studios in 1913. Finally, Carl Laemmle hired a popular performer, Florence Lawrence, away from Biograph where she was known to the public only as "The Biograph Girl." Laemmle offered the woman not only a higher salary but also her own name in his IMP (Independent Moving Picture) Company productions.

Feature films became another weapon in breaking the Trust domination. There had, of course, been movies before that overran the 1-reel dictum. Enoch Rector, friend of the Lathams, documented the Corbett-Fitzsimmons fight at Carson City, Nevada 1897 on 11,000 feet of film, and it played that year at the Academy of Music in New York for a one dollar admission. The next year, W. B. Hurd, who represented Lumière in the United States, reasoned that if a prizefight appealed to men, the Passion Play might do as well with women and children. He purchased rights to the Oberammergau version. After an unsuccessful attempt to film the actual performance in Bohemia, Hurd staged the play for camera on the roof of the Grand Central Palace. The 3-reel film ran successfully in New York accompanied by choir and lecturer, interspersed with intermissions.

Motivated now to expand into broader audience markets by new merchandising techniques, Adolph Zukor imported another kind of production. France's Film d'art and Séries d'art were movie documentations, often tediously pretentious, of traditional prose, poetry, and theater pieces as well as "imports" like Oliver Twist. Under Zukor, American audiences were treated to Eleonora Duse and to Sarah Bernhardt's Queen Elizabeth in 1912. More important than the stage gesture and emoting, many French and Italian "screen-plays" ran from 4 to 8 reels, confronting the Trust's limitations on programming, and implicitly, theater capacities, not once but on a regular basis.

The other trust-busting strategy was a literal escape from the East's overseeing eye. Film companies followed the lead of Bronco Billy and sought locations along the California coast, a continent between themselves and cries of patent infringement. Where Anderson had chosen Niles, other producers eschewed the questionable weather of the San Francisco area and turned southward. Lower California (the Flying A Studio on State and Mission streets in Santa Barbara, for example) had an unpolished air, but promised near-constant sunlight. Also, should patent litigation threaten, Mexico gave refuge to filmmaker and film. A small, quiet Los Angeles suburb called Hollywood played host to eastern émigrés in 1913.

The Trust's hold was altogether broken by 1915. Most significant about the insurgence of the independents, led by Laemmle and Fox, was the fact that their success derived not so much from legal maneuvers and shrewd business practice as from a competitive under-standing of film audience appetites—how to create and indulge them. The independents expanded the limits of film more easily to "meet" audience dispositions toward story, star and length. The filmgoer wanted to stretch his experience beyond ten minutes.

FRANCE

Remarkably soon after his first public exhibition, Louis Lumière recruited and dispatched agents. A camera was set up on a gondola traveling the Grand Canal in Venice in Spring, 1896. Less then three months after Koster and Bial's vitascope premiere, 200 people each paid an exhorbitant two rupees to watch movies at Watson's Hotel in Bombay.

Lumière's representatives exhibited at Za-van's Café in Alexandria in 1896. The kinetoscope was privately exhibited to Japan's Imperial Highness in his hotel bedroom. In 1897, residents of Osaka saw Edison's film of Crissie Sheridan's Butterfly Dance, but Lumière's men had scooped Edison by an appearance one week earlier.

Lumière's agents exhibited in Austria in 1896. Lumière played Brussels in 1896, and Malmö, Sweden the same year. The Swedish scene was itself documented by the *cinématographe* in 1897. Lumière film appeared at the Sponek beer house in Istanbul in 1896 or 1897.

Two Lumière men documented the coronation of Tsar Nicholas II in seventeen shots during May, 1896. Other Lumière films were exhibited at the annual fair at Nizhni-Novgorod in June. In attendance was the author Maxim Gorky. He wrote a report of his experience for the local press.

Without fear of exaggeration, a wide use can be predicted for this invention, because of its tremendous novelty. But how great are its results compared with the expenditure of nervous energy that it requires? Is it possible for it to be applied usefully enough to compensate for the nervous strain it produces on the spectator? A yet more important problem is that our nerves are getting weaker and less reliable, we are reacting less to natural sensations of our daily life and thirst more eagerly for new strong sensations. The cinématographe gives you all these—cultivating the nerves on the one hand and dulling them on the other. The thirst for such strange, fantastic sensations as it gives will grow ever greater and we will be increasingly less able and less willing to grasp the everyday impressions of ordinary life. This thirst for the strange and the new can lead us far, very far.[13]

[13] *Quoted in Jay Leyda*, Kino, *(London, 1960), pp. 20-21.*

ENGLAND

Many exhibitor-producers came to English film by way of the magic lantern. In the century's first decade, traveling showmen often documented local events or else staged little story films. A British cameraman captured the siege of Port Arthur during the Russo-Japanese war (January, 1905), and one company made advertising films for cigarettes, custard, whiskey, and soap. Like the Americans and the French, the British "reenacted," too, exploiting current events. Take, for example, Sheffield Company's advertisement for its *Russo-Japanese War—Attack on a Japanese Convoy* (1904):

A party of Cossacks is seen chasing a Coolie spy, from whom they endeavor to obtain information respecting a Jap Convoy. After threatening him with a pistol, the information is given and the Cossacks ride away, dragging the Coolie with them by his pigtail.

The next scene shows the Convoy with its escort hotly pursued by a Russian Patrol. Seeing escape hopeless, the Japs halt, dismount, open fire on the Cossacks, wounding one and driving the rest away for a time. Before proceeding, the Japs dress the wounds of the injured Cossack and place him in a convoy waggon.

Last scene, laid in beautiful rugged scenery, shows the Convoy crossing a drift. When in midstream, the advance rider comes in contact with a Cossack party, on whom he promptly fires, the remaining Japs ride up to his assistance and succeed in putting the Cossacks out of action. During the excitement, the wounded Russian makes his escape from the waggon, but on reaching the bank he is seen and promptly shot.

The plucky Japs with the Convoy are then seen mounting the opposite bank of the river and disappear round the bend.

THIS IS WITHOUT DOUBT THE FINEST WAR FILM ON THE MARKET.

The greatest care has been exercised in producing the above picture, every detail having been considered. The Japanese, Russians, and Coolies being perfect representations.[14]

ITALY

Enterprising Italian exhibitors took movies and projection equipment to Bombay in 1897. An early national production was *La Presa di Roma* (The capture of Rome) (1904) made by Filoteo Alberini. Italy's influence on the international market was effected by a series of 1913 historical epics, first a 10-reel *Last Days of Pompeii*, then *Quo Vadis,* ninety minutes of extravaganza. George Kleine, a member of the Trust, imported *Quo Vadis* into the United States, booking it at New York's Astor Theater. At one dollar admission, the picture ran twenty-two weeks, proceeding to like success in other large cities.

Quo Vadis provided a middle-class public spectacle, religion and impressive settings, time-tested ingredients of nineteenth-century melodrama, like the story itself. *Cabiria* followed in 1914.

Cabiria's credits imply that it was prepared by Italy's patriotic writer Gabriele D'Annunzio. In fact, the film was designed by its producer-director Giovanni Pastrone, who paid D'Annunzio for titles. Maciste, a popular actor, appeared as a slave. The film was said to cost more than a million dollars, originally ran 12 reels, and alternates between pompous posturing, speechmaking, action, and still-comic bits. Grandiose architectural and mountain sets and an exploding volcano are impressive if unstable in look. *Cabiria* is noteworthy, too, for Pastrone's camera movement, some-

[14] *Rachel Low and Roger Manvell,* The History of the British Film 1896-1906, *(London, 1948), p. 70.*

times skirting expanses of stone plaza to relate individual characters to crowds and events. A striking set is the immense bronze statue of Baal, whose gaping mouth houses a great flame. Children are sacrificed here, the image a harbinger of later set designs in *Intolerance* (1915) and *Metropolis* (1926).

THE FILMS

By the time film exhibition had blanketed the United States — the Trust in retreat — movies themselves were separating into distinct types. Differing modes foreshadowed production specializations and audience enthusiasms for years to follow.

Actualities, movies of unstaged (or purportedly unstaged) reality, appear as early as the medium. Such Lumière films as *Feeding the Baby* (1895) suggest posed, amateur events timed to the length of the camera reel. This was Lumière's heritage as a manufacturer of photographic equipment. Films like *Workers Leaving the Lumière Factory* (1895) document daily life itself, seemingly unaffected by camera presence.

Both approaches provide the germ of travel movies as well as films that explain or demonstrate process, like the English Country Life series, which dates from 1899 and includes titles like *Seed-threshing* and *Blacksmiths at Work — Tying a Cartwheel.*

Topical films recorded events: public and ritual like the Lumières' Coronation of Czar Nicholas II; or else, spontaneously, they recorded "news":

Robert W. Paul's *Disaster* (1898)

The launching of H.M.S. *Albion,* followed by the scene of the rescuing of the persons submerged in the water by the collapse of the staging. The only view of this terrible and affecting scene taken.[15]

Filming from the ship *Anita,* a Biograph cameraman covers the Spanish-American War. For Vitascope, Albert E. Smith and J. Stuart Blackton faked a naval battle and a flag raising, but they also covered the Rough Riders' assault on San Juan Hill in actuality. Teddy Roosevelt loved publicity. (The Byron Collection, Museum of the City of New York)

These films range from war footage to prize fights. Like the actualities, they underline the film's capacity to provide affecting yet vicarious relations to distant places and occurrences.

As early as the popularity of the topical film was that of pseudo-topical film. At the time of the Spanish-American War, Edison concocted *Raising Old Glory over Morro Castle* (1899). Early in 1900, on the Omaha Exposition Midway in Austin, Texas, the "Warograph" (Lumière's cinématographe) devoted itself exclusively to Spanish-American War titles.[16]

[15] *Ibid., p. 62.*
[16] *Burnes St. Patrick Hollyman, "The First Picture Shows: Austin, Texas (1804-1913)," Journal of the University Film Association (Summer 1977), pp. 3-8.*

When Roosevelt emerged as a public figure, Edison invented a tongue-in-cheek hunt movie, *Terrible Teddy, the Grizzly King* (1901). Many such films made little effort to delude audiences. Rather, they "reenacted" history or anecdote. Other titles went to lengths to simulate the real thing, like English shorts depicting the assassination of King Alexander and Queen Draga of Serbia in 1903 and a Pathé eruption of Mt. Pelée in 1902. In its own fashion, fakery initiated the whole tradition of special effects.

Stage pieces reflect Edison's impulse to record theater for home enjoyment and posterity. Carmencita, a Spanish dancer than appearing at Koster and Bial's, journeyed to West Orange, New Jersey to be filmed in 1894, followed by a succession of stage figures. The famous May Irwin-John C. Rice *The Kiss* of 1896 came out of a play in which the actors were appearing, *The Widow Jones*. While the literal documentation of theater disappeared as actors and performers learned to adapt to the newer medium, the absorption of stage into screen was pervasive, not only in terms of narrative itself, but also by way of actors, from Mary Pickford to Marlon Brando, and comics, Chaplin, W. C. Fields, the Marx Brothers, whose film appeal rested in a charismatic presence and sometimes in routines that had been polished before live audiences.

Fiction film resolved itself into genres identical with earlier popular entertainments: dime novels, boys' books and stage melodrama. Comedy excepted, film lost its improvised air, and as this happened, older vehicles reappeared. Prose had first provided *Sherlock Holmes, Uncle Tom's Cabin, The Clansman, The Prisoner of Zenda, The Corsican Brothers, The Count of Monte Cristo* and *The Sign of the Cross*. They reemerged on stage and then were followed by movie versions, usually more than one. Screen followed theater with: animal drama, *Rescued by Rover* (1905); patriotism, *The Call to Arms* (1902); thrillers, *A Den of Thieves* (1905); suspense, *Falsely Ac-*

cused (1905); westerns, *The Great Train Robbery* (1903); criminals, *The Life of Charles Peace, the Notorious Burglar* (1905); social criticism *The Kleptomaniac* (1905), and so on. Fireman stories were especially popular in the early film period, *The Life of an American Fireman* (1903), *Fire* (1902) and, earliest of all, *Plucked from the Burning* (1898).

One of the first Lumière efforts, *L'Arroseur arrosé* (1895) is a simple gag: Gardener waters lawn. Boy steps on hose. Gardener looks into nozzle. Boy releases water and wets gardener. Gardener squirts boy. Comic actors also brought their stage presences. The stage comic John Bunny was an early name to be publicized when the independents broke the Trust's anonyms, but even earlier, Bunny had been featured in a series of Vitagraph comedies with Flora Finch. In 1909, he appeared with the animator Winsor McCay in *Little Nemo*. Much early comedy depended on stage-derived types, like *Uncle Josh at the Moving Picture Show* (1902), and *The Widow and the Only Man* (1904).

Salacious film made an early appearance. Some of the documented stage performances were themselves titilating, incredible as this may seem to jaded perceptions of today: *Fatima's Coochee-Coochee Dance* (1901), for example. Just as film proffered safe adventure, it promised vicarious sex clothed in darkness. Unconfirmed reports suggest that pornography was shot as early as 1904 in Buenos Aires bordellos; films for smokers were soon available. Diluted, comedies about flirtation and the troubles between married couples were regular fare in the nickelodeons.

Usually comic and sometimes theatrical, the trick film was a speciality of Georges Méliès; his French productions date from 1896. Influenced by Méliès, whose films were successfully distributed throughout the world, English filmmakers like G. A. Smith, *Photographing a Ghost* (1898) and Robert Paul, *Voyage of the "Arctic," or How Captain Kettle Discovered the North Pole* (1903) soon learned to pass apparitions through doors and cause people to disappear on screen. Edwin S. Porter made *The Dream of a Rarebit Fiend* in 1906. Emile Cohl, a French filmmaker associated with animation, made trick films of rich and extraordinary inventions like *The Automatic Moving Company* (1911).[17]

Shuffling, stammering blacks, raucous Irish, knife-wielding Italians and sly, hand-rubbing Jews frequented the Victorian stage, particularly the music halls, popular fiction and even Edison cylinders. The conventions often served to account for treacherous behavior in melodrama, as when swarthy "foreigners" would menace youths and kidnap children, finally bested by courageous, tall, Nordic males. Early films absorbed the racial and national stereotypes. Such old movies provide curious artifacts in evidence of national taste and values, if we remember, too, that many were produced, and responded to, by immigrants, so that the entertainments comprise a first-generation's estimation of the American sensibility. The advertisement of an early exhibition at Vitascope Hall is typical.

[17] *Cohl worked briefly in the United States, became destitute after World War I, and died in 1938 in a hotel fire.*

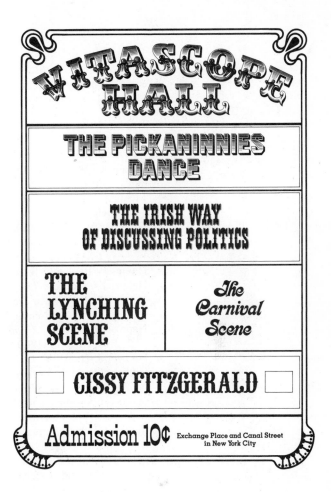

Summary

Within a very few years after Lumière's public cinématographe debut in 1895, motion pictures had been witnessed throughout the world. During that same period, distinct traditions were already forming: historical spectacle in Italy, actualities in Britain, cross currents of documentation and stage event in France.

By the end of the new century's first decade, fictional, entertaining movies showed unexpected, resilient appeal. Film had begun to pervade national topography and cultural landscape; film's popularity outdistanced any possible domination by those figures who birthed it.

In the United States, pragmatic relations between exhibitor and filmmaker developed from the early appearance of businessmen like Zukor and Fox. Such direct, commercially based experience with audiences soon encouraged production efforts to determine future successes by tailoring the subject matter to conform to the widespread appeal of strongly narrative films. The next chapter details how and where narrative evolved, starting from views and snippets, soon confidently exploiting a developing sense of "story" whose strength grew out of audience empathy and the capacity to believe.

Bibliography

Bardeche, Maurice and Robert Brasillach. *The History of Motion Pictures.* Translated and Edited by Iris Barry. New York, 1938.

Ceram, C. W. *Archaeology of the Cinema.* London, 1965.

Cook, Olive. *Movement in Two Dimensions.* London, 1963.

Fielding, Raymond. *A Technical History of Motion Pictures and Television.* Berkeley, 1967.

Grau, Robert. *The Business Man in the Amusement World.* New York, 1910.

————. *The Stage in the Twentieth Century.* New York, 1912.

————. *The Theater of Science.* New York, 1914.

Hampton, Benjamin B. *A History of the Movies.* New York, 1970.

Hendricks, Gordon. *The Edison Motion Picture Myth.* Berkeley, 1961.

————. *Beginnings of the Biograph.* New York, 1964.

————. *The Kinetoscope.* New York, 1966.

Hepworth, Cecil M. *Animated Photography the A B C of the Cinematograph.* 2nd ed. London, 1900.

Hopwood, Henry V. *Living Pictures.* London, 1899.

Hulfish, David S. *Motion-Picture Work.* Chicago, 1913.

Jacobs, Lewis. *The Rise of the American Film.* New York, 1939.

Jenkins, C. Francis and Oscar B. Depue. *Handbook for Motion Picture and Stereopticon Operators.* Washington, D.C., 1897.

Jowett, Garth. *Film the Democratic Art.* Boston, 1976.

Klaw and Erlanger Present Famous Plays in Pictures. Los Angeles, 1976.

Leyda, Jay. *Kino.* London, 1960.

Low, Rachel and Roger Manvell. *The History of the British Film 1896-1906.* London, 1948.

MacDonald, Kevin. *Eadweard Muybridge The Man Who Invented the Motion Picture.* Boston, 1972.

Munkhouse, Bob. *Picture Pioneers.* Newcastle upon Tyne, 1971.

Muybridge, Eadweard. *The Human Figure in Motion.* 1887. Introduction by Robert Taft, New York, 1955.

North, Joseph H. "The Early Development of the Motion Picture (1887-1909)". Ph.D. dissertation, Cornell, 1949. Facsimile ed. New York, 1973.

Noxon, Gerald. "Pictorial Origins of Cinema Narrative in Pre-Historic and Ancient Art," *Cinema Studies 2,* Spring 1968.

Porta, John Baptista. *Natural Magick.* London, 1658. Facsimile ed. New York, 1957.

Quigley, Martin *Magic Shadows.* Washington, D.C., 1948.

Ramsaye, Terry. *A Million and One Nights.* 2 vols. New York, 1962.

Richardson, R. H. *Motion Picture Handbook: A Guide for Managers and Operators of Motion Picture Theaters.* New York, circa 1911.

Sadoul, Georges. *French Film.* London, 1953.

Stanford University. *Eadweard Muybridge: The Stanford Years 1872-1882.* Palo Alto, 1972.

Sklar, Robert. *Movie-Made America a Cultural History of American Movies.* New York, 1975.

Slide, Anthony. *The Big V: A History of the Vitagraph Company.* Metuchen, N.J., 1976.

Talbot, Frederick A. *Moving Pictures: How They Are Made and Worked.* Philadelphia, 1912.

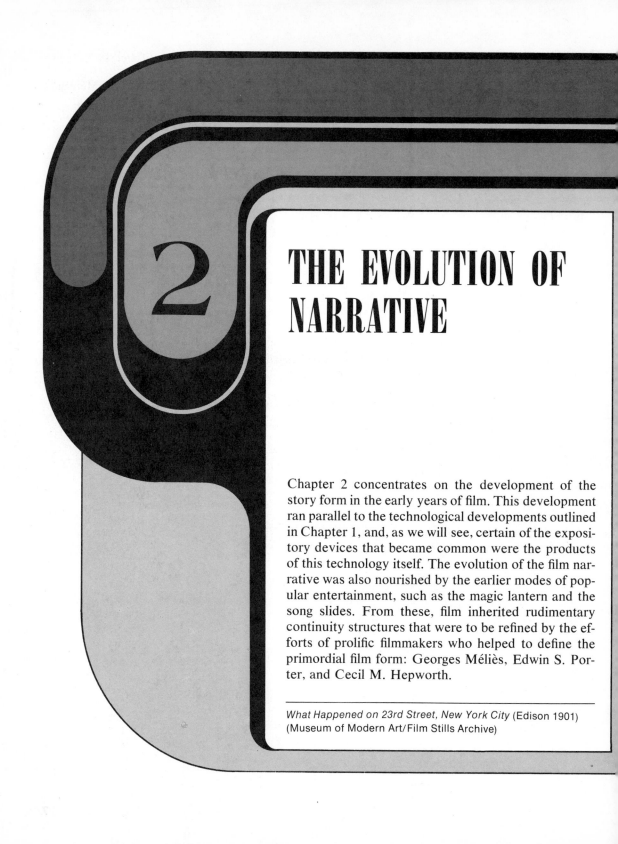

THE EVOLUTION OF NARRATIVE

Chapter 2 concentrates on the development of the story form in the early years of film. This development ran parallel to the technological developments outlined in Chapter 1, and, as we will see, certain of the expository devices that became common were the products of this technology itself. The evolution of the film narrative was also nourished by the earlier modes of popular entertainment, such as the magic lantern and the song slides. From these, film inherited rudimentary continuity structures that were to be refined by the efforts of prolific filmmakers who helped to define the primordial film form: Georges Méliès, Edwin S. Porter, and Cecil M. Hepworth.

What Happened on 23rd Street, New York City (Edison 1901) (Museum of Modern Art/Film Stills Archive)

1

EXPOSITORY FORM

Film's technological evolution coincided with industrial developments in printing: photo engraving, rotary presses, and three-color processes. These developments made it possible to publish and market illustrated books, magazines, and newspapers on a large scale. While learning to read prose, a mass audience simultaneously acquired visual literacy. The use of word and picture together as storytelling agents redeployed certain expository devices from entertainments like the peepshow and the magic lantern. These two entertainments were, in fact, outgrowths of oral storytelling that funneled through nineteenth-century theater and the popular press to become narrative conventions.

Urban workers and semiliterate country people who became the genesis of a popular audience had made a silent pact—one still honored by television viewers—with performance. A story might be patently make believe, but it was accepted as "true" for its duration. The characters' behaviors, producing a change of condition (for example, a rescue) or understanding (the dawn of love) transported actors and viewers/readers together through a predictable sequence of rising expectations and agreeable resolutions.

Plots might proceed straight ahead in continuous time but reveal discontinuous space. They could skip from place to place, smoothing transition with chapter breaks, stage lighting change, or visual similarities between sequential pictures as in a comic strip ("matching" action and composition between adjacent panels). When time pressed forward, a switchback in space, as in the last minute rescue, might engender suspense. Alternately, stories could jump backward or forward in time, as when an enacted memory supplied motivation for present behavior. Theater called this a "vision scene," film a "flashback." In either case, the viewer was confronted with simultaneous moments of time: the dreamer (present) and his recollected images (past). *Let Me Dream Again* (1900) and *The Tramp's Dream* (1901) provide early instances of dreams appearing full-frame, rather than shown simultaneous with the dreamer, like comic "dream balloons."

An audience expected that it held an ideal perspective on the action. In boys' stories and dime novels, the reader was privy to the private thoughts of the characters as well as their deeds. Comic drawings pulled viewers in to closer "shots," or "followed" characters in motion. Photography adapted the skills of painterly composition with regard to angle of view, lighting and foreground-background relationships and was, therefore, able to present the characters and events in a very convincing way.

Character defined itself through action more often than speech. Action was simply coded so as to shorthand plot relationships, and "types" explained motives. Heroes rescued; factory owners threatened. Tramps, farmers and immigrants were comic. Brave girls were boyish. Reserved, flat-chested women in Edwardian skirts fainted under stress. Gypsies kidnapped children. A story with a tramp, a farmer and a cowboy would take one turn. Substitute a feisty heroine for the farmer and the plot would veer predictably elsewhere.

SLIDE SHOWS

Photography vastly expanded the resources of the magic lantern, evolving story sets: series of sequential photos that followed the usual patterns of exposition. In 1894, Alexander Black, an amateur photographer, extended drama further into slide entertainment. Black wrote an adventure about a plucky young woman reporter, then photographed his story in New York City with actors staging the incidents in part on location. In performance,

A four-slide sequence from *Miss Jerry.* The heroine reminisces with Pink, an old companion from her mining-camp childhood. The cluttered décor of table, chairs, and set dressing establishes a field where apparent figure movement seems the more pronounced. (Courtesy of The New York Public Library: Astor, Lenox and Tilden Foundations)

Black narrated his tale, *Miss Jerry,* while projecting its images. The projections ran four per minute. Where an episode was confined to a single set, Black held to one camera setup, moving his characters minimally from picture to picture against a constant background. Thus, when the pictures were "dissolved" from one to another by way of two magic lantern projectors, a momentary impression of movement resulted. Interestingly, the plot "cuts" from place to place: villain offers hero a bribe in a business office while, at the same moment, Miss Jerry conducts an interview in a lower Manhattan tenement.

The song slide was another expository medium that preceded early film. It consisted of series that came in sets ranging from four to sixteen images, each illustrating the lyric of a current popular song, so that in a curious fashion the song slide echoes oral narrative while imposing its own graphics on story. Examination of existing song slides indicates that their producers anticipated a variety of motion picture techniques, including the very notion of scripting a story beforehand and shooting it out-of-sequence. Pictures show the use of camera-angle shifts from far to near, movement to follow a subject and parallel editing—like Alexander Black's design—to tell a story simultaneously in two locations.

PRIMORDIAL FILM FORM

Little researched until recently, the dozen years between premiere motion picture projections and D. W. Griffith's directorial ap-

The Morning Bath, or Bathing the Baby (Edison 1893). Centered, symmetrical compositioning in an unadorned set is typical of early Edison kinetoscope reels. The performances—though unscripted—paced themselves to footage capacities, thereby increasing a viewer's sense of "performance." (Museum of Modern Art/Film Stills Archive)

may unexpectedly, momentarily erupt. Debts to theater, popular fiction, magic lanterns and still photography are apparent; some conventions adapted to the new idiom with little strain. Others appear to have provided temporary, false leads, from which motion pictures withdrew, as from expository paths untaken.

Because of its very naïveté, earliest film projects an unselfconscious energy and charm that will never be recaptured. Among fiction films, the events are curiously lively. At times they suggest directions that narrative may not take for decades to come. However commercially motivated, most footage clearly possesses the characteristics of play. These early films, as short as a single shot in duration, may imply proscenium performances not only by staging, but because they are entire, self-contained events that the camera records, controlling performance by the limitations of the reel capacity.

Likenesses between early film and theater have been seen to suggest theater's domination over film esthetics, but they can often be explained in terms of technology. Film actors exit screen left and screen right, as if entering

pearance have only recently begun to yield their secrets.[1] Today, reports can only be preliminary and speculative. The material is fascinating. In truth, a study of surviving films,[2] which range from snippets to full-scale productions, extends to the onlooker the rare privilege of witnessing technology giving birth to new narrative possibilities. Among the most mundane entertainments, some innovative employment of a traditional narrative device

[1] In the fall of 1977, relevant early film from the Library of Congress, the Museum of Modern Art, the National Film Archive of Great Britain, and Eastman House was made available for study in preparation for a Spring Conference of the International Federation of Film Archives. This section is deeply grateful to the generosity of these institutions and to the scholars with whom the author shared a week of viewing pleasures: Eileen Bowser, Lucy Fisher, John Gartenberg, Tom Gunning, John Hagan, Jay Leyda, David Levy, Charles Musser, and Paul Spehr. Barry Salt's paper, "The Evolution of Film Form up to 1906," proved especially

helpful with its references to some unviewed British materials.
[2] A vast number of early motion pictures have been preserved only because each was submitted to the Library of Congress for copyright in the form of a paper-print roll copying the original film in its entirety. Over a ten year period, Kemp R. Niver transferred the images back onto motion picture film, thus making the material again available for viewing. The more-than-3000 restored films are described and indexed in Kemp Niver, Motion Pictures from the Library of Congress Paper Print Collection, 1894-1912 (Berkeley, 1967).

32   The Evolution of Narrative

or departing a proscenium, in part to accommodate the earliest studio camera's disinclination to pan (swivel horizontally on its base). Actors played in profile, avoiding movements that would distance them from the camera because available lenses, lighting and film speed contributed to a short depth of field, which limited the area what could be held in focus. But such limitations were short term. Diagonal movements toward or from the camera, as in Lumière's *The Train*, became increasingly common by the turn of the century, and camera pans became almost a fetish during the first decade.

Film Space

Before space was separated by discrete shots and rejoined through editing, other techniques at times serve the purposes of multishot continuity without resorting to any change in camera placement.

Simultaneous playing areas, a theatrical convention dating at least from the early nineteenth century, required that action in one area be overseen from an adjacent location that sustained secrecy. This convention was used in *In a Raines Law Hotel* (American Mutoscope and Biograph, 1905), *The Bridal Chamber* (AM&B 1905), *The Abductors* (AM&B 1905), and *Blackmail* (AM&B 1905). In point of fact, the first three titles were copyrighted on the same day and use an identical set, dressed with minor variations. *Blackmail* is slightly more complicated. Two women enter the outer room of a business office. While one passes into the adjoining private quarters and kisses a man at his desk, her companion photographs the proceedings. Unnerved, the man pays for the picture. While he sits disconsolate at his desk, both women move to the outer area and split the profits. Here, exits and entrances between the two spaces are obscured. A performer disappears momentarily from one office room before reappearing in another. The stagings of the other three films amount simply to cross-sectional views. In each case, the story's "point" requires audience omniscience toward behaviors unbeknownst to all the actors.

Tracking shots, as from a moving vehicle, appear in *The Runaway Match* (1905) where a shot from a moving car is followed by one from the auto chasing it.

Pans seem most often either to widen a purview of vision, that is, to serve the purpose of more distant camera angles, or else functionally to follow action. Another, more occasional, employment substitutes, as it were, for a cut. In *The Little Train Robbery* (Edison 1905), a parody of *The Great Train Robbery* (Edison 1903), performed largely by children and apparently directed by Edwin S. Porter, the bandit gang stops a narrow-gauge railroad train and robs its passengers. One horizontal camera movement follows the escaping bandits on horseback, then pivots back to the victims, bereft in their abandoned railroad car.

Deep space might have produced a like effect in *The Little Train Robbery,* had the camera setup composed a railroad track running from foreground to background in sharp diagonal. Such staging characterizes several Edison war reenactments. For *Charge of Boer Cavalry* (Edison 1900), the camera's high angle encompasses a vast area between two hills where uniformed Boer army cavalry approach the camera, sabres in hand. Distance lends a sort of anonymous authenticity to the staged maneuver, whose seeming actuality is emphasized by passages of horses horizontally across screen, right to left, between camera and soldiers. Similarly, *Red Cross Ambulance on Battlefield* (Edison 1900) — same location, same camera setup — stages involved oval movements in the field, supplemented by the arrival of Red Cross wagons (left to right), repositioning of figures on the field and exits of the vehicles (right to left), all in one shot.

The space-creating techniques of these two war films bear interesting comparison with those used in *The Battle of the Yalu* (*Russo-*

Japanese War) (AM&B 1904). Filmed by William Bitzer in the light snows of New York's Mohawk Valley near Syracuse, separate shots alternate camera angles so that Japanese and Russian troops switch foreground-background relationships, as if one shot were the reverse angle of its precedent. The five-shot "sequence" carries four copyrights, so that one must timidly estimate how often the episodes which are sequential on the Library of Congress Paper Print Roll may actually have been exhibited in such combination.

Attaching separately photographed shots together dates from the earliest days. The step is implicit in the Latham Brothers' Leonard-Cushing prizefight, although kinetoscope capacities required separate machines for each round. Events like Queen Victoria's Diamond Jubilee (1897) were covered with several cameras, and Robert Paul's 1898 catalogue of forty-foot films includes a notation that *Colonial Troops Passing Westminster* can be joined to *Troopers—Continuation of.* We remember that Lumière's agents filmed the coronation of Tsar Nicholas II in seventeen shots during May, 1896. In such events, public performance requires its own continuity, although separate shots do not demand different camera angles. *Admiral Dewey at State House, Boston* (Edison 1899) consists of nine shots and four different setups. There is an implicit narrative progression independent of the fiction movie structure that imposes sequence upon separately shot moments. In contrast, Lumière's boy-and-gardener gag has one-shot autonomy, because it can be staged and executed to the "convenience" of a camera. Early among fiction films, Méliès' *La Lune à un metre* (the moon at one meter) (1898) consists of three like-angled shots.

We find a kind of intermediate stage of continuity in the record of the 1899 Royal Henley Regatta filmed by two British photographers, G. A. Smith and James A. Williamson. There, onshore shots of the race were intercut with others, filmed from a boat, of the cheering crowd. Then, rather than attempting an altogether faithful record, the filmmakers indulge a minimal "liberty" with the event: they organized the different filmed moments to maximize their effect. It is immaterial whether in actuality a cheering crowd applauded those moments that precede and follow it on screen. Such an editing decision suggests early stirrings of film's capacity to create and to impose independent organizing principles upon a world in which photography has required fidelity in the recording of experience.

Edison exploited such techniques and some examples are still available. *Strange Adventures of New York Drummer* (1899) places a traveling salesman in a haunted hotel room. Objects appear and disappear. The salesman unaccountably changes his clothing instantly. To accomplish these effects, a filmmaker stopped his camera midway in an action, re-costuming, say, a performer, Repositioning him on the same spot in identical pose, the cameraman-director recommences action and photography. Projected, the constant-speed succession of images appears to effect a miraculous, inexplicable change, except that the transition usually had to be smoothed over by cutting out excess and inappropriate film frames. Examination of the actual film shows primitive splicing marks between the pivotal images. The notion that shifts may be smoothly managed without viewer awareness of the change is born here.

Strange Adventures of New York Drummer demanded preplanning, sets, and the considered direction of actors; even further, the dramatic film required appearance to inform spectators with a developing awareness of story. While we associate early Edison filming with studio settings, a surprising number of titles, like *Elopement on Horseback* and *Red Cross Ambulance on Battlefield,* were executed out of doors.

Made in 1899, *Love and War,* filmed by the Edison Company and probably executed by James H. White, runs seventy-one feet, again

Two shots from James Williamson's *Fire!* More dramatically composed than like moments in *Life of an American Fireman* (1903), the stagings are otherwise strikingly identical. But similar designs also appear in 1904 song slides for a popular ditty, "The Man With the Ladder and the Hose." (British National Film Archive/Stills Library)

in four scenes: (1) Hero leaves for Spanish-American War; (2) battle; (3) hero wounded and removed from battlefield; (4) hero recuperates in field hospital and is returned to family. Another James A. Williamson film, *Fire!*, dates from 1901 or 1902. The British film breaks action into a sequence of scenes, too: (1) Policemen spots a fire and seeks help; (2) policeman rouses firemen at station; (3) horse and engine hurry to fire; (4) inmate of building trapped by flames is rescued by fireman who breaks through window; (5) fireman descends escape with rescued man; fireman rescues child; another inmate jumps to safety. To enhance effects, portions of the film were dyed or painted red.

With such evidence, we realize that episodic, manipulated narrative structure never sprang full blown from any individual at any

moment. Such design emanated from myriad, scattered worldwide figures, anonymous outside their immediate worlds, unknown to one another except as the circulation of prints increasingly developed a mainstream of storytelling resources.

The appearance of an expository device, often a product of technical experiment, will interrupt unexpectedly. Functional closeups, for example, occur in yet another James Williamson film from 1901 or 1902, *A Big Swallow* (also known as *Englishman Swallows Photographer: Eaten Alive*). Reading in the park and interrupted by a nosy photographer, a gentleman approaches the camera threateningly, until his open mouth encloses the lens itself. A second scene shows cameraman and camera plunging down the throat. Finally, the gentleman is seen again, happily munching.

Bridging Time and Space

In cases where sequentially presented locations are connected by a character's movements from one place to another, i.e., an exit and an entrance, time may sometimes be seen to overlap the two scenes. Thus, during an interior in *The Firebug* (AM&B 1905), a pyromaniac escapes through a basement window pursued by another male figure. The following shot presents an exterior of the same window, and each man reenacts the escape and pursuit. *The Tunnel Workers* (AM&B 1906) carries even more interesting shot pairings. A workman on a tunnel construction gang observes his wife being kissed by the gang's foreman. Later, a tunnel construction is evoked with two sets, one a reverse angle of the other with a background door linking an anterior ready room to a digging site. On the former set, the foreman exits through the door. The workman pauses to gesture his rage toward the camera in a melodramatic aside, then follows. The next scene reenacts the passage of both figures through the door from the adjacent set. At this point, the two fight, and there is an explosion that buries them beneath rocks. Fellow workers rescue both men, carrying them through the door. Then, reverting to the earlier set, we resume the rescue as if continuously — that is, the action reasonably matches what has preceded and time seems smoothly to bridge the cut. A like employment of one door connecting adjacent rooms and scenes figures in *Rounding Up of the "Yeggmen"* (Edison 1904).

A similar instance of continuous time bridged by matching action manifests itself in the cut-in: closer-shot magnifications of elements visible in a preceding, more distant shot. In *Gay Shoe Clerk* (Edison 1903), a salesman adjusting the footwear of a young woman customer is accentuated by a following closeup. Whether action matches is problematical. The continuity of movement may be clumsy or it may be unintentional. *The Little*

Doctors, made by G. A. Smith in 1901, cuts — also inexactly — from long shot to closeup of a kitten being given medicine by two small children. Other cut-ins, although more distant, can be seen in *Life Rescue at Long Branch* (Edison 1901) and *Caught in the Undertow* (AM&B 1902). In each case, the nearer shot maintains the same visual axis as the more distant shot that precedes.

The Strenuous Life; or, Anti-Race Suicide (Edison 1904) complicates matters by implying different intentions for the cut-in. A businessman arrives home with an obstetrician. (The father's passage from foyer to living room suggests continuous time while reversing screen direction; he exits from right to left then enters from left to right.) A maid brings a newborn child downstairs, presenting it to the father, who mimes the baby's heaviness. The maid brings in a scale on which the infant is placed. The father happily gesticulates his offspring's weight. Ambiguously this may be read as seven or twelve pounds. The scale's pointer isn't discernible. A closer shot follows. The father's hand movements are repeated clearly in such a way that his gesticulation should not be read as continuous with the earlier movement, but rather as a restaging of the last expression. So closeups might sometimes be considered as inserts intended to emphasize detail through enlargement and repetition. In *How Old Is Ann?* (Edison 1903), a cut-in is followed by a reversion to its preceding shot. Changes of camera angle thus prove capable of pressing narrative forward as well as providing information.

One of the clearest time-space matches occurs in Porter's *Dream of a Rarebit Fiend*. A long shot of a man flying through space, clinging to the footboard of his bed, culminates in his losing hold and falling, snagging on a weather vane. In medium close shot, the man is then seen hanging from the perch in his nightshirt. A similarly matched continuity appears in Méliès' *Le Voyage à travers l'impossible* (1904). Here, a loose train car plummets over a cliff, followed by a closer shot that preserves speed, screen direction and studio geography with convincing fidelity.

In *The Widow and the Only Man* (AM&B 1904) — which also suggests, like *The Firebug*, that closeups may introduce characters at the beginning of a film — a widow admires her suitor's bouquet, first in long shot then closeup, but her flower-sniffing actions do not match. In *Stolen by Gypsies* (Edison, directed by Porter 1905), the closeup of a baby being diapered advises us of an identifying butterfly birthmark on the child's shoulder, a mark that will later prove important to the story logic. In *The Seven Ages* (Edison 1905), a film distinguished by functional "fireplace" lighting accomplished with an arc floodlight, four of the episodes ("Playmates," "Soldier," "Judge," "Second Childhood") appear with closeup inserts of embracing couples. The "Soldier" material mismatches actor positions from its ear-

lier shot. The discrepancy strikes us by its very unabashed presence.

The schemes that organize multishot films of this period themselves confront problems posed by contiguous space. Notions like a day's experience — *Fun on the Farm* (British 1905) — and famous locations — Coney Island in *Ruby and Mandy at Coney Island* (Edison 1903); *Boarding School Girls* (Edison 1905) are defiantly episodic. Further, they ignore the continuity of proceeding from a geographic overview to the particular. In contrast, an event film, *Execution of Czolgosz wth Panorama of Auburn Prison* (Edison 1900), creates temporal ellipses by telescoping separate moments into a progressive passage from prison exterior to the electric chair within. *Storm at Sea* (Edison 1900), which contains three shots, may be viewed either as a triad of distinct moments, sustained by the idea of atmosphere, or else as showing blustering ocean

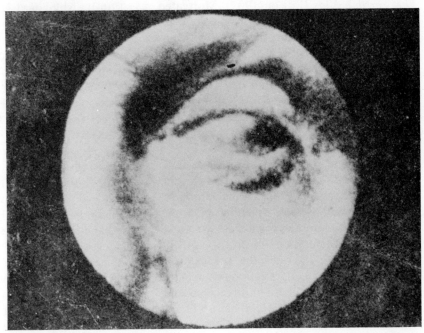

A still from G. A. Smith's *Grandma's Reading Glass*, variously dated between 1898 and 1900. Like Biograph's 1902 remake, *Grandpa's Reading Glass*, the film betrays primitive beginnings of the motivated point-of-view shot: a camera matte simulates a child's subjective perspective. (British National Film Archive/Stills Library)

movements that could be "as seen" by an initially documented shipboard passenger at the railing.

Another way in which the treatment of spatial relationships may be seen to evolve is in terms of physical oppositions presented in certain films. At first, a physical confrontation is visualized in a general manner: an entire prize-fight ring with both antagonists in frame. For example, in *Capture of the Biddle Brothers* (Edison, Porter 1902), mounted men approach the camera from a distance, riding in snow through a forest. Then a sleigh enters, coming from behind the camera and approaching the horsemen. The sleigh's two occupants stop, descend and shoot it out with the approaching figures.

The separation of opposing figures may first transpire in chase films, although pursuer and pursued generally pass diagonally before the viewer in the same shot. An early instance is *The Terrible Kids* (Edison 1902). Motivated by theft or affront, the chase was easy to invent and combined dramatic action with unpretentious mime. It also encouraged convincing shot-to-shot continuity, as long as screen direction was vaguely matched. Early variations on the theme appear in *Maniac Chase* (Edison 1904), which adds trick effects, and in *The Gentleman Highwayman* (AM&B 1905), which uses automobiles. It might be argued that out-of-door filming was a necessary condition for radical shifts in camera angle, the kind that amounted to more daring editing rationales than the mere enlargement of a previous image, because the visual field was freed from studio-set limitations.

Parallel editing intercuts the scenes from one action with those of an action occurring at the same time as in a chase or a rescue scene. This technique was in use long before D. W. Griffith in *The Hundred-to-One-Chance* (Vitagraph 1906), where we shift several times from a racing car to incidents at the spot toward which the car is bound.

Motivating a subsequent shot by glance, often an off-screen look, suggests the overlaying of a subjective vantage onto off-stage theater space. As late at 1904, in *Western Stage Coach Holdup* (Edison), a robbery is preceded by one bandit's peering offscreen in anticipation of the arrival of a stage. The in-camera matted shot appears at least as early as G. A. Smith's *Grandma's Reading Glass* (1898). Children borrow an old lady's magnifying lens. As each holds the glass to his eye, we see an enlargement of what is viewed, a framing black cardboard cut to suggest the glass. The technique is repeated in *As Seen Through a Telescope* (1900) and in *Scenes on Every Floor* (1902); AM&B aped Smith with *Grandpa's Reading Glass* (1902). *A Search for Evidence* (AM&B 1903) simulates keyholes through which a woman spies activities in various hotel rooms while seeking her husband. In *Battle of Chemulpo Bay* (Edison 1904), a shipboard gun crew fires at Russian battleships. One sailor raises binoculars to his eyes, and we cut to a circular matte that encloses a flag closeup. Gunfire devastates the flag, and we cut back to shipboard.

In *Tour du monde d'un policier* (A policeman's world cruise) (Pathé 1905), a shipboard detective views Suez Canal traffic with binoculars, and we see the scene ourselves through a two-circle matte. A like technique appears, more fully developed, in *Revolution en Russe* (Pathé, directed by Lucien Nonguet 1906). In this eight-shot film, which recounts the Potemkin mutiny, a deckboard officer, telescope in hand, views the besieged, burning town of Odessa. Then, as if seen through the telescope, a family flees the bombardment. Cut back to deck officer, who lowers his instrument and speaks to the gun crew. He raises the telescope. The "subjective," matted telescope view is repeated, followed again by an objective shot of its user on deck. A skillful simulation of the subjective point-of-view through an apparent keyhole matte appears in animation as early as 1912. Ladislas Starevitch's *The Revenge of the Kinematograph Cameraman,* a puppet film executed in Russia, evokes *A Search for Evidence,* but has its fictional cinematographer actually filming through the aperture (see Chapter 15).

Evidence of predesign can help to distinguish the self-conscious efforts at bridging time and space from the fortuitous ones. As shots increase in single films, their sequence can be designated as nonrepeating or else to be rescheduling earlier camera setups. In Porter's *The White Caps* (Edison 1905), Shot 1 consists of an exterior cottage entrance, through which a drunken man enters. Shot 2, cottage interior, shows the man beating his wife. Shot 3 exactly repeats the composition of Shot 1. Woman and daughter flee. A famous case in point is *The Great Train Robbery,* in which the same railroad station interior appears as shots 1 and 10.

In *The Suburbanites* (AM&B 1904), a 14-shot story filmed both on location at Asbury Park, New Jersey and in Biograph's New York studio, repeated shots of the same sets (a kitchen, a living room) are checkerboarded with one another. Further, the final shot, an exterior, is separated from any earlier exterior by 5 shots. Such reliance on script suggests increasing awarenesses that spatial relationships can be realized through editing, which is to say, through preconception.

Relation of Angle to Narrative Agent

The sum total of more complex employments of narrative devices generated a sometimes unanswerable question, one relevant today, namely: "Who is telling the story?" Closeups generally suggest a kind of facilitating agency maximizing our understanding. Distant shots, as with Edison's Boer War films, pretend to candor and accident by clever stagings of horizontal movements contrary to the primary, vertical screen directions. The compositions of Biograph's seemingly least-talented cameraman, one Weed — *Novel Way of Catching a Burglar* (1904), *A Windy Day on the Roof* (1904) — are composed of single shot gags with bottom-frame figures cut off intentionally at the torso, maximizing our interest in what remains unseen.

If pans serve most often as bridging agents, there is a provoking moment in *Stolen by Gypsies.* A gypsy kidnaps a baby untended on the family lawn. He skulks left into a carriage and exits. Camera then pans right to a distant side of the house. Here, different, new robbers appear, escaping with a bag of chickens. This pair is pursued by the household, some of whom mistake the thieves for the kidnappers. As audience, with fore-knowledge independent from and superior to the experience of the performers, we occupy a seemingly unique relation to the unfolding events. Narrative approaches a new level of complication when Porter manipulates, rather than merely easing, the order of our perceptions.

Because of general unavailability, materials of Vitagraph, Selig and Lubin, as well as many French, British and Italian titles have so far been less carefully considered than Edison and Biograph work. Whether further study will radically shift current schemes of early film "history" remains unclear and is perhaps unlikely, but the very anonymity of much early work underlines one's sense that noteworthy achievement rests not so much on technical innovation as in putting technique to use through a coherent integration of narrative conventions. The early filmmakers of developing stature, Méliès, Porter and Hepworth, answered this challenge successfully. Further, they mounted many productions of increased ambition. However primitive their work may look to modern eyes, these men contributed most heavily to film's emergence from the innocence of birth.

Georges Méliès (1861–1938)

Une partie de cartes/Playing Cards	1896
Cortège du Tzar allant à Versailles/The Czar's Excursion to Versailles	1896
Séance de prestidigitation/Conjuring	1896
Le Cabinet de Mephistophélès/ The Laboratory of Mephistopheles	1897
Le Cuirassé Main/The Battleship Maine	1898
L'Homme de tête/The Man of Heads	1898
La Lune à un mètre/The Moon from One Meter Away	1898
Guilliame Tell/William Tell	1898
La Caverne maudite/The Cave of the Demons	1898
Le Christ marchant sur les eaux/Christ Walking on Water	1899
L'Affaire Dreyfus/The Dreyfus Affair	1899
Cendrillon/Cinderella	1899
La Danse de feu/The Pillar of Fire	1899
Le Miroir de Cagliostro/Cagliostro's Mirror	1899
Jeanne d'Arc/Joan of Arc	1900
Barbe-bleu/Bluebeard	1901
Le Voyage de Gulliver à Lilliput et chez les géants/Gulliver's Travels	1902
Les Adventures de Robinson Crusoe/ Robinson Crusoe	1902
Le Voyage dans la lune/A Trip to the Moon	1902
Damnation du Dr. Faust/The Damnation of Faust	1903
Le Royaume des fées/The Kingdom of the Fairies	1903
Le Voyage à travers l'impossible/The Impossible Voyage	1904
Benvenuto Cellini	1904
Le Barbier de Seville/The Barber of Seville	1904
Le Raid Paris-Monte Carlo en deux heures/Paris to Monte Carlo	1905
Le Palais des Mille et une nuits/ The Palace of a Thousand and One Nights	1905
Les 400 farces du diable/The Devil's 400 Tricks	1906

GEORGES MÉLIÈS

Son of a well-to-do family, Georges Méliès learned the tricks of conjuring and managed a magician's theater in Paris, the Robert Houdin. He was also a caricaturist, scene designer, and actor. A demonstration of the cinématographe impressed the thirty-four year-old Méliès, and he tried to buy one. He was undiscouraged by Louis Lumière's response, which echoed Edison. Viewing film as a passing fad, a novelty, Lumière warned that the motion picture might enjoy short popularity as a curiosity, but its commercial value was most certainly transient. Unable to obtain the cinématographe, Méliès bought a Bioscope projector from Robert Paul in England. Until death, Lumière held Méliès accountable for usurping his own success, but Lumière lived to comfortable retirement; his competitor died poverty-stricken.

Méliès installed the Bioscope in his theater. He secured a camera from Georges Demeny, an inventor, and incorporated as Star Film, whose first production was *Une partie de cartes/Playing Cards* (1896), in which its director acted a player.

In 1897, Méliès constructed a film studio on his estate at Montreuil-sous-Bois. Named Atelier de Poses (Modeling Studio), this first full-fledged production center in film history employed glass walls and roof to maximize sunlight. Inside, a moveable stage accomodated sets designed for rapid scene changes and stage machinery, as well as trap doors, strings and pullies for flying effects. In many respects, the studio recreated the Robert Houdin theater. To the theatrical resources, the filmmaker added trick film techniques as he learned or invented them, but for Méliès film was always an extension of the magician's stage. Méliès played his trickery to the camera. For example, in creating the impression of a head (his own) expanding grotesquely, or a rocket ship moving toward the moon, the director mounted his subject on a cart that rode by tracks to approach or recede from a stationary camera. (In contrast, Paul mounted his camera on a railed trolley in his New Southgate studio.)

Like those of Lumière, many early efforts were shot out of doors, but Méliès' work soon became studio-bound. Most fell into three idioms: contemporary events, historical recreations and fantasy. Following the famous Dreyfus trial, Méliès capitalized on a second court-martial that disclosed that false evidence had sent Captain Dreyfus to Devil's Island, *The Dreyfus Affair* (1899) was Méliès' first ambitious attempt—650 feet. Reenactments included *Joan of Arc* (1900) and *Shakespeare Writing Julius Caesar* (1907). Méliès also made films of *The Czar's Excursion to Versailles* (1896), *Benvenuto Cellini* (1904), and *The Barber of Seville* (1904). Trickery elaborated biblical anecdote in *Christ Walking on the Waters* (1899), but Méliès' most common ventures and his most successful were out-and-out fantasies.

Often such films originated in literature (*Faust, Gulliver's Travels*), fairytale (*Blue Beard*), and myth (*Jupiter's Thunderbolts*). Méliès was the first film personality consistently to "adapt." One of his most effective genres was science fantasy, most closely associated with Jules Verne: underground, underwater and interplanetary travel.

Understandably, many special effects are associated with Méliès. He effected a transformation in *La Danse du Feu/The Pillar of Fire* (1899), based on the scene in Rider Haggard's novel *She*, in which a beautiful, ageless woman suddenly grows ancient. Superimpositions are said by Maurice Bessy, a Méliès biographer, to appear first in *La Caverne maudite/The Cave of the Demons* (1898). These were created in the camera by rewinding the exposed footage from one scene, then filming another, separate action on the same film. Ghostly apparitions materialize in *Séance de prestidigitation/Conjuring* (1896). More important, this technique facilitated the dissolve, that is, the introduction of a new scene simultaneous with the gradual disappearance on screen of what has preceded.

Méliès' very titles, his selection of significant moments, evidence scenes chosen for

L'Atelier de poses. Fifty-five by twenty feet with roof peak twenty feet above, Méliès' studio intentionally resembles a greenhouse. When withdrawn to an adjoining shed, the camera could accomodate thirty-six foot compositions. The director is at right. The vehicle prop will soon appear in *Off to Bloomingdale Asylum* (1901). (French Cultural Services)

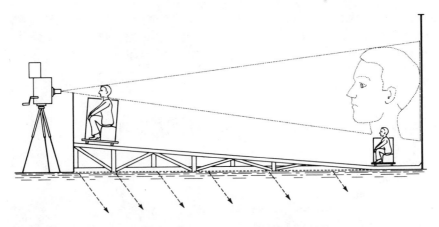

Méliès' movement of the performer rather than the camera figures less importantly as an illustration of filmed theater than as a technique of special effects. This staging was used in *L'Homme à la tête de caoutchout/The Man With the Rubber Head* (1901). (From Bessy and Lo Duca, *Georges Méliès, Mage.*)

spectacle and magic effect. By now, the capacity of motion pictures to mystify had been somewhat explored worldwide. Copy the sequence of frames backwards in the printer, or else run film through the camera in reverse (so that on projection, movement would appear to go backward), overcrank rapidly on exposure (so that the projected image would appear in slow motion), and undercrank (for a speeded-up effect). If an object were slightly moved between exposures, it would appear to have a life of its own (pixilation). If a card matted out all but one portion of a scene, as in *Grandma's Reading Glass,* and then that scene were rewound and reexposed with only the unexposed portion now visible (in-camera matte), two separately photographed scenes would seem to be one.

However elaborate in their effects, however often the camera might stop and start in preparing them, early Méliès films still look like one-shot, one-angled productions: an act at the Robert Houdin seen from a center-aisled, orchestra seat. Indeed, of all filmmakers, Méliès most identified movies with theater. He prepared his titles and credits on drawings that simulated theater curtains. Stage sets used period theatrical designs including backcloth, friezes and wings. At key moments during the performance and on its conclusion, he and other actors might bow and wave at the camera, acknowledging the presumed laughter and applause. The filmmaker drew on dancers and other performers from the Folies-Bergère and the Châtelet for his casts.

As ventures grew more ambitious, they required breaking up action into separate scenes. Descriptively, "scene" fits Méliès, for characteristically (but not always) he connected each shot to its neighbor by a dissolve, equivalent to a theater curtain's traditional indication of a passage of time and/or a shift in location.

A Méliès version of *Cinderella* (1899) staged the fairytale in twenty scenes:

1. *Cinderella in the Kitchen*
2. *The Fairy*
3. *The Transformation of the Rat*
4. *The Pumpkin Changes to a Carriage*
5. *The Ball at the King's Palace*
6. *The Hour of Midnight*
7. *The Bedroom of Cinderella*
8. *The Dance of the Clocks*

Georges Méliès   **43**

Like Méliès' other fantasies and extravaganzas, *Cinderella* used theatrical timing, staging and display. Conceived as mime, the material had little of the exaggerated, inexplicable confusions of Sarah Bernhardt's silent emoting. *Cinderella* proved successful in France and abroad. *Joan of Arc,* which followed, held to twelve scenes, but boasted a costumed "cast of five hundred." In 1902, Méliès produced his most ambitious work to date, *Le Voyage dans la lune/A Trip to the Moon.*

A Trip to the Moon has a casual relation to one of Jules Verne's stories, *From the Earth to the Moon and Around the Moon.* Essentially it is a light satire of science and of contemporary notions on space travel and extraterrestrial life. The film cost 10,000 gold francs, and ran 845 feet with thirty scenes.

Méliès commences his story with a meeting of the Scientific Congress at the Astronomic Club. Here, sober-faced professor types in frock coats are reduced from discussion to frenzy by the intrusion of a manic academic, played by Méliès. A moon expedition is planned, and Méliès' stage-bound imagery is most evident in a rocket construction scene in which workers hammer at their tasks like little animated figures in a windup toy. Still frock-coated, the astronomers are led by Méliès into their rocket shell, which is pushed into a cannon by a leggy chorus line. The gun is fired, followed by a shot of the man in the moon,

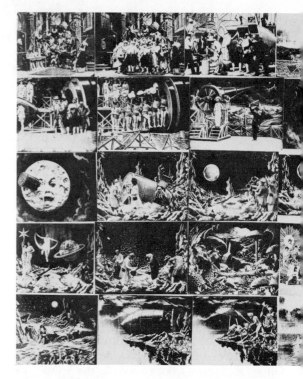

A Trip to the Moon. Some scenes are repeated here at different stages; others are omitted. Selenites were Folies-Bergère acrobats, the gunners Châtelet dancers. *The Astronomer's Dream, or The Man in the Moon* (1898) preceded, and *An Impossible Voyage* (1904) used an identical plot to yet more remarkable effect. (Museum of Modern Art/Film Stills Archive)

whose size increases to fill the screen until the rocket lands in his eye. Astronauts disembark and fall asleep on the ground. In the sky appears a collective dream of planets and constellations, peopled with pretty girls and Saturn. The men wake in a snow storm and are attacked by moon men (Selenites), who hop alarmingly on all fours. Méliès strikes some with his umbrella; each disappears in a wisp of smoke. Overpowered, the scientists are brought to an underground grotto. Breaking free and popping more Selenites, Méliès leads his astronauts to the ship, which drops off a precipice back to the earth. The projectile falls into the ocean, and is drawn to the surface; the explorers return in a ship. At this point, most known versions of *A Trip to the Moon* conclude, although Méliès lists additional episodes in his Star catalogue: the Great Fête; Triumphal March Past; Crowning and Decorating the Heroes of the Trip; Procession of Marines and the Fire Brigade; Inauguration of the Commemorative Statue by the Manager and the Council; Public Rejoicings; and Exhibition of the Selenite.

Although Méliès considered *A Trip to the Moon* one of his lesser works, its extravagant invention augured quick success. Méliès' popularity, however, proved a mixed blessing, for worldwide pirates illegally duplicated prints of the film. Lacking copyright protection and victimized by his own policy of selling rather than leasing prints, the Frenchman lost huge sums to film bootleggers despite appeals to customers in his catalogue.

Méliès followed his science fiction entertainment in 1903 with an even longer sixteen-minute film. *Le Royaume des fées/ The Kingdom of the Fairies* was made up of thirty-two "tableaux," and included cartoon work, miniatures on tabletop, sliding sets, underwater effects shot through fishtanks and the combination of slide projections with live-action photography. Its undersea cavern and models of swimming monsters are even more wildly conceived than the Selenites.

Méliès' success reinforced public interest in film story and through his films audiences learned what might be expected from a movie. In point of fact, his linkage of effects by means of a simple, witty dramatic thread aped story inventions that supported the stage technique of an English conjurer, John Nevil Maskelyne. Abundantly imagined productions continued — 500 in Méliès' lifetime — but two factors finally outdistanced his skills. One was the rapid evolution of movie storytelling during the next ten years, when movies became a largely out-of-doors medium and rejected mechanisms of the nineteenth-century stage. In his Montreuil-sous-Bois studio, Méliès lost touch with new techniques and tastes.

The second factor in Méliès' decline was a growing ruthlessness and sophistication among rival film businessmen: Pathé and Gaumont in particular. They not only stole Méliès' ideas and sometimes his films, but also developed great monopolistic enterprises that dwarfed and finally bested Star Film. A profit-sharing contract with Pathé in 1911 had failed by 1913 and the Montreuil-sous-Bois property was lost to creditors. Later, Méliès sold candy and toys in a little Paris shop. He had marginal relations with the film industry during the late twenties and thirties, and died of cancer in 1938.

Above all else, Méliès demonstrated that the motion picture need not fall servant to what it photographs but rather can create an independent reality. At its beginnings, film history is illuminated by Méliès' presence and sadly diminished because he destroyed all Star Film negatives in 1923.

Méliès' rivals, Pathé and Gaumont, both made film equipment like Lumière. Each entered production, Pathé moving into the manufacture of motion picture film as well. By 1912, Pathé's profits had risen to 8 million francs. The two companies dominated much of world film until World War I.

EDWIN S. PORTER

Edwin Stratton Porter left the US Navy in 1896 with some skill as a mechanic and electrician and found employment operating vitascope projectors in New York. Soon he bought a "Projectorscope" from the International Film Company, joined a partnership, and journied to San Jose in Costa Rica, where Porter rented a theater and exhibited excitements like *Annabelle's Butterfly Dance* to the populace under the imposing pseudonym of Thomas A. Edison, Jr.

Porter later worked Nova Scotia and Quebec, then joined the Edison Company itself as a mechanic and handyman. He was soon working with James H. White in the production of motion pictures. Their first major venture was *The Life of an American Fireman* (1903).

The Life of an American Fireman suggests close familiarity with the Englishman James Williamson's *Fire!* In seven scenes, a fireman first dozes in his chair, dreaming of a mother and child, perhaps his own family. A fire alarm is rung, and firemen rush from their beds in response. Horse and hose carts speed from the engine house to the fire. On arrival, the original fireman breaks through the door first to save a mother and then her child (who look like those he had dreamed in the first scene).

Contrary to popular opinion, the Porter-White film may not have been made up in part from "stock footage" of fire department activi-

ties,[3] but proves interesting as narrative for other reasons. Between Shot 1 (fireman asleep) and Shot 3 (fireman aroused), Porter relates the fire alarm closeup to its context by implication, the three episodes assuming a single meaning because of their sequence. What the Edison catalogue describes as "Scene 7, Arrival at the Fire" is still more instructive. It consists not of a single shot, like the preceding scenes and like all Méliès' "tableaux," but rather, action has been dismantled into separately staged, separately photographed components, so that we begin to experience a notion that the time and pace of an actual behavior need not coincide with its perception on screen. A filmmaker may choose to

[3] *Jack Spears, "Edwin S. Porter,"* Films in Review *(June-July 1970).*

The Life of an American Fireman. The first two frames capture a theatrical "vision scene," just as Porter simulated other stage devices in *Uncle Tom's Cabin.* Left half of the composition reads first, like facing comic book pages. Action match (or mismatch) connects the final two scenes. (Museum of Modern Art/Film Stills Archive)

regulate how long we will watch an event and, too, how we shall see it, that is, our angle of view.

In fact, *The Life of an American Fireman* exists in more than one Edison version. This was not uncommon in early film days, because copying a print in the laboratory soon damaged the original's perforations, causing slippage and blur, so that a popular film was often restaged or else recut from extant but as yet unused footage, or simply reprinted and then re-edited. The two versions of *Fireman* are essentially alike, however, but for the manner of their editing in Scene 7. (Both differ from Edison's catalogue description.) One stages the camera view of distressed mother and daughter from within the trapped bedroom; here we view the mother's rescue. This is followed by a repeat of the same action as seen from outside. The fireman mounts the ladder and carries the woman down to safety. The other version escapes the problem of repeated action by varying point-of-view in time with the rescue movement itself. Thus, the fireman carries the woman to the window, seen from inside, then, allowing for a somewhat clumsy mismatch between the shots, we see the action continue from outside as he steps from window to ladder and carries his burden to safety (In staging, the continuity and action "match," here echo *Fire!*). Fireman then returns to save the child.

It is as if the first version (if it was first) constituted a kind of learning stage for Porter, the editor, for on viewing the results he would seem to have realized that however often a continuous action must be restaged from different camera angles, it needs finally to flow continuously forward, without backtracking.

Now Porter seems to have assumed more complete responsibility for the Edison productions. His next venture was *Uncle Tom's Cabin* (1903), based on the many Tom shows that had toured ever since the Civil-War success of Harriet Beecher Stowe's novel. By the twentieth century, *Uncle Tom's Cabin* had degenerated into a few required scenes. Audiences attended stage performances confident of anger and tears that would attend the death of Tom, Eliza's escape across the ice and Little Eva's ascent to heaven.

Porter keeps faith with the Tom shows, and provides a fascinating artifact of turn-of-the-century melodrama, including an escape across ice floes, which must have resembled the stage machinery of second-class theaters. There are, too, conventional vision scenes, as in *The Life of an American Fireman,* Scene 1, when a man's revery was projected above his head like a "dream balloon" in the comics. While Uncle Tom dies, we see visions of Little Eva and of Abraham Lincoln emancipating the slaves. Eva's angelic rise to heaven is done with double exposure instead of ropes, her ascending, nightgowned body an overlaid picture appearing in the death scene.

Edwin S. Porter (1870–1941)

The American Cup Race	1899
The Life of an American Fireman (with James H. White)	1903
Uncle Tom's Cabin	1903
Gay Shoe Clerk	1903
A Romance of the Rails	1903
The Great Train Robbery	1903
The Ex-Convict	1904
Jack and the Beanstalk	1904
The Kleptomaniac	1905
The Dream of a Rarebit Fiend	1906
The Seven Ages	1906
Rescued from an Eagle's Nest	1907
The Prisoner of Zenda	1913
In the Bishop's Carriage	1913
Hearts Adrift	1913
A Good Little Devil	1913
Tess of the Storm Country	1914
The Dictator	1915
The Eternal City (co-director Hugh Ford)	1915
Partial listing	

Gay Shoe Clerk and *A Romance of the Rails* (1903) followed *Uncle Tom*. The latter is an advertising venture for the Lackawana Railroad,[4] "proving" that a pretty, white-gowned woman can ride smoky trains without fear of dirt. Even tramps dressed in evening clothes ride the rods free of cinders or soot. Based on his work with the railroad, Porter negotiated the loan of a train for *The Great Train Robbery* (1903).

Filmed in the fall, *The Great Train Robbery*

[4] *Edison and AM&B were shooting cigarette commercials as early as 1896.*

develops Porter's narrative skills one more step. As with *Fireman*, he capitalized on topical interest, this time western outlaws and railroad thefts. Such events figured heavily in dime novels of the period, associated often with glamorized badmen like the James Boys, or a new hero, the cowboy detective. They also played in popular melodrama, and Porter adapted his movie from Scott Marble's *The Great Train Robbery*, which had appeared at New York's Bowery Theater seven years before.

The film opens with two masked outlaws breaking into a railroad telegraph office. They

The Great Train Robbery. The holdup. Opinion remains divided whether the apparently exterior railroad train was accomplished by in-camera matting (blacking out appropriate sections and double exposing these) or with an optical printer (which might accomplish special effects in the course of printing the original picture on new film stock). The latter must have been used for *Uncle Josh at the Moving Picture Show* (1902), for an earlier Edison film appears there. Later, the bandits' baggage-car holdup uses the above set with a similarly placed matte. (Museum of Modern Art/Film Stills Archive)

force the operator to signal an oncoming train to stop, then bind and bludgeon him. When the train pauses to take on water, the bandits sneak aboard. In the baggage car, they shoot an attendant, blow up a strongbox and seize the valuables. The badmen then hold up the engineer and subdue the fireman, throwing him off the speeding train. The train stopped, the bandits force the passengers outside, rob them, and shoot one attempting to escape. They flee in the uncoupled locomotive, and then escape into the woods where confederates are waiting with horses. At the telegraph office, the operator is revived by his young daughter. He alarms the patrons of a local dance hall, who form a posse. Posse chases bandits, killing one man on horseback, then dispatching the rest as they are apprehended dividing their loot.

What is novel about *The Great Train Robbery* is the choice of locales and camera angles, for even though the camera keeps at middle distance, it angles compositions in the exterior shots to maximize diagonal movement. But for the return to the telegraph office, each location progresses the story by its appearance. More important, the story lends itself to mime and a forward-thrusting action because it is exciting. Altough Porter allows each shot to complete its own movement, rather than cutting in anticipation of the next scene, the elements of assault, murder, robbery, pursuit, and vengeance press the plot along. More ably than in *The Life of an American Fireman,* Porter cuts from studio sets, the office, and the dance hall to exteriors; even though the Old West as seen from the speeding locomotive is belied by Patterson, New Jersey telephone poles, the view from a speeding train enforces its own appeal. When the outlaws leap from the locomotive down an embankment to the woods, Porter's camera swivels and angles diagonally to follow the action. Some prints of *The Great Train Robbery* were hand painted with red to intensify gunshots and the dynamite explosion.

The film has disconcerting moments: the daughter pausing to pray before throwing water in her unconscious father's face; the sagging bundle that is supposed to be a fireman pitched overboard; the murdered passenger dies with alarming histrionics, and one bandit, mounting from the wrong side, has a dreadful time getting on his horse. Porter's direction of actors is execrable. At the same time, story moves with unaccountable ease for the period. Porter substituted sensation for Méliès' spectacle. The difference is epitomized in a shot of outlaw George Barnes firing a pistol directly at the audience in closeup. Edison's catalogue said: "The resulting excitement is great. This scene can be used to begin or end the picture."

Noteworthy, too, in Porter's film is the lapse allowed between the two telegraph office shots. As audience, we are unconcerned whether this time corresponds exactly to what happened in the interim: robbery, murders and escape. Dramatic necessity returns us to the office when necessary. Similarly, we do not care about unaccounted time and movement between the operator's exit from his office and his entrance into the dance hall, or between that scene and its follow-up, the chase. It is evident that Porter had suspected that dramatic incident can stretch or contract clocktime with impunity, so long as audience anticipation is satisfied with its "rightness."

The Great Train Robbery was the country's first hit. It even initiated a cowboy career for Max Aronson, "Bronco Billy" Anderson, who took so long to mount his horse. Sigmund Lubin paid Edison his usual tribute to success by immediately preparing another *Great Train Robbery* (1904), soon followed by *The Bold Bank Robbery* (1904).

After this success, Porter made *The Ex-Convict* (1904) and *The Kleptomaniac* (1905), both hinting social criticism, if covertly. In one, an industrialist refuses to hire an ex-convict; in the other a well-to-do woman is apprehended for shoplifting while a poor mother is caught stealing bread to feed her starving children. Porter underlines his messages by intercutting for the sake of contrast. *The Ex-Convict* ends happily; he is rewarded for saving a little girl's life. In *The Kleptomaniac,* a statue of justice is seen peeking over her bandage; on her scale, a bag of gold outweighs a feather.

Other Porter work imitates the Méliès style: *Jack and the Beanstalk* (1904), *The Dream of a Rarebit Fiend* (1906). Either from edict or inclination, Porter never elaborated his narrative skills further. He left Edison and formed an independent company, Rex, in 1911, then moved the next year to Adolph Zukor's Famous Players Company where he directed its first feature, *The Prisoner of Zenda* (1913). Porter's last film, *The Eternal City,* was shot in Rome in 1915, after which he retired, a wealthy man who lost his money in the crash of 1929 and returned to mechanical work in the machine shop of an appliance corporation.

CECIL M. HEPWORTH

Unlike Porter, the British Cecil Hepworth grew up in a middle-class atmosphere and many of his films reflect the experience; before Griffith, he was a "class" director. Hepworth entered filmmaking by way of his father, devising a lighting system for magic lantern projection during the older man's science lectures. The design was integrated into the motion picture projector of Robert W. Paul.

Young Hepworth secured some of Paul's discarded film footage and it won his heart. In his father's footsteps, Hepworth developed a film-and-slide presentation with which he toured lecture halls. He joined the company Maguire and Baucus, Edison's English agents, where he developed first a flickerless projector then an early film developing tank. He began a film processing laboratory at Walton-on-Thames and commenced producing fifty-foot

titles. The first was *Express Trains in a Railway Cutting* (1898). Within two years, the company was producing about one hundred films a year, two hundred by 1906.

An apparent Hepworth innovation was the use of earlier footage for different story purpose. *Peace With Honour* (1902) intercuts news film from the Boer War with a newsboy proclaiming the peace and then an allegorical encounter between Britannia, Lord Kitchener and the dispirited Boer. *Alice in Wonderland* (1903) followed the Tennial illustrations, running sixteen scenes and 800 feet.

Like other Englishmen, Hepworth's disposition was to film out of doors at first, and most of his earliest subjects are unstaged. A traveling shot resulted from mounting a camera on the front of a locomotive for *View from an Engine Front — Shilla Mill Tunnel* (1900). The first studio was a ten-foot by six-foot wooden platform bounded on one side by uprights against which to rest the scenery flats. The 1903, indoor studio combined open-arc lamps with muranese glass to diffuse the sunlight. The same year, audience and revenue were expanded when Hepworth, along with other major British companies, entered into a system of reciprocal film exchange with American Mutoscope and Biograph. At this stage, the American width and sprocket hole dimensions were agreed upon as standard both by the British and the French filmmakers.

Hepworth filmed *Rescued by Rover* in 1905, a movie that sold more than 400 prints over a four to five year lifetime. Again, *Rescued by Rover* exists in several versions, but the earliest is also the most effective. The plot was conceived by Mrs. Hepworth. It is said to be the first British film for which actors were paid.

Wheeling a baby carriage along the street, a nurse is accosted by a gypsy woman asking for charity. Rebuffed, the gypsy steals the baby while the nurse is chatting with a boyfriend. Nurse is next seen bursting into the parents' home to break the news. Rover, the family collie, listens, licks the nurse's face, and leaps out the window. Rover runs through the neighborhood, coming to a stream, which he swims. In a slum area, he checks each entrance until he finds the right house, pushing the door ajar and entering. In the basement, he finds and comforts the baby. Her kidnapper returns and chases Rover away. The collie runs home by the identical route, informs the grief-stricken father with insistent barks, and leads him to the hideaway. The child is rescued and returned to the mother. Rover licks everybody.

In design. *Rescued by Rover* differs little from Porter's epics. The rebuff to the gypsy sets off the action like the *Fireman's* alarm box or the attack on the telegraph operator in *The Great Train Robbery*. What impresses in the film are its editing skills and the choices of camera position. More fully than his predecessors, Hepworth fashions his little story to indulge a continuous forward thrust. Hepworth draws on rescue and retribution conventions, but it is the continuity of action itself, carrying over from shot to shot with the collie's bounds, that earns audience involvement.

Further, Hepworth has learned a technique that D. W. Griffith was often to exploit. Mrs. Hepworth's tale is structured to repeat itself in identical shots with contrary movement, that is: Rover jumps from his window, fords the stream, and enters the gypsy's house moving left to right, left to right. He returns through the same locations and like or near-identical setups right to left. He leads his master to the rescue in a repetition of the first screen patterns. The locales, distances and routes become familiar to a screen audience after a first exposure, and they, too, invest the story with meaning. We even know that a boat waits at riverside for the father to use. (A nearby bridge is unaccountably ignored throughout.)

Hepworth's success stems, also, from his editing decisions. The dog's movements shot-to-shot are so thoughtfully matched in terms of screen direction and rhythm that we accept

a fiction of apparent continuity between the separate locations. We are undisturbed by spatial ellipse just as we are unaffected by the truncation of passing time between the moment the baby is kidnapped and the moment

Cecil M. Hepworth (1874–1953)

the nurse bursts into the house. Omitted time and space become irrelevant because of audience anticipation. Rover continued to rescue for the Hepworth company until 1914, abetted by a pony, a pigeon and, once, an elephant.

Falsely Accused (1905) ran fourteen minutes, about twice as long as *Rescued by Rover*. A business clerk is given bank notes to lock up. Their numbers are noted by the audience (closeup), and their value by another clerk who makes a wax impression of the safe's key. That night the criminal clerk steals the notes, leaving two of them and the wax in the first clerk's drawer. In the morning, theft and incriminating evidence are discovered (closeup of wax). Momentarily believed through the fervor of his innocent protestations, the clerk returns home, where he is arrested. Working in a prison quarry, he escapes through the help of sympathetic prisoners, fleeing to a vicar's study. The vicar apprehends him, but believing his story, disguises the clerk as a curate when prison officials arrive. The vicar lends him money. The criminal clerk goes to a gambling den, which has earlier been spotted by police who now surround it. They raid the game, apprehending the villain with the bank notes in his hand. A policeman recognizes the notes' numbers. At the innocent clerk's home, where he is comforting his wife, the policeman arrives and announces the criminal's capture. A final scene shows the criminal raging behind bars.

Falsely Accused sustains a far more involved plot than anything that had preceded, perhaps too much story for its length. The film makes use of enough little "bits" (clerk as curate sitting with unsuspecting pursuers, villain taunted by fellow gamblers so that he defiantly uses the stolen notes) to suggest directions fiction film was to take as it approached feature length. *Falsely Accused* is a feature film in miniature, lacking only more clearly drawn characterizations of future films. A similarly involving story appears in *A Den of Thieves* (1904 or 1905).

Hepworth withdrew from production for a period, to return in 1913. He made fifty features, increasingly producing rather than directing work up until 1923 when the company went bankrupt through overexpansion. The Englishman spent much of the remainder of his life making trailers (previews) for his country's National Screen Service.

Summary

Méliès, Porter and Hepworth won reputations in film history by organizing expository techniques into coherent narrative patterns.

Certain narrative conventions—such as switching from place to place for the sake of suspense or "visualizing" thought by vision-scene images—traveled directly from fiction and theater into film. In other respects, motion pictures evolved unique techniques: astonishing by way of special "effects" (*A Trip to the Moon*), creating meaning through juxtaposition (*The Life of an American Fireman*), using motion to bridge continuity (*Rescued by Rover*).

Yet the speed of change quickly converted such past accomplishment to cliché. By the second decade of the new century, narrative film had so evolved that the films just recounted looked woefully dated in comparison to new work of greater ambition. During the next years, the length, scope, complexity and skilled execution of motion pictures were amplified by many figures, but the most notable of these was D. W. Griffith, whose story follows.

Bibliography

Bessy, Maurice, "Méliès." *Anthologie du Cinéma,* 1966.

Bessy, Maurice and Lo Duca. *Georges Méliès.* Paris, 1945.

Fell, John L. *Film and the Narrative Tradition.* Norman, Okla., 1974.

Gessner, Robert. "The Moving Image." *American Heritage* 11 (April 1960).

Hammond, Paul. *Marvelous Méliès.* New York, 1975.

Hollyman, Burns. "Alexander Black's Picture Plays: 1893-1894." *Cinema Journal* 16 (Spring 1977).

Jacobs, Lewis. *The Rise of the American Film.* New York, 1939.

Jowett, Garth S. "The First Motion Picture Audiences," *Journal of Popular Film,* Winter, 1974.

Low, Rachel. *The History of the British Film 1906-1914.* London, 1949.

Low, Rachel and Roger Manvell. *The History of the British Film 1896-1906.* London, 1948.

Malthête-Méliès, Madeleine. *Méliès l'enchanteur.* Paris, 1973.

National Film Library Catalogue. Part I: Silent News Film 1895–1933. London, 1951.

Niver, Kemp. *In the Beginning: Program Notes to Accompany One Hundred Early Motion Pictures.* New York, n.d.

———. *Motion Pictures from the Library of Congress Paper Print Collection: 1894-1912.* Berkeley, 1967.

———. *The First Twenty Years a Segment of Film History.* Los Angeles, 1968.

Perry, George. *The Great British Picture Show.* New York, 1974.

Ramsaye, Terry. *A Million and One Nights.* 2 vols. New York, 1962.

Sadoul, Georges. *French Film.* London, 1953.

———. *Dictionary of Film Makers.* Berkeley, 1972.

Salt, Barry. "The Early Development of Film Form," *Film Form,* Spring 1976.

Spears, Jack. "Edwin S. Porter." *Films in Review,* June-July 1970.

Wenden, D. J. *The Birth of the Movies.* London, 1974.

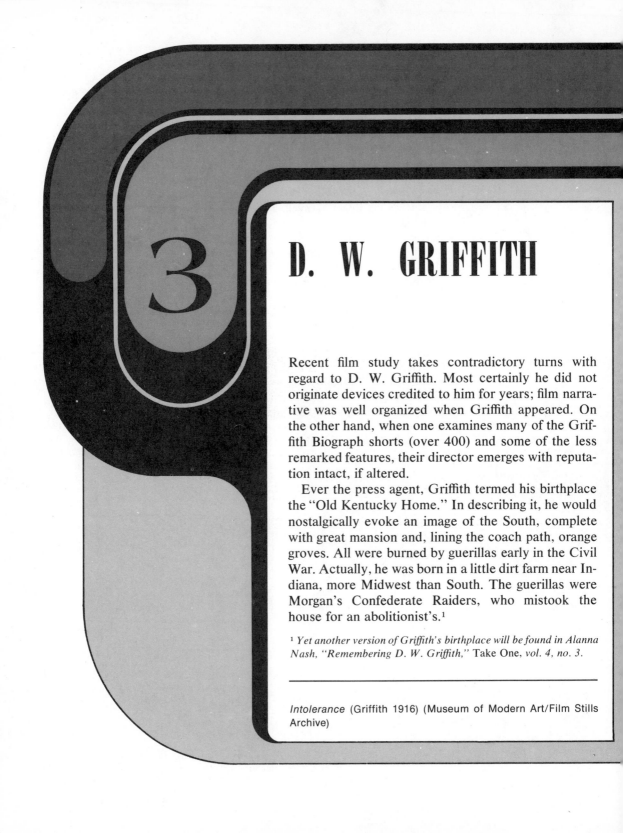

3   D. W. GRIFFITH

Recent film study takes contradictory turns with regard to D. W. Griffith. Most certainly he did not originate devices credited to him for years; film narrative was well organized when Griffith appeared. On the other hand, when one examines many of the Griffith Biograph shorts (over 400) and some of the less remarked features, their director emerges with reputation intact, if altered.

Ever the press agent, Griffith termed his birthplace the "Old Kentucky Home." In describing it, he would nostalgically evoke an image of the South, complete with great mansion and, lining the coach path, orange groves. All were burned by guerillas early in the Civil War. Actually, he was born in a little dirt farm near Indiana, more Midwest than South. The guerillas were Morgan's Confederate Raiders, who mistook the house for an abolitionist's.[1]

[1] *Yet another version of Griffith's birthplace will be found in Alanna Nash, "Remembering D. W. Griffith," Take One, vol. 4, no. 3.*

Intolerance (Griffith 1916) (Museum of Modern Art/Film Stills Archive)

D. W. Griffith 1875-1948

The Adventures of Dollie	1908
The Call of the Wild	1908
For Love of Gold	1908
Where the Breakers Roar	1908
After Many Years	1908
An Awful Moment	1908
Betrayed by a Handprint	1908
The Redman and the Child	1908
The Lonely Villa	1909
The Country Doctor	1909
A Corner in Wheat	1909
Ramona	1910
In Old California	1910
His Trust	1910
His Trust Fulfilled	1910
The Lonedale Operator	1911
Enoch Arden	1911
The Battle	1911
The Musketeers of Pig Alley	1912
The Girl and Her Trust	1912
The New York Hat	1912
Man's Genesis	1912
The Battle of Elderberry Gulch	1913
Judith of Bethulia	1913
The Escape	1914
The Battle of the Sexes	1914
The Avenging Conscience	1914
Home Sweet Home	1914
The Birth of a Nation	1915
Intolerance	1916
Hearts of the World	1918
True Heart Susie	1919
Broken Blossoms	1919
Way Down East	1920
Dream Street	1921
Orphans of the Storm	1921
Isn't Life Wonderful	1924
Sally of the Sawdust	1925
Abraham Lincoln	1930
The Struggle	1931

Partial listing

Griffith was especially proud of his father, "Roaring Jake" Griffith, who was sewn up without anaesthetic on a battlefield and led a cavalry charge in a buggy when he was too incapacitated to mount. His father died when Griffith was ten, and poverty mingled with the folklore of the defeated South to form a personal mythology of courage, gentility, and triumph over adversity that permeated the director's movie stories and personal life.

Moved to Louisville, Griffith worked in a bookstore, which held informal literary soirées with figures like James Whitcomb Riley, the poet, in attendance. Here Griffith, whose short-lived formal education was insubstantial, listened; he decided to become a playright. Later, Griffith once confessed that some of his ideas on structure and pace came not from Dickens but from Walt Whitman. In those days the poet was too scandalous to acknowledge.

The route to stage authorship was considered to be acting. After taking vocal lessons, Griffith joined a little traveling company, "The Twilight Revellers," first among a series of stock companies that took the young man from New York to Chicago and San Francisco, a journey intercut with flophouses and free lunch counters. Griffith's actual writing has become a matter of conjecture. Certainly he conceived the important films, although writing little down. He spoke of helping to translate *Ramona* into a stage play, and pointed to *The Wild Duck,* a poem published in *Leslie's Weekly,* and to the manuscript of a play, *A Fool and a Girl.* But Griffith's first wife, Linda Arvidson, once testifying in court over alimony, swore she alone had written both poem and play. She was an actress whom Griffith met and married on the West Coast in 1905. They sold *A Fool and a Girl* for $1000, but it opened and closed quickly at Ford's Theater in Washington.

Indigent in New York City, Griffith sustained himself with occasional film parts. He is seen in Porter's *Rescued from an Eagle's Nest* (Edison 1907) and in several Biograph Company films dating from early 1908, *At the French Ball* and *A Calamitous Elopement,* for example. He also began to sell story ideas, "most borrowed from the very best authors," at $5 apiece. In June, Griffith became an assistant director. Alone, he directed his first film, *The Adventures of Dollie,* the next month: shooting schedule two days, cost $65, retail price $99.82 per print.

Until 1913, Griffith was responsible for approximately one hundred Biograph pictures per year, some eleven to sixteen minutes, others eight minute "half-reels." With the increasing success of these pictures the director, anonymous like his actors in terms of screen credit, gained nonetheless prestige and power. He assembled a group of sympathetic players who became in time a kind of repertory group, some stereotyped in role (Mack Sennett was the principal slapstick figure), some refined to fit Griffith's Victorian-southern sensibility. Blanche Sweet, Mae Marsh and the Gish sisters were imperiled and usually plucky heroines; Bobby Harron, Henry B. Walthall and Frank Grandin played heroes. Griffith was quick to recognize and to nurture the talents of Mary Pickford and Florence Lawrence and his later productions became training grounds for directors Erich von Stroheim and Raoul Walsh. Increasingly, he worked with Billy Bitzer, a photographer long associated with American Mutoscope and Biograph, soon called simply Biograph.

Griffith's pictures covered a range of modes. He was an able period comedy director. He had strong interest in translating the cultural "greats" onto film, writers like Tennyson, Dickens, and Browning, as well as contemporary novelists Jack London and Frank Norris. The most notable Griffith successes, those that Biograph executives encouraged him to repeat, were melodramas: rescues and escapes, which drew from theater pieces for

FORM NO. 132t   BULLETIN No. 151. RELEASED July 14, 1908

THE ADVENTURES OF DOLLIE

HER MARVELOUS EXPERIENCE AT THE HANDS OF GYPSIES

LENGTH, 713 FEET.   PRICE, 14 CENTS PER FOOT.

One of the most remarkable cases of child-stealing is depicted in this Biograph picture, showing the thwarting by a kind Providence of the attempt to kidnap for revenge a pretty little girl by a Gypsy. On the lawn of a country residence we find the little family, comprising father, mother and little Dollie, their daughter. In front of the grounds there flows a picturesque stream to which the mother and little one go to watch the boys fishing. There has come into the neighborhood a band of those peripatetic Nomads of the Zingani type, whose ostensible occupation is selling baskets and reed ware, but their real motive is pillage. While the mother and child are seated on the wall beside the stream, one of these Gypsies approaches and offers for sale several baskets. A refusal raises his ire and he seizes the woman's purse and is about to make off with it when the husband, hearing her cries of alarm, rushes down to her aid, and with a heavy snakewhip lashes the Gypsy unmercifully, leaving great welts upon his swarthy body, at the same time arousing the venom of his black heart. The Gypsy leaves the scene vowing vengeance, and the little family go, back to the lawn, where the father amuses little Dollie with a game of battledore and shuttlecock. During the game the mother calls papa to the house for an instant. This is the Gypsy's chance, for he has been hiding in the bushes all the while. He seizes the child and carries her to his camp where he gags and conceals her in a watercask. A search of the Gypsy's effects by the distracted father proves fruitless and the Gypsy with the aid of his wife gathers up his traps into his wagon, placing the cask containing the child on the back. Down the road they go at breakneck speed, and as they ford a stream the cask falls off the wagon into the water and is carried away by the current. Next we see the cask floating down the stream toward a waterfall, over which it goes; then through the seething spray of the rapids, and on, on until it finally enters the quiet cove of the first scene, where it is brought ashore by the fisherboys. Hearing strange sounds emitted from the barrel, the boys call for the bereft father, who is still searching for the lost one. Breaking the head from the barrel the amazed and happy parents now fold in their arms their loved one, who is not much worse off for her marvelous experience.

No. 3454   CODE WORD—Reverso

Produced and Controlled Exclusively by the

American Mutoscope & Biograph Co.

11 East 14th Street, New York City.

PACIFIC COAST BRANCH,   312 California Street   Los Angeles. Cal

Licensees
{ Williams, Brown & Earle.   Kleine Optical Company.
   Society Italian "Cines"   Great Northern Film Company.
   American Mutoscope & Biograph Company.

We will protect our customers and those of our licensees against patent litigation in the use of our licensed films.

American Mutoscope and Biograph's release notice for *Adventures of Dollie* (1908). Griffith's acting career with the company began in January of the same year. *Dollie* was shot at Sound Beach, Connecticut. Linda Arvidson played the mother. Biograph's hyperbolic description betrays the value-lashed stereotypings that customarily "sold" a story and underlined the minimal characterizations. (Museum of Modern Art/Film Stills Archive)

narrative substance and form. Interiors were staged in the company's brownstone studio at 11 West 14th Street, but Griffith ventured afield for new locations, appropriate to his stories and different one from another: in rural Connecticut, the Pallisades, the New Jersey shore and New York state forests. First condescending about the flickers, a vulgar entertainment form hardly comparable to "legitimate" theater, Griffith soon became deeply committed. He examined lighting, makeup, the Biograph camera, and the work of his predecessors and competitors with studied interest.

In 1910, Griffith persuaded Biograph to finance a journey with the troupe to California for winter filming. Biograph was not the first film company to inhabit Los Angeles. Selig had been there for two years, and a pair of one-time bookmakers who eventually became Mack Sennett's partners had taken over a deserted grocery store for a studio a year earlier. As before, Griffith moved afield for scenery: to Pasadena, the San Gabriel Mission, the Sierra Madres, and Pacific beaches. He returned to New York in the Spring.

After his sojurn in the west, Griffith's ambitions rose. Still turning out the Biograph staples, he made fewer films and even fewer half-reel quickies. His impulse was toward developed, longer productions but he was thwarted and sometimes had to cut back on the footage shot for a film so as to stay within the Trust's 1-reel dictum. A late 1910 venture was released in two parts, *His Trust* and its sequel, *His Trust Fulfilled,* which included a synopsis.

The troupe returned to Los Angeles in 1911. Among the films of that year was a 2-reel remake of Tennyson's *Enoch Arden,* which finally appeared in theaters as one picture. This was a minor triumph over Biograph's efforts to separate it into individual reels, each making up a separate day's show. At this date within the Trust, Griffith's interest in longer pictures was not unique. Selig released the three-reel *Two Orphans* (1911) on three consecutive days, and the *The Coming of Columbus* complete (3¼ reels) in 1912.

As movie directors went, Griffith was well paid by 1911. He earned about $2000 a month (salary and commission on the footage of his own films sold or leased). Although his output continued to decrease, Biograph production was maintained by passing the comedy films on to Mack Sennett and Frank Powell, with Griffith as overseer.

Again back in New York, Griffith viewed the Adolph Zukor-Marcus Loew-Edwin S. Porter-sponsored *Queen Elizabeth,* starring Sarah Bernhardt. This production, unmovingly stage bound, was 3 to 4 reels long and made impressive profits. Griffith obtained Biograph's permission to make more 2-reelers, none longer. The company was unwilling to make the higher investments required of more ambitious filming. In Southern California he made more 1- and 2-reelers, the most effective of which was *The Battle of Elderberry Gulch* (1913), also known as *The Battle at (or of) Elderbush Gulch.*

Griffith then undertook his most ambitious venture to date, *Judith of Bethulia* (1913). Despite the New York office's protests about cost—$36,000—he proceeded with a 4-reel design, concluding its shooting and editing in Biograph's new Bronx studio. At this stage of production, Griffith may have seen the 8-reel Italian import *Quo Vadis,* which was playing in New York. That fall he left Biograph and joined Mutual, a new distribution company, as an independent producer.

THE BIOGRAPH FILMS

The hundreds of Griffith Biographs have provided an extraordinary resource for film study. All but eight survive. A reassuring number remain available, along with Biograph advertising copy, which provided synopses and usu-ally stills for prospective buyers and leasees. Made at upmost speed, the shorts mirror a mind in process: innovations side by side with lacklustre conventions. Griffith's growing narrative sophistication and his mixed, sometimes conflicting impulses toward what was both entertaining and "good for" his audience.[2]

The production schedule of Griffith's early films usually averaged two days. Impressive moments of story execution appear and pass; year by year plot complexities grow and with them the editing skills. Thus, while the early Biographs may employ a dozen or fewer camera positionings in their entirety, the later ones often use eighty to one hundred setups for a film of equal length. It might even be speculated that the 1- and 2-reel lengths to which Griffith was restrained finally worked in his favor. Circumscribed by length, narrative conceptions break out into fragments that require more complicated editing to realize themselves.

Structure grew from Griffith's pragmatic sense of audience receptivity when dealing with the problems he faced in translating a narrative into film: (1) how to deal with the passage of time; (2) how to tell the story quickly; (3) how to emotionalize the material without histrionics in the absence of sound; (4) how to take maximum advantage of location and set; (5) how to control audience perceptions; (6) how to resolve the drama. Griffith's narrative accomplishments are in the noncomic modes: adaptation, drama, and melodrama.

Some of Griffith's experiments were with punctuating devices, which is to say experi-

[2] *The following considerations owe particular debts to Kemp Niver,* The Battle of Elderbush Gulch *(Los Angeles, 1972),* Biograph Bulletins 1896-1908 *(Los Angeles, 1971),* D. W. Griffith: His Biograph Films in Perspective *(Los Angeles, 1964) and to William Johnson, "Early Griffith: A Wider View,"* Film Quarterly, *vol. 29, no. 3 (Spring 1976).*

Blanche Sweet in *The Lonedale Operator* (left). Dorothy Bernard in the remake, *The Girl and Her Trust* (right). Isolated and in danger, the women desperately telegraph for help. At the climax of *The Lonedale Operator* Griffith cuts into a closeup of Blanche using a monkey wrench as a pretend pistol to ward off the villians. In the remake, Dorothy explodes a cartridge through the keyhole, shown in tight closeup withdrawing to a head and shoulders shot. Her effort unsuccessful, Dorothy is kidnapped. The cutting frequencies and traveling shots of the chase outdistance the earlier film. (Museum of Modern Art/Film Stills Archive)

ments with the representation of time. The fade (light's diminished entrance into the camera) was first accomplished by controlling the lens aperture in the course of actual filming. This is not original to Griffith but to Billy Bitzer. (Later, this effect was achieved easily more often in laboratory processing and printing.) As on the stage, Griffith and Bitzer used fades both to provide a sense of conclusion to final scenes and, within the film, to show the passage of time. In *The Battle of Elderberry Gulch,* Shots 1 and 2 (two orphans being sent from their home; the children on a cart in transit) are separated by a fade. The transition required by the story would otherwise have been an overly abrupt transition in time. The alternative to such technique would be a title card (intertitle), but, although he used titles with increasing frequency, Griffith tried to avoid them where picture alone could carry

the story. Fades were generally not to total but to relative black. Sometimes Griffith betrays the theatrical origins of his technique by dimming lights on a last scene rather than using Bitzer's camera, as in *A Baby's Shoes* (1909).

With shorter, more frequent shots, Griffith manipulated time by representing simultaneous events related by plot but taking place in different locations, e.g., the last-minute rescue. Such parallel action, sometimes termed cross cutting or the switchback, allowed Griffith as editor to control audience perception in process. If a girl is protecting herself from thieves while an engineer rides to the rescue, as in *The Lonedale Operator* (1911), Griffith found that an audience will accept as much fictional time passing, great or small, as the drama sustains. Incongruity itself makes the engineer's rush unbearably slow. Such paralleling is hinted in *The Great Train Robbery,* the speedups through smooth editing in *Rescued by Rover,* but is employed repeatedly in early Griffith films in more complex designs. Two or three stories are intercut in a manner designed to intensify the climax when they come together.

Griffith emotionalizes his material visually. Most elementary is his habit of planting an object early in the story, like a gun triggered to kill the heroine when a door is opened in *An Awful Moment* (1908). This gives the audience a tangible object of suspense that is tied to the unpredictability of plot resolution. More inventively, Griffith uses an actor's relation to setting to objectify feeling and intensify characterization. Beseiged by villains, Blanche Sweet in *The Lonedale Operator* desperately telegraphs for help while a window curtain blows behind her head, tremors of the cloth spelling out her mounting anxiety. Describing a 1910 film called *As It Is in Life,* a seventies critic writes:

. . . [a] widower gives up the woman he loves in order to look after his small daughter, who later deserts him for the man she loves. The widower works at a pigeon farm, and there are stunning scenes filled with thousands of pigeons, some flashing past the lens in blurry close-ups, others circling as dots in the distance, and the rest flocking in a dense mass in between. But Griffith offers more than pretty pictures. There are repeated scenes of the widower with his daughter, both as a small girl and grown up—pushing a feed cart through the farm. As they move, the flocking pigeons edge away to leave a clear circle of ground around them—and this shifting no-man's land projects a vivid image of the seeming transience of the widower's life, which contains nothing he can hold onto.[3]

[3] *William Johnson, "Early Griffith: A Wider View,"* Film Quarterly, *vol. 29, no. 3. (Spring 1976), p. 6.*

Indeed, Griffith's sense of narrative is structured by his conception of drama: "All drama must of necessity be conflict, battle, fight. How are we to depict the right unless we show the wrong?"[4] In war film, such conflict may be externalized. Elsewhere, it can lurk in restrained imagery, but Griffith thrives on contrasts and comparisons that at best have the strength of implied metaphor buried in story elements.

Griffith's interest in location filming makes evident both his quest for scope and verisimilitude and the practicalities of Biograph production, where two or three studio sets were the maximum for any film. Country, seaside and mountains encouraged long-shot settings and their geographies allowed more imaginative groupings and character movements than might be organized inside. Thus, the beach in *Where the Breakers Roar* (1908) lets Griffith divide his characters into simultaneous foreground-background action. Even his first venture, *Adventures of Dollie,* filmed in Connecticut, gains strength from the vertical and diagonal movements of a barrel floating down river, over a falls, and to waters' edge with a little girl trapped inside.

Control of audience perceptions figures in camera positionings, in lighting, focus, iris, and editing tempos. These determine what is to be seen, how it shall be viewed and for how long. As Griffith increased the frequency of camera setups, he allowed greater variety in their angles of view and sometimes their movement. The distance between camera and subject had a narrative relation to the behaviors of the actors and to their interrelationships. Although the Biograph camera rebelled against anything but pans and tilts (movement on a horizontal or a vertical axis), these appear impressively in *The Call of The*

[4] *Quoted in Jean Bernique,* Motion Picture Acting *(Chicago, 1916), p. 199, and in Robert Henderson,* D. W. Griffith: The Years at Biograph, *(New York, 1970), p. 164.*

Wild (1908) and *The Country Doctor* (1909). Most often, Griffith moved his camera between shots, but movement to follow action is seen in *The Girl and Her Trust* (1912) (a remake of *The Lonedale Operator*). This was achieved by mounting a camera on an automobile that rode parallel to the tracks to follow a speeding handcar. More impressive yet is *A Beast At Bay* (1912) in which a racing car and an automobile are both filmed from another vehicle.

Closeups are common in Griffith, usually to advise the audience as to what is happening and to dramatize it; the shot, for instance, of the jewels hidden in a bar of soap in *Betrayed by a Handprint* (1908) and the rigged gun in *An Awful Moment*. Bitzer disliked the out-of-focus closeup backgrounds, and such shots are often filmed against near, flat drops as in *The Sacrifice* (1908) or black, *The Curtain Pole* (1908).

Griffith and Bitzer experimented with additional ways to direct attention. Theater lighting techniques, both for compositional and naturalistic effect were used. In *Fools of Fate* (1909), a girl extinguishes her lantern and the screen goes black. The 1910 *Ramona* shows that Bitzer was using reflectors to separate actors from their mountain settings in the California sunlight. Another device was the matte-box mask. Like *Grandma's Reading Glass*, *The Redman and the Child* (1908), one of Griffith's earliest ventures, simulates the view through a surveyor's transit scope by masking the picture into a circle. (Thus it becomes a subjective point-of-view shot as well.) A development of this technique was the use of an exterior iris, which substituted a variable aperture for the cutout and so enabled the photographer to diminish the field of vision on the screen from its usual full rectangle down to a circle of variable size located anywhere on screen. Another variation of the use of a matte mask was called vignetting, which blurred picture edges into soft focus, like period portraits.

Although the Biographs are full of editing bloopers, as an editor, Griffith gave special attention to pace. Although its importance becomes more evident as films lengthen, the design of Griffith tempos originate in the Biographs. As shot frequency increases, the authority over a performance shifts from actor to editor. When action was broken down into components, it became the editor who decided the order of an event's perception and its duration. In 1925, Griffith wrote:

The pace must be quickened from beginning to end. This is not, however, a steady ascent. The action must quicken to a height in a minor climax, then slow down and build again to the next climax, which should be faster than the second and on to the major climax, where the pace should be fastest. Through the big moments of the story, the pace should be like the beat of an excited pulse.[5]

In the 1-reelers, Griffith was learning to organize one climax at a time.

The story resolutions show some of Griffith's weakest and some of his most interesting conceptions. He had a predilection for returning audience emotion to the stasis of beginnings. Beginnings were appropriately slow.

In the opening passages of a photoplay, the tempo is usually maintained in multiples of three counts—six, nine, twelve. This is the cadence of the waltz, tranquil, soothing, almost hypnotic to the senses.[6]

Sometimes a film concludes on the same scene as it began, framed in long shot. After-climax scenes may degenerate into clichéd or bizarre clashes of style, as when the two bandits doff their caps and bow to pay mock homage to Blanche Sweet when outwitted in *The*

[5] *D. W. Griffith, "Pace in the Movies," Liberty (April 18, 1925).*
[6] Ibid.

Lonedale Operator. In some cases, like *A Corner in Wheat* (1909), which is loosely based on Frank Norris' novel *The Octopus,* a concluding scene of grain sown in the fields gives ironic repetition to the cycle of poverty introduced at the beginning of the film in a similar scene. In *The Battle of Elderberry Gulch,* a final long shot of cavalry departing from a little cabin places an action-paced rescue drama back into the contexts of its historical setting, a notion of growing interest to Griffith.

THE BIRTH OF A NATION

Leaving Biograph for more money, prestige, and the chance to make features, Griffith based his choice to join Mutual on personal estimation of Harry Aitken, a midwest distributor who ran the company. Aitken was a nimble, fast-thinking businessman who had broken from the Trust and, in the absence of Trust product, now sought to develop a combination production-distribution agency. He promised Griffith money and independence.

Griffith took along the essential members of his company of players: the Gish sisters, Blanche Sweet, Mae Marsh, Donald Crisp, Bobby Harron, and George Siegman. Lionel Barrymore returned to the stage, and Mary Pickford had departed Biograph earlier to play the lead in a Broadway comedy directed by David Belasco, *A Good Little Devil.* Mack Sennett left with the comedy team to start his own production company, which was named Keystone after the Pennsylvania Railroad insignia.

Battle scene in *The Birth of a Nation.* Griffith's circular matte is evocative of *The Redman and the Child,* for "spyglasses" figured in Civil-War military strategy and journalism coverage. More likely here, however, the manipulated composition intends to intensify its "objective" point of view. (Museum of Modern Art/Film Stills Archive)

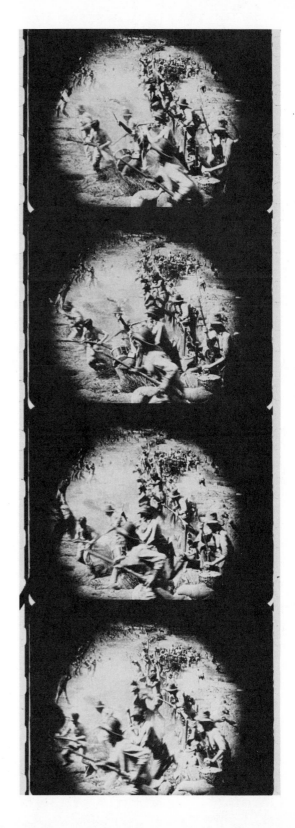

Griffith's first Mutual films were 4- and 5-reel features, designed at minimal expense ($5000 per film) for quick production and fast profit. Aitken's business was precariously financed and overextended, with profits from one production supposedly underwriting the next. Griffith, however, insisted on first runs in legitimate Broadway theaters, which, with promotion and advertising costs, delayed returns. The players made *The Escape* and *The Battle of the Sexes,* before they moved to Sunset Boulevard. There Griffith filmed *Home Sweet Home* and a version of Poe's "The Tell-Tale Heart" and "Annabel Lee" called *The Avenging Conscience.* At the same time he was at work on a design for *The Clansman,* a fervid tale of Reconstruction by Thomas Dixon which appeared first as a novel and was then adapted for the stage. (Historians notwithstanding, another Dixon novel, *The Leopard's Spots,* does not figure in Griffith's film.) On Griffith's suggestion, Aitken bought the rights to *The Clansman* for $10,000, although he could only pay $2500 down; in a monumental piece of good fortune, Dixon chose profit sharing rather than the remaining $7500.

The Clansman detailed the birth of the Ku Klux Klan as an heroic response to carpetbagger depredations on the fallen South. Blacks were seen as a millstone about the neck of the white race, and the worst villainies attributed to opportunistic and hypocritical New Englanders and power-hungry mulattoes. Self identified as fallen gentry, with memories of Colonel Roaring Jake Griffith, scarred by a poverty-stricken boyhood, Griffith found the story personally agreeable and meat to his imagination. The film was scheduled for 10 reels at a budget of $40,000.

Much has been made of Griffith's disposition to work "without a script," but his pictures were sometimes weeks in rehearsal. Further, he had become enthusiastic about historical research, and, although his partisan sources tended to reinforce Dixon's views of the period, Griffith viewed scholarship as a support to authenticity. The director made much of the dapple gray coloring on General Lee's horse Traveler and the fact that a pen had to be passed through several inkwells before signatures were appended to the surrender at Appomatox. His film would be history reborn.

Shooting took from nine to twelve weeks, ridden with financial crises as costs mounted. Griffith sought out small private investors, including Billy Bitzer. Crowd scenes sometimes involved 200 extras; Griffith staged great battles with smoke bombs and volleys of blanks. He burned Atlanta and assassinated Lincoln at Ford's Theater. The spectacle was more epically staged, more painstakingly reproduced than anything before, including the Italian histories. *The Clansman* opened in Los Angeles in February, 1915 and then in New York under a new title, *The Birth of a Nation.*

Aitken's strategy was to roadshow the extraordinarily successful picture, first in the big cities, pulling fast profits at two dollar admissions. The film was then leased on a territorial basis to state distributors, who paid a percentage for the rights. Aitken underestimated the remaining audiences, and the picture's owners lost great sums because of slipshod accounting procedures for state distributors. Louis B. Mayer, who had been managing nickelodeons in Massachusetts, made his first million in part from under-reported revenue from that state. Nevertheless, overall grosses on showings of *The Birth of a Nation* in 1915 and later ran from eighteen to twenty million dollars.

Attendance at the epic was fanned by the controversy it aroused, for *The Birth of a Nation* fed on white America's racial prejudices and southern resentments. Griffith's very talents in snaring and accelerating audience empathy combined with a vision of American history that tapped the value systems of nineteenth-century melodrama. The polarizing framework of villain, heroine, and hero were doubly reinforced by Dixon's white-black story, and Griffith made the most of it, using all the resources at his command.

The Birth of a Nation was, and still is, attacked by civic groups. Screenings in Boston led to race riots and unsuccessful efforts to revoke exhibition licenses. The recently formed National Association for the Advancement of Colored People issued a pamphlet, *Fighting a Vicious Film,* and embittered controversy, which first attended the 1905 publication of *The Clansman,* was revived. President Woodrow Wilson's office quickly denied film publicity that he had endorsed the movie.

The story separates into two parts. A well-to-do Southern family, the Camerons, are visited by Pennsylvania friends, the Stonemans. War breaks out and the families part. A young Cameron son falls beside a Stoneman boy on the battlefield. Ben Cameron, the Little Colonel (Henry B. Walthall), is nursed from a war wound by Elsie Stoneman (Lillian Gish), whom he loves. Following the surrender, Ben returns to the Piedmont family home, and Lincoln is assassinated.

In the second section, the elder Stoneman, a United States senator, comes to Piedmont with a black mistress and a mulatto protégé, Silas Lynch, the lieutenant governor. Lynch falls in love with Elsie Stoneman. Blacks win the election and dominate the town. They flog a Cameron servant who has remained loyal to the family. They carrouse in the legislature. A renegade black soldier, Gus (Walter Long), chases the youngest Cameron daugher Flora (Mae Marsh) to a cliff, where she chooses suicide before rape.

Ben Cameron conceives of and forms the Ku Klux Klan, which engages in guerilla conflict with the black community. The Klan catches, tries, and executes Gus. Discovering his membership, Elsie rejects Ben, and Margaret Cameron (Miriam Cooper) cannot

The Birth of a Nation. The assassination at Ford's Theater. Griffith's interior was the largest film set built before 1915. When he had completed the Lincoln role, Joseph Henabery played thirteen additional bit parts. Besides shooting the president, Raoul Walsh worked as an assistant for Griffith and, later, Thomas Ince.

The Birth of a Nation 65

accept the advances of Phil Stoneman (Elmer Clifton) because of war's bitter memories.

Enraged by the Klan and infatuated with Elsie, Silas Lynch arrests the Cameron father and presses his suit on Elsie, who reacts as if Lynch were threatening to pull out her fingernails. Senator Stoneman approves Lynch's marriage intentions until he discovers that Lynch wants his daughter. Lynch imprisons Elsie and blacks attack Cameron, Phil Stoneman, Margaret Cameron, and the faithful servants who have all escaped and sought refuge in a small cabin occupied by two Yankee veterans. In the nick of time, the KKK rescues the beseiged party, subdues rioting black mobs in Piedmont, and frees Elsie. The film concludes with a double marriage—Margaret and Phil, Elsie and Ben—followed by an allegorical epilogue where the god of war is replaced by the figure of Christ. A title reads:

Liberty and Union,
One and inseparable,
now and forever

Fade to

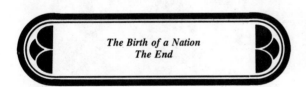

The Birth of a Nation
The End

The film has passed through a variety of versions, in part because of deletions forced on it by censorial municipalities, in part because of Griffith's own disposition to tinker with his footage at any stage of distribution, sometimes even in a projection booth as a feature was being played! Some of the most virulent material may now be altogether lost.[7]

[7] *Extant but not available for study are nitrate-stock outtakes from* The Birth of a Nation *in the Library of Congress.*

In many respects, *The Birth of a Nation* "reads" like a great, three-hour Biograph in which all of the skills of 1-reel melodrama have been expanded to countenance a grandiose, violent scheme peopled with the full Griffith troupe. Certainly one of his triumphs was the ability to inflate earlier designs of a single climax into many. In part, this is accomplished by pacing. In part, Griffith is successful because he has the wisdom to fall back on verities of the poetic epic, a narrative scheme that plots individual actions so that they either cause or show the effects of great, transcending events. Thus, the Civil War and Reconstruction are checkerboarded, or intercut, with individualized stories of imperiled love and threats to a society's way of life. The successes of the Klan's final rescues rest on customary Biograph climaxing, resolving finally in an intermingling of history and individualized plot: a quasi-military battle where North and South unite against a common enemy and triumph together. A nation is born through the resubjugation of uppity blacks.

At his best, Griffith joins "big" and "little" pictures in moving images. One of the most reknowned connectives in film history is the scene preceded by the title "While women and children weep, a great conqueror marches to the sea." An irised close shot of huddled forms on a hillside opens out while the camera pans right to a long shot of Sherman's army marching through Georgia. Bitzer says the first part of the sequence was a family group he shot candidly while working on another project. The two images were joined in the laboratory.

Griffith is least successful when he depends on contrived coincidences to make his connections. For example, at the battle of Petersburg, Ben Cameron thrusts a Confederate flag into a Yankee cannon barrel, then faints in the arms of his Northern pal, Phil Stoneman. The strength of the film is also diminished by many of its intertitles, both because of their racist editorializing and because they resort to prose for motivation. An example of this follows a scene in which Ben Cameron refuses to shake the hand of Silas Lynch, who had earlier treated Ben's sisters rudely:

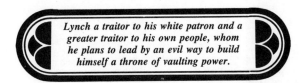

Lynch a traitor to his white patron and a greater traitor to his own people, whom he plans to lead by an evil way to build himself a throne of vaulting power.

Recalling theatrical spectacle scenes in which horses, ships, and artillery sometimes appeared on stage, Griffith's battles contribute some of the film's most awesome moments. The plains of southern California provided immense staging areas, and Bitzer's evocation of Civil-War photography is masterful. Most impressive is Griffith's capacity to move masses of men in panoramic patterns so that the entire screen fills with conflict. The Biograph training ground for staging planes of action (keeping all the playing areas busy with contrary movement) reaches fruition. Such grandiose shots also draw strength from their contexts. As Griffith patterns the epic against individualized story, he juxtaposes multiple-figured compositions with single ones. After signing the heavily witnessed order for Union volunteers, Lincoln sits alone in his office. Bidding her brothers farewell, Margaret Cameron is left in a garden.

Griffith uses equal sophistication in support of the film's racism. Gus's bent animal-like pursuit through the forest contrasts with Flora's dainty retreat. Lillian Gish, white gowned and hair disheveled, in the arms of Silas Lynch is a moving composition of blacks and whites, like that of Gus crouching over the broken figure of Flora. Further, the plot carries emblematic overtones. Black rape is the Northern rape of the South. In the opening sequence, the South appears as a kind of feudal agrarian utopia, the nation's "heart," in contrast to a hard, industrial North, signified at its worst by Senator "Stone-man."

Other factors accounted for *The Birth of a Nation's* impressive box office. One was its war theme, undertaken at a time when patriotism was seen by exhibitors to be a shrewd response to European film spectacles. American releases in early 1914 include Universal's *Washington at Valley Forge* (4 reels) and *The Spy* (4 reels), Kalem's *The Swamp Fox* (3 reels), Mutual's own *Battle at Gettysburg* (5 reels), Edison's *The Southerner* (3 reels), and Vitagraph's *The Night Riders of Petersham* (3 reels), the latter including the Ku Klux Klan.[8]

Another significant contribution was film music, compiled by Griffith and Joseph Carl Breil. Breil had earlier scored *Queen Elizabeth* and *Cabiria*. Months before the premiere, the two men worked together to organize operatic, symphonic, folk, and original materials. Like the film, this music was more ambitious and more sophisticated than what had preceded, assigning themes to major characters and situations: the *1812 Overture* accompanied battle, and the Klan raced to *The Ride of the Valkyries*. Breil's original love theme for Ben Cameron and Elsie Stoneman was published as sheet music; ironically, a later generation remembers it as the theme for radio's *Amos and Andy,* two white men in blackface like most of the blacks in Griffith's movie.

INTOLERANCE

Griffith wrote a pamphlet titled "The Rise and Fall of Free Speech in America," arguing for freedom of expression in movies and maintaining the historical accuracy of his Civil-War film. While throwing his energies into the

---

[8] *A. Marshall Deutelbaum, "Re-assessing* The Birth of a Nation," *in* The Birth of a Nation and 1915, *(Society for Cinema Studies, 1976), p. 12.*

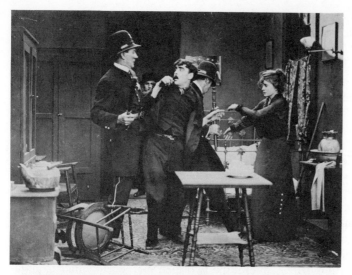

Intolerance. Reading from top to bottom, police apprehend The Boy while the Dear One, now his wife, stands by; Catherine de Medici pressures Charles IX to take brutal action against the Huguenots; Christ speaks to bystanders who would prosecute a "fallen woman." For the Babylonian (see page 55) and medieval stories, a special railroad brought materials to the set and food to the extras. A camp was built to house all the players. (Museum of Modern Art/Film Stills Archive)

growing controversy over *Birth,* he turned to a smaller subject, *The Mother and the Law.* Increasingly, Griffith saw the new film as one element among several stories that might be bound by a common theme: intolerance through the ages. The idea assumed massive proportions, but, with the success of his previous film, financing was easier, and Griffith had his own profits to invest.

As the concept of *Intolerance* grew, so did the carpentry; residents living many miles from Hollywood witnessed hundred-foot walls of Babylon in construction. Built without an art designer, Babylon stood defiantly for one year before it was demolished. It was the most massive but only one of many sets, which included the quarters of Louis IX, the streets of Paris, and biblical Judea. The enormity of the production with its attendant publicity exploitation taught Hollywood a new lesson. Costs were awesome. One magazine, referring to Griffith's own auditors, spoke of $1,900,000, including $250,000 for the Banquet Hall scene from the Feast of Belshazzar. This was the famous Babylon set whose intimidating heights led the director to construct a new mechanism to house Bitzer and his camera. With the help of Alan Dwan, later to become a director himself, Griffith built a combination elevator and truck, which descended as it approached the actors far below.

The first cut of *Intolerance* ran eight hours. Griffith explored ideas for a two-part version, then settled for single-showing length. Like *The Birth of a Nation, Intolerance* is known now only in a truncated form, further complicated in this case by the fact that the original negative was disassembled to separate out two of its four stories, later to be reordered, as far as this was possible, by Griffith. With another Breil-Griffith musical score, *Intolerance* opened in New York in September, 1916 and laid a colossal egg.

The film endeavors to tell four stories separated not only in space, like many Griffiths,

but in time as well: Babylon's fall to Cyrus the Great in 538 A.D., the story of Christ, the Saint Bartholomew's Day Massacre of 1572, and a contemporary American crime drama. The tale's common theme—human intolerance—links stories, and a recurrent image of a woman (Lillian Gish) rocking a cradle intends to signify life's continuity in the midst of change and pain.

In a gesture of religious tolerance, the rulers of Babylon allow the introduction of Ishtar, a rival goddess, into the city. This enrages the High Priest of Bel. Prince Balshazzar, son of King Nabonidus, loves the Princess Beloved and is in turn loved by the Mountain Girl who is herself adored by the Rhapsode, who works for the High Priest. Cyrus the Great attacks the city and is repulsed at the great wall, but the High Priest opens Babylon's gate of Igur-Bel. Despite the Mountain Girl's heroic effort to warn her Prince, the city falls. Prince and Princess commit suicide, and the Mountain Girl dies fighting.

The Judean and French sections are least developed. Three episodes of Jesus' story are told, concluding with the Crucifixion. The Saint Bartholomew's Day Massacre is explained as the work of Catherine de Medici who persuades Charles IX, her effeminate son, to authorize it. The violence is personalized in the slaughter of a Huguenot family whose older daugher, Brown Eyes, is loved by Prosper Latour. He is shot down with Brown Eyes in his arms.

Originally *The Mother and the Law,* the modern story is most developed. It centers around the inhabitants of a tenement: the Boy, the Dear One, and the Friendless One. Rendered fatherless by the violence of a strike, the Boy becomes a petty gangster, working for the Musketeer of the Slums whose mistress is the Friendless One. The Dear One's own father dies, and she marries the Boy. However, the Musketeer incriminates the Boy with false evidence, and the Boy is imprisoned for a crime he did not commit. Do-gooders financed by the Jenkins Foundation, whose money comes from the mill where the Boy's father died, seize the Dear One's baby, claiming she is not a fit mother, and place it in an institution. The Boy returns from prison to find the Musketeer pressing his attentions on the Dear One. Jealous, the Friendless One shoots her lover through an open window and flees. The Boy is convicted of the crime and sentenced to hang. After lengthy efforts to delay execution fail, a policeman secures the Friendless One's confession, and the Boy is saved from impending death.

The four tales were not presented separatedly, but intercut one with another, sometimes for the sake of contrast, more often to point up likenesses of human motive and behavior which transcended the ages. Thus the intolerance of the Jenkins Foundation women is likened to the Pharisees, to Catherine de Medici, and to the High Priest of Bel. For example, Griffith moves from the modern social workers to Christ's rebuke to the vindictive townspeople who would punish the adulterous woman, "He that is without sin among you, let him first cast a stone at her."

Each story deals with innocence betrayed, and placed in jeopardy of life. Griffith paces his exposition and plots his intercutting so that situations parallel one another across the ages. As the Huguenots barricade themselves from attack, Jesus is condemned to death. A taxi rushes to advise the Governor of the Friendless One's confession so that he can stay the execution while "at the same time" the Mountain Girl rides horse and chariot to warn Babylon, pursued by Cyrus' army. The Saint Bartholemew's Day Massacre is completed, and Griffith mounts intensity by underlining the tragic outcomes of the other stories: Babylon lies in carnage; the Boy's march to the gallows is paralleled with a shot of the crosses on Calvary Hill. Then, when the Boy is about to join every other victim, he is saved by the Governor's reprieve. Like *The Birth of a Nation, In-*

tolerance concludes in an apocalyptic sequence: battlefields, a bombing of New York City, and imprisoned men. These are followed by angels. Soldiers on the field freeze in their actions; a great ray of light frees the prisoners; and grassy fields are peopled with happy children, this preceded by the intertitle "And perfect love shall bring peace forever" followed by the woman and cradle.

A common response to *Intolerance* is total exhaustion, bemusedly mingled with conflicting emotions. Period reviews sometimes complained of the film's incomprehensible structure, but it is not at all difficult to follow; earlier, longer versions may have posed their own problems. The actor who played Christ said the Judean story originally ran to thirty episodes but was cut when "Jewish authorities" in Los Angeles insisted.

The chase editing in particular assumes a torrential emotionality for any sympathetic viewer, as if four tributaries had joined into a raging Mississippi. The onrush of images (some flash across the screen at enormous speed) draws one into a fictional sense of causality; intercutting suggests that the Mountain Girl seems to be trying to save both Belshazzar and the Boy. Griffith thus accomplished one of his essential intentions: linking behavior across the years. Some acting is both restrained and impassioned, Mae Marsh as the Dear One in particular. The Babylonian sets still awe, especially the scenes of night fighting on the wall, done with magnesium flares. (Griffith's features were sometimes tinted to emotionalize effects even further). The very thought of a picture inspired and designed by an idea wins our admiration.

At the same time, *Intolerance,* for all its grandeurs rarely fully satisfies any but that small, unreserved group who still find it the greatest of motion pictures. Epilogue apart, Griffith's notion of intolerance simply does not satisfy one's understandings about the destruction of Babylon, and if the Jenkins Foundation women are hypocrites like the Pharisees, the modern crime story is still an incredible melodrama. All human history seems to depend upon the insubstantial jealousies of the Friendless One (Meriam Cooper). Acting styles war together, ranging from the bravura chest-thumping Mountain Girl (Constance Talmadge) to Little Brown Eyes (Margery Wilson) who is somewhat sweeter than whipped cream.

Seeking to universalize by drawing characters out of time with stereotyped roles and choice of names, Griffith falters when humans become too allegorical to be real. The cultural disparity between Victorian conception and detailed, concrete performance of which Griffith was so capable elsewhere, here constitutes its own melodramatic conflict.

THE OTHER FEATURES

He never again enjoyed the success of *The Birth of a Nation* or the indulgences of *Intolerance,* but Griffith continued to make features, some on order, some as he wished, until 1931. In recent years, distributors have acquired a number of these and, through retrospectives, they have become increasingly available. The overall effect of this exposure has been the revision of earlier verdicts that found the director declining, like one of his melodramas, at accelerating pace. Where the first two features carried their own brands of extraordinary fantasy, some later films, often in the very modesty of their conceptions, held Griffith's energies in salutory check.

Certain pictures remain lost, and others repay the viewer with only occasional moments of brilliant effect. For all its peculiar allegory of good (the street preacher) against evil (the masked violinist) in Limehouse, *Dream Street* (1921) interestingly poses the notion that our dreams somehow relate functionally to life; in consequence, Griffith designs his parallel editing at places so that life is alternately "real" and "revery."

Hearts of the World (1918) is an unexceptional World War I drama of lovers reunited in a French village recaptured from the Germans, but the battle scenes (documentary footage combined with staged reenactments) are noteworthy. One long shot in particular is thrilling: troops move forward in foreground; others are stationary in the distance; and one contingent shifts screen right in mid-screen.

A commercial failure, *Isn't Life Wonderful* (1924) more effectively sustains audience interest today than many more successful Griffith features. Exteriors for the production were filmed in Germany. Its simple story concerns conditions of famine and inflation after the war; the very squalor of the starving Polish family's existence gives realistic substance to Griffith's usual pathos. Rooted in mundanities of day-to-day survival, *Isn't Life Wonderful* bears legitimate comparison to post-World War II Italian features, but for some smiling-through-the-tears optimisms.

Lillian Gish worked with Griffith until the filming of *Orphans of the Storm* (1921). Arguably the finest American player in silent film, her performances are marked by that kind of mimed detail that most effectively deepened character. She acted with all her body. Her roles have great variety, and the most exceptional are *True Heart Susie* (1919) and *Broken Blossoms* (1919).

True Heart Susie secretly finances the education of her neighbor and friend, William Jenkins without his knowledge. When William returns to their country town, her romantic hopes are dashed, because he marries a frivolous, dissipate milliner, Bettina Hopkins. Susie knows of Bettina's cheating, but, even after Bettina's death, Susie conceals the truth from William. Finally, he discovers Bettina's real character and proposes to Susie.

With such unpromising material, Griffith builds a restrained, lyric film freed for once both from great clashes of good and evil and from last-minute rescues. The rural settings sanction and endorse an innocence that strikes discord in Griffith's metropolitan locations. Lillian Gish excels. She develops characteristic little gestures such as a quick, contained kick of her foot, which suggests both her shyness and an exhuberant, almost manic emotionality that can erupt only in privacy. Her face masterfully plays out contrary emotions, as in the scene when William advises her of his love for Bettina while she herself anticipates a proposal. Done in one unrelenting take, Gish's expression concludes with a kind of wistful, self-deprecating admonishment to her own presumptions.

In *Broken Blossoms*, Lillian Gish plays Lucy, the victimized daughter of Battling Burrows, who is a sadistic, local prizefighter. They live in a shack in Limehouse; Lucy scrounges for food and is beaten for her ef-

Hearts of the World. After a French village is bombarded, German troops occupy it, killing Lillian Gish's grandfather. Fiancé Robert Harron returns in time to save her from ravishment by Stroheim. The still makes evident Griffith's manipulation of nonrectangular compositions by use of a matte box. (British National Film Archive/Stills Library)

Blanche Sweet, Dorothy Gish, Griffith, and Bitzer. When Griffith took his troupe away from Biograph, the company never recovered. In 1915 it went into liquidation. (Museum of Modern Art/Film Stills Archive)

forts. She faints in the shop of Cheng Huan, a young Chinaman who had journeyed to London from China years before to teach the lessons of the Buddha. Disillusioned, he has taken to opium, but Lucy's beauty wins his heart and Cheng Huan nurses her to health in his upstairs quarters. The two are seen there by Evil Eye, a Chinese heavy, who advises Battling Burrows. The fighter is overcome at the interracial implications and destroys Cheng

Huan's richly decorated quarters. He drags Lucy home to squalor. She hides in a closet, but Burrows breaks in and beats her to death. Cheng Huan discovers his ravaged room, finds Lucy's body, and shoots Burrows. He returns with Lucy to his store and stabs himself.

Here Lillian Gish, reluctantly it is said, plays a frightened creature more child than woman. The major parts are few, and like *True Heart Susie*, the story avoids the plot

Robert Harron and Lillian Gish in *True Heart Susie*. The film escapes the usual sense of history to which Griffith was more often victim than managing agent. *True Heart Susie* afforded Gish a kind of ultimate innocence, as well. It contrasts with such post-Griffith roles as Vidor's *La Bohème* (1926) and Seastrom's *The Wind* (1928), which makes her performances seem even the more remarkable. (Museum of Modern Art/ Film Stills Archive)

ures moving silently in long shot on solitary missions.

Gish plays the pathos of her role against the practicalities of poverty. Asleep and secure in Cheng Huan's bed, dressed in his opulent robe against velvet pillows, her fragile beauty is resonated by Bitzer's experimentations in soft focus photography. Gish's most remembered "bit" is a frightened effort to prop her mouth up into a grimace when ordered by her father to "put a smile on her face." Her most exceptional moment is the remarkable scene in which Lucy is crouched in the closet while her maddened father breaks down the door. She is hysterical. She has no place to go, and, in the frenzy of her fear, she clenches her hands and revolves around and around on the little spot of floor—trapped.

The performance of the actresses is fundamental to the work of Griffith and the most memorable images of his films are those of women. We associate a certain kind of slender, girlish, Edwardian figure with "Griffith actresses." He chose his actresses carefully, passing over those who threatened to reach a greater level of physical or emotional maturity than his conception of the female role would allow.

While the Biograph repertory players knew that one day's star would have a minor role in the next story, the developing popularity of "names" made featured performers requisite to financial success. With shifts in cultural values that characterized the American twenties, small changes in acting styles are apparent. Carol Dempster is more buxom, and her movements are freer than the Biograph girls, but even she may fall into that strange, flapping exuberance that one associates with early Mary Pickford, Griffith's now-bizarre vision of feminine innocence and free spirit.

Along with these simple stories and potboilers, Griffith made epics and melodramas. Two of the most successful were *Way Down East* (1920) and *Orphans of the Storm* (1921).

complexities and manipulations of other Griffith drama. Both Richard Barthelmess as Cheng Huan and Donald Crisp as Battling Burrows give strong, containing performances; Barthelmess allowing rage to break the subservience of his role in the shooting scene; Crisp adding a truly offensive ego to the cruelty of his character. The exceptional sets, filmed in the studio, are brilliantly lit and photographed to capture the wharf's river mists clinging to the bleak horizontals of the boats and waterline. Much of the picture's strength grows from the portrayal of cold, huddled fig-

Way Down East was based on a turn-of-the-century play and little was changed for the postwar audience, but, despite its creaky sentimentalities, the director drew maximum effect from the material. Deceived and abandoned, Lilian Gish has a child who dies. She tries to start a new life, but is ordered into the snow when her sinful past comes to light. Caught in the breaking river ice, she is rescued by a man who marries her. Noteworthy, if archetypal melodrama, is the river sequence in which Lillian lies senseless on a slab rushing toward a waterfall. Griffith made interminable shots of the Connecticut River and included footage of Niagara Falls to build his final cut, which is said to have influenced the Russian filmmaker Pudovkin when making *Mother* years later. Ms. Gish said, "Whenever Mr. Griffith saw a chunk of ice that winter he wanted to put me on it."

In *Orphans of the Storm,* the Gish sisters (Dorothy blind in the film) are victims of the French Revolution. Danton rescues Dorothy from the guillotine and she recovers her sight. Like *Judith of Bethulia,* the picture slows to pageantry under weights of costume and decor, although Dorothy's rescue carries the usual thrills.

Griffith completed two sound features, *Abraham Lincoln* (1930) and *The Struggle* (1931). The Lincoln film was originally written by poet Stephen Vincent Benét, although little of his work reached the screen. As completed, the film acts out great moments in a president's life, never betraying actual character through the façade of popular legend.

The Struggle undertook a study of alcoholism. (Griffith was himself drinking heavily at this time.) Although received with laughter, viewed as an anachronistic *Ten Nights in a Barroom* prohibition tract, *The Struggle* is not without interest. Occasional histrionics aside, the film is remarkably well acted, and speech in the early soundtrack holds up well. Sections were shot on location in the Bronx.

They carry the out-of-door flavor of Griffith's best work into a modern city environ. If *The Struggle* proves to be less than masterful, it is hardly a disasterous conclusion to an illustrious career.

Through the thirties, Griffith continued to announce projects, journeying from his Kentucky home to an increasingly alien Los Angeles when directing jobs were dangled. He had gained a reputation for unreliability as well as financial irresponsibility; he was thought to dominate productions in what had become an industry where writers, actors, and directors were now minions of powerful studio heads. On rare occasions, Griffith would be honored by testimonial or award, but this brought no work, and he died in 1948, rushed to a hospital from the lobby of a Hollywood hotel where he had been living alone.

Donald Crisp and Lillian Gish in *Broken Blossoms.* Battling Burrows' victimization of Lucy evokes the dark side of Victorian consciousness: father-figure sadism and a melodrama that only escapes caricature because of the remarkable performances. Like his costar, Crisp develops small, controlled mannerisms and gestures. (British National Film Archive/Stills Library)

Griffith instructs Zita Johann, who plays Florrie in *The Struggle*. Weak in characterization, although written by Anita Loos and John Emerson, the film's city scenes and its factory sequence in Connecticut are sharply etched. In its early use of location sound, *The Struggle* followed close on the heels of *Trader Horn* (1931). (Museum of Modern Art/Film Stills Archive)

Summary

Reappraisals of Griffith's fame will surely continue, his Biographs rising on a tide of critical affirmation as the features recede. Inextricably tied to the substance and fortunes of American entertainment film, the director's reputation is also subject to ongoing controversy over just how far any successful filmmaker can be said to fashion audience sensibilities, or to exploit the ideological determinants of any given period. Griffith moves confortably in both spheres. He was uniquely qualified to spill the country's nineteenth-century melodramatic conventions and expectations into movie studios. An exemplary manipulator of the elements of film narrative before a critical vocabulary had been developed, Griffith also honed the medium into a functioning design that differs very little from today's product.

In more material terms, Griffith taught film producers that ambitious investment might accrue rewards as spectacular as his staging and sets. One overambitious Griffith biography title is *The Man Who Invented Hollywood,* but in large measure, southern California's film capital became legendary because of developments in the motion picture industry that are evident in the work of Griffith. Chapter 4 spells the consequences of these developments on the community: financial, legal, industrial, and esthetic.

Bibliography

Adams Jr., Robert L. "D. W. Griffith and the Use of Offscreen Space," *Cinema Journal,* Spring 1976.

Aitken, Roy E. and Al. P. Nelson. *The Birth of a Nation Story.* Middlebury, Vt., 1965.

Barry, Iris. *D. W. Griffith: American Film Master.* New York, 1940.

Barry, Iris and Eileen Bowser. *D. W. Griffith: American Film Master.* New York, 1965.

Bitzer, G. W. *Billy Bitzer: His Story.* New York, 1973.

Boston Branch of the National Association for the Advancement of Colored People. *Fighting a Vicious Film: Protest Against The Birth of a Nation.* Boston, 1915.

Bowser, Eileen. "The Reconstruction of *A Corner in Wheat.*" *Cinema Journal,* Spring 1976.

Brown, Karl. *Adventures with D. W. Griffith*. New York, 1973.

Brownlow, Kevin. *The Parade's Gone By*. New York, 1968.

Cadbury, William. "Theme, Felt Life and the Last-Minute Rescue in Griffith after *Intolerance*." *Film Quarterly,* Fall 1974.

Casty, Alan. "The Films of D. W. Griffith: A Style for the Times." *Journal of Popular Film,* Spring 1972.

Cook, Raymond Allen. *Fire From the Flint: The Amazing Careers of Thomas Dixon*. Winston-Salem, 1968.

Dixon, Thomas W. *The Clansman*. New York, 1905.

———. *The Leopard's Spots*. New York, 1902.

Door, John. "The Movies, Mr. Griffith and Carol Dempster." *Cinema* 7 (Fall 1971).

———. "The Griffith Tradition." *Film Comment,* March-April 1974.

Geduld, Henry M., ed. *Focus on D. W. Griffith*. Englewood Cliffs. N.J., 1971.

Gerien, Michael Terrence. "D. W. Griffith: The Women in His Life and the Women in His Films." Master thesis, San Francisco State University, 1975.

Gish, Lillian with Ann Pinchot. *The Movies, Mr. Griffith and Me*. Englewood Cliffs, N.J., 1969.

Goodman, Ezra. *The Fifty Year Decline and Fall of Hollywood*. New York, 1957.

Griffith, David Wark. "Pace in the Movies." *Liberty,* April 18, 1925.

Griffith, Linda Arvidson. *When the Movies Were Young*. New York, 1925.

Hart, James, ed. *The Man Who Invented Hollywood*. Louisville, 1972.

Henderson, Robert W. *D. W. Griffith: His Life and Work*. New York, 1972.

———. *D. W. Griffith: The Years at Biograph*. New York, 1970.

Hutchins, Charles L. "A Critical Evaluation of the Controversies Engendered by D. W. Griffith's The Birth of a Nation." Master's thesis, University of Iowa, 1961.

Johnson, William. "Early Griffith: a Wider View." *Film Quarterly* 29 (Spring 1976).

Loos, Anita, *A Girl Like I*. New York, 1966.

Merritt, Russell. "The Impact of D. W. Griffith's Motion Pictures from 1908 to 1914 on Contemporary American Culture." Ph.D. dissertation, Harvard University, 1970.

———. "Dixon, Griffith and the Southern Legend." *Cinema Journal,* Winter 1972.

Miller, Kelly. *As to the Leopard's Spots*. Washington, D.C., 1905.

Morse, David. "Every Article on the Cinema Ought to Talk About Griffith," *Monogram* 4 (1972).

Niven, Kemp. *The Battle of Elderbush Gulch*. Los Angeles, 1972.

———. *Biograph Bulletins 1896-1908*. Los Angeles, 1971.

———. *D. W. Griffith: His Biograph Films in Perspective*. Los Angeles, 1964.

———. *Mary Pickford Comedienne*. Los Angeles, 1969.

O'Dell, Paul. *Griffith and the Rise of Hollywood*. New York, 1970.

Petric, Vladamir. *A Corner in Wheat*. Cambridge, Mass., 1975.

Pratt, George C. *Spellbound in Darkness*. rev. ed. Greenwich, Conn., 1973.

Silva, Fred. *Focus on The Birth of a Nation*. Englewood Cliffs, N.J., 1971.

Society for Cinema Studies. *The Birth of a Nation and 1915*. (discussion panel outline), April 22, 1976.

Stern, Seymour. "Griffith: I. The Birth of a Nation," *Film Culture* 36 (Spring-Summer 1965).

Wagenknecht, Edward. *The Movies in the Age of Innocence*. Norman, Okla., 1962.

Wagenknecht, Edward and Anthony Slide. *The Films of D. W. Griffith*. New York, 1975.

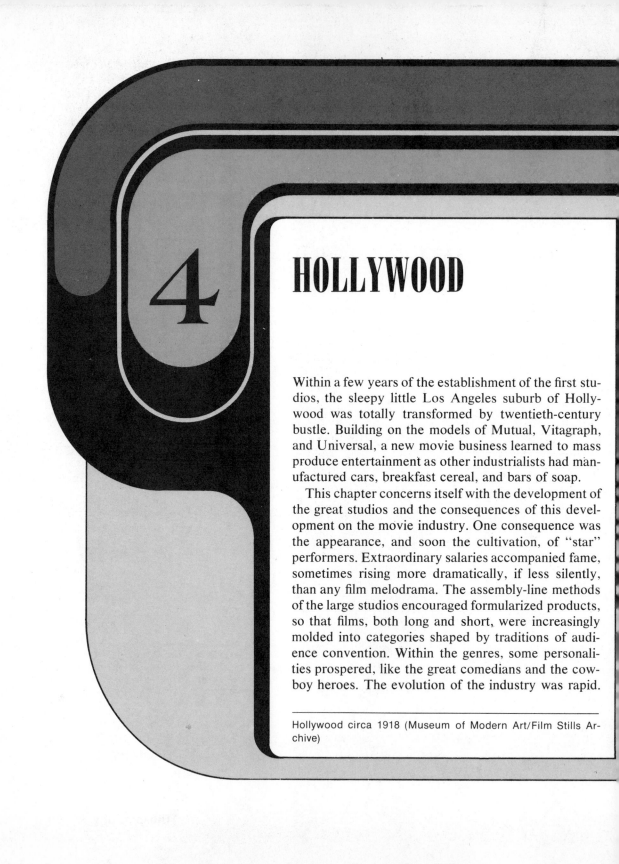

HOLLYWOOD

Within a few years of the establishment of the first studios, the sleepy little Los Angeles suburb of Hollywood was totally transformed by twentieth-century bustle. Building on the models of Mutual, Vitagraph, and Universal, a new movie business learned to mass produce entertainment as other industrialists had manufactured cars, breakfast cereal, and bars of soap.

This chapter concerns itself with the development of the great studios and the consequences of this development on the movie industry. One consequence was the appearance, and soon the cultivation, of "star" performers. Extraordinary salaries accompanied fame, sometimes rising more dramatically, if less silently, than any film melodrama. The assembly-line methods of the large studios encouraged formularized products, so that films, both long and short, were increasingly molded into categories shaped by traditions of audience convention. Within the genres, some personalities prospered, like the great comedians and the cowboy heroes. The evolution of the industry was rapid.

Hollywood circa 1918 (Museum of Modern Art/Film Stills Archive)

In a very short time, Hollywood was born, it blossomed, and then threatened to go into a decline as the result of public reaction to scandals created by members of the motion picture community. Before there was legal intervention, however, into the matter of making movies, the movie tycoons initiated a peculiar form of self-censorship that dictated the moral code of Hollywood and of the pictures it produced.

INDUSTRIAL CONSOLIDATION

Los Angeles was not bereft of filmmakers in 1913, although production was still centered in the New York City area with outposts in Philadelphia, Chicago, Oakland, San Diego, and Santa Barbara. Known for its oak and holly trees, Hollywood existed largely as a realtor's blueprint. (Some say that the development was named for a summer home near Chicago.) Because of inexpensive real estate ($400 an acre), and low construction costs (labor and material) a second generation of motion picture financeers found the spot ideally suited to studio operations. These men were independents who challenged the Trust's production-distribution controls. When Jesse Lasky — in league with Samuel Goldfish, Cecil B. DeMille, and stage-actor Dustin Farnum — bought ten acres at Sunset and Vine, Hollywood was underway.

Cognizant of profits realized by long European imports, William Selig of the Trust produced *The Spoilers,* a popular novel by Rex Beach about Alaska, which premiered at the new Strand Theater in New York City in April 1914. *The Spoilers* (8 reels) filled the Strand's three thousand seats for five daily shows through a seven-day week. These "feature" films (the name given movies greater than 3 reels) made certain demands on the studios. They would cost more to make and fewer could be produced. They needed larger audiences, and audiences would have to pay more money. The roadshowing principle of *The Birth of a Nation* worked effectively for one-shot blockbusters; a theater like the Strand regularized exhibition. Prices rose from nickels and dimes to quarters and higher, as audiences proved to be willing to pay for particular kinds of entertainment in certain sorts of luxurious atmospheres, served by obsequious, uniformed ushers and sonorous pipe organs. With the development of picture palaces, distribution ran to graded patterns of attractiveness: first-, second-, and third-run houses. Best location won best picture first and paid most for the priority.

Negative costs of feature films, the investment required to have a finished original in hand, initially ran $10,000 to $20,000, and this sort of investment required financing different from that of $500-a-reel ventures. Although films were no longer sold outright, Harry Aitken's policy of marketing "states right" ownerships to individual distributors was a common practice. If the film was successful, much of the profit reverted to local men. Increasingly, distributors invested their own money in production. William W. Hodkinson, an executive, regularized this system. He persuaded states-rights distributors to lend capital to designated filmmakers in order to insure the supply of feature films. By working for percentages, both factions shared in a film's popularity. Hodkinson named his organization Paramount; Paramount depended upon Adolph Zukor's Famous Players for many of its pictures, as well as on the Lasky-Goldfish-DeMille team. Similar, rival organizations were Universal, Fox Film Company, Lewis J. Selznick Pictures Company, and Metro Pictures, who produced their own films rather than contracting out like Paramount. Metro's secretary was Louis B. Mayer, and Universal was controlled by Carl Laemmle of IMP.

Soon, ambitious film executives saw the writing on the wall. Separation of filmmaking and of filmmarketing functions clearly fostered risks that might be overcome through alliance. At Paramount, a corporate effort was undertaken to combine production and distribution functions into one enterprise for the sake of business efficiency. In the ensuing infighting, Hodkinson was forced out; Zukor, a man of immense craft and energy, took control. Such arrangements served to link the film business cross-country, connecting studio with theater and shifting the nature of investment capital by placing it in the hands of exhibitors.

As profits and costs mounted, so did the very size of film companies that filled back lots with property storage and personnel. Overhead began to assume significance in the industry, which was developing attributes of big business. By the early twenties, studios were being listed in the stock exchanges, which meant, too, that their financing had gone public.

Yet, because of the popularity of film, Hollywood's sprawling giants and corporate struggles dominated but never excluded smaller kinds of productions. Companies ranged from slick, executive-desk studios to little transient production units on Poverty Row, fronting Gower Street off Sunset Boulevard. As theater chains and first-run palaces developed their caste system of exhibition, small companies sometimes organized independent film exchanges that could provide films at less expense to side-street theaters across the country. A unit like Tiffany Productions specialized in society films and entered the sound era with small-budget westerns and soap opera. Sometimes a single figure would pass through different corporate lives, like W. Ray Johnson (Big Productions, Monogram, Rayart). Often a company leased space in the quarters of a larger studio or else commandeered deserted spots, as Republic did with Mack Sennett's vacated property. Columbia Pictures started as C.B.C. Film Sales on Poverty Row.

William Fox gave name and energies to his own company in 1915 at a time of consolidation, but lost control in 1931. Four years later, the Fox Company merged with Twentieth Century, a recent creation of Joseph Schenck and Darryl Zanuck. Harry, Sam, Jack, and Albert Warner, distributors and exhibitors, absorbed Vitagraph, aging member of the Trust, in 1924 and First National in 1929 under the name of Warner Brothers. Metro-Goldwyn-Mayer came into existence when Marcus Loew, who used Metro Pictures to produce for his New York film chain, merged with Goldwyn, itself a unit composed of the Selwyn brothers and Sam Goldfish, who had been forced out of the Famous Players-Lasky combine by Zukor. Goldfish so liked the new name that he took it for his own, although he only held stock in the firm. Until the early fifties, Mayer supervised production arms of MGM's business.

THE STARS

Big business in Hollywood considered its money invested not risked and expected guaranteed returns. Since profit originated in the pockets and pocketbooks of movie-going millions, audience "predispositions" became matters of increasing concern, sometimes anxiety. Clearly, people responded to certain personalities.

Any relation between screen success and ordinary measures of talent is muddied by contradiction. Some performers brought stage training to the studios; others did not. Some gained reputations on the basis of skills, such as dancing, or of moods projected with a minor litany of facial expressions. Unstudied naturalness (sometimes a cultivated art) engendered audience trust. Sometimes, because of photography, a silent star exuded a unique presence to which onlookers might relate in private fantasy. A rapid examination of movie personalities shows that the motivations for these identifications varied greatly.

Filmgoers were not attracted to the stories

Mary Pickford in *Fate's Interception*. In three years' time her salary leaped upward from $500 to $19,000 per week. World War I saw some of Pickford's best efforts including *Rebecca of Sunnybrook Farm* (1917), *The Little American* (1917), and *M'liss* (1918). (British National Film Archive/Stills Library)

of *Poor Little Peppina* (1916) or *A Romance of the Redwoods* (1917), but rather to "the new Mary Pickford." Her expressions and manner were ritualized performances to be reexperienced with each new title. A director's job amounted less to molding her performance than making her maximally charming and accessible to the audience, working in all the requisite scenes and emotions.

She was, in fact, so successful at defining a screen presence that, like Chaplin, she could not escape it. Carefully filing her nails after a sharp-eyed young spectator saw her on screen and commented that "she's no girl," Little Mary first tried to preserve her pre-adolescent image. But even when roles belied the little-girl character—an unwed sexual liaison in

Fate's Interception (1912), an illegitimate mother in *Hearts Adrift* (1914)—the public held to a breastless, long-curled, popular image of youth. In fact, Pickford grew younger in the twenties. Her use of the baby spot (aimed from below to smooth lines and flatter features) was said to lead to standard practice in Hollywood.

Pickford's charm was nostalgic. She reminded a generation entering a postwar world with transient values and ephemeral standards of a time when parents, minister, and teacher stood for and spoke to stability. Words like *impish, wholesome,* and above all *innocent* described her appeal. Poet and film critic Vachel Lindsay compared her face to a Botticelli painting.

Douglas Fairbanks was a man of uncommonly cheerful energy and a tendency to play to the camera. His early comic success grew in large measure from director John Emerson and scriptwriter Anita Loos, who concocted stories that took advantage of the actor's restless acrobatics. His films celebrated American vulnerabilities, like the urge toward publicity in *His Picture in the Papers* (1916) or crassness about social distinction, *American Aristocracy* (1916). The movies were so bracing, so filled out by Fairbanks' ingratiating energy and optimism that he served equally to reinforce and to ridicule his subject. He became a kind of up-dated Theodore Roosevelt, celebrating the virtues of the West and the strenuous life.

His features provided escape and reassurance that American optimism might hold its own in any exotic setting. Some of the most charming moments in a film like *The Black Pirate* (1926) come from the conspiratorial relation between actor and audience. Both know the story is little more than a flimsy vehicle to support Fairbanks' stunts, and pleasure is shared in the exercise. Yet, while Douglas Fairbanks is skilled enough to be self-deprecating, he has, too, the competitiveness of a deeply ambitious man.

Rodolpho d'Antonguolla started to become Valentino when cast as the lead in *The Four Horsemen of the Apocalypse* (1921), an Argentine playboy celebrated for his Tango. Graceful, handsome, and adored by women, he is yet brave and strong enough to assert his manhood against jealous masculine sneers.

Douglas Fairbanks in *The Mark of Zorro* (1920). The lavishness of Fairbanks' set designs betrayed both his own exuberant pleasures and an executive's interest in every facet of production. Pickfair, home of Pickford and Fairbanks from which they ruled Hollywood society, was emblematic of the twenties film capital. Later remarried and living in England, Fairbanks withdrew from filmmaking in 1934 when encroaching age became visibly evident. (Museum of Modern Art/Film Stills Archive)

Based on a popular novel, the film was written and produced by June Mathis, who recognized Valentino's un-American appeal to American women and tailored subsequent roles to the specifications of that fantasy in *The Conquering Power* (1921), *Blood and Sand* (1922), and *The Young Rajah* (1922). A powerful force in creating Valentino, Mathis's efforts to sustain him with appropriate stories also pioneered in

Lon Chaney as Mr. Wu, a sinister, cultivated mandarin who reverts to vengeance when white miscegenation threatens his family. A child of deaf and dumb parents, Chaney's grotesque make-ups reinforced his mimed skills at characterization. But for a throat cancer, he would have played Count Dracula in 1931. (Movie Star News)

pressing for studio recognition of the scriptwriter's importance.

Valentino's grace, restraint, and surprising flair for comedy were natural skills, but his box-office strength lay in the characterizations of European, Arab, or South American heroes; the sexuality of these foreigners was acceptable while it would have been embar-

rassing in an American male character. Particularly successful was *The Sheik* (1923) in which Ahmed captured Diana Mayo, a beautiful English girl who refuses to submit to him. Ahmed frees Diana, then rescues her from bandits; he is wounded. Nursing him, Diana realizes her love. This was the stuff for American wives.

For twenties filmgoers, Lon Chaney *was* acting. For his roles, he combined a range of characterization with exceptional, sometimes startling makeup. He learned pantomime early. From comic and dance parts on stage, he graduated to slapstick short films in Chicago.

William S. Hart cast Chaney as a heavy in *Riddle Gawne* (1918). Successful, he undertook Frog, a fraudulent cripple in *The Miracle Man* (1919). From this Chaney proceeded to a legless criminal in *The Penalty* (1920), Fagin in *Oliver Twist* (1922), a clown in Victor Seastrom's *He Who Gets Slapped* (1924), a marine in *Tell it to the Marines* (1927), a Chinese mandarin in *Mr. Wu* (1927), and an armless knife thrower in *The Unknown* (1927). Two notorious parts were Quasimodo in *The Hunchback of Notre Dame* (1923) and the scarred composer of *The Phantom of the Opera* (1925). For the hunchback he wore a seventy-pound contrivance, a harness that held him to a crouch, and a skin-tight rubber covering laced with animal hair. Chaney's dedication and energies transcended the vehicles in which he appeared. The Phantom was accomplished with false teeth, discs behind his cheeks, and a wired mechanism which lifted his nose and spread his nostrils. Of all the stars, Chaney was best able to maintain a private life, unrecognized on the street.

If women had Valentino, they shared Greta Garbo with men, although again she fitted a certain type of women's fictions more easily: the beautiful heroine, exotically mysterious, who sacrifices everything for a doomed love. As Valentino's Italian background "allowed" him special erotic behavior, Greta Garbo showed in *Flesh and the Devil* (1927) and *Love* (1928) that her Swedish commitments to passion were without calculation or reservation. Aided by cameraman William Daniels, who did most of her pictures, she projected a sexual openness, while a natural reserve and detachment could imply anything from world-weariness to passive, masochistic suffering. Garbo had the skill to sustain ambiguity. She could be what any man wanted, absorbing in her calculated inexpressiveness the separate needs of an audience.

Hollywood of the silent feature slowly evolved into a new and unique social phenomenon, where the "stars" made more annually than a spectator could earn in a lifetime; where company owners were learning to buy and sell talent the better to hold lucrative fantasies in place; where writers, directors, and cameramen became servants both to actors and owners, while developing the skills on which the others depended.

Salaries

When Mary Pickford's Belasco play, *A Good Little Devil,* was wearing out its run, Zukor contracted to film it, paying Pickford an exceptional $500 a week. Her substantial success in the Famous Players films enriched both the company and Pickford. The salary rose to one, then $2000 dollars weekly.

Samuel Goldwyn said he first heard Mary Pickford's voice as she spoke to Adolph Zukor. Little Mary was saying, "They've offered me five hundred for the use of my name, but do you really think that is enough? After all, it means a lot to those cold cream people."[1] Reinforced with her mother's determination, Pickford knew her worth. Only Chaplin rivaled her popularity. In 1916, both stung and inspired by Charlie Chaplin's Mutual contract of $13,000 a week, Mary Pickford, ably

[1] *Samuel Goldwyn,* Behind the Screen *(New York, 1923), p. 30.*

abetted by her mother, negotiated $10,000 every Monday plus a $300,000 bonus to be given when her pictures had earned that sum beyond the initial investment.

Salary increases reflected the box-office appeal of certain popular stars. The rise in actors' salaries paralleled inflation in other wages. Directors, cameramen, and writers never rivaled Chaplin and, at best, they earned several hundred dollars a week. If top stars appeared, negative costs regularly rose as high as $100,000 to $125,000.

To compensate for these enormous expenditures and to realize continuing profits, Zukor increasingly dominated Paramount's distribution. He raised the rents on his features and gave preferential treatment (access to the most popular films) to those first-run theaters who would additionally accept anything else Zukor made. Rebelling, wealthy exhibitor chains created a rival organization that successfully recruited membership in every major city; its aim was to distribute films which were either independently produced or purchased outright. The group called itself First National; its control of a hundred major theaters threatened principal Zukor outlets. To secure product, First National entered the bidding for high-priced stars and wrote an exceptional contract with Chaplin who would conceive, produce, and direct his own features.

NEWSREELS

As production costs rose, studios were forced to limit the variety of their product, formularizing their output into a specific type of film: a Keystone comedy, a western, a Charlie Chaplin. Small companies and production units within the larger firms often specialized in order to corner pieces of the market that had not been preempted by high budget features. The animated cartoon, comic short, serial and newsreel emerged.

Parades, races and the prize fight had figured early in filmmaking. The 1898 Spanish American War was both documented and staged; W. K. L. Dickson photographed some of the best Boer War material for a British subsidiary of American Mutoscope and Biograph.

After the mass dissemination of photographs through halftone printing, newsreels served more effectively than any other medium to bring events, albeit sensational ones, directly to a vast public. Through the efforts of movie cameramen, theater audiences saw the army of Pancho Villa, trench warfare and torpedoed ships in World War I, earthquakes, presidential campaigns, and Lindbergh's flight. The gravity of these topics was offset by others such as bathing beauty contests, Niagara Falls, and the world series.

In fact, news coverage predates the drama as a high-investment product. The Jeffries-Johnson heavyweight championship at Reno, Nevada on the Fourth of July, 1910 was filmed for General Film Company at a reported $150,000 for exclusive rights and may have realized twice that. Pathé introduced a regular release of events footage in Europe around 1910: literally a news-reel. This was followed by *Britain's Topical Budget,* the *Williamson News, Warwick Chronicle,* and the *Eclair Journal.* An American version of *Pathé's Weekly* appeared in 1911, followed by the *Vitagraph Monthly of Current Events* and the *Gaumont Animated Weekly.* In 1914, Hearst journalism combined with filmmaking to create *Hearst-Selig News Pictorial,* a semi-weekly. *Fox News* appeared in 1919. This was highly capitalized and survived longer than all the rest in the form of *Fox Movietone News.*

SERIALS

The idea of one cast of characters appearing continuously in story episodes had been institutionalized by the nineteenth-century dime

Fantômas. He first appeared in a thirty-two novel detective series written by Pierre Souvestre and Marcel Allain. The movie serial was released in three parts. Like comic superheroes to come, Fantômas cloaked daredevil escapes and rescues beneath criminal guise, his adversaries detective Juve and reporter Jerôme Fandor. (Museum of Modern Art/Film Stills Archive)

novel. Nick Carter, Buffalo Bill, and the James Boys appealed to audiences of predictable size. Since the audience was well aquainted with the particular hero and sometimes villain (Professor Moriarty, for example), a writer could slip more easily into fast, conventionalized plotting without repeating or rethinking characterization.

Movie serials evolved from complete, sequential stories into separate but plot-connected segments which were linked by the manipulation of suspense and resolution. The Edison Company filmed *What Happened to Mary* in 1912, while the story ran concurrently in a popular magazine, *The Ladies' World. What Happened to Mary* could be read monthly and viewed during the week it had appeared in print.

Closer to our own sense of the serial was a French production that appeared in the summer of 1913. This was *Fantômas,* directed by Louis Feuillade. (An important influence on Feuillade appears to be a Vitagraph series,

Scenes From Real Life.) Fantômas was a black-caped bandit, and Feuillade staged his stories, which later appeared in feature length, all over Paris. Even today the combination of real location and fantastic crime and rescue is appealing. Resourceful with gadgets like an early James Bond, Fantômas was well received by the public and, curiously, by avant-garde writers.

For American companies the serial not only carried melodramatic appeal, it afforded a compromise between the 1-reel Trust requirement and the independents' success with longer work. Serial conventions required spe-

cial studio resources. *The Perils of Pauline* (1914) was produced in Jersey City Heights at the Pathé studio, which had a thirty-by-thirty foot tank into which a set might be lowered if the heroine was threatened by rising water. Pearl White sometimes performed her own stunts—on occasion dangerous ones—often more trying on the cameraman than on the actress. *The Perils of Pauline* ran twenty chapters and was "serialized" in Hearst papers. Serials were sometimes condensed and reedited into features at a later date; the ease of this transition testifies to a certain puffiness in the original. Louis B. Mayer's first

"*The Perils of Pauline* is a clean photoplay from beginning to end. You can bring the children and know that they will see only that which is beneficial to them. There are many thrills, many spectacular accidents and many dramatic situations in *The Perils of Pauline* which will keep your interest at fever pitch through the whole episode. Some spectacular accident occurs in each episode, something which you would imagine would be almost impossible for human beings to enact and survive. We will be very much pleased indeed to have you attend the showing of *The Perils of Pauline*." Eclectic Film Co., 110 W. 40th St., New York City. (Museum of Modern Art/ Film Stills Archive)

movie was a serial, *The Great Secret* (1916).

Like pulp-magazine stories, serials often capitalized on national prejudices. Pearl White's villains were menacing Orientals. Other heavies were Mexicans and Huns. The serial was somewhat later than the feature in heeding censors' concerns for national feelings, although gypsies, lacking diplomatic channels, often figured on the dark side of the plots, and sound-era villains from outer space served as politically neutral scapegoats.

In 1915, Pearl White appeared in *The Exploits of Elaine*. A rival heroine, Helen Gibson, outdistanced Ms. White if only in duration: *The Hazards of Helen* ran to 119 chapters. Silent serials concentrated on brave young women, often wealthy, in recurrent danger. The stories were heavily plotted and directed at adults as well as children. Sometimes poorly made (*Pauline's* director Louis Gasnier was abysmal), the serials served as training ground for such performers as Boris Karloff, Carole Lombard, and Jennifer Jones. Serial directors sharpened their skills on action and spectacle, usually with miniscule budgets; some graduated to the position of second-unit directors on expensive features, B. Reeves Eason, for example, who burned Atlanta for *Gone With the Wind* in 1939.

WESTERNS

As in popular literature, the movie western combined action, history, the out-of-doors, and a national preoccupation with overcoming evil by superior skill. Even before *The Great Train Robbery,* Edison did a snippet of western picturesque titled *Cripple Creek Barroom* (1898). Bronco Billy Anderson's cowboy series helped to equate a star with a screen character. Buffalo Bill's Wild West Show had earlier fixed garishly leathered, sequinned costumes in the popular imagination. Buffalo Bill had cowgirls, too. The formula was popular even in Europe, where, for example, Denmark made an early Texas Tex. *The Virginian,* a 1902 novel by Owen Wister, sold 30,000 copies in two years and contributed many conventions. Its hero, a quiet, noble displaced Southerner, lived by a feudal code. Mocked by his enemy, Trampas, who called him a son of a bitch, the Virginian murmured, "When you call me that, smile."

Everyone tried a hand at westerns, but Griffith was first to press the material into a pattern. In *The Last Drop of Water* (1911), US cavalry rescue a wagon train beseiged by Indians. In *Fighting Blood* (1911), the cavalry saved women and children under Indian attack in a cabin. Mary Pickford appeared in a number of Biograph Indian films, such as *A Pueblo Legend* (1912). Griffith allowed Indians to be seen as heroic, but, like Mexicans and other foreigners, they were commendable when behaving most like whites.

Thomas Ince, whose story follows in Chapter 5, further defined what we call the western. He hired William S. Hart, a stage actor friend, in 1914 to appear as a villain in a pair of 2-reelers. These were followed by western features, one of which Hart wrote in part, *The Bargain* (1914). Its success led to a spate of Hart directed-acted stories. The best history of western films points up one significant shot in *The Scourge of the Desert* (1916) that:

. . . became something of a Hart trademark: a slow pan from the villain's face, in full close-up, across to Hart's grim and defiant face, also in close-up. In this instance, the pan continued past Hart's face to take in a rifle hanging on the wall, panning down to the anxious face of the heroine, desperately afraid, but trusting Hart to protect her.[2]

---

[2] *George Fenin and William K. Everson,* The Western *(New York, 1962), p. 79.*

The Aryan. William Hart turns to an outlaw life among Indians after having been cheated of his gold claim by an unscrupulous woman. Finally, the trust and confidence of actress Bessie Love wins him back. Hart's heyday was the decade following *The Squaw Man. Tumbleweeds* tried, and failed commercially, to equal the epic proportions of *The Covered Wagon.* (Museum of Modern Art/Film Stills Archive)

To our eyes, Hart's films seem a mixture of the realistic and the sentimental. He played a variety of unsympathetic roles, from gambler to outlaw accomplice. Staging was remarkably authentic and unpretentious, and Hart would often die at the end, yet he was dangerously prone to reform, either through a child's adoration or the love of a good woman. His affection for his horse was enormous. Hart would sometimes journey to the East to rescue or avenge someone, then turn back with a title like, "I'm goin' back to the country where I belong." Hart's titles were quite something.

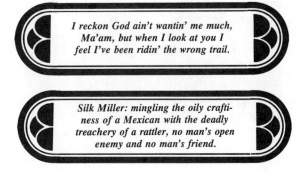

I reckon God ain't wantin' me much, Ma'am, but when I look at you I feel I've been ridin' the wrong trail.

Silk Miller: mingling the oily craftiness of a Mexican with the deadly treachery of a rattler, no man's open enemy and no man's friend.

Hart continued to make films for years, *The Aryan* (1916) was noteworthy, although later production evidenced advancing age and inclination toward cliché. *Tumbleweeds* (1925), his last, featured the opening of the Cherokee Strip to the land rush, edited with precision and beauty.

The other silent western star was Tom Mix, one-time soldier, wrangler, rodeo contestant, Texas Ranger, sheriff and US deputy. Mix joined Selig as an animal trainer and double, then became a screenwriter, director, and star. In 1917, he moved to Fox, who gave him his own crew. Mix made more than sixty features for Fox, establishing his personal pattern.

I ride into a place owning my own horse, saddle, and bridle. It isn't my quarrel, but I get into trouble doing the right thing for somebody else. When it's all ironed out, I never get any money reward. I may be made foreman of the ranch and I get the girl but there is never a fervid love scene.[3]

Mix's screen presence was far more easygoing than Hart's. Many of his Selig films were comedies. His wonder horse, Tony, figured heavily in the stories and made the transition to sound more easily than his master. In 1932, Tom Mix married for the fifth time, quit film, and joined Sells Floto Circus.

Douglas Fairbanks brought another kind of dashing, energetic comedic personality to westerns he made for Triangle. The form became increasingly stylized, and western scriptwriting a skilled specialty. Charles Alden Seltzer, for instance, wrote forty-six novels and scripts for Tom Mix, William S. Hart, and Buck Jones. Jones was one of the next crop of featured performers, which included Harry Carey and Hoot Gibson.

Director John Ford commenced early with westerns for Universal. He also wrote and starred, as Jack Ford, in *The Scrapper* (1915). *The Outcasts of Poker Flat* (1919) was praised for its photography. Ford's most noteworthy silent film was *The Iron Horse* (1924), shot in the deserts of Nevada. It ran two hours and forty minutes, and was distinguished by its carefully built action sequences and the special placement of a camera to capture movement from atop the train.

The Covered Wagon, directed by James Cruze in 1923, proved even more successful than *The Iron Horse*. It was epic in conception, weak in plot, and impressively photographed. The story traced a wagon trip to California, with predictable villainy and love interest. If diminished by some studio simulations, the film used Utah and Nevada locations for effective, documentary flavor. Its popularity helped to insure the well-budgeted western feature into early sound years.

SHORTS

After Hollywood's turn to features, what had earlier been complete entertainment projects now were known as "shorts." So long as the single feature was booked in theaters, shorts led a healthy commercial existence, increasingly inflected by specialization and series design. Besides Sennett, certain studios came to devote full attention to such films: Hal Roach, for one, and Educational Pictures. The latter foresook the intentions that its name implied and turned to comedy. Large companies also had shorts units, often used to train production crews and performers.

The short provided a basic vehicle for artists like Laurel and Hardy and Our Gang, both by way of Hal Roach. Shorts first exposed film audiences to Will Rogers. They were a special vehicle for screen comics, figures like Larry Semon, Ben Turpin, Charley Chase, and Harry Langdon, as well as those

---

[3] *Ibid. p. 117.*

graduating to feature length. Keaton and Langdon offer the additional cases of stars who returned to shorts in the sound period. Shorts-buffs can trace a figure like Edgar "Slow Burn" Kennedy from Keystone Kop days through Laurel and Hardy, Charley Chase and Our Gang productions to his own series and then feature credit in films like *Duck Soup* (1933), *Twentieth Century* (1934), and *San Francisco* (1936).

KEYSTONE COMEDY

Before Mack Sennett went bankrupt in the thirties, he had established a unique reputation for a peculiarly identifiable American comedy. More than actor, writer, or director, Sennett was catalyst to an eccentric collection of clowns and straightmen who composed Keystone, whose trademark became grotesque slapstick. He worked with major comedians like Chaplin, Harry Langdon, and Buster Keaton, but these men moved on, and Keystone was best known for minor clowns like Al St. John, Ben Turpin, Ford Sterling, and Chester Conklin, as well as the Sennett Bathing Girls.

Sennett's shorts, which number in the hundreds with titles like *Love, Speed and Thrills* (1915) and *Teddy at the Throttle* (1916), usually involve chases, for which the Keystone Kops were preeminent. Featuring Gloria Swanson and Wallace Beery. *Teddy* satirizes both Griffith rescues and *Rover* dog stories. The chases did not so much serve the narrative climaxes as exist like vulgar circus ballets with choreographies that shone strangely independent of story. Sennett's characters are the loosest sort of funny masks, and it is their invention that matters. The movement is especially important, for at best, Keystones are remarkable for their odd, frenetic pace. As overseer of an anarchic troupe, Sennett had a tower constructed in the middle of his lot. High above, with windows on all sides, he looked down from an office equipped with bathtub and masseur. His wild comedy declined in the twenties. Early in the thirties,

The Keystone Kops in a tight moment. Sennett restored out-of-fashion chases both by ridiculing and choreographing their movements, in particular the indignities visited on both pursuer and pursued. Keystone used trained racing drivers. In combination with camera undercranking and soap-slicked roads, their feats were prodigious. (British National Film Archive/Stills Library)

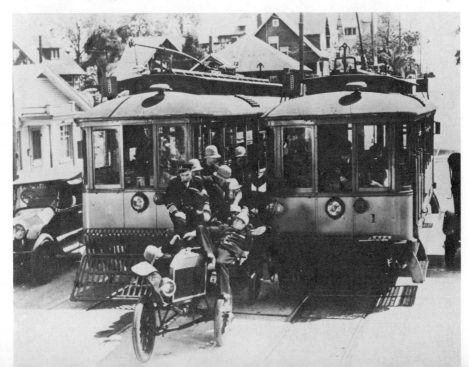

Sennett made sound shorts, including three 1933 W. C. Fields classics: *The Fatal Glass of Beer, The Pharmacist* and *The Barbershop*.

THE FUNNYMEN

Silent film, particularly well-suited to pratfalls and anticipations, played host to a remarkable number and variety of comics. In name or spirit, the best of the funny men wrote and directed their work; of all the early filmmakers, they learned the silent film prosody best, manipulating audience perceptions the better to support gags and story lines. Like early dramatic stars, comedians fall into two classes, those whose masks transform and disguise through caricature alone and those whose screen presence extends a more complex, personality, a broader world view.

In the cases of Harold Lloyd, we witness an apprenticeship behind the mask. He is seen gradually to become Harold Lloyd. In early Hollywood days, Lloyd and Hal Roach had scurried about the studios looking for extra work. When Roach entered filmmaking, the pair developed a character out of low-comic materials—silk hat, mustache, padded coat— and named it Willie Work. Lloyd quit when he discovered a dramatic lead working for Roach was earning ten dollars a day against his five.

Lloyd moved to Keystone where he learned from the knockabout frenzies. Then he returned to Roach at fifty dollars a week and conceived another Chaplin variation: big

Harold Lloyd on the flagpole in *Safety Last.* While a double, Bill Strothers, appeared in some shots, Lloyd executed most himself, playing to camera angles that stressed the street below. A platform stood ready three flights down, but, when a dummy was dropped, it bounced directly onto the street. (Museum of Modern Art/Film Stills Archive)

shoes, tight striped pants, too-small vest, collar, hat, and sleazy tie. As Lonesome Luke, Lloyd made a hundred 1-reelers. In time he "wanted to be a fellow who wouldn't be ridiculous on the screen if the story of a boy-and-girl romance came along. I wanted to wear decent, or at least appropriate clothes."[4] In part, the impulse was a response to feature-length plots.

Lloyd termed the character he devised a "comic Frank Merriwell," a young man of boundless energy, trust, naïveté and faith in the system. He pursued success, winning the girl, making money, becoming popular, but there were obstacles. The greatest obstacle was himself, for Lloyd was alternately so unbelievably brash as to alienate everyone he met, or else he was a "mama's boy," insecure, inept, and cowardly.

To identify this figure, Lloyd settled on what he called the Glass Character; he wore horn-rimmed glasses, heavy enough for distinctive cast, small enough to allow expressions to play on his face. A flowing tie was later discarded. The Glass Character exaggerated, to the degree of satire but not caricature, middle-class America. Lloyd's work blended a restrained slapstick with enough believability to nurture a kind of situation comedy that survives today in many television series: an optimistic mirror of the American Dream. In the end, Boy Gets Girl because at the climax he successfully breaks from inhibitions that constrained or distorted his behavior earlier.

In *The Freshman* (1925), Lloyd becomes enraged when he comes to understand that he has been water boy all season, rather than a playing team member, so he throws himself into the big game, and wins it with a manic speed that expresses all the furious energy that had been only implicit until then, guised in his urge for popularity. In *Safety Last* (1923), Lloyd plays a store clerk who is forced by circumstances to assume the role of a human fly, scaling a many-storied office building. Elaborated from an earlier short, the situation is ideal for the comedian. He faces a tennis net, scaffolding, pigeons, and finally a wall clock whose hands and face thwart every inventive upward thrust. As with most Lloyd humor, both the clerk's objective and obstacles to its achievement are apparent to the audience. He triumphs through physical skill, with gags paced to build like the increasing thrills in an acrobatic act. Lloyd *earns* his laughs, as ambitious and eager to please as the Glass Character.

The director Frank Capra learned writing at Keystone. Puzzling over comedy one day, he concluded that what he termed "fixes" on the stars decreed Chaplin to think his way out of difficulties, Lloyd to overcome them with speed, Keaton to suffer stoically.[5]

Like Lloyd, Buster Keaton plotted his films with an eye to the "normal." Buster characteristically plays a young man in love who may, often as not, win the girl. His obstacles come not from personal inadequacies but a manic world that consistently betrays him through chance, misunderstanding, and perverse coincidence.

[5] *Frank Capra*, The Name Above the Title, *(New York, 1971), p. 62.*

Harold Lloyd (1893–1971)

Grandma's Boy	1922
Dr. Jack	1922
Safety Last	1923
Why Worry?	1923
The Freshman	1925
Speedy	1925
Professor Beware	1938
Mad Wednesday/The Sins of Howard Diddlebock	1947
Harold Lloyd's World of Comedy (compilation)	1961
Partial listing	

[4] *William Cohn,* Harold Lloyd's World of Comedy *(New York, 1964), p. 83.*

The Funnymen   **95**

While Lloyd satirizes but embraces his society, Buster Keaton creates a total environment whose ultimate cruelty is to encourage our trust. In *Cops* (1922), a 2-reeler, Buster finds a wallet of money, is rebuffed by the dapper figure who dropped it, retrieves the wallet's money, and departs in the owner's taxi. He is tricked into buying a cart of furniture, which really belongs to a policeman in process of moving. He makes the investment in order to become a successful businessman, the condition his girl places on marriage. Driving the cart, Buster becomes involved in a municipal police parade. Business, money, and police merge into a logic gone awry, a system based on false impressions. Riding in the parade, Buster searches for a match. At that moment, a bearded anarchist pitches a bomb that lands, sizzling, next to Keaton. Unknowing, he lights his cigarette with the fuse, and pitches the bomb overboard. It explodes, and Keaton is pursued by the entire police parade.

As a child, Buster learned every kind of fall from vaudeville while performing as the Human Mop with his parents in their act, The Three Keatons. His father flung Keaton about the stage, teaching him to endure. The essence of his comedy rests in Buster's extraordinary grace in confronting, surviving, then overcoming the world's ominous perfidies. He was called "The Great Stone Face," because his apparent expression was so unchanging, but the body is eloquent. Really, there is nothing inexpressive about Keaton; he is totally a subtle instrument of response. Just as close examination of the eyes and mouth show us that Buster *is* feeling most deeply, the postures of his figure betray intense human dispositions, such as trust, when he holds the position of a sailor looking out to sea as a boat sinks steadily in *The Navigator* (1924). In *Seven Chances* (1925), the body is altogether panicked, fleeing a pursuit by women and boulders, both of whom carry an equal sense of inevitability about them.

Keaton's best sequences were painstakingly constructed out of comic intuition, an enthusiasm for mechanics, and a mastery of timing and physical control. The entire wall of a house falls on Keaton and he survives because an open window coincides with the spot where he stands. The stunt was done "live" in *Steamboat Bill, Jr.* (1928). Unlike Lloyd, Keaton is not motivated by competitiveness, but rather by a steady, almost unconscious perseverence, which perhaps explains the continuing popularity of his films.

Resurgent interest in Keaton implies no inevitable decline in Charlie Chaplin's standing, although sentimentality is increasing apparent in Chaplin's work. Like Griffith he inhabits the far side of World War I where some emotions, such as pity, appear to require highly conventional plot contrivances.

Chaplin's childhood reads like Dickens. He grew up in the slums of London, born of unsuccessful music hall artists, commencing on stage in 1895 at age six. The success of a pantomime company produced by Fred Carno led to an American tour, which in turn brought Chaplin to Hollywood as one of Sennett's clowns. The Englishman's technique suffered in Keystone's quick, frenzied productions, but in thirty-five films, Chaplin developed a basic

Buster Keaton (1895–1966)

Cops	1922
The Balloonatic	1923
The Three Ages	1923
Our Hospitality	1923
Sherlock Junior	1924
The Navigator	1924
Seven Chances	1925
Go West	1925
The General	1926
Steamboat Bill, Jr.	1928
The Cameraman	1928
The Railrodder (actor)	1965
Film (actor)	1968
Partial Listing	

Buster in *The Frozen North* (1922) (left). This sequence opens the picture, partly a burlesque on William S. Hart's deadpan heroics. Charlie in *The Gold Rush* (right). Keaton said The Little Tramp was ultimately a bum with a bum's philosophy, while—in contrast—he played an honest working man. The comparison conveniently ignores such incidents as Buster's pilfering a billfold in *Cops*. (Museum of Modern Art/Film Stills Archive) (Movie Star News)

style and costume: oversized, ragged shoes, baggy pants, vest and jacket that were tight under the arm and spreading at the waist, derby hat too small and high on the head, frayed shirt, shabby tie, worn gloves, and cane. His tramp figure, pathetic, pretentious, shy and inventive, cascades with the versatility of a great improviser.

Worldwide audience response to Charlie, the comic figure so different from the man and yet so inseparable, was immense. The humor grew out of situations so basic that mime bypassed language and culture. Chaplin moved from Essanay to Mutual to United Artists. His salary skyrocketed so wildly that a contract with First National guaranteed one million dollars for eight films of any length. In 1918, Chaplin occupied his own film studios, which he inhabited as long as his tenure in Hollywood. As early as Keystone, Chaplin had gained writer-director control of his work. When the projects grew in length and ambition, Chaplin developed increasingly painstaking, time-consuming approaches to the rou-

Charles Chaplin (1889–1977)

Kid Auto Races at Venice	1914
Tillie's Punctured Romance	1914
The Tramp	1915
A Woman	1915
One A.M.	1916
Easy Street	1917
The Cure	1917
A Dog's Life	1918
Shoulder Arms	1918
Sunnyside	1919
The Kid	1921
A Woman of Paris	1923
The Gold Rush	1925
The Circus	1928
City Lights	1931
Modern Times	1936
The Great Dictator	1940
Monsieur Verdoux	1947
Limelight	1952
A King in New York	1957
A Countess from Hong Kong	1966
Partial listing	

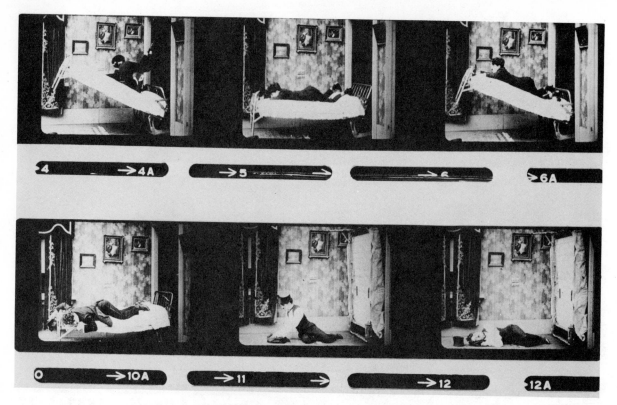

The Murphy bed in *One A.M.* Excepting Albert Austin's moment as a taxi driver, Chaplin's fourth Mutual was a solo tour de force, which resuscitated early Karno Company English pantomime bits. Wildly drunk, Charlie challenges the bed and loses. An upstanding leg will shortly drop directly onto the hat. (Museum of Modern Art/Film Stills Archive)

tines, shooting endlessly until the apparently unstudied performance was refined to perfection.

At first, the shorts range from Keystone comedy to music-hall routines. Then they become stories invented for the camera. Most establish archetypal comic figures—the Girl, the Villain—who operate as pivots against whom Charlie can play inventive variation.

Chaplin material draws on first generation American experience: immigration, employment in a pawnshop, a dishwasher, working with a paperhanger. Other stories fantasize vagabond adventures on the road, and sometimes Chaplin burlesques the pretensions of his costume by playing a count, a floorwalker, or a policeman. He is always an underling at heart, pathetic in his need, inconsonant with the mundanity of his surroundings. In a fight Chaplin outwits. As a drunk in *One A.M.* (1916), he staggers with a dancer's grace. A policeman in *Easy Street* (1917), he bests the villains, pirhouettes to embrace Edna Purviance, narrowly escapes falling into an open manhole, and wipes beads of sweat from his brow into the sewer.

Like stage mime, Chaplin comedy depends on creating an imagined scene with gesture alone. He watches a masseur in *The Cure* (1917), then raises the pummeling hands, inasmuch saying: "The winner." In *Shoulder Arms* (1918), he identifies his origins to Edna by acting out the stars and stripes. Excepting the uneven 6 reel *Tillie's Punctured Romance*, directed by Sennett in 1914, Chaplin made eleven features. But for small bits, he directed but did not appear in two, the dramatic *A Woman of Paris* (1923)[6] and *A Countess from Hong Kong* (1966). Until the last, humor is bittersweet. Pity mingles with the laughs, and this becomes increasingly true as Chaplin's story lines develop human character for the Tramp in the longer works. Charlie's very fantasy-inducing skills blind him to the realities of human relationship. At one point in *The Gold Rush* (1925), he mistakes Georgia Hale's smile when it is intended for a man standing behind him; later when she actually does address him, he cannot believe it.

Sometimes he wins, as in *Modern Times* (1936), but the most-remembered conclusions grow out of pathos, like the famous ending to *City Lights* (1931). The blind flower girl has recovered her sight and now sees her benefactor, Charlie. His fingers in his mouth, Chaplin stares into her eyes, waiting to discover whether his fantasy or the world's realities will prevail.

City Lights was Chaplin's first sound venture, but he rejected speech in favor of music and sound effects. He allowed himself a nonsensical patter song in *Modern Times,* and did not give himself regular language until *The Great Dictator* (1940), in which Adolph Hitler replaced the Tramp's presumptions. In *Monsieur Verdoux* (1947), Chaplin essayed a bitter, ironic comedy about an out-of-work clerk who marries, then murders wealthy women to support his crippled wife. Verdoux sees murder as the logical extension of business. At the expense of humor, Chaplin's later films grew increasingly prone to philosophical monologues. From earliest times, he showed a penchant for social criticism, but his barbs were more effective when they were the slyest, as in a dream of slum heaven in *The Kid* (1921), where all is white and drinks are free and dogs have wings, but a vamp's temptation and the police never change. Angered at American affairs and beseiged by bad publicity, Chaplin left the United States in 1952, denied reentry by the government.

MOTION PICTURE PRODUCERS AND DISTRIBUTORS OF AMERICA, INCORPORATED

Local and regional outcries at lasciviousness in film (more often innuendo than not) date from nickelodeon times. Then, women stripped to underwear or leotards. Skirts blew up above the knees and middle-class husbands kissed servants and typists. Edison's *Passion Dance* (1896), performed by Dolorita in ponderous emulation of North African exotica, led to one cancelation from Atlantic City's Boardwalk when a Kinetoscope owner wrote:

The authorities request us not to show the Houchi Kouchi, so please cancel order for new Dolorita, also order for Amy Muller, colored. The emulsion on the *Rope Dance* is coming off in large pieces.[7]

In 1907, a Chicago judge announced that nickelodeons "cause, indirectly or directly, more juvenile crime coming into my court than all other causes combined."[8] At the same time, civic groups were willing to oppose municipal censorship of short films with the argu-

[6] *All Chaplin's work has not stood the test of time equally well. Except for its dance sequence,* Sunnyside *(1919) is dreadfully contrived.* A Woman of Paris *tries to wring drama out of situations that might better have served comedy. The emotions are incongruous, subtleties clichéd, resolutions pat, ironies banal. Some lost films are better lost.*

[7] *Terry Ramsaye,* A Million and One Nights *(New York, 1962), vol. I, p. 256.*
[8] *Ibid. p. 474.*

ment that such action amounted to inequitable class legislation which judged the people's cheap theater far more harshly than what might be permitted on "legitimate" stages.[9]

Yet, until the early twenties, motion pictures were relatively free of serious threats to their unfettered exhibition, even despite occasional nudity and unpunished philandering. At that time, two separate pressures brought about a turn of events.

In September of 1921, Hollywood recoiled in trepidation from the Fatty Arbuckle scandal. Arbuckle was a successful comedian accused of accidentally killing a young woman in a San Francisco hotel-room. Wallace Reid, a popular star, died in a sanitorium trying to break his drug addiction. Then an English director named William Desmond Taylor was shot in his home, and the ensuing new stories involved comedienne Mabel Normand and actress Mary Miles Minter as well as drugs. If movies were becoming as Jazz Age as the society, popular evidence now suggested that filmmakers acted no differently offscreen than on.

The outcry from national religious leaders, public figures, and legislators coincided with an unexpected downturn in movie profits. The decline might be explained in terms of newly-competitive radio broadcasts, increased sales of automobiles, and the closing of older store-front theaters; it might equally be considered a public response to Hollywood misbehavior.

Under similar pressure, major league baseball had inaugurated Judge Kenesaw Mountain Landis as "czar" in the wake of the 1919 World Series, which gamblers had fixed. Landis was a conservative, midwestern jurist. The filmmakers set their eyes on President Warren Harding's Postmaster-General and onetime national chairman of the Republican Party, Will H. Hays.

[9] Russell Merritt, "Nickelodeon Theaters 1905-1914," in Tino Balio, ed., The American Film Industry (Madison, 1976), p. 63.

Hays assumed office in 1922 as president of the Motion Picture Producers and Distributors of America, Inc. He continued in that capacity until 1945, salary soon raised from $100,000 to $150,000 a year. The MPPDA was a successful diplomatic effort not only to avoid legislative edict by imposing self-censorship on the industry but also to appease Protestant American criticisms of a business that was largely controlled by Jews. Hays' organization was stocked with Christians and situated in New York, where the financial seat of film power still rested, because of exhibitors' headquarters and of Wall Street financing. Hays was also markedly successful in reassuring financeers that Hollywood's intensely competitive production empires were in fact responsible business ventures whose expansions deserved the investment capital of the East.

The MPPDA Production Code spelled out in detail what could or could not be included in films produced by member corporations, articulating the acceptable in terms of plot, speech, costume, and subject. Crime, sex, religion, profanity, cruelty to animals, and "national feelings" were areas of particular concern. In the back of everyone's mind, offense to no one meant maximum sales, domestically and abroad. Scripts were submitted to the MPPDA so that problems could be resolved before the expense of production. Failure to secure a Seal of Approval thrust an offending film into the outskirts of film exhibition, beyond the pale of theaters and distributors controlled by the MPPDA, which became the MPAA, Motion Pictures Association of America, Inc. in 1945.

In theory, the Production Code sternly regulated screen morals. In practice, it led to some unanticipated results. Many code fiats imposed prohibitions and values common only to selected portions of the broad audience. (Much of it was composed by Martin Quigley, a power-wielding trade publisher and Catholic layman.)

Unsuppressible scandal erupts in Hollywood and San Francisco. After further trials, Arbuckle was ultimately found innocent, but by then the damage was done to his career and to the film capital. Some students of comedy view Lloyd's star rising in genteel reaction to Fatty's screen vulgarities. Following on implications of orgy and rape, the Taylor case added clear evidence of hard drugs. (Newspaper Collection—The New York Public Library: Astor, Lenox and Tilden Foundations)

Melodramatic formulae that permitted misbehavior by finally punishing it encouraged perfunctory endings, or else attributions of motive helped to substantiate suspicions that some parts of a story might be "truer" (more consistent and closer to experience) than others. Especially after the advent of sound, efforts by scriptwriters and directors to sneak their intentions around the regulations sometimes encouraged new subtleties. At their best, the style of some directors constituted a creative response to the Motion Picture Producers and Distributors of America's moral admonitions.

Summary

Impressive transitions from 2-reelers to "features" gave rise to Hollywood as an industrial film capital. Consolidating production and exhibition, major studios regularized the financing of ambitious projects and systematized assembly-line production.

With higher commitments at stake, both stars and generic formulae came quickly to be regarded as potential guarantees of a predictable audience size. Figures such as Pickford and Chaplin, who enjoined personal appeal with audience fantasy, met with unprecedented success. Ever cautious of public opinion, the industry took steps in the early twenties to regulate motion picture behavior, on screen and off, in response to the scandals that threatened to blacken Hollywood's name and, worse, to reduce audience size.

The twenties constituted Hollywood's silent heyday, built on a stable narrative design, comfortably financed, sometimes self-indulgent with its own dream factory evocations. Chapter 5 singles out the decade's outstanding directors for more detailed examination.

Bibliography

Allvine, Glendon. *The Greatest Fox of Them All*. New York, 1969.
Asplund, Uno. *Chaplin's Films*. South Brunswick, N.J., 1976.
Balio, Tino, ed. *The American Film Industry*. Madison, 1976.
Balio, Tino. *United Artists: The Company Built by Stars*. Madison, 1975.
Balshofer, Fred J. and Arthur C. Miller. *One Reel a Day*. Berkeley, 1967.
Barbour, Alan G. *Cliffhanger*. New York, 1977.
Berg, Charles Merrell. *An Investigation of the Motives for and Realization of Music to Accompany the American Silent Film: 1897-1927*. New York, 1976.
Blesh, Rudi. *Keaton*. New York, 1966.
Crowther, Bosley. *The Lion's Share*. New York, 1957.
———. *Hollywood Rajah*. New York, 1960.
Drinkwater, John. *The Life and Adventures of Carl Laemmle*. New York, 1931.
Eames, John Douglas. *The MGM Story*. New York, 1975.
Easton, Carol. *The Search for Sam Goldwyn*. New York, 1976.
Edmunds, I. G. *Big U.: Universal in the Silent Days*. New York, 1977.
Fenin, George and William K. Everson. *The Western*. New York, 1962.
Fernett, Gene. *Poverty Row*. Satellite Beach, Fla., 1973.
French, Philip. *The Movie Moguls*. Chicago, 1969.

Goldwyn, Samuel. *Behind the Screen*. New York, 1923.

Green, Fitzhugh. *The Film Finds Its Tongue*. New York, 1929.

Hampton, Benjamin. *History of the American Film Industry*. rev. ed. New York, 1970.

Harmon, Jim and Donald Glut. *The Great Movies Serials*. Garden City, N.Y., 1972.

Higham, Charles. *Warner Brothers*. New York, 1975.

Huettig, Mae D. *Economic Control of the Motion Picture Industry*. Philadelphia, 1944.

Huff, Theodore. *Charlie Chaplin*. New York, 1951.

Jobes, Gertrude. *Motion Picture Empire*. Hampton, Conn., 1966.

Johnston, Alva. *The Great Goldwyn*. New York, 1937.

Kennedy, Joseph P., ed. *The Story of the Films*. Chicago, 1927.

Koszarski, Richard. *Hollywood Directors 1914-1940*. New York, 1976.

Lahue, Kalton C. *Kops and Custard*. Norman, Okla., 1968.

————. *Dreams for Sale: The Rise and Fall of the Triangle Film Corporation*. South Brunswick, N.J., 1971.

————. *Motion Picture Pioneer: The Selig Polyscope Company*. New York, 1973.

Larkin, Rochelle. *Hail, Columbia*. New Rochelle, N.Y., 1975.

Lasky, Jesse. *I Blow My Own Horn*. Garden City, 1957.

Lyons, Timothy J. *The Silent Partner: The History of the American Film Manufacturing Company*. New York, 1974.

McCaffrey, Donald. *Four Great Comedians*. New York, 1968.

Maltin, Leonard. *The Great Movie Shorts*. New York, 1972.

Marx, Samuel. *Mayer and Thalberg, the Make-Believe Saints*. New York, 1975.

Moews, Daniel. *Keaton: The Silent Features Close Up*. Berkeley, 1976.

Moley, Raymond. *The Hays Office*. New York, 1945.

North, Christopher. "U. A.'s 35th Birthday." *Films in Review*, April 1954.

Pratt, George. *Spellbound in Darkness*. 2nd ed. New York, 1966.

Robinson, David. *Hollywood in the Twenties*. New York, 1968.

Seabury, William. *The Public and the Motion Picture Industry*. New York, 1926.

Sennett, Mack. *King of Comedy*. Garden City, N.Y., 1954.

Sklar, Robert. *Movie Made America*. New York, 1975.

Spears, Jack. *Hollywood the Golden Era*. New York, 1971.

Stedman, Raymond W. *The Serials: Suspense and Drama by Installment*. Norman, Okla., 1977.

Thomas, Bob. *King Cohn*. London, 1967.

Warner, Jack. *My First Hundred Years in Hollywood*. New York, 1965.

White, Pearl. *Just Me*. New York, 1919.

Zukor, Adolph. *The Public Is Never Wrong*. New York. 1953.

5

DIRECTORS OF AMERICAN FILM: SILENT

During 1922, 40 million Americans frequented movie theaters weekly; by 1928, that number had risen by half. In the earlier period, more than 300 million dollars went to tickets, well beyond a half billion by the time of commercial sound.[1] Through this epoch, thousands of motion pictures came and went, most as interesting and long-lived as a daily newspaper. At the same time, some personalities—as often emigrés as not—shaped the outline, the substance, and the style of execution for the undefined medium. From among this group, eight appear below.

Cecil DeMille combined directing skill with a talent to predict lascivious shifts of audience taste. Thomas Ince imposed the studio producer's role on ensuing decades. King Vidor and Henry King imbued commercial film product with their personal visions.

[1] *Garth Jowett,* Film The Democratic Art *(Boston, 1976), pp. 192-5.*

Thomas Ince (left) (Museum of Modern Art/Film Stills Archive)

Like fruit trees, European directors might or might not take to the native soil. Some, like Mauritz Stiller, Paul Leni, Benjamin Christiensen, Paul Fejos, and Ludwig Berger, made seemingly little contribution to American screens, although Fejos' *Lonsome* and *The Last Moment* received strong critical support in 1928. In contrast, Erich von Stroheim and Josef von Sternberg became the stuff of Hollywood legend, due in large part to their own crafty devising. Each developed a kind of impermeable public façade, the better to protect a relation to the "industry" which was at odds with Hollywood's sense of entertainment. Lodging vulgarity in delightful comic froth, Ernst Lubitsch had more of DeMille about him. Seastrom seems almost to have made Swedish films in America.

Cecil B. Demille (1881–1959)

The Squaw Man	1913
The Virginian	1914
The Girl of the Golden West	1915
The Warrens of Virginia	1915
The Arab	1915
The Golden Chance	1915
The Cheat	1915
The Trail of the Lonesome Pine	1916
Joan the Woman	1917
Male and Female	1919
Don't Change Your Husband	1919
For Better or Worse	1919
Why Change your Wife	1920
The Ten Commandments	1923
King of Kings	1927
The Sign of the Cross	1932
Cleopatra	1934
The Plainsman	1938
Union Pacific	1939
The Greatest Show on Earth	1952
The Ten Commandments	1956
Partial listing	

CECIL B. DEMILLE

The DeMille from the time of *Joan the Woman* (1917) is one of movie spectaculars, historical and biblical epics, impressive crowd scenes, weak story lines, wooden acting, and a judicious mix of titillating sin with stern moral retribution so that a viewer enjoys the best of both worlds. Without the evidence of earlier films, it is difficult to realize that there was a previous, better DeMille who dates from the very birth of Hollywood.

The Great Train Robbery was still exhibited in 1913 and, however dated, it inspired Cecil B. DeMille. He formed a New York partnership with Jesse Lasky, with whom DeMille had collaborated on some operas; in earlier life, Lasky had been a vaudeville musician. With Sam Goldfish as salesman, the Jesse L. Lasky Feature Play Company hawked states rights sales to build front money for a feature. Their property was a successful play called *The Squaw Man*. DeMille, with acting and playwrighting experience, prepared an adaptation and shared the directing with Oscar Apfel, who had done "some film work."

The group envisioned Flagstaff as their location, but on arrival found Arizona so unlike the fictional Wyoming they had in mind that they continued to the end of the train line, which happened to be Los Angeles. *The Squaw Man* (6 reels) was shot in 1914 on southern California locations and in a Hollywood barn that became headquarters. The staging and performance, if stiff, profited from the geography and from honest efforts to substitute action for lengthy, explanatory intertitles. Goldfish's $60,000 worth of contracts grew during exhibition to $250,000.

DeMille's early films were alternately westerns, society dramas, and comedies. Cecil's brother William adapted plays, like David Belasco's *The Girl of the Golden West* (1915) and *The Warrens of Virginia* (1915). Battle scenes and panoramic views aside, the early DeMilles have effective if melodramatic story lines, unfatted with pomposity.

One of the best of these early films is *The Cheat* (1915), which concerns Edith Hardy, a frivolous society woman, who gambles away charity funds, secures a loan from Tori, a wealthy Burmese, and is about to pay the usual Victorian price for such generosity when her husband makes Edith a gift of the same sum. She returns the money to Tori; he is dissatisfied with the new turn and brands the woman with an Oriental emblem of personal ownership. Edith shoots Tori. Her husband assumes the guilt. The whole story comes out in court, and Tori, now recovered, is attacked by the spectators. The story is not without racial overtones, but Sessue Hayakawa as Tori triumphs in a superior performance.

The film foreshadows DeMille's later strategies, for he said he wanted to confront contemporary social issues, such as prejudice, by "pointing out incidents that shouldn't happen." Cameraman Alvin Wyckoff photographed key scenes in a high-contrast lighting that intensifies the branding, the shooting, and the trial in deep blacks and whites. A man of immense will, DeMille was filming a second feature, *The Golden Chance* (1915), in the evening while he made *The Cheat* during the day.

His penchant for starless films eventually trained future celebrities who started as unknowns, Gloria Swanson in particular, who appeared in *Don't Change Your Husband* (1919), *For Better or Worse* (1919), and *Why Change Your Wife* (1920). Swanson's most entertaining vehicle, *Male and Female* (1919),

The Cheat. Fanny Ward and Jack Dean both appear to be immensely pleased in this publicity still reenacting his gift of bank notes, which will replace Red Cross funds she gambled away. DeMille's sensational scenes were abetted by cameraman Alvin Wyckoff; his chiaroscuro effects became renowned as "Lasky lightning." (Museum of Modern Art/Film Stills Archive)

The hero of *Civilization* is a submarine commander. When he refuses to torpedo a passenger liner, the crew mutinies. Dying when his vessel sinks, the commander yields his body to Christ, who returns to earth and persuasively shows war's horrors (as above) to a militant, vaguely Teutonic, ruler. Ince made a mint. (British National Archive/Stills Library)

combined social comedy with scanty costume; in a somewhat inexplicable Babylonian flashback, she is suggestively pawed by a friendly lion.

DeMille bears interesting comparison to Griffith. They made similar pictures and built reputations as dominating figures. Griffith's tack was toward the exploration of narrative devices and methods of eliciting acting performances. DeMille had a prescience that Griffith lacked: he was able to estimate the shifting states of audience interest and receptivity at particular moments. Only six years younger, DeMille more easily inhabited this side of World War I, a master at genteel vulgarity. He had the wisdom to understand that revealing dress was justified in historical epics, that "sin" made sense if it led to repen-

tance or punishment. He was famous for elaborate bathrooms, which reached something of an apotheosis when Claudette Colbert inhabited a pool of asses' milk in *The Sign of the Cross* (1932).

A Brussels film festival asked DeMille to note the ten best films of all time. Excepting one Bing Crosby feature. DeMille's titles were all epics: eight were historical and four his own.

THOMAS H. INCE

Ince's career resembles Griffith's and DeMille's; indeed, most first generation directors entered film from the theater and music hall.

Ince toured the country as a young actor in western melodramas. Disdaining film, he still did bit work for Edison, Vitagraph, and Biograph. His first directing was at IMP where Ince was charged with their Mary Pickfords, including some filmed in Cuba, where the company hid out for a time.

Kessel and Bauman (Kay-Bee) hired Ince to make westerns in southern California. The success of a 2-reel *War on the Plains* (1912) enabled the purchase of 18,000 acres that became Inceville, first of the great studio cities. He hired the Miller Brothers 101 Ranch Circus to supply cowboys and horses, and he made governmental arrangements to employ a tribe of Sioux.

Between 1911 and 1913, Ince executed more than a hundred short films as well as the 5-reel *Battle of Gettysburg* (1913). In 1915, he joined Mack Sennett and Griffith in the Triangle Film Corporation. Like his partners, Ince turned to supervising productions.

Before unionization and specialization of production crews in the thirties, jobs shifted freely among workers. The activities of producing, directing, camera operation, editing, set design, and set construction sometimes outnumbered the employees. This gave rise to ambiguities of responsibility and an increasing need for a central authority for coordination. The term "produced by" in early film credits very often literally means "directed by," a usage still employed in British theater. For Lasky films, Cecil B. DeMille is often awarded a "picturized by" credit, which implies adaptation and script writing. "Producer-Director" might mean that one man assumed all of both functions or else that he undertook certain tasks and delegated others. Produced sometimes meant that a director would take time from another job to write scenes, then return the project to a fellow worker.

Inceville developed five shooting stages and Ince oversaw simultaneous productions. He took credit for developing shooting scripts into elaborate and detailed blueprints. Scripts in hand, Ince succeeded in designing productions to his satisfaction while delegating their execution to others. He required employees to shoot film as written, later viewing the day's rushes and making editing and title decisions.

With such authority, Ince maintained consistency, imposing qualities identifiably his own. The westerns made for Ince by William S. Hart and others struck critics and foreign audiences, the French particularly, as remarkable for their attention to natural detail, especially the spare backgrounds on which elemental dramas played. Ince worked closely with his scriptwriters, first Richard Spencer, then C. Gardner Sullivan, to weave plots whose variations themselves became identifiably the producer's. Some of Hollywood questioned Ince's range of talents. Buster Keaton satirized Ince in *The Playhouse* (1921) where the credits read: Written by Keaton/Directed

Thomas H. Ince (1882–1924)

Director

Little Nell's Tobacco	1911
War on the Plains	1912
For Freedom of Cuba	1912
Custer's Last Fight	1912
The Battle of Gettysburg	1913
The Despoilers	1915
Civilization (with Raymond West and Reginald Baker)	1916

Producer

The Coward	1915
Hell's Hinges	1915
The Aryan	1916
The Patriot	1916
Flying Colors	1917
Vive la France	1918
Carmen of the Klondyke	1918
Human Wreckage	1923
Anna Christie	1923
Partial listing	

by Keaton/Costumes by Keaton. Finally, the cast was entirely played by Keaton.

Ince's most direct challenge to Griffith was *Civilization* (1916), directed by Raymond B. West and Irvin Willet, and made at the same time as *Intolerance*. The producer sought to capitalize on pacifist American sentiment and the film, tapping Christian sentiment, is said to have aided Woodrow Wilson's reelection. Grandiose, *Civilization* is noteworthy for editing skills that relate a range of characters and events; it is diminished by a vagueness untypical of Ince in the characterizations. *Civilization* cost a tenth of *Intolerance*. More important to Hollywood, it returned the investment eightfold.

Typical and more pleasing is another 1916 venture, *The Deserter*, directed by Scott Sidney, screenplay by Spencer and Ince. A western, it concerns a young army officer who goes bad, deserts, then returns to a certain court-martial in order to rescue a beseiged wagon train, and, finally, dies a hero's death. Long shots distinguish the film, skillfully lit effects (dust, campfires) combining the picturesque with the functional. These features and tight editing—Ince mercilessly cut his films to advance story, carefully eliminating all but the essential—show the producer-editor-writer at his best and help a viewer to identify what is most likely to be Ince in Hart as well as to foresee what will happen to the western in other hands.

Curiously, Ince did not easily survive the regimented studio system he conceived. Some credit the decline to a parting with writer C. Gardner Sullivan. Ince moved to an independent contract with Paramount in 1918, again building new studios, but later films disappointed. Because of stern efficiencies, Ince was not popular. He died on board William Randolph Hearst's yacht in 1924; gossip suggested mysterious circumstances, but the cause appears to have been a thrombosis.

Henry King (1896?–   )

Who Pays	1916
Tol'able David	1921
Stella Dallas	1925
The Winning of Barbara Worth	1926
State Fair	1933
Way Down East	1935
In Old Chicago	1937
Alexander's Ragtime Band	1938
Jesse James	1939
Stanley and Livingstone	1939
The Song of Bernadette	1943
Wilson	1944
A Bell for Adano	1945
Twelve O'Clock High	1949
The Gunfighter	1950
The Snows of Kilimanjaro	1952
Carousel	1956
The Sun Also Rises	1957
The Old Man and the Sea (completed by John Sturges)	1958
This Earth is Mine	1959
Tender is the Night	1961
Partial listing	

HENRY KING

A stage producer and actor, King entered film to direct for Pathé in 1916. Later, working for Ince, King found himself in personal sympathy with western and period dramas. *Stella Dallas* (1925) and *The Winning of Barbara Worth* (1926) carry emotional themes in unsentimentalized images, but his deservedly famous feature is *Tol'able David* (1921).

The film is a contemporary story of David and Goliath set in a little farming village. The Hatburn brothers terrorize the area and kill a farmer whose son David (Richard Barth-

Richard Barthelmess, Joseph Hergesheimer and Henry King (right) confer on the *set of Tol'able David*. Some of the picture's climaxes reappeared fleetingly as silent background to a later, squeally denouement. It occurs in a revival movie house in William Castle's *The Tingler* (1959). (Museum of Modern Art/Film Stills Archive)

elmess) finally defeats them despite his fears. *Tol'able David* is touched by the affectionate candor with which King, himself a southerner, elaborates his mountain community and by the care spent in establishing David and developing his will to brave the Hatburns. Based on a novel by Joseph Hergesheimer, the story was originally purchased by D. W. Griffith as a vehicle for Barthelmess. When the star departed, Griffith sold him the rights. King had clearly studied Griffith, and achieved a personal, tightly constructed, engrossing film. The Russian director-theoretician Vsevolod Pudovkin pointed to King's ability at characterizing players with behavior rather than resorting to titles.

KING VIDOR

Vidor was young enough to commence his film career as a schoolboy projectionist in Texas, where he studied the screen. Apprenticing on 2-reelers at Universal, Vidor started his own studio, then moved to Metro, soon to be MGM. He was a successful commercial director who, at the same time, interjected ideas into his pictures, avoiding Stroheim's pitfalls by his choice of issues: Vidor tended to select the positive.

The Big Parade (1925) established Vidor's reputation. As with Griffith, Vidor personalized world event (World War I) with a love story, this one about a young American whose ideas of battle are disabused by experience, and whose faith is rekindled by a French peasant girl. He returns home a invalid. The director has a keen eye for detail and composition, and, for all its naïveté to modern eyes, *The Big Parade* is marked with stark images of troops moving in and out of combat and by skillfully edited battlefront footage, some of which is staged by veterans.

Vidor's other major silent feature was *The Crowd* (1928), markedly obliged to German Expressionism. He wrote and independently financed the story of an "ordinary American" and family. *The Crowd* begins as it ends, with a long, oblique, vertical camera movement that picks one young man out of a great expanse of like figures seated at their desks in a metropolitan office. In conclusion, the camera

distances from the same figure, now in the midst of a large auditorium, laughing and applauding a clown. Between these two shots, the man marries, finds work, and has a child who dies in a meaningless street accident. *The Crowd* is uncompromising about the protagonist's self-delusions, which are gradually stripped away, but its usual ending is unaccountably optimistic. Like Sternberg's *The Salvation Hunters*, *The Crowd* implies a generalizable subject, one man's story that is like many others. It is a technique that sits more easily among its German progenitors.

ERICH VON STROHEIM

Erich von Stroheim[2] is one of the most colorful, legendary directors in film history as well as one of the most talented. Because his right to work was so often revoked—irrevocably in the thirties—he carries something of the aura of a lyric poet dying young, even though Stroheim the actor continued in film and on stage until late in life.[3]

The director invented many of his legends. He was not the child of Viennese aristocracy with a mother who served as lady-in-waiting to the empress. Rather, Erich Oswald Stroheim was the son of a Jewish hat manufacturer from Poland, and he joined the army not as an officer but a private. He appears to have deserted Austria's forces and come to the United States about 1906.

The actor played his part so well that it

[2] *Born Erich Oswald Stroheim, he tacked on the "von" upon leaving Germany.*
[3] *Jon Barna's english language biographical study of Stroheim will document the director's past in great detail. Barna's premise is that Stroheim's early experience can be seen to have exercised an intractable, repetitive pattern on all his work.*

became effectively indistinguishable from mundane truth. By Stroheim's testimony, he washed dishes, laid railroad tracks, sang in beer gardens, and sold magazines and fly paper. Griffith hired him to play various Negro parts in blackface for *The Birth of a Nation,* and Stroheim became one of several assistants to the director, a role he resumed in *Intolerance.* He held Griffith in reverence. However different in content, Stroheim's own films bear obvious formal similarity to his mentor's.

While studying directing, Stroheim contined to act, often as a despicable Prussian officer: *Hearts of the World* (1918), *The Hun Within* (1918), *the Heart of Humanity* (1919). The role, one Stroheim developed offstage as well, is definitively portrayed in *Grand Illusion* (1937). While acting, Stroheim devised a feature screenplay, which he sold to Carl Laemmle, supposedly persuading Laemmle that, with Stroheim as director and star, the venture would cost no more than $25,000. Production expenses ran considerably higher, but the film, titled by Laemmle *Blind Husbands* (1918), proved successful. Set in the Austrian Alps, the movie pits Stroheim, a seductive Austrian officer on holiday, against a bored American wife and her neglectful husband. The husband kills the seducer by cutting his rope on a mountain height. The man then descends to find his wife was faithful after all, and the two reconcile.

If Stroheim's exposition was like Griffith (the quiet introduction, careful compositions, characterizing closeups), he is far more ironic

A part of the James Murray-Eleanor Boardman courtship in *The Crowd.* Vidor's production combined studio interiors and special effects with location filming in New York City. The film was sent to exhibitors with two alternative endings. Contrary to some reports, it was not a commercial failure. (Museum of Modern Art/Film Stills Archive)

Erich von Stroheim   113

in the execution. What DeMille might have made a melodrama of social conventions is skewed by Stroheim's cynicism. Unconscious of their own motives, the characters behave in ignorant self-service. The wife's seduction is interrupted by circumstances beyond her control; when making her decision to be unfaithful, the innocence of her behavior belies her awareness of its consequences.

The Devil's Passkey (1919) concerns an American playwright in Paris who writes a play based on gossip he has heard about an infidelity, only to discover the deceived husband to be himself. Strengthened by new awareness, he cancels the successful production and forgives his wife. Longer and more expensive, Stroheim's film again made money. *Foolish Wives* (1921) completes a trilogy of triangles. Once more a continental seducer, Stroheim victimizes and blackmails wealthy wives. He rapes the daughter of a counterfeiter who has supplied him with currency. Stroheim is killed by the girl's father, and his body is thrown into a sewer.

From an original 21 reels, which would have run four hours, *Foolish Wives* was cut on Laemmle's order to 14, some say 10. Where Stroheim had been budgeted at $50,000, Laemmle said he spent a million. The director disagreed, but Laemmle erected promotional signs in major cities which spelled out *$troheim* and kept a running billboard tally on expenses to date. Critics and industry spokesmen were dazzled by the performances in *Foolish Wives* and outraged by the sordid candor. It was not the sort of film to impress Kansas, whose board of review required substantial excisions.

When *Merry-Go-Round* (1922) was in production, Laemmle left a twenty-four year old assistant, Irving Thalberg, in charge of the studio while on a European trip. Thalberg discharged Stroheim for overspending his budget and hired another man to finish the production. Stroheim claimed that he had shot half the film and only six hundred feet were used in the release.

He moved to the studios of Sam Goldwyn, who was then operating an independent production unit. There, he produced *Greed* (1924), a version of Frank Norris' novel *McTeague*. The story progressed from a mining camp to turn-of-the-century San Francisco to Death Valley, and the director's penchant for realistic detail assumed devastating proportions. He required locations, costumes, and furniture that exactly duplicated the book's descriptions. Always demanding, he drove performers to excruciating lengths in order to intensify and emotionalize behavior.

McTeague, a self-taught dentist in San Francisco, marries Trina, who wins money in a lottery. Marcus, McTeague's friend, grows envious and reports McTeague to the authorities. The dentist loses his license and becomes a derelict. Trina is obsessed by greed. When she consistently refuses to aid McTeague, who has taken to drink and deserted her, he kills Trina. Marcus pursues McTeague into Death Valley, where the two die, handcuffed together.

Erich von Stroheim (1885–1957)

Stroheim's original version was 47 reels. On demand, he cut it to 42, then 24, then, with help, 18. By this time Goldwyn had joined MGM and instructed June Mathis to cut further. She reduced the film to 10 reels. It was released in 1924.

Even so truncated, *Greed* is exceptional. Sequences play like a nineteenth-century novel come alive. If in retrospect the characters seem singly motivated, this is a limitation of naturalism itself. No sordid detail is spared, as when McTeague in anger bites Trina's clasping fingers, and she loses them from infection. Zasu Pitts and Gibson Gowland as Trina and McTeague are outstanding; one imagines the two in countless incidents quite independent of the footage that contains them.[4]

More difficult to accept are the interminable intertitles (a heritage of Griffith at his most literary), and Stroheim's heavy symbolism, particularly a hand clutching at gold coins in overbearing repetition of the story's theme. These scenes, like those involving gilt picture frames, gold teeth, and a canary in its cage, were originally tinted yellow—a device that added even more weight to the symbolism.

Stroheim viewed the fate of his masterpiece with despair and vowed to work now only to support his family. Nonetheless, *The Merry Widow* (1925) carries biting perceptions of Viennese aristocracy that are absent from the Franz Lehar operetta on which it is based. Stroheim encountered his usual studio difficulties. Thalberg was now at MGM. Troubles were intensified by Mayer's insistence that the film include contracted players Mae Murray and John Gilbert. To Stroheim, actors were not stars but tools. Once he walked off the set. The crew refused to work with a new

[4] *This impression is furthered by Herman G. Weinberg, comp.,* The Complete Greed *(New York, 1973), which organizes production stills to reconstruct the original film version as far as this is humanly possible.*

director, and Stroheim only returned when Mae Murray apologized for calling him a dirty Hun. *The Merry Widow* was cut from 14 to 11 reels.

The Wedding March (1928) encountered further disasters. It was well financed by Pat Powers, an entrepreneur of low-budget films, but nevertheless exceeded the $750,000 allocation. Again the producers, this time Paramount who had bought controlling interest, assigned editing to another man. With Stroheim's apparent agreement, Josef von Sternberg cut the film by a fifth. Paramount tried to separate out a second part, *The Honeymoon* (1928), into an additional feature, but Stroheim had never completed shooting and the sequel was only sporadically released in Europe.

The Wedding March again portrays a decadent Austria, where bordellos are frequented by royalty, and industrialists haggle over dowries. Prince Nicki (Stroheim) falls in love with a commoner but is forced to marry a wealthy cripple. In *The Honeymoon,* he is killed by a vengeful butcher in love with the commoner. Aristocratic trappings are lavishly displayed, including a colored, Corpus Christi parade sequence. By now, Stroheim's plot conventions have become depressingly obvious: love across class barriers, the betrayal (usually learned by a newspaper account), the attempted rape, smoking as a coded clue to a character's decadence.

Stroheim undertook to make a film with Gloria Swanson, financed by herself with the backing of Joseph Kennedy, John F. Kennedy's father. The actress falls in love with a German prince who is betrothed to a tyrannical queen. (Their meeting is a minor variation of the plot in *The Wedding March.*) The queen discovers them together and whips Gloria Swanson out of the palace. Swanson attempts suicide but is brought back to her convent-school to discover that her aunt, mistress of a bordello in Africa, is dying and wants her there. Swanson inherits the establishment, becomes its madam and marries. The husband dies, the queen is assassinated, and Swanson and the Prince are reunited in the palace. Filming halted when the advent of sound put into question the profit potentials of silent films in production. Gloria Swanson also realized that the whorehouse sequences could never be shown anyway. She, therefore, shot an ending to tie up what had been already filmed and released *Queen Kelly* (1928) in

The bordello scene in *The Wedding March*. In love with a poor girl, Prince Nicki (Stroheim) accedes to his parents' orders ("Marry money!") and suffers an arranged betrothal to Zasu Pitts, the crippled daughter of a rich, corn-plaster manufacturer. The marriage contract is negotiated by the two drunken fathers. Here the magnate applies his medication to the feet of Prince Ottokar. (Museum of Modern Art/Film Stills Archive.

Europe: Kitty Kelly drowns and the Prince kills himself at her bier.

Erich von Stroheim's last directing venture was to have been *Walking down Broadway* for Fox. Again it was taken from him. It was reshot, and a version quite different from his intentions was released as *Hello Sister!* (1933). The story deals with a love affair between displaced midwesterners living on 47th Street and Ninth Avenue. Through misunderstandings, the boy rejects his pregnant girlfriend, then saves her from a tenement fire. *Hello Sister* looks like a Stroheim sketch that has been filled in by a sign painter.

The career of "Erich von Stroheim" presents film study with a depressing conjunction of fable, obsession, accomplishment, and mutilated footage. Hardly any of his work exists intact. *The Devil's Passkey* has disappeared entirely. *Walking down Broadway* was largely reshot by Sol Wurtzel and released as *Hello Sister*. *The Honeymoon* had only limited circulation. Almost every other film was egregiously cut. The only complete Stroheims available are his first, *Blind Husbands,* and a recently reassembled *Foolish Wives.*

At best, the filmmaker's extraordinary disposition toward authenticity and detail encapsulates social history, alternately Vienna and working-class America. His willingness to defy social mores and audience convention provides portions of his films with a kind of contemporaneity rare among fifty- and sixty-year-old motion pictures, which are more often imprisoned in the culture of their times. Stroheim elicited exceptional acting performances. If Zasu Pitts' avarice at its nadir defies belief, she is outstanding in the courtship and marriage scenes of *Greed,* and pathetically empty headed in *Hello Sister*. Whatever Mae Murray's altercations with the director, her performance in *The Merry Widow* was never equalled in her other films.

Stroheim's directing sense combined an autocrat's vision with intense dedication.

They call me hateful, and say I talk to my people as if they were dogs, that I am in truth the typical pre-war German. But I know what I am doing. It is my method. I must undermine this surface of acquired false technique and bring out the real feeling that is like a kernel beneath a girl's superficial charm. I glower at them. Never in their lives have they been spoken to as roughly as by me. I crush them, break them down with satire, with harsh words, with scorn. They are ready to quit. Then I get at the real soul and guide its natural unfoldment. . . . Mae Murray's artificiality in most of her films, her self-consciousness and cuteyisms had to be torn away, gossamar garments that concealed her genuine capacity for feelings and her capability for expressing it.[5]

[5] *Period interview for* Picture Play; *quoted in Peter Noble,* Hollywood Scapegoat *(New York, 1972), p. 59.*

Another whorehouse, here in *Queen Kelly*. Gloria Swanson has become a barmaid in her aunt's east African "hotel." The product of an orphan's convent school, her manner provokes the nickname of Queen Kelly. Swanson unwillingly marries a wealthy planter, who quickly expires. None of these episodes ever reached American screens. (Museum of Modern Art/Film Stills Archive)

Erich von Stroheim   117

Stroheim's films with European settings indict a decaying, class-ridden society for its perversities and oppressions. At the same time, like Griffith in his violence and DeMille in his sin, Stroheim takes obsessive personal delight in dwelling on the human failings he condemns: seductions and orgies and near rapes. They hold a fascination only partly explained by the moralist's gesture of a finger pointed in horror. He disclaimed producers' complaints of extravagance as studio publicity, but Stroheim was clearly unconcerned with cost and with the time his obsessive dedication to detail required. Among all feature filmmakers, he best epitomizes a tension between film as personal vision and film as commerce. Money he was give to make films was after all not Stroheim's own, and one cannot escape the least sympathy for Irving Thalberg who, seeing incessant *Merry Widow* footage taken to document the closet of an aristocrat with a preoccupation for shoes, described the director as a footage fetishist.

ERNST LUBITSCH

Lubitsch worked in Max Reinhardt's theater company and entered film at German Bioscope, directing comic shorts in which he sometimes appeared. Early features made for Ufa [*The Eyes of the Mummy Ma* (1918), *Carmen* (1918)] were spectacles, and coupled with Polish actress Pola Negri, the success encouraged further collaborations: *Madame Dubarry* (1919), *The Flame* (1923). On the basis of these historical epics, which combined melodrama (Dubarry at the guillotine) with the concupiscent (Dubarry in the bedroom),

Lady Windemere's Fan. Although posed, the publicity still demonstrates Lubitsch's luxurious employment of space. He eschewed Oscar Wilde's witticisms, even in intertitles, although Lubitsch invented others, like "The relations between a man and a woman can be told by the way he presses her doorbell." (Museum of Modern Art/Film Stills Archive)

Ernst Lubitsch (1892-1947)

Fräulein Seifenschaum/Miss Soapsuds	1914
Blinde Kuh/Blind Man's Buff	1915
Schuhpalast Pinkus/Show Salon Pinkus	1916
Ein Fideles Gefängnis/The Merry Jail	1917
Die Augen der Mummie Ma/The Eyes of the Mummy Ma	1918
Carmen/Gypsy Blood	1918
Madame Dubarry/Passion	1919
Die Puppe/The Doll	1919
Anne Boleyn/Deception	1920
Die Bergkatze/The Mountain Cat/The Wildcat	1921
Das Weib des Pharao/The Wife of Pharaoh	1922
Die Flamme/The Flame	1923
Rosita	1923
The Marriage Circle	1924
Forbidden Paradise	1924
Kiss Me Again	1925
Lady Windemere's Fan	1925
So This is Paris	1926
The Student Prince	1927
The Patriot	1928
The Love Parade	1930
Monte Carlo	1930
The Smiling Lieutenant	1931
The Man I Killed	1932
Trouble in Paradise	1932
If I Had a Million	1932
The Merry Widow	1934
Desire	1936
Angel	1937
Bluebeard's Eighth Wife	1938
Ninotchka	1939
The Shop Around the Corner	1940
That Uncertain Feeling	1941
To Be or Not to Be	1942
Cluny Brown	1946

Partial listing

Lubitsch's reputation crossed the Atlantic. American audiences enjoyed history reduced to court flirtations, and Emil Jannings who had starred as Louis XV, returned as Henry VIII in *Anne Boleyn* (1920).

Lubitsch crested on the first wave of Hollywood Europeans. Mary Pickford hired him. He rejected the first script, but agreed to *Rosita* (1923). Well enough received, the production experience was wrenching—a miniature staging of the director-star prizefight that Stroheim and Mae Murray played to even larger effect.

Lubitsch began making a series of sophisticated comedies in 1924 that skirted risqué sex so playfully as to confound censorship and delight audiences. He generally worked with substar performers. Where DeMille mixed the prurient with the spectacular and Stroheim confronted innocence and decadence, Lubitsch viewed sex as a game whose rules must be fully understood by all parties if it is to be well played.

The so-called Lubitsch Touch evidences how far his films capitalized on minimal, indirect visual clues to unexpressed feelings and undescribed events. Although the titles are often witty in *Lady Windemere's Fan* (1925), glances and Lubitsch's relentless eye supersede the epigrams of Oscar Wilde. If a woman is conscious of her age, Lubitsch points at a flabby forearm. If a millionaire buys off his revolutionary opponents, like the chancellor in *Forbidden Paradise* (1924), he writes a check with the flourish of a businessman consumating a wise and enjoyable deal.

Beyond injecting frivolity into the deadly serious subjects (sex, class, and politics), Lubitsch is remembered for another singular trait. His motion pictures eschewed ornate, busy, overstuffed period sets. A theater heritage in Hollywood was the employment of luxurious props to convey luxury. In Lubitsch's spare but stylized designs, decor is minimized, and the effect points up expression and body nuance as well as establishing the *implication* of opulence in *Kiss Me Again* (1925) and *So This is Paris* (1926). This was accomplished by deep staging which emphasized height and uncluttered floorspace that only the rich could afford anyway.

JOSEF VON STERNBERG

Born in Vienna, Josef Stern was brought to the United States as a child, then returned to Austria where he attended school. He worked as editor, writer, and assistant director for the World Film Company in Fort Lee, New Jersey,[6] and made training films for the Signal Corps during World War I. After the war, he took advantage of apprenticeships with film directors in England, Paris, Prague, Naples, and Berlin.

Like Stroheim, after leaving Germany, Stern changed his name. He surfaced in Hollywood in 1924 as Josef von Sternberg, where he persuaded George K. Arthur, a British actor, to finance *The Salvation Hunters* (1925) with $4800 of savings. Responses to the film, which featured Arthur and Georgia Hale, were extreme. On the enthusiastic side were Max Reinhardt and Charlie Chaplin, who bought it for United Artists. *Salvation Hunters* was filmed in the San Pedro mud flats and features three symbolic characters, a Boy, a Girl, and a Brute. The emblematic connotations, amplified in distressing detail by the intertitles, bear the test of time nearly as well as an overripe banana. Nevertheless, the film is an effectively told story of two young people who live on a barge with a child and seek a

[6] *Scriptwriter Frances Marion remembers meeting Joe Stern at the World Studios in 1914. He was an official "greeter." Frances Marion,* Off With Their Heads *(New York, 1972), p. 31.*

better life. The photography is exceptional; Sternberg was especially accomplished as a cameraman and always insisted that he totally control the camerawork on his films, whoever received nominal credit. Further, the location infuses the footage with mud, dirt, poverty, and a seascape that ascribes feeling by juxtaposition with the often-expressionless actors.

The director's next film is a curiosity of history. An enthusiastic Chaplin commissioned Sternberg to make a serious drama that might bring his onetime leading lady, Edna Purviance, out of retirement. The picture was filmed in Monterey, and Chaplin chose not to release it, either because he did not like *Women of the Sea* or because of some disagreement between the two men.[7]

In another seaside story, *The Docks of New York* (1928), a stoker rescues a drowning girl, then marries her during an evening's drinking, or perhaps the ceremony is a sham. The girl is accused of shooting a ship's engineer who had tried to assault her. Freed of this charge, she is arrested for theft, but her husband returns from his ship to confess and face imprisonment in her place. Again the photography imparts a special flavor to the waterfront, especially at night and in fog.

Considered together, the waterfront stories characterize an unstated premise of the director's sound work. Plots are melodramatic and undistinguished; they seem far less important to Sternberg than the creation of both an embracing, consistent atmosphere and faces that are lit and composed like paintings, independent of linear exposition. As Stroheim

was obsessed with natural detail, Sternberg dedicated himself to screen images that posed on screen, autonomous and unbeholden to any other world. Of all his work, the remaining two silent films most effectively reconciled this propensity of Sternberg with ordinary narrative.

Often cited in résumés of the gangster genre, *Underworld* (1927) was written by Jules Furthman and Ben Hecht, men who became highly successful screenwriters. Bull Weed goes to prison for shooting a rival who has forced his attention on Bull's girl, Feathers. Feathers and Bull's subordinate, Rolls Royce, love one another but remain loyal to Bull and arrange his breakout. Recognizing their situation, Bull sends them away and confronts the police alone. The Hecht plot

[7] *By Geraldine Chaplin's testimony, her late father literally burned* Women of the Sea *because, he said, he thought it so poorly made. In her own opinion, Chaplin was wildly jealous of a production he had neither directed nor acted in, and which featured a woman he loved. See Natalie Gittelson, "My Father, Charlie Chaplin,"* McCalls *(March 1978).*

Josef von Sternberg (1894–1969

The Salvation Hunters	1925
Women of the Sea/The Sea Gull (unreleased)	1926
Underworld	1927
The Last Command	1928
The Docks of New York	1928
Die Blaue Engel/The Blue Angel	1930
Morocco	1930
Dishonored	1931
An American Tragedy	1931
Shanghai Express	1932
Blond Venus	1932
The Scarlet Empress	1934
The Devil is a Woman	1935
Crime and Punishment	1935
I, Claudius (abandoned) (Britain)	1937
Shanghai Gesture	1941
Jet Pilot	1950
The Saga of Anatahan	1953
Partial listing	

Publicity run amok! The following caption accompanied this *Photoplay Magazine* cut: "GIRL FLEES BLAST! But the cameraman had to stay behind and photograph the blast in this scene from *Underworld*, where Evelyn Brent fled from a gang lair dynamited by the police. Otto Pierce, Paramount cameraman, however, was prepared for whatever the blast blew up by having on a cast-iron business suit, three-rivet double breasted. These Hollywood cameramen will go to any extremes to 'get the picture.' " (Museum of Modern Art/Film Stills Archive)

is violent and impulsive enough to sustain viewer interest, while Sternberg creates a visual style, striking in itself, that yet sustains and furthers story. Feathers' sensuality is carefully built by costume, lighting, and decor to culminate in a wild party scene when she is attacked by Kohler, Bull's enemy. Details, such as jewelry ripped from a store window, press the story on; by selective camera focus, Sternberg chooses as much or as little background as the narrative regulates.

If Lubitsch sustains audience comprehension with glances and space, Sternberg accomplishes similar ends through lighting and set dressing. A central sequence in *Underworld* takes place in Bull's hideout. Rolls Royce works there as a kind of butler-lieutenant, and

Bull brings Feathers by to introduce her, then abruptly leaves the two together when he goes out to "get" something Feathers had admired (the jewelry in the window).

Feathers flirts with Rolls. Their attraction to one another is obvious. Finally, he rejects her advances and Bull returns. With masterly control, Sternberg defines the relationship by compositions which balance the twosome and threesome against pictures on the walls. When Rolls and Feathers have only themselves in mind, camera setups pose two figures against two pictures. When Bull enters their thoughts, compositions are readjusted to introduce a third visual element. Emotions are underlined and amplified by every screen area. An actor once said of Sternberg that he "thought no

more of people than he did of the pictures on the walls," and he was quite correct.

On the request of Emil Jannings, Sternberg prepared a film to feature the German actor, *The Last Command* (1928). The story follows a White Russian general who escapes the revolution and becomes a Hollywood extra. There he reencounters a Red leader who is now directing a film about the revolution. The general, Jannings, relives his military role and dies on the set. The film combines *Underworld*'s visual subtleties with unique, self-reflexive features. When the fictive, "Hollywood" film is being shot, Sternberg gives particular attention to the mechanics of its studio staging, clearly in order to encourage us to rethink the scenes back one further step toward the artificiality of what we ourselves are witnessing. Before he dies, Jannings hallucinates the earlier, "real" battle of the revolution, but his images of dead comrades merge with actual shooting conditions of the mock battle. The circumstances of the Hollywood extra are ironically paralled to military life. He is assembled at attention, inspected, ordered, and herded through a supply room, quite like a conscript.

Again, Sternberg uses props to underline relationships. During a scene in which Jannings and a Communist spy, Natasha (Evelyn Brent, who also played Feathers), both try to seduce and to outwit one another in his quarters, the state of affairs can be traced by the compositional importance that Sternberg invests in three sexually suggestive mantel decorations: two candles and an urn. As Jannings presses his suit, a candle locates itself closer to his head, the urn beside and behind the girl. Sternberg uses cigarettes to elaborate a power motif. As the general blew smoke in the face of the Communist leader/director, the latter

Underworld. As Bull Weed departs, Rolls decorates his boss's lapel. Alone together, Rolls rejects Feathers' flirtatious advance. On each occasion, a painting is displaced or disclosed so as to manipulate visual motifs of two's and three's.

Josef von Sternberg   123

(William Powell) now blows smoke at his servile extra. The authoritarian hierarchy of a Hollywood studio, where underlings rush to light their director's cigarettes, is slyly reproduced by a diagonal of pictures on the wall, suggesting a chain of command. Sternberg said that when he worked in New Jersey, one of his jobs was to light the director's cigarettes.

VICTOR SEASTROM

Sjöström in his native Sweden, the director is rivalled only by Ingmar Bergman in national preemminence and known to Bergman audiences for his role as Professor Isak Borg in *Wild Strawberries* (1957). Seastrom began as a stage actor and manager. His early films, often based on Scandinavian saga and literature, were marked by spare, stylized sets and an economy of acting. Some of his Swedish pictures have structural devices that have a modern ring, such as the episodic division of story in *Give Us This Day* (1913) and the differing versions of a remembered incident told by flashbacks in *The Kiss of Death* (1916). *The Outlaw and His Wife* (1917) foretells Seastrom's magnificent *The Wind* (1928).

Seastrom came to the United States in the twenties where work for MGM included two remarkable adaptations of American fiction, *The Scarlet Letter* (1926) and *The Wind*. Both have extraordinary performances by Lillian Gish, who said that Seastrom led her through the Swedish school of acting, which was one of repression. For the screen, Nathaniel Hawthorne's indictment of Puritan persecutions cast Lars Hanson as the Reverend Dimmesdale against Gish's Hester Prynne. Despite the fact that Hanson spoke no English, his acting impressed everyone and one impassioned speech in Swedish even prompted a burst of applause from the crew.

Based on a novel by Dorothy Scarborough, *The Wind* set Gish, a sensitive Virginian, in the midst of a Texas prairie. To escape the resentments of her cousin's crude wife with whom she is living, Gish marries a cowboy and moves to a lonely cabin. There she kills a man who has tried to molest her.

Despite Louis B. Mayer's trepidation that the Texas market would resent labelling its climate so cruelly windswept, the film was produced under tryingly realistic settings in the Mojave Desert. Seastrom plays scenes in long takes without detailing closeups, an approach shared by Ince, King, and often Stroheim. But for the uncluttered sets, *The Wind* has something of the quality of *Greed* with its accumulating atmosphere and ensemble performances.

Victor Seastrom (1879–1960)

Trädgardsmästern/The Gardener	1912
Ingeborg Holm/Give Us This Day	1913
Dödskyssen/The Kiss of Death	1916
Berg-Ejvind och hans hustru/The Outlaw and His Wife	1917
Karin Ingmorsdotter/Karin, Daughter of Ingmar	1920
Körkarlen/The Phantom Chariot/Thy Soul Shall Bear Witness/Clay	1920
He Who Gets Slapped	1924
Confessions of a Queen	1925
The Tower of Lies	1925
The Scarlet Letter	1926
The Divine Woman	1927
The Wind	1928
Masks of the Devil	1928
A Lady to Love	1930
Markurells fran wadköping	1930
Under the Red Robe (British)	1937
Partial listing	

The Scarlet Letter. With daughter Pearl as witness, the Reverend Dimmesdale confesses his fatherhood and collapses, dying, in the arms of Hester Prynne. Lillian Gish figured closely in the film's production, including the selection of Lars Hanson (based on his performance in *The Saga of Gösta Berling*) and the approval of Victor Seastrom. Gish's later silent films forcefully eroticize the naïve Griffith image. (Museum of Modern Art/Film Stills Archive)

The story itself is brutal. Lillian Gish drags the body of the man she has killed out into the howling windstorm and buries it under a bulwark that her husband had dug to keep blowing sand from their cabin. The wind shifts its course and proceeds to uncover the body, which so unnerves Gish that she runs from the cabin, herself caught in the lashing torrents. MGM's eastern financeers, however, objected to the ending and it was reshot. After the murder, Gish's husband (Lars Hanson) returns.

He is well pleased with her actions and they bury the corpse together. This time it stays put.[8]

[8] *Double endings, sometimes different for European export, sometimes a recasting to satisfy someone's idea of box office, were common. Vidor had two conclusions to* The Crowd, *and Gloria Swanson's end for* Queen Kelly *had no relation to Stroheim's story. Stroheim's* Wedding March *also had alternate conclusions at different stages.*

Summary

DeMille excepted, it would be tempting but misleading to imply that the work of the filmmakers sketched here exercised an appreciable effect on Hollywood's daily product. Commercial film was effectively regulated by conventions, schedules, and the dominating presences of stars or stolid performance or both. What the Stroheims and Sternbergs did suggest was that movies might move in directions different from the Saturday-night fare of the Bijou. In thirty years' time, silent film had become a supple instrument capable of evocative power and immense variety.

Foreign productions proved film's versatility with even greater force. Following chapters trace the evolution of film in other motion picture capitals, where different cultures and traditions gave rise to quite different modes of expression and production.

Bibliography

Barna, Jon. *Erich von Stroheim*. Vienna, 1966.

Bergut, Bob. *Erich von Stroheim*. Paris, 1960.

Bickford, Charles. *Bulls, Bells, Bicycles, and Actors*. New York, 1965.

Bowser, Eileen, ed. *Film Notes*. New York, 1969.

Brownlow, Kevin. *The Parade's Gone By*, New York, 1968.

Castello, Guilio. *Erich von Stroheim*. Lyon, 1963.

Curtis, Thomas Q. *Von Stroheim*. New York, 1971.

DeMille, Cecil B. *Autobiography*. Englewood Cliffs, N.J., 1949.

———. "After Seventy Pictures." *Film in Review,* March 1956.

Essoe, Gabe and Raymond Lee. *DeMille: The Man and His Pictures*. South Brunswick, N.J., 1970.

Everson, William. "The Lubitsch Legend." *Film Library Quarterly,* Spring 1969.

Fernandez, Cuenca. *Erich von Stroheim*. Madrid, 1964.

Finler, Joel. *Stroheim*. Berkeley, 1968.

Gilliatt, Penelope. "The Scabrous Poet from the Estate Belonging to No One." *The New Yorker,* June 3, 1972.

Gobeil, Charlotte, comp. *Hommage à Erich von Stroheim: A Tribute*. Ottawa, 1966.

Green, Calvin. "Lubitsch: The Trouble with Paradise," *Film Society Review.* vol. 4, no. 4 (1968).

Higham, Charles. *The Art of the American Film*. Garden City, N.J., 1974.

———. *Cecil B. DeMille*. New York, 1973.

Koszarski, Richard. "*Hello Sister.*" *Sight and Sound,* Autumn 1970.

Koszarski, Richard and William K. Everson. "Stroheim's Last 'Lost' Film." *Film Comment,* May-June 1975.

Koury, Phil. *Yes, Mr. DeMille*. New York, 1959.

Marion, Frances. *Off with Their Heads*. New York, 1972.

Mitchell, George. "Thomas H. Ince." *Films in Review,* October 1960.

Mourlet, Michelle. *Cecil B. DeMille*. Paris, 1968.

Myers, Eric. "Stroheim and *Queen Kelly*." *Cinema Journal,* Spring 1976.

Noble, Peter. *Hollywood Scapegoat*. New York, 1972.

Pensel, Hans. *Seastrom and Stiller in Hollywood*. New York, 1969.

Pratt, George. *Spellbound in Darkness*. 2nd. ed. New York, 1966.

Ringgold, Gene. *The Films of Cecil B. DeMille*. New York, 1969.

Sarris, Andrew. *The Films of Josef von Sternberg*. Garden City, N.J., 1966.

Shibuk, Charles and Christopher North. "The Life and Films of Henry King." *Films in Review,* October 1958.

Spears, Jack. *Hollywood the Golden Era*. New York, 1971.

Tibbetts, John. "Sternberg and *The Last Command*." *Cinema Journal,* Spring 1976.

Turner, Charles L. "Victor Seastrom," *Films in Review,* May-July 1960.

Von Sternberg, Josef. *Fun in a Chinese Laundry*. New York, 1965.

———. "On Life and Film." *Films in Review,* October 1952.

Von Stroheim, Erich. *Paprika*. New York, 1937.

Von Stroheim Issue. *Film Culture* 19 (1959).

Weinberg, Herman G., comp. *The Complete Greed*. New York, 1973.

———. *The Complete Wedding March*. Boston, 1974.

Weinberg, Herman G. *Josef von Sternberg*. New York, 1967.

———. *The Lubitsch Touch*. New York, 1968.

———. *Stroheim a Pictorial Record of His Nine Films*. New York, 1975.

6

SILENT GERMAN FILM

Max and Emil Skladanowsky exhibited their own film projector—the Bioscope—at the Wintergarten, Berlin's great music hall, as early as November 1895. Featuring street scenes and parades as subjects, early German film exhibition was confined to fairgrounds until small theaters emerged around 1905. Most films were imported, and the popularity of Asta Nielsen, a reputable Danish actress, was symptomatic of Scandinavian interest and accomplishment in the upstart medium.

SCANDINAVIAN ROOTS

While many noteworthy Scandinavian film figures enhanced their reputations outside of Scandinavia (Nielsen, Dreyer, Seastrom, Stiller), the early output of Sweden and Denmark was outstanding, particularly as judged for the quality of the pictures' image. In the

The Cabinet of Dr. Caligari (Wiene 1919) (Movie Star News)

century's first decade, Danish films employed lighting techniques far more advanced than most lighting being done elsewhere, and Seastrom's impressive use of Swedish landscape, even in World War I vintage titles, appears curiously modern to today's eye.

Through the efforts and foresight of Charles Magnussen, an exceptional producer-executive, Seastrom and Maurice Stiller joined Svenska Bio, soon to become Svensk Filmindustri, the leading Swedish production company, in 1912 and succeeded in shifting production toward national themes and preoccupations. Selma Lagerlöf provided numerous source materials for films from both directors.

Seastrom, the more severe of the two, shows his early control of actors and of stark, unadorned emotional display in *Give Us This Day* (1913). The film exposes Sweden's poor laws, which decreed that children of destitute parents be auctioned as forced labor. A son finally returns to restore his mother's sanity. *Terje Vigen/A Man There Was* (released 1917) derives from Ibsen. In wartime, a Swedish fisherman is captured and imprisoned by a British sea captain. The apprehension, cutting from matching shots of pursuers and pursued at their oars in a stormy sea, is brilliantly visualized. *The Outlaw and His Wife* (1917) emotionally executes a precipice rescue that could have dissolved to greasepaint heroics in a Griffith film or flash-frame hysteria if done by Abel Gance (see Chaper 7). *The Phantom Chariot* (1920) is sordid melodrama with brilliant photography by Svensk Filmindustri's Julius Jaenzon, notably in its fantasy sequences and the depictions of slum life.

While highly successful with sophisticated comedy, Mauritz Stiller also drew on the talents of Julius Jaenzon and his peer, Henric Jaenzon, to execute national sagas that rivalled Seastrom in emotionality while differing in graphic display. *Erotikon* (1920) is an infidelity comedy that titillated with its cigarette smoking and leggy women; Ernst Lubitsch ac-

knowledged the film's tongue-in-cheek suggestiveness as a considerable influence.

Gösta Berling's Saga (released 1923) is based on a Lagerlöf novel and sometimes suggests soap opera, but its abbreviated version (shortened from three hours) exploits the young beauty of Greta Garbo and possesses an extraordinary scene in which a major's wife, dispossessed for infidelity, confronts her toiling mother whom she had struck earlier.

Stiller's great achievement is *Herr Arnes Pengar/Sir Arne's Treasure,* again from Lagerlöf, a sixteenth-century fable of murder, theft, and sacrificing love. The film carries striking images: a fish peddler drives his cart across the ice to an ice-locked English ship; a horse and sleigh fall through the ice and sink. The director carefully stages small details as well: a guilt-ridden Scottish mercenary and his Swedish lover duplicate postures after she learns he has killed her foster sister. The final sequence mounts a long, black-costumed procession of women and young boys who carry the Scot's slain girlfriend's body off the ship, back to her home. It suggests processions — like the peasants in Eisenstein's *Ivan the Terrible* — to come, but Stiller's images are beholden to no one.

Alliances between Sweden and Germany to coproduce features during the twenties resulted in undistinguished products. Like Denmark, Sweden suffered from language barriers with the coming of sound. Denmark, in fact, never recovered from World War I's effect on an international market.

GERMAN CONSOLIDATION

In Germany, plays and fiction were adapted early to film: *The Other One* (1913), and *The Student of Prague* (1913). Soon, cut off from French, British, Italian, and American resources, wartime Germany encouraged the development of a native industry. Recognizing film's utility as entertainment and propaganda, the Reich, in 1917, helped to underwrite Universum Film A.G., known as Ufa (or UFA). An affiliation of major production companies, exhibitors, and the Projection Union, Ufa financed such expensive postwar endeavors as Lubitsch's *Madame Dubarry* (1919). In 1921, Ufa merged with a major competitor, Decla-Bioscope, to gain further power. Soon, most major German films appeared under its aegis, many originating in the huge, modern studio facility at Neubabelsberg, but Ufa was only one among several active production companies (6.2 to 7.1 percent of total output between 1926 and 1929). In the twenties, Germany's feature output was prodigious, outnumbering the rest of the continent by 1927.

The Weimar government tried to counter what were thought to be dangerous influences on German film: pornography and foreign domination. After the Republic had abolished censorship in the early twenties, a spate of "educational" movies appeared, exploiting homosexuality, veneral diseases, prostitution, and what were then considered esoteric sexual behaviors. In consequence, the Reich Film Act established examining boards who certified titles acceptable to the twelve-to-eighteen-year-old age group. Beyond eighteen there were no restrictions, and the act care-

Ufa's modern studios. Until 1921, Social Democrats in power first hid, then disguised government ownership of one-third the company's stock. During the few silent-film years when it showed a profit, Ufa realized much revenue through theater chains, distribution, and rental of equipment and studio space. In essence, the company linked subsidary units in a loose, cartel-like corporate structure. (Museum of Modern Art/Film Stills Library)

fully placed decisions concerning political issues in films beyond the governance of the board, until Naziism fostered a reinterpretation of censorial functions and the introduction of political standards of value. Other examiners evaluated German film in terms of artistic merit. Exhibitors who booked well-regarded productions earned reductions in the entertainment tax. Because foreign imports, American especially, threatened the survival of German production, the Reich imposed import quotas.

The output of exceptional silent German films can more easily be understood if we center attention on certain esthetic and cultural preoccupations, in particular the Gothic, expressionism, and Kammerspiel. Only England and Scandinavia rival Germany in determined fascination with mystery, the devil, magic, and madness; with romantic leanings toward ghosts, transformations, and supernatural pacts.

Certain themes permeate German expression of this period: (1) surpassing his own nature, man becomes inhuman, not godlike; (2) the separation of man's good-and-evil nature into two autonomous personalities leads to his destruction; (3) what man creates mirrors himself; (4) civilized man treads an uneasy balance between his natural impulse (the animal) and its artifical modification (tradition and reasoned thought). Stories of E. T. A. Hoffmann reappear literally or indirectly in countless German films.

The Gothic mode veers toward horror and fantasy. Its impulse to deny a rational, explicable world view found reinforcement in expressionism. Expressionism proposed that nature's forms might be distorted, exaggerated, and intensified better to present emotional content and subjective experience. On theater sets, expressionism led to sharp-edged, often black-lined, heavy designs. In performance, acting was emotive, large gestured, and sometimes pointed straight toward the audience as a character shared thoughts and feelings without fictional mediation. In league, expressionism and the Gothic denied apparent reality to emphasize the invisible and the unexpressed.

As expressionists condemned naturalism, they derogated psychology, for psychology claimed to explain the inexplicable. An influential theatrical producer and director named Max Reinhardt assumed a contrary esthetic. Although Reinhardt was responsible for pageants and epics, and even though he staged expressionist plays, he encouraged a different, intimate theater by way of the Kammerspiele, which he built in 1906. If large auditoriums asked large gesture for visibility, the Kammerspiele, seating only three hundred, encouraged easy communication with subtle expression. Reinhardt's productions, which carried over into Kammerspielfilm ventures, employed sophisticated lighting techniques to resonate psychological aspects of character. Shading effects echoed gradations of feeling and thought in naturalistic productions. Stepping in and out of light pools, themselves motivated ("coming" from a high window, say), gave dramatic emphasis. Figures in German film who studied with Reinhardt included Paul Wegener, Ernst Lubitsch, Emil Jannings, F. W. Murnau, William Dieterle, and Conrad Veidt. German film, then, developed in an atmosphere of conflicting esthetics as well as traditions of superstition and fantasy intensified by the blood bath of World War I and the instability of the short-lived Weimar Republic.

The Doppelgänger

The Other One used a theme of personality change: a Jekyll/Hyde transformation. Wegener's *The Student of Prague*, which was remade in 1926, concerned a poor student who makes a pact with the devil for wealth. In exchange, he parts with his mirror reflection. Freed, the double disgraces him. Finally, the student traps the errant Other back into the mirror and shoots it, only to destroy himself. *The Student of Prague* combined preoccupations with social acceptability, good and evil, and youth and age, linking such themes as appeared in E. T. A. Hoffman ("The Devil's Elixer"), Oscar Wilde (*The Picture of Dorian Grey*), and Edgar Allen Poe ("William Wilson"). Wegener's next film, *The Golem* (1915), revived an old legend about a rediscovered clay statue, created in ancient times by a rabbi to wreck vengeance on enemies of the Jews. Brought alive again, the Golem falls in love and rampages a city in anger when he is spurned, finally falling to his destruction. A serial, *Homunculus* (1916), told the story of an artificial man, hence a man without a soul. Rejected by his fellows, Homunculus becomes a dictator, starts a war, and is punished by God.

This theme of the destructive and vengeful monster was expressed most successfully in *The Cabinet of Dr. Caligari* (1919). The film was made for Decla-Bioscope, derived from a story submitted by two young men, Carl Mayer and Hans Janowitz. Based on a sex-murder trial he once reported, Janowitz, a Czech poet and journalist, conceived the idea of a carnival figure who publicly exhibits a somnambulist but secretly directs him to carry out murderous night-time orders. Mayer, an Austrian, wrote the script in part as a satire of German authoritarianism, which "changed men into robots." The Decla producer, Erich Pommer, added a framing story which located the tale itself in the mind of a madman; the German narrative frame was a common device that even has a name: *Rahmenhandlung.*

Pommer proposed that the story, now distorted by its narrator, should be represented in the radical expressionist form espoused by a group called Der Sturm.[1] Sets were executed

by two painters and a designer from Der Sturm: Walter Reiman, Walter Röhrig, and Herman Warm. *Caligari* was located in a small town, Holstenwall, which is striking because of its veering, angled roofs, grotesquely elongated furniture, and walls with painted lights and shadows.

Two students attend a fair exhibit, where the somnambulist, Cesare, tells one he will die at dawn. This happens, and the surviving man, Francis, suspects Dr. Caligari, who exhibited Cesare. Caligari sends Cesare to murder Francis' girlfriend Jane, but Cesare carries Jane away instead, finally falling dead from exhaustion when he is chased by townspeople. Francis discovers Caligari to be the insane director of a mental institution. The film concludes with Jane, Cesare and Caligari reappearing in the asylum and Francis identified as the madman. "Ah," says Caligari, "I understand. He thinks me to be Caligari. Now perhaps I can cure him."

Inadequacies of performance mar *Caligari,* and attention in the story flags as a result of poorly concerted script, directing, and editing. But visual impact is strong. Expressions and movements linger, as when Cesare first raises his eyelids, and when Cesare crawls gracefully against an expressionist wall. One scene, where Cesare, who wears a kind of black leotard, carries the white-gowned Jane, now fainted, through the bedroom window, became a required convention of monster movies.

The expressionist sets are graphically vivid and artificially at odds with flesh-and-blood actors inhabiting them. At one point in the film, Caligari the asylum director decides to "become" the legendary Dr. Caligari of medieval times, and jagged letters spell "I must become Caligari" in the sky. A successful promotional advertisement announced "You must become Caligari," proposing that the audience would share Caligari's fancies through the agency of the picture's expressionist staging. It is sometimes argued that *Caligari*'s conclusion, placing the story in an unreliable

[1] *Another version has the artists persuading Pommer, motivated in part by an electricity shortage. See Herbert Luft, "Carl Mayer,"* Films in Review *(November 1972).*

mind, has deftly cancelled any qualms about the representation of willful authority and blind obedience. Yet Dr. Caligari's last sly glance at the camera suggests otherwise, whatever the trouble with poor Francis. Robert Wiene, the director of *Caligari,* tried unsuccessfully for the remainder of his career to duplicate his accomplishment.

FRITZ LANG

The direction of *Caligari* was originally offered to Fritz Lang, who entered film through script writing and editing, his specialty being the gangster-detective thriller. At the time, however, he was engaged in a serial: *The Spiders* (1919-1920). Lang's first critical success was *Der Müde Tod* (the weary Death) (1921), known in the United States as *Destiny;* the picture is subtitled *A German Folksong in Six Verses.* Although it is a story of fate, appearing in the figure of Death, the German title is significant, for Death tires of enacting his morbid duties on mankind.

A young man is about to die, and his lover tries to save him by dissuading Death. Death tells her three stories, set in Baghdad, Venice, and China. All concern the boy and girl seeking to escape a tyrant; each time the tyrant is successful. Deaths are represented by burning candles that always extinguish. The girl pleads for her friend. Death says that if she can bring him another volunteer for death he may spare the boy. She tries in vain to convince forsaken and doomed figures she encounters to give up their lives. Finally, the girl herself dies saving a child and thus joins her lover who has died during her search.

Trained as an architect and conscious both of Reinhardt's staging effects and of expressionism, Lang infuses *Destiny* with a high degree of stylization that places intense, low-angled lighting sources to intensify shadows on walls and arches. His patterned crowd movements balance compositions in action against great gothic arches and stairways.

Like his other German films, *Dr. Mabuse, the Gambler* (1922) was written by Lang's wife, Thea von Harbou. The central figure is a mastermind criminal whose organization victimizes well-to-do, postwar German society. With his mistress, Mabuse battles a public Prosecutor, Wenk, who has enlisted a millionaire's wife, Countess Told, in aid. Mabuse falls in love with the Countess and kidnaps her after forcing her husband, through hypnotic power, to cheat at cards and then destroy himself in despair. Mabuse orders his mistress who is imprisoned by the police to take poison. Then he hypnotizes Wenk to press him to suicide. Wenk, however, escapes death for he is apprehended by the police while driving at an insane speed. The law lays siege to Mabuse's quarters and Wenk frees the Countess. Mabuse crawls to an underground retreat, a raving lunatic.

The mad, powerful Dr. Mabuse captured public imagination in Germany and abroad. His ability to hypnotize is a constant danger to anyone who approaches too close; he escapes apprehension by slipping, disguised, from one to another personality. The film was released in two parts in Germany, and Lang subtitled the first "Images of Our Times" and the second "Men of Our Times." The nightclub, criminal world that figures heavily in the story mirrors postwar Germany's inflationary, cynical, bitter milieu of idle wealth, intense poverty, and raucous entertainment. Placing the arch-criminal Mabuse "behind" this lifestyle provided a concrete, fascinating figure on whom audiences might locate their anxieties. Further, Mabuse is indicated as being sometimes almost an unwilling party to his own urges.

The dark city streets of Mabuse's world were effectively represented by Lang's high-contrast, expressionist graphics: overly-bright streetlights spotted on asphalt. A gambling casino has painted walls that look like a flat out

Dr. Mabuse the Gambler. Attracted to the Countess Told, Mabuse is about to dominate her husband (third from left) with such powerful mental projection that the count will clumsily cheat during his card game. Mabuse equivocates, his infatuation shifting between a fatal character flaw and villainous lust. (British National Film Archive/Stills Library)

of *Caligari.* Lang sketches bit-part characters with significant mannerisms so that they project vivid instants of the seeming "real:" an ugly old woman on the street scratches herself with a knitting needle. *Mabuse* is essentially pulp-sensational melodrama combined with skillful staging and structuring (exemplary editing) and subtle social commentary that raise the film above the limitations of the genre.

Again issued in separate parts, the director's next project draws on Nordic mythology:

the legend of the Nibelungen: *Die Nibelungen* (1924). In *Siegfried,* the hero battles and destroys the dragon, then bathes himself in its blood to gain invulnerability, excepting a spot on his back that is covered by a leaf. He visits Burgundy, ruled by King Gunther and there proposes to Gunther's sister, Kriemhild. To win Kriemhild, Siegfried is required to defeat the forces of Queen Brumhild. At Brumhild's castle, Siegfried assumes his magic hood. Invisible, he tricks Brumhild into marrying Gunter by falsifying Gunther's strength and

Hero and dragon in *Siegfried*. Inside the reptilian body a crew steered wheels, pulleys, and treads to articulate each threatening movement. Ufa built the forest in a zeppelin hanger. Its fantastic decor dominates depersonalized characters who act on vengeful emotions at an inexorable pace. (Museum of Modern Art/Film Stills Archive)

skill. On discovering the truth from Kriemhild, Brumhild demands that Siegfried be killed, and this is done by Hagen, the evil agent of King Gunther. Kriemhild swears vengeance at the bier of her husband.

In *Kriemhilds's Revenge,* she marries Atilla, the black knight and ruler of the Huns. Gunter and Hagan are invited to Atilla's castle. Kriemhild commands the Huns to attack the visitors during a banquet. Gunther and his men are trapped in a hall that Atilla sets on fire. In the ensuing battle, Kriemhild kills both Gunther and Hagan and is slain. To his own destruction, Atilla carries his wife's body back into the flaming hall.

Die Niebelungen is based on mythic sources earlier than Wagner's *Ring of the Niebelung* and was intended both to evidence the inexorable consequences of an evil deed and to celebrate a national cultural heritage. Ufa's disposition was to execute everything, "exteriors" included, in the studio. Where Langs's sets transcended even Ufa's resour-

ces, they were built outside. In consequence, the film has an extraordinary, consistent artificiality, for everything from trees to boulders is designed to graphic specification. The pagan world recreated in the film evokes the work of Arnold Böcklin, whose romantic paintings inspired the set design. Expressionist light and composition glorify the legend. If figures are sometimes dwarfed by their settings in *Destiny*, they are reduced to near obscurity in *Die Niebelungen*.

Seen as a harbinger of Naziism with its idealized heroics, this strange national celebration offends many; the Nazis continued to exhibit *Siegfried* but withdrew *Kriemhild's Revenge*. Both films are at times so slow moving as to defy endurance: Wagner without the music. However, Lang's grand designs, the mists of the forests, and the great archetectonic scheme of castles, archways, bridges, and banquet halls cannot be denied. Pace accelerates somewhat in Part II, where the violent action dictates a certain speed, but even here, figures are inclined to hold poses not only in satisfaction of Lang's compositional needs, but as if their statuesque quality might communicate the significance of the legend they mime.

Some believe that Ufa, itself vulnerable to major German industrialists such as Krupp and Farben, produced *Die Niebelungen* as part of a concerted effort to encourage national self-consciousness. If this is so, Lang's next film ostensibly challenges a world dominated by industrial self-interest. *Metropolis* (1926) is subtitled *Mankind's Destiny in 2000* A.D. In the millenium, two classes have evolved. An all-powerful industrialist, John Frederson, lives in a beautiful garden together with his son Freder, managerial assistants, and servants. He rules his business-empire

from a skyscraper, one of many in a modernist city where airplanes are a common means of transportation.

The workers, who man the machines that support Metropolis, live below ground and trudge in lockstep to benumbing labors, shuttling in great elevators. At rest, they listen underground to a beautiful girl, Marie, who exhorts them to wait patiently rather than rebel. The industrialist sneaks below and listens; then he orders a mad scientist, Rotwang, who has designed Metropolis, to construct a robot in the guise of Marie. The real Marie is captured, the false Marie goes below and incites the workers to revolt and destroy the machines. This is accomplished, but in the act of destruction, rioters cause the release of underground waters that threaten to drown their

Metropolis. Rotwang brings his robot to life in the guise of Maria, harbinger of innumerable monsters yet to be born. In Thea von Harbou's garish allegory, a coalition (implicitly Christian Party and Social Democrats) might together defeat a revolutionary force whose first victims would be the workers' own children. "The ending is false," Lang said later, "I didn't like it even when I made the picture." The director can be seen beneath the table. (Movie Star News)

families. Freder rescues Marie and the two save the workers' city. At the conclusion, Freder and Marie are betrothed and their union signifies a new coalition between management and labor. Marie had urged the

Fritz Lang (1890–1976)

Halbblut	1919
Die Spinnen: I Der goldene See	1919
Die Spinnen: II Das Brillantenschiff	1920
Der Müde Tod/Destiny	1921
Dr. Mabuse der Spieler/Dr. Mabuse, the Gambler	1922
Die Nibelungen	1924
Metropolis	1926
Spione/Spies	1928
Die Frau in Mond/Woman in the Moon	1929
M/M the Kidnapper	1931
Das Testament des Dr. Mabuse/The Testament of Dr. Mabuse/The Last Will of Dr. Mabuse	1933
Liliom	1933
You Only Live Once	1936
You and Me	1937
The Return of Frank James	1938
Western Union	1940
Man Hunt	1941
The Ministry of Fear	1943
The Woman in the Window	1944
Scarlet Street	1945
House by the River	1950
Rancho Notorious	1951
Clash by Night	1952
The Big Heat	1953
While the City Sleeps	1956
Der Tiger von Eschnapur/The Tiger of Bengal	1958
Die tausand Augen des Dr. Mabuse/The Thousand Eyes of Dr. Mabuse	1960
Partial listing	

workers to wait for a mediator to come. The industrialist announces: "The path to human dignity and happiness lies through the great master of us all, the great Mediator, Love."

Like Caligari and other pieces of German Gothic, *Metropolis* perpetuates themes of the manmade monster, good and evil in self-destructive combat, and the danger of denying humanity's past. Here, the story is cloaked in a costume of modernity, and its bland conclusion ineffectively resolves social and political issues through the obvious contrivances of melodrama.

Our understanding of *Metropolis*, particularly of Rotwang's role and why Frederson wants to wreck his own machines, are frustrated by the fact that 7 of 17 reels were cut from the American release.[2] However, for all its squeaky plot machinery, Lang's film continues to amuse and visually to impress viewers. The striking city of the future was accomplished by Eugene Shuftan (originally Eugan Schuffan). Shuftan had been working as a film animator and designed a technique for combining models, mirrors, and photography to create the impression of elaborate sets. Models and camera were positioned at forty-five degree angles from a mirror. The mirror reflected in the camera lens the desired visual image reproduced from the model. The rest of the mirror's surface was clear glass which exposed a rear-projected image that merged with the mirrored image to "place" one image in the midst of the other.

Industrial operations of *Metropolis* are facilitated by science fiction machinery and television. Work is stylized into mechanical, expressionist movement. When Freder first discovers the horrors of the workers' lot, Lang dissolves from the giant machinery into a lurid image of the god Moloch devouring his victims. The riot and the threatening flood are

[2] *Apparently Rotwang and Frederson had once competed for the same woman and the scientist's incongruous house with its cabalistic symbols, evidences a background in magic.*

staged with patterned crowd movements Lang manages so effectively. Rotwang's creation of the false Marie generates another convention requisite to future Frankensteins, like her destruction later.

Lang said that he conceived *Metropolis* when first viewing the cityscape of New York at night from his ocean liner. He produced two more pulp, science-fiction silent features: *Spies* (1928) and *The Woman in the Moon* (1929). Completing a second Dr. Mabuse film in the early thirties, Lang was invited by Goebbels to supervise motion picture work for the National Socialist Party. Lang elected to flee instead, spent a short time in France, and departed for Hollywood. Thea von Harbou remained behind and became a Nazi.

G. W. PABST

George Wilhelm Pabst moved from expressionism to psychological, realist films, although both varieties were sharpened by a penchant for romanticism. An early actor in film and theater, Pabst directed his first movie, *The Treasure*, in 1923. The contrived story of love, gold, greed, and jealousy, staged in painted sets, shared the qualities of expressionist films of the period.

Pabst became a spokesman for what was described among a group of German painters of the time as *die Neue Sachlichkeit,* or the New Realism. They espoused a sharply detailed rendering of representational forms, assuming a stance esthetically at odds with expressionism's distorting abstraction, more agreeable to the similarly motivated Kammerspiel.[3]

[3] *Richard Byrne dates the end of German expressionism in film at 1924, although this neglects the workers in* Metropolis *and the professor's dreams in* Secrets of a Soul. *See "German Cinematic Expressionism: 1919-1924" (Ph.D. diss., University of Iowa, Ames, 1962).*

Success came with *The Joyless Street* (1925), also known as *Street of Sorrows,* a dispiriting view of the people who live on one Viennese block in the postwar period and are tormented by the alarming inflation. A petty government official loses his job, and his daughter (Greta Garbo) almost becomes a prostitute to support the family. She is saved by a young American. Asta Nielsen plays a prostitute who commits a murder, reports it as a suicide, but later confesses to the police.

The drab, desperate life of the poor clashes

G. W. Pabst (1885–1967)

Der Schatz/The Treasure	1923
Die Freudlosse Gasse/The Joyless Street	1925
Geheimnisse einer Seele/ Secrets of a Soul	1926
Der Liebe der Jeanne Ney/ The Love of Jeanne Ney	1927
Abwege/Crisis	1928
Die Büchse der Pandora/ Pandora's Box/Lulu	1928
Tagebuch einer Verlorenen/ Diary of a Lost Girl	1929
Die Weisse Hölle vom Piz Palü/The White Hell of Pitz Palü (co-director Arnold Fanck)	1929
Westfront 1918/Four from the Infantry	1930
Die Dreigroschenoper/The Threepenny Opera	1931
Kameradschaft	1931
Die Herrin von Atlantis/ L'Atlantide (France/Germany)	1932
Don Quichotte (France)	1933
Der Prozess/The Trial	1947
Der Letze Akt/Ten Days to Die/The Last Ten Days	1955
Partial listing	

with the forced gaieties that take place in a flat where pleasure can be brought by those able to pay. A principle client is the gross butcher, in front of whose store lines of women stand for hours. Excepting the sensationalism of the plot and the foolish, false ending, Pabst manages his material with seeming objectivity, calling details to the viewer's attention while appearing to avoid editorial decisions about their significance.

Pabst next elected to make a film which would evidence and dramatize the techniques of psychoanalysis. *Secrets of a Soul* (1926)

today seems rather tidy therapy, but it was in part designed with two members of Sigmund Freud's inner circle: Doctors Karl Abraham and Hanns Sachs.

Freud himself viewed the world of commercial film with some amusement. Earlier, Samuel Goldwyn had offered him $100,000 for his cooperation in the production of a feature that would trace famous love stories through the ages, beginning with Anthony and Cleopatra. Freud declined, and it was said that his telegram to Goldwyn caused greater publicity than the publication of *The Interpretation of*

The Joyless Street. Based on factual incident, the film's inflated pathos was tempered by performances from Asta Nielson and from Greta Garbo, fresh out of *Gösta Berling.* Pabst's film was radically altered abroad. France cut two thousand feet. Vienna excised Werner Krauss, a central character. Russia made Garbo's savior, an American lieutenant, into a doctor and pinned the murder on Werner Krauss. (Museum of Modern Art/Film Stills Archive)

Dreams in New York.[4] Ufa then approached Karl Abraham with the idea of making a movie that would explain some therapeutic techniques of psychoanalysis. Freud suspected film's capacities to elucidate his theory and refused any personal authorization, but did not try to dissuade his colleague. Abraham was unable to participate in the making of the film due to severe illness, so major collaboration fell to Hans Sachs. The reaction of psychoanalytic circles to *Secrets of a Soul* was underenthusiastic.

In the film, a chemistry professor (Werner Krauss, who played Dr. Caligari, the butcher in *The Joyless Street,* and anti-Semitic roles in Nazi films) learns of the impending arrival from India of a boyhood friend. This prompts dreams of attacking his wife with a dagger. Still possessed of the impulse on waking, the professor seeks psychoanalytic help. In therapy, free association and fragments of dreams coalesce in the discovery of Krauss' difficulties. Jealous since childhood of the wife's preference for his friend, her cousin, the patient had developed inferiority feelings, which

[4] *Ernest Jones.* The Life and Work of Sigmund Freud. *(New York, 1957), vol. 3, p. 114.*

erupted in the phallic urge to attack. Freed by his capacity consciously to confront the repressed emotions, Krauss emerges cured in the remarkably efficient case history.

The movie's dream sequences have special interest, for expressionism, which consistently translated emotion onto the screen at the expense of a more objective perception, lent itself easily to the night world of the mind. In *Secrets of a Soul,* Pabst seems to have found an effective alliance of expressionist and naturalist tendencies that more commonly were at odds in the twenties. The daylight professor is cooly observed, his gestures in particular, as they betray inner tensions aroused by Krauss' knife phobia. Interestingly, recollections recounted to the analyst are seen by Pabst to constitute a half-way point betwen dream and reality, so they are played against white backgrounds, which serve as well to withdraw them from the original environment and context.

The Love of Jeanne Ney (1927) derives from a rather trashy communist romance written by Ilya Ehrenberg. It follows a liaison between Andreas, who is a Russian Communist dispatched by his government around the major cosmopolitan centers of Europe, and

One moment of Werner Krauss's nightmare combines authoritarian threat and vertigo during *Secrets of a Soul.* On the film's appearance, the British press accused Freud of forsaking his profession for show business profits. (Museum of Modern Art/Film Stills Archive)

Jeanne, the daughter of a French bourgeois industrialist. Their love is engulfed in the social turmoils of great events and periodically endangered by a scurrilous villain, Khalibiev, who betrays either side for money and lusts not only after Jeanne but also after a gentle, beautiful blind girl played by Birgitte Helm, the Marie/robot heroine of *Metropolis*.

Ehrenberg's novel concludes with the execution of Andreas for the political murder of Jeanne's father. The author clucks his tongue and comments to the reader that his is not a Dickins novel and cannot distort reality for the sake of last-minute reprieves. Pabst's film manages a happy ending, like many of his efforts, and further sanitizes Andreas' politics by cutting down on his agitational work and suggesting at one point that he may become a good Catholic.

Unlike many Ufa productions, *The Love of Jeanne Ney* manages something of a documentary flavor by the use, in part, of real locations. Thus, the social turmoil, which gives background to the romance, is more firmly and realistically founded; some of the most affecting scenes, as when Jeanne runs to meet her lover along a city sidewalk, draw stength from this sense of individual story blending in and out of overpowering, unmanageable events.

Pabst's eye for detail is well supported by the work of Fritz Arno Wagner, a skilled Ufa cinematographer who, working with set designers, is responsible for the look of many major films: *Destiny, Nosferatu, Spies, Westfront 1918, The Threepenny Opera, M, Kameradschaft* and *The Testament of Dr. Mabuse.* Wagner was especially adept at diffused lighting effects, mimimizing the contrasts and shadows by reducing the illumination of his subject so that the screen image appeared in a rich spectrum of intermediate grays, a quality that lent itself especially well to Pabst's own inclinations toward the contrived appearance of unstaged reality.

The other feature of special interest in *The Love of Jeanne Ney* is the editing, for, at this stage, Pabst had become a master of continuity within scenes. In this respect, his work surpasses other twenties directors. Pabst organizes his cuts on movement, that is, an action initiated in one shot will continue into the next: a change of camera angle bridges a connection between the shots, avoiding any abruptness or jarring effect by the smoothness with which the two are matched. Further, Pabst cleverly breaks his sequences down into choices of angles that are motivated by the glances of his actors. In consequence, shots will be positioned so as to simulate the point of view of someone whose directed attention the audience has just seen, often in closeup. Because we see "with the eyes of" one, then another participant, we gain a special intimacy with the frame of reference of both. What an actor sees helps to define the psychology that has controlled his perception; a famous example is Khalibiev's introduction to Jeanne when he watches her cross her father's study. Finally, by separating his sequence into so many segments that vary both in length and in camera angle, Pabst gains significant control over audience attention.

Also known as *Lulu, Pandora's Box* (1928) derives from two plays by Frank Wedekind, a German forerunner of the expressionists. Wedekind saw sex as an elemental power that determined men's lives, and he wrote plays that combined fantasy with critiques of social values. This material (it also constuted the basis for an opera by Alban Berg) lent itself well to Pabst's own pattern of fabricated story and social concern.

Lulu is the mistress of a gross figure named Schön (beautiful). His son and Lulu fall in love and shoot the father on his wedding night with Lulu. She is apprehended and tried, but the two escape and flee to London. There, moneyless, Lulu becomes a prostitute. One of her clients is Jack the Ripper who murders her grotesquely.

The photography, not Wagner's is more high key than other Pabst work (the visual ele-

Dangerous moments in *The White Hell of Pitz Palü*, performed rather than acted, contribute to the film's documentary appeal. Once a ski instructor, Fanck trained a production crew of skiers and climbers. His films helped to extricate German shooting from studio domination. (Museum of Modern Art/Film Stills Archive)

ments are in higher contrast with fewer intermediate tones), emphasizing the dark sides of its characters as well as their night world, and giving special play to the erotic power of Lulu. She is played by Louise Brooks, an American of extraordinary beauty whom Pabst saw in a Hollywood feature by Howard Hawks. Brooks is the emotional center of the film; her attraction seems to transcend protocols or ordinary behavior. She is like a jungle flower consuming what it touches, man or woman, and one of the strongest scenes depicts a dance between Brooks and another woman, the lesbian bond but another facet of Lulu's exuding sexuality. While Brooks has an immobile quality to her expression, this only serves to emphasize the eroticism beneath, as if she disdained women's ordinary agitated efforts to attract. Pabst's skill at shifting points of view works to special effect here, for it allows us to understand Lulu's unarticulated perceptions and finally to view her as Jack the Ripper sees his victim. The high key lighting also makes special use of light sources and reflections to reinforce the atmosphere: street lights, lamps, and stage illumination. The reflection of a bread knife instigates Jack the Ripper's brutalities, a device that can be traced through a succession of later Expressionist-inflected film including Lang's *M* and Alfred Hitchcock's *Blackmail* (1929) and *The Thirty-Nine Steps* (1935).

Pabst's second collaboration with Louise Brooks, *Diary of a Lost Girl* (1929), presents her in quite a different light, as victim rather than cause. She is seduced by her father's pharmacy assistant, Fritz Rasp, the evil Khalibiev of *Jeanne Ney*. Mothering a child, the girl goes from a cruel correctional institution to a whorehouse. She marries a nobleman who commits suicide, then is taken into her uncle's home.

The sordid, sensational script, which bears curious resemblances to *Queen Kelly*, carries social criticism as well. Here, Pabst characters almost seem to act out a case history. (He is quoted as once saying, "What need is there for romantic treatment? Real life is too romantic, too ghastly.")[5] Events appear to support his views, although one cannot help feeling, too, that Pabst writes pulp in the guise of sociology. Perhaps the problem is that so few Louise Brookses exist in real life.

[5] *Paul Rotha*, The Film Till Now *(Bedford, England, 1949), p. 269.*

Pabst's last silent film was a collaboration with Arnold Fanck, himself responsible for a popular series of films about mountain climbing and skiing. *The White Hell of Pitz Palü* (1929) combined plane acrobatics with climbing skills in a melodramatic adventure story whose interest lies in the action sequences.

Exceptional shots staged by stand-ins are intercut with closeups to supply drama by identification with the characters, as when imperiled climbers are viewed from a distance, then from near-by. Such a technique does not always coordinate the shots effectively (a rope broken by an avalance, followed by its frayed end), but one sequence works especially well. This involves the efforts of an airborn search team to locate a lost ski party by flying dangerously close to mountain peaks. Strong shots from the skirting plane match dramatically with the climbers' points-of-view. Rescue efforts, sometimes shot in deep verticals, sometimes straight on, sometimes sharp-angled, give an unnerving sense of height and sheer precipice drops. A storm sequence, where the screen is whited out by torrents of snow, provides its own dramatic shading, the snow's brilliance replacing Pabst's blacks and shadows in *Pandora's Box. The White Hell of Pitz Palü* features Leni Riefenstahl, who gained her initial filmmaking experience as an actress for Fanck's mountain films.

With the introduction of sound, Pabst continued to make films at home, then worked in France and the United States. He was caught in Germany at the outbreak of World War II and executed what emerged as unremarkable, routine work during and after the hostilities.

F. W. MURNAU

A Reinhardt pupil, Murnau became a feature director in 1919. His *Nosferatu* (1922), subtitled "A Symphony of Horror," was loosely based, quite without authorization, on Bram Stoker's *Dracula*. The vampire is equated with a deadly plague that devastates any spot he inhabits. He dies, finally, because a young woman sacrifices herself by spending the night with Nosferatu, tricking him into facing the deadly rays of sunlight.

Much of the film's acting is forced or amateurish, and the story lags, particularly at the beginning and up to the point when Jonathan Harker, called Granach in German prints, reaches Transylvania. Nevertheless, Nosferatu himself is a singular monster as played by Max Schreck with pointy, hairy ears, great white almond-shaped eyes that peer from a skull-like bald head, and long, gently curving talons that give insect dimension to his jerky, lurching movements, particularly when viewed in the shadows and silhouettes that Murnau creates. If Nosferatu carrying his coffin across the Bremen landscape has slightly the look of Bugs Bunny, he is otherwise properly menacing and intimidating, particularly on shipboard. When horses and carriage move through the Carpathian forest, Murnau uses two effective devices. He locates the coach against a rear-projected background of trees shown in negative, so that the footage assumes an inexplicable whiteness, and elsewhere, he photographs the horses' passage intermittantly, so they and the carriage have a jerky, magic, unnatural movement that evoke the mystery of Nosferatu himself. Against the negative projections, the coach goes at normal speed, as if time had two gears.

Murnau's most famous silent production was done as a collaborative effort with scriptwriter Carl Mayer, photographer Karl Freund and, in some measure, Emil Jannings, although Jannings does not seem to have been a favorite among his associates. *Der Letzte Mann* (1924) translates as "the last man" and more accurately describes the film than its American title, *The Last Laugh,* which speaks only to the ending, a tacked-one affair that Murnau said satirized American movie resolutions, but Jannings may have required to give his part more appeal.

Murnau's earlier films were often marked with expressionist technique, sometimes alleviated by humor. In *The Last Laugh,* these inclinations balance against the Kammerspiel style invoked in Carl Mayer's script. Murnau and Jannings built up the Jannings doorman figure in careful detail, but he is played against other characters so little developed as to compose almost a background.

Jannings proudly serves as a doorman for a luxury hotel. Dressed in resplendent uniform, his jocular condescension gives neighborhood status not only to himself but, by reflection, to his sister and her daughter. Because of age, Jannings is relieved of his duties and assigned to tending a lavatory. Such disgrace leads to ridicule and humiliation from the very people, including his own sister, who had earlier placed him in such esteem. Jennings withdraws to this bathroom and is sympathetically covered with a wrap by a night watchman. Then the film is interrupted by its first and only title, announcing a millionaire's bequest to the last person who had served him, which proves to be Jannings. He returns to the hotel as a guest with the night watchman in tow, dispensing good humor and largess to all the dining room's uniformed flunkies.

The story proved an exhilerating vehicle for Emil Jannings who, Josef von Sternberg said, enjoyed nothing more than being humilated on screen. More broadly, it satirized the national inclinations toward uniforms and status. Further, the film used exceptional, imaginative technique to identify and amplify the meaning of Jannings' porter figure in the scheme of things.

Carl Mayer's two previous film scripts, *Shattered* (1921) and *New Year's Eve* (1923), emphasized an unharmonious division of society into incompatible, class-based echelons. For *The Last Laugh,* he visualized the porter as a figure whose petit-bourgeois pretensions delude him into believing that, in some personal way, he mediates between the wealthy hotel clientele and his apartment house and neighborhood. As doorman he officiates the connection between interior lobby luxury and the city street life, and the revolving door is emblematic of this role.

Like other entrances, the hotel door figures recurrently in Murnau's imagery, both for its connecting function and because the movement suggests, with cyclically reflecting surfaces, the inevitability of each act in a social scene that appears altogether ritualized. To emphasize movement and its relation to feeling and audience perception, Mayer investigated radical camera mobility, an extension of his work in *New Year's Eve.* An open-grilled escalator had already been built for the Ufa lobby set.

"Now at last we know why you built an open lift," Murnau said to me, smiling. The camera was attached to a bicycle and made to descend, focused on the hotel vestibule; the bicycle went across the hall to the porter, and then, with a cut between shots, continued into the street, which had

F. W. Murnau (1888–1931)

Der Knabe in Blau/The Blue Boy	1919
Satanas	1919
Der Januskopf/Janus Head	1920
Schloss Vogelöd/Vogelöd Castle	1921
Nosferatu	1922
Phantom	1922
Der Letzte Mann/The Last Laugh	1924
Tartüff/Tartuffe	1925
Faust	1926
Sunrise: A Song of Two Humans	1927
The Four Devils	1928
Our Daily Bread/City Girl	1929
Tabu	1931
Partial listing	

been built on the lot. Sometimes the camera was fixed to Freund's stomach, sometimes it flew through the air attached to a scaffolding, or moved forward with Freund on a rubber-wheeled trolly I had built.[6]

---

[6] *Robert Herlth, "With Murnau on the Set," in Lotte Eisner,* Murnau *(Berkeley, 1973). Like most innovation, the device of moving a camera relative to the behavior photographed so that it seems to have a kind of independence is better considered in terms of usage than "firsts." Fred Balshofer, who started as a cameraman for Lubin in 1905, described one technique devised for* The Second in Command *(1915). "We decided to plan the action of some scenes to make it possible to follow the actors . . . and to move into a close-up without making a cut. We . . . drew a rough sketch of a platform large enough to set the tripod on with the camera and cameraman that could be moved on four wheels. When it was constructed, we found we would have to enlarge it to accommodate a second person. As the platform was pushed forward, it became difficult for Alder to crank the camera, watch the actors to judge distances as the platform moved, and follow the focus all at the same time. . . . The platform was an underslung affair that hung from the axles and rode about four inches from the floor. We began calling the moving camera "trucking shots" and the platform a truck. . . .*
"Of course the scenes had to be planned precisely in order to coordinate the movement of the truck with the panning and tilting of the camera, and it was most important that the actors cooperate for they were part of the entire planned movement of the scene. . . . Making a film this way took more time but after looking at the rushes, we thought it worthwhile." Fred J. Balshofer and Arthur C. Miller, One Reel a Week *(Berkeley, 1967) pp. 117-18.*
With Wagner, Freund was a germinal figure in German cinematography. He worked on The Golem, Tartuffe, Metropolis, Variety, *and the documentary* Berlin, Symphony of a City. *In the United States he was responsible for the impressive first-reel moving camera in* Dr. Jekyll and Mr. Hyde *(see Chapter 10) and* Dracula *(1931). He directed* The Mummy *(1932) and* Mad Love *(1935). Freund concluded his career as cinematographer on the* I Love Lucy *television series.*

Karl Freund credited this exploitation of camera to Mayer. Such innovation had several effects on narrative exposition. Substituting a continuous run of film for what would otherwise have been negotiated by cuts, it withdrew from the kind of clipped control that Pabst explored later in *Jeanne Ney*. At the same time, mobility injected choreographed performance into the viewer's experience, for, if actors moved relative to the camera, now the camera could shift relative to performance. Its independent behavior gave the viewer a new, liberating spatial ubiquity.

Murnau took advantage of other options available to a filmmaker who wants to manifest a particular attitude toward his material. When the camera draws back from Jannings in his lavatory (Freund crouched on a fireman's ladder pointing the camera diagonally upward. The camera was then withdrawn from the original location, rising as it withdrew), the shot's increasing distance "generalizes" about the human condition as the attendant becomes smaller and less identifiable; the intention is analagous (and superior) to Vidor's later *The Crowd*.

Camera mobility also identified with character point of view. Jannings, partying in his flat, is simulated by a lurching camera whose focus and multiple exposure suggest drunkenness and dreams. These techniques have virtuoso fascination, but fail to hold an audience for any length of time or to maintain any intensity of feeling.

Tartuffe (1925) was scripted by Mayer, after the Molière play. It is interesting for staging, lighting, and, depending on individual relish, the performance of Emil Jannings. (In the passage of time, Jannings' expressions sometimes become an acquired distaste; with their theatrical asides, Tartuffe and the devil's role in *Faust* finally bludgeon the mind.)

The same dramatic strategy that Mayer used in *The Last Laugh* is evident in *Tartuffe*. He is willing to play the aniticipated "high" moments of the plot, but seems to take greater interest in seemingly insignificant incidents. Without Molière's dialogue to amplify the hypocritical Tartuffe, Mayer takes advantage of Jannings' behavior when no one is watching except the audience. The story is played in sparse, classic decor, uncharacteristic of German films; fragile effects of light and texture (the gowns and hangings) contaminated by the vulgarity of Tartuffe.

It is unfortunate that so many available copies of *Faust* (1926) are made from late generation prints, far removed from original picture quality, because a strength of the film rests in its visual beauty, independent of the conglomerated, simplifed version of Goethe,

Marlowe, and folk tale. Because this legend lies so close to many German silent film themes, it seem curious that Faust itself is done in stilted cliché. Murnau appears to indulge himself the same reverence for his material that Lang did in *Die Niebelungen*.

Ufa outdid itself in constructing entire landscapes viewed from above by photographer Carl Hoffmann[7] on a trolley arrangement that simulates the aerial tour Mephistopheles give Faust when their pact has been consumated. The most impressive moments stem from spe-

[7] *Freund is sometimes falsely credited with* Faust.

A publicity still. George O'Brien, Janet Gaynor, and the boat in *Sunrise*. William Fox wired Murnau: "I hope it will contain pathos, thrills, well-timed and well-celebrated comedy situations intermingled with the other emotions which I am certain every large picture requires." The film's financial failure placed Murnau in subservience to Hollywood studios for the remainder of his short life. (Move Star News).

cial effects: a burning parchment of Faust's agreement, the invocation of the devil by the drawing of magic circles, and Gretchen's execution at the stake. Best of all is the prelude in which the devil looms like a colossal vulture over the world, over light itself, so that his great wings obscure the sun and cast a pall of black clouds across Faust's village, bringing storm and plague.

Murnau moved to the United States where he made *Sunrise* (1927) for Fox, again written by Mayer who remained in Europe. While *Sunrise* was filmed, sound arrived, and Fox added a synchronized music track, but *Sunrise* is a silent film. Mayer's script concerns a married couple whose rural life is unsettled when the man becomes entranced by a vacationing city woman. On her order, the husband tries to drown his wife, but cannot. The wife flees to the city; he meets her there and they reconcile. A storm overturns their boat on the way home. Thinking his wife has died, the man nearly strangles the city woman in rage, but he is interrupted by news that his mate has survived.

In Hollywood, Murnau reconstructed the circumstances of his Ufa productions, working in studio sets that reproduced the most ambitious exteriors. He built a city street with buildings, crossings, automobiles, a trolley, and an overhead viaduct on the Fox lot as well as a German lakeside village nearby. It is difficult to recall another film that has so many complicated, multidirectional movements, particularly those of the city scenes, which are totally controlled by the director for his ulterior purposes.

After she has fled earlier in fear, the man and woman meet in the city and rediscover one another. Murnau develops an elaborate visual parallel to their evolving feelings. The pair is so self-absorbed that they are oblivious of traffic, diners, playground, and passersby behind them. Murnau uses this background to externalize the rekindling trust and commitment. It culminates in a restaurant scene where background dancers seem to explode into weightless shapes, and the lyric mode is sustained in shoreline figurations as the pair returns home in their boat.

Murnau's tracking shot as the man walks from his farmhouse to where he will meet the city woman in the marshes is stunning, both in its virtuosity and the unexpected turns given to our spatial expectations, undermining our confidence in what to anticipate. *Sunrise* is, in style, the most characteristically German film made in Hollywood. After its financial failure, Murnau made another silent, originally *Our Daily Bread,* now known only in a shortened version to which sound had been added called *City Girl* (1929). He completed a film in Tahiti, which had been initiated with Robert Flaherty: *Tabu* (1931). Shortly after, Murnau died in an automobile accident.

THREE FURTHER FILMS

Major in themselves, three additional features also represent the outstanding work of the director: Dupont, Leni and Robison. The American prints of Dupont's *Variety* (1925) differ from longer German versions. In the original length, Boss Haller (Emil Jannings again) runs away from his aging wife with a beautiful girl, working second string circuses in an aerial act until they are hired to team with a star, Artinelli, at the Winter Garden. Artinelli has an affair with the girl, is discovered, and dies at Haller's hands. Our versions omit Haller's wife and represent his relationship to the girl as married. In consequence Haller seems the more innocent and wronged. Both versions are framed by Haller in the process of being pardoned from prison for his crime.

Photographed by Freund, *Variety* impresses with its gaudy camera subjectivities, swinging above the music-hall audiences as from a high trapeze. Director E. A. Dupont is equally skilled at holding the camera steady and moving actors in and out of frame, pacing their screen absences with special care.

There is much eye work among the principals. Jannings runs the gamut from ecstatic lover to raging cuckold. As the girl, Lya de Putti alternates genuine seductiveness with hypocritical charm. Although the climax now draws unintended laughs, *Variety* is a virtuoso performance never repeated by Dupont, an early film critic who finally became an American talent agent.

Another Reinhardt protégé, Paul Leni made *Waxworks* (1924) an apogee of the German tyrant-horror-expressionist thrust, featuring Jannings as Haroun el Raschid, an Oriental potentate, Werner Krauss as Jack the Ripper,

and Conrad Veidt, the Cesare of *Caligari*, as Ivan the Terrible. The episodic story concerns a young poet hired to invent lurid stories about figures in a wax museum. A final episode links historical fantasy and personal history when the poet falls asleep and dreams he is pursued on the fairground by Jack the Ripper.

Leni was a set designer, and *Waxworks* blends naturalist fairgrounds, expressionist Russia, and a sort of "near-east Baroque." The dream sequence, which takes place in the deserted amusement park, is outstanding. Merry-go-round and ferris wheel whirl empty; signs flash, and the shifting shadows imply a surrounding so untrustworthy that its very surfaces may not be depended on. Leni proceeded to the United States, where he applied

Warning Shadows. In fact, the count (left) is unseen by his wife and her lover, who will soon embrace. Like Robison the director, an itinerant showman in the film "captures" his subjects' shadows. They are sometimes trustworthy, sometimes illusory. He plays them back, perhaps in hope that the images may instruct an audience as well as amuse it. (Museum of Modern Art/Film Stills Archive)

his graphic and directing skills to the horror-comic genre, notably *The Cat and the Canary* (1927), before an untimely death.

Arthur Robison, also spelled Robinson, was born in Chicago, became a German physician, then entered the movies. His most memorable film, *Warning Shadows* (1922), is subtitled "a nocturnal hallucination." It seizes on expressionist shadow images as the distorted evidence of feelings, and develops a story in which the shadows act out fears and desires among a dinner party's hosts and guests. A traveling conjurer performs a shadow play for the diners, staging an oriental fable that serves as an analogue to their own situation. In the play, the wife deceives her husband with a lover-guest. The conjurer then readjusts his light so that the dinner audience, who appear to fall asleep, are silhouetted on his screen. A fantasy is enacted during which the host forces his wife's admirers to stab her to death and is himself killed. Returning to the oriental fable, the showman depicts a wife who begs forgiveness. The performance concluded, husband and wife are reconciled and the conjurer rides off on a pig.

Interesting for the effects themselves, photographed by Fritz Arno Wagner, *Warning Shadows* exposes the plot through a particularly complex and successful intermingling of the different means of film expression on many levels. Early in the story the wife's lover and her admirers amuse themselves by caressing her shadow as she stands admiring herself in a mirror. Shadows and reflections are both narcissistic and errant, like film screen surfaces. Servant to the manipulations of an artist, they sometimes threaten to escape human control. Audiences both sleep and watch alertly. The film commences with a conjurer in a prompter's stage box introducing characters through the agency of a magic lantern, and of course the magician himself is introduced to us by the lamp of a film projector. Robison's last work was yet another version of *The Student of Prague* (1935).

Summary

In varying proportions, the best of silent German films evidence national preoccupations with the Gothic, expressionism, and psychological realism. Lang's work often encases legend and national aspiration in pulp narrative. Pabst betrays a shift from expressionism toward the New Realism, maintaining, however, his penchant for attributing the motives of characters in an oversimplified, sensationalist way. Murnau encompasses vampires, Goethe, and Molière, *The Last Laugh,* and *Sunrise* especially enhanced by Mayer's scripts. The country's industry is characterized by highly skilled technical execution and by unique emphasis on and control over graphic stylizations.

As in the United States, accomplished German directors accounted for merely a small percentage of total output, which was prodigious. Yet Germany's "Golden Age" films had consistency and consequence, in part because their studio origins emphasized "looks" at a time when both expressionism and psychological realism fostered easily identifiable visual conventions. The best of these films filtered across German borders, just as Ince and DeMille had come to be known in Europe. German technicians invaded Hollywood in large number, particularly as a consequence of a mid-twenties pact between Ufa, Paramount, and MGM that worked to Ufa's singular disadvantage.

Unlike Germany, the French film industry suffered disasterously from World War I, yet, as will be seen in Chapter 7, the neighboring culture was still capable of nurturing foundations for a unique narrative tradition.

Bibliography

Atwell, Lee. *G. W. Pabst.* Boston, 1977.

Brooks, Louise. "Meeting with Pabst." *Sight and Sound,* Autumn 1967.

———. "Pabst and Lulu." *Sight and Sound,* Summer 1965.

Bauche, Freddy. *G. W. Pabst.* Lyon, 1965.

Bucher, Felix. *Screen Series: Germany.* New York, 1970.

Byrne, Richard. "German Cinematic Expressionism: 1919-1924." Ph.D. dissertation, State University of Iowa, 1962.

Eisner, Lotte. *The Haunted Screen.* Berkeley, 1969.

———. *Murnau.* Berkeley, 1973.

———. "The German Films of Fritz Lang." *Penguin Film Review* 6 (1948).

———. *Fritz Lang.* London, 1976.

Fantastique et réalisme dans le cinéma allemand: 1912-1933. Brussels, 1969.

Guillermo, Gilberto Perez. "Shadows and Substance: F. W. Murnau's *Nosferatu.*" *Sight and Sound,* Summer 1967.

Horak, Jan-Christopher. "Brecht vs. Pabst." *Jump Cut* no. 15 (July 20, 1977).

Kraszna, Krausz A. "Proletarian of the Film." *Close Up* 6 (1930).

Kracauer, Siegfried. *From Caligari to Hitler.* Princeton, 1947.

Lang, Fritz. *Metropolis.* New York, 1973.

Luft, Herbert G. "Carl Mayer." *Films in Review,* March 1963.

———. "Carl Mayer." *Films in Review,* November 1972, May 1973, January 1974.

———. "Karl Freund." *Films in Review,* February 1963.

Manvell, Roger. *The German Cinema.* New York, 1971.

Melnitz, William. "Aspects of War and Revolution in the Theater and Film of the Weimar Republic." *Hollywood Quarterly* 3 (1948-49).

Monaco, Paul. *Cinema and Society.* New York, 1976.

Titford, John S. "Object-Subject Relationships in German Expressionist Cinema." *Cinema Journal,* Fall 1973.

Von Harbou, Thea. *Metropolis.* New York, 1963.

Whitford, Frank. "Expressionism in the Cinema." *Studio International* 179 (1970).

Wollenberg, H. H. *Fifty Years of German Film.* London, 1948.

Wood, Robin. "Murnau's Midnight and *Sunrise.*" *Film Comment,* May-June 1976.

7 SILENT FRENCH FILM

Filmmaker-critic Louis Delluc heralded France's movie future after World War I, but his vision appeared optimistic to the industry. Economic hardship touched film as it did the rest of French commerce. By the end of the twenties, production had become more of a national than an international business.

The effect of such withdrawal was, in terms of quality, saluatory. Filmmakers not only produced subtler, more "French" products, they established unique working relationships with actors, stage directors, artists, poets, and novelists. Also, the lower production budgets, necessary because of the shrunken markets, had no serious ill effects.

Entr'acte (Clair 1924) (Museum of Modern Art/Film Stills Archive)

INDUSTRIAL CONSOLIDATION

Before the war, boundaries had been less intimidating. Méliès' brothers, Gaston and Paul, made films for the Méliès Manufacturing Company in Chicago; Fort Lee, New Jersey; San Antonio; and Sulphur Mountain Springs, California between 1909 and 1911. But the prospering fortunes of Pathé and Gaumont had counterpointed Méliès' decline. In the century's early years, Pathé drew heavily on backing from banks and industrial capital; by 1908, the company led a world market in film production. Gaumont, Pathé's nearest competitor, used Louis Feuillade both for comedies and for its successful serials. The prodigious Pathé output, popular and unimpressive, eminated not only from France but Fort Lee, a center of French-American filmmaking for the Eclair Company.

Ferdinand Zecca and Lucien Nonguet were supplanted at Pathé by comic director-actors, in particular Prince Rigadin and Max Linder. Rigadin worked largely in imitation of Linder; Linder, a Bourdeaux performer with a background from the music halls, achieved international fame in the years before World War I. He developed a foppish, elegantly dressed character whose self-assurance is continually undercut by impossible, sometimes fantastic, situations. Linder's elegant costume was mirrored in reverse by the shabby garb of Charlie Chaplin, and Linder's small, subtle gestures were elaborated in the satire of Chaplin, who termed Max "The Professor" and credited him with the inspiration for the Chaplin style.

Linder made hundreds of comedies for Pathé, most quickly improvised, like Feuillade's serials. He came twice to the United States, producing features there in the early twenties. *Seven Years' Bad Luck* (1921) traces the unhappy consequences that follow breaking a shaving mirror. *The Three Must-Get-Theres* (1922) satirizes Fairbanks' *The Three Musketeers* with Linder as Dart-in-Again. Done in period costume, the film cavalierly includes motorcycles and an effigy of Napoleon. However, the features were less successful commercially than his earlier shorts. By then, the competition, Chaplin, Keaton, and Lloyd, had adapted more successfully to tightly-knit plots and to disciplined production methods. Linder and his wife died in a suicide pact in 1925.

War closed all but domestic markets to French production, which had so vigorously dominated international distribution earlier. When hostilities ceased, French businessmen concluded that the country, victorious in battle, had surrendered its economic supremacy. After unsuccessfully trying to coerce film producers into competing with Hollywood on America's own thematic terms, Charles Pathé withdrew from motion pictures. He sold American distribution offices to the Chase Bank of New York and his Jersey City laboratories to DuPont. Eclair Film abandoned production in 1924. Such disinclinations to gamble were evidence of shrinking French economic power for years to come. Although, among all the allies, France had profited most by reparations, the twenties were a period of economic strain in which the country significantly was incapable of making good its war debts. At the same time, attendence in French movie houses boomed, just as it did in Germany.

LOUIS DELLUC

During hostilities, a bond was made that helped to shape film production: a tie between movies and the artistic community. Feuillade's serials had entertained painters and writers for years; around 1918, a playwright, novelist, and critic, Louis Delluc, inititated a series of articles on the motion picture, later founding a journal called *Cinéma* and publishing several books on film. Delluc thought well of Thomas H. Ince, his scriptwriter Gardner Sullivan, and Cecil B. DeMille; *The Cheat* had inspired him to engage in film study. (Griffith was little known in Europe until the twenties.) Delluc also respected expressionism, Chaplin, and the Swedish filmmakers, but his dream was to develop a school indigenous to his own country: "The French cinema must be *cinema;* the French cinema must be *French.*" (From such usage we can begin to discern semantic inflections that today would claim to distinguish *cinema* from *movies* or *film.*)

To accomplish his aims, Delluc advocated an approach that later, forties critics sometimes questionably termed impressionist, singling out directors whose work appeared to further the development of a French esthetic: Abel Gance, Marcel L'Herbier, Germaine Dulac, and Jean Epstein. In his own scripts and the films he directed, Delluc emphasized the elaboration of pervasive, dominant atmosphere, even to the subordination of plot and character, a sort of Gallic equivalent to what Kammerspiel dramatists called *stimmung* (mood).

In *Fièvre* (1921), set in a Marseille saloon, one of the regular patrons murders a visiting

Fièvre. Character types gather in a Marseilles sailors' bar: an unprepossessing clerk, a grey-hatted man, an oriental girl, a Frenchwoman named Patience. After a fight, a murder, and a police interrogation, the oriental girl examines a flower that she has admired until then from a distance. It is artificial. (Museum of Modern Art/Film Stills Archive)

sailor who has been making advances to the bar's owner. Like the scripts of Carl Mayer, Delluc's story is not intended to individualize characters. Rather, they act out a typical night in a typical locale. The time of the film's projection closely coincides to the time it reports. In other ways, too, the director's ability to manipulate viewer experience is underplayed. Delluc alternates near shots of the bar's habitués with deep-focused shots that encompass the place itself. The close shots tend to withdraw our interest in the specifics of the drama, substituting, rather, a commitment to pervading mood. Significantly, Delluc wanted to title his film *La Boue* (Filth), but was prevented by the censors.

Eldorado. The painter and the dead dancer. L'Herbier's film alternates from documentary-like style, as in an Andalusian Holy Week procession, to highly subjective points of view. The latter visions shift between those of dancer, painter, and drunk, their views distorted by the characters' states of mind. (British National Film Archive/Stills Library)

In *La Femme de nulle part* (1922), Delluc turns to a little rivertown community, but his immersion in atmosphere continues to be evident. Delluc's wife, Eve Francis, plays a middle-aged woman who returns to her early home, one she had fled to escape the stifling conventionality. There, the woman convinces a girl not to reenact her own past, then leaves for the city because she can no longer recapture a way of life so distant now from what she has become. Dying at thirty-four, Delluc was a tireless advocate of film study and a proselytizer for noteworthy films. He founded a ciné-club and brought *The Cabinet of Dr. Caligari* to Paris for exhibition. Delluc is the root of a filmmaking coterie (Epstein, Gance) whose concepts of film were essentially more intellectual than pragmatic, as in the commercial milieu, even though some of the Delluc-influenced group (like Vigo and early Renoir) drew on private sources for financing, while others worked through the movie industry.

MARCEL L'HERBIER

Delluc's highest patriotic film enthusiasms were bestowed upon Marcel L'Herbier, a playwright and poet. L'Herbier began his career as a scriptwriter, but his special pleasure rested in graphic aspects of film, and his productions are marked by pictorial beauty and the most careful composition.

Eldorado (1921) transplants a *Fièvre*-like melodrama (many such French scenarios resemble Ince westerns) into Seville, where a Swedish painter meets a Spanish dancer who is raped by an ominous clown figure and kills herself. L'Herbier concentrates on the Spanish countryside and the bar where the girl performs. Innovative in *Eldorado* was the director's employment of distortion to make evident the subjective perceptions of characters. The painter's view of the Alhambra is softened in focus, shifting with the sunlight so that it has the quality, for example, of the Impressionist Claude Monet's sequential pictures of the Cathedral at Rouens. Similarly, when the bar patrons are drunk, their perceptions distort and go out of focus, like those of the porter in *The Last Laugh*.[1]

L'Herbier's other success was *The Late Matthew Pascal* (1925), set in Italy and based on a Pirandello novel about a man who seizes advantage of a mistaken account that he has died. One of its special features was the use of ceilinged sets, designed by Alberto Cavalcanti, who became a director himself within the year. Such enclosure permits angled shots impossible otherwise and also readjusts lighting balances which ordinarily operate from lamps attached to the tops of the set's wall flats. With Fernand Leger's help on properties, Cavalcanti's sets also evoke a cubist tension between surface flatness and photographed depth. *The Late Matthew Pascal* introduced Michel Simon, who figures so often in major films of the thirties, and starred the émigré Russian, Moszhukin, a famous actor associated with Kuleshov's experimental work described in Chapter 8.

L'Herbier continued to make films until the fifties, largely undistinguished but for a remake of DeMille's *The Cheat* in 1937. During World War II he founded IDHEC (Institut des Hautes Etudes Cinématographiques), the Paris film school that has systematized and extended the study of film begun by Delluc.

---

[1] *A useful distinction can be made here between impressionism and expressionism: when the representation of the external world reveals a distortion of objective reality due to the projection of an subjective worldview—the expression of a state of mind—the mode is expressionist. When the representation reveals a distortion that results from a desire to reproduce literally a fleeting impression of a specific moment, impressionism is at play.*

JEAN EPSTEIN

Slightly younger than the other "impressionists," who have sometimes been termed the first French avant-garde,[2] Jean Epstein worked with Abel Gance and Delluc. *Coeur Fidèle* (1923) concerned two rivals for the same woman. In a fast-cut fairground sequence, a fight between the men is staged against a merry-go-round background whose accelerating pace intensified the human action. *The Beauty from Nivernaise* (1923) furthered Epstein's interest in working-class life with a documentary-like story about bargemen on the canals and rivers. *Six and a Half by Eleven (a Kodak)* (1927) was a more contrived story in which the discovery of an old, undeveloped camera roll leads to a husband's realization that his wife is loved by his brother.

The Fall of the House of Usher (1928) integrates a Poe story, "The Oval Portrait" [which figures, too, in Godard's *Vivre sa vie*, (1962)] into an atmospheric evocation of gloom, mystery, and the macabre, mixing misty-focused subjectivities with some of the expressionist qualities of *Nosferatu*. In his choice of materials, Epstein veers between the most contrived kinds of emotional and poetic stories and the unstructured documentary. Whatever his subject, the character and story, in the traditions of impressionism, subordinate themselves to the creation of a dominant, atmospherie sense of place. This quality is paramount in *Finnis Terrae* (1929), which has little narrative at all, and clearly shows Epstein's response to Russian films that had then reached European audiences. *Finnis Terrae* was made on an island off the coast of Brittany and concerns a quarrel among island fishermen as a result of one man's hand injury. Ep-

---

[2] *Other highly experimental work from France and elsewhere that departs most dramatically from orthodox narrativity is discussed in Chapter 18.*

stein's control of rhythm and pace blends happily with the island life, particularly in a kelp harvesting sequence. He worked intimately with the islanders whose obliviousness to camera intrusion testifies to a skill Epstein shares both with Russian filmmakers and the documentarian Robert Flaherty.

JACQUES FEYDER

Feyder, a Belgian, left theater to direct films, and moved from the lofty intellectual concerns of theater circles into the more commercial realm of film, often adapting popular literature whose appeal helped to guarantee success. He argued that anything could be translated into screen images if one had a cinematic soul.

A case in point is Feyder's first commercial hit, *L'Atlantide* (1921), based on a popular novel that recounts the exotic situation of an ancient city unknown to civilization and surrounded by desert, ruled by the beautiful, man-destroying Queen Antinea (who bears striking resemblance to H. Rider Hagard's *She*). The expensive Feyder version (G. W. Pabst made one among other *L'Atlantide*'s) was filmed in the Sahara, with interiors in Algiers. The desert scenes were impressive, and box office abroad monentarily revived French investor hopes.

Crainquebille (1922) comes from an Anatole France novel about a pushcart vegetable peddler arrested for supposedly calling a gendarme a fathead. The combination of studio naturalism and expressionist hallucination during a courtroom sequence reminds the viewer of later German films like *Überfall* (1929) and *Variety*. Cobbled roads, proletarian gestures, streetlit rain, and underlying sentimentalities foreshadow the Carné-Prévert sound features to follow.

Feyder attempted to capitalize on the suc-

The Fall of the House of Usher. Poe's title story is preceded by "The Oval Portrait" tale; Lady Madeline expires when her picture is completed. Here her body is transported to the family vault on a distant shore. Filmmaker Luis Buñuel commenced his first production experience as assistant director, but he was repelled by Epstein's admiration for Abel Gance and withdrew from the project.

cess of Lubitsch's *Carmen* with another costly version filmed in Spain in 1926. More successful was a German production of *Thérèse Raquin,* the Zola novel, as *Du Sollst Nicht Ehebrechen/Thou Shalt Not* (1928), prints of which have disappeared. The story parallels that of *The Postman Always Rings Twice.* A sensual shopkeeper persuades a lover to murder her feeble husband and then to move in with her. Period reviewers were struck by Feyder's combination of sexuality and social observation.

Best known among Feyder's silent features is the satiric *Les Nouveaux Messieurs* (1928). It recounts a romance between a trade union official and a pretty dancer. The man becomes a cabinet minister and takes the girl away from a count to be his mistress. The government shifts; the count becomes a minister. He secures a diplomatic post abroad for his rival and wins back the girl. Like René Clair comedies that followed, *Les Nouveaux Messieurs* derived from the stage. His cynical view of politicians in the film is achieved through skillful timing and imaginative visual gags. Peopling parliament with ballerinas in their tutus during a dream sequence, Feyder aroused government indignation that withheld the film's release for a year. In the interim, he left for the United States where he worked on Garbo pictures including her first sound venture, *Anne Christie* (1929), before returning to further success in France.

ABEL GANCE

Gance's career spans from early serials (*Barberousse,* 1916) up to seventies features; his grandiose *Napoleon* was redesigned in 1971 as *Bonaparte et la révolution.* Gance moved from theater to script writing and formed his own film company in 1911. An early comedy, *La Folie du Docteur Tube* (1914), played with mirror distortions. He drew from Ince and

DeMille, interested in fast-paced editing and the metaphoric juxtaposition of images, (e.g., an aging, blind railroad engineer dies as his train model falls from a table). The manner recalls Griffith, and Griffith was immensely moved by Gance's work.

Mater Dolorosa (1917), a drama in which an unfaithful wife is reunited with her husband when her child falls ill, established Gance's commercial potentials. The use of light (as in *The Cheat*) to throw actors' expressions into accentuated relief was particularly effective. Gance is a grandiose, romantic figure who never shied from powerful feeling and extravagant technique. A production similar to *Mater Dolorosa* was *The Tenth Symphony* (1918) wherein the ostensible subject of the film—the tribulations of a composer and his second wife—figure less importantly than Gance's interest in building atmosphere and characterization by his editing and light.

J'Accuse (1919) was filmed with the aid of

Jacques Feyder (1885–1948)

M. Pinson, Policer	1915
L'Atlantide	1921
Crainquebille	1922
Visages d'enfants	1925
L'Image	1925
Carmen	1926
Thérèse Raquin/Du Sollst Nicht Ehebrechen	1928
Les Nouveaux Messieurs	1928
The Kiss (United States)	1929
Anna Christie (United States)	1929
Daybreak (United States)	1931
Le grand jeu	1934
Pension Mimosas	1935
La Kermesse héroïque	1935
Knight Without Armour (Britain)	1937
Une femme disparaît	1941
Partial listing	

the French army's photography service, combining patriotic motif with a horror of war and war's aftermath. Gance reconciled the two by claiming that his film was an accusation of German militarism as it had devastated the civilizations of Europe.

Jean and François love the same girl, but François is married to her. They become soldiers. During war the wife, Edith, is captured and sent to Germany. François dies at the front. Jean is driven insane by the carnage. Edith is made pregnant by a German. In an allegorical climax, the mad Jean renames himself J'Accuse and evokes all the dead French soldiery to rise in vengeance. Sensing the approach of another war, Gance remade *J'Accuse* in 1937. But for excerpts, the original version appears to be lost.

La Roue (1922) realized one of Eric von Stroheim's ambitious dreams of scope; it was 32 reels in length, released in three parts. Later, the material was edited down to a single feature. A melodramatic and sprawling railroad story traces relations between a retired engineer, his son, and the adopted daughter both love. The son dies spectacularly in the Swiss Alps. The father loses his eyesight. Again, Gance's material (as customary, he wrote the script) is less interesting than the use to which he puts it. Responding to the single-showing version, Louis Moussinac, critic and theoretician, wrote:

This film is a combination of forces. In it, the purity of the water matters less than the power of the gushing forth. We should have the courage to forget that which is unbearable and even odious: the exaggerated effects, the visual excesses, literature that only appears in these bits of visuals, and the extreme bad taste, because it is the price we have to pay for the dazzling glimpses of something to admire. It matters little whether we are mistaken. It is sufficient that it is ventured. Gance is the first to have captured, and, albeit confusedly, he *has* captured, exhuberance, movement, depth — in a word, original beauty.[3]

Gance worked on *La Roue,* originally called *La Roue du rail* (the railroad wheel) for three years, shooting in the Alps and the station yards at Nice. Some studio work was done, but more often the director constructed sets on location. Editing assumes new functions in *La Roue.* Scenes cut rapidly, one to another, to show the son's flashing thoughts of past life before he falls to his death. The central theme of the railroad is emphasized by referential

Abel Gance (1889–   )

La Digue	1911
La Folie du Docteur Tube	1914
Barberousse	1916
Mater Dolorosa	1917
La Dixième Symphonie	1918
J'accuse	1919
La Roue	1922
Napoléon	1927
Mater Dolorosa	1932
Napoléon	1934
Lucrèce Borgia	1935
Un grand amour de Beethoven	1936
J'accuse	1937
Quatorze juillet (multiscreen short)	1953
Austerlitz	1960
Bonaparte et la révolution (different edited version of Napoléon)	1971
Partial listing	

[3] *Georges Sadoul,* Dictionary of Films, *trans. Peter Morris, (Berkeley, 1972), p. 321.*

J'accuse (above, 1919; below, 1937). The pacifist poet, shell-shocked and insane in Gance's earlier version, becomes an inventor haunted by his comrades' deaths in the remake. He sets up living quarters in the soldiers' cemetery. In 1922, Gance reedited his film to contrast the "Return of the Dead" sequence with the post-World-War I Victory Parade of Joffre. Foch, and Clemenceau. (British National Film Archive/Stills Library) (Museum of Modern Art/Film Stills Archive)

cuts to locomotive machinery. Gance was impressed by the time's esthetic involvement in technology, as on the part of Fernand Leger and the Constructivists. So far as anything holds the story together, cyclic movements of the trains and their travels supply Gance's underlying theme.

The next venture consumed the director's attention from 1923 to 1927, finally resulting in *Napoleon*, also known as *Napoleon seen by Abel Gance* (1927). Despite the production time span, only one section was realized in a project that had intended to follow all Napoleon's history in six motion pictures. The only completed work traces Bonaparte's early life and school, the period of the Revolution, and the Italian Campaign.

Long interested in motion picture technology, Gance had experimented as early as *La Folie du Docteur Tube* with a triptych effect, breaking the image into three segments, separately but simultaneously projected on adjacent screens. For *Napoleon*, Gance conceived this application in four sequences, each a climax in the long biography. Gance employed the three screens in several ways. On some occasions, pictures blend with one another, like an early version of Cinerama, except since each image retains the high-verticals of the 3:4 aspect ratio,[4] in combination they give an even more striking, mural-like effect. This impression figures strongest when Gance stages Napoleon's inspirational confrontation with his troops as they prepare to enter Italy.

Alternatively, Gance counterposed left and right screens as frames to central action. What had been metaphoric sequential images in *J'Accuse* and *La Roue* now appeared simultaneously. A recurrent motif is the face of Napoleon, whom Gance viewed with unqualified approval, in the middle while events rage around him.

Gance experimented with color as well. He combined the process of film tinting with toning. Tinting was accomplished either by projecting the black and white image through a colored gel or dying film in the course of processing. In toning, blacks assumed color while whites stayed white. In combination, a two-color appearance might be achieved. When Napoleon views the English fleet burning in Toulon harbor, the reds reflect in his face while he stands against a deep blue sky.

Gance knew, too, that film sound was shortly forthcoming. With this in mind, so far as possible he cast Napoleon with stage actors whose voices would lend themselves to the rhetoric. Thus Robespierre and Danton were filmed actually speaking their lines. Gance himself played Saint-Just, and Antonin Artaud, playwright and critic, Marat. In 1934, Gance added sound, and some additional scenes, to *Napoleon*, reconvening almost all his original cast to dub voices against their own silent images. This version of *Napoleon* originally appeared in stereophonic sound as well. Later sound versions incorporate portions of the three screen material.

An impressive sequence is one in which Gance intercuts a storm at sea (Napoleon is escaping pursuers off the coast of Corsica in an open boat to which he has lashed the tricolor as sail) with the Convention, now falling into disarray in the face of the competing arguments from Danton, Marat, and Robespierre. Gance likens Napoleon's plight to the developing emotions of the assembly, implying that as Napoleon saves himself he will soon rescue France. To do this, Gance fits the lurching, water-threatened boat against high-angled views of the Convention that seem to mirror waves of water with the crowd's behavior. Then the camera itself starts to move as if swaying on a trapeze, sweeping down toward the assembly in an arch that is intercut with the boat knifing through the waves. The effect combines vertigo, mass fervor and the furies of nature.

Another exceptional multi-image effect is accomplished by Gance early in the film during young Napoleon's schooldays. On a single screen, through multiple exposure, Gance combines nine images, lined three by three, each viewing a pillow fight from a different angle. Since both perspective and time intermingle, one's impression is that of a moving cubist picture, more so indeed than in any more recent experimentation with multiple screens.

Throughout the film, Bonaparte is associ-

---

[4] *With minor exceptions, the general pattern of projected images until the widescreens of the fifties has been approximately 3:4. For example, a screen picture thirty feet tall would be forty feet wide.*

ated with the eagle. As a boy he has a sentimental attachment to one and starts the pillow
fight described above when some schoolmates
release the bird. In *Napoleon's* ecstatic conclusion, the General's face is replaced by a
huge, militant, three-screen eagle. Originally,
Gance tinted his left screen red and his right
screen blue to create a mighty, patriotic backdrop to the bird. The version viewed by this
writer was black and white. Even so, a young,
San Francisco audience whose interest in Napoleon and French chauvinist expression can
fairly be described as minimal, roared in unqualified approval.

Gance's *Napoleon* was an unwitting victim
of its innovations. Unfortunately, the three-
projector versions of Napoleon demand both
exceptional coordination and luck for their execution. Worse, when MGM brought the film
for distribution it was decided after a very few
metropolitan exhibitions that the three-screen
"Polyvision" stood to endanger the industry
by imposing further requirements of technical
renovation at a time when theaters and production companies already faced expensive
adaptations required for sound. In consequence, *Napoleon,* even in its 17-reel, four-
hour version, has been little shown, although

Napoleon (General Houch, Josephine's lover, plays chess with Bonnaparte).
Napoleon: "Be careful, or I shall take your queen." (Hoche is checkmated, as Josephine studies
her lover from behind her undulating fan, then turns to Napoleon.
Josephine: "Tell me, General, what weapon do you fear most?"
Napoleon: "Fans, madam." (Museum of Modern Art/Film Stills Archive)

recent reconstruction efforts have been undertaken. Sound versions undercut something of the experience because much of the action, particularly crowds and battles, is unduly accelerated to accomodate the higher projection speed.[5]

Viewed silent with resounding Wurlitzer organ accompaniment, the experience of *Napoleon* proves wearing, cumulative, and exhilarating, like listening to several Beethoven symphonies uninterrupted, concluding with the Ninth. Much of the staging, accentuated by theatrical performance, has the quality of pageant, and powerful, patriotic rhetoric does not always sit easily today. Gance's visual effects still command audience enthusiasm. The panoramic, triptych shots executed with 14mm wide-angle lenses carry special grandeur.

---

[5] *Most sound equipment standardizes projection at 16 frames per second for silent film, 24 frames per second for sound. This equates to about 11 minutes, 7 seconds for a sound reel, sixteen minutes 40 seconds silent. However, there is no true standardization of how fast silent film was photographed and hence how it should be projected. Before cameras were actuated by electric, governed motors, speed of passage depended on the cameraman's arm. Speed was something adapted to story: slow for comedy so action would speed up on projection, fast for drama. Some filmmakers objected to the rate at which their films were projected and shifted exposure speed to compensate.*

One indication of appropriate projection speed for silent film, presuming a projector can facilitate it, is indicated on the music cue sheets made available to first run houses for orchestral accompaniment to the picture. These vary in the extreme, and James M. Card, Curator of film at George Eastman House, has supplied reel speeds specified in minutes for particular films: Male and Female *(14),* The Sheik *(12),* The Three Musketeers *(14),* Robin Hood *(12),* Blood and Sand *(14),* Sherlock Jr. *(11),* Seven Chances *(11),* Sally of the Sawdust *(12),* Phantom of the Opera *(14),* Lady Windemere's Fan *(11),* The Merry Widow *(11).*

Paris qui dort, also known as *Le Rayon invisible/The Crazy Ray/At 3:25.* The Eiffel Tower figures in avant-garde French visions since its construction in 1889, first a harbinger of technological salvation, later symbolizing industrial menace. At about the same time as Clair's film, Jean Cocteau wrote a one-act comic play set on the tower. (Museum of Modern Art/Film Stills Archive)

RENÉ CLAIR

Clair experienced the war, monastery life, and journalism before entering film, first as an actor in Feuillade's serials. His earliest work shows an awareness of France's film traditions and an immersion in twenties esthetics. *Paris qui dort* (1923) has something of a *Fantômas* about it and a touch of dada as well. The city is paralyzed. Time stops because of a ray gun directed by an eccentric scientist. Six people escape, a guard high in the Eiffel Tower, an airplane pilot and his four passengers who include a detective bringing in a thief, a business magnate, and a young woman. Living on the Eiffel Tower, they roam the city, enjoying its unguarded favors and growing restive until they find the scientist, and the ray gun is set again in motion, this time to restore life. Clair's visual gags arise from an amused, cynical vision of what might be discovered in public and private if we were all zapped into immobility. Beneath the fun lies a premise of Clair the film critic. He conceived a story that might throw film back onto its own basic properties (moving pictures telling a story), what he called "the external movement of the objects and the internal movement of the action."

Entr'acte (1924) was produced for a special occasion, the intermission entertainment separating two acts of a dadaist ballet. It features avant-garde artists of Paris: Man Ray, Francis Picabia, Marcel Duchamp, and Eric Satie. Satie wrote music both for the ballet and film. His film accompaniment exists on some prints, charming and idiosyncratic; passages are cued to particular visual moments as they appear on screen. If *Paris qui dort* reverted film to primitive functions, *Entr'acte* removed it from the characteristics of story.

The film is made up of sequences, each possessing an alogical consistency. The opening introduces images alternately startling in magnification (a head of hair), playfully manipulated (a row of cigarettes rises to assume the colonnade design of the Parthenon, then becomes the Parthenon), and hints of material to follow (an ostrich egg is suspended at the top of a column of jetting water). Images are edited together either through similarity of form (matches, cigarettes) or else they are juxtaposed to provide unexpected associations.

Throughout, the image of a ballet dancer, shot through glass from below in slow motion, combines voyeurism with a depersonalized beauty as the costume billows and contracts like a blossoming flower. Once the camera slowly tilts down the dancer's upraised arms to reveal the bearded face of a man wearing pince-nez. Anecdotal fragments piece together. Man Ray and Marcel Duchamp try to play a game of chess on a rooftop but are disturbed by a water jet. A hunter dressed in Tyrolian hat is shot by Francis Picabia (who had scribbled the ideas of *Entr'acte* on a piece of stationery in a few minutes' time) with a gun that looks like a clay pipe.

The most developed episode commences with a funeral procession in which mourners, curiously dressed, are filmed in slow motion, the party headed by a camel. As the cortege proceeds, the hearse breaks loose. The pace accelerates until all becomes a manic chase. A seemingly legless man who has been riding on his cart leaps off and runs. Finally the coffin

René Clair (1898–   )

Paris qui dort/The Crazy Ray/ At 3:25	1923
Entr'acte	1924
Le Fantôme du Moulin-Rouge	1924
Le Voyage imaginaire	1925
Un Chapeau de paille d'Italie/ The Italian Straw Hat	1927
Le Deux Timides	1928
Sous les toits de Paris	1930
A nous la liberté	1931
Quatorze juillet	1932
Le Dernier Milliardaire	1934
The Ghost Goes West (Britain)	1935
I Married a Witch (United States)	1942
It Happened Tomorrow (United States)	1943
And Then There Were None/ Ten Little Indians (United States)	1945
Le Silence est d'or	1947
La Beauté du diable	1949
Les Belles de nuit	1952
Les Grandes Manoeuvres	1955
Porte des Lilas	1957
Les Fêtes galantes	1965
Partial listing	

The Italian Straw Hat. Fadinard (Albert Préjean) holds Anaïs de Beauperthuis (Olga Tsche-chowa), just fainted, while her lover, Lieutenant Tavernier (Vital Geymond), threatens destruction of the residence. Deaf Uncle Vésinet (Paul Olivier) is oblivious to the comotion. Finally Uncle Vésinet will save the day for everybody by presenting an identical straw hat as a wedding present. (Museum of Modern Art/Film Stills Archive)

rolls out into a field. Its top flies open and the corpse sits up, a magician with a wand. He makes each of the party disappear, finally himself. The movie is over, except that a man bursts through the *Fin* title, which is drawn on paper.

Entr'acte was Clair's closest affiliation with experimentation and the graphic arts. Although its elements reoccur, particularly the Sennett-like chases and competitions, later Clair joined film elements aimed at mass audiences to comic story lines. The dispositions can be seen drawing together in *Le Fantôme du Moulin-Rouge* (1924), which is about a soul that has become separated from its body.

Clair's silent masterpiece, one of the most successful of all silent comedies, appeared in 1927, *The Italian Straw Hat*. It was based on a stage farce written by a comic opera team, Marc Michel and Eugene Labiche, and set in mid-nineteenth century France. Clair was unenthusiastic about the assignment because he disagreed in principle with the idea of adapting material from other media into film. He moved the period to the turn of the century.

Enroute to his wedding, a young man, Fadinard, unknowingly lets his horse eat the straw hat of a married woman engaged in a tryst behind bushes. Fadinard is charged by the lover, an officer, with locating a similar hat so the husband's suspicions will not be aroused. As a result, Fadinard must leave his wedding at odd moments and search the town because the impetuous officer threatens to destroy his house. More importantly, however, the hat must be recovered because the hat itself means respectability, a part of the middle-class guise, and so it assumes special significance for everyone. Fadinard tirelessly seeks to preserve the married woman's false innocence while he prepares to enter the same treacherous social institution himself. The fact that a hat is finally located among the bride's wedding presents speaks impishly of the couple's own future. At the same time, the bridegroom is eager to get underway.

On so simple a farce, Clair builds a world of comic types, caricatures of the self-important, provincial middle class so dear to French satirists. Each figure has one or two distinctive characteristics: the deaf uncle with an ear trumpet, the henpecked husband whose tie keeps slipping down his shirtfront. It is the beginning of that parade of "typical" men and women that made Clair the "French" filmmaker for foreign audiences. His talent lay in organizing a play whose humor rested on verbal exchange (Labiche's work is superbly witty) into visual contrivances. A famous wedding episode has the domineering, impatient wife signalling to her husband to adjust his necktie while all the men about him fiddle with their own and the husband sits complacent. *Paris qui dort* bared human foibles by freezing their execution; *An Italian Straw Hat* exposes the philanderings of pompous bourgeois in action.

Finally, the marriage is cancelled by the bride's father, who discovers the hatless older woman in his son-in-law's quarters. Wedding guests force their way into the house to retrieve their presents. The father-in-law grabs his prized possession, the daughter. At last, a hat appears and resolves everyone's conflicts. Bride and presents are returned. And in tidy design, each figure reverts to his special problems. The deaf uncle has his ear trumpet unplugged. The cuckold with too tight shoes takes them off. The wedding guest who has spent all day looking for one glove finds it. The little man with the skewed tie wakes in terror to check his throat. The errant wife has a hat. Bride and groom are in bed. This film set Clair in the direction he pursued for the remainder of his career, except for those productions geared to the commercial requirements in England and the United States.

DIMITRI KIRSANOFF

During the twenties, Kiransoff emigrated to France from Estonia and made films outside the mainstream of the industry, which featured his wife, Nadia Sibirskaia. The most fully developed and impressive is *Ménilmontant* (1925), which tells the story of two sisters left bereft by a violent murder in their country village. They find work in the city making artificial flowers. Sibirskaia falls in love with a young man who seduces and abandons her for her sister and others to follow. Under great hardship, Sibirskaia has a child and is finally reconciled to her sister, now a whore. The seducer is killed in a last act, which frames the story with violence.

Ménilmontant is notable for Kirsanoff's immensely thoughtful employment of his camera and for the expressive face of Sibirskaia. The

Dimitri Kirsanoff (1899-1957)

L'Ironie du destin	1923
Ménilmontant	1925
Sylvie-Destin	1926
Sables	1927
Brumes d'automnes	1928
Rapt	1934

story is told without titles, adapting picture to narrative exigencies with great imagination. A hand-held, mobile subjective movement lends strong emotion to the young mother's lonely walk through the city and her contemplation of suicide in the Seine. When feeling requires, Kirsanoff edits sequences in flashing pastiches, and he maximizes expression in tight closeups that sometimes become even tighter.

In the seduction scene, Kirsanoff puts together a series of masculine, kneeling beseechments by connecting dissolves so that the entire campaign is quickly, effectively, and ironically laid out. One sequence locates Sibirskaia on a park bench starving in the chilly Paris afternoon. An old man quietly eating his lunch cuts his small piece of salami and passes it to her without comment or a meeting of the eyes. Chewing, the woman looks at him with the skin hanging from her mouth; the moment is exceptionally moving.

Like Feyder's *Crainquebille,* Kirsanoff's film is another precursor of the poetic realist school of French film that followed in the next decade. Kirsanoff made other films. *Brumes d'automme* (1928) visualizes the thoughts of a lonely woman, again played by Sibirskaia. A last personal work, *Rapt* (1934), thoughtfully counterpointed sound to images. In his remaining years, Kirsanoff supported himself with sponsored films and professional work in the industry until 1956.

JEAN RENOIR

Renoir fought in World War I and abandoned ceramics for film. His early work alternates commerciality with fantasy and experimentation. *La Fille de l'eau* (1924) features his wife, Catherine Hessling, who had been a model for Auguste Renoir, the director's father. Its story, not written by Renoir, is garish. Hessling lives with her uncle, a drunk who

Ménilmontant. The park bench sequence. Kirsanov's film appears without intertitles, its lurid plot deftly muted by performance. Nadia Sibirskaia reappears in Renoir's *The Crime of Monsieur Lange* in 1935 as a pretty laundress in love with the concierge's son. Kirsanov's *L'Ironie du destin* (1923), which also featured his wife, seems to be lost. (Museum of Modern Art/ Film Stills Archive)

Jean Renoir (1894–   )

La Fille de l'eau	1924
Nana	1926
La petite marchande d'allumettes/ The Little Match Girl	1928
Tire-au-flanc	1928
On purge bébé	1931
La Chienne	1931
Boudu sauvé des eaux/Boudu Saved From Drowning	1932
Madame Bovary	1934
Toni	1934
Le Crime de Monsier Lange/The Crime of M. Lange	1936
La Vie est à nous	1936
Une partie de campagne	1936 (released 1946)
Les Bas-Fonds/The Lower Depths	1936
La Grande Illusion/Grand Illusion	1937
La Bête humaine/The Human Beast	1938
La Règle du jeu/The Rules of the Game	1939
Swamp Water (United States)	1941
This Land is Mine (United States)	1943
The Southerner (United States)	1945
The Diary of a Chambermaid (United States)	1946
The Woman on the Beach (United States)	1947
The River (India)	1951
Le Carosse d'or/The Golden Coach (France/Italy)	1952
French Cancan	1954
Elena et les hommes	1956
Le Déjeuner sur l'herbe	1959
Le Testament du Dr. Cordelier/Experiment in Evil	1959
Le Caporal épinglé	1962
Le Petit théâtre de Jean Renoir	1971

Partial listing

threatens her sexually. She runs away and joins forces with a gypsy and his mother: the Ferret and Crazy Kate. Georges, son of local gentry who live on an estate, falls in love with Hessling. Animosity flares between Georges and the Ferret, and the gypsy sets fire to a haystack. Hessling is frightened into delirium by the events, and is abandoned by the gypsies. After various misunderstandings, Georges rescues her from the alcoholic uncle, and she leaves for Algeria with the family.

In countryside scenes, *La Fille de l'eau* hints at Renoir's later talents, extravagant plot notwithstanding. He savors the spontaneous movements and interactions of his characters, although these behaviors alternate with dated aspects of twenties experimentation—multiple exposures and pyrotechnic editing flashes. The latter are at their height during Catherine Hessling's period of hallucination, in a way justified like the drunken sequence of *The Last Laugh,* but this is the least interesting episode. Renoir's celebration of nomadic life is tempered by a view of the gypsies as opportunistic and untrustworthy, although their freedom of human movement and expression clearly intrigues him.

His next production adapted Emile Zola's *Nana* (1926) and followed on Renoir's having seen *Foolish Wives.* Perhaps for this reason *Nana* is more unemotionally observed than many Renoir films; the greatest sympathy rests with a horse burned to death by an enraged youth. As with other productions Renoir financed his own film, largely with money left by his father. Again Catherine Hessling was featured.

Nana was expensively mounted. Hessling is difficult to view as a lower-class woman who exists to revenge herself on wealthy lovers, but she is a beautiful, able actress. Another motif of the director's work becomes apparent in *Nana:* his fascination with the stylizations of convention-ridden performance—life as theater. Nana's success as a kept woman

evolves from her ability to play parts appropriate to the needs of each lover. Renoir quietly calls attention to our spectator's relation to events by designing several scenes with hints of the proscenium, whether through a visible frame, like a window, or through the exits and entrances of his players that evoke stage performance.

Following on Delluc's ciné-club, others appeared, including the Vieux-Colombier Cinéma, which invited Renoir to administrate its studio laboratory, designed to experiment with film. Catherine Hessling appeared again in *The Little Match Girl* (1928). Renoir took a cue from Gance's *Napoleon,* shooting with hand-held cameras on galloping horseback, and he recorded some scenes with five cameras set at different angles.

The Little Match Girl is one of Renoir's most interesting early films, for its Hans Christian Anderson story integrated realist and fantasy impulses. Street life is filmed in diffused focus, while the fairy-tale dreams have visual clarity; the invented reality is more real, sharper, and more meaningful than ordinary experience, an irony that permeates other Renoir films.

The film consists largely of the match girl's dream as she lies dying, huddled in snow on a city street. Figures from her waking life reappear as toys, and she is pursued by Death who finally overtakes. Passersby think the girl has foolishly tried to keep herself warm with matches. Renoir does little to make the toy-like illusions of the apparitions appear "real." Although the film catches something of a child's innocent pleasures in fantasy, it is permeated by the imminence of Death. One is reminded of Hessling's delirium in *La Fille de l'eau,* but here the restorative powers of a rainstorm are replaced by cold snow.

With the coming of sound, a rather ineffective music track has been added. Apparently a different, happy ending existed at one time, although this is difficult to imagine. The film also marks Renoir's experimentation with panchromatic film stock. Before this time (until about 1918), most motion pictures had been filmed on monochromatic and then orthochromatic (1918-1925) emulsions. The former did not respond well in the green-to-red area of the light spectrum. Orthochromatic still converted reds to black on screen. (This accounts for many of the curiosities of makeup in early motion pictures). Panchromatic responded well to a broader range of color, but was adversely affected by the violet hues in mercury lamps and arc lights, common studio tools. Renoir compensated with incandescent lighting, a practice that became increasingly common with the advent of sound, since arcs also emitted an audible hiss.

Tire-au-flanc (1928), whose title suggests good-for-nothing or ne'er-do-well, has affinities with Chaplin and *The Italian Straw Hat*. Like Clair's film it is based on a nineteenth-century music hall piece. Significantly, Renoir cast a dancer instead of an actor in the leading role. Although the film is not altogether successful, it has received less critical attention than merited and echoes another Renoir preoccupation: the ironies inherent in class-based human relationships.

Master and servant are conscripted. In process, the servant renounces his subservient role, and, without his customary protection and support, the aristocrat becomes increasingly a victim. Each pursues a courtship. The master redeems himself by besting a barracks

The Little Match Girl. Catherine Hessling among the toys of her dream fantasy before Death threatens. "We constructed a plant that is that basis of every studio, and we also made our own sets, make-up, costumes, and so on. We did the developing and printing. The end result was a film, in the fantasy sequences, not worse than any other." Jean Renoir. (British National Film Archive/Stills Library)

bully. The servant interrupts his own wedding to work at his master's nuptials. Renoir advances the time to World War I and play his story in a style moving from farce to slapstick, but *Tire-au-flanc* is not without elements of sadness.

JEAN VIGO

The Basque son of an anarchist who died in a French prison, probably strangled with his own shoelaces, Jean Vigo grew up in schools like the one he recreated in *Zéro de conduite* (1933). His film output is meagre. Even the feature films are short. The complete works amount to little more than the time of a double feature, yet Vigo's reputation and influence have been immense. Because indignation and rebellion figure centrally in *A propos de Nice* (1929) and *Zéro de conduite,* he is sometimes heralded as a revolutionary voice. Because experimentation, humor and deep affection for his subjects are so present in the work, he fits, too, into other French traditions. Much abused, the adjective *lyric* describes Vigo with accuracy.

Vigo met his wife in a sanitorium for tubercular patients. He worked in a Nice film studio and *A Propos de Nice* was subsidized by a 100,000 franc gift from his father-in-law. While planning his film he met Boris Kaufman[6] who helped to shape it and executed a large part of the finished camera work. Rejecting an early, pedestrian conception, the two men elaborated their imaginative approach (which nimbly sidesteps categorization) to the subject, the resort of Nice. Vigo and Kaufman roamed cemeteries and beaches. They hid their secondhand camera in a cardboard box to catch pedestrians unaware. The carnival was documented, but efforts to film gambling in the casinos proved unsuccessful.

Most available prints of *A propos de Nice* are considerably shorter than the original, intended length. As it stands, the film constitutes a documentary of the Mediterranean town, heavily shaped by indignation toward rich, idle tourists, indignation imbued with a satiric eye for vulgarities of dress and manner. Death punctuates much of the footage, for Nice is a refuge for old people who seek to deny age with frivolity. Vigo was interested in all film history, and moments of his first film gesture toward Stroheim, Clair, expressionism, and the Russian experimentalists, but these are passing footnotes. For all its veering enthusiams, *A propos de Nice* retains an integrity of its own, heavily charged with individual, or, with Kaufman, a paired, sensibility.

After aerial shots of Nice, the gambling theme is introduced with dolls. A toy train and its passengers are swept from a table by a croupier's rake, then resort hotels, the promenade, sport and harbor are shown, along with shots of Carnival. The cemetery appears. Festive celebration intercuts with Nice's factory buildings, on which the film concludes.

Because *A propos de Nice* recapitulates many playthings of a young filmmaker, it is sometimes dismissed today for cinematic techniques (slow motion, creating amusement

---

Jean Vigo (1905–1934)

A propos de Nice	1929
Jean Taris, champion de natation/Taris, roi de l'eau	1930
Zéro de conduite	1933
L'Atalante	1934

---

[6] *Boris Kaufman is the brother of Dziga Vertov, but not to be confused with Mikhail Kaufman, another brother, who worked with Vertov in Russia.*

by unexpected juxtapositions) that have justifiably passed into cliché. The film's deeper character rests in Vigo's ability to coalesce a resort atmosphere, the fear of death, and the cheap eroticism of aging, wealthy women into personal statement. Vigo knows Nice so thoroughly that its variety, which includes slums, warships, manikins, cripples, and statuary, each come finally to assume meanings which reflect off of each other. Vigo exhibited the finished film at Vieux-Colombier in Paris, but it was little seen in his life.

He made a short, sponsored film for Gaumont in Paris, again with Kaufman's photography. *Jean Taris, champion de natation* (1930) simply shows a champion swimmer demonstrating various strokes. A soundtrack with music and narration was added. Vigo was not taken with the work excepting the shape of certain underwater shots, filmed in slow motion through glass portholes in the swimming pool. These were to reappear in *L'Atalante*.

CARL DREYER

The Danish Dreyer entered film in his own country as a journalist-critic, then wrote scripts and titles and worked as an editor. His early work shows a developing austerity of staging, and unwavering interest in human features as these may reflect inner states. *Leaves from Satan's Book* (1919) begins a lifelong preoccupation with diabolism. *Love One Another* (1922) was filmed in Germany and follows the situation of Russian Jews during the 1905 revolution. Apparently it now exists in a print held by the Soviet film archive.

Again in Denmark, *Master of the House* (1925) was a domestic drama that showed a family's successful efforts to best a tyrannical father. The complete studio set, built to simulate a two-room flat, included gas, electricity,

and running water. Dreyer's concerns rested in the intimate, psychological detail of close relationships. "What interests me—and this comes before technique—is to reproduce the feelings of the characters in my films, to reproduce, as sincerely as possible, feeling which are as sincere as possible."[7] The success of *Master of the House* led to an invitation from a French firm, Société Générale des Films, to make a film for them. Considering Joan of Arc, Catherine de Medicis, and Marie-Antoinette as subjects, Dreyer decided on Joan.

He spent months in preparation for *The Passion of Joan of Arc* (1928), which was partly based on a contemporary novel, but largely on actual trial records of Joan's interrogation. A great set was constructed, although it is never seen in its entirety, and the film itself eschews extreme long shots. As in the *Master of the House* flat, Dreyer sought

[7] *From an interview with Dreyer conducted by Michel Delahaye for* Cahiers du Cinema *(September 1965): quoted in Tom Milne,* The Cinema of Carl Dreyer *(New York, 1971), p. 85.*

Carl Dreyer (1889–1968)

Praesidenten/The President	1919
Blade af Satans Bog/Leaves from Satan's Book	1919
Die Gezeichneten/Love One Another	1922
Du Skal Aere din Hustru/ Master of the House	1925
La Passion de Jeanne d'Arc/ The Passion of Joan of Arc (France)	1928
Vampyr (Germany/France)	1931
Vredens Dag/Day of Wrath	1943
Ordet (Denmark)	1955
Gertrud (Denmark)	1964
Partial listing	

maximum environmental authenticity for its effect on his actors. (His *The Word* required a rural kitchen to be stocked with all necessary, if unused, utensils and tools). The impulse reminds one of Stroheim, but even more than the American director, Dreyer sought authenticity beyond the appurtenances of naturalism.

Dreyer achieved a stark white against which to play much of his interior action and closeups by painting walls pink and filming on panchromatic stock, which photographs light pink as white. Set design was by Hermann Warm, who collaborated on *Caligari* and did *Destiny, The Love of Jeanne Ney* and Dreyer's later *Vampyr* (1931). The film merges Joan's several questionings into one, her last. Actors perform without makeup, a policy Dreyer followed thereafter and perhaps an outcome of the obvious and distracting cosmetics in *The Master of the House*. As the

The Passion of Joan of Arc. "We were as touched as if the mark of infamy were truly being applied and we were in the grip of ancient prejudices. The electricians, the mechanics held their breaths and their eyes were full of tears. . . ." Falconetti cried. "Then the director slowly walked toward the heroine, caught some of her tears on his finger and touched them to his lips." *Ciné-Miroir* (November 11, 1927). (Museum of Modern Art/Film Stills Archive)

one sympathetic priest, he cast Antonin Artaud. Joan is played by Maria Falconetti, an Italian actress whom Dreyer had seen in a light comic role in a Paris theater.

Dreyer followed chronological unity in his production schedule. The story moves from Joan's interrogation through her scourging and execution. Dreyer's efforts to replace behavior that is unsimulated and arises genuinely from inner feeling were extreme. He drove Falconetti unmercifully for his effects and required endless repetitions of gesture. Her performance is unquestionably one of the highpoints of silent film, radiating by the least movement Joan's immense suffering and torment. Falconetti's eyes work to greatest effect, and their tears are real. Dreyer enhances performance with intense closeups, low-set camera angles, and compositions that isolate Joan in space as she is alienated from her spiritual refuge. Bending at the stake to pick up a fallen rope with which she is being tied, Joan prepares all of us for the final escape from her tormenters.

Although the lengthy series of question-response closeups in mid-section are best remembered, these are carefully prepared by a preceding sequence which uses tracking shots to introduce the courtroom and judges. The last episode carries Joan through the market to her death and introduces soldiers, alert to a crowd's mood, and underlying tones of violence, compounded by cruel weaponry. The emotion breaks into the authority's cathartic viciousness when a spectator cries, "You have burned a saint."

Spiritually preoccupied, Dreyer's view of Joan is still deeply human. Her suffering and the film's strength stems from the tension on Falconetti's face, an agony resting between what she knows and what the world understands. Here rest the powers of Dreyer's closeups and of his somber pace. It is sometimes proposed that the interrogation's lengthy intertitles destroy natural rhythms and double screen length without esthetic purpose. Contrary to some reports, Dreyer did not wish to do *Joan* in sound. In any case, one finds it hard to believe that speech might have added to such images. Stylized and cursory in relation to the speech titles, the mouthings themselves further testify to Dreyer's skill at implying the deeply meaningful through art's falsities. Falconetti made no other films.

Summary

Underfinanced by American standards and lacking the cavernous studio resources of Ufa, silent French film pursued different ends, with subtleties of dramatic reading, comedy and evocation of atmosphere central ingredients. If Gance might be thought France's Griffith, Linder its Chaplin, Feyder perhaps a Gallic Lang, the presound output sustained far too many individual voices to support generalization. Further, with Renoir, Epstein, and Vigo in the forefront, a thrust toward out-of-doors staging and unaffected performance gained momentum. Had he lived, Dulluc might contentedly have acknowledged his country's contribution to have become both cinema and French. The next chapter will describe the efforts of another culture—that of Russia —to define a film esthetic not in terms of film tradition, but of a new society.

Bibliography

Abel, Richard. "The Contribution of the French Literary Avant-Garde to Film Theory and Criticism (1907-1924)." *Cinema Journal,* Spring 1975.

Amangual, Barthélemy. *René Clair.* Paris, 1969.

Analyse des films de Jean Renoir. Paris, 1966.

Analyse des films de René Clair. Paris, 1965.

Anthologie du Cinéma. V. 2 (Vigo, Feyder). 1967.

———. V. 6 (Dreyer). 1971.

———. V. 7 (Delluc). 1973.

Armes, Roy. *French Film.* New York, 1970.

Bazin, André. *Jean Renoir.* New York, 1973.

Blumer, Ronald H. "The Camera as Snowball: France 1918-1927." *Cinema Journal,* Spring 1970.

Braudy, Leo. *Jean Renoir: The World of His Films.* Garden City, N.Y. 1972.

Buache, Breddy. *Hommage à Jean Vigo.* Lausanne, 1962.

Cinemages (1955). Jean Epstein.

De la Roche, Catherine. *René Clair: An Index.* London, 1958.

Dreyer, Carl Theodor. *Four Screen Plays.* Bloomington, 1964.

Durgnat, Raymond. *Jean Renoir.* Berkeley, 1974.

Dyssegaard, Søren. *Carl T. Dreyer: Danish Film Director.* Copenhagen, n.d.

Feldman, Joseph. *Jean Vigo.* London, n.d.

Gallez, Douglas W. "*Entr'acte*: A Model of Film Music." *Cinema Journal,* Fall 1976.

Gomes, P. E. Salles. *Jean Vigo.* Berkeley, 1971.

Jean Renoir. (numéro special 22-23-24 of Premier Plan). Lyon, n.d.

Jean Vigo. Paris, 1966.

Jean Vigo. Paris, 1967.

Jeanne, René. *Cinéma 1900.* Paris, 1965.

Kaufman, Boris, Interview. *Film Culture* 4 (1955).

Kelman, Ken. "Dreyer." *Film Culture* 35 (1964-65).

Kramer, Steven Philip and James Michael Walsh. *Abel Gance.* Boston, 1978.

Leprohon, Pierre. *Jean Renoir.* New York, 1971.

Masterworks of the French Cinema. New York, 1974.

Michel, Walter. "In Memory of Dimitri Kirsanov." *Film Culture* 14 (1957).

Milne, Tom. *The Cinema of Carl Dreyer.* New York, 1971.

Mitry, Jean. *René Clair.* Paris, 1960.

Monaco, Paul. *Cinema and Society.* Ph.D. dissertation, Brandeis University, 1973.

Renoir, Jean. *My Life and My Films*. New York, 1974.

Sadoul, Georges. *French Film*. London, 1953.

Schofer, Peter. "See *Fantômas*." *Velvet Light Trap* 9 (Summer 1973).

Smith, John M. *Jean Vigo*. New York, 1972.

Welsh, James M. and Steven Kramer. "Abel Gance's Accusation Against War." *Cinema Journal,* Spring 1975.

8

SILENT RUSSIAN FILM

From the time of the Revolution, Russian silent film traces a unique effort to reconceive narrativity in terms of theoretical constructs, allied to socio-political theory. Simultaneously, a mainstream, naturalist tradition produced exceptional work. No country more carefully crafted and developed the motion picture into an effective conveyer of ideas of cultural need and aspiration.

Early film in Russia derived from Lumière, Pathé, and Gaumont cameramen. When small native studios developed, around 1907, French, American, and British influence dominated, both in terms of foreign investment and style. In terms of acting style, the emerging Russian industry was beholden to Danish and Italian films. In the time of Alexander Kerensky's provisional government, one out-of-the-ordinary feature appeared, *Father Sergius* (1917), based on a work of Tolstoy's and directed by Yakov Protazanov. Set in the time of Nicholas I, *Father Sergius* episodically

Earth (Dovzhenko 1930) (Museum of Modern Art/Film Stills Archive)

traced a prince's career from court life to religious conversion, and finally the wandering existence of a holy man. Protazanov exposed czarist corruption; more important, the director strove for natural characterizations and cultivated visible authenticity by filming, where possible, in Tolstoy's historic settings. Russian film historian Jay Leyda favorably compares *Father Sergius* to Victor Seastrom's *The Outlaw and His Wife* (1917), whose spare decor and psychological precision led Louis Delluc to term it. "The most beautiful film in the world."

Rebellion in Russia was promoted by a repressive autocracy, religious persecutions, and corruption that was revealed during the Russo-Japanese War of 1904–5. Peasant outbreaks, strikes, riots, and assassinations broke out during 1905; these included the mutiny of the battleship *Potemkin* and the uprising in Odessa. Ruthless repression only temporarily quelled revolutionary ardor.

When World War I erupted, Russia joined the allies. By 1917 food shortages, military defeats, and rumors about secret dealings between the aristocracy and Germany led to further strikes and riots. Czar Nicholas II abdicated and was replaced by a provisional government that included Alexander Kerensky, who became minister of war. Germany permitted Lenin and other revolutionary leaders to return to Russia, hoping that their presence might undermine war efforts.

Lenin galvanized the Bolsheviks, a radical Marxist proletarian party, into action. Under Bolshevik pressure, disorder erupted again, and Kerensky assumed greater power at the head of a coalition cabinet that included Mensheviks, a more conservative proletarian political group. Between summer and fall of 1917, the Bolsheviks won broader bases of support from peasant, intelligensia, and military factions. On October 24, Lenin and Leon Trotsky effected a coup d'état and seized control of government buildings and the winter palace in St. Petersburg, Kerensky fled.

From 1918 to 1920, Russia was torn by civil warfare between Bolshevik-dominated factions and anti-Bolsheviks whose support included Allied military contingents: British, French and American (American troops did not participate in the fighting.) At great cost, the Red forces triumphed.

Speculation over film's revolutionary role preceded the Bolsheviks' seizure of power; in November 1917, the Second All Russian Congress of Soviets initiated moves toward the nationalization of film. At the time of the Revolution, the Futurist poet Mayakovsky and, for a short while, novelist Maxim Gorky rallied to the new state with a few other artists; most of the first generation of Soviet filmmakers were still youths or committed to other, more mundane national concerns.

With nationalization, movies fell under the People's Commissariat of Education. One early commissariat decision was the mass distribution of *Intolerance;* Griffith's editing schemes consequently had an effect on a new, foreign generation. Production was hampered by a total absence of indigenous Russian film equipment or film stock. Manufacture of movie film began in Summer 1919, but its scarcity contributed to a cannibalization of old films, their emulsions stripped so that the base might be used again.

Film's status blossomed under Lenin's vision of the medium's utility for propaganda and education. In Swiss exile, he had frequented small movie theaters and learned both the movies' power and their capacities to reach illiterate populations. In 1922, advocating censorship of "counter-revolutionary and immoral films" and the development of new film approaches, Lenin advised the commissar of education: ". . . [Y]ou must well remember that, of all the arts, for us the cinema is the most important."[1]

[1] *From a letter written by Lunacharsky to Boltyansky, January 9, 1925. Quoted in Jay Leyda, Kino (London, 1960), p. 161.*

Stalin, too, placed motion pictures coequal to other arts. A film school was established during the twenties and experimentation was encouraged. In principle, motion pictures lent themselves to the ideology of the socialist state. Like Marxism, they were a modern form, an outgrowth of the Industrial Revolution, new to practical application. As film might organize the consciousness of the people, it could itself be shaped by experiment. Also, film could record and celebrate the fresh pages of history. In a country that envisioned future progress and prosperity through industrialization, the very technology of film seemed to echo a modern spirit, reinforced by experimental art movements at home and abroad: constructivism, futurism, and the prevailing avant-garde fascination with machines. It is hardly surprising that early Soviet editing designs encouraged departures from narrative usages that were already becoming conventions in capitalist societies.

LEV KULESHOV

Kuleshov joined the film industry early enough to aid in its revolutionary reorganization. He had worked as a stage designer and brought to film an awareness of how set plans and actor movements were basic to narrative effect. His first theoretical writings appeared in 1917. Kuleshov prepared hortatory documentaries during the civil war. When the Polish army threatened Kiev, he produced *On the Red Front* (1920), a short war-spy melodrama, its structure patterned in the mode of *The Mother and the Law*.

Kuleshov's special interest rested in editing: to reduce the image to components that acceded their significations to the filmmaker's will, then connecting shots to develop new meanings. Confronting the possibilities of editing while producing his first film, *Engineer*

Prite's Project (1918), Kuleshov realized the material lacked an episode of men observing some electric cable strung on poles. He hypothesized that the same effect might be accomplished by filming actors looking off camera, then cutting to the cables as if the second shot were the object of their glance. This thesis proved true, and since the shots had been taken at points in Moscow, quite separate from one another, Kuleshov described his phenomenon as "artificial landscape" or "creative geography."[2]

The director held classes that evolved into the Kuleshov Workshop. The workshop included many soon-to-be-central figures in Soviet filmmaking, among them Vsevolod Pudovkin and, briefly, Sergei Eisenstein. With

[2] *See Ronald Levaco, Introduction, in Lev Kuleshov,* Kuleshov on Film, *trans. Ronald Levaco (Berkeley, 1974). It should be noted that Kuleshov's "discovery" was practically antedated in Abel Gance's* The Folly of Dr. Tube *(1914) as well as the matte shots discussed in Chapter 2 and in Griffith's* The Redman and the Child.

Lev Kuleshov (1899–1970)

Engineer Prite's Project	1918
Newsreels	1919–1920
On the Red Front	1920
The Extraordinary Adventures of Mr. West in the Land of the Bolsheviks	1924
The Death Ray	1925
By the Law	1926
Horizon	1932
The Great Consoler	1933
Theft of Sight	1935
The Siberians	1940
The Oath of Timur	1942
The Young Partisans	1943
We are from the Urals	1943

their teacher, students extended creative geography to encompass a sequence in which two figures appeared to approach one another although in actuality they were filmed in different parts of the city. They meet at a third location and seem to ascend the steps of Washington's White House, which is mixed in with a Moscow building. In another exercise, Kuleshov combined closeups of separate parts of different women's bodies to create a composite person who existed only in the film. The most quoted Kuleshov encounter with film space and time (perhaps it never occurred at all) was said to involve the famous actor Mozhukhin, who left Russia and later surfaced in Europe. Kuleshov, it is proposed, intercut a closeup of Mozhukhin's expressionless face with such other subjects as food, a coffin and a child. In combination, the effect led audiences to remark on Mozhukhin's subtlety of response, implying the different emotions suggested in fact by the objects of his apparent gaze when, in fact, his face remained expressionless.

With his workshop, Kuleshov undertook a comedy modeled after Mack Sennett and the serials, titled *The Extraordinary Adventures of Mr. West in the Land of the Bolsheviks* (1924). It capitalized on the need for humor in a somber time, poking fun at American attitudes toward the USSR, parading workshop skills, and seeking to compete on their own terms with the output of foreign producers. Mr. West, president of the YMCA, is duped by the Muskovites into believing his own xenophobic fantasies. He falls into acrobatic

The Extraordinary Adventures of Mr. West in the Land of the Bolsheviks. Captured by Moscow criminals, Mr. West (in the glasses) is here rescued by government agents. Pudovkin assistant directed, designed sets, and cowrote the scenario. He's in the black suit behind West. (British National Film Archive/Stills Library)

pitfalls, like Harold Lloyd in *Safety Last,* until the hosts finally relent and show him their real city. The film proved immensely successful in Russia, although it was not distributed elsewhere for many years.

A science fiction thriller, *The Death Ray* (1925), was unsuccessful, and Kuleshov turned to an adaptation of Jack London's "The Unexpected." *By the Law* (1926) was written by Victor Shkolvsky, a formalist critic whose linguistic studies helped to shape Kuleshov's approach to film structure. It begins with an Alaskan mining expedition in which one man shoots two companions because he thinks they intend to steal his share of gold. The rest of the action is confined to a one-room cabin. The survivors, a married couple, subdue the murderer and feed and tend to his needs during the winter months. In spring, they hang him after a grim trial. The rope breaks; the hanged man staggers away into the rain.

Kuleshov employs his editing skills in *By the Law* not to artificialize setting, but to provide intensity. The acting is realistic, emotional, and sustained, and Kuleshov's staging, particularly in the murder and hanging sequences, singles out details (an overturned, dripping soup bowl; the woman's feet sliding in the mud as she tries to carry out the execution). In their isolation, these moments reinforce meaning like metonymies in rhetoric. Despite its quality, *By the Law* was ill-received by the Soviet press. But for *The Great Consoler* (1933), the remainder of Kuleshov's work was undistinguished. He spent much of his time teaching and writing about film, and suffered during the thirties for his interest in ideas of the Formalists. When the Congress of Soviet Writers adopted socialist realism as a national esthetic in 1934, a final damper was put on the verve and experimental enthusiasms of the early revolutionary filmmakers. Kuleshov felt the effects of the Congress for the rest of his life.

DZIGA VERTOV

Vertov occupies an extreme position relative to film's commitment toward narrative continuity and to fiction. As a twenty-year-old experimental poet, he supported the Revolution by editing film on the first agit-train in 1918. The agit-train included a theater troupe, journalists, a printing press, and a film unit. It journeyed to the Eastern front to inform and entertain troops.

In 1918, Vertov assumed supervision of Kinonedelia, the official Soviet newsreel, producing more than thirty issues. In 1919, he initiated a series of feature-length productions: *Anniversary of the Revolution* (1920), *Instructional Steamer 'Red Star'* (1920), *Agit-Train of the Central Committee* (1921), *Trial of the Revolutionaries* (1921), and *Department Store* (1921). From the experience, Vertov evolved notions he termed "Kino-Pravda"—a term equivalent to cinéma-vérité. Kino-Pravda began in 1922 as a motion picture series, modeled like a journal and construed to advise citizens of national problems, needs, failings, and accomplishments. Twenty-three installments appeared.

Vertov saw himself not as field director, but a kind of newspaper editor. He organized and commissioned cameraman-correspondents to cover the country with portable film equipment, feeding reports to a dingy basement office where, theoretically, he would assemble publication in final form. The series seems to have been visualized along organizational lines like network television news. In fact, most of Vertov's films derived from the photography of his own film unit.

His dedication was immense, his editing dazzling, and Vertov's absolute commitment to unstaged reality aroused impassioned controversy and dissension in radical artistic circles. Whatever their allegiance to fragmentizing innovation, the theater-derived personalities, Mayakovsky, Kuleshov, and Eisenstein included, believed in invented narrative. The polemics focused film's attention on ideas that had been fomenting elsewhere for years. In different ways, the creation of new concepts through an imaginative regrouping of fragmented materials figures in cubism, in formalist prose such as Shklovsky's in avant-garde poems, in futurist sculpture, collage, and surrealist games. Vertov himself had investigated the mixing and blending of dissimilar sounds through phonograph recordings in a "Laboratory of hearing" as early as 1916 in Saint Petersburg.

Among the radical left branch of Soviet filmmakers, futurism exerted substantial influence. The futurists proposed abandonment of words' meanings in poetry, arguing that the texture of sounds, the melody of intonation provided the essential communicated messages in song and poetry. Futurism's fascination with machinery, echoed in European avant-garde artistic circles (see Chapter 18), meshed with the impulses of constructivism in the USSR. The constructivists allied the artist-worker to machinery and to modern architectural forms. In part, film's rejection of theater was a rejection of traditions contaminated by prerevolutionary influences.

Lenin's own esthetic figures paradoxically in the history of Soviet film, for he seems to have supported both "documentary" and "realist" impulses. He weighted Vertov's case in early 1922 by issuing an edict that set a ratio of entertainment to factual film in Soviet theaters. Kino-Pravda controversies were intensified by Vertov's disposition toward manifestoes. His attack on literary films was signed by the "Council of Three." That group renamed itself Kino-Eyes in 1922, further pressing for a national film movement that would celebrate work, technology, and the poetry of machines. Vertov came to call his esthetic the Kino-Eye.

With an accumulating backlog of reference materials, Vertov's Kino-Pravda experiments juxtaposed past and current footage executed all around the country. If Kuleshov manipulated time and geography for story purpose, Vertov used editing to explicate theses and motifs independent of fiction. *Kino Eye* (1924), for example, his first feature length production, contrasted the new and the old, the country and the city, health and disease, sloth and bravery. Vertov used intertitles to emphasize his points, employing cadence, typography, and duration to build on rhythms and audience interest. *Stride, Soviet!* (1926) further contrasts Soviet life with society else-

Dziga Vertov (1896–1954)

Cinema Weekly	1918-1919
Anniversary of the Revolution	1919
Agit-Train	1921
History of the Civil War	1922
Goskinocalendar (55 issues)	1923-1925
Kino Pravda (23 issues)	1923-1925
Kino-Eye	1924
Stride, Soviet!	1926
The Man with a Movie Camera	1928
Symphony of the Don Basin/ Enthusiasm	1929
Three Songs About Lenin	1930
Lullaby	1934
Sergo Ordhonikdze	1937
Glory to Soviet Heroines	1937
Three Heroes	1938
In the Region of Hill A	1938
Newsreel Cameraman Under Fire	1941
For You, The Front!	1942
In the Ala-Tau Mountains	1944
Young People Vow	1944
News of the Day (55 issues)	1944-1945

Partial listing

where, war's devastation with accomplishment and reconstruction.

A Vertov film is challenging to describe. Editing pace is often furious. Camera trickery abounds, for Vertov believed that the mechanical eye could see much that was inaccessible to normal vision. *The Man With a Movie Camera* (1928) is his silent tour-de-force. Like other Vertov work, parts are photographed by brother Michael Kaufman. (Vertov changed his name from Denis Kaufman to a slang expression meaning "spinning top," some say in acknowledgment of the sound of a camera hand crank.)

The film's introduction shows a screening in preparation at a village meeting hall. The audience arrives, and with them we begin the show, which becomes our own movie. The subject of the film is the production process of Vertov's films. A cameraman explores his city and responds to its activities and alarms, recording what occurs. This material is presented in bursts of images; one realizes why Vertov was likened to the staccato outcries of Mayakovsky's poems. At one point a multi-image effect pictures the cameraman towering over a metropolitan crowd; in conclusion, the camera on its tripod is pixilated, dancing before the audience and finally bowing farewell. The film concludes. The audience leaves and we reenact their departure.

Man With a Movie Camera exalts the energy and multiplicity of city life, especially its varieties of work. The production of a film is

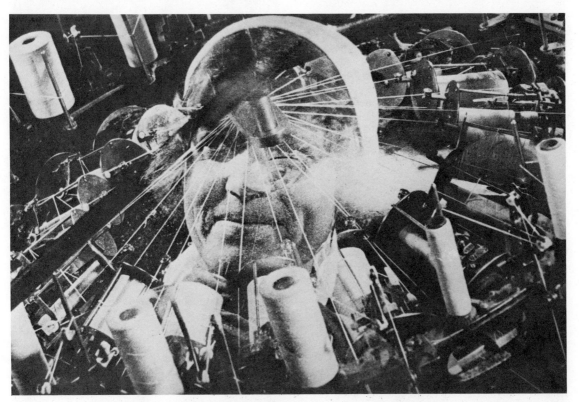

The Man With a Movie Camera. "WE discover the soul of the machine, we are in love with the worker at his bench, we are in love with the farmer on his tractor, the engineer on his locomotive. WE bring creative joy into every mechanical activity. WE make peace between man and machine." Dziga Vertov (Museum of Modern Art/Film Stills Archive)

fitted into the dynamics of other labor processes, examined with equal verve but no greater adulation. A barber's skills are likened to the film editor. Typewriters and sewing machines are compared to the editor's equipment. A woman throwing a slip over her head is cut against a camera gaining a lens.

As Vertov moves from the photographic stage into editing, he creates a self-reflective design that provides a contemporary aura to *The Man With a Movie Camera* and helps to explain why Dziga Vertov has evoked special interest during the past several years. Vertov likens his camera eye to the projector eye and to the eye of the spectator. We are the cameraman, and in this equation customary distinctions between observation and event become blurred. We see figures in a carriage photographed by the cameraman. We see the event as photographed. Then the movement itself stops, freezes, and withdraws to disclose its own celluloid mode, the footage we had seen earlier now examined and catalogued by a film editor, who studies, as well, footage that is yet to "appear" in the movie.

We cannot, however, consider the Vertov esthetic as "democratic" even though it encourages audience "participation" and demystifies film's production process. Vertov viewed the camera eye as different from human perception; its mechanical vision surpasses and need not emulate human perception. The film camera "draws the eyes of the audience." In what he termed the "System of

The Man With a Movie Camera, Vertov was attracted to hidden cameras—life caught unawares—especially after brother Mikhail Kaufman joined his work in 1922. In the presence of an unconcealed photographer, behavior sometimes measured the commitment of Kino Eye subjects: outcasts, reactionaries, and bureaucrats might mug; good workers went about their business. While serving on the agit-train *Lenin* in 1920, Vertov commenced a strategy of filming audience responses to his work, then cutting this footage into the movie itself. (Museum of Modern Art/Film Stills Archive)

Consecutive Movements," Vertov asked film not to recapitulate random, incoherent visual impressions, but rather to force the spectator's eyes onto those successive details that "must" be seen.

The Man With a Movie Camera audience, the group that gives a framing narrative to the film, is not cosmopolitan but rural, thus audience and subject (city life) merge different parts of the Soviet Union into a cohesive portrait. Vertov anticipated the coming of film sound without the foreboding of other, story-telling filmmakers, for he foresaw a new medium that could only extend Kino-Eye's possibilities.

SERGEI MIKHAILOVICH EISENSTEIN

The son of a bourgeois shipbuilder, Eisenstein studied architecture and engineering. He worked as an engineer during the civil war and then became a designer for the experimental theater developing during the twenties, an ardent pupil of Mayakovsky. Of all silent film-makers, Eisenstein was most committed to establishing his practicing methods on a theoretical basis. His multilingual skills — French, German, and English — supported myriad enthusiasms, and his research provides a scholarly intonation to Eisenstein's writing and teaching that is not apparent in the work of other early film essayists.

After designing sets and costumes for the Proletkult Theater, Eisenstein undertook to direct a free adaptation of a nineteenth-century play by Alexander Ostrovsky, *Enough Simplicity in Every Wise Man,* during 1923. In the performance he intermixed film with action and used it as an epilogue. Eisenstein termed his own concepts of organizing fragmentized material *Montage of Attraction* and published his conclusions in *Lef,* a radical journal (in the same issue with one of Vertov's

manifestoes). The Ostrovsky production displayed current experimental interest in such popular entertainments as the music hall and circus, besides employing techniques of the eccentric actor. Eccentricism, which was a circus term for novelty acts that indulged the illogical, the unanticipated, and the ludicrous, had, in fact, helped to shape an entire new approach to performance, one that rejected

Sergei Eisenstein (1898–1948)

Enough Simplicity in Every Wise Man (footage)	1923
Strike	1924
The Battleship Potemkin	1925
October/Ten Days that Shook the World	1927
The General Line/Old and New/The Old and the New	1929
Que Viva Mexico! unfinished footage released as:	1931
Thunder Over Mexico (Don Hayes, editor)	1933
Death Day (Sol Lesser, producer)	1934
Eisenstein in Mexico (Sol Lesser, producer)	1934
Time in the Sun (Marie Seton)	1939
Mexican Symphony (five educational documentaries by W. Kruse)	1941
Provisional Rough Editing (Jay Leyda, editor)	1954
Eisenstein's Mexican Project (three-hour uncut assemblage of all available material Jay Leyda)	1958
Bezhin Meadow (unfinished)	1935-1937
Alexander Nevsky	1938
Ivan the Terrible, Part I	1944
Ivan the Terrible, Part II	1946 released 1958

Stanislavskian naturalism and used devices like American slapstick to evoke meanings by oblique appeals to audience receptivity.[3]

With these techniques, which implied breaking down the esthetic distance between audience and performance, Eisenstein's montage of attractions argued that the spectator himself should be revolutionary theater's focus, that stylized, new skills well outside naturalist tradition could best serve a worker's theater devoted to making socialist principles understood. Ostrovsky was rewritten to include novelty acts, a tightrope, popular songs, and a mockery of original bourgeois values. Besides furnishing continuities to the play, the film material parodied Vertov's voguish newsreels.

Eisenstein's design for *The Mexican,* adapted from Jack London, included a prize-fight staged as an actual sports event in a ring before the audience. Then he situated a play, *Gas Masks,* in a real Moscow chemical factory. Thus, eccentric performance vied with "authentic" mise en scène, and Eisenstein was soon drawn into the film world. With the editor Ester Shub, he prepared a Russian version of Fritz Lang's *Doctor Mabuse the Gambler,* one in which the final battle between Mabuse and Wenk is converted, through editing and titles, into a street rebellion. Eisenstein's first film, *Strike* was completed in 1924. Drastically revised in process, *Strike* retained its original intention to depict revolutionary struggle before 1917. In developing a story that forsook individual characterization, with police, workers, and criminals represented stereotypically, Eisenstein broke with Lev Kuleshov, who required particularized, psychologically underlined performances, as in *By the Law.* Eisenstein separated himself, too, from Dziga Vertov, saying, "I don't produce films to please the eye but to make a point." *Strike* follows the history of a collective action

by workers that is defeated as a result of starvation and police brutality. It concludes with the authorities savagely attacking the workers' community, Eisenstein intercutting this material with the slaughter of animals.

Critical response to *Strike* was mixed, and Eisenstein met his first accusations of deviationism, but his film was exported and won a prize at a Paris Exposition. Eisenstein was next commissioned to prepare a study of Russia's earlier rebellion, to be titled *The Year 1905.* With scriptwriter Nina Agadzhanova, he journeyed to Odessa to reconstruct a sailor's mutiny on the Potemkin, one of eight episodes. Scenes on the Odessa steps did not figure in the original scenario, but Eisenstein's first view of them led to a drastic revision of *The Year 1905,* singling out the ship's mutiny for emphasis.

The Battleship Potemkin (1925) as the film came to be named, is structured by what Eisenstein terms five "acts." Sailors on the ship object to putrified meat, but a medical officer identifies the maggots as flies and the meat is prepared for soup. The sailors refuse the food. They are called to the upper deck. About twenty are chosen to be covered with a tarpaulin. Ordered to fire, the riflemen hesitate when the sailors cry "Brothers! Who are you going to shoot?" and rebellion is triggered. The leader of the mutiny, Vakoulintchouk, is killed, his body taken to shore where citizens of Odessa come to sympathize with the rebel cause. Townspeople send provisions to the battleship in a flotilla of little sailboats. Gathered on the steps of the czar's Winter Palace, the citizens are attacked by the czar's troops, who fire without warning and descend, shooting. Fleeing, the townspeople are cut off by Cossacks on horseback, slashed by sabres. The Potemkin's guns blow up the gate of the Odessa Theater, and shoot at the winter palace. The battleship then turns to confront admiralty ships that threaten. A battle is anticipated, but admiralty sailors refuse to fire on the Potemkin, and it sails past the squadron.

[3] *Daniel Gerould, "Eisenstein's* Wiseman," The Drama Review *T-61 (March, 1974).*

Sailors on the *Potemkin*. In historical truth, Odessa was in revolt when the mutinous battleship appeared offshore. Many deaths occurred on the steps, but quite unlike Eisenstein's vision. The director did not invent the tarpaulin episode as he claimed; it actually happened. After being shot at from shore, crewmen returned fire. Shells from the battleship missed their target, the theater where czarist authorities were in conference and damaged a nearby apartment. (Museum of Modern Art/Film Stills Archive)

The Battleship Potemkin proved an immense success in Russia and abroad. To his compositional sophistications, the director added a new skill in the use of faces; significance emerged not from individualized characterizations but because of conventional expectation. Each performer in *Potemkin* strikes us as a *kind of* person: courageous man, malicious priest, cruel captain, bewildered student, ineffective teacher.

Action was compounded from dramatically shot, minutely edited sequences, violence fragmented with extreme care. Some bits are as short as a single frame (less than a sixteenth of a second), and many run two, three and four frames. In the famous steps sequence, Eisenstein imposes a dramatic confrontation so effective that we unwittingly suspend judgment on what real experience would challenge. Eisenstein punctuated his violences with carefully paced interludes. The slaughter is preceded with calm, symmetric images, announced when the point of a parasol lunges toward the camera, our eye further attacked by plunging, dynamic, skewed diagonals of the scene that follows.

The director's next commission was the October Revolution. Eisenstein worked with

Gregory Alexandrov, an actor and his assistant dating from the time of Ostrovsky, to compound a scenario for *October* (1927) inspired by the American author John Reed's *Ten Days That Shook the World*. Again, a broad, episodic overview was condensed to one episode: Petrograd between February and October of 1917. The production was well supported. Some scenes employ literally thousands of extras, and city resources were placed at the filmmakers' disposal. Before the release of *October* the next year, Leon Trotsky's expulsion from the Party and his exile required drastic changes, expurgating him from most of the final version.

October begins on the uprising against Imperial forces. Workers overturn a statue of Alexander II. Russian and German soldiers depart trenches to fraternize. When the Kerensky government resumes hostilities, and

A still attributed to *October,* but unfamiliar to American prints. Since 1920, citizens of Leningrad annually reenacted the storming of the czar's winter palace, and Eisenstein seized advantage of the episode for his film, which was made to commemorate the revolution's tenth anniversary. *October's* applications of theory to practice were suspiciously received. They triggered early accusations of "empty formalism." (Museum of Modern Art/Film Stills Archive)

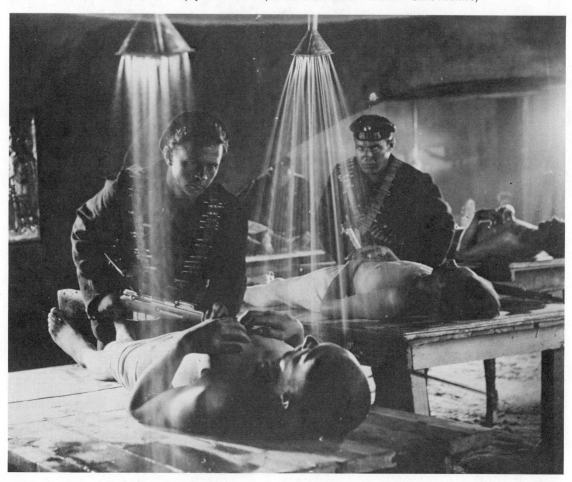

the civilians' situation is little changed, Lenin returns from exile, urging revolt. Government troops fire on a workers' peaceful march. Kerensky occupies the czar's palace and reestablishes the death penalty. The Bolsheviks organize, rebel an attack of White Russians leading Tartar troops, and befriend the Tartars. Kerensky flees, and the Congress of Soviets assumes control, ignoring soothing homilies of the Mensheviks. Bolsheviks storm the palace, arresting ministers of the provisional government. Lenin announces victory.

Eisenstein's film reconstructs events with such apparent fidelity that one recognizes actual excerpts taken from *October* in television documentaries that pretend to newsreel veracity. Again, the people are types, with the partial exception of Lenin (hero) and Kerensky (villain).

Beyond a dynamic representation of history, *October* interests the student of film for its efforts to apply theory in practice. Vertov had prefigured Eisenstein's intent when he proposed that, through editing, the expression of abstract ideas was possible in the film medium. Eisenstein adapted the premise to classical Marxism. As Kuleshov had argued that film might be construed like grammar, Eisenstein found in the shot a "nucleus" from which broader relationships emerged. Within shots, between shots, and between groups of shots, he argued, conflict (what Hegel and Marx described as the dialectic) could result in a synthesizing understanding on the spectator's part. The notion extended elements of Eisenstein's earlier montage of attractions into film's narrative pattern.

Ordering of the cellular shots follows definite design, Eisenstein said. It might be organized in terms of length (metric montage), interior rhythms (rhythmic montage, credited to Vertov), denotations of the image (tonal montage), broader connotations (overtonal montage), and even with shot-meanings pointed to direct thought processes (intellectual mon-

tage).[4] As an example of intellectual montage, Eisenstein cited a sequence from *October:*

Kornilov's march on Petrograd was under the banner of "In the name of God and Country." Here we attempted to reveal the religious significance of this episode in a rationalistic way. A number of religious images, from a magnificent Baroque Christ to an Eskimo idol, were cut together. The conflict in this case was between the concept and the symbolization of God. While ideas and image appear to accord completely in the first statue shown, the two elements move further from each other with each successive image. Maintaining the denotation of "God," inevitably leading to individual conclusions about the true nature of all deities. In this case, too, a chain of images attempted to achieve a purely intellectual resolution, resulting from a conflict between a preconception and a gradual discrediting of it in purposeful steps.[5]

October was conceived in two parts, but reedited into a single feature for public release. By 1927, and until after Stalin's death, John Reed's book was outlawed in the Soviet Union, although various foreign distributors assigned *Ten Days That Shook the World* as the film's title.

Begun in 1926 but interrupted by *October, The General Line* (also known as *The Old and the New*) (1929) repeated earlier Eisenstein patterns by drastically refocusing scope and intentions, in the process, narrowing from theoretical concepts down to a close study of rural life. (*October*'s intellectual montage had been received in many quarters, particularly

[4] *Sergei Eisenstein,* Film Form, *(New York, 1949), pp. 37-40, 45-58. 54-56, 66-67, 72-82.*
[5] Ibid, *p. 62.*

rural areas with puzzlement.) Marfa, a peasant woman cannily played by Marfa Lapkina, suffers under the poverty and superstition of a farm community. After government encouragement, she is the first to join a *kolkhoz;* when the new commune receives a butter separator, it wins more converts. Sale of butter results in the purchase of a bull and, through Marfa's urging, a tractor. Marfa and the trac-

tor mechanic convert holdouts to the new system by hooking all the village carts together and hauling them with the new machine.

Departing for the first time from revolutionary violence, Eisenstein paces his simple story with key sequences: the peasants parading and praying for rain, jubilation at the cream separator, and the bull. Working with Edouard Tisse, the exceptional photographer who collaborated on all his ventures, Eisenstein gives particular attention to picture tonalities. The cream separator sequence is notable, its machinery a glistening celebration of technology, overrun by the sensuous whiteness of milky product. In the character of Marfa, Eisenstein draws a fine line between the nonprofessional *types* cast in earlier films and individualized characterization. A simple peasant in fact as well as fiction, Marfa emerges as a popular, ingratiating personality, in striking contrast to the one-dimensional peasants (superstitious), kulaks (selfish), governmental organizer (noble), and tractor driver (ebullient).

With friends Alexandrov and Tisse, Eisenstein received permission to investigate filmmaking and sound technology abroad, each allotted thirty-five dollars in expense money! After Berlin, Paris, and London, the party came to Hollywood. MGM, United Artists and Universal considered engaging the Russian director, but Paramount finally settled on a six-month contract, an experience distinguished by lack of productivity. Paramount rejected every Eisenstein film proposal: for a psychological study to be called *Glass House;* for *Sutter's Gold,* a treatment of the California gold rush; and for Theodore Dreiser's *An American Tragedy,* later undertaken by Josef von Sternberg. Conservative factions in Los Angeles pressed to oust the Communists from southern California and expressed public outrage.

On Chaplin's suggestion, Eisenstein contacted Upton Sinclair. The novelist contracted

Eisenstein in New York (May 1930). At a Manhattan cocktail gathering, Eisenstein was asked, "Do Russians ever laugh?" "They will," Eisenstein replied, "when I tell them about this party." He soon formed a close friendship with Chaplin in Hollywood. (Museum of Modern Art/Film Stills Archive)

with Eisenstein to produce a film with Mexico as its subject, one which would be apolitical, rights reverting to the Sinclairs excepting those for Russian distribution. Eisenstein, Alexandrov, and Tisse journeyed from Mexico City to Yucatán. A script was approved and shooting undertaken. Production ran slowly; controversy developed. Finally, Sinclair withdrew support and retained the footage that had been shot.[6] Ill received by its administration, the Russians returned to their country. Eisenstein was not permitted another production until 1935, and never managed to resume work on the Mexican footage, although it exists in different versions completed by others.

Based on script plans and the footage produced, *Que Viva Mexico* consists of a prologue that introduces the people and rituals of the Yucatán. A Christian ceremony of the Passion is enacted, then a marriage. Next, during the days of the dictator Porifiro Diaz, a peon couple in Maguey goes to the master to ask permission to marry. At the hacienda, the boy is beaten, the girl raped. The boy returns with friends to free his fiancée, but they are captured, buried in sand and trampled to death by horsemen. Finally in an epilogue, a celebration of All Saint's Day expresses the life-affirming spirit of Mexican youth as they reveal smiling faces from behind skeleton masks. The footage is marked by highly dramatic, often symbolically patterned compositions, as when the execution of the peasant trio is equated with that of Jesus and the thieves. Assembled versions provide little indication of Eisenstein's characteristic editing designs, and his scenarios give no clear indication of how he himself intended specifically to assemble the material.

---

[6] *Contrary reports notwithstanding, Sinclair supported Eisenstein against Stalin's growing suspicions. See Ronald Gottesman, "Sergei Eisenstein and Upton Sinclair,"* Sight and Sound *(Summer, 1965).*

VSEVOLOD PUDOVKIN

Eisenstein's friendly, sometimes not-so-friendly, rival during the twenties was Pudovkin, who studied chemistry before enlisting in the artillery during World War I. He was captured, and then escaped from a German prison camp, completing his studies and entering the State Film School, inspired by *Intolerance*. Pudovkin acted in various film projects, and continued acting through his life, including an appearance in Eisenstein's *Ivan the Terrible, Part I* (1944). He joined Kuleshov's workshop and participated in *The Extraordinary Adventures of Mr. West* as actor, designer, writer, and editor. Pudovkin wrote the unsuccessful *The Death Ray* as well.

Because of his scientific background, Pudovkin was commissioned to make an educational film on the conditioned reflex experiments of Ivan Petrovich Pavlov. *The Mechanics of the Brain* (1926) is clear, careful, stolid exposition. While it was in process, Pudovkin made a 2-reel, Sennett-like comedy, *Chess Fever* (1925), satirizing Moscow's preoccupation with the game.

Mother (1926) derives from the novel by Maxim Gorky, although it freely reconstructed the story so that its central character, a woman who develops political consciousness, is more concisely defined and thrust into prominence. At the time of the 1905 revolution, the woman (Vera Baranovskaya) is married to a brutalized, drunken strike breaker who is killed in an encounter with workers. Pavel, the son (Nokolai Batalov), is apprehended by the police for participation in the strike. Because the police promise her son's freedom in exchange for a confession, his mother betrays Pavel and his fellows; instead, he is tried, found guilty, and imprisoned. She joins the workers and helps to organize Pavel's escape at the time of a May Day celebration. Firing on the parade, authorities kill

Mother. Pavel's hidden propaganda leaflets are disclosed to the authorities by his mother. According to the director, Vera Baranovskaya refused to act unless he stood beside the camera responding to her work. Since the spectacled police officer in this scene is Pudovkin himself, the actress's need poses a perplexing quandary. (Museum of Modern Art/Film Stills Archive)

Pavel. The mother seizes a banner and bravely faces a charge of mounted police.

In the production of *Mother*, Pudovkin was forced to abdicate some of the precepts of Kuleshov that had influenced him, for what Kuleshov espoused shifted control of an actor's intentions from performer to director-editor. Pudovkin began to view Kuleshov's direction of actors as "purely mechanical mimicry."[7] Baranovskaya and Batalov were members of the Moscow Art Theater, devoted to Stanislavskian naturalism. This approach was anathema to the radical left among socialist artists, and by his action, Pudovkin separated himself from controversial, experimental

esthetics. He studied Stanislavsky method, and Baranovskaya's performance testifies to the skill with which Pudovkin adapted theatrical techniques to the screen.

In many respects, *Mother* reminds one of a Griffith film (not *Intolerance*) in which socialist fervor has replaced genteel love, with violence retained. In two sequences, Pudovkin experiments in his own fashion with narrative exposition. One shows Pavel in prison, informed of the impending escape. The director constructs a joyful "vision" of water rippling and reflecting sunlight, Pavel's exultant eyes, and a laughing baby. The success of this scheme is arguable, for it unexpectedly throws an incongruent style into the material.

Later, at the time of the workers' assembly for May Day, the director reverts again to water images. Solitary protestors merge into

[7] *"Pudovkin on his Early Films,"* in Peter Dart, Pudovkin's Films and Film Theory *p. 60.*

little groups and these into larger units, finally a crowd, as the people determinedly approach a bridge. As background to these shots, Pudovkin uses water streams feeding a river at the time of the spring thaws. The stream's mounting rush underlines and supports a foregrounded human determination, and both energies merge at river's edge. Pavel escapes across the ice breaking on the river. His success confirms another bond between natural forces and a spirit of revolt. Following as it did on *Potemkin, Mother* consolidated the emerging status of Soviet film.

While Eisenstein attacked the czar's palace for *October*, Pudovkin bombarded its roof from another angle filming *The End of Saint Petersburg* (1927), both scheduled for the Revolution's tenth aniversary. Where Eisenstein concentrated on the ideological implications of historical events, Pudovkin's film personalized a story that again carries a naïve rural consciousness into political awareness. A peasant youth leaves his farm, forced by poverty and the death of his wife to appeal for help from a cousin in St. Petersburg. The cousin is planning a strike, and the peasant ignorantly joins strike breakers and betrays the workers. Faced with the indignation of his cousin's wife, the peasant realizes in limited fashion what he has done. He attacks the factory boss, is jailed, and then conscripted to the Western front. Now fully understanding the human consequences of war and of capitalism, the peasant persuades his battalion to desert. They join the Bolsheviks, storm the palace, and overthrow Kerensky's government. The worker's wife forgives and commends her cousin, now brother.

Even more effectively than *Mother, The End of St. Peterburg* projects its protagonist's developing awareness in images. This heightened consciousness progresses from his entrance to the city, where buildings, monuments, people, and industry overcome and awe, to the strike and his angry rebellion in the factory; he is attacking the accoutrements of capitalist industry. Pudovkin invokes the Griffith of *A Corner in Wheat* when contrasting the horrors of the Russian-German warfare with figures at the stock exchange who rejoice at war's profits.

Storm over Asia (1928) began inauspiciously, a vacation project. It developed, largely, out of the performance of Valeri Inkizhinov, a Mongolian who plays the central character.

In 1920, Bair, a simple fur trapper, brings his catch to market and is cheated by the English trader, who ignores the value of a silver fox skin. Bair attacks the trader and escapes. The time is the civil war and the English occupation army, unsuccessfully disguised as "White Russians" in English intertitles, captures Bair. He is shot by a young soldier and left to die in the snow. Bair's possessions include an amulet, left at his home by a lama. Its inscription discloses the bearer to be a direct descendent of Genghis Kahn. Learning

Vsevolod Pudovkin (1893–1953)

Hunger Hunger Hunger	1925
Chess Fever	1925
The Mechanics of the Brain	1926
Mother	1926
The End of St. Petersburg	1927
Storm over Asia	1928
A Simple Case	1932
Deserter	1933
Victory	1938
Minin and Pozharsky	1939
Twenty Years of Cinema (co-director Ester Shub)	1940
Suvorov	1941
In the Name of the Fatherland (co-director Dmitri Vasiliev)	1943
Admiral Nakhimov	1946
The Return of Vassili/The Harvest	1953

Vsevolod Pudovkin **195**

this, the English find and revive Bair, establishing him as a puppet leader of the Mongols. As he regains strength, Bair realizes the use to which he is being put, his awareness crystallized when he sees his silver fox worn by the English colonel's daughter. Bair escapes, gathers the Mongols and drives the invaders from Mongolia, the rout accompanied by a giant wind storm which blows all before it.

With different setting and performers, *Storm over Asia* recapitulates the successful formula of its predecessors. The naïf learns how capitalist exploitation grinds his people. He joins and leads the mass, which triumphs in a resolution of apocalyptic violence. The film uses its windstorm with something of the intentions of the water in *Mother,* but *Storm over Asia* lacks the earlier film's verisimilitude; one wonders where the storm emerged from so suddenly and withdraws from the huffing symbol while yet marveling at its effects.

A Simple Case (1932) was conceived as a sound film but produced silent. An early figure to commit his theory and technique to publication, Pudovkin's two books, *Film Technique* and *Film Acting* were published in English in 1929 and 1931.

ALEXANDER DOVZHENKO

Older than Eisenstein, Dovzhenko started his film career late in life. After a childhood and youth in the Ukraine, he threw his energies toward that area's liberation at the time of revolution. Like other patriots, Dovzhenko pressed for Ukrainian cultural autonomy in the early years of the Soviet; all suffered when Stalin's collectivization policies formented peasant resistance in the late twenties.

First a diplomat, art student, and writer, Dovzhenko made a dramatic, unexplained change in June, 1926:

I sat up all night at my studio, assessed my thirty-two unsuccessful years of life, and in the morning picked up cane and suitcase, leaving behind my canvasses and painting supplies, and departed from the house, never to return. I went to Odessa and got a job at the film studio as a director. You could say that I stood a naked man on the Black Sea Coast.[8]

Two comedies and a spy thriller proved to be unimpressive, but Pudovkin and Eisenstein immediately recognized *Zvenigora* (1928) as an exceptional work. The two established directors were invited by the Ukrainian Film Studio to explain a new film that no one could make head or tail of. In Dovzhenko, Eisenstein and Pudovkin found an ally who did not "beg for alms from West-minded filmmakers."

Approbations notwithstanding, audiences found *Zvenigora* perplexing, especially in foreign distribution prints that cut out explanatory flashback sequences. The film blends myth, history, and comedy in a tale about two brothers who are entranced by their grandfather's stories of a treasure that legend says lies buried in the mountain Zvenigora. Timosh understands the treasure to be the heritage of the Ukraine, and when revolution commences, he defends his homeland. Pavlo succumbs to love of wealth and flees to Paris. Adopting capitalistic schemes, he sells tickets to a theatrical event that will be climaxed by Pavlo's onstage suicide; instead he runs off with the box office take and returns to the Ukraine to fight against the revolution. In Pavlo's mind, the grandfather stands for a conservative past. When the old man fails to sabotage a revolutionary train, Pavlo finally does shoot himself. Grandfather joins Timosh to fight for the new society.

[8] *Quoted in Marco Carynnck's introduction to Alexander Dovzhenko,* The Poet as Filmmaker *(Cambridge, 1973), p. xiii.*

If Dovzhenko's story was reasonably cogent, its exposition proved to be unique. The grandfather's tales of Viking gold are clouded in slow motion and soft focus, fantasy imbued with self-serving humor as the old man, still ancient in his own recollections, imagines himself a superhero. In Paris, the suspense of Pavlo's advertised suicide resolves in Chaplinesque anticlimax.

Dovzhenko's next film centered on revolution in the Ukraine and continued to trace exploits of Timosh. While this supplies a certain continuity, *Arsenal* (1929) departs story orthodoxy even further, in expanses of poetic exposition. Sometimes, relationships between images are in high contrast, as when an aging woman working in the fields falls exhausted, while elsewhere Czar Nicholas writes in his diary, "I shot a crow. The weather is fine." At other times, the connections are associational. Enraged by the poor harvest, a man beats his horse; the exhausted woman beats her children. Other images draw on local history. Counterrevolutionaries resurrect the memory of a deceased Ukrainian poet as their inspirational hero. Contemptuous, the nineteenth-century patriot leans from his portrait and spits out an icon lamp lit in his honor. One sequence is built on the rush to bring a dead comrade's body to his mother for burial. Horses sing patriotic songs as they race across the snow and admonish the driver for pressing them beyond endurance. Land, horses, and people signify as one in the Ukraine.

Arsenal is filled, too, with brutal war images. Death constantly figures in all Dovzhenko's films, a moment in life's cycle, but here it is compounded with violent horrors. Timosh, played by the same actor as in *Zvenigora,* emerges finally as invincible, a kind of folk hero, not because he is personally immortal, but because he is a Ukrainian worker, whose defiance transcends individualism.

Dovzhenko's last silent film is his finest. He foresook mythology in favor of a paean to the Ukraine that succeeds with a photography absent of special effects. Images are brilliantly realized by the cameraman, Danylo Demutsky, who worked on the director's earliest two films as well as in *Arsenal*. No film captures natures fecundity to greater effect than *Earth* (1930).

An old man dies in his apple orchard, calm, chewing a fruit, surrounded by grandchildren. With this prelude of past yielding to present, a generational dispute ensues. Vassily, the old man's grandson, presses for a tractor and the agricultural reform that mechanism implies. His father cannot agree to such innovation. Nevertheless, Vassily becomes chair of the collective. A tractor is purchased, and the local kulak's (landowner's) security threatened. The kulak's son murders Vassily. Vassily's father rejects a religious funeral and calls for burial by the people. The body is carried through the fields, under the apple trees. A

Alexander Dovzhenko (1894–1956)

priest curses the procession, and the murderer, tormented, tries to confess, but both men are ignored, for the young people are interested only in the future; this is the way Vassily's death will be given meaning.

On its first showing, *Earth* triggered the attack of a proletarian poet whose pen name was Demyan Byedny. Byedny's critical hatchet work, which termed *Earth* defeatist, led to cuts that significantly diminished Dovzhenko's triumph. In one sequence, the tractor had run out of water and stalled in the fields. The peasants all urinate into the radiator, restoring the machine to use; thus Dovzhenko intended to extend the community of the Ukraine quite literally into its technology. During Vassily's funeral, his fiancée, naked and despairing, moans in her room, and at the same moment a mother suffers the pains of childbirth. The director meant to match life's cycles, including the anguish which accompanies their passages.

Excisions aside, *Earth* carries great force, much of it developed from the central portion when harvesting is completed and couples make love in the light of harvest moon. Vassily leaves his girl and dances on the way home. As he leaps for joy, the murderer's bullet drops Vassily to the ground, and horses look up momentarily from their grazing.

THE OTHER RUSSIAN CINEMA

Mainstream narrative approaches continued throughout the first revolutionary decade, sometimes marked by their own efforts toward innovation. Yakov Protazanov, who had directed before the Revolution, returned from France (where many men of like experience had fled) to make *Aelita* in 1924, a science fiction piece that wed Marxism to a Mars of constructivist sets and costumes.

The first film by Sergei Yutkevich, *Lace* (1928) a story of factory workers, provided foreign audiences a view of ordinary life and dress in the postwar years. *Fragments of an Empire* (1929) by Friedrich Ermler had a man amnesic since wartime returning to St. Petersburg, now Leningrad. Images of past and present evidenced cosmopolitan change and gradually merged to restore the hero's memory in a film whose intentions were often comic.

Abram Room was responsible for two exemplary silent features. Equally satiric and psychologically shrewd, *Bed and Sofa* (1927) deals with ordinary life in Moscow in the postwar period when families were encouraged to accept lodgers because of the housing shortage. Room's *The Ghost That Never Returns* (1929) is a fantasy about a political prisoner in Latin America who is given one day's freedom, ignorant that authorities will shoot him when it is over. Instead of trying to flee, he leads a revolt against the country's dominant oil interests.

Close study of *The Ghost* will help to dissuade film students from any notion that Russia's silent epoch can easily be summarized by considerations of Eisenstein, Pudovkin, and Dovzhenko alone. Room's extremely sophisticated editing employments compare easily with the Pabst of *Jeanne Ney* and develop point-of-view subjectives that Eisenstein managed only to talk about in his Hollywood period.

The present generation best knows director Grigori Kozintsev for *Hamlet* (1964) and *King Lear* (1972). In a sense, his earlier career, shared in part with Leonid Trauberg, traces a shift from radical experimentation to psychologically sharpened naturalism, which encountered greater success, both esthetic and personal, than more famous peers. During the early twenties, Kozintsev and Trauberg founded the Factory of the Eccentric Actor (FEKS), whose futurist, circus excesses attracted Eisenstein and others. Tempered, too, by expressionism, the pair's exuberant early films included such adventures as a mass of

Fragment of an Empire. Fyodor Nikitin, a victim of the war, is haunted by vague and unresolvable memories of his wife, his employer, and his battle trauma. The new city, blending with the old, restores continuity to his consciousness. Director Friedrich Ermler continued to produce films until 1964. *Katka's Reinette Apples* (1926), featuring Nikitin again, made use of Kozintsev's FEKS troupe. (Museum of Modern Art/Film Stills Archive)

bicyclists scurrying across rooftops in *The Adventures of Oktyabrina* (1924).

The New Babylon (1928) marks a high point of Russian silent film as well as evidenc-ing an untypically effective merger between symbolic conception and dramatic execution, the latter depending on sharp-etched characterizations. The time is 1870, when Paris workers take up arms and form a commune, only to be betrayed by bourgeois shopkeepers. The New Babylon is a luxury department store. Louise, one of the salesgirls (Yelena Kuzmina) represents a link between the two classes, and her demise proves the social irreconcilabilities; Pudovkin effectively plays another clerk. The film's sets, particularly the department store are stunningly apt, and Kozintsev and Trauberg capture a sardonic edge whose wit escapes the heavyhandedness of most Marxist views toward capitalism. Dimitri Shostakovich wrote his first film score to accompany *Babylon* in theaters.

By the time of sound's appearance in 1930, Soviet film had shifted dramatically away from the experimental beginnings. Scheduled in coincidence with the first five-year plan, a Congress on Film Matters in 1928 betrayed deep suspicions about decadent influences on non-Party directors (neither Eisenstein, Alexandrov, nor Pudovkin, for example, were Party members). Formalism was also held in disdain: undue emphasis on technique and narrative innovation at the expense of subject. A stage was being set for socialist realism, and films from this point on show an increasing inclination toward "beautiful" salon photography, as if to armor themselves against any suspicion of self-indulgence or ideological deviation.

Summary

If finally subdued by party-line socialist realism, the experiments of Kuleshov, Vertov, Eisenstein, and Dovzhenko mark high achievements in motion picture history. Unlike one another, sometimes at stylistic and theoretical odds, these directors commonly sought to introduce expository designs, often based on linguistic models, which might inspire a new society with a new esthetic. At the same time, succinct, sophisticated naturalism found expression in other productions by Yutkevich, Room, Kozintsev, and — on occasion — Pudovkin and Kuleshov.

Here our consideration of silent film concludes. In time, it has occupied about one third of all motion picture history. In terms of narrative design, the conventions of silent film continue to dominate movie entertainment today. And much of the experimentation done in the silents, Vertov, for example, has seen little to supersede it. Our attention returns to the United States, and to the events that gave film a voice, whether Hollywood wanted it or not.

Bibliography

Abbott, Jere. "Eisenstein's New York." *Hound and Horn,* 1972.

Barna, Jon. *Eisenstein.* Bloomington, 1973.

Bashky, Alexander. *The Path of the Modern Russian Stage.* London, 1916.

Baskalov, Vladimir. *Soviet Cinema.* Moscow, n.d.

Bond, Kirk. "Spoilation of *Que Viva Mexico.*" *Hound and Horn,* 1972.

Bordwell, David. "Dziga Vertov." *Film Comment,* Spring 1972.

Byrrher, Winifred (Annie Winifred Ellerman). *Film Problems of Soviet Russia.* London, 1929.

Carter, Huntly. *The New Theater and Cinema of Soviet Russia.* New York, 1925.

Cohen, Louis. *The Cultural-political Traditions and Developments of the Soviet Cinema 1917-1972.* New York, 1974.

Dart, Peter. *Pudovkin's Films and Film Theory.* New York, 1974.

Dickinson, Thorold and Catherine de la Roche. *Soviet Cinema.* London, 1948.

Dovzhenko, Alexander. *The Poet as Filmmaker.* Cambridge, 1973.

———. *Earth.* London, 1973.

Eisenstein, Sergei. *The Battleship Potemkin.* London, 1968.

———. "The Birth of a Film." *The Hudson Review,* Summer 1951.

———. *The Complete Films of Eisenstein.* New York, 1974.

———. "Eisenstein on Mayakovsky." *Artforum,* January 1973.

———. *Film Form.* New York, 1949.

———. *Film Essays and a Lecture.* New York, 1970.

———. *The Film Sense.* New York, 1947.

———. *Notes of a Film Director.* London, 1959.

———. *Three Films.* New York, 1974.

Feldman, Seth R. *Evolution of Style in the Early Work of Dziga Vertov.* New York, 1977.

Gerould, Daniel. "Eisenstein's Wiseman." *The Drama Review* T64 (March 1974).

Gottesman, Ronald. "Sergei Eisenstein and Upton Sinclair." *Sight and Sound,* Summer 1965.

Hill, Stephen P. "Kuleshov: Prophet Without Honor?." *Film Culture 44* (Spring 1967).

Kovacs, Stephen. "Kuleshov's Film Aesthetics." *Film Quarterly,* Spring 1976.

Kepley, Vance. "The Evolution of Eisenstein's *Old and New.*" *Cinema Journal,* Fall 1974.

Kuiper, John. "An Analysis of the Four Silent Films of Sergei Mikhailovich Eisenstein." Ph.D. dissertation, State University of Iowa, 1960.

Kuleshov, Lev. *Kuleshov on Film.* Translated by Ronald Levaco. Berkeley, 1974.

Lennig, Arthur. *The Silent Voice*. Albany, 1966.

Levaco, Ronald. "The Eisenstein-Prokofiev Correspondence." *Cinema Journal,* Fall 1973.

Leyda, Jay. *Films Beget Films*. New York, 1964.

———. *Kino*. London, 1960.

Michelson, Annette. "Camera Lucida/Camera Obscura." *Artforum,* January 1973.

———. *"The Man with the Movie Camera." Artforum,* March 1972.

Montagu, Ivor. *With Eisenstein in Hollywood*. New York, 1967.

Moussinac, Leon. *Sergei Eisenstein*. New York, 1970.

———. "Sergei Mikhailovich Eisenstein." *Penguin Film Review* 7 (1948).

Nizhny, Vladimir. *Lessons with Eisenstein*. New York, 1962.

Oms, Mardel. *Alexandre Dovjenko*. Lyon, 1968.

Potamkin, Harry. "Eisenstein and the Theory of Cinema." *Hound and Horn,* 1972.

Pudovkin, Vsevolod. *Film Technique and Film Acting*. London, 1954.

———. *Mother*. London, 1973.

Rimberg, John. *The Motion Picture in the Soviet Union*. London, 1959.

Schnitzer, Luda and Jean Schnitzer and Marcel Martin, eds. *Cinema in Revolution*. New York, 1973.

Seton, Marie. *Eisenstein*. London, 1952.

Vertov, Dziga. "From the Notebooks of Dziga Vertov." *Artforum,* March 1972.

———. "The Notebooks of Dziga Vertov." In *Film Makers on Film Making,* by Harry Geduld. Bloomington, 1967.

———. "The Vertov Papers," *Film Comment,* Spring 1972.

Wollen, Peter. *Signs and Meaning in the Cinema*. Bloomington, 1969.

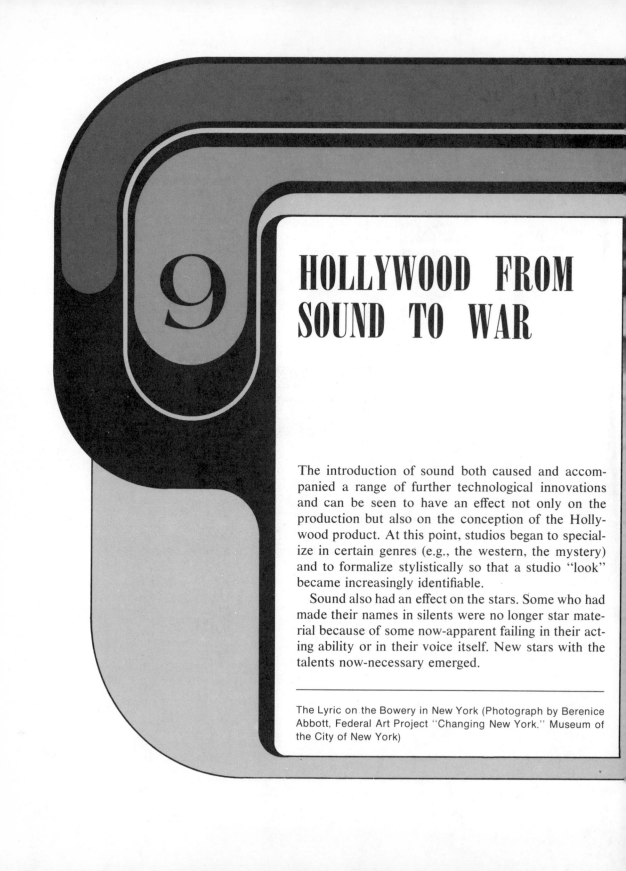

9 HOLLYWOOD FROM SOUND TO WAR

The introduction of sound both caused and accompanied a range of further technological innovations and can be seen to have an effect not only on the production but also on the conception of the Hollywood product. At this point, studios began to specialize in certain genres (e.g., the western, the mystery) and to formalize stylistically so that a studio "look" became increasingly identifiable.

Sound also had an effect on the stars. Some who had made their names in silents were no longer star material because of some now-apparent failing in their acting ability or in their voice itself. New stars with the talents now-necessary emerged.

The Lyric on the Bowery in New York (Photograph by Berenice Abbott, Federal Art Project "Changing New York." Museum of the City of New York)

It is during this period, coinciding with the introduction of sound, that the characteristics of the American feature become sharpened and increasingly visible.

Early film was usually accompanied by music and sometimes effects, so that what is meant by film sound really amounts to synchronous speech capacities, however the technology may be applied. Edison's efforts to wed the kinetoscope to his kinetophone are remembered from Chapter 1; the two machines were jointly available to peep show customers in 1893, wired by accoustic headsets to the individual spectator. Such technique had no need for amplification. In order to provide sound without the use of headsets, efforts to adapt phonograph discs in synchronization with picture were undertaken in Berlin in 1896 by Oscar Mester. These efforts failed, however, to produce adequate volume. Edison unsuccessfully sought amplification by using banks of phonographs in 1899. Another effort

by Pineaud in France tried to notch the film edge so that sound could be reproduced in the same way as a pianola roll.

SYNCHRONOUS SOUND

Synchronization between disc and film also posed problems of maintaining a successful speed relationship, and difficulties were compounded by the possibility of film breaking or a needle skipping grooves. Griffith's *Dream Street* premiered in 1921 with a phonograph accompaniment synchronized to the projector by a connecting device and included a prologue with the director discussing "The Evolution of the Motion Picture," but the effort was abandoned after the first run.

Eugene Lauste in England and Lee De Forest in the United States researched sound-on-film systems. De Forest's development of

The old Manhattan Opera House served as studio for Western Electric when accompanying music was recorded for *Don Juan*. Here singer Anna Case and the Casinos dancing team rest between takes of an operatic film short. (Courtesy of Western Electric)

the audion amplifier finally provided volume that might be achieved by electronic means; he sold his patents to American Telephone and Telegraph and turned his attention to ways to locate the sound recording on the picture film's edge. Independently, the Germans Günther Vogt, Ehrich Engl, and Josef Massolle evolved a sound-on-film technique in 1918–19. This was termed Tri-Ergon; it was controlled by Tobis-Klangfilm.

In 1924, the Western Electric Company, a subsidiary of American Telephone and Telegraph, made several efforts to promote its systems, which were sound-on disc, to the major Hollywood companies, but studio executives could visualize no more than the inconvenience of technical failure and theater-conversion cost when thinking in terms of sound as opposed to the continued profits of the silent feature.

San Francisco's Embassy played host to Vitaphone. Besides Barrymore in the feature, Giovanni Martinelli sang Pagliacci and the Vitaphone Symphony Orchestra, seventy-five strong, played the overture to the third act of *Lohengrin*.

One of the smaller production firms, Warner Brothers, suffered from the lack of a first-run theater chain. Warners reasoned that sound might provide a competitive edge if it were possible to outfit little independent neighborhood houses with reproduction equipment. In this way, Warner outlets could boast musical accompaniments to match the big orchestras of the picture palaces.

Warners publicized the innovation with a trio of features in 1926[1]: *Don Juan, The Better 'ole,* and *When a Man Loves.* These provided synchronous music support, and their success helped to develop an audience. In the same year, more than a hundred sound shorts, including voice-synchronized vocals by entertainers like George Jessel and Al Jolson, were

completed. They served as an experimental ground for technical training. When *The Jazz Singer,* a sentimental, turgid drama about a cantor who forsakes synagogue for stage, proved successful in 1927, other major Hollywood companies fell into line. Obviously sound had to be accommodated.[2]

Even before sound-on-disc had prospered,

[1] *Western Electric had made earlier shorts as demonstration pieces. A Eubie Blake-Noble Sissle performance dates from 1923.*

[2] *J. Douglas Gomery indicates that the majors played a careful, waiting game, taking full advantage of Warner's and Fox's gamble, and riding out an apparent dip in sound's popularity during 1928. The "Big Five" maneuvered RCA against Western Electric to secure the most favorable royalty terms. J. Douglas Gomery, "The Coming of Sound to the American Cinema: a History of the Transformation of an Industry," Ph.D dissertation (Madison: The University of Wisconsin, 1975). Summarized in J. Douglas Gomery,* "The Warner-Vitaphone Peril," Journal of the University Film Association *(Winter 1976).*

The Jazz Singer. Jolson is the son of a Jewish cantor played by Warner Oland, who later adapted himself to the role of an oriental detective, Charlie Chan. Jolson forsakes the stage for religion and his parents, but the film ends on another theatrical triumph. Warner's remake of the film in 1952 was even worse. (Movie Star News)

William Fox was pursuing a sound-on-film system, one developed by the Case Laboratory working with De Forest patents. When its capacity to operate out of doors was demonstrated, Fox committed sound-on-film to the newsreel as well as to musical and comic shorts. A Fox Movietone cameraman recorded Lindbergh's take-off from Roosevelt Field with shouts from the crowd, and the film was shown five days later as part of an all-Movietone program in New York City along with *Seventh Heaven* (1927), which had a sound-on-film music track.[3] The next several years witnessed open and behind-the-scenes fights over different systems, the wiring of theaters for sound, antitrust actions, international complications, production conversions, and royalty impositions.

The Electrical Research Products, Inc., ERPI, became Western Electric's motion-picture subsidiary. If Hollywood made money from the new system, so did Western Electric; they charged royalties on every sound negative produced, royalties on copyrighted music, royalties even on the distribution of pictures made with other sound systems. Soon ERPI was confronted by Radio Corporation of America. RCA devised the Photophone Sound System through Westinghouse and General Electric, and entered production, distribution, and exhibition by way of the new Radio-Keith-Orpheum Corporation. Then, RCA and ERPI combined to challenge Klang-film-Tobis-Tri-Ergon for the international market. William Fox sold his rights for $18,000,000, and the result was a cartel, not unlike the Trust but worldwide, with territories assigned or split for royalties. By late 1929, the last major American silent film had appeared: *The Kiss* with Greta Garbo. Sound-on-film won the day over the bulkier, less reliable sound-on-disc technique.

The Effects on Production

Nine thousand movie houses had converted to sound by 1929. Production corporations adjusted to a new medium that required far greater research and more advanced technology. Faster, fine-grained film stocks permitted superior in-focus depth in studio photography because smaller aperture lens settings could be used. A new camera, the Mitchell BNC, finally accommodated wide-angle lenses whose use had been restricted while photography was confined to sound-proofed boxes or sound-cushioned mobile cameras. Maneuverable camera dollies encouraged greater flexibility in shooting. Tungsten lighting gave softer effects; it focused less harshly on the subject matter. Techniques were devised to aid in sound editing, which was far more involved than silent. Because of editing complications, early sound was inclined to long camera takes.

Because primitive sound production was studio bound, new efforts were made to stimulate exteriors by way of background projecting, miniatures, and special effects accomplished in the laboratory. (This accounts in part for the number of disaster and spectacle films in the thirties.) New microphones maximized the speech qualities of performers and eventually could work from distances great enough to free an actor's movements relative to mike placement; greater skill in localizing the microphone pickup field and in amplifying sound signals helped to return film to location

[3] *More specific details of Fox's early screenings help to provide a setting for optical sound's appearance. The first Fox Movietone was shown at New York's Roxy Theater May 2, 1927 with the silent feature* Yankee Clipper. *The newsreel featured cadets marching at West Point. Lindbergh joined* Seventh Heaven *on May 25. June 14 saw Lindbergh's reception in Washington by Calvin Coolidge and the silent feature* Secret Service. *Lindbergh was reshown on September 23 at the Times Square Theater with Murnau's* Sunrise, *which had a music and effects track, plus shorts of the Italian Army on parade and of the Vatican Choir.*

shooting. Sound editors became more adept at cutting dialogue so that transitions were less noticeable: most often toward the end of a speech, not on the final syllable and not between lines. Techniques gradually permitted mixing several sound tracks at post-shooting stages so that some elements might be "added."

Such skills had affected film's narrativity. The possibility for speech to originate from a source beyond the image permitted subjectivized, interior monlogue and narration that might comment on the picture. Performers could, on the other hand, address the audience directly, thus stepping out of the story in which they were acting and disrupting the illusion being created in the film. These interruptions in the narrative can be seen as sound counterparts to Dziga Vertov's visual interruptions of screen illusion. Since sound possessed its own independent continuities, it might be used to develop an independent voice with no necessary relation to picture at all, although this was seldom undertaken. Sound could bridge narrative transitions by smoothing over connections with music or speech; it could motivate a forthcoming appearance, or mislead audiences into anticipating one event (a scream) while providing another (a telephone ring).

COLOR

In one sense, all film is committed to color, for every black and white emulsion reacts uniquely to a spectrum of light waves. The replication of hues other than black, white, and gray was first approximated by handpainting, frame by frame, as many as six colors on a black-and-white, silent projection print. This practice began before the twentieth century, on Méliès prints for example, and continued through the silent era. The flag raised by Po-temkin sailors to hail Odessa's citizens was sometimes red, and Eisenstein intercut red flashes into his bull mating sequence for *The General Line.*

Pathé applied its still photography color process, termed *Pathécolor,* in 1905, accomplished by separate stencils, cut out of each frame, then used to print dye on a black-and-white copy. Such techniques, while often striking, were expensive and confined to shorts or to excerpts from features. Tinting, toning, and combinations of the two (recall *Napoleon*) were less expensive and less selective. Color itself could be selectively photographed through filters, and this technique was demonstrated as early as the mid-nineteenth century. Dual projection systems, reproducing the same procedures for viewing purposes, were employed by the Englishman G. A. Smith in 1908 as *Kinemacolor.* Later systems expanded Smith's separate red/blue-green filtration to red/blue/green.

Projection problems entailed in such designs were overcome by Eastman Kodak as early as 1915. Eastman devised a front-and-back emulsioned film on which each side was separately processed for a combined image that had restricted color range. Led by Herbert Kalmus, the Technicolor Motion Picture Corporation learned to separate colors onto two different black-and-white films, and then to combine the images into a composite by dyeing each during processing and then literally fastening the two films together. This technique was used on Douglas Fairbanks' *The Black Pirate* in 1926, and later modified so that each color printed separately on one unlayered film base. Later, the Corporation devised a three-color printing method that first appeared in a Walt Disney "Silly Symphony" titled *Flowers and Trees* (1933), then most notably in *The Three Little Pigs* (1933). Animation easily conformed to the limitations of the Technicolor technique because each image could be prepared with separately colored cellulose overlays. Technicolor redesigned a camera capable of photographing live action on its three film reels and produced a short, *La Cucaracha,* and a feature, *Becky Sharp,* in 1935. Color use escalated in 1952 when Eastman introduced *Eastmancolor,* a technique that was easier to control, less expensive to print, and applicable to widescreen formats.

Seemingly affording the motion picture a closer alliance to the world it documented, the advent of color, like that of sound, had its own effects on lighting and camera mobility. In the measure that a screen image was open to stylization, color introduced further variables that might be applied to narrative purpose, but these were rarely exploited until more recent times.

THE STUDIOS

With corporate ties between production, distribution, and exhibition to guarantee outlets, American producers, from the thirties until after World War II, adopted a policy of maximized output. The fast turnover in theaters, often twice a week, compounded by the depression-inaugurated, two-feature programs, encouraged quantity production that was responsible, in part, for sustaining mediocre product.

Such mass production had its own effects on story substance. Dialogue ranked foremost in importance, and fully predesigned scripts, therefore, preceded each production. Their approval placed further controls in the hands of executives and producers, and writer-director functions became increasingly separated, like the other craft jobs of editing, cinematography, and sound. The thirties were a period of emerging guilds and unions. Returning to neighborhood theaters week after week, the public was thought to require repeated experiences: the same star, identical stories, fa-

miliar settings. As far as it existed at all, such conventionalized reactions to the same conventionalized entertainment were further shaped by the success of Hollywood fan magazines which fed at the trough of studio publicity handouts.

While these factors encouraged a standardization of product, Hollywood films were, at the same time, evolving and developing new characteristics. One was a stylistic specialization within each studio, the product of particular personalities and working methods: an intensification of twenties procedures. Another was the pronounced individual expression of contract directors working within the system and its requirements while yet having some personal way with their assigned productions. Twentieth Century Fox and RKO were less identifiable than most studios in terms of institutional or director styles except by way of stars (Shirley Temple) or set design (the Astaire-Rogers musicals). United Artists was a distribution agency rather than a studio, but other corporations assumed distinctive images.

Warner Brothers

Warner decided to gamble on the popularity of sound and followed *The Jazz Singer* with *The Lights of New York* (1928). It seems amazing that audiences continued their interest in sound film when one considers the abysmal dialogue and acting of this film. Soon talking was followed by talking and singing, and Rin-Tin-Tin, an old standby in the silents, now barked vigorously.

The Wonder Dog had been made successful by Darryl Zanuck, a young writer who moved into production responsibility and helped to formularize the Warner pattern. Pictures moved fast, beginning with an absorbing episode of action and sensation. Lines were spat out like old chewing gum, and stories often centered around exposé, prisoners, mystery, and social problems. Although the company finally produced its share of musicals, comedies, romances, and westerns, a depression era specialty of Warner was crime and gangster films.

The first notable success of this type was *Little Caesar* (1930), directed by Mervin Leroy. Its scenes now look stiff and staged. The genre has been so emulated that what was then original now seems most clichéd, but Edward G. Robinson's Rico was a deft variation on Al Capone at a time when the ganglord figured heavily in popular mythology and sometimes in American experience. *Caesar*'s success led to such films as *Public Enemy* (1931), *The Hatchet Man* (1932), and *Three on a Match* (1932).

Corrupt journalism was exposed in *Five Star Final* (1931), Georgia prisons in *I Am a Fugitive from a Chain Gang* (1932), and criminal lawyers in *The Mouthpiece* (1932). The Warner film gave birth to the Warner star. James Cagney, Pat O'Brien, Barbara Stanwyck, and Joan Blondell developed fast-talking, wisecracking images. Edward G. Robinson and Paul Muni were the "actors" of the studio, and their screen agonies were sometimes the product of down beat endings marked with somber despair.

The Warner audience was conceived as working class, like the Warner movie protagonist. Issues of real-life audience concern were alternately dramatized or avoided. The latter was achieved through romance and musicals, but even the pictures committed to making social comment had fuzzy solutions. Before moving on to Fox, Zanuck pressed for a sophisticated wave of musicals, which resulted in Busby Berkeley's *Gold Diggers of 1935* (1935), *I Live for Love* (1936), and *Hollywood Hotel* (1937). *Forty-Second Street* (1933) and *Dames* (1934)—Berkeley directed both of these musical extravaganzas—had established a style that combined backstage fantasy (the star breaks her leg, and a budding dancer is called out of the line to replace her) with sharp vignettes of hard-working chorus girls who face an unfeeling world with cynical good humor.

When portraits of gangsters fell into disfavor, the studio turned to law enforcers: *'G' Men* (1935), *Bullets or Ballots* (1936). A drift toward European adaptations or themes, like *A Midsummer Night's Dream* (1934) codirected by William Dieterle and his teacher Max Reinhardt, might be viewed as a momentary lapse on Warner's part, but actually reflected an effort to capitalize on what Warner's presumed to be their audience's climbing aspirations toward "high culture." The mode soon combined biography with social comment in such films as *The Story of Louis Pasteur* (1936), *Jaurez* (1939), and *Dr. Ehrlich's Magic Bullet* (1940). Errol Flynn's adventures were effective sound equivalents to the last decade's Fairbanks films: *The Charge of the Light Brigade* (1936), *The Adventures of Robin Hood* (1938). The Warners cast Olivia de Haviland against Flynn for romance. *Robin Hood* was distinguished by an ambitious musical score from Erich Wolfgang Korngold, who assigned leitmotifs to characters and events. The wartime Warners welded traditional plot formulae to patriotism. Criminals adopted Axis or Vichy accents in *Casablanca* (1942). The treatment of social problems became global in *Mission to Moscow* (1943). The musical evolved into *This is the Army* (1943).

In the mid-thirties, the Warner look shifts somewhat from high-key, studio tenements, apartments, and city streets (sometimes dark to disguise breakneck set construction) to softer lit, more lavish locations. Warner's attention to social detail was keener than other studios and its sexual candor sometimes bypassed the Hays Office without the latter realizing that anything was amiss. "Classy chassis," George Raft, a truck driver, murmurs to Ann Sheridan across a lunch counter in *They Drive By Night* (1940). "You couldn't," she replies, just a little sadly, "even pay for the headlights." Hot stuff.

For all its predictabilities and ruthless management, Warner Brothers was a base at one time or another for such able directors as William Wellman, Michael Curtiz, William Dieterle, Marvin LeRoy, and Raoul Walsh. Its cameramen (Hal Mohr, Barney McGill, Ted McCord) and writers (Albert Maltz, W. R. Burnett, John Bright, Sheridan Gibney) contributed unique character to studio product. Performers like James Cagney, Humphrey Bogart, and Bette Davis developed their screen selves on Warner stages; films like *The Maltese Falcon* (1941) and *White Heat* (1949) combined studio genre with more transcending aspirations.

Metro-Goldwyn-Mayer

If the Warner ethos was gritty, MGM veered between spic-and-span family pictures and the candelabra of wealthy drawing rooms. In investment and output (forty films a year), Louis B. Mayer's enterprise ranked first; he held power from 1924 to 1951, backed by the eastern financing of Chase National Bank. MGM set quality standards for its sound, lighting, and design and developed a stable of contract actors whose names sold films: Joan Crawford, Myrna Loy, Clark Gable, Jean Harlow, Spencer Tracy, William Powell, Norma Shearer. Some, like Greta Garbo, were carefully groomed into special commodities through a combination of talent, casting, and press release. Mickey Rooney and Judy Garland literally grew up at MGM. Mayer's special forte was the Andy Hardy series, which he watched closely, regulating Rooney's screen prayers, kisses, and heart-to-heart talks with his father, the judge.

Production during MGM's early period was channeled in large measure by Irving Thal-

berg, with Mayer seated above, regulating business interests. On the formation of MGM, Thalberg moved in as production director, working independently in his last years before death at age thirty-seven in 1936. Thalberg evidenced the qualities admired in the able supervisor. He mixed spectacle, *Ben Hur* (1926), with prestigious experiment (MGM released *The Crowd,* although Vidor paid for most of it). *Trader Horn* (1931) was filmed in Africa, the first sound feature to work effectively out-of-doors. *Anna Christie* successfully delivered Greta Garbo across the sound barrier by casting her in a role that accommodated her Swedish accent. Studio investment in stars was seriously threatened by the demands sound made on voices, and some figures such as John Gilbert, Garbo's silent costar, and Pola Negri were defeated either by vocal inadequacies or speech that was simply incongruent with the fantasized qualities audiences had invested in their wordless images. (Gilbert's daughter believes that Mayer sabotaged her father's sound tests out of personal enmity.)

MGM directors included Woodbridge S. Van Dyke II, Howard Hawks, Victor Fleming, Sidney Franklin, and Clarence Brown. Some of Ernst Lubitsch's best sound features, such as *The Merry Window* (1934) and *Ninotchka* (1939), were done for the company. In retrospect, nevertheless, much MGM product seems either to powder or to petrify under one's eyes. The Andy Hardy series becomes an embarrassing artifact, a testament to Hollywood's image of small-town, middle-class, white America, which was drawn by family magazines of the time, like *The Saturday Evening Post* and *Collier's.* Some extravaganzas—*The Wizard of Oz* (1939) and *Gone With the Wind* (1939)—have a larger-than-life inevitability now, like a Brahms symphony.

A curious byway in MGM's archive is the depression film that bears similarities to

Conquest. Charles Boyer was vaguely listless as Napoleon, despite Garbo's presence as a Polish countess. The lavish sets of MGM are evident. A moonlit exterior sequence in *Conquest* looks equally artificial. (Museum of Modern Art/Film Stills Archive)

Warner's, while retaining a studio identity. *Washington Masquerade* (1932) attacks a Congress corrupted by private interests. *Gabriel over the White House* (1932) shows a conservative president led to authoritarian actions in order to save the country. (The film was released but not produced by MGM.) Fritz Lang's *Fury* (1936) attacked lynchings, although its melodrama is inclined to approach social issues with something of Lang's old *Metropolis* resolution: simplistic solutions to complex problems.

Other major studio ventures, like *Conquest* (1937), a Napoleon-Marie Walewska romance, or *A Tale of Two Cities* (1935), lack either the integrity of history or the power of coherent fantasy. They occupy a strange nether world that can only be described as MGM. Sometimes the acting still holds, often in comedies such as *Too Hot to Handle* (1938), in which Clark Gable and Myrna Loy

as newsreel reporters fight and make up against backgrounds of China and the Amazon jungle. The MGM Marx Brothers, *A Night at the Opera* (1935) and *A Day at the Races* (1937), both directed by Sam Wood, fit the comedians' specialties more closely than usual into a story line, which may or may not be to the viewer's taste.

Female stars, Garbo and Norma Shearer especially, profit enormously from the high-key lighting which was a studio specialty, designed, too, to display the sumptuous sets, and expertly controlled by cameramen George Folsey, Harold Rosson, William Daniels, and Karl Freund from Ufa. Jean Harlow's brassiness seems half-acted, half-not in films like *Bombshell* (1933) and *Reckless* (1935). Thalberg sometimes kept his contract stars occupied with multitalent productions such as *Dinner at Eight* (1933) and *Grand Hotel* (1932) in which one may compare performances of Harlow, Garbo, Wallace Beery, John and Lionel Barrymore, and Joan Crawford. One of the most durable and entertaining MGM products is the series that grew from a W. S. Van Dyke version of Dashiell Hammett's novel and starred William Powell and Myrna Loy in *The Thin Man* (1934). As Nick and Nora Charles, Powell and Loy play so effectively against one another that their boozy affection and mugging still overcome the aging detective story plots in *After the Thin Man* (1936), *Another Thin Man* (1939), *Shadow of the Thin Man* (1941) and *Song of the Thin Man* (1947).

Paramount

In contrast to Warner and MGM, Paramount elected European themes and sophisticated mannerisms. Studio ties to Ufa account for the number of technicians and of directors who left their own countries for American work. Paramount's directing stable included Robert Florey, Cecil B. DeMille, Wesley Ruggles, and Michael Leisen, but its major talents were Josef von Sternberg, Rouben Mamoulian, and Ernst Lubitsch.

The Paramount look is attributable in great measure to its head designer, Hans Dreier, formerly of Ufa; his counterpart at MGM was Cedric Gibbons, Anton Grot at Warner.[4] Dreier excelled at European evocations and can be seen to good advantage in *Monte Carlo* (1930), *Dr. Jekyll and Mr. Hyde* (1932), and *The Devil is a Woman* (1935), all directed by Europeans. He worked, too, with DeMille on his spectaculars. Gloria Swanson's deteriorating mansion in *Sunset Boulevard* (1950)

[4] *At long last studio designers received their proper due in a sumptuously illustrated book. Leon Barsacq, Caligari's Cabinet and other Grand Illusions: A History of Film Design. revised and edited by Elliott Stein (New York: Graphic House, 1976).*

mixes German visual busyness with aging Hollywood decadence.

Paramount's stars were fewer than the major competition: Gary Cooper, Frederic March, Claudette Colbert, and Miriam Hopkins. Like stories and visual style, they were more varied as well. Cinematographers Victor Milner and Theodore Sparkuhl achieved a warm, diffused light that maximized the Dreier design and costumes.

Less financially stable than others, the company gambled its future on individual ventures at times, and comedy helped to insure Paramount's survival in the early sound years. The first Marx Brothers films were Paramounts, made between 1929 and 1933. *The Coconuts* (1929) and *Animal Crackers* (1930) derived from Broadway reviews. Like the voices of W. C. Fields and Mae West, the individualized patter of Groucho and Chico easily lent itself to sound. Harpo refined mime into sight gags and girl chasing. The brothers' first film drew almost $2 million and *Animal Crackers* was the studio's top attraction of 1930. *Monkey Business* (1931), *Horsefeathers* (1932), and *Duck Soup* (1933) followed.

While the Marxist response to society was anarchic zeal, Mae West satirized the country's values in exaggeration that veered from caricature to innuendo. She worked for Paramount through the thirties and her first films, *Night after Night* (1932) and *She Done Him Wrong* (1933), are said to have rescued the company again. *She Done Him Wrong* was based on West's self-authored Broadway success and introduced a young unknown she picked to play against her, Cary Grant.

W. C. Fields' *Million Dollar Legs* (1932) adopted something of the Marx Brothers formula, eccentric behavior, gags, and Sennet-like antics loosely glued to a skeletal farce. Klopstockia's king and champion weight lifter, Fields triumphed over the wiles of a shimmy dancer and the cross-eyed spying of Ben Turpin. As an unwitting testament to its times, *Million Dollar Legs* bears careful scrutiny.

Cecil B. DeMille's Paramount product shifted from history-*cum*-sin and religion in *The Sign of the Cross* (1932), *Cleopatra* (1934), and *The Crusades* (1935) to nineteenth-century American themes like *The Plainsman* (1937), *The Buccaneer* (1938) and *Union Pacific* (1939). All the DeMille product had assumed a stiffness of pageantry, and an unplanned humor sometimes attended his personalized history, but the impact of some of the visual effects cannot be denied, like Cleopatra's barge and her orchestrated seduction of Mark Antony. In Charles Laughton and Frederic March, DeMille accomplished interesting impersonations of Nero (*The Sign of the Cross*) and Jean Lafitte (*The Buccaneer*).

The World War II years saw Paramount's own version of low-key-lit urban melodrama in the films of Alan Ladd: *This Gun For Hire* (1942), *The Glass Key* (1942); Ladd went to war in *China* (1943), like other Hollywood heroes. Their return to civilian crimes brought home some of the screen violences that had been condoned in fighting the Nazis and Japanese.

The war also saw a series of comedies directed by Preston Sturges, a screenwriter who made exceptional features for the studio. Sturges was especially adept at pace and dialogue, reverting to slapstick when the occasion suggested. His conversations have a surreal quality of the slightly skewed, as when McGinty, an aspiring politician, talks with the city boss in *The Great McGinty* (1940):

The Boss: Where I come from is very poor, see.
McGinty: What makes this bus so quiet? You don't hear nothin' in here.
The Boss: It's armored. So everybody lives by. . .
McGinty: Armored for what?

In 1936, Frank Forest records a solo for *The Big Broadcast of 1937*, a Paramount release. Beside Forest is Borris Morros, then musical director of the studio. Later, Forest will mouth visuals to conform to his sound track. (Museum of Modern Art/Film Stills Archive)

The Boss: So people shouldn't interrupt me. So everybody lives by chiseling everybody else. It seems to me very natural. If I lived five hundred years ago, I guess I'd be a baron and everybody call me boss. *McGinty:* I get it. Bulletproof, huh?

Sturges satirized slogan contents in *Christmas in July* (1940), "If you can't sleep, it isn't the coffee. It's the bunk." *Sullivan's Travels* (1942) had as its protagonist a Hollywood director who wanted to forsake comedy for significant films, one to be called *Brother Where Art Thou? The Miracle of Morgan's Creek* (1943) resolved an apparently illegitimate birth (it wasn't really) by having Betty Hutton produce socially admirable sextuplets. *Hail the Conquering Hero* (1944) even looked askance at patriotism and mother love. Sturges' Paramounts are peopled with a repertory group of supporting players like William Demarest, Franklin Pangborn, Jimmy Conlin, and Frank Moran. They are sharp-edged, one-dimensional grotesque characters from whose mouths anything can issue, a shifting, bizarre background against which featured players carry the plot.

Columbia

Closely identified with studio head Harry Cohn, Columbia Pictures was equally dependent on Frank Capra for commercial resilience: each man found in the other a support and resource. The creation of no particular studio, the screwball comedies emanated more often than not from Columbia, beginning with Howard Hawks' *Twientieth Century* (1934). *Twentieth Century* was written by Ben Hecht and Charles MacArthur, screenwriters adept at pell mell, antic dialogue. A light romance provided the plot, and situations grew out of misunderstandings and the scheming of John Barrymore. The male-female relationships thrived on light-hearted banter in which sexual innuendo served merely as a means to one-up the other and to secure a competitive edge. Hawks' later Columbia comedy, *His Girl Friday* (1940) came from another Hecht-MacArthur stage play, *The Front Page,* and Hawks gave the vehicle its screwball formula by casting Rosalind Russell in the Hildy Johnson role that, on stage, had belonged to a newspaperman.

Other Columbia comedies included *The Whole Town's Talking* (1935) directed by John Ford, which married murder to farce, as in the MGM *The Thin Man* series, and starred the archetypal Columbia heroine, Jean Arthur. Screwball offered good women's parts, because the female lead had to be self-reliant, clever, and comic. Two of the best were *Theodora Goes Wild* (1936) and *The Awful Truth* (1937), both Irene Dunne pictures. Director George Stevens' flair for working in this genre is apparent in *The Talk of the Town* (1942) and *The More the Merrier* (1943).

Columbia lacked the size or bankroll to maintain and to train potential stars, although notable contracted Harry Cohn players began to appear in the fifties: William Holden, Judy Holliday, Kim Novak, and Jack Lemmon. The development of these stars was similar to the career of Rita Hayworth who began as a dancer. She was worked into small but attention-provoking parts, as in Hawks' *Only Angels Have Wings* (1939), then carefully set off in glamour roles, epitomized by *Gilda* (1946). A rising star was like bullish stock, for the studio that leased her/him out to other lots profited both financially and by the publicity of someone else's expensive production. Cohn capitalized on such moments and withdrew from the high-paid performers at their peak, when their salaries were, of course, at their highest. "We get them on the way up and we get them on the way down," he said.

GENRE

Some Hollywood films can be understood most easily as the predictable product conforming to a studio's image; other films are most easily approached through a consideration of their genre. In American film language, the term does not carry the literary connotation of expository mode (the poetic genre) or of broader scope such as national idiom (the Russian genre). Rather, genre suggests types of films with common content, like westerns or horror films, which are characterized by sets of conventions, themselves drawing on plot design, costume, setting, certain recognizable artists, locales, and constellations of values (e.g., gangster as self-made man, or cowboy as noble innocent). Such formularizing approaches lent themselves to the rapidly made, strictly controlled studio product for obvious reasons, not the least of which was a premise practically confirmed at the box office: if audience expectations followed patterns established by convention, then attendance might be assured when the expectations were satisfied. This is one reason why movie posters, displayed on theater fronts and in newspaper advertising, are themselves so garishly stereotyped.

Musicals

Over the years, the musical was nourished as much by noise as song, the result of a desire to exploit fully synchronous visibility. In time, tap dance chorus lines and stand-up or kneeling singers became part of story designs that integrated musical performance with drama to the extent that song and dance had some relation to situation and motive. The Busby Berkeley Warner Brothers films managed effectively to match the concept of a review (the

story involves a musical in rehearsal) with the depression (everybody is broke and the show will fold) and cultural optimism (backing is withdrawn but the show must go on). Such a pattern was later adapted to the Mickey Rooney-Judy Garland MGM musicals, sometimes directed by Berkeley. His extravaganza revue numbers in the Warners films depersonalize the women dancers by the very size of the production and by the geometry of the choreography. The abstraction of the human figure is further emphasized by startling camera angles, which may run between dancers' legs or peer down on the stage from great height for the unique purpose of creating a startling image. In fact, Berkeley was remarkably effective at removing his big production numbers from any stage at all. Typically, as in *The Gold Diggers of 1933,* a performance commences in a theater during rehearsal or on opening night. The camera draws in to some detail, then proceeds along to reveal that the fictitious setting has become real. At the sequence's end, singers and dancers will be returned to the proscenium and stage audience. By such devices Berkeley injected geographic fantasy in the voyeurism of his technique. Kuleshov created an artificial woman by building her out of closeups, i.e., his "artificial geography"; Busby Berkeley did something similar with long shots.

In contrast, RKO's Fred Astaire-Ginger Rogers musicals employed story to establish an emotional basis for song and dance performance. Stories were comic-romance, and musical performance usually portrayed a stage in the stars' wooing: "A Fine Romance With No Kisses," "I Won't Dance," "You're Easy to Dance With," "Let's Call the Whole Thing Off," "Change Partners," "I'm Putting All My Eggs in One Basket." True love overcame misunderstanding in the film's big number, which drew on lavish RKO sets and male/female chorus lines that echoed the Rogers-Astaire routines. The stars were accomplished performers; Astaire's grace, based like Chaplin's on painstaking preparation, gave a personal, sardonic twist to the excellent songs provided by composers like Gershwin and Kern. The ten Astaire-Rogers films have an individuality that grew out of the compatibility of the stars in speech as much as in song.

Columbia made interesting musicals in wartime and after, although they had the quality of star showcases: Astaire in *You'll Never Get Rich* (1941) and *You Were Never Lovelier* (1942) with Rita Hayworth; *The Jolson Story* (1946), *Jolson Sings Again* (1949). Increasing investment is evident in the MGM musical, which embraces the Rooney-Garland series, *Babes in Arms* (1939), *Babes on Broadway* (1941) and *Strike Up the Band* (1940); the Garland pictures, *Meet Me in St. Louis* (1944), *The Harvey Girls* (1946), *In the Good Old Summertime* (1949); the Garland-Kelly's, *For Me and My Gal* (1942), *The Pirate* (1948), *Summer Stock* (1950).

Especially interesting is the series done by Kelly with director Stanley Donen, beginning with *Cover Girl* (1944) at Columbia and including *On the Town* (1949) and *Singin' in the Rain* (1952). As in his collaborations with Vincente Minnelli in *An American in Paris* (1951), Kelly choreographs his dancing in close harmony with the professional resources of MGM. The finale of *An American in Paris* is noteworthy for showcasing a studio look that includes an element of out-and-out pomposity. As antidote, the "Beautiful Girl" number in *Singin' in the Rain* is tongue-in-cheek Busby Berkeley.

Musicals betray a cloudier pattern than some other generic forms, although they clearly trace a path away from the early reviews (themselves an outgrowth of Victor Herbert's adaptation of European light opera into an American idiom) to more carefully plotted comedies in which music figures both as functional to the story and in counterpoint to the emotions of the principals.

Crime

Since *Underworld* (1927), gangsters made money in Hollywood. The recent history of prohibition and a spate of Public Enemies Number One promised that each new film would be topical. *The Lights of New York* demonstrated the effective collaboration of sound and crime. *Little Caesar* (1930), *The Public Enemy* (1931), and *Scarface* (1932) were only the most compelling of dozens of gangster biographies. The pattern traced a hoodlum from apprenticeship to top-of-the-heap. Censorship required his punishment and the total absence of redeeming good deeds, but the ironic Horatio Alger aspect of his success story could not be avoided, even if he "turned yellow" when the chips were down. Intimidation and corruption on which the underworld fed were detailed to coat sensationalism with authenticity, and one early spinoff of the gangster movie was the exposé: *The Big House* (1930) on the penitentiary; *The Power of the Press* (1931) on journalism; *Mayor of Hell* (1934) on reform school.

By the time of Roosevelt's presidency, the pressure from city and federal agents shifted earlier crime biography to good guy-bad guy plot forms in *'G' Men* (1935) and *Bullets or Ballots* (1936). Edward G. Robinson and James Cagney, who had earlier played the heavies, could now shift to law-enforcement figures, combining more sympathetic characterization with the legitimitized violence of a ruthless war on crime. With the additional facet of patriotism, this pattern served effectively for many wartime and postwar political dramas, such as *Confessions of a Nazi Spy* (1939) made early by Warner Brothers, *The House on 92nd Street* (1945), and *Whip Hand* (1951) in which communists ran a prison camp in an outlying, rural American community. Another combination of crime and exposé was the juvenile-delinquency film which established the city as a sordid environment that spawned criminality by stunting the human spirit. Such films spawned the Dead End Kids out of *Dead End* (1937). The young hoodlums were significantly refreshed and rejuvenated, if temporarily, by country living in *They Made Me a Criminal* (1939), a film directed by Busby Berkeley!

Echoing something of the subculture it portrayed, the crime film had its own conventions of speech, dress, and manner. A gangster's status was defined in part by the quality of his clothes and his way of taking orders from The Boss. A German tradition dating from Berthold Brecht's *The Threepenny Opera* on stage and Fritz Lang's *M* (1931) had criminal gangs and police cooperating for some common purpose, and directors, following Lang's example, might surreptitiously suggest parallels between cop and criminal by composing group shots that made visual equivalents of the two and by reflecting the similar power-base of their organizations. By the time of *Pickup on South Street* (1953), commie ''gangsters'' and city police pose an equal threat to the pickpocket loner, Richard Widmark.

Often low budgeted, the crime genre kicked off audience reaction with violence—violence that might appear with unnerving suddenness by way of the criminal's erratic personality. Because it was a kind of urban war film, the form also lent itself to visually stimulating action as well as atmospheric lighting and even expressionist design. For example, director Robert Siodmak came to Hollywood from Germany and several of his crime films—*Phantom Lady* (1944), *The Suspect* (1944), *Crisscross* (1949)—make use of Ufa-like effects, shifting the gangster genre toward what came to be categorized as film noir. Of course, film noir can be traced back into many other wartime idioms.

Detective

Detective stories may be distinguished from crime stories by way of plot, which requires that the misdeed precede the detective story proper. The act of discovery with its attendant unmasking steps establishes detective conventions. Like every other generic form, detective formulae precede the motion pictures, buried deep in the popular ephemera of nineteenth-century entertainment. The detective Hawkshaw was a gallant, tough master of disguises in an 1863 play, and most detectives have first appeared in print, directly as with Spade, Marlowe, Holmes, Chan, Marple, Poirrot, Archer (Harper in film), Charles and Vance, or indirectly as in television's Columbo, modeled after the Police Inspector in *Crime and Punishment*.

Nevertheless, the detective idiom lends itself gracefully to film. The very concept of clues is a visual one, and the process of search facilitates the use of different, interesting locations to which the detective must journey in order to locate witnesses and follow up leads. Two traditions compete and coalesce in the detective form. One is predominantly British, essentially a puzzle. The criminal will be discovered by problem-solving skills much as one might respond to challenge in chess or bridge. This is the form of the early detective talkies, such as William Powell as Philo Vance in *The Canary Murder Case* (1929), *The Greene Murder Case* (1929), *The Benson Murder Case* (1930), and *The Kennel Murder Case* (1933). As with Charlie Chan and Hercule Poirot, the formula requires that all suspects be assembled in finale, perhaps at a dinner party, for most such stories are equally concerned with social conduct. The detective may then explain the murder and identify its perpetrator after eliminating the other suspects by tracing out his evidentiary logic. *The Thin Man* films end this way, and the murderer is always to be seen behind Nick Charles in the final scenes, usually behind his left shoulder, as the search climaxes.

The alternative detective story is ''hard boiled,'' less class bound, and more action packed. The protagonist is often placed in dangerous confrontation with the criminal, who may even be professional, rather than a caddish gentleman in disguise. Beatings temporarily set back Sam Spade: *The Maltese Falcon* (1941); and Philip Marlowe: *The Big Sleep* (1946), *Murder My Sweet* (1944), *Lady in the Lake* (1946), and *The Brasher Doubloon* (1947). This violence often interferes with the process of detection; Marlowe usually stumbles about, only piecing the puzzle together in a last moment of intuitive insight. At worst, such adventure abdicates the detective form in favor of the crime story form or that of less-structured adventure melodramas.

Detective films endure because their form can be adapted to contemporary events. Holmes and Watson spent an embarrassing period fighting the Nazis during World War II. Police work sometimes requires enough investigation to remove the story from battlefield to laboratory. A popular variation on straight detection is the hero as victim, an innocent whom chance has thrust into personal danger that can only be removed by solving an attendant mystery. The form is a Hitchcock favorite, openly acknowledged in *The Wrong Man* (1956).

Horror

Thomas Edison filmed a *Frankenstein* in 1910. *Dr. Jekyll and Mr. Hyde* appeared silent (1920) and again in Rouben Mamoulian's early sound version of 1932, the transformation accomplished by lighting changes gradually engineered to reveal different makeup to the camera. Many of the Lon Chaney grotesqueries fall under the horror category, but sound fostered a new reign of monsters and the supernatural, affording inexpensive spectacle and seizing advantage of the pleasure in secure anxiety that is one important attraction in popular film viewing.

By objectifying unacknowledged audience anxieties in the form of frightening images, Hollywood horror externalized such themes as our concerns about sanity, conformity, and the sacred, as well as our fear of science, and, above all, of death's inevitability. Again Ufa contributed, not only in terms of expressionism's murky stylistics, but by way of a heritage of legend and cultural motifs, mostly variations on the *Faust* myth. Whatever its current life as an MCA subsidiary, Universal Studios survives in memory as home to the horror film, even though horror constituted no large percentage of its output. Made in 1931, both *Frankenstein* and *Dracula* helped Universal to survive the early thirties slump that threatened attendances alarmingly—Hollywood's own horror story.

Dracula was directed by Tod Browning, onetime Griffith assistant who had worked with Lon Chaney on both silent and sound versions of *The Unholy Three* and other silents. Bela Lugosi and Transylvania are now such casualties of familiarity and camp that one can do little more than admire the count's cobwebbed basement, but Browning's *Freaks* (1932) and *The Devil Doll* (1936) still have impact. James Whale's *Frankenstein* survives in large part because of Karloff's early innocence mimed behind the exceptional makeup of Jack Pierce. Here the monster comes closest to Mary Shelley's romantic design: the noble primitive still uncorrupted by Europe's decadence. *The Bride of Frankenstein* (1935), again made by Whale, is a better movie, blending a subcurrent of satire with the menace. Karl Freund, who photographed *Dracula*, began his short directing career with *The Mummy* (1932), a variation on *The Golem* that congeals resurrection, profanation, and rampant sexual energy into the form of a bandaged Egyptian corpse. With the burning of tanis leaves, the mummy appears on call like an old firehorse who hears the alarm.

The last of Freund's own films was *Mad Love* (1934), a remake of Wiene's *The Hands of Orlac* (1924). It provided one of Peter Lorre's best parts, and Lorre's first American

"There was a mocking smile on the bloated face which seemed to drive me mad. This was the being I was helping to transfer to London, where, perhaps, for centuries to come he might, amongst its teeming millions, satiate his lust for blood, and create a new and everwidening circle of semidemons to batten on the helpless." Bram Stoker, *Dracula*. (Movie Star News)

venture. He plays a mad surgeon who sews the hands of a knife murderer onto an injured pianist with predictable results. Lorre's unrequited love for the pianist's wife suggests a sadism born of impotence. One of the most grotesque depression horrors was Edgar Ulmer's *The Black Cat* (1934). It pits Boris Karloff against Bela Lugosi in a Gothic castle that is the locus of a black mass, necrophilia, madness, and hideous torture.

Far more effective than Burt Lancaster in *The Island of Dr. Moreau* (1977) was the other outstanding mad scientist, Charles Laughton, in Paramount's *The Island of Lost Souls* (1933). The film is an adaptation of the H. G. Wells story in which humans are created from jungle beasts that are led by Lugosi. The earlier version can be seen as an ironic comment on evolution, religion, and Marxism, as the beast-men discard the Law ("We walk on two legs. We do not eat meat.") and turn on their perverse creator in his dwelling, the House of Pain.

King Kong (1932) was made by two documentary directors, Ernest Schoedsack and Merian Cooper, and allowed RKO to capitalize on special effects produced under the hand of Willis O'Brien, who had earlier animated models in *The Lost World* (1925). Hired to reorganize RKO, Cooper sold its stockholders on a full-year production schedule for *Kong*, mostly with intricate models and complex combinations of glass shots, rear projection, traveling mattes and optical printing.[5]

Imaginative horror reappeared at RKO for a short period during World War II when Val Lewton produced a series of films that economically combined tight, suggestive scripts with clever staging and careful employment of sound. Best were a transformation story, *The Cat People* (1942) and a resurrection, *I Walked With a Zombie* (1943), both directed by Jacques Tourneur, and *The Body Snatcher* (1945), directed by Robert Wise with Boris Karloff and a cast of corpses.

Soon afterward, horror's grand guignol aspects became increasingly preempted by more garish crime and detective stories; in the next generation, horror turned with relief to outer

[5] *A layman's survey of special effects trickery will be found in John Brosnan,* Movie Magic *(New York, 1974). More technical explanations appear in Raymond Fielding,* The Technique of Special Effects Cinematography *(New York, 1972).*

space. All genres must remain in touch with their times, one reason why satanism-today themes show popularity in the seventies.

Western

A comprehensive summary of the western reflects much of American film history. The genre's status as ambitiously financed features falls into trends. Early sound westerns—*In Old Arizona* (a Cisco Kid), *The Virginian* (1929) and *Cimarron* (1931)—succeed as modernized versions of "classics," but the form loped through a good part of the thirties in "B" pictures and serials (the true homes of genre), with colorfully costumed cowboys riding an endless procession of ponies down dusty streets.

The western is one of the most flexible of forms, so long as it maintains the basic pattern of the skilled man and his code resolving moral and ethical complication with "pure" acts of violence. In *The Plainsman* (1937), Cecil B. DeMille first shifted his attention from pagan and Christian myth to American, casting Gary Cooper and Jean Arthur as Wild Bill Hickok and Calamity Jane. Another way station of the thirties western was operetta: Jeanette MacDonald and Nelson Eddy in

The Virginian. Gary Cooper and Mary Brian. As leader of a posse, Cooper must supervise the hanging of his best friend for rustling. Trampas (Walter Huston) had led the thieves and abandoned Cooper's friend. A lively shoot-out finally compensates for some stiff drama. (British National Film Archive/Stills Library)

Rose Marie! (1936) and *The Girl of the Golden West* (1938). Rescripted, Eisenstein's *Sutter's Gold* was finally undertaken by James Cruze in 1936. John Ford's *Stagecoach* (1939) was essentially an unacknowledged deMaupassant short story, but John Wayne's Ringo sustains requirements of the western form by doing what a man must do in a shotgun crescendo.

Westerns can also absorb the criminal biography, as those of Jesse James and Billy the Kid testify. Three of Fritz Lang's American films are westerns, *The Return of Frank James* (1940), *Western Union* (1941) and *Rancho Notorious* (1952). Ostensibly a study of the mounting of the telegraph, *Western Union* concentrates on badman Randolph Scott. The outlaw as protagonist challenges a western's code, for he must simultaneously die and resolve the moral issues. This may be accommodated by betrayal, as in *Jesse James* (1940), or sentimentalizing, as in *The Okla-*

Stagecoach. Atop the Overland Stage, Ringo joins shotgun Curley Wilcox, driver Buck, and gambler Hatfield (inside) in warding off the Cheyenne menace. Wilcox is bringing Ringo to Lordsburg for trial. By his gallantry, Ringo wins the chance for a shoot-out with the Plummer brothers and for future happiness with Dallas, a reformed prostitute. Poorly redone in 1966. (British National Film Archive/Stills Library)

homa Kid (1939). In *The Return of Frank James,* Lang has Henry Fonda as Jesse's brother withhold the bullet from his final shootout and thus avoid social retribution. But, even though he bests the villain, Frank doesn't get the girl.

Westerns have always been attractive by virtue of panoramic exteriors and the idiom's capacity to show America's self-image of frontier expansion. When developed as an overt theme, the legends usually require bad-men and Indians, separately or together, as threats to "civilization," which often presents its case in the form of a young schoolmarm (a tradition probably derived from Owen Wister's *The Virginian*). The theme is common to John Ford, who also plays variations on popular conventions in *My Darling Clementine* (1946), the military, *She Wore a Yellow Ribbon* (1949), and lifestyles in *Wagonmaster* (1950).

Adapted from Walter Van Tilburg Clark's

Tom Mix in an early, unknown western. With horse Tony's usual assistance, Mix manages a goodbye, while the girl's male companion remains determinedly oblivious. Western buffs rank Mix's *Rider of Death Valley* (1932) with *Stagecoach* and *Shane* (1953). (Movie Star News)

Mildred Pierce. Exceptionally competent as a business woman, Mildred projects her social ambitions onto her daughter, Veda. Mildred's agony stems mostly from Veda, who taunts her with educated, spoiled tastes and punishes her mother by reverting to low-status nightclub singing, a step beneath Mildred's own social origins. The daughter murders her mother's fiancé. Bert Pierce, the ineffective divorced first husband, returns to stand by his wife. (Movie Star News)

novel, *The Ox-Bow Incident* (1943) was used by William Wellman to challenge the notion of vigilante justice. Echoing the pulp magazine's technique of rejuvenating wheezing formulae with sex, a satiric *Destry Rides Again* (1939) played James Stewart (an apparently timid sheriff) against Marlene Dietrich. Although Dietrich at this stage had made four films without Josef von Sternberg, her exotic image had been ossified and her role as "dance-hall girl" showed off both her legs and her humor.

Like Watson and Holmes in their World War II adventures, the Range Busters helped to subdue the Axis in *Texas to Bataan* (1942) and *Cowboy Commandos* (1943).

"Women's" Pictures

A less remarked generic form showcases the brave and suffering woman, at best a pillar of strength in a world of weak males and children, at worst more sinned against than sinning, like Goneril in *King Lear*. This genre does not possess as many tradition-bound overtones as other genres, but bears a clear relation to the thirties soap operas: radio's quarter-hour homage to house-bound wives. In the soap opera, genre expresses its canny employment of fictionalized star personalities to support a pattern of conventions. The scenes of Greta Garbo touching the furniture of her lover's room in *Queen Christina* so that she may always remember it or saying goodbye to Count Vronsky in *Anna Karenina* (1935) have qualities of the weepie, but the strongest representatives of this genre are figures like Joan Crawford and Bette Davis.

Both Crawford and Davis worked well in other kinds of vehicles. (Crawford started as a roaring twenties, dancing-on-the-pianos flapper). Yet each projected qualities of endurance that raised suffering in women's pictures to noble heights. Directed by the very able Dorothy Arzner, Crawford "smouldered with indecision, consumed with talk of love and fashion" (in the words of *The New York Times*) in *The Bride Wore Black* (1937). She suffered from disfigurement in *A Woman's Face* (1941). In *Humoresque* (1946), she loves but knows she would only corrupt protégé violinist John Garfield. In *Torch Song* (1953), Crawford is a neurotic, tough musical comedy star in love with a blind pianist. *Mildred Pierce* (1945) was quintessential Crawford, a self-sacrificing mother whose hard-won success serves only to spoil a daughter who spurns her mother's gifts and steals her lover.

Bette Davis' style was more nervous, the bitchy woman whose neurosis made life hell for her. In *Marked Woman* (1936), she is persuaded by Humphrey Bogart to testify against her underworld boss. She brings on her own downfall, stealing her sister's husband in *In This Our Life* (1942). Davis is her noblest as a spoiled rich girl who faces early death in *Dark Victory* (1939). The most rounded Davis personality was Margo Channing in *All About Eve* (1950), an aging actress threatened by her insecurities, counterpart to Crawford's *Torch Song*.

Like film noir, the women's picture may be more style than substance. It thrives on closeup, alienating compositions, and intimacy built of interiors and long camera takes. It is dialogue-based and resolves its dramatic confrontations more through emotive scenes than by action. Dorothy McGuire inherited some of the temper in *The Enchanted Cottage* (1945) and *Till the End of Time* (1946). It is a kind of interiorized melodrama played on a landscape of private pain, punctuated with cigarette stubs and coffee cups.

Summary

The study of the evolution of American film during the period from sound's appearance to the postwar, pretelevision world, reveals an almost overwhelming quantity of information often resulting from technical advances and industrial consolidation. As Chapter 10 will show, many out-of-the-ordinary films were accomplished, but the study of these alone fails altogether to accommodate the comprehension of this era for, as we have seen in this chapter, studio-defined and genre film constitute a significant portion of film product. The most serious cases for genre and studio study customarily draw on this period's films. Further, the wit, energy, and charm of many titles that boast neither star nor pantheon director make good arguments for other analytic approaches besides that of authorship. Unlike so much else regarding film history, there are many opportunities to study this period because American sound film constantly reappears on late television for everyone with the patience to seek it out and the endurance to stay awake.

Bibliography

Baxter, John. *Hollywood in the Thirties*. New York, 1968.
Bergman, Andrew. *We're in the Money*. New York, 1971.
Brosnan, John. *Movie Magic*. New York, 1974.
Budd, Michael. "Notes on Preston Sturges and America." *Film Society Review*, January 1968.
Butler, Ivan. *The Horror Film*. Cranbury, N.J., 1967.

Cameron, Ian. *A Practical History of Crime Films*. New York, 1975.

Cawelti, John. *The Six Gun Mystique*. Bowling Green, Ohio, 1971.

Clarens, Carlos. *An Illustrated History of the Horror Film*. New York, 1967.

Corliss, Richard. *Talking Pictures*. Woodstock, N.Y., 1974.

Crowther, Bosley. *Hollywood Rajah*. New York, 1960.

Dillard, R. H. W. "Even a Man Who is Pure at Heart." In *Man and the Movies*, edited by W. R. Robinson. Baton Rouge, 1967.

Elsaesser, Thomas. "Tales of Sound and Fury." *Monogram* 4 (1972).

Everson, William. "A Family Tree of Monsters." *Film Culture* 1 (January 1955).

Ericcson, Peter. "The Films of Preston Sturges." *Sequence* 4 (Summer 1948).

Farber, Manny and W. S. Poster. "Preston Sturges: Success in Movies." *Film Culture* 26 (Fall 1962).

Fenin, George and William Everson. *The Western*. rev. ed. New York, 1973.

Fordin, Hugh. *The World of Entertainment!* New York, 1975.

Fox, Julian. "Dangerous Games." *Films and Filming*, June-August 1976.

Geduld, Harry. *The Birth of the Talkies*. Bloomington, 1975.

Gomery, J. Douglas. "The Warner-Vitaphone Peril." *Journal of the University Film Association*, Winter 1976.

Higham, Charles. *Warner Brothers*. New York, 1975.

Higham, Charles and Joel Greenberg. *Hollywood in the Forties*. New York, 1968.

Houston, Penelope. "Preston Sturges." *Sight and Sound*, Summer 1965.

Huss, Roy and T. J. Ross. *Focus on the Horror Film*. Englewood Cliffs, N.J., 1972.

Johnston, Claire. *The Work of Dorothy Arzner*. London, 1975.

Jonsson, Eric. "Preston Sturges and the Theory of Decline." *Film Culture* 26 (Fall 1962).

Kaminsky, Stuart M. *American Film Genres*. Dayton, 1974.

Kirstein, Lincoln. "James Cagney and the American Hero." *Hound and Horn*, 1972.

Kitses, Jim. *Auteur and Genre*. BFI seminar discussion paper. London, 1969.

———. *Horizons West*. London, 1970.

Kobal, John. *Gotta Sing, Gotta Dance*. London, 1970.

Larkin, Rochelle. *Hail, Columbia!* New Rochelle, 1975.

MacArthur, Colin. *Underworld USA*. New York, 1972.

McVay, J. Douglas. *The Musical Film*. New York, 1967.

Maiden, Benjamin. "The Paramount Films of Preston Sturges." Master's thesis, San Francisco State University, 1972.

Nachbar, Jack. *Focus on the Western*. Englewood Cliffs, N.J., 1974.

Ross, Lillian. *Picture*. New York, 1962.

Sennett, Ted. *Warner Brothers Presents*. New Rochelle, 1971.

Siegal, Joel. *Val Lewton*. New York, 1972.

Silke, James R. *Here's Looking at You Kid*. Boston, 1976.

Solomon, Stanley, *Beyond Formula*. New York, 1976.

Taylor, John Russell. *The Hollywood Musical*. New York, 1971.

Thomas, John. "Freaks." *Film Quarterly*, Spring 1964.

Thomas, Lawrence. *The MGM Years*. New York, 1972.

Tuska, Jon. *The Filming of the West*. Garden City, N.Y., 1976.
"Warners Revisited." *Velvet Light Trap* 15 (Fall 1975).
"The Western." *Velvet Light Trap* 12 (Spring 1974).
Westmore, Frank. *The Westmores of Hollywood*. New York, 1976.
Wright, Will. *Six Guns and Society*. Berkeley, 1975.

10

HOLLYWOOD DIRECTORS

Outside the categories of generic mode and studio ambiance, many films produced in the heyday of Hollywood studio operation are undistinguished and unmemorable. Some, however, show consistent patterns of stylistic integrity, the mark of individual directors. These men stood apart from their peers; each had distinguishing qualities. Such men were undiminished by the economic and administrative boundaries staking their work, which transcends ordinary "professionalism" when it successfully defines cultural values by way of an individual film esthetic.

For the sake of organizational coherence, this chapter seeks to describe directors whose significant work commences or continues in the American sound era, which was otherwise described in Chapter 9. The design presents obvious insufficiencies. Alfred Hitchcock began and refined his work outside the United States; *The Blue Angel* and Fritz Lang remain in a later, German sound section. Clearly, too, the organization of feature film history by directors will inescapably de-emphasize other perspectives that range from the effect of social, economic, and ideological factors on narrative to the movies' own consequences on esthetics and society. Against such reasonable criti-

Camille (Cukor 1936) (Museum of Modern Art/Film Stills Archive)

cism, it may be noted that social history and broader esthetic issues figure implicitly in the work of any filmmaker, and are there for the taking though they are often not easily identified. The present history, emphasizing as it does a somewhat detailed consideration of individual works, has found the present course comparatively most effective, if sometimes distressingly encyclopedic.[1]

FRANK CAPRA

Gagman for Sennett, Frank Capra directed the comic Harry Langdon's best features, *The Strong Man* (1926) and *Long Pants* (1927). His contact with Columbia in the late twenties initiated a career at that studio in which the director enjoyed support and latitude uncommon to thirties and forties employees in Harry Cohn's disciplined camp.

Capra's forte was the humorous, sentimental drama, supportive of "American" ideals, humane and somewhat naïve, especially in story resolution. The style can be seen in formation in *Platinum Blonde* (1931), a Jean Harlow vehicle about a newspaper reporter who falls in love with a society girl. The reporter is blind to the affections of his fellow newspaperperson, Loretta Young, whom he can only see as a coworker. Awakened, the reporter forsakes luxury for Loretta. The wisecracking hat-on-the-back-of-the-head jargon (an idiom Capra refined into good-but-disillusioned journalism *types* later) and a

[1] *Readers who wish to consider other perspectives such as those concerned with sociology, economics, and ideology in the American film are encouraged to examine such additional works as Garth Jowett,* Film the Democratic Art *(Boston: Little, Brown, 1976); Robert Sklar,* Movie Made America *(New York: Random House, 1975); and, perhaps, John L. Fell,* Film and the Narrative Tradition *(Norman: University of Oklahoma Press, 1974).*

parade of eccentric, boozing reporters, are harbingers of *You Can't Take it with You* (1938) and *Meet John Doe* (1941).

Much of Capra's success grew out of collaborations with scriptwriter Robert Riskin, as John Ford's did with Dudley Nichols. Riskin wrote *American Madness* (1932), *Lady for a Day* (1933), *It Happened One Night* (1934), *Mr. Deeds Goes to Town* (1936), *You Can't Take it With You*, and *Meet John Doe*. Together, Capra and Riskin evolved a sophisticated, satiric approach that easily fitted aspirations and values of the New Deal. Typically, a depressed country is further threatened by loss of faith when some trusted innocent is revealed or seems to be revealed

Frank Capra (1897–)

The Strong Man	1926
Long Pants	1927
Submarine	1928
Platinum Blonde	1931
The Miracle Woman	1931
American Madness	1932
The Bitter Tea of General Yen	1933
Lady for a Day	1933
It Happened One Night	1934
Mr. Deeds Goes to Town	1936
Lost Horizon	1937
You Can't Take it with You	1938
Mr. Smith Goes to Washington	1939
Meet John Doe/John Doe Dynamite	1941
Arsenic and Old Lace	1944
Why We Fight (episodes)	1942–1944
It's a Wonderful World	1946
State of the Union	1948
Riding High	1949
A Hole in the Head	1959
A Pocket Full of Miracles	1961
Partial listing	

You Can't Take It With You. A publicity still encapsulates each eccentric player in the adapted George Kaufman-Moss Hart Broadway hit. The happy abnormalities of an extended family are threatened by hard-headed "real life," epitomized by Edward Arnold. Performers include James Stewart and Jean Arthur (far left), Lionel Barrymore (seated, mouth open), Spring Byington (with sampler), Ann Miller (arm upraised), Misha Auer (on floor), and Donald Meek (balding). (Movie Star News)

as fraudulent. Through an energetic act of public self defense or contrition, the bond of trust is restored and optimism asserted. In *American Madness,* Walter Huston is a banker who represses a panic at great personal risk and simultaneously discovers he has been neglecting his patient wife. In *Mr. Deeds Goes to Town,* which introduces both the archetypal Capra innocent, Gary Cooper, and wisecracking woman, Jean Arthur, Deeds is a newlyrich poet (!) who convinces a judge that he is not insane simply because he chooses to give his fortune to the poor. In *Mr. Smith Goes to Washington* (1939), James Stewart plays a Boy Scout leader appointed to the senate by the political machine. Discovering he has been a naïve front, Smith wins massive public support with a monologue filibuster.

Meet John Doe provides interesting evidence about the implications of the Capra-Riskin pattern. A derelict John Doe (Gary Cooper) is party to newspaper exploitation, then manipulated by the politically minded rich to develop popular support in order to provide a power base for Edward Arnold's ambition. Forsaking the usual, believable, hero's innocence, Capra made Cooper a knowledgeable party, at least in part, to the corruption. How then to resolve his story in an upbeat way? Alternative endings were filmed and tried. The final solution, which has John Doe's public confess its mean-spirited disloyalty to Doe and his ideals, fails.

Capra's design accommodated a particular American decade and remains to be seen as a skillfully crafted artifact of that moment in the society's consciousness. He was, too, a vigorous, early spokesman for the director's rights to exercise final authority over his films, rather than abdicating that prerogative to studios and assembly-line production schedules. Capra's outstanding accomplishment is *It Happened One Night,* in which he departs the innocent-corrupt convention and allows both a reporter (Clark Gable) and a debutante (Claudette Colbert) human foibles and strengths equally.

GEORGE CUKOR

Cukor approached film by way of Broadway, serving as dialogue director for *All Quiet on the Western Front* (1930); early on he worked with Lubitsch. Most often, Cukor serves as an effective interpreter of novelists like Dickens and dramatists like Shaw and Shakespeare. His work reveals a special aptitude for the direction of actresses, which was a collaborative endeavor that extends equally to writers, crew, and, indeed, choice of story material.

Cukor films have polish that at best sets off the wit and energy of refined, often backstage, stories. At worst, the films betray a gloss akin to slickness, but this impression is offset by sharp, sometimes eccentric characterizations, such as Roland Young as Uriah Heep and W. C. Fields as Mr. Micawber in *David Copperfield* (1934). Cukor often thinks in theatrical terms, so that a scene is played in long shot, its meaning deployed by physical relationships and details rather than cutting, as in Garbo's bedroom scenes in *Camille* (1936) and Vivien Leigh's in *Gone With the Wind* (1939), a film from which Cukor was discharged, in part at least for his slow and painstaking attention to minutiae of performance and staging.

Cukor works well with light comedy and such an articulate performer as Katherine Hepburn in films like *Holiday* (1938), *The Philadelphia Story* (1940), *Adam's Rib* (1949), *Pat and Mike* (1952). He places high

value on the expression of emotional candor. Whether shown erotically, as in *Camille,* or in aggressive wit, *The Women* (1939), it is revealed through the patterns of cultural repression. His direction of musicals—*A Star is Born* (1954), *Les Girls* (1957) and *My Fair Lady* (1964)—show a capacity to sustain extravagance with intimate detail. Cukor enjoys depicting close relations between the sexes, always expressed with what he (and Lubitsch) regarded as "taste," as in the warm overtones of the Aldo Ray-Judy Holliday family history in *The Marrying Kind* (1951). Like five other Cukors, the polished script came from Garson Kanin and Ruth Gordon.

George Cukor (1899–)

Grumpy (co-director Cyril Gardner)	1930
A Bill of Divorcement	1932
Dinner at Eight	1933
Little Women	1933
David Copperfield	1934
Romeo and Juliet	1936
Camille	1936
Holiday	1938
The Women	1939
The Philadelphia Story	1940
A Woman's Face	1941
Keeper of the Flame	1943
Gaslight	1944
Adam's Rib	1949
Born Yesterday	1950
The Marrying Kind	1951
Pat and Mike	1952
It Should Happen to You	1954
A Star is Born	1954
Bhowani Junction	1955
Les Girls	1957
The Chapman Report	1961
My Fair Lady	1964
Justine	1969
Travels With My Aunt	1972
The Blue Bird	1976
Partial listing	

JOHN FORD

Ford's *Steamboat Round the Bend* (1935), *The Whole Town's Talking* (1935), and a Shirley Temple, *Wee Willie Winkie* (1937) are untypical comedies in a productive career, although he often used humor to relieve drama. The sound films run from Irish stories, literary adaptations, war tales, and adventure to westerns. Typically they are convention-exploiting stories of betrayal, loyalty, patriotism, and institutions. Individual mettle is tested in crisis, while sexuality is absent or subordinated. Many of these films have epic ambitions, not so much through any literal tracings of historic movements, but by the employment of legends, such as Wyatt Earp, and in photography that uses open space for grandiose effects. Ford's forty-eight year career as a director traversed generations of shifting audience values and enthusiasms. He was an avowedly commercial filmmaker, and some of his appeals, as to the military in *The Long Gray Line* (1955), hardly sit easily with contemporary viewers. What once seemed liberal appears paternalistic, like the plight of Indians in *Cheyenne Autumn* (1964) with whom Ford was clearly in deep sympathy. The rewards of a Ford film are most accessible to an audience that allows itself some latitude of feeling.

Ford's work is often characterized by an eye for pictorial values that sustain a story in an environment that is both picturesque and narratively appropriate. The Monument Valley background to the Indian attack in *Stagecoach* (1939), its first employment, is a classic example, but the same could be said about the desert in *The Lost Patrol* (1934) and the Irish countryside of *The Quiet Man* (1952).

Stagecoach plays popular images of the "regenerated badman" (John Wayne) and the "whore with the heart of gold" (Claire Trevor) into another conventional scheme, that of diverse personalities thrust together on a dangerous journey. As customary, the stage's constituency is a society in microcosm: gambler, officer's wife, drunken doctor, corrupt banker, and traveling salesman. Ford's dictum requires people to reveal themselves under stress, and part of the film's appeal rests in his ability to manipulate our responses to character traits that comment ironically on society. Thus Thomas Mitchell, the alcoholic doctor, after performing nobly, reverts to his whiskey.

My Darling Clementine (1946) locates Wyatt Earp, Doc Holliday and the OK Corral at a moment in time when the frontier outpost of "civilization" is Tombstone. Figuring in the sequences are a church dedication and the appearance of an itinerant theater troupe. Dancing at the church inauguration, amenable to barbers and to storebought clothes, Henry Fonda's Earp is clearly interested in establishing relations with the emerging social order. While undeveloped in this film, the passage of an earlier way of life, supplanted by everything that accompanies law and order, figures increasingly in later Ford, as his protagonists' age and lifestyle become increasingly incongruent with new ways. The knowledge of how to behave at pressured moments is finally muddled by society's confused values and expectations. In *The Man Who Shot Liberty Valance* (1962), James Stewart, the new breed, a lawyer, becomes governor and senator because people believe he bested the town badman in confrontation, but John Wayne, who dies as the town bum, had really shot Liberty Valance. Years later, a newspaper editor rejects the true story because "the legend has become fact."

Some of Ford's later films exploit the microcosm/macrocosm devices of epic by casting the situations of individuals against a background where the issues no longer seem comprehensible in terms of their inner needs. In *The Horse Soldiers* (1959), John Wayne is a northern colonel sent to sabotage confederate supply lines. His forces occupy a southern mansion maintained by a loyal southern woman (Constance Towers). Her impetuous efforts betray an uncritical allegiance, while Wayne is torn by disillusionment about human integrity and anguished by his own destructive mission. The acting of Towers and Wayne is bravura, but scenes of seige and of primitive medical treatment at Newton Station remain effective.

Sergeant Rutledge (1960) recounts through flashback the rape-murder of a young white woman for which Rutledge, a soldier in the black Ninth Cavalry, is held accountable. One might argue that the sergeant's innocence depends on his uncalculated disinterest in pretty young white girls, but the film has interesting complexities. It shrewdly parallels and compares different social strata. The Indian's suicidal attack on the Ninth proves to be a despairing gesture to prove their manhood. The relation of the black troops to their white officers denies, too, some of these men's self-respect, but because Rutledge, well played by Woody Strode, finds his self-realization in the military code, he rejects the temptation of flight without vindication. The film blends unsentimentalized overlays of racial prejudice, ranging from fort civilians to Rutledge's white friends; each group working from certain untested premises about the sergeant's nature.

Two later Ford westerns, variations on a common theme, show something of his diminishing faith. *The Searchers* (1956) and *Two Rode Together* (1961) center on efforts to recover white captives from the Indians. In the former case, an alienated hero must, in the process, come to terms with his own rage and grief so that his travels constitute a kind of metaphor for an interior search. Written, like many post-World-War-II Fords by Frank Nugent, *Two Rode Together* views even more scornfully the white settlers' bigotry toward women's "contamination" by Indian capture. In either case, the Ford hero is no longer singly motivated but vulnerable and confused. Finally, Ford withdraws his own confidence in the significance of human effort, leaving us with the landscape.

HOWARD HAWKS

Like Raoul Walsh, Hawks excels in action pictures with adventurous male camaraderie. Many, not all, his comedies have shown remarkable longevity as well. Hawks differs from similar studio directors more in degree than in kind. Working with assigned, formu-

John Ford (1895–1973)

The Tornado	1917
The Iron Horse	1924
Arrowsmith	1931
The Lost Patrol	1934
Judge Priest	1934
The Long Gray Line	1935
The Whole Town's Talking	1935
The Informer	1935
Steamboat Round the Bend	1935
The Prisoner of Shark Island	1936
The Plough and the Stars	1936
Wee Willie Winkie	1937
Stagecoach	1939
Young Mr. Lincoln	1939
Drums Along the Mohawk	1940
The Grapes of Wrath	1940
The Long Voyage Home	1940
How Green Was My Valley	1941
The Battle of Midway	1942
My Darling Clementine	1946
She Wore a Yellow Ribbon	1949
Wagonmaster	1950
Rio Grande	1950
The Quiet Man	1952
The Searchers	1956
The Last Hurrah	1958
The Horse Soldiers	1959
Sergeant Rutledge	1960
Two Rode Together	1961
The Man Who Shot Liberty Valance	1961
Cheyenne Autumn	1964
Seven Women	1965
Partial listing	

larized plots and characters, or sometimes inventing stories himself in collaboration with assigned writers, his highly stereotyped principals seem to emerge from primordial genre like creatures crawling in an effort to become human.

This quality is intensified by a Hawksian scheme that elicits dramatic tensions from calls to duty or professional commitment that may be at odds with other loyalties or attractions. The Hawks protagonist, whether Hildy Johnson in *His Girl Friday* (1939) or Bat, the once cowardly pilot in *Only Angels Have Wings* (1939), is inexorably drawn toward what he/she was trained, if not born, to do. In the process, male loyalties or true male-female sexual bonds are confirmed. Endings somtimes release a man from sexual lures either by revealing a woman's destructive effect on male integrity or by converting her to the status of "pal" in the male group. Such story conventions may nudge or even abrade contemporary sensibilities. At his best, Hawks accomplishes his intentions with sharp, unobstrusive style.

A fighter pilot in World War I like William Wellman, Hawks passed through editing and scriptwriting phases at Paramount before directing his first film, *The Road to Glory,* in 1926. His association with such writers as Ben Hecht: *Scarface* (1932), *Viva Villa!* (1934), *Twentieth Century* (1934), *Monkey Business* (1952); and William Faulkner: *The Road to Glory* (1936 remake), *To Have and Have Not* (1944), *The Big Sleep* (1946) indicates a commitment to incident and dialogue. Speech with Hawks is laconic, shrewdly paced when it is stacatto-idiomatic as in *Scarface* or timed for manic delivery as in the comedies.

The Big Sleep. Philip Marlowe and Vivian Sternwood await the arrival of Eddie Mars. Mars has been blackmailing Vivian because he knows her sister, a dope addict and nymphomaniac, murdered their father's bodyguard. Marlowe will soon force Mars to expose himself suicidally to his own gang's ambush. Then Marlowe will win Vivian and propose that her sister be institutionalized. Unevenly remade by Michael Winner in 1978. (Copyright © 1946 Warner Bros. Pictures, Inc. Copyright renewed 1973.) (Movie Star News)

In *Dawn Patrol* (1930), a wartime squadron leader of volunteer American pilots escapes through promotion his onorous, despised task of sending men on suicidal morning raids. He is replaced by his severest critic who dies heroically, followed in command by a best friend. Here, weakness is the failure to carry out odious, self-destructive military orders. Other Hawks airplane films trade on the same, inexorable situation, but with variations. In *Ceiling Zero* (1936), a brash, flashy James Cagney finally subordinates himself to mundane, demanding requirements of modern aviation. The individuality of barnstorming days must accede to shared, cooperative endeavor. In *Only Angels Have Wings,* Cary Grant directs a little crew of pilots from a South American airport across the Andes through dangerous fog. Heroism and emotions are underplayed with Hemingwayesque muteness. The sparring courtship between Grant and Jean Arthur is conducted obliquely. She knows he cares for her after discovering he has flipped a two-headed coin in order to determine the outcome of a bet.

Hawks' love stories emerge in the vehicles created for Humphrey Bogart and Lauren Bacall and the comedies: *Twentieth Century, Bringing Up Baby* (1938), and *His Girl Friday. Twentieth Century* has John Barrymore, amusingly self-conscious in his hamming, as a Broadway producer who must woo his former wife, Carole Lombard, into signing a contract before their Chicago train reaches Grand Central Station. In such a setting, hysterics and deceit become permissible behavior. *Bringing Up Baby* sets Katherine Hepburn as eccentric debutante against a staid museum scientist, Cary Grant; a pet leopard becomes confused with a wild one escaped from the circus. Breaking down Grant's pompous reserve, Hepburn surrenders the antic behavior resulting from her own social conceits at the same time.

In *To Have and Have Not* and *The Big Sleep,* Hawks surrounds the sex relationship with adventure and murder-detection, but the Bogart-Bacall fulcrum rests on power. Designing *To Have and Have Not,* the director is said to have advised Bogart of his intention to create a woman more insolent than the actor himself. The wit has an aggressive bite, each partner vying for position. In fact, an irrelevant dialogue sequence was written into *The Big Sleep* after its completion further to sharpen the sparring. In a night club scene, Bogart and Bacall are discussing horse racing. Bacall explains how she likes to be ridden. The dialogue serves to provide thinly-disguised sexual jostling and to equate that banter to power relationships.

Howard Hawks (1896–1977)

The Road to Glory	1926
A Girl in Every Port	1928
Trent's Last Case	1929
Dawn Patrol	1930
The Criminal Code	1931
Scarface	1932
Tiger Shark	1932
Viva Villa!	1934
Twentieth Century	1934
The Road to Glory	1936
Ceiling Zero	1936
Bringing Up Baby	1938
Only Angels Have Wings	1939
His Girl Friday	1939
Sergeant York	1941
Ball of Fire	1941
To Have and Have Not	1944
The Big Sleep	1946
Red River	1948
A Song is Born	1948
I Was a Male War Bride	1949
Monkey Business	1952
Gentlemen Prefer Blondes	1953
Land of the Pharaohs	1955
Rio Bravo	1959
Hatari!	1962
El Dorado	1967
Rio Lobo	1970
Partial listing	

Hawks' westerns come closest to reconciling his various aptitudes, for they usually contain humor and the development of male-female relationships within formula locations and shoot outs. *Red River* (1948) traces a cattle drive from Texas to Missouri. Father (John Wayne) and surrogate son (Montgomery Clift) fall out. Their final showdown resolves amicably (and rather ridiculously) when Clift's girlfriend stops the fight. The relationship between the men on the cattle drive is carefully worked into patterns of shifting alliances depending in part on issues (some desert the overly demanding Wayne), partly on loyalties, partly on skill (who can draw or fight the best). Slipping in and out of genre is done for effect, particularly in the Wayne part, which contrasts vengeful indignation at having his cattle taken from him against expectations of loyalty that reveal a certain attractive, human vulnerability.

Rio Bravo (1959) casts Wayne again as a sheriff. Supported only by the aid of a cripple and a drunk, he is obliged to secure a prisoner from rescue by his gang. Feathers (Angie Dickenson) proves her mettle by helping Wayne escape capture. The reform of Martin, the drunk, and the Wayne-Dickenson relation are unstable elements here, like the issue of whether a new gunfighter may prove to be more skillful than Martin. *Rio Bravo* bears interesting comparison with Sternberg's *Underworld,* from which Feather's name, some of the plot situations (e.g., both openings) and much of the three main characterizations derive.[2]

Rio Bravo. "In 1958, Jack Warner asked me what I wanted to do, and I said, 'Make a western,' and he said, 'Oh, no.' And I said, 'O.K., I'll go make it for some other place,' and he said, 'No, make it here, but do you really think you can make it work?' I said, 'I'm going to make it the exact opposite from the way they're making westerns today.' They were making westerns like *High Noon* with Gary Cooper. He plays a sheriff who runs around like a chicken with his head cut off, trying to get everybody to help him and finally his Quaker wife saves him. That isn't a sheriff. If a sheriff is any good and somebody comes and asks him if they can help him, he says, 'How good are you? Can you go up against the best man they've got?' and if you said, 'No,' he'd say, 'Stay out of it; I'd just have to carry you.' " Howard Hawks. (Museum of Modern Art/Film Stills Archive)

---

[2] *Likenesses between* Underworld, Rio Bravo, *and* To Have and Have Not *can be accounted for by the presence of scriptwriter Jules Furthman on all projects. Such evidence seriously puts into question the concept of the director's primacy in film authorship. Some issues of plot in the three films are examined in John L. Fell, "Vladimir Propp in Hollywood,"* Film Quarterly *(Spring 1977). For a contrary opinion on Furthman, see Richard Corliss,* Talking Pictures *(Woodstock, N.Y., 1974), pp. 268-69.*

ALFRED HITCHCOCK

Hitchcock entered film as a designer of title cards; he made his first silent feature, *The Pleasure Garden* (1925) in Ufa facilities in Munich, then did the first British talkie, *Blackmail* (1929). Originally, *Blackmail* was silent but, with foreknowledge of sound's imminence, it was reconceived in process with dialogue. Off camera, an English actress spoke the lines of the leading lady, Anny Ondra, into a microphone as Ondra mimed the same speech.

Blackmail concerns a detective's girlfriend who commits a crime he must investigate. The theme is characteristic Hitchcock and his explanation of the film's conception gives some sense of the director's organizational strategy.

The hazy pattern one saw beforehand was duty – love – love versus duty – and finally either duty or love, one or the other. The whole middle section was built up on the theme of love versus duty, after duty and love had been introduced separately in turn. So I had first to put on the screen an episode expressing duty.[3]

Hitchcock experimented with "impressionistic" sound, heard distortedly by the heroine. More precedent setting was the climax in the British Museum. Hitchcock draws on establishment landmarks against which to stage his confrontations, as if the world were an impassive witness to the melodrama. In contrast to the American films, Hitchcock's British work profits from a sharp-eyed perception of class behaviors and relationships; on his return to England after many years, the talent reemerges in *Frenzy* (1972).

Sean O'Casey's *Juno and the Paycock*

(1930) was made with Dublin's Abbey Theater Players and was largely a documentation of the play that is notable for the actors' performance. *Murder* (1930) was a thriller with theater and circus background; *The Skin Game* (1931) and *Rich and Strange* (1932) comedy-dramas of manners.

Mid-thirties Hitchcocks show a refinement in the murder thriller, usually with espionage overtones. Itself a British genre, the form requires innocent, middle-class figures to be accidentally drawn into a web of spies and underground hostilities. *The Man Who Knew Too Much* (1935), *The Thirty-Nine Steps* (1936), *Secret Agent* (1936), *Sabotage* (1937), and *The Lady Vanishes* (1938) introduce to the genre contrivances on which Hitchcock played variations for the next forty years.

Unlike the mystery, the Hitchcock films reveal, indeed require, a villain's identity. From such prescience suspense is engendered. The plot confirms from the start the inevitability of an act that the hero must perform, thus thwarting the intrigue. A foreign diplomat will be assassinated in the Royal Albert Hall at the moment of a cymbal clash during the concert he is attending. Such classic Hitchcock, enacted in both versions of *The Man Who Knew Too Much* (1935, 1955), titillates by maneuvering the audience skillfully toward the moment of anticipated catastrophe. In *Sabotage,* a boy travels across London carrying a film case. He is unaware that it contains an activated time bomb, but we know.

The director's good-natured deflation of his own melodrama is available to the knowing spectator. Spies in *The Secret Agent* are provided with headquarters in a Swiss chocolate factory. In the opening of *The Thirty-Nine Steps,* a woman asks Robert Donat to take her home with him. "Well, it's your funeral," Donat says, and by early morning she has expired with a knife in her back.

Hitchcock films are peopled with false leads, false suspects, false motives; action is propelled by some tangible fragment of infor-

[3] *Alfred Hitchcock, "Direction (1937)," in Charles Davy, ed.,* Footnotes to the Film *(London, 1937).*

Alfred Hitchcock (1899-   )

Always Tell your Wife (codirector Seymour Hicks)	1922
The Pleasure Garden	1925
The Lodger	1926
The Ring	1927
The Manxman	1929
Blackmail	1929
Juno and the Paycock	1930
Murder	1930
The Skin Game	1931
Rich and Strange	1932
The Man Who Knew Too Much	1935
The Thirty-Nine Steps	1936
The Secret Agent	1936
Sabotage/A Woman Alone	1937
Young and Innocent/A Girl Was Young	1938
The Lady Vanishes	1938
Jamaica Inn	1940
The Foreign Correspondent	1940
Rebecca	1940
Mr. and Mrs. Smith	1941
Suspicion	1942
Saboteur	1943
Shadow of a Doubt	1943
Lifeboat	1945
Spellbound	1946
Notorious	1947
The Paradine Case	1948
Rope	1949
Under Capricorn	1951
Strangers on a Train	1954
Dial M for Murder	1954
Rear Window	1954
To Catch a Thief	1955
The Man Who Knew Too Much	1955
The Trouble with Harry	1956
The Wrong Man	1957
Vertigo	1958
North by Northwest	1959
Psycho	1960
The Birds	1963
Marnie	1964
Torn Curtain	1966
Topaz	1969
Frenzy	1973
Family Plot	1976

Partial listing

mation that focuses the quest, what Hitchcock terms the Maguffin. An English governess in *The Lady Vanishes* drinks a particular brand of tea, and a short Balkan folk melody threads the story. The hero of *The Thirty-Nine Steps* is haunted by a tune he heard in a music hall and seeks a man with a missing finger joint. The tangibility of elements on which audience foreknowledge is based is wittily embodied in *The Girl was Young* (1938), known in the United States as *Young and Innocent*. Hero and heroine seek a man who blinks in nervous spasms. She and a cooperating witness are dancing in a crowded room. In a virtuoso boom execution, the camera moves from a long shot of all the environment down and in, past tables and floor to center on the drummer of the blackface band. In closeup he blinks furiously. English Hitchcocks display his bag of tricks and hint at overlays of innocence and guilt that will add moral dimension to the American versions yet to come.

Hitchcock is in the curious position of a director who has chosen to make the kinds of films to which lesser men are generally assigned: murder and spy stories. He signed his first Hollywood contract in 1939, wooed finally by Selznick to do a Titanic story. Instead, he directed an atypical *Rebecca* (1940). Since then, a comedy, *Mr. and Mrs. Smith* (1941) and the Australian-set *Under Capricorn* (1949) have been Hitchcock's only excursions away from the usual generic path.

Of all directors in America, Hitchcock most effectively unwinds the yarn so that plot and character follow predestined roles, simultaneously misleading and satisfying audience expectations. Casting in a Hitchcock film often employs an actor's image to confuse the audience. The actor chosen to portray a villain, for example, may have a more charming image than the actor chosen as the hero. Hitchcock stars augment generic conventions with their own. A Cary Grant or James Stewart brings a history of earlier films into each new assignment, although it is difficult to include moral guilt as an element in their images which spoils the endings of such works as *Suspicion* (1942) and the British silent *The Lodger* (1926).

Pervasive themes and preoccupations run through Hitchcock productions. Apparent guilt is based on misunderstandings that society and its agents of authority, the police, quickly infer, but a deeper personal sense of misdeed may underlie all the appearances. A Hitchcock protagonist is himself pursued and must solve a problem to establish his innocence, like Cary Grant in *North By Northwest* (1959), who, in hopes of clearing himself, travels the country looking for a man who does not exist, one invented by federal authorities.

Often the hero is subject to infirmity, a broken leg in *Rear Window* (1954), or personal foibles, the urge to "cure" in *Marnie* (1964). Such dispositions give contrary impulses to motive, and a climax requires the hero to confront both exterior enemy and himself. While this takes place, Hitchcock is also having fun with his own inventions: cuing the spectator, often on second viewing, with the whole contrivance, as when Anthony Perkins confides, "Mother's not quite herself tonight" to Janet Leigh early in *Psycho* (1960). Hitchcock toyed with, but rejected, the thought of having Cary Grant and Eva Marie Saint subject to sneezing fits when hiding in the nose of a Mount Rushmore president in *North By Northwest*.

Sex relations in Hitchcock may be openly (lengthy kisses) yet ambiguously stated. Suspicion figures essentially in plot turns because either party's ability to place her trust in a partner further convolutes the question of where evil will be finally unmasked. A characteristic heroine is blonde, cool, and disdainful, yet seething with erotic juices. In *The Birds* (1963) Tipi Hedron steps out of role, actually pursuing Rod Taylor, and her behavior seems obscurely connected with the birds' turning on mankind. Retribution in Hitchcock is inevitable, often unbearably disproportionate to the crime, like Janet Leigh's shower death in *Psycho*.

There is a voyeuristic quality in Hitchcock, shared with his audience so that we become party to a character's guilty secret. The subject is central in *Rear Window* and implicit in many other films. Sometimes it figures in the detailed exposition of behavior that seems to depart from the plot as when Perkins cleans up after his mother in *Psycho* or Paul Newman faces a series of unexpected practical difficulties to killing a man violently in *Torn Curtain* (1966).

The Hitchcock world is paranoid and untrustworthy especially when it is most reassuring. A landscape of windmills in *Foreign Correspondent* (1940) shows on examination that one runs backward. Hitchcock's is a world of chance as well, the director a jovial, deist god. In the remake of *The Man Who Knew Too Much*, a bus swerves, a little boy accidentally pulls the veil from a woman's face, and this promotes a conversation with someone who will figure ominously later on. In *North By Northwest*, Cary Grant calls for a bellboy at the moment the bellboy is paging Mr. Kaplan, which leads foreign agents to believe that Grant is Kaplan, who does not really exist.

Such manipulations derive from tight production, so closely scripted and designed that problems of composition, pace and continuity have been resolved long before their literal execution in shooting. Hitchcock brings imaginative sophistication to the employment of color as when James Stewart and Kim Novak first kiss in *Vertigo*. The camera takes a near 360° arc about the pair while a light coming through a window changes hue to emotionalize the experience for Stewart, the background recalling an earlier moment between the pair. Special effects are used to sensationalize catastrophe. A passenger plane crashes into the sea in *Foreign Correspondent* and we are astonished to see water plunging through the pilot's window in one uninterrupted shot.

Vertigo (1958). "Actually I have been quoted as saying all stars are cattle, which I believe they are in a nice way. They're really children and need nurturing. . . . It's a very funny profession, really. You know, a man has to put paint and powder on his face and, shall we say, strut his wares—gaze in faces, you know." Alfred Hitchcock (Museum of Modern Art/Film Stills Archive)

The Hitchcock universe has characteristics of the comic strip, not only in terms of composition, form, and subject, but because nothing is wasted. Every economical brush stroke is used either to lead or mislead. There is no unnecessary or overabundant "reality." Sensing this, we suspect from the outset that everything has meaning. In consequence, we hold it all under suspicion.

Alfred Hitchcock   **241**

JOHN HUSTON

John Huston alternates between incisive plots whose momentum does not disfigure subtle characterization and commercial assignments that anger some viewers because they seem to indicate Huston's noncommitment. Huston entered Hollywood as a screenwriter and did *Jezebel* (1938) for William Wyler, *Juarez* (1939) for William Dieterle, and *High Sierra* for Raoul Walsh.

John Huston (1906–   )

The Maltese Falcon	1941
Across the Pacific	1942
Report from the Aleutians (documentary)	1943
The Battle of San Pietro (documentary)	1944
Let There Be Light (documentary)	1946
The Treasure of the Sierra Madre	1948
Key Largo	1948
The Asphalt Jungle	1950
The Red Badge of Courage	1951
The African Queen (British)	1951
Moulin Rouge (British)	1952
Beat the Devil (British/Italian)	1953
Moby Dick	1956
The Roots of Heaven	1958
The Misfits	1961
Freud	1962
The List of Adrian Messenger	1963
The Night of the Iguana	1964
The Bible (Italy)	1966
Reflections in a Golden Eye	1967
The Kremlin Letter	1969
The Life and Times of Judge Roy Bean	1972
Fat City	1972
The Mackintosh Man	1974
The Man Who Would Be King	1976
Partial listing	

Closely faithful to Dashiell Hammett's novel, *The Maltese Falcon* (1941) has survived because of its actors' supple identification with their roles; Peter Lorre, Sidney Greenstreet, Barton MacClane, and Ward Bond exist as definitively as Bogart's Spade and Mary Astor's Brigid. The experience of viewing an earlier version of *The Maltese Falcon* made in 1931, may leave a viewer outraged to see Bebe Daniels, say, "impersonating" Mary Astor. Huston elicits similarly keen performances from Tim Holt in *The Treasure of the Sierra Madre* (1948) and John Dierkes, the Tall Soldier, in *The Red Badge of Courage* (1951).

Huston's failures unreasonably disappoint because of our expectations. *The Roots of Heaven* (1958) and *The List of Adrian Messenger* (1963) seem not so much inadequate as incomplete, films that might have been different. Much of Huston's successful conception is touched by Hemingwayesque portrayals of grace under pressure when it succeeds, like the Katherine Hepburn English spinster, Rose, in *The African Queen* (1951) and Clark Gable in *The Misfits* (1961). Humphrey Bogart's cowardly flight in *Beat the Devil* (1953) satirizes the esthetic. *Fat City* (1972) and *The Man Who Would Be King* (1976) suggest that age has allowed John Huston a maturity to infiltrate characters' pristine motives with increasing irony.

FRITZ LANG

While Lang's German films often pitted criminal figures against the institutionalized police, his American ventures substitute accident and environmental pressures for purposeful law-breaking as the plot-generating forces of the films. The Lang protagonist is pursued as in a nightmare in *You Only Live Once* (1937), lit-

Key Largo (1948). Humphrey Bogart, Claire Trevor, and Lauren Bacall. "Who am I?" Trevor asked Huston. "You're the kind of a dame," he said, "whose elbows are always a little too big. Your voice is a little too loud. You're a little too polite. You're very sad, very resigned." (Copyright © 1948 Warner Bros. Pictures, Inc. Copyright renewed 1975.) (Museum of Modern Art/Film Stills Archive)

erally a nightmare in *The Woman in the Window* (1944). He is subject to a mob's violence in *Fury* (1936) and the victim of passions beyond his control in *Scarlet Street* (1945).

The director spent a year in Culver City learning English and studying production. His separation from Germany suggests that Lang underwent a self-reappraisal of his cultural allegiances and human values, and many of his American films have critical and reformist views about social conditions. His expressionist vision sees the individual oppressed by pressures of conformity or by an inexorable universe, and, in his films, this translates into plots in which a protagonist is likely to be condemned to failure and destruction.

Such dispositions, imposed on genre westerns and crime stories and glossed with Lang's technical skills provide curiously convoluted work that veers from posture to posture without always integrating a coherent view. Lang operates most effectively when, as in *The Big Heat* (1953), a reformer's drive to expose big city corruption, abetted by a bad-girl-turned-good, encases the director's allegiances in a form with which he is comfortable.

ERNST LUBITSCH

With sound, Lubitsch discovered yet more fertile fields for his displaced, European comedy, enhanced now with clever, frivolous dialogue. He developed a series of musicals, more often comedies with song interludes, which numbered among the early innovative employments of sound. *The Love Parade* (1929) was Lubitsch's first Maurice Chevalier film and introduced Jeannette MacDonald, a mixed blessing. Set in mythic Lylvania, it involves a prince consort who overcomes the regal domination of his queen to win both her love and her subservience, while maid and valet parody the state of regal affairs. Rather than using his camera in strict, synchronous liaison with the sound source in the manner of Busby Berkeley, Lubitsch plays with his operetta format with flowing visuals. The location is party to the music, rather than merely serving as a stage set for a singer. A palace dog, for example, barks a coda to one song. In their early-reversed roles, MacDonald sings a rousing military song in one section of the castle while Chevalier sleeps in another wing.

Monte Carlo (1930) repeats the formula with even greater imaginative attention to sound-picture relationships. The finale involves MacDonald and Chevalier separated in space but simultaneously singing "Beyond the Blue Horizon" as she approaches him in a train. Unmotivated singing, especially performed with fervor on film, always borders on the ludicrous. This time the humor is compounded by Lubitsch's very conception. The engine's chugging and the rattling tracks enter into the number with sound effect synchronicity, as if the earth itself had suddenly elected to share the Richard Whiting tune, MacDonald joyfully belting its lyric out the window to rows of jolly peasants who chorus back.

After these musicals, Lubitsch made an uncharacteristic military drama, *The Man I Killed* (1932), also known as *Broken Lullaby.*

The story is set after the war and involves a French boy who is guilt-ridden at having killed a German during the hostilities. He visits the dead boy's father, is accepted by the family, and elects to remain there without betraying his secret. While speeches, motives, and story are difficult to accept, Lubitsch's orchestration of effects in the film's introduction is powerful. The armistice has been declared. Cathedral bells sound victory. A parade is viewed between the leg and crutch of an amputated veteran. In a church, uniformed soldiers kneel to receive the priest's sanction of their deeds, and the camera tracks down rows of swords and spurs that sparkle under light pouring through stained glass windows. Outside, guns shoot in celebration, and the explosions supply a transition to a convalescent hospital where a frightened soldier starts up in bed and cries out.

MacDonald and Chevalier returned in *One Hour With You* (1932), a musical version of *The Marriage Circle*. The same year Lubitsch produced one of his best comedies, *Trouble in Paradise*. A pair of swindlers enter the employment of a rich widow, the man falls in love with her but, for the sake of everyone's well-being, elects to return to his accomplice, whom he has decided he loves anyway. The dialogue is brilliant, mixing with its humor a thorough irony that views mankind, at least the wealthy and thieves, as altogether without integrity, each a charming proof of the fatal demands social institutions impose on human possibility. To view a film like *Trouble in Paradise* is to realize what skill and care are required to sustain an impression of lightness and shallow ease.

Throughout his career, Lubitsch continued with comedies, sometimes skirting drama as in *Angel* (1937) and *The Shop around the Corner* (1940), sometimes finding humor in politics as in *Ninotchka* (1939), and even in the gestapo as in *To Be Or Not To Be* (1942). *The Merry Widow* (1934) bears interesting comparison to Stroheim's version. While each departs from the operatic original to concen-

Ninotchka (left). Garbo arrives in Paris to confront the apprehensive Soviet agents. *Silk Stockings* (right). This time Cyd Charisse interviews the trio, Peter Lorre on left.

Ninotchka: How much does this cost?
Iranoff: Two thousand francs.
Ninotchka: A week?
Iranoff: A day.
Ninotchka: Do you know how much a cow costs, Comrade Iranoff?
Iranoff: A cow?
Ninotchka: Two thousand francs. If I stay here a week I will cost the Russian people seven cows. Who am I to cost the Russian people seven cows?
(Movie Star News)

trate on the sexual ironies, Stroheim's vision maintains an implicit outrage at the decadence he so enjoys enacting, while Lubitsch allows nothing to offend him because he operates from no ground of moral judgment. Chevalier's sexual prowess is funny because no one takes it seriously, he least of all.

The last major Lubitsch success was *Ninotchka,* a story of a Soviet worker dispatched to France to discipline and coordinate the errant behavior of three earlier agents. Like her predecessors, Ninotchka (Garbo) is corrupted by Paris. She falls in love with a capitalist. If one does not find the director's approach to politics opportunistically simple, the film has immense charm, highlighted by Garbo at her most relaxed. She said that Lubitsch was the only great director she ever worked with in Hollywood.

Rouben Mamoulian (1898–   )

Applause	1929
City Streets	1931
Dr. Jekyll and Mr. Hyde	1931
Love Me Tonight	1932
The Song of Songs	1933
Queen Christina	1933
We Live Again	1934
Becky Sharp	1935
The Gay Desperado	1936
High, Wide and Handsome	1937
Golden Boy	1939
The Mark of Zorro	1940
Blood and Sand	1941
Rings on Her Fingers	1942
Summer Holiday	1948
The Wild Heart (replaced Michael Powell but uncredited)	1951
Silk Stockings	1957
Porgy and Bess (replaced by Otto Preminger)	1959
Cleopatra (replaced by Joseph Mankiewicz)	1963

ROUBEN MAMOULIAN

A Russian émigré, Mamoulian's preparation for sound rested in operatic and stage work. A 1927 nonmusical theatrical *Porgy* presaged his later skills in the employment of noises, as distinguished from speech. The beats of a shifting rhythmic prelude were made up of morning sounds, like a shoemaker, a knife sharpener, and a woman cleaning rugs.

Mamoulian's first film assignment was *Applause* (1929), a backstage soap opera about a burlesque queen's sacrifices for her daughter. Enhanced by the performance of Helen Morgan as the aging mother, *Applause* overcomes many camera-sound limitations by restoring both camera movement and some of the conciseness and economy of silent editing. Until then, sound tracks were mixed and balanced by separately miked sources at the time of shooting. By mixing tracks that were first recorded on different reels of sound film, Mamoulian helped to unchain the camera, which had until than been held a slave to sound-stage necessities.

City Streets (1931), is based on a Dashiell Hammett story, and uses an underworld setting but proves more humanly dramatic than criminal-genre in tone. It marks Mamoulian's excursion into sound as subjective experience, like Hitchcock's *Blackmail.* In prison, a girl "hears" her absent boyfriend's voice expressed in unrealistic speech pattern. The technique has not stood the test of time, but other sequences still work, punctuating swift continuities with economic, well-spaced dialogue, as when a gangland killing is planned and executed with no speech except for idiomatic mumblings which bridge time gaps between the scenes.

Dr. Jekyll and Mr. Hyde (1931) carries subjectivity into the visual realm by way of its lengthy opening, all photographed as if from Jekyll's eyes. The Murnau-Mayer-Freund idiom is strengthened here by conversations

Applause. Runway of the burlesque house where Helen Morgan shares the stage with aging dancers to entertain aging men. The determination of Morgan's daughter to follow in her footsteps leads the mother to suicide. (Museum of Modern Art/Film Stills Archive)

between Hyde and, successively, a butler, a policeman, and doormen. Before his mirror, the doctor sees himself as he dons a hat and cloak, and the sequence progresses from Jekyll's study where he is practicing a Bach fugue on the organ, out to a waiting coach, down cobbled London streets, and into a vast lecture hall. Jekyll commences to lecture, and at his opening salutation the camera, which has arced about the room, cuts to the audience's point of view and we view Frederic March for the first time "objectively." Mamoulian intensified the visuals of the unedited

transformation scene by filming March's face in an apparently continuous camera take, and by building an accompanying sound track out of his own heartbeats, a gong played backward to reverse reverberations, and sounds synthesized by painting directly on the optical sound track.

Love Me Tonight (1932) was Mamoulian's variation on Lubitsch's MacDonald-Chevalier musicals, casting the same stars in a Paris story. In playful acknowledgment of *Monte Carlo,* Mamoulian ends his film with a brilliant sequence that has MacDonald on horseback racing to a railroad track where she faces down an oncoming train in order to reunite with her lover. Again, all the earth, including requisite fieldside peasants, bursts into song; Mamoulian's version additionally parodies melodramatic rescues and Eisensteinian editing effects with its pastiche of rails, wheels, hooves, and exhuberant vocalizing.

The Song of Songs (1933) and *Queen Christina* (1933) successively pair Mamoulian with Marlene Dietrich and Greta Garbo. While Dietrich is somewhat more humanized than Sternberg allowed, the narrative progresses from the unlikely (Dietrich as shy and innocent country girl) to the expected (Dietrich, corrupted, singing in a Berlin nightclub). Her very artificiality has its own charm when we watch the actress assume this and that emotion as if trying on the clothes she wears so well. Since the story involves a nude statue of Dietrich, it is even possible that the conceit of costume changes, identical to the conceit of changing roles, underlays the Mamoulian conception.

Queen Christina's furniture-stroking bedroom sequence, in which Garbo commits the room to memory so that it may sustain her in years to come, was filmed to a metronome, the actress rhythmically choreographed to movements and pauses. The conclusion is another tour-de-force: Garbo on shipboard, staring ahead while the audience accumulates all that has brought her to this state and the bleak future she faces. Mamoulian recounted:

Garbo asked me, "What do I play in this scene?" Remember, she is standing there for 150 feet of film, 90 of them in a closeup. I said, "Have you heard of *tabula rasa?* I want your face to be a blank sheet of paper. I want the writing to be done by every member of the audience. I'd like it if you could avoid even blinking your eyes, so that you're nothing but a beautiful mask." So in fact there is *nothing* on her

face; but everyone who has seen the film will tell you that she is thinking and feeling, and always it's something different.[4]

In *Becky Sharp* (1935), Mamoulian was the first director to investigate at feature length three-color Technicolor's resources. He used color toward narrative effect in a ballroom sequence when guests leave under the threat of battle. Costumes were cued to exit, so that blacks and whites, browns, blues, greens, yellows, oranges and finally reds trace a spectrum of mounting intensity, allying history to the personal fates of the players, for the nearby fighting is the first skirmishes of Waterloo. Becky Sharp's costumes correspond throughout to her self-advancing strategies.[5]

Golden Boy (1939) valiantly fights but finally succumbs to the rhetoric of Clifford Odets. ("Be glad you're rid of him. You're free. Now you can go back to yourself, to your music. Nothing can stop you when you do what's in your heart.") *The Mark of Zorro* (1940) fails to surpass or to supply an alternative to Fairbank's earlier gymnastics. *Blood and Sand* (1941) effectively evokes the color schemes of Goya, Valasquez, and El Greco. *Silk Stockings* (1957), based on the Broadway musical version of *Ninotchka*, again asks comparison with Lubitsch, although the forms are vastly different. Playing Ninotchka, Cyd Charisse invests great emotion in her dancing. Mamoulian's camera sense serves Fred Astaire well. The choreographed routines fit brilliantly into the continuity, as if Astaire were doing a Gene Kelly scenario, an ideal combination.

---

[4] *Tom Milne,* Rouben Mamoulian *(London, 1969), pp. 74-75.*
[5] *As with many early color films, a viewer should be cautioned that dyes fade from early prints, and recent ones, especially when made as a second generation on Eastmancolor or other stock, altogether fail to realize the picture quality of the original.*

LEWIS MILESTONE

Russian born, Milestone worked under Sennett, Henry King, and Thomas Ince. He first directed silent features and established his reputation with *All Quiet on the Western Front* (1930). Production of the pacifist war film was begun silent and preserves in many of its unromanticized battle scenes the freedoms silent film had developed by the end of its period, here scored with artillery and machine-gun sound effects. Sometimes larger than life, performances by Louis Wolheim and Lew Ayres as German soldiers are remarkably underplayed at key moments.

In *The Front Page* (1931), Milestone honed the deliveries of his actors, whose accelerated dialogue established a precedent for later screen journalists in the Hecht-MacArthur opus. Subsequent films were less successful until *The General Died at Dawn* (1936), a Chinese warlord adventure, and *Of Mice and Men* (1939), based on John Steinbeck's novel, which afforded Lon Chaney's son a rare escape from monster makeup.

Much of the later work of Milestone was undistinguished, excepting *A Walk in the Sun* (1945) and *The Strange Love of Martha Ivers* (1946). Both films were written by Robert Rossen, who becomes a director himself. The war movie deals with the Allied Salerno landing, following a platoon into the beachhead. It is marked by unglamorized incident and restrained performance, one of the few American World War II films maintaining a certain amount of integrity, and departing from Milestone's earlier pacifism. *The Strange Love of Martha Ivers* is often noted in sociopsychological studies of forties films for its complexity of national stereotypes (the good/bad girl) and themes of corruptive success and sexual domination. Given the melodrama and coincidence of his story, Milestone sustains credibility admirably until a suicide-confessional-lovers' rejection ending throws it all to the winds.

Lewis Milestone (1895–   )

Seven Sinners	1925
All Quiet on the Western Front	1930
The Front Page	1931
Rain	1932
Hallelujah I'm a Bum	1933
The General Died at Dawn	1936
Of Mice and Men	1939
The North Star	1943
The Purple Heart	1944
A Walk in the Sun	1945
The Strange Love of Martha Ivers	1946
Arch of Triumph	1948
The Red Pony	1949
Les Miserables	1952
Melba	1953
Pork Chop Hill	1959
Mutiny on the Bounty (replacing Carol Reed)	1962
Partial listing	

JOSEF VON STERNBERG

Thunderbolt (1929), Sternberg's first sound venture and another gangster film, used off-screen sound, a technique that was used again in a more complicated manner in *The Blue Angel* (1930), his next production, made in Germany. With the coming of dialogue, the director's inclination toward highly stylized, personal narrative becomes increasingly evident. However criminals speak, they can hardly talk in the contorted idiom of Snapper and Bad Al in *Thunderbolt*. At the same time, Sternberg is learning to punctuate dialogue with actors' movements tuned to the camera rather than by theatrical gesture.

After the success of *The Blue Angel*, Sternberg and his star, Dietrich, embarked on a series of five films for Paramount. Increasingly, the characters in the Paramounts lose their natural dimension and weight. Rather, Dietrich and her male leads become players in Sternbergian worlds that string together high moments of theatrical situation along preposterous story lines. To seek correspondence to known behaviors in these films is to mire in quicksand. The movies bear as much resemblance to naturalism as Bizet's *Carmen* might to a documentary on Spanish cigarette manufacturing.

Morocco (1930) has Dietrich as a night club singer, Gary Cooper a Legionnaire, and Adolphe Menjou a wealthy artist. After requisite rejections and misunderstandings, Dietrich's love for Cooper overpowers everything else and she follows his troop into the desert, running across the sands on three inch heels. Dietrich's cabaret feature is done in top hat, white tie, and tails. She shocks the Moroccan audience by fondling the hair, then planting a kiss full on the face of a young woman at ringside. Thus Sternberg introduces that bisexual, beautifully decadent Dietrich image that he refines in later films. At the same time, Dietrich, like Garbo, suffers for her feelings, for giving way to impulses that only result in pain. *Morocco* marks the first of several collaborations between Sternberg and photographer Lee Garmes. Its unique result is distinguished by long, undarkening, lingering dissolves and extraordinary traveling shots. The face of every American actress of long standing has its characteristic lighting, and Dietrich's is hollowed and smoothed away from her pudgier German image. Morocco itself becomes a studio contrivance built of picture postcard sand dunes and electric fan desert winds; the artificiality suggests style rather than insufficiency.

Dishonored (1931) has Dietrich as a Viennese officer's widow who becomes a prostitute recruited to spy against Austria. Carrying out various assignments, she falls in love with a czarist Russian secret serviceman, Victor McLaglen of all people. She allows him to escape, and is sentenced to execution. When the rifleman refuses to shoot a woman, Dietrich, dressed in the costume of her earlier profession, checks her lipstick. The execution proceeds.

Shanghai Express (1932) is the actress's Shanghai Lily phase, the White Flower of the Chinese Coast, riding from Peking on a train that contains an old flame, Clive Brook, as well as a Chinese rebel leader. Brook is held hostage. Lily offers herself to the rebel in exchange for her lover's freedom. The rebel is stabbed and the couple continue toward Shanghai. In *Blonde Venus* (1932), Dietrich sells herself to Cary Grant to finance medical treatment for Herbert Marshall, her husband. She introduces one night club number in a rather astonishing gorilla costume. *The Devil is a Woman* (1935) is based on the same Pierre Louys novel that Luis Buñuel used in *That Obscure Object of Desire* (1977), although few films could be more different. Dietrich is Concha Perez, a Spaniard who seduces both father and son, finally leaving the younger man for what may or may not be a permanent liaison with his father.

The Scarlet Empress (1934) has Sternberg at the apex of visual flamboyance, posing Dietrich as Catherine II of Russia against Byzantine icons and candelabra to achieve a gargoyled expressionism that exists nowhere else in time and space. Married to an insane, impotent Grand Duke, she distributes her favors to the military with such effect that in crisis their support awards her the monarchy. The director's equation of sex with power here takes the form of palace diplomacy, but the emotional consequences are less often expressed in speech or plot than in the images themselves, as when Duke Peter thrusts a knife toward Catherine that she parries and disposes with a flick of lace. If Dietrich-Sternberg is a specialized pleasure, *The Scarlet Empress* becomes its litmus test.

The Scarlet Empress. Dietrich and Sam Jaffe. Catherine gains the throne after the assassination of Grand Duke Peter, demented son of the Empress Elizabeth. Clothed in a hussar's uniform, Dietrich's requisite male-dress scene is rationalized as symbolic of the power she will assume as ruler. (Movie Star News)

Between Dietrichs, Sternberg made *An American Tragedy* (1931). The artistic meeting of Sternberg and Dreiser led the author to sue Paramount. He lost, but so does the story, which becomes another temptation theme without the eroticism of Dietrich. *Crime and Punishment* (1935) suffered a somewhat similar fate.

Uncompleted, *I, Claudius* (1937) promised to have been one of Sternberg's most effective projects, based on surviving British footage of Charles Laughton as the Roman King. As if silent film had helped to hold his stories in place and Dietrich provided his sound films with an emotional center, two later ventures, *The Shanghai Gesture* (1941) and *The Saga of Anatahan* (1953), have a curious, abstracted quality. Characters are no more than personifications of feeling, acting out a succession of moods that evoke, in various forms, sex, authoritarianism, pride, and longing.

KING VIDOR

His sound ventures uneven, Vidor's successes still remain impressive peaks. *Hallelujah!* (1929) appeared in the same year as *The Love Parade* and *Applause,* beholden to neither. The film combines excellent use of music and sound with sometimes stereotyped characterizations. Using an all-black cast, Vidor's southern story has hand-waving prayer meetings, dice-rolling temptations, sex-incited murder, and a tearful spiritual rebirth. It gains immeasurably from location filming: mass river baptism, cotton fields, and shanty town slums belie easy character motivations.

Nina Mae McKinney, who might have become the first black movie star but for bad luck and an overhealthy ego, plays a vigorous, sensual quasi-prostitute, and blues affecionados are surprised by the somewhat incongruous appearance of Victoria Spivey as a sweet-faced, nineteen-year-old Missy Rose, the long-suffering good girl. Vidor post-synchronized his more difficult sound in the studio, which facilitated both superior quality and expressionist exaggerations, especially in a swamp pursuit with its bird screeches, deep panting, and murky splashes.

Not to be confused with Murnau's film, *Our Daily Bread* (1934) became Vidor's depression statement. Unemployed city dwellers (out of the ethos of *The Crowd*) form a rural co-op and triumph finally over hardship in a climactic scene showing the building of an irrigation project, edited to Eisenstein's notions of rhythmic montage.

Duel in the Sun (1946) revived Vidor's flagging reputation with an emotional, engaging, high-budget improvement on Niven Busch's raunchy novel about lust and murder on a Texas ranch. Clearly, Vidor possessed the skills to mount grandiose projects, and his final films were highly ambitious. *War and Peace* (1955) looks most Russian in its battle scenes. *Solomon and Sheba* (1959) turned to the Bible more for inspiration than plot.

RAOUL WALSH

Walsh entered film as a western heavy and worked as a Griffith assistant in early California days. (He played John Wilkes Booth in *The Birth of a Nation*). Features he directed precede World War I. Walsh was early noted for masculine adventure-action stories, many of which he wrote. Some of his films are better known as vehicles for stars like Errol Flynn, James Cagney, and Humphrey Bogart, but the best of them emerge as somewhat involved studies of male figures whose psychological

Raoul Walsh (1892–   )

The Regeneration	1915
Carmen	1915
The Thief of Bagdad	1924
What Price Glory	1926
The Loves of Carmen	1927
Sadie Thompson	1928
Me, Gangster	1928
In Old Arizona	1929
The Big Trail	1930
The Man Who Came Back	1933
The Bowery	1933
Artists and Models	1937
The Roaring Twenties	1939
They Drive by Night	1940
High Sierra	1941
Strawberry Blonde	1941
They Died With Their Boots On	1941
Gentleman Jim	1942
Background to Danger	1943
Objective, Burma!	1945
The Horn Blows at Midnight	1945
Cheyenne	1947
White Heat	1949
A Lion is in the Street	1953
Battle Cry	1955
The Naked and the Dead	1958
A Distant Trumpet	1964
Partial listing	

complexities and society's pressures have turned into desperate, often antisocial anachronisms. To locate such characterization in a gangster film or western serves to shift codes so that anticipated conventions may take on unexpected meanings. In *High Sierra* (1941), Bogart is a criminal fugitive who faces inevitable death or capture when he has for the first time made himself psychologically vulnerable. Made shortly before *The Maltese Falcon, High Sierra* is interesting as a study of the "Bogart" persona in the process of formation.

White Heat (1949) characterizes James Cagney as a psychopathic gangster, subject to epileptic fits and fixated on his brutish mother. The tensions surface in an extraordinary prison scene where Cagney's usual exuberance finds its outlet in hysterical violence. *White Heat* ends with an apocalyptic shootout on an exploding gas tank whose mushroom cloud symbolism would oppress were Walsh not so down-to-earth a filmmaker.

ORSON WELLES

Approaching Hollywood with skills he developed in theater and radio, Welles integrated elements of each into the motion picture, an intermediary between the first generation of Hollywood directors and a younger group who found its voice during and after the war.

Welles afforded the country expressionist-tinged visions of human power and psychological aberration. He incorporated these into American themes and into an overall view of characters no longer good or bad but increasingly corrupt with age. That conception is recurrent in Welles' work, whether invented in original scripts or skewed into literary adaptations, including the organization of Shakespeare's Falstaff appearances that comprised *Chimes at Midnight* (1966).

Under his RKO contract, Welles brought

A production still from *Citizen Kane*. "I believe it is necessary to give all the characters their best arguments in order that they may defend themselves, including those I disagree with. That's what gives the impression of ambiguity: my being chivalrous to people whose behavior I do not approve of; the characters are ambitious but the significance of the work is not." Orson Welles (Movie Star News)

west a repertory group called the Mercury Theater with which he had worked on radio and Broadway. Actors like Joseph Cotten, Dorothy Comingore, Everett Sloane, Ray Collins, and Agnes Moorehead began in films as Mercury Players. Early plans to do Joseph Conrad's *Heart of Darkness* as a subjective camera experiment were shelved and Welles' first RKO film became *Citizen Kane* (1941).

Kane is so well-known now, so remarked as innovative, that the very study of this film obscures it. The narrative begins with death, and, again like a detective story, investigates the personal life of the long-lived newspaper tycoon to find his "secret." A reporter questions people who knew Charles Foster Kane only to conclude that his life had no explana-

tion or that it could never be known. Clues to which only the film audience is privy suggest that Kane's ruthlessness and impulsiveness may have grown from an early sense of being abandoned.

Citizen Kane is staged with a strong element of theater design and of film's capacities to expose by camera movement, editing, and sound. An often-cited sequence capsulates the relation between Kane and his first wife through a succession of exchanges at the breakfast table. These appear to have the continuity of one conversation but in fact span several years. Elsewhere, Welles adapts the Russian and German stage technique of sequence transition by manipulating light pools; in this case, scenes displace one another in the manner of nineteenth-century vision scenes. Expressionist camera angles, evocative of Murnau's silent period, help to define power relationships. Decor incarnates Kane's emotional states, as when he wanders among the debris of a failed political bid. In cooperation with Gregg Toland, a cinematographer who had performed similar work with John Ford in *The Long Voyage Home* and *The Grapes of Wrath* a year before, Welles combined lighting, a wide-angle lens and set perspective to establish extreme deep-focused compositions. This allowed space to assume additional psychological ramifications, for example, Kane's exaggerated distance from his second wife in the great hall of their castle. Further, the technique enhanced theater-like staging in which foreground-background effects in combination produced a narrative that would ordinarily have been broken into a sequence of separate, closer shots. Welles encouraged his actors to let their speeches overlap one another, and he developed a stylized delivery which, like Lewis Milestone's journelese, carried a sense of natural intonation.

The group turned to *The Magnificent Ambersons* (1942), a Booth Tarkington novel that relates a family's dissolution to the industrialization of its mid-western community. Here, Welles subdues his effects with greater effect. A ball is meticulously choreographed against camera movement so that characters appear, speak, and exit with apparently spontaneous impulse. The town's evolution is quietly demonstrated by changes in exterior backgrounds, vehicles, storefronts, and signs. Although the film differs little from, and only improves upon, Tarkington's ending, its conclusion is hurried and undeveloped. RKO appropriated the unfinished production while Welles was absent on other assignment.

Later Welles work ranges from adventure-melodrama, *Lady From Shanghai* (1947), to Franz Kafka, *The Trial* (1967) and Shakespeare: *Macbeth* (1948), *Othello* (1951), and *Chimes at Midnight*. Whatever the source, Welles redesigns his material into a personal vision. His life is spotted with infrequent assignments because commercial success has always eluded him. Like Stroheim before, Welles sustains himself by acting.

Welles' films often develop an hallucinatory quality, partly because of the expressionist staging (the funhouse sequence of *Lady From Shanghai* easily compares to *Waxworks*), and partly because the stamp of the director's subjectivity on the narrative has the effect of distancing speech and behavior from their apparent base in experience. *Mr. Arkadin* (1963) has something of the quality of the Sternberg-Dietrich Paramounts. To get in touch with this part of Welles, we must defer the uneasy suspicions of contrivance and place our confidence in intentions that are less beholden to

Orson Welles (1915–   )

Citizen Kane	1941
The Magnificent Ambersons	1942
Journey into Fear (credited to Norman Foster)	1942
The Stranger	1946
Lady from Shanghai	1947
Macbeth	1948
Othello (Morocco)	1951
Mr. Arkadin/Confidential Report	1955
Around the World with Orson Welles (Britain TV)	1955
Touch of Evil	1957
The Method (Britain TV documentary)	1958
Voyage to the Country of Don Quixote (Italy TV documentary)	1961
Le Procès/The Trial (France)	1962
Falstaff/Chimes at Midnight (Spain/Switzerland)	1966
Une Histoire immortelle/The Immortal Story	1968
F for Fake	1976

naturalism. Another constant Welles preoccupation has been magic, patterns of illusion that serve ulterior purpose. Arkadin is a further Welles figure who grows old harboring a secret past. He is seen as if in a series of roles, each with qualities of impersonation that are obvious both to himself (Welles) and to the audience. The old man investigates his own history, killing anyone left to bear witness, finally destroying himself because the truth can no longer be withheld from his young daughter.

Touch of Evil (1957) casts Welles as a corrupt police sergeant whose pursuit of justice disguises a pathological sadism. He is finally unmasked by a somewhat pompous Mexican official. Again the exposition has nightmare qualities, characters eccentrically one-dimensional, dialogue bizarrely related to story.

Through the eyes of Marlene Dietrich who plays a bit as a madam, Sergeant Quinlan's guilty secret is that he was once good.

F For Fake (1976) purports to be a documentary-like study of Howard Hughes' fraudulent biographer Clifford Irving, an art forger named Elmyr de Hory, and of Welles himself. At further remove, the film plays on illusion within illusion. Welles appears as a magician, a stage profession he has always enjoyed. Irving is purportedly Hory's biographer. Hory signs Welles' name to one of his works. Welles tells the audience, "I promised to tell you the truth for an hour, but for the past seventeen minutes I've been lying my head off." The film incorporates documentary footage by French filmmaker François Reichenbach, but we cannot be confident that this material is used the way it was intended. *F For Fake* is a meditation on film's untrustworthiness as witness to anything beyond itself. In a short film made for French television, *The Immortal Story* (1968), Welles plays an aging businessman who concocts a series of real events in order to make a fictive story he has heard really come true. His success is partial, like Welles' own film career.

WILLIAM WELLMAN

Although films in his later career never seemed to fulfill the early promise, Wellman was comfortable with a range of material and specially accomplished in *Wings* (1927) with its spectacularly photographed aerial dogfights. He succeeded, too, with gangster-depression era stories. The feel of *Public Enemy* (1931) is dated by studio sound, although the same aspect seems to afford the film a period authenticity as well. *Wild Boys of the Road* (1933) oversimplifies a story of teenagers who become depression vagabonds, but develops a sharply-drawn vagrant atmosphere as well as sympathy for the boys when

illiam Wellman (1896–   )

Wings	1927
Public Enemy	1931
Wild Boys of the Road	1933
The President Vanishes	1934
Stingaree	1934
Call of the Road	1935
A Star is Born	1937
Nothing Sacred	1937
Beau Geste	1939
The Light That Failed	1939
The Great Man's Lady	1941
The Ox-Bow Incident	1943
The Story of GI Joe	1945
The Iron Curtain	1948
Battleground	1949
Yellow Sky	1949
The Next Voice You Hear	1951
Across the Wide Missouri	1951
The High and the Mighty	1954
Track of the Cat	1954
Blood Alley	1956
Lafayette Escadrille	1958
Partial listing	

Public Enemy. James Cagney acts out three prototypical gangster film conventions: the new suit which evidences his initiation into the mob (top); riding shotgun on a haul of contraband goods (middle); the intimidation of a bar owner (bottom). (Museum of Modern Art/Film Stills Archive)

they are attacked by police. *The President Vanishes* (1934) makes a taut mystery melodrama from a political tale in which war is averted by a brave leader who employs what now appear to be very questionable methods to fight local fascism.

The Ox-Bow Incident (1943) slips into the idiom of a "literary" film, as if its painted exteriors were fashioned from the novel's book jacket, but *Track of the Cat* (1954), another adaptation, sustains. *Nothing Sacred* (1937) is one of the best of the screwball comedies. Carole Lombard has a field day as a Vermont woman who first wins New York City's heart, then prompts its morbid impatience by pretending to be bravely facing death from an incurable disease.

William Wyler (1902–   )

Anybody Here Seen Kelly?	1928
Counselor at Law	1933
Dodsworth	1936
These Three	1936
Dead End	1937
Jezabel	1938
Wuthering Heights	1939
The Westerner	1940
The Letter	1940
The Little Foxes	1941
Mrs. Miniver	1942
The Memphis Belle	1943
The Fighting Lady	1944
The Best Years of Our Lives	1946
The Heiress	1949
Detective Story	1951
Carrie	1952
Roman Holiday	1953
The Desperate Hours	1955
The Big Country	1958
Ben Hur	1959
The Children's Hour	1962
The Collector	1965
Funny Girl	1968
Partial listing	

WILLIAM WYLER

Like others in human history, William Wyler entered Hollywood by way of relatives: his uncle was Carl Laemmle, Uncle Carl to many. Unlike many, Wyler proved his talent after working through minor assignments, until the mid-thirties when he took full advantage of three Lillian Hellman properties: two plays, *These Three* (1936) and *The Little Foxes* (1941); one an adaptation, *Dead End* (1937).

Wyler's strengths have rested in a capacity to adapt theater pieces and fictions to the screen, preserving the integrity of his sources while affording them reasonable autonomy as movies. *The Best Years of Our Lives* (1946) combined sentimentality, liberal sympathy, and some understanding of problems faced by returning servicemen. *The Little Foxes, Jezabel* (1938), and *The Letter* (1940) convincingly develop, through employments of Bette Davis' hothouse emotions. Wyler's relation to warhorses and to major capital investments like *Ben Hur* (1959) and *Funny Girl* (1968) should not mitigate his earlier accomplishment.

Summary

The principal directing figures in Hollywood's sound era have shown remarkable longevity, and, Welles and von Sternberg excepted, output. Some, like Capra and Hitchcock, personally shaped generic formulas. More broadly, Ford and Hawks apply ethical designs onto diverse materials. Such figures may profitably be considered in terms of their individual relations with studios and with production heads such as Harry Cohn, for each man evolved a strategy which allowed him to effect some appreciable personal control on assigned projects. At the same time, we ought to be wary that distortion can accompany undue emphases on the commerical film as an expression of highly individual values. In many respects, the most effective Hollywood sound directors were most like the culture to which they catered. Chapter 11 describes European and Russian accomplishments with early sound narrative.

Bibliography

"Alfred Hitchcock: A Friendly Salute." *Take One* 5 (1976).

Auriol, Jean-George. "Chez Ernst." *Cahiers du Cinéma in English* 9 (March 1967).

Baxter, John. *The Cinema of John Ford*. New York, 1971.

Bazin, André. *Orson Welles*. Paris, 1972.

Belton, John. *Howard Hawks*. New York, 1974.

Bellour, Raymond. "On Fritz Lang." *Sub-Stance* 9 (1974).

Bessy, Maurice. *Orson Welles*. New York, 1971.

Bogdonovich, Peter. *The Cinema of Orson Welles*. New York, 1965.

———. *Fritz Lang in America*. London, 1968.

———. *John Ford*. Berkeley, 1968.

Brantley, Robin. "What Makes a Star?" *New York Times*, Sunday January 22, 1978.

Cameron, Ian. "Suspense and Meaning," In *Movie Reader,* by Ian Cameron. New York, 1972.

Canham, Kingsley. *Lewis Milestone.* New York, 1974.

Capra, Frank. *The Name Above the Title.* New York, 1971.

Carey, Gary. *Cukor and Co.* New York, 1971.

Clark, Paul Sergeant. "Hitchcock's Finest Hour." *Today's Film Maker,* November 1972.

Cobos, Juan. "A Voyage to Don Quixoteland." *Cahiers du Cinéma in English* 5 (1966).

Cowie, Peter. *The Cinema of Orson Welles.* New York, 1965.

———. *A Ribbon of Dreams.* South Brunswick, N.J., 1973.

Davis, Paxton. "Bogart, Hawks in *The Big Sleep.*" *The Film Journal,* Summer 1971.

Dickens, Homer. *The Films of Marlene Dietrich.* New York, 1968.

Durgnat, Raymond. "Six Films of Josef von Sternberg," In *Movie Reader,* by Ian Cameron. New York, 1972.

———. "Hawks Isn't Good Enough." *Film Comment,* July-August 1977.

Dynia, Philip. "Alfred Hitchcock and the Ghost of Thomas Hobbes." *Cinema Journal,* Spring 1976.

Feinstein, Herbert. "Interview with Lewis Milestone." *Film Culture* 34 (1964).

Gallagher, Tag. "John Ford: Midway." *Film Comment,* September–October 1975.

Gili, Jean. *Howard Hawks.* Paris, 1971.

Glatzer, Richard and John Raeburn. *Frank Capra: The Man and His Films.* Ann Arbor, 1975.

Gottesman, Ronald, ed. *Focus on Citizen Kane.* Englewood Cliffs, N.J., 1971.

Hardiquet, Philippe. *John Ford.* Paris, 1966.

Hardy, Phil, ed. *Raoul Walsh.* Edinburgh Film Festival, 1974.

Hawks, Howard. "Hawks on Film, Politics and Childrearing." *Jump Cut* 5 (January–February 1975).

Higham, Charles. *The Films of Orson Welles.* Berkeley, 1970.

———. "Hitchcock's World." *Film Quarterly,* Winter 1962-63.

Higham, Charles and Joel Greenberg. *The Celluloid Muse.* Chicago, 1969.

Hitchcock, Alfred. *Dialogue on Film* (no. 8). American Film Institute, 1972.

Jensen, Paul. *The Cinema of Fritz Lang.* New York, 1969.

Johnson, William. "Orson Welles: of Time and Loss." *Film Quarterly,* 1967.

Kael, Pauline. *The Citizen Kane Book.* Boston, 1971.

Kezich, Tullio. *John Ford.* Parma, 1958.

La Valley, Albert, ed. *Focus on Hitchcock.* Englewood Cliffs, N.J., 1972.

Lambert, Gavin. "Fritz Lang's America." *Sight and Sound,* Summer 1955, Autumn 1955.

McBride, Joseph and Michael Wilmington. *John Ford.* New York, 1975.

McBride, Joseph. *Focus on Howard Hawks.* Englewood Cliffs, 1972.

———. *John Ford.* New York, 1975.

———. *Orson Welles.* New York, 1972.

Madsen, Axel. *William Wyler.* New York, 1973.

Milne, Tom. *Rouben Mamoulian.* New York, 1969.

Missiaen, Jean. *Howard Hawks.* Paris, 1966.

Mitry, Jean. *John Ford.* Paris, 1964.

"Morocco." *Cahiers du Cinéma* 225 (November–December 1970).

Noble, Peter. *The Fabulous Orson Welles*. London, 1956.

Overstreet, Richard, "Interview with George Cukor." *Film Culture* 34 (1964).

Paul, William. "Hawks vs. Durgnat." *Film Comment*, January–February 1978.

Perkins, V. F. "Hawks' Comedies," In *Movie Reader*, by Ian Cameron. New York, 1972.

Perry, George. *Hitchcock*. Garden City, N.Y., 1975.

Place, J. A. *The Western Films of John Ford*. Secaucus, N.J., 1974.

Poague, Leland. *The Cinema of Frank Capra*. South Brunswick, N.J., 1975.

Richards, Jeffrey, "Frank Capra and the Cinema of Populism." *Film Society Review*, February 1972, March–April 1972.

Sarris, Andrew. *The John Ford Movie Mystery*. London, 1976.

———. *The Films of Josef von Sternberg*. Garden City, N.Y., 1966.

Schary, Dore. *Case History of a Movie*. New York, 1950.

"Semiotics and Citizen Kane." *Film Reader* 1 (1975).

Spoto, Donald. *The Art of Alfred Hitchcock*. New York, 1976.

Steen, Mike. *Hollywood Speaks*. New York, 1975.

Sternberg, Josef von. "Acting in Film and Theater." *Film Culture* 5-6 (1955).

———. *Fun in a Chinese Laundry*. New York, 1965.

Truffaut, François. *Hitchcock*. New York, 1967.

Walsh, Raoul. *Each Man in His Time*. New York, 1974.

Weinberg, Herman G. *Josef von Sternberg*. New York, 1967.

———. *The Lubitsch Touch*. New York, 1968.

Wellman, William. *A Short Time for Insanity*. New York, 1974.

Willis, Donald. *The Films of Frank Capra*. Metuchen, N.J., 1975.

———. *The Films of Howard Hawks*. Metuchen, N.J., 1975.

Wood, Robin. *Hitchcock's Films*. Cranbury, N.J., 1969.

———. *Howard Hawks*. London, 1968.

11 EUROPE, RUSSIA, AND SOUND

Countries other than the United States, while each producing sound film with distinct characteristics, all struggled with a depression economy, often one more restricted than that of the United States. Sound required financing not only for production equipment and for royalties, but also to enable each movie house, large or small, to exhibit the new product. The amount of capital that sound technology required of its investors served to locate control of production centers even more firmly in the hands of financial power: investment houses and banks. In France, for example, the name Pathé re-emerged in a Pathé-Natan-Cinéromans trust, underwritten by Bauer and Marshall, a banking firm. Its rival was Gaumont-Aubert-Franco Films, whose money came from the Industrie Electrique Suisse and the Crédit Intrustriel et Commercial. Ultimately, much of the investment reverted to the international RCA-Western Electric-Tobis sound cartel.

Les Enfants du paradis (Carné 1945) (Museum of Modern Art/Film Stills Archive)

Because of dialogue, a language barrier also threatened international distribution. One solution was to stage multiple versions of the same film with different performers. Thus, G. W. Pabst made Brecht's *Three Penny Opera* (1931) in German and French, and *Don Quixote* (1932) in French and English. Both films operated with the somewhat preordained dialogue of previous authors; other filmmakers, often working with original stories, investigated more imaginative ways to escape the boundaries imposed by language.

GREAT BRITAIN

Dominated by such visitors as E. A. Dupont (production supervisor at Elstree), Paul Czinner and Elizabeth Bergner in *Catherine the Great* (1933), Jacques Feyder, *Knight Without Armour* (1937), and René Clair, *The Ghost Goes West* (1935), Britain found it difficult to develop a coherent, English sound-film tradition. Its quota system, which perscribed how many English features had to be produced relative to the imports (largely American), encouraged an outpouring of inexpensive films, little admired by audience or producer, that paid lip service to the regulations. Aging Hollywood performers were often cast into these features until a revision of the Film Act in 1938 encouraged fewer, more expensively mounted projects. At this time, Warner, RKO, MGM, and Twentieth Century Fox began to finance their own projects in Britain, using English technicians and first-echelon American stars. The new practice met Britain's quota restrictions, while Hollywood companies retained control of overseas distribution. Examples include King Vidor's *The Citadel* (1938) and *Goodbye Mr. Chips* (1939). British corporations gradually consolidated into large production-distribution-exhibition combines.

Alexander Korda

Some of the most interesting English films came from Alexander Korda, Hungarian-born director-producer who passed through Ufa, Hollywood, and Paris before settling in Britain. His studios at Denham began their career housing extravagantly mounted productions with *The Private Life of Henry VIII* (1933). Like *Catherine the Great* (1934), *Don Juan* (1934), and *Rembrandt* (1936), the narrative concentrates on idiosyncratic privacies of the famous, bending history as necessary to accommodate drama or romance. Paul Robeson was featured in *Sanders of the River* (1935). Patriotic subjects figured in *The Scarlet Pimpernel* (1934), *Four Feathers* (1939), and *Lady Hamilton* (1941), where British composure under the most trying situations rivaled the cool of American cowboys and detectives.

Two of the most entertaining Korda ventures were H. G. Wells stories. *The Man Who Could Work Miracles* (1936) permitted divine intervention to test the mettle of an unprepossessing clerk, Roland Young. Young finds he has the power to change anything in the world simply by command. As his ambition grows, so does the production, until Young is a supreme ruler with the audacity to demand that the very earth stop its rotation.

Even more grandiose was *Things To Come* (1936), for which Wells himself wrote a scenario. The film traces history from a new world war through its feudal society aftermath to a futurist metropolis, ruled by science and facing rebellion from workers who suffer from the constant striving of their leaders for godlike power. Flamboyant performance, Wells' pessimistic imagination, and the direction-staging of William Cameron Menzies create a spectacle that is uniquely thirties and characteristically British. Menzies designed Douglas Fairbanks' *Thief of Bagdad* in 1924 as well as the Korda remake of 1940, along with *Gone With the Wind* (1939) and *For Whom the Bell Tolls* (1943). In *Things To Come,* his visualization of detailed, deep-perspective architecture is seen to advantage in the cityscapes of "Everytown," executed in miniatures and mirror shots. Of all film designers, Menzies most closely fitted a vivid imagination to clear understandings about the relation of set to story.

Anthony Asquith

If any figure stood for a British counterforce to Korda's pageantry and spectacle, it was Anthony Asquith. Spanning four decades, his films combined original, unpretentious storytelling — *Tell England* (1930) — with friendly, often quietly mocking examinations of English character: *A Cottage on Dartmoor* (1929), *Forever England* (1935).

Where other directors turned to prose, As-

quith became especially adept at adapting theater pieces to film: George Bernard Shaw, *Pygmalion* (1938); Oscar Wilde, *The Importance of Being Earnest* (1952); especially Terrence Rattigan, *French Without Tears* (1939), *While the Sun Shines* (1946), *The Winslow Boy* (1948), and *The Browning Version* (1951). Asquith's concerns with the moral implications of individual responsibility are highlighted in *Orders to Kill* (1958).

Carol Reed

With Hitchcock's departure to the United States, Carol Reed and David Lean emerged as Britain's major directors. Reed's early films have working-class settings. The best is *The Stars Look Down* (1939), which takes place in a mining town. It is based on an A. J. Cronin novel and the strike-love-catastrophe story is less significant than Reed's sympathetic portraits of miners and their families. Although England's more recent pictures of working-class life have more intensive dialogue and resentment, Reed's film maintains its integrity and is easily more effective than John Ford's *How Green Was My Valley* (1941).

After the war, Reed's films focused on the perspective of an outsider — a protagonist isolated by childhood, social pressures, or crime. *A Kid for Two Farthings* (1955) used low angles and optical distortion to approximate a child's perception of adult behavior, but *The Fallen Idol* (1948), less visually self-conscious, was better realized. A young boy's imagination leads him to misunderstand the actions of his hero, the family butler, and to implicate him unjustly. *Odd Man Out* (1947) and *The Third Man* (1949) exemplify Reed's skills. Each develops an escape-pursuit motif, paying constant attention to the motives of friend and foe. In *Odd Man Out*, Johnny MacQueen (James Mason) is wounded in a bank robbery and flees Dublin police while the organization and his girl seek him. A priest wants Johnny's soul, the girl his body, a

thony Asquith (1902–1968)

Shooting Stars (codirector A. V. Bramble)	1928
A Cottage on Dartmoor	1929
Tell England (codirector Geoffrey Barkas)	1930
Dance, Pretty Lady	1932
Forever England	1935
Pygmalion (codirector Leslie Howard)	1938
French Without Tears	1939
We Dive at Dawn	1943
Fanny By Gaslight	1944
The Way to the Stars	1945
While the Sun Shines	1946
The Winslow Boy	1948
The Browning Version	1951
The Importance of Being Earnest	1952
Court Martial	1954
Orders to Kill	1958
Libel	1959
Guns of Darkness	1962
The Yellow Rolls Royce	1964
Partial listing	

The Stars Look Down. Miners in a northeast English village strike for safety improvements. The coal owners respond with brutal repression. A worker's son unsuccessfully seeks the kind of education that may support the struggle. Finally, a cave in and rescue solidify the men's spirits without alleviating their condition. (Museum of Modern Art/Film Stills Archive)

Carol Reed (1906–1976)

painter his expression, an informer the reward, the organization his silence. Townspeople, often cast from the Abbey Theater, mix human concern with a fear of involvement, give Johnny a drink and send him along his way. Alcohol and pain foster nightmarish hallucinations, as his dishabille tatters and life slips away in the dirty, wet, Dublin streets.

Turning to Vienna and again to Graham Greene, who wrote *The Fallen Idol, The Third Man* poses questions of motives and moral responsibility. Holly Martins (Joseph Cotten), a western writer, comes to the city to work for his friend Harry Lime (Orson Welles). He is informed that Lime is dead, and that he was a racketeer whose drug smuggling led to children's deaths. Holly falls in love with Lime's girl and faces a conflict of allegiances when Lime turns up alive. Like Dublin in *Odd Man Out*, Vienna so contributes to the story that it assumes a character's role, personified by zither music that counterpoints the plotted action with mocking improvisations.

Brief Encounter. Laura Jesson (Celia Johnson) and Alec Harvey (Trevor Howard) are comfortably married middle-class spouses whose chance meetings trigger depths of feeling that excite and frighten each. Here, typically, a barmaid interrupts their declarations; an act that simultaneously relieves and frustrates the incipient affair. (Museum of Modern Art/Film Stills Archive)

David Lean

In Which We Serve (1942) and *This Happy Breed* (1943) painted British determination and stiff-lipped courage. The frustrations of a suburban pair who desire to commit, but cannot bring themselves to, adultery in *Brief En-*

David Lean (1908–   )

In Which We Serve (codirector Noel Coward)	1942
This Happy Breed	1943
Blithe Spirit	1944
Brief Encounter	1945
Great Expectations	1946
Oliver Twist	1947
The Passionate Friends	1948
Madeleine	1950
Breaking the Sound Barrier	1952
Hobson's Choice	1953
Summertime	1955
The Bridge on the River Kwai	1957
Lawrence of Arabia	1962
Doctor Zhivago	1964
Ryan's Daughter	1970

counter (1945) defy a modern age, but the hesitations and anxieties of Celia Johnson and Trevor Howard still work, somehow almost independent of the emotions they reflect. *Great Expectations* (1946) and *Oliver Twist* (1947) are illustrated Dickens that create a shabby, raucous London, particularly in *Oliver Twist* with Alec Guinness's Fagin and Robert Newton's Bill Sykes.

In later years, Lean incorporated thoughtful character into the wide-screen extravagance of *The Bridge on the River Kwai* (1957) and *Lawrence of Arabia* (1962). In contrast to his wartime films, Lean seems less confident of the motives of Colonel Nicolson (Alec Guinness) and of T. E. Lawrence (Peter O'Toole) and of the effect of their actions on future history.

By the end of the forties, Britain had finally developed a tradition of dialogue film distinguished by bravura performance and by imaginative style in conceiving naturalistic sets, which often evoked earlier times or distant places. But their industry's dependence upon literary sources and historical evocations clearly circumscribed the British film's relation to both internal and foreign audiences; a harbinger of post-World-War-II problems.

The Bridge on the River Kwai. After supervising the construction of a bridge, Colonel Nicholson (Alec Guinness) deludedly believes his effort has sustained prisoner morale. He ignores its contribution to a Japanese offensive. A reluctant American commando (William Holden) returns to destroy the construction. At this moment, he emerges from the water, to Nicholson's astonishment and outrage. (Museum of Modern Art/Film Stills Archive) (Produced by Horizon Pictures, Inc. Sam Spiegel Producer.)

FRANCE

In the suburbs of Joinville le Point, a new, American-dominated (Paramount Pictures) sound studio mass produced multi-language versions of cosmopolitan stories, employing figures like Korda, Cavalcanti, and Marcel Pagnol to little artistic effect, excepting Pagnol's Marseilles trilogy of plays. Closer to Paris at Epinay, Tobis constructed its own facilities. Their product rivaled Joinville in commercial success and mediocrity, but Tobis had the distinction of fathering René Clair's early sound comedies.

For reasons of cost, the ciné-clubs figured less importantly as a financial resource for sound productions than they had for silent experimentation, but they continued to supply outlets, however minimal, for imports and independent films whose commercial appeal was clearly limited. Although he found industry financing for his sound films, Vigo's relation to the ciné-clubs continued through his short life. Experimental French film, a tradition that is discussed in Chapter 18, had few other sources for exhibition.

Sound also attracted theater personalities: actors and playwrights such as Sacha Guitry and Pagnol. The performers Pierre Fresnay, Fernandel, Raimu and Louis Jouvet (himself a stage director) ennoble the thirties and forties, often side-by-side with actors like Jean Gabin and Michel Simon who established their primary reputation on the screen.

Automation and unemployment are central

issues in *A nous la liberté* (1931), and Popular-Front optimism underlies *Le Crime de Monsieur Lange* (1936). A blend of anarchy and confidence spills across René Clair's *Le Million* (1931), Jean Renoir's *Boudu sauvé des eaux* (1932) and Jean Vigo's *Zéro de conduite* (1933). The disillusions of writer Charles Spaak in Duvivier's *Pepé-le-Moko* (1936) reflect equally in Marcel Carné's *Quai des brumes* (1938). In occupied France, maliciousness takes similar turns in Carné's *Les Visiteurs du soir* (1942) and Henri Clouzot's *Le Corbeau* (1943). Such generalizations always threaten to descend into glibness, but France's sound films seem to evidence, more visibly than many countries, social dispositions of their times.

René Clair

Sous les toits de Paris (1930), *Le Million* (1931) and *A nous la liberté* (1931) are pinnacles of early sound comedy. The second a farce, the third a satire of the machine age, Clair's films use speech and song as elements equally integrated with the comic narrative he organized so effectively in *The Italian Straw Hat*.

Clair took sound no more seriously than situations required, refused to accede its domination, indeed ridiculed the lip-synchronization, as when dialogue is muffled behind doors or apparently live singing is found to emanate from a phonograph. Clair's films have the operatic qualities of Lubitsch and Mamoulian. Song plays ironic counterpoint to action. While all hell erupts backstage in an opera house, the grotesque soprano and tenor are singing "We are alone in the forest." When a crowd grapples wildly for a million franc lottery ticket, the melee is punctuated with sounds of a rugby game.

Clair moved to England for a period, then, interrupted by the war, Hollywood. His later films, in particular *Le Silence est d'or* (1947) and *La Beauté du Diable* (1950), preserve

much of the early skill while further humanizing character. A seduction comedy, *Le Silence est d'or* is placed in the century's first decade, the hero a director in the style of Feuillade. *La Beauté du Diable* casts Michel Simon both as an elderly Faust and as the devil, the better to interiorize Faust's temptation. The price of Faust's soul is atomic energy. Redeemed by Marguerite, Faust rejects his pact and leads a revolt against the forces that will lead to a catastrophic future.

Jean Vigo

Impressed with Warner's *I am a Fugitive from a Chain Gang*, Jean Vigo wanted to make a prison picture and settled finally on *Zéro de conduite* (1933). Where Mervyn LeRoy's exposé viewed jail as a strangulation of the human spirit, Vigo made a film that celebrates people's capacities to survive restraint. Three youths return to a small, oppressive boarding school. It is ruled by a tiny, authoritarian principal, abetted by a sneaky teacher-spy. Despite the efforts toward amelioration by a new instructor, the boys join forces with Tabard, a fourth student, whose mother dresses him effeminately. They rebel. Small gestures of dissent precede a dream-like pillow fight and a parade in the dormitory. The boys revolt openly during a courtyard ceremony. They raise a skull and crossbones on the roof and hurl rubbish at assembled dignitaries.

Zéro de conduite mixes intimate, affectionate memories of childhood with a narrative that allows the students a free, fantasized display of exuberant indignation. Because the revolt touches so closely on basic human indignations, the film is sometimes regarded as revolutionary. Because the students' actions show Vigo's highly personal stylizations, the film is often described as poetic. *Zéro de conduite*, like *L'Atalante* (1934), ties form to function. The boys become real because we believe their needs and behaviors to be complete and unfalsified. Their actions find speech and gesture that express, rather than document, intentions. Triggered by a fat, shabby chemistry teacher's physical interest in the long-haired Tabard (this is the ultimate expression of older generation corruption), the rebellious students unite. Quite intentionally, the slow motion of the pillow fight evokes both *Entr'acte* and Gance's multi-image *Napoleon* sequence. The beauty of its feathered shambles asserts human impulse against reductive academic dignity. The film's exhibition was banned in France for years.

L'Atalante transposes much the same design into a plot with a more detailed story line, peopled with more developed characterizations. The captain of a Seine barge marries a peasant girl. They live aboard ship with a re-tarded boy and an aging mate. She grows bored, quarrels with her husband and finds herself alone in Paris. With the mate's gruff assistance, the couple is reunited. Using such ordinary material, Vigo and Boris Kaufman develop images of exceptional beauty, particularly as they touch on the young bride, whose grace and sexual receptiveness bouquet the weatherbeaten, creaking boat. Just married and immediately before joining her husband below, the girl walks along the boat's deck, gown blowing, composed against the distant riverside and another boat, the shot so framed that the barge seems to move backwards with the wind.

As Père Jules, Michel Simon embodies a grumbling, disheveled, half-civilized mate whose aging reminiscences prattle about old

Zéro de conduite. In the yard, their principal, an officious midget, admonishes boarding-school students. While the boys are drawn with affectionate candor, Vigo stylizes authority figures, like the principal and his lackey, a spying instructor known as Sourpuss, into middle-class grotesques. (Museum of Modern Art/Film Stills Archive)

adventures and romantic self-indulgences. His cabin is a hodge-podge of toys and mementos, gross and sensual, imbued by touch and featuring a jar of preserved human hands. Distributors cut Vigo's film and added a popular ballad, "Le Chaland qui passe" as a theme. This became the film's first title. It opened in Paris on the day that Vigo, dead from protracted, debilitating disease, was buried, and remains one of the few authentic masterpieces of film.

Marcel Carné

First a film critic, Carné apprenticed with Feyder and Clair. His early sound films extend the popular themes and settings of Feyder's *Crainquebille*. Romantic and pessimistic, emotionally they anticipate the coming war. *Quai des brumes* (1938) was one of several very successful collaborations with Jacques Prévert, poet and scriptwriter, whose influence was equally important on Renoir's *Le Crime de Monsieur Lange* (1936). An army deserter (Jean Gabin) falls in love with an orphan (Michele Morgan). Her cruel guardian (Michel Simon), in league with criminals, attacks Morgan. Gabin kills the guardian, only to be shot himself by a criminal rival for Morgan. The lover's relationship is subtly developed, and Carné's film is permeated with a somber, defeated sense about possibilities for individual happiness. This pessimism stems both from the aura of underworld corruption and by way of certain recurrent Carné-Prévert figures, here a painter and a bum, who seem to express inexorable fate. Eugen Shuftan contributes a dour, waterfront face to the film.[1]

Le Jour se léve (1939) locates Gabin alone in his room, besieged by police for killing his girl's seducer. Gabin spends the night recalling his past. At dawn he kills himself. Again,

Prévert and Carné posit a man of good impulse pressed beyond endurance by circumstance. The term *poetic realism* was applied to these films: poetic because the mood is reinforced by characters with symbolic resonance (here a blind man is fate), realism because the mode is working-class, nineteenth-century naturalism. Pabst's *die neue Sachlichkeit* is recalled by Carné's concern for artificial detail. He built an elaborate studio set to isolate the hotel properly in its proletarian neighborhood, a significance he regarded essential to Gabin's alienation.

Les Visiteurs du soir (1942) was made during German occupation and the Prévert-Carné collaboration replaced their earlier tales about destiny with allegory of Nazi domination. Here, set in the fifteenth-century, the devil turns two lovers to stone, but he cannot still their beating hearts, an image popularly seen at the time to represent France under Vichy.

Released at war's end, *Les Enfants du paradis* (1945) is the most original, ambitious Prévert-Carné work. It is a complex mid-nineteenth-century interweaving of several characters' lives as they are played out in romantic Paris. More than three hours, *Les Enfants du paradis* enjoys a major performance by Jean-

[1] *Shüftan also filmed Franju's* Eyes Without a Face *(1959) and Robert Rossen's* The Hustler *(1961) and* Lillith *(1964).*

Marcel Carné (1909–   )

Jenny	1936
Drôle de drame	1937
Quai des brumes	1938
Le Jour se lève	1939
Les Visiteurs du soir	1942
Les Enfants du paradis	1945
Les Portes de la nuit	1946
La Marie du port	1950
Thérèse Raquin	1953
Les Pays d'où je viens	1956
Trois chambres à Manhattan	1965
Les Assassins de l'orde	1971
Partial listing	

Louis Barrault who plays the mime, Duberau. Duberau loves a minor actress whom he alternately possesses and loses. Certain of the characters, Duberau among them, are based on actual people, but the film itself is contrived in special and involved ways, employing theater settings to pose, but not to resolve, a variety of conceptual relationships. Central to these is the theme of the lover and the loved, and around this revolve questions of reality and artifice, comedy and tragedy, acting and non-acting, even sound and silent film (Barrault's mime is silent film). The organization of the narrative is more fugue-like than theatrically dramatic, and the spectacle of the historical settings and character guises the movie's intellectual sub-surfaces.

Jean Renoir

Jean Renoir's contribution to sound film are so many and so varied that no historical survey can do justice. *La Chienne* (1931) has Michel Simon as a nagged husband whose escapes from his wife and his work are painting and a mistress. When jealousy demands, Simon's repressed personality gives way to the passion which had always been implied in his paintings.[2] *Boudu sauvé des eaux* (1932) casts Simon as a derelict rescued from suicide by a middle-class bookdealer. As a household guest of the dealer, Boudu's anarchic, disordered vision of life produces chaos. He seduces every available woman, finally escaping marriage and the bourgeois world by again falling into the water. *Toni* (1934) is a melodrama of love and murder among Italian peasant workers in a French quarry. *Le Crime de Monsieur Lange* (1936) has workers in a Paris print shop forming a cooperative when their exploitive boss flees creditors. On his return, the boss is murdered and his executioner, M.

[2] *Fritz Lang remade the story as* Scarlet Street *in 1945.*

Lange, escapes with a loving woman. *La Vie est á nous* (1936) was produced for French communists to affect the year's elections. Its episodes deal with unemployment, fascist brutalities, and communism's defense of the poor. Mussolini is edited into shots of war dead; Hitler speaks, but his voice is a dog barking. The Communist Party aids the bankrupt and out-of-work. The film concludes on marching crowds singing the *Internationale*.

Une Partie du campagne (1936 but not released until 1946) was never completed. It finally appeared as a forty minute short. A family goes on a country picnic. The daughter falls in love with a young man. The mother dallies with another. Years later, the daughter, now tediously married, returns and meets her lover. *The Lower Depths* (1936) sets Gorky's play in a French courtyard. *La Marseillaise* (1937) follows a corps of revolutionary volunteers from Marseille to Paris. *La Bête humaine* casts Gabin as a railroad worker whose inherited madness leads him to strangle his girl.

Such résumés do no justice to the films and serve only to locate them by way of time and subject. Each production evidences an extraordinary artist, attentive to themes of freedom and restraint, individuality and organization, the beauty and often the transcience of human affection, aggressive impulse warring with self-protective instinct. Renoir's actors develop an unassumingly natural style whose verve compares only to the Simon role in *L'Atalante*.

Renoir's films have a look of improvisation that is, on analysis, predetermined. In *Une Partie du campagne,* the director is most clearly Auguste Renoir's son, spotting countryside and costume with textures and compositions of the Impressionist nineties. Elsewhere, locale and period are carefully rendered through considered attention to design, like the bereft countryside of *Toni* and the studio courtyard of *Le Crime de Monsieur*

Lange. Even moments such as the meeting in the Club des Jacobins in the commercial *La Marseillaise* still have a documented flavor.

More important yet to the sense of immediacy of these films is Renoir's choreographed staging. By the time of *Lange,* he is experimenting with camera takes of increasing length, conducted both on location and sets, complete enough to maximize camera and actor movements and playing foreground and background against one another. Camera mobility works not to shift attention (as in a customary pan) or to follow (as in a usual tracking shot) nor to reveal clues (as in Hitchcock's discovery of the blinking drummer in *Young and Innocent*). Rather, it is used to preserve the naturalness and life-like tempo of performance while maintaining a fluid, visual ambiance by exiting actors out-of-frame and entering them back in subtle concert with the story. The camera does not so much dominate as participate in proceedings. While Renoir's depth-of-field does not (for reasons of his lenses' optical properties) approximate the Toland Ford and Welles films of 1939-41, Renoir stages shots with unique, often superior forethought from the time of *Lange*.

The Popular Front, a short-lived alliance between French Radical Socialists, Socialists and communists against rightwing forces, also inflects Renoir's films of the midthirties. It underlines the sense of commune in *M. Lange* (as in Duvivier's *La belle équipe,* released the same year), of oppression in *The Lower Depths* and of nationalism in *La Marseillaise,* but Renoir's deep sympathy for almost anyone in almost any circumstance lies even closer to the center of his work.

Grand Illusion (1937) is the first of the director's two great accomplishments, drawing on Renoir's own experiences as a prisoner of war. Three French officers are moved to a German fortress-camp administered by von Rauffenstein (Erich von Stroheim). The men are an aristocrat Boeldieu (Pierre Fresnay), a Jewish, middle-class banker Rosenthal (Marcel Dalio) and a Paris mechanic Maréchal (Jean Gabin). Together with von Rauffenstein they constantly betray class relationships as affected by military and cultural change. Von Rauffenstein confides to Boeldieu, the only Frenchman with whom he will speak (and then often in English) because both are career officers, that whoever wins, war's end will bring the end of the von Rauffensteins and the Boeldieus.

Maréchal and Rosenthal escape, and von Rauffenstein regretfully shoots Boeldieu whose ruse assured the success of the escape plan. The fugitives pause at a German farm where Maréchal has a love affair with the widowed wife. Finally the two men cross the border to Switzerland.

Each figure is drawn in close detail. Von Rauffenstein, von Stroheim's best performance, is encased in a body that is almost half metal as a result of injuries. His burned fingers, hidden by gloves, carefully tend the only flower in the prison. Rosenthal is resented both for his Jewishness and because his background is Polish and German. Boeldieu worries about a spot on his gloves and dons the final pair before sacrificing himself so that the others may escape. As in *Boudu,* where actors demonstrate something of their character by attitudes toward cats, behaviors play off one another in *Grand Illusion* so that each major figure is better understood by his sense of performance. Class roles serve to write each man's dialogue without altogether compromising his individuality.

The Rules of the Game (1939) describes a weekend houseparty in the country chateau of a Marquis. As Octave, Renoir joins the cast, a self-confessed failure who lives off his friends and always wanted to be an orchestra conductor. Renoir conceived the film as a candid view of bourgeois decadence, its players ensnared in rules of conduct that most resemble the conventions of an elaborate game. Behind

Rules of the Game. Christine (Nora Grégor) discusses men with her maid Lisette (Paulette Dubost). "Rules of the Game," Renoir said, "are those which must be observed in society if one wishes to avoid being crushed." The women's conversation centers on men: what they want, and how to survive disaster by outwitting them. (Museum of Modern Art/Film Stills Archive)

the society's adultery, intrigue and jealousies, exists a longing for some other life. This is unacknowledged by most and epitomized in Octave whose out-going generosities vie with self-pity. The film's climax occurs during a dress ball for which guests provide comic entertainment. A servant's intrigue erupts into real-life vengeance and the drunken party can no longer distinguish between what is real and what are staged frivolities. At its conclusion, the film abruptly dispenses with comedy when an aviator, a public hero, is mistakenly shot by the enraged gamekeeper. Social rules and class distinctions have been breached, but they are quickly healed by the Jewish Marquis' gracious speech. Misunderstanding the incident (he believes a lovers quarrel has prompted the shooting), a conservative general finally forgives the Marquis his Jewishness and concedes him style.

For all the film's view of decadence, the players can no more escape Renoir's understanding, and hence his forgiveness, than inhabitants of any of his other films. When war was imminent, Renoir intended to make a commentary on the country's state of mind; now the film stands more independent of historical reference. Broadly, *The Rules of the Game* seems to suggest that participation in any society requires one's cautious understanding. The price of naïveté can be self-destruction. Hypocrisy may prove yet more useful for survival. Reviled and rejected at release, the film was revived in 1946 and now stands as Renoir's greatest achievement. In the guise of a loose, even an improvised comic spoof, it carries so many subterranean reflections that *The Rules of the Game* bears repeated viewings.

After war years spent in Hollywood, Renoir made *The River* (1951) in India and then a series of French features. *French Can Can* (1954) and *Le Dejeuneur sur l'herbe* (1959) again evoke an earlier period when feelings seemed more closely allied to the social forms that contained them. One remembers Octave's most telling statement in *The Rules of the Game:* "There's one thing, do you see, that's absolutely terrifying, and that is that everybody has his reasons." Renoir's later work continues an affectionate lower-keyed perspective toward human behavior, mixing humor with ironic wisdom about pleasure's impermanence and life's poignancies.

Further French Films

While the motives of playwright-producer Marcel Pagnol in filming *Marius* (1931), *Fanny* (1932) and *César* (1936) appear to have been no more than to "can" exemplary versions of his plays for wide distribution, the movies' location shooting in Marseilles and natural performances by Raimu transcend original intention. Pagnol himself directed *César* and in 1938 *The Baker's Wife,* again with Raimu.

Julien Duvivier, a prolific filmmaker, did his best work in the thirties, *Poil de carotte* (1932) in particular, the study of a sensitive child who kills himself, and *La Belle Équipe* (1936). In the latter film, five Parisians win a lottery and start a cooperative restaurant, *La Belle Équipe* had two conclusions, one for first run distribution that ends pessimistically, the other for general release with a Popular Front reassertion of the cooperative. In *Pépé-le-Moko* (1936), Duvivier provided a curious, partially successful mixture of gangster film (one thug is directly out of George Raft in

Scarface) and Carné-shaded pessimism. For love of a girl (the love interest is mawkish), a French criminal (Gabin) leaves his Casbah retreat in Algiers to be shot down by police.

Devil in the Flesh (1947) by Claude Autant-Lara was based on a famous French novel, set in World War I and sympathetically tracing the love between a student and a married woman whose husband is in the army. Henri-Georges Clouzot developed a personal, tense thriller idiom that made use of provincial suspicion, *Le Corbeau* (1943); police work, *Quai des Ofrevres/Jenny l'Amour* (1947), trucking explosives, *The Wages of Fear* (1953), and schemes to induce madness, *Les Diaboliques* (1955). René Clément replicated Resistance operations in *La Bataille du rail* (1945) and directed one of Jean Cocteau's best scripts, *Beauty and the Beast* (1946). *Forbidden Games* (1952) depicted two children's wartime efforts to understand and come to terms with death. *Gervaise* (1956) adapted the Zola novel with special attention to the flavor of nineteenth-century Paris.

Jacques Becker assisted Renoir through the thirties and spent part of the war in a German prison camp. The postwar films he completed before an early death are, at their best, intense character studies that emerge from a highly detailed environment and social milieu. *Casque d'or* (1952) is Becker's most fully realized film, a turn-of-the-century drama set in Paris in which murder and retribution are not so much plot devices as they are seemingly natural outgrowths of behavior and style among the workers and petty thieves.

Jacques Tati, the finest comic in France's post-music hall tradition, developed a series of polished, minutely controlled films beginning with *Jour de fête* (1948). Tati's M. Hulot character combines Chaplin's insouciance with Keaton's relationship to objects, which Tati encounters in confident ignorance. Alternately, he suffers, benefits, or escapes technology through complex planning or sheer luck. M. Hulot deals with his environment in darts

M. Hulot's Holiday. Joining Keaton and Chaplin in the upper reaches of comic mime, Hulot survives a vacation in an out-of-the-ordinary boarding house. Mechanical contrivance and chance sometimes defeat, sometimes rescue him, and always anonymously. "I mean to suggest a return to gentleness," Tati said, "through a defense of individuality." (Museum of Modern Art/Film Stills Archive)

Jacques Tati (1908–   )

of exuberant improvisation. Tati's ability to design his settings surpasses understanding in *Monsieur Hulot's Holiday* (1953), *Mon Oncle* (1958), *Playtime* (1967), and *Traffic* (1971).

Carl Dreyer's single French sound film was *Vampyr* (1931), bearing closer relation to the stories of Sheridan le Fanu than to Bram Stoker's *Dracula*. In fact, *Vampyr* has little connection with either, but is an atmospheric vampire story whose most powerful scenes are undercut by an erratic continuity in available prints. Dialogue is used so sparingly that it has the quality of interrupting pictures. Like *The Passion of Joan of Arc, Vampyr* was photographed by Rudolph Maté, who became a Hollywood cameraman and later a director.

Certain shots, such as the aged vampire haltingly moving across the landscape with her cane, are haunting. Throughout, Dreyer develops a value scheme in which the greying white of mists and gravestones suggest oppressive forces. The design culminates with a vampire's live burial, suffocating in a deluge of mill flour like the factory owner in Griffith's *A Corner in Wheat*.

Max Ophüls

Like Lubitsch in other respects as well, Ophüls escapes national classification, but he is arguably more French than German. Born in Germany, he produced at the Vienna Bergtheater before entering film. His first movie work linked the newer medium with opera and operetta. *The Bartered Bride* (1932) and *Lieberlei* (1933) as well as many later films join story theme to a musical motif. With the Nazi rise to power, Ophüls worked in France, the Netherlands, Italy, and Switzerland, coming finally to the United States. After years of unemployment, he returned to filmmaking, with the help of Preston Sturges, directing *The Exile* (1947), *Letter From an Unknown Woman* (1948), *Caught* (1948), and *The Reckless Moment* (1949). His last, finest films were completed in France.

Ophüls' characteristic story involves a woman whom impulse and an emotional integrity toward love have carried to an impossible state of nonfulfillment — "weepies," as it were. But Ophüls' films raised themselves beyond this genre by qualities of personal performance, psychological insight, and execution. Ophüls' women might figure in contemporary murder melodrama as in *Caught* and *The Reckless Moment,* but the director operated with greatest skillful zeal in the nostalgic, romanticized recreations of aristocratic Vienna. Like Lubitsch and von Stroheim, he is aware of the decadence and incessant frivolity of the period, using the flirtations and grand manner

as background to impossible love affairs rather than satire or indignation.

La Ronde (1950) traces sex with or without affection through a round of couples that finally comes full circle so that a young prostitute (Simone Signoret) who introduced the film marks its conclusion. The passage of coupling hints ever so slightly at venereal disease, to provide a mocking undercurrent throughout.

Le Plaisir (1951) is the adaptation of three de Maupassant stories, each putting in relief pleasure and its impermanence. An aging husband attends a dance hall masked to disguise his wrinkles. To the town's indignation, a brothel is closed so that the girls may attend the first communion of the madame's niece. Playing the part of a young innocent, one girl enjoys a short affair with a farmer. A model jumps from a window for love of an artist. She becomes crippled, and the painter marries her. *The Earrings of Madame de. . .* (1953) traces a set of earrings through their several owners. As in *La Ronde,* they return to Madame de. . .,

Max Ophüls (1902–1957)

Dann schol lieber Lebertran	1930
Die Verkaufte Braut/The Bartered Bride	1932
Lieberlei	1933
La Tendre Ennemie	1936
The Exile	1947
Letter from an Unknown Woman	1948
Caught	1948
The Reckless Moment	1949
La Ronde	1950
Le Plaisir	1951
Madame de. . ./The Earrings of Madame de	1953
Lola Montèz	1955
Partial listing	

Lola Montès. Introduced by ringmaster Peter Ustinov. Lola (Martine Carol) is questioned by the audience about her scandalous past. Ophüls based the queries on material he heard on the radio. Opulently expensive, the failure of the film bankrupted Gamma Films. It passed through unsuccessful rerelease stages of re-editing and rearrangement until the original version appeared again in 1969 and met with critical acclaim. (Museum of Modern Art/Film Stills Archive)

but here, rather than making the rounds of all the characters, attention is concentrated on the original owner throughout. Aware of his wife's deception. Monsieur de . . ., yet in love, plays a hypocritical game. Finally, he kills his wife's lover in a duel. Forsaken, exposed, she dies. *Lola Montès* (1955) introduces its principal as a circus performer, recalling her early marriage, her romance with Franz Liszt, and an affair with the King of Bavaria that induced his abdication. Lola is

placed in a cage. Spectators are encouraged to ask her questions and to kiss her hand for the price of an extra dollar.

Ophüls' films are constructed as a series of episodes linked by a motivating character, object, emotion, or idea. A woman is always central, her pain a consequence of rejecting one kind of human relation for another. To develop an ethos that is strong enough to sustain such romanticism, Ophüls employs highly stylized and exceptionally mobile camera trackings, which often observe, without pausing on, entire successions of detail: the closet of Madame de . . ., the costumes and decorum of a ball, the actions in a brothel as seen from outside. These help to locate the conditions of a world that is so governed by men, class, and rules that a heroine's very efforts to satisfy her own needs expose her vulnerabilities. Ophüls' camera movements, too, are highly emotional in their own terms, a kind of authored expressionism that is heightened in *Lola Montès* by striking, non-natural employment of color and by complexities of composition in a Cinema-Scope screen that have not been equalled elsewhere.

GERMANY

Germany had a head start in the sophisticated use of sound, profiting from early Tri-Ergon research in sound technology. Dietrich appeared in an early musical, *I Kiss Your Hand, Madame* (1929), and, before Nazi power was consolidated, some sound pictures were outspoken in their opposition to militarism, e.g., *The Captain of Köpenick* (1931) and *War is Hell* (1931). *Mädchen in Uniform* (1931), directed by Leontine Sagan, touched on both lesbianism and authoritarianism in a girl's school, its style effectively balancing repression, hysteria, and sensitive interchanges between students and one affectionate teacher. *The Blue Light* (1932), featuring and directed by Leni Riefenstahl, combined legend and mountain climbing, Riefenstahl's energetic beauty supportive of the German romantic mystique amidst the panoramic photography. An unlikely collaborator in the venture was the Hungarian filmmaker-theoretician Béla Balázs.

Kühle Wampe?/Whither Germany? (1932) appeared under communist sponsorship, co-operatively produced by a group that included writer Bertold Brecht, composer Hanns Eisler, and director Slatan Dudow. Heavily censored in Germany and elsewhere, *Kühle Wampe?* exists now only in an incomplete form. Its narrative both fictionalizes and documents with unstaged footage the condition of unemployed German workers, hopelessly victimized by social and political events of the period. In the manner of Brecht's plays, ballads are interjected now and again, here somewhat unsuccessfully. The playwright fled to Denmark soon after *Kühle Wampe?* was banned by the Nazis in 1933.

As Minister of Propaganda and Public Enlightenment soon after Nazi takeover, Joseph Goebbels grouped film with theater, newspapers, books, and radio. Offensive material, domestic or imported, was banned. Jews were hounded from the industry. Many who had not already departed for Hollywood or other film capitals left: Lubitsch, Carl Mayer, Peter Lorre, Max Reinhardt. In various combinations of fear and indignation other figures like Fritz Lang, Marlene Dietrich, and Conrad Veidt departed; some important names, Werner Krauss, Emil Jannings, and Hans Albers among them, remained.

Dominated before World War II hostilities and then nationalized, companies like Ufa and Deulig turned to history, biography, and trivial amusements. Hitler understood film's capacity to shape ideology; indeed, *The Battleship Potemkin* impressed him especially. While Nazi films tended toward heroism and celebration, many promoted anti-Semitism, *Jud Süss* (1940) in particular. However unbe-lievable, it has been revived in Europe in recent years. History sometimes took curious turns; *Titanic* (1943) became a German captain's struggle against capitalistic irresponsibility. *Kolberg* (1945) was a lavish call to German resistance against invaders, set in the time of the Napoleonic War.

At war's end, various parts of the film industry fell under the supervision of different Allies, depending on their location in East or West Germany. In early postwar years, a kind of genre dubbed "rubble films" sought to deal with current problems and the haunting issue of national guilt, for example, *The Murderers Are Amongst Us* (1946) and *Film Without Title* (1947). But only in recent years has Germany repeated the achievements of its pre-Nazi sound period.

The Blue Angel

Josef von Sternberg's single German production, *The Blue Angel* (1930), proved to be one of its most famous, although its story, partially based on a novel by Heinrich Mann, has not altogether withstood time's ravages. A petty, authoritarian boys' school teacher (Emil Jannings), whose bedroom sign reads "Do right and fear no one," falls in love with a club singer, Lola Lola (Marlene Dietrich). They marry and Professor Rath deteriorates into a shuffling, humiliated lackey, forced to appear onstage as a clown before his former students and peers. Maddened, Jannings tries to strangle his wife, then retreats to his old schoolroom where he collapses at his desk.

Jannings seems to suffer better in silence (*The Last Laugh, Variety, The Last Command*). Dietrich's maneating appetites were refined in the subsequent von Sternberg collaborations so that Lola has something yet-unformed about her, but her songs are marvels. More effective yet is von Sternberg's use of offscreen sound; the patriotic tune of a village clock provides a mundane, traditional comment on Jannings' decline. The doors to Die-

The Blue Angel.
Lola: "If you don't like it, you can always go."
Rath: "Yes, I'll go away. I've had enough. I'd rather die like a dog than carry on like this."
(National Film Archives, Ottawa)

trich's dressing room in the Blue Angel night-club open and close to punctuate action within by offscreen sounds from the stage. In the German atmosphere, von Sternberg's interests in authority's cruel expressions are developed in elaborate visual codes, such as the Professor's choice and employment of hats.

G. W. Pabst

Pabst's sound output is extremely impressive, employing sound to intensify the naturalism of his silent period, whose social concerns continue in *Westfront 1918* (1930), *Threepenny Opera* (1931), and *Kameradschaft* (1931).

Like Milestone's *All Quiet on the Western Front* (an inferior film), *Westfront 1918* sought to punctuate mobile, silent camera footage with war's noise. Mixing was yet unknown in German studios, and separate tracks were printed superimposed to blend the effects. Pabst's film has an especially documented feel with respect both to its battles and to the case history stories about four German soldiers on the French line. Pabst's staged horror is unrhetorical for all its violence, and thus the more powerful. Mutilation, death, and home front demoralization (the civilian scenes are as strong as the battles) are viewed fatalistically, ruled by events beyond human volition. The director refused to use music in his film.

In contrast, Kurt Weill's music sit more easily than Berthold Brecht's words in *Threepenny Opera*, which provoked indignation from both. The savage satire of Brecht's theatrical adaptation from *The Beggar's Opera* is muted. *Threepenny Opera* departs Brecht's broken shifts from fiction into collusive discussions with a live audience, so that the ballad singer becomes a part of the narrative more than he is an intermediary. The film adds an entire new episode with Polly, wife to Mack the Knife, founding a bank firm in which her father, king of the beggars, and the police commissioner eventually become partners. The location is a Berlin-like Victorian London whose flavor is absorbed by Mackheath as he walks down city streets, tracked by the camera. Although her part is diminished, Lotte Lenya again plays the prostitute Jenny. Whatever else, the film documents Lenya, Weill's wife, at the height of her power.

Kameradschaft is the more remarkable for its studio staging. It has the authentic look of a mine on the French-German border. An explosion traps French workers, and unem-

Kameradshaft. The mine rescue is based on an actual 1906 disaster when German workers rescued their comrades across the Franco-Austrian border. On first release, the film's final scene, when a new barrier is erected, was sometimes omitted. (Museum of Modern Art/Film Stills Archive)

ployed Germans enter through their own shafts to break past a Versailles barrier, a wall marking the natural boundary, and rescue the men. After expressions of thanks and friendship, the Germans depart. A new wall is erected. Like Pabst's other sound ventures, *Kameradschaft* is distinguished by the camera work of Fritz Arno Wagner and by Erno Metzner's underground sets. In the collapse of the mine shaft and the ensuing rescue attempts, sound acquires special intensity, and we find it difficult at times to remember we are watching a studio construction.

Fritz Lang

Provisionally titled *Murderer Among Us, M* (1931) considers the crimes of a child-murderer, a city's hysterical response, apprehension by criminals, a kangaroo court trial, and final capture by police. Much of the film's power rests in Peter Lorre's representation of the psychologically twisted criminal whose quiet exterior guises a psychic swamp of anxiety and sadism. Lorre studied under Brecht, and his controlled hysteria slips easily into Lang's expressionist ambiance and shadowed urban sites. Violence is the more stark for the restrained manner in which it is implied: an abandoned child's ball rolling in the grass, a balloon caught among telephone wires. Underworld and police operate with parallel organizations, and Lang underlines the point by cuts that emphasize visual similarities. Sound is used with economic skill. The melody of a whistle is identified with the murderer. Trying to open a warehouse lock, his knife scratches betray Lorre to the criminals. Lang cuts speech from a previous scene against the shifted locale, so that, for example, police speculation about the unknown, demented criminal is voiced as we watch Lorre making mad faces in a mirror.

Framing Lang's American period were Dr. Mabuses. *The Testament of Dr. Mabuse* (1933), also known as *The Last Will of Dr.*

Mabuse, was said to have been intended as an allegory to Hitler's growing power, but such a conceit appears strained. Now mad, Mabuse "escapes" his asylum by death, and then assumes spiritual control over Dr. Baum, the asylum's administrator. His plans to seize power through terrorism are executed through criminal agents who take orders from a darkened silhouette in a underground chamber. The script is Thea von Harbou at her most lurid, leavened by Lang's production skills. Promoted from Superintendent to Chief Inspector, Lohmann returns from a policeman character in *M* to foil the mad doctor's plans. Again, sound overlaps contrast strategies of police and criminals. As distant sirens were used in *M* to evoke city desolation, here they blend with fire, motors, falling buildings, and train noises to crescendo a sabotage of the city's gasworks. Mabuse is associated with mechanical and electronic technology, a Langian motif out of *Metropolis* and *Spies*, but one that might have commented, too, on Hitler's use of the media. The director departed Germany soon after the completion of *The Testament* with a print of his new film.

USSR

Before sound, there were rumblings among Communist Party members in the Soviet film industry. Moscow sophistication, as in Abram Room's *Bed and Sofa* (1927), engendered suspicion among peasant audiences. Eisenstein's *October* and Dovzhenko's *Zvenigora*, however applauded by Western critics, were not popular. Coincident with the technical changes engendered by sound, the administration and financial organization of the film industry were consolidated under Boris Shumyatsky, who became an increasingly stern critic of artistic deviation.

Russian had researched sound-on-film early enough that the method was understood in 1930. Absent by then in Mexico, Eisenstein had previously joined with Pudovkin and Alexandrov to warn against a total exploitation of naturalistic, talking picture synchrony at the expense of work "along the lines of (sound's) distinct non-synchronization with the visual images."[3]

In fact, such approaches were only occasional in ensuing years. As elsewhere, Soviet sound took the direction of filmed drama, but in the USSR the disposition toward the "natural" was further promoted by a political vision of the esthetic: socialist realism. Charged to applaud and to motivate efforts toward national goals, i.e., the first five-year plan, simple dramas now seemed best able to effect such ends. With the fifteenth-anniversary celebration of Soviet cinema in 1934, experimentation was officially over.[4]

Typically, the first sound feature (as distinguished from silent films with added tracks) was *Road to Life* (1931) by Nikolai Ekk, a kind of *Wild Boys of the Road*. One of the early successes was *Chapayev* (1934), a first film by Sergei and Georgi Vasiliev. Chapayev was a Red Army commander. Together with his ingratiating, pipe-smoking companion, Comissar Furmanov, the two were harbingers of Shumyatsky's thorough allegiances to simple stories with indentification-inducing heroes.

Dziga Vertov

Vertov's experimentation with recording had preceded the sound film by years. Hindered by the lack of portable recording equipment,

---

[3] *Appendix A, Sergei Eisenstein*, Film Form.
[4] *Jay Leyda*, Kino, *pp. 317-19. Ronald Levaco cogently locates the origins of ideological conflict in the pervasive formalist esthetic that preceded the Socialist state and emphasized artistic style and the manipulation of conventions. Lenin himself, like Stalin and those who followed, regarded art as a substitute reality, possessing the potential of either moral uplift or decay. See* Introduction to Kuleshov on Film, *by Lev Kuleshov.*

Vertov nevertheless considered an accumulation of aural records quite as he did his visuals. Further, the Vertov films were already unencumbered by story orthodoxies, fragmented and shifting in subject and point of view. Of all the Soviet filmmakers, Vertov's approach most clearly lent itself to imaginative exploitation of sound. His preparedness undoubtedly helps to explain how *Enthusiasm* managed to be produced at all.

The intention of *Enthusiasm,* (or *Symphony of the Don Basin*) (1931) was to show the Don miners' progress toward realization of Russia's first five-year plan. This is accomplished in part by documentation of the underground operation, its modernization a fruition of the new industrialization. What is most memorable, indeed stunning, in *Enthusiasm* is the opening sequence, built of newsreel images and one of the most exceptional sound tracks in film history. Sound is blended and mixed from documentary recordings, radio excerpts, factory noises, workers' voices, music, crowds, tools, and trains. Vertov organizes this array with an attention equal to his complex, segmented pictures, so that each element possesses both autonomy and a contrapuntal, denotational relation to the other. The sequence itself traces the dismantling of Russian Orthodox churches and their conversion to workers' clubs, where the men relax and study. What is most astonishing is that a viewer innocent not only of this period in Russian history but equally ignorant of the language can find himself so remarkably moved by the experience, which lacks subtitles or other explanatory information.

Truly, Vertov created a symphony. But the authorities felt otherwise and he was not to make another film for three years. *Three Songs of Lenin* (1934) is built around folk songs that celebrate the dead leader's own life and his effect on the new country. Somewhat dependent on an understanding of the music's words the film is yet moving and evocative, concentrating especially on changes the Revolution had effected in women. It makes maximum use of a small amount of Lenin footage, organizing this and other images as a composer might develop motifs and patterned repetitions. Vertov's last feature film, *Lullaby* (1937), is unknown to the author. He then returned to newsreel editing during World War II and worked in the front lines. Vertov died in 1954; little is known about his last years or why his film credits had become so infrequent, except that Vertov was out of esthetic favor.

Vsevolod Pudovkin

Pudovkin's *A Simple Case* (1932) was also known as *Life is Very Good*. It is a story of a husband's desertion of his wife for another woman and then his return. The film was ill received and much revised to accommodate audience criticism and ideological suspicions. *Deserter* (1933) comes closer to approximating something of the Eisenstein-Pudovkin sound manifesto, especially in its opening sequence. Here, as in a later police-worker confrontation, image is edited against sound to develop a dramatic intensity without resorting to synchronous speech, at least without conforming to the regimens of lip-sync. What may start as photographed speech will be interrupted by crowd noises and traffic sounds, movements punctuated to coincide with vocal rhythms and phrases. A later section, during which police break up a workers' demonstration, uses music not to support the drama (a banner rises anew after being torn down) but rather to supply an underlying theme of confidence in the face of police brutality. Here Pudovkin's sound work has something of the quality of Vertov, if more beholden to ordinary narrative continuity.

His last film work, interrupted by a five year's illness, is little known outside the USSR, perhaps little known there. Many of the films were historical epics. *The Harvest* (1953) is said to invoke something of Pudovkin's earlier power.

One of Eisenstein's many sketches for *Ivan the Terrible*. Camera angle, decor, and costume are denoted, but emphasis rests on Ivan's posture and its central purpose in the overall composition. Shooting closely followed Eisenstein's design, a cause of some discomfort to Nikolai Cherkassov, who played the Czar. (British National Film Archive/Stills Library)

Sergei Eisenstein

On return from Mexico, Eisenstein spent much of his time teaching at the Moscow Film Institute. *Bezhin Meadow* was in production, on and off, for three years beginning in 1935, constantly confronting Shumyatsky's mount-

ing opposition to the director's plan. Eisenstein appears to have conceived imaginative sound employments, shifting and blending effects so that they might gain broader significance. With much of the project finally completed, production was halted by order of the Central Administration of the Cinema Industry. *Bezhin Meadow* exists now only in the form of a short made up from stills culled from clips of shot heads and tails which were filed with the production script.

Eisenstein recanted his misdeeds:

. . . Unripened revolutionary feelings, which should have been replaced long ago by disciplined Bolshevik consciousness, is (sic) the source of errors that, subjectively mistaken, become objectively harmful, despite affirmative intentions and purposes . . .[5]

He was allowed to write and film *Alexander Nevsky* (1938), surrounded with co-workers dedicated to insuring that Eisenstein did not again fall prey to deviant formalism. Nevsky was a thirteenth-century prince, chosen by the people to drive the Teutonic knights out of their homeland. The film was designed to alert and prepare its viewers to the growing threat of German forces.

Eisenstein made *Nevsky* a highly stylized, operatic performance, its protagonist nobler than noble, the Germans blacker than black. The film's power grows from a designer's imagination and the director's capacity to develop the deepening sense of great historic forces approaching inevitable confrontation. Sergei Prokofiev worked in close collaboration with Eisenstein, so that sound and picture echo one another intimately. Most notable is the climactic battle between Teutons and Nevsky's forces, seemingly fought on the frozen ice of Lake Peipus, in fact along a Moscow shore covered with sand, chalk and asphalt under hot, July sun.

Ivan the Terrible had been planned as a trilogy. Part I was finished during the war (1944). Eisenstein completed Part II in 1946, but

[5] *Sergei Eisenstein, "The Mistakes of Bezhin Lug,"* International Literature, *no. 8, 1937. Quoted in Marie Seton,* Eisenstein, *p. 373.*

Stalin prohibited release and the film did not appear until 1958. Ivan assumes the throne, marries, defeats the Mongols and abdicates after boyar treachery. In Part II, the citizens of Moscow call him back, and Ivan bests boyar plots by causing the assassination of their intended replacement, the weak Vladimir. *Ivan* is the most deeply Russian of all Eisenstein's films, its Byzantine costume and decor a constant reminder of non-European patterns of thought. The two parts profit from being viewed together, and there is a prologue. Ivan's childhood, which exists as a self-sufficient piece but is seen only in excerpt in Part II. Again, Prokofiev collaborated on a score that resonates the passionate, suspicion-ridden, sometimes bloody atmosphere. Eisenstein appears to be more committed to a system of stylized graphic display than to opera. The films are rich in detailed compositions that are effected by (sometimes unbearably slow) actors' movements which culminate in hieratic postures. A banquet and dance sequence in Part II is filmed in Agfacolor (the Russians seized the process from Germany during the war). Part III was to have been made entirely in color, but Eisenstein died from a second heart attack in 1948 before it could be completed.

Alexander Dovzhenko

Dovzhenko's sound films ran another gauntlet of political criticism and obstruction. *Ivan* (1932) is set in a hydroelectric project on the Dneiper in the Ukraine. Dovzhenko developed a new Soviet man, good humored and unassuming, who opposes a retrogressive anarchist. Unfortunately, the handsomely shot celebration of the dam construction failed to offset audience puzzlement at the director's elliptical, mood-shifting style.

Aerograd Frontier (1934) finally moved Dovzhenko away from the Ukraine to a Siberian frontier where soldiers guard the borders from penetration by Japanese espionage agents. *Shchors* (1939) is the most emotionally accessible of the director's sound films. It was commissioned by Stalin as a Ukranian *Chapayev,* and the central character, a partisan leader in the time of the Revolution, bears distinct similarities to an idealized Stalin. However, Dovzhenko balances this picture with other deft portraits of Ukrainian life and a peasant who has something of the comfortable quality of the old grandfather in *Zvenigora,* something of the undisciplined, warm farmers in *Earth*.

More Films

The end of experiment in Russian film ought no more to cloud realist accomplishments in the USSR than elsewhere; Griffith, Renoir, and Pabst were naturalistic directors, too. A psychological study, *Baltic Deputy* (1937), directed by Alexander Zharki and Josef Heifitz, describes the life of an actual Russian scientist, a 72-year-old professor who comes to discover his role in the new regime. It is distinguished by a performance from Nikolai Cherkassov, then 32, in the professor's part. Cherkassov soon impersonated Nevsky, then Ivan for Eisenstein.

Lenin in October (1937) was made by Michael Romm in response to the state's twentieth anniversary. Despite a fanciful premonition of Lenin's suspicions toward Trotskyite deviations in 1917, the film escapes easy categorization and inaugurated a series of further Lenin stories. *Professor Mamlock* (1938) derives from a play by the German Friedrich Wolf, an associate of Brecht's who fled the Nazis and settled in Russia. It documents the villifications of a Jewish physician and German patriot at the time of Hitler's rise, codirected by Adolf Minkin and Herbert Rappoport, the latter an assistant to Pabst.

Outstanding among filmed biographies was the trilogy of films directed by Mark Donskoy and based on the life of Maxim Gorky: *Childhood* (1938), *Out in the World* (1939), and *My University* (1940). Material derives from Gorky's autobiography and traces his life from czarist childhood to a revolutionary (perhaps exaggeratedly revolutionary) writer's commitment.

Gregory Kozintsev and Leonid Trauberg took another turn in biographical studies: the creation of a kind of composite fictional revolutionary biography. The Maxim Trilogy consists of *The Youth of Maxim* (1935), *The Return of Maxim* (1937), and *The Vyborg Side* (1939). It was developed from close study of prewar revolutionaries and eschewed romantic adventure for a more penetrating, episodic design whose scope is effectively contained by recurrent themes, a breadth of emotion, and even devices from eccentric theater (discussed in Chapter 8).

A further example of the Soviet's withdrawal from contemporary themes was the musical. Alexandrov made three that reflected his sojourn in Hollywood: *Jazz Comedy* (1934), *Circus* (1936), and *Volga-Volga* (1938). Finally, Boris Shumyatsky, himself a symptom of Stalinist repression of dissidence, failed to develop a subject appropriate to the twentieth anniversary. He disappeared from the scene early in 1938.

Summary

While conversion to sound in Britain, France, Germany, and the USSR almost consistently supported reversions to naturalist, theatrical traditions, film product soon demonstrated narrative accomplishments quite as unique as what had preceded. Attitudes toward cinematic styles ranged from Russian and German dedication to recreated authenticity (as in the Maxim Trilogy and *Kameradschaft*) to Renoir's vision of film as an extension of the proscenium equipped with new aural and visual subtleties. In the hands of skillful writers and directors, sound film soon became a medium that might amplify representational images to evoke further dimensions without sacrifice to "story." A different conception of film, one which elected to subordinate plot to social purpose, will be considered in the following chapter on documentary.

Bibliography

Armes, Ray. *French Cinema Since 1946*. Cranbury, N.J. 1970.
Balcon, Michael. *Twenty Years of British Film*. London, 1947.
Betts, Ernest, *Inside Pictures*. London, 1960.
Beylie, Claude. *Max Ophuls*. Paris, 1963.
Buache, Freddy. *G. W. Pabst*. Lyon, 1965.
————. *Hommage à Jean Vigo*. Lausanne, 1962.
Carné, Marcel. *Les Enfants du paradis* (based on Jacques Prévert shooting script). London, 1968.
Chazel, Robert. *Marcel Carné*. Paris, 1965.
Clair, René. *A nous la liberté*. New York, 1970.
DeFelice, James. *Filmguide to Odd Man Out*. Bloomington, 1975.
Diehl, Digby. *"The Grand Illusion," Action* (May-June 1972).
Durgnat, Raymond. *A Mirror for England*. London, 1970.
————. *Jean Renoir*. Berkeley, 1974.
Eisenstein, Sergei. *Ivan the Terrible*. New York, 1970.
Eisner, Lotte. *The Haunted Screen*. Berkeley, 1969.
Everson, William K. "Vampyr," *Cinemages* 4 (May 1, 1955).
Feldman, Joseph. *Jean Vigo*. London, n.d.
Feldman, Seth. "Cinema Weekly and Cinema Truth," *Sight and Sound* (Winter 1973–74).
————. *Evolution of Style in the Early Work of Dziga Vertov*. New York, 1977.
The Film Society Programs 1925-1939. New York, 1972.
Fisher, Lucy. "René Clair and the Coming of Sound," *Cinema Journal* (Spring 1977).
————. *"Enthusiasm," Film Quarterly* (Winter 1977–78).
Film Comment 7 (Summer 1971). (Several articles on Ophuls.)
Fowler, Roy. *The Film in France*. London, 1946.
Fofi, Goffredo. "The Cinema of the Popular Front in France," *Screen* (1972).
Gilliatt, Penelope. *Jean Renoir*. New York, 1975.
Gomery, J. Douglas. "Children of Paradise," *Sub-Stance* 9 (1974).
Gomes, P. E. Salles. *Jean Vigo*. Berkeley, 1971.
Greene, Graham and Carol Reed. *The Third Man*. New York, 1968.
Hammond, Robert M. "Writer vs. Director: an interview with Charles Spaak," *Film Culture* 15 (1957).
Hill, Stephen. "A Quantitative View of Soviet Cinema," *Cinema Journal* (Spring 1972).
Hull, David Stewart. *Film in the Third Reich*. Berkeley, 1969.
Johiel, Edwin. "Mädchen in Uniform," *Film Society Review* (February 1968).
Kracauer, Siegfried. *From Caligari to Hitler*. Princeton, 1947.

Kulik, Karel. *Alexander Korda*. London, 1975.

Leiser, Erwin. *Nazi Cinema*. London, 1974.

Leyda, Jay. *Kino*. London, 1960.

Litle, Michael. "Sound Track: *The Rules of the Game*," *Cinema Journal* (Fall 1973).

Maddock, Brent. *The Films of Jacques Tati*. Metuchen, N.J., 1977.

Manvell, Roger. *The German Cinema*. New York, 1971.

———,ed. *Three British Screen Plays*. London, 1950.

Minney, Rubeigh James. *The Films of Anthony Asquith, etc*. South Brunswick, N.J., 1976.

Mazzocco, Robert. "That's Entertainment," *New York Review of Books* (October 3, 1974).

Neergard, Ebbe. "Vampyr," *Cinemages* 4 (May 1, 1955).

Oakley, Charles. *Where We Came In*. London, 1964.

Perry, George. *Hitchcock*. Garden City, N.Y., 1975.

———. *The Great Britian Picture Show*. New York, 1974.

Pratley, Gerald, *The Cinema of David Lean*. South Brunswick, N.J., 1974.

Ralmon, John. *"Béla Balázs in German Exile,"* *Film Quarterly* (Spring 1977).

Renoir, Jean. *La Grande Illusion* (based on the script by Charles Spaak) London, 1968.

———. "How I Came to Film Boudu," *Film Society Review* (February 1967).

Richards, Jeffrey. *Visions of Yesterday*. London, 1973.

Roseen, Clarice. "Jean Vigo's Comic Vision," *Velvet Light Trap* 9 (Summer 1973).

Roud, Richard. *Max Ophuls*. Cincinnati, 1976.

Sadoul, Georges. *French Film*. London, 1953.

Sarris, Andrew. "Boudu Saved from Drowning," *Cahiers du Cinéma in English* 9 (March 1967).

———. "Carol Reed in the Context of His Time," *Film Culture* 10, 11 (1956, 1957).

Simon, Bill. "Renoir Re-Viewed," *University Films Study Center Newsletter Supplement* 5 (1975).

"Six Talks on G. W. Pabst," *Cinemages* 3 (May 1955).

Smith, John M. *Jean Vigo*. New York, 1972.

Sternberg, Josef von. *The Blue Angel*. New York, 1968.

Thompson, Kristin. "Ivan the Terrible and Stalinist Russia," *Cinema Journal* (Fall 1977).

Tuillermo, Gilberto Perez. "Jacques Becker: two films," *Sight and Sound* (Summer 1969).

Truffaut, François. *Hitchcock*. New York, 1967.

Vertov, Dziga. "From the Notebooks of Dziga Vertov," *Artforum* (March 1972).

———. "The Notebooks of Dziga Vertov," in Harry Geduld, *Film Makers on Film Making*. Bloomington, 1967.

———. "The Vertov Papers," *Film Comment* (Spring 1972).

Warfield, Nancy. "Notes on *Les Enfants du paradis*," *The Little Film Gazette of N.D.W.* (March 1967).

Weinberg, Herman. *Josef von Sternberg*. New York, 1967.

———. "Michel Simon," *Film Society Review* (March 1968).

Whitaker, Richard W. *The Content Analysis of Film: a Survey of the Field, An Exhaustive Study of Quai des brumes, and a Functional Description of the Film.* Ph. D. dissertation, Northwestern University, Evanston, 1966.

Willig, Robert. "Boudu and Satyrs," *Velvet Light Trap* 9 (Summer 1973).

Wollenberg, Hans H. *Fifty Years of German Film.* London, 1948.

Wood, George A. "Game Theory and *The Rules of the Game,*" *Cinema Journal* (Fall 1973).

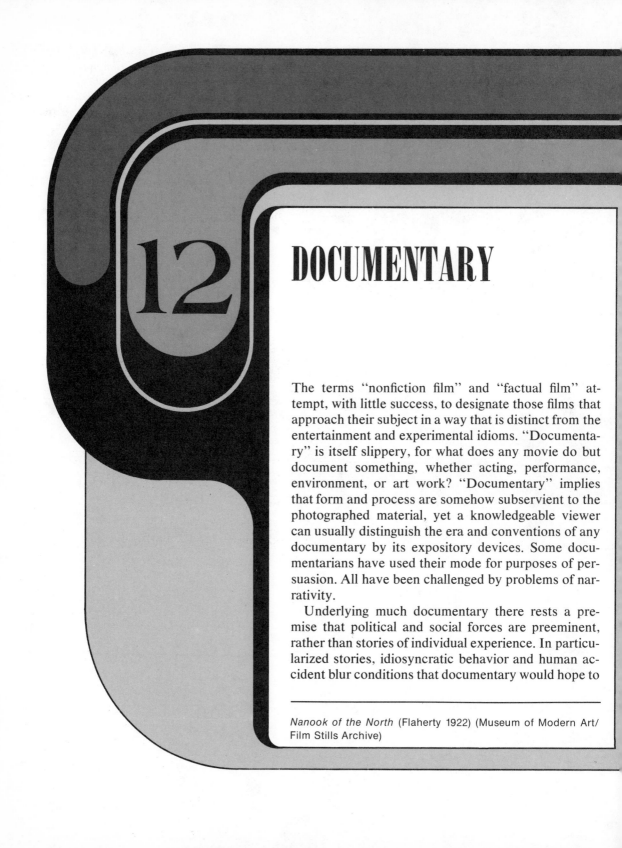

DOCUMENTARY

The terms "nonfiction film" and "factual film" attempt, with little success, to designate those films that approach their subject in a way that is distinct from the entertainment and experimental idioms. "Documentary" is itself slippery, for what does any movie do but document something, whether acting, performance, environment, or art work? "Documentary" implies that form and process are somehow subservient to the photographed material, yet a knowledgeable viewer can usually distinguish the era and conventions of any documentary by its expository devices. Some documentarians have used their mode for purposes of persuasion. All have been challenged by problems of narrativity.

Underlying much documentary there rests a premise that political and social forces are preeminent, rather than stories of individual experience. In particularized stories, idiosyncratic behavior and human accident blur conditions that documentary would hope to

Nanook of the North (Flaherty 1922) (Museum of Modern Art/ Film Stills Archive)

express more clearly through generalizations, made or implied. Documentary sometimes distinguishes between the staged event and one captured unawares, unaffected by camera presence. An evocation of the Revolution with "real" street people and locations, Eisenstein's *October* falls into the staged idiom, while most of Vertov's work does not. Inasmuch as the recreated film is peopled with those who enact common, unexceptional behavior, individualized performance may be subsumed into cultural roles. Thus, Gance's employment of soldiers for the battle scenes of *J'accuse* has a particular sort of authenticity.

Documentary's relation to experimentation has been periodic. Committed to certain kinds of visuals and hampered by recording equipment, British documentarians gave imaginative attention to sound during the thirties. Invention was encouraged by social-problem documentary filmmakers who feared when audiences equated their work with boring, prosaic uplift. Some consider documentary prefigured by broad, nonfilm ideas and propagandistic intention, regardless of the means employed. However, experimentation may itself threaten to cloak a film's persuasive capabilities with over-visible technique. The issue underlay Eisenstein's, Vertov's and Dovzhenko's difficulties with Boris Shumyatsky (in control of education and in position to censor), who viewed with greater favor a straightforward hortatory documentary like *Turksib* (1928) by Victor Turin, in which the Turkistan-Siberian railway is energetically constructed against pressures of time and forces of nature. More recently, the relation of illusion to persuasion defined Jean-Luc Godard's differences with the Brazilian filmmaker Glauber Rocha. In Godard's opinion, revolutionary ideas required revolutionary technique, uncorrupted by bourgeois traditions of narrative. Rocha believes that persuasive film must necessarily accommodate itself to the narrative conventions of its audience to meet with positive reception.

ACTUALITY EXPRESSIONS

Incipient documentary locates itself in the actuality films, real and staged, that were described in Chapter 1. Many of the earliest Lumière ventures—filmed from train windows and platforms and hand-developed in enameled buckets—still carry immense visual pleasure as they innocently shift camera perspective, depth, and foreground-background composition to beautiful effect. As the motion picture cannibalized and replaced nineteenth-century theater and pulp fiction, it also took over functions of the educational slide shows. The early history of Cecil Hepworth is a case in point, for England supported many itinerant presentations like his father's. Both travel and educational films derive from these beginnings, as well as from the still photography records of exploration and experimentation that found broad audiences when photogravure printing methods inexpensively facilitated more pictures in magazines and journals during the nineties. Enthusiasm for Hale's Tours and for the newsreel grew from that tradition; indeed, newsreels sometimes had direct affiliations with journalism, as with Hearst-Selig News Pictorial.

Percy Smith, a minor civil servant in the British Ministry of Education, developed nature photography out of a hobby. Before World War I, the *World Before Your Eye* series of fifty-four films, produced for Charles Urban, documented processes of natural growth; one film on the gladioli was made in Kinemacolor. Smith developed time lapse photography and microphotography to make the silent *Secrets of Nature* and the sound *Secrets of Life* films that first familiarized large audiences with the functionings of plants and micro-organisms.

Jean Painlevé, French creator of science documentaries as well as entertainment features, combined interests in surrealist film with his enthusiasm for underwater photography, so that *La Pieuvre* (1928), *Crevette* (1930), and *L'Hippocampe* (1934) became highly poetic visions of aquatic biology. Painlevé's original approach to documentary has been little explored since.

TRAVEL AND ADVENTURE

A documentation may be organized by the continuity and drama of events themselves. Scott's expedition to the antarctic in 1911-13 was photographed by Herbert Ponting, and *Scott's Antarctic Expedition* (1913) became an early, theatrically exhibited feature. World War I was covered by many motion picture photographers, viewed as newsreel shorts and, in *The Battle of the Somme* (1916), as a British feature executed by Geoffrey Malins and J. B. McDowell. Griffith's *Hearts of the World* war footage eventually showed up in government archives and newsreel stock footage libraries.

Feature length travel-adventure films, *Hunting Big Game in Africa* (1923), exploration, *With Byrd at the South Pole* (1930, and exotica, *Wild Beauty* (1927), vied with entertainment films for theater audiences. The careers of Ernest B. Schoedsack and Merian C. Copper consolidated and then exploited such films' relation to Hollywood.

Schoedsack and Cooper were wartime friends, Schoedsack a combat photographer. They filmed an extraordinary trek by 50,000 Baktyari tribemen in search of pasture land for their herds in Persia and Turkey. The migration is climaxed by a barefoot climb over the 12,000 foot Zardeh Kuh mountain, covered with ice and snow. This effort, along with an involved and dangerous fording of the river Karun, carried out on simple hand-hewn crafts, is spectacularly filmed in long shots that gain, like the Riefenstahl-Fanck mountain films, from their panoramas and awesome inclines. The film appeared as *Grass* (1925) and still carries impact. Its antiquated intertitles provide young audiences unintended di-

Grass. Schoedsack and Cooper in the forefront of the expedition. The Baktyari carried not only their own supplies but the filmmakers' equipment as well! The migration was filmed again by Anthony Howarth for a two-hour documentary released as *People of the Wind* in 1976. (Museum of Modern Art/Film Stills Archive)

version when tribesmen finally reach their goal, grass, and settle contentedly into pipe smoking.

Schoedsack and Cooper then made *Chang* (1927) in a Siamese village, developing a minimal story about the threat of wild beasts in surrounding jungle. Its exhibition was enhanced by employment of a wide-angle projection lens, dubbed a magnascope, which dramatically expanded a climactic elephant charge onto a great, enlarged screen. Both films were released by Paramount, who then incorporated the filmmaker's reality with Hollywood artifice in a version of *Four Feathers* (1929) that tied Sudan footage to studio adventure. Like *Rango* (1931), which followed, the combination helped neither idiom. More effectively, Schoedsack and Cooper were absorbed in a papier-mâché jungle that had its own charms, *King Kong* (1933), and insubstantiality, *Mighty Joe Young* (1949).

Personalized Travel

As it is usually described in histories, documentary's romantic progenitor was Robert Flaherty, son of a prospector who explored Canadian hinterlands for minerals. The young man was encouraged by Sir William Mackenzie to bring a camera on a 1913 exploration of Hudson Bay. Later, editing the film, Flaherty dropped a cigarette and lost his footage in flames.[1] In any case, it had been screened and rejected by the cameraman for its impersonality. On the next trip, Flaherty again brought photographic equipment. The result was *Nanook of the North* (1922).

Nanook profits enormously from its detailed attention to a single Eskimo of immense charm, and to his family. The film develops sequences of ordinary life, including a visit to the trading post, but its strongest moments come from specific observations of Eskimo skills, as in building an igloo and spearing fish and seals. Production costs of *Nanook* were underwritten by a furrier, Revillon Frères. After rejection by various distributors, it finally opened to commercial success, gaining Flaherty a Paramount contract. He journeyed to Samoa, encouraged by Jesse Lasky to make a Nanook without the snow.

Flaherty's view of non-European cultures isolated each society from effects of foreign intrusion. He was interested not in what deterioration had resulted from exploitation, but rather in the integrity of the uncontaminated culture. Nanook's life depended on his own skills; in fact, he died of starvation on a hunt two years after *Nanook of the North* appeared. *Moana — a Romance of the Golden Age* (1925) captured a society who faced no grueling challenge. To impose drama, Flaherty filmed an initiatory tattooing ceremony that had not been practiced for years. The film lacks *Nanook*'s intensity, but it is a delight to watch. Flaherty was now a practiced cameraman with great visual sensitivity (although some Hollywood cameramen, Floyd Crosby for example, decry his professional skill).[2] Flaherty's experimental employment of panchromatic film in exteriors captured the Polynesian skin tones to beautiful effect. His familiarity with ritual movements allowed the photography a confident, mobile ease which, as in all his films, avoids both unexpected and unanticipated movement. Flaherty once proposed that a good cameraman could find drama in a left-to-right pan across a map of the United States-Canada border.

[1] *Frances Flaherty once advised me that she never knew what actually happened to the film's original, since her husband was editing a workprint at the time of the accident.*

[2] See *Nicholas Pasquiriello*, Oral History of Floyd D. Crosby, A.S.C. *American Film Institute Oral History Series. Crosby worked with Flaherty on* Tabu, The Land, *and an unfinished project,* Acoma, The Sky City *(1928). He considers Flaherty ignorant of elementary photographic skills and technical expertise and uncomfortable with any sort of staged performance at all.*

Anticipating more sex and less joy, American audiences failed to support *Moana* and Flaherty never again shared a successful relation with any Hollywood studio. He teamed with F. W. Murnau and commenced a Tahitian film, but the two disagreed on story line, and *Tabu* (1931) is clearly dominated by Murnau's Germanic fatalism. *Man of Aran* (1934) was supported by Gaumont-British and documents the arduous life of a society of islanders off Ireland. As in *Moana*, Flaherty intensified narrative by reviving custom, in this case the harpooning of a basking shark. Its sound is murky, but *Man of Aran* captures the people's dignity and humor with respect and affection.

In the adaptation of *Elephant Boy* (1937), Kipling and Flaherty fought to a draw, Alexander Korda as spectator and only Sabu, a young Indian discovery, the winner. *The Land* (1942) has been the least seen of the director's major films. It was commissioned by the Department of Agriculture to call attention to the consequences of over production in the midwest, and while the intention is not persuasively argued, Flaherty develops strong sequences about the effect of mechanization on farmworkers.

Louisiana Story (1948) was Flaherty's last feature, the adventures of young Cajun in the Louisiana bayous and his relation to an oil crew who are constructing a derrick nearby. The film was sponsored by Standard Oil without restraints and with all rights reverting to Flaherty. It represents a kind of reconciliation between the director and civilization (or at least with Standard Oil), but more important are the bayou sequences, exquisitely photographed by Flaherty and his assistant, the young Richard Leacock.[3]

THE FILM AS SOCIAL FORCE

John Grierson, son of a Scottish schoolmaster, viewed film as Calvinists saw the Bible, a means to grace and salvation. In the midtwenties, he investigated mass media in the United States on a study grant. Grierson saw film's potential for propaganda as similar to that of political newspaper cartoons: a way to inform and to sharpen political and social sophistications among great audiences in industrialized democracies. Semi-literate or non-readers, these people might not be effectively approached by print, and their minimal instruction was essential to the survival of any political process that required wide spread public judgement and participation. He was an ardant, highly articulate polemicist for the use of the documentary to this end, viewing propaganda not as necessary dissimulation, but rather an energetic informational service that combined emotion with fact to call attention and to arouse sympathy.

Grierson returned to Britain and became Films Officer of the Empire Marketing Board.

obert Flaherty (1884–1951)

Nanook of the North	1922
Moana—A Romance of the Golden Age	1925
The Twenty-Four Dollar Island (short)	1926
Tabu (codirector F. W. Murnau)	1931
Industrial Britain (completed by John Grierson)	1932
Man of Aran (Britain)	1934
Elephant Boy (codirector Zoltan Korda)	1937
The Land	1942
Louisiana Story	1948

[3] *The Museum of Modern Art Film Department distributes a film made up of footage shot for bayou sequences with accompanying discussion by participants in the production. Paeans to Flaherty aside, the film is interesting as a study guide to work in progress.*

The favorable reception to *Drifters* (1929), his film on the North Sea herring fleet, helped Grierson to concentrate on the organization and training of a production unit that might turn out strong, effective documentaries with intelligence and imagination, and without the vagaries of one-shot productions and financing. Crews were successfully trained, first under the Marketing Board sponsorship, next under the General Post Office and later at the Canadian Film Board (which Grierson helped to organize and to administrate) and UNESCO.

Grierson's prose on the subject of documentaries must be balanced against his product, for, without the experience of his films, one may distort the toughminded, hardheaded Scottish argument into notions of the prosaic information film. It is also a mistake to overcredit Grierson on films where his role was secondhand as producer, advisor, or inspiration, even though his strategy pervades prewar British documentary.

In fact, British documentary is surprisingly varied both in subject and execution. *Drifters* emerges as a strong emotional experience, however one feels about barrels of herring. Grierson was influenced by Soviet films, and the drama of sea life, labor, and fishing success is translated into heavy, massed images whose composition, movement, and tempo lyricize the labor process.

In one manner or another, this quality permeates a great number of the period's documentaries, which otherwise vary in subject matter. Further experimentation was fostered when Alberto Cavalcanti assumed supervision of many productions. Both *Coal Face* by Cavalcanti (1936) and *Night Mail* by Basil Wright and Harry Watt (1936) edit sequences to prerecorded music and to poetic commentary that exalts the workers. *Housing Problems* (1935) bypassed the usual dramatized incident or omniscient narrator and let slum tenement dwellers talk directly to the camera-audience, taking us on tour through decaying buildings. A recurrent motif was the character and resilience of the English worker. Grierson hired Flaherty to make one short film, *Industrial Britain* (1933). Typically, Flaherty concentrated on craftsmen rather than assembly-line employees.

Song of Ceylon (1935) directed by Basil Wright, is one of the time's most ambitious documentaries, a celebration of Ceylonese culture constructed in four parts, ranging from modern commerce to religious ritual. Sound commentary is often played against, rather than congruent with, the picture, as when the sound track of export finance dealings accompanies shots of elephants pushing down jungle trees.

Paul Rotha, author of silent film's most perceptive early history, *The Film Till Now*, joined documentary as a screen writer. His self-directed documentary, *The Face of Britain* (1935), investigated national planning for coal and electricity production. *The World of Plenty* (1943) combined stock footage, interviews, and a strong commentary composed of many voices in order to impress audiences with the dimensions of international hunger. These techniques were further refined in *Land of Promise* (1945) and *The World is Rich* (1948).

THE CITY FILM

A Propos de Nice was one expression of the city documentary, designed to record a cosmopolitan environment, often one day's experience, and styled by the esthetic of a filmmaker. Still photographer Paul Strand made an early experimental study of New York with Charles Sheeler, *Manhatta* (1921), depersonalized into abstracted compositions similar to those of photographer Alfred Steiglitz.

The designs of Walter Ruttmann in his documentary *Berlin, Symphony of a City* (1927) are suggested by the title. With the aid of Karl Freund, Ruttmann photographed the city, much of it in early morning and by way of concealed cameras. Another collaborator, Carl Mayer, withdrew from the project in disagreement with Ruttmann's depersonalized notions. His departure is significant, for, where an individual story for Mayer epitomized social forces, *Berlin* concentrates less ideologically on crowds, institutions, and transportation. The film traces one day, as if Berlin had a life somehow expressed through, but not determined by, its inhabitants. Juxtapositions, like crowds and cattle, provide heavy-handed equivalents to some of the notions of *The Man With a Movie Camera*. Prismatic lenses sometimes break one image into identical reflections, an expressionist convention one also finds in *Variety* and *Metropolis*.

Simultaneously, *Rien que les heures* (1926) was produced in Paris by the Brazilian Alberto Cavalcanti. Again, passages of a city day are depicted, although Cavalcanti gives more attention to thematic development, as when a staggering, starving woman derelict reappears, cut against images of affluence. Cavalcanti is somewhat closer to Vertov's spirit than is Ruttmann.

An introductory sequence begins with a glamorous shot of attractive women modishly walking down a flight of stairs. The picture is then frozen and withdrawn from the camera field so that we may see it now as a still photograph. The photograph is torn and discarded as if such fantasy must be openly rejected before we can witness real behavior. Labor process in the city's life is referred to in a scene where a man chews his restaurant steak; superimposed on the plate we see a steer's abbatoir slaughter.

A final scene departs the Kino-Eye approach to explore a French preoccupation: time and simultaneity. The times of cities throughout the world are shown on clocks while people dressed in costumes of different nationalities rush past the camera in a kind of wind-swept effort to overcome the passage of time. Cavalcanti's film is lovelier and wittier than *Berlin,* but it is also less consistent.

The city film engendered visual records of Moscow, Mikhail Kaufman's *Moscow* (1925); Amsterdam, Joris Ivens' *Rain* (1929); and Ostend, *Images of Ostend* (1930) by Henri Storck. It continued into such sound productions as Arne Sucksdorf's *People of the City* (1947) of Stockholm and *Waverley Steps* (1948) of Edinburgh.

NEW DEAL DOCUMENTARY

Hopes for social change under Franklin Roosevelt were reflected in a growing enthusiasm of politically minded artists about the use of still and motion photography to document injustice and poverty in the interest of reform. The Film and Photo League in New York City fostered similar organizations in other cities and encouraged familiarity with such theorist-filmmakers as Eisenstein and Vertov and with Leon Moussinac, who had worked with Delluc in the formation of French ciné-clubs. Experimentation and documentation would be put to use by filmmakers in the name of social reform.

Pare Lorentz, a journalist and film critic, became involved in documentary production when he undertook a small-budget study of the dust-bowl crisis, *The Plow That Broke the Plains* (1936). Based on its reception, Lorentz was commissioned by the Department of Agriculture to do a film on the Mississippi River and flood control. *The River* (1937) established the notion of documentary for generations of American school children: sonorous, urgent narration ("*down* the Monongehela, *down* the Yellowstone, the Milk, the White and the Cheyenne"), stern admonitions, rising excitement followed by ponderous explanation. At the same time, *The River* was well photographed, skillfully edited, and enhanced

The Plow That Broke the Plains. As with *The River,* Lorenz used commentary and a didactic ending to mount his argument. However, it lacked the dramatic narrative of *The River* and the second film's humanization of the ecological drama. (Museum of Modern Art/Film Stills Archive)

by the rousing score from Virgil Thomson. Response to *The River* helped to promote another government-sponsored documentary on rural electrification, *Power and the Land* (1940), directed by the Dutch Joris Ivens. Pressed by the New Deal to book the documentaries, film distributors resented such competition in theaters, and Republican adversaries further suspected a film program enlisted in the service of government policy. Appropriations were voted away in 1940.

The City (1939) directed by Willard van Dyke and Ralph Steiner was privately sponsored for exhibition at the New York World's Fair. All thirties American documentaries carry messages like envelopes; the message of *The City* concerned municipal planning. In the style of *The River,* it was constructed in terms of Problem/Solution. Noteworthy are humorous sequences on eating a standup lunch and crossing the street in New York City, events that assume monstrous dimensions through clever editing.

Spanish Earth (1937) was sponsored by a group of American artists who commissioned Joris Ivens and Ernest Hemingway to make a report on the Spanish Civil War supportive of the Loyalist cause. The film follows a contingent of volunteers who join the Loyalist soldiers while their families work to produce food at home. It includes powerful battle footage, and Hemingway's narration emotionally disports itself in a style that he somehow never managed in his screen fiction dialogue. *Spanish Earth* exists in a commentary version spoken by Orson Welles and one by Hemingway himself.

An outgrowth of the Film and Photo League, Frontier Films made documentaries in the period between 1937 and 1942. *Heart of Spain* (1937) was assembled from newsreels, material secured by a neophyte cameraman, and a bit of Joris Ivens' footage to celebrate the Loyalist cause and to make known the work of a Canadian medical unit's blood transfusions to soldiers just out of combat.

Native Land (1942), Frontier's last production, was edited, like *Heart of Spain,* by Leo Hurwitz, who shared directing credits with Paul Strand. Like Renoir's *La Vie est à nous,* it assembled a series of reenactments, some quite poorly simulated, depicting abridgement of American civil liberties and applauding the developing labor movement. Lacking either the popular fantasy elements of Hollywood films or the support of government pressure in distribution, Frontier Films were seldom seen by the general public.

With the inauguration of *The March of Time* in 1933, Time, Inc. capitalized on its news-gathering organization. Conceived in a magazine format, sometimes with separate sections, sometimes held together by a theme, *The March of Time* ranged in subject from studies of American music to news events and social issues, some searchingly reported for the times. As with *The River,* its visuals were organized and "explained" by a strident narrator, and sometimes recorded "reenactments" by professionals. Appearing with increasing infrequency in later years, *The March of Time* was discontinued in 1951.

TRIUMPH OF THE WILL AND OLYMPIA

Before she became a star in the mountain films, Leni Riefenstahl was a dancer. Under Arnold Fanck and Pabst, who codirected *The White Hell of Pitz Palü,* she learned film production. Hitler admired Riefenstahl and persuaded her to make a short based on the 1933 Nazi rally, *Victory of Faith* (1933).

The experience was debilitating. Riefenstahl felt she had been harassed by Goebbels. When Hitler requested a bigger documentary of next year's more ambitious rally, she tried to substitute Walter Ruttmann in her place. On the führer's insistence, Riefenstahl agreed, with the condition that she be allowed total freedom of execution. *Triumph of the Will* (1934) runs two hours, executed by some reports with sixteen chief cameramen and a

Triumph of the Will. Whether the woman in a loose coat with hand on camera dolly is Riefenstahl remains unclear, but the photograph dramatizes effective coordinations between staged event and its "documentation." (Museum of Modern Art/Film Stills Archive)

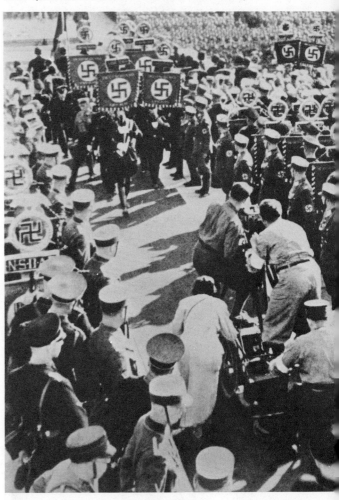

crew of 120. Not only production resources but the event itself was adapted to Riefenstahl's filmmaking purposes, parades and ceremony cued to camera positions. The result is a wearing, impressive spectacle that, even more than similar ceremonies, combines public ritual with its documentation so that distinctions between reality and fiction falter. *Triumph of the Will* overwhelmingly accomplishes its purpose, which was publicly to consolidate National Socialism and to relate the Nazi takeover to German aspiration and traditions.

An out-of-the-way, minor Riefenstahl project was *Tag der Freiheit/Day of Freedom* (1935). It was photographed in a single day by six cameramen and assembled by Riefenstahl because the army felt itself inadequately represented in *Triumph of the Will.* Following an opening sequence of night sentinels, a garrison waking, and the introduction of maneuvers staged for an audience, which includes Hitler, Hess, and Himmler, a military attack proceeds. With smoke grenades, automatic and semi-automatic weaponry, and cars from which riflemen leap, the entertainment has somewhat the look of a Buffalo Bill Wild West show. The short film ends with anti-aircraft units firing at overhead planes, concluding on swastika flags and uniformed soldiers in stern diagonals.

Riefenstahl proposed to film the 1936 Berlin Olympics with similar resources and cooperation. Under persistent urgings, game officials concurred, and *Olympia* (1938) was shot from towers, pits, and tracks specially constructed for the cameramen. Some material was automatically photographed beneath free-floating balloons and cameras mounted in boat prows. Cameramen trained themselves to film high divers in the air, then to submerge and complete the executions underwater.

As before, Riefenstahl accumulated vast footage. It required eighteen months to edit, appearing in two parts, with different language versions cleverly adapted to the distribution areas. *Triumph of the Will* celebrates military precision, uniforms, and determination; *Olympia* is dedicated to the human body and its controlled performance. The intimacy of the cameras and the performance they record personalizes athletes' experience. Sequences are constructed out of events, like the marathon torch-carrying prologue, so that physical exertion and beauty are developed by editing into emotionalized, cumulative incidents. *Olympia* has a propensity for heavy-filtered dramatic graphics, bodies poised against explosions of cumulus clouds, which give the viewer a further, uneasy sense that ideology permeates the physical, non-anecdotal experience. After the war, Riefenstahl never engaged in further successful film production, excepting *Tiefland* (1952), based on an opera.

Leni Riefenstahl (1902–   )

WARTIME FILMS

Germany made vast records of its military campaigns, cloaking rhetoric with the apparent candor of newsreels in *Baptism of Fire* (1940), *Campaign in Poland* (1940), and *Victory in the West* (1941). Russian cameras, seeking to offset defeat with evidence of heroism and determination in the early years, reported hostilities in *Leningrad at War*

(1942), *Moscow Strikes Back* (1943), and *The Fight for Our Soviet Ukraine* (1943). Major directors participated (Dovzhenko made the last cited film), and more than a hundred Russian combat cameramen died in action.

Early American war documentaries were conceived as motivational, designed as in the *Why We Fight* series produced by Frank Capra, to acquaint first recruits and later civilians with recent political history and rhetorical calls for aggressive response. ("Free men are like rubber balls. The harder they fall, the harder they bounce.") Seven such films appeared. They were constructed out of Hollywood footage, enemy film including parts of *Triumph of the Will,* and stark, dramatically animated maps. *The Battle of Russia* (1943) and *The Battle of China* (1944) were later withdrawn as political circumstances shifted, but postwar soldiers remember required viewings of *Why We Fight* long after hostilities.

As the United States engaged more fully in the fighting, single films emerged, often made by Hollywood figures. John Ford did *The Battle of Midway* (1944), Louis de Rochement *The Fighting Lady* (1943) on an aircraft carrier in the Pacific, and William Wyler *Memphis Belle* (1944), the record of a bombing mission.

John Huston made moving documentary films. *Report from the Aleutians* (1942) is less taut and ordered than subsequent work, but already shows Huston's interest in the reactions of individual soldiers and a laconic, Heming-

Divide and Conquer, the third episode in the *Why We Fight* series. Captured German footage documents the Nazi blitz. Here paratroopers over Belgium undertake a new form of aerial offensive with brutal efficiency. (Museum of Modern Art/Film Stills Archive)

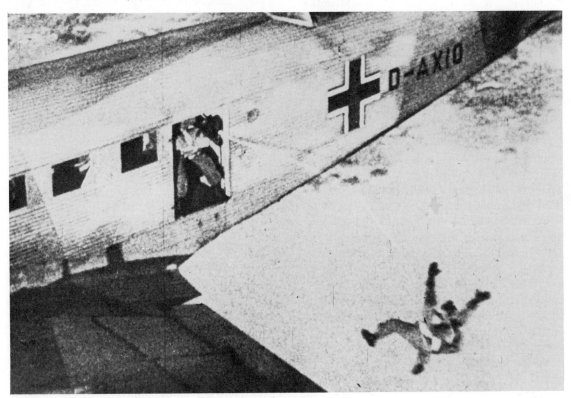

wayesque narrative style that is often effective although sometimes bordering on the cliché of tough-sentimental. *The Battle of San Pietro* (1944) details, with strategic explanation, an American assault in Italy, bogged by winter mud and vicious crossfire. The film's uncompromising view of war's cost, however mitigated by the infantry's extraordinary courage, led to Pentagon-induced cuts. *Let There Be Light* (1945) views rehabilitation at a military hospital. It was intended to promote civilian understanding of neuropsychiatric damage, and Huston recorded therapy with concealed cameras. The deeply moving film has been little seen beyond psychiatric circles.[4]

England's battle documentaries include records of the Rommel campaign in *Desert Victory* (1943) and *Tunisian Victory* (1944). Harry Watt, a Grierson associate since 1931, recorded a Royal Air Force bombing mission in *Target for Tonight* (1941). Cavalcanti's *Three Songs of Resistance* (1943) was produced for underground resistance fighters, and parachuted to partisans in Europe.

The most personalized British documentaries came from Humphrey Jennings, a Cambridge-educated figure whose backgrounds in music, poetry, and painting nurtured structural complexities and sound employments that now account for the viability of his films when almost all World War II films from any country are difficult to accept. In *London Can Take It* (1940), *Listen to Britain* (1942), *Fires Were Started* (1943), *The Silent Village* (1943), and *A Diary for Timothy* (1945) Jennings resonated British pride and understated determination without bombast or devious argument. Although his subleties did not sit well with Grierson, Jennings argued for the country's ability to endure German bombings without irrevocable sacrifice of its humane values. The premise of *Listen to Britain* is that

[4] *A script for* Let There Be Light, *made from the film, will be found in Robert Hughes,* Film: Book 2. *New York, 1962.*

England can be understood by her wartime sounds, and Jennings accompanies his picture with the BBC, a Blackpool dance band, workers in an assembly line, birds, and airplanes overhead. Pictures are largely illustrations to the sounds. They include a concert by Myra Hess who, significantly, is playing Mozart.

Narration on *A Diary for Timothy* was written by the novelist E. M. Forster, viewing Britain at war's end in a report to a newborn child. Words effect radical transitions from scene to scene by free association, as from bombing rubble to the graveyard episode in Hamlet. While equating the two sequences with death, Forster draws on English traditions to provide meaning for the war casualties.

Full-length documentary war features in World War II were able, at their best, to impose meaning, through a narration's broader comprehensions, on material that would otherwise strike observers, like participants, as distressingly fragmented. *Stalingrad* (1943) by L. Valamov drew great emotionality in the portrayal of the heroic defense of the city. In a broader context, *The True Glory* (1945) supplied an overview of the Allies' European campaign. It was commissioned by General Eisenhower, produced in Britain, and jointly supervised by Carol Reed and the American Garson Kanin.

POETRY AND POVERTY

Spanning much documentary history, Joris Ivens' work does not comfortably fit the ethos of any particular time or place, a sensitive photographer's vision in *The Bridge* (1928) and *Rain* (1929), hardened by the inspiration of Vertov and a visit to Russia. *Borinage* (1933) was made in a Belgian mining region during a debilitating strike. A staged demonstration was itself suppressed by police. Ivens commented that in filming *Borinage* he rea-

Joris Ivens (1898–)

lized beautiful photography might detract from a filmmaker's intentions.

New Earth (1934), like *Drifters,* owes its success to the effective harnessing of dramatic energies to mechanical process. The movie deals with the reclamation of the Zuiderzee. Although its second-reel conclusion, the closing of a dike, is highly effective, *New Earth* in fact includes a third reel, less often seen, which shows farmers pouring their grain back into the sea to support food prices.

After helping to film *Spanish Earth,* Ivens journeyed to China with many members of the same crew and made *The 400 Million* (1939) about China's war with Japan. Its battle footage is even starker than the Spanish film. Ivens made *Power and the Land* (1940), wartime films in the United States and Canada, and went to the East Indies as Dutch Film Commissioner, there to switch sides, join the Indonesian rebels, and make *Indonesia Calling* (1946). Since that time, he has worked in the USSR, France, China, Cuba, Chile, the Netherlands, and Vietnam.

CONCENTRATION CAMPS

Germany's defeat disclosed concentration camp horrors. Masses of film footage, surprisingly thorough and including "home movies," were used for war-crime trials and in the assemblage of many long films. Pare Lorentz made *Nuremberg* (1948) and the Russians *Judgement of the Nations* (1946). In East Germany, Andrew and Annelie Thorndike have devoted their lives to studying Nazi film archives and preparing films from this material to document German war crimes and military-political collaborations. The field of new films cannibalized from old has roots in traditions of the newsreel and "stock shot" libraries, its progenitor Ester Shub.[5]

[5] *See Jay Leyda,* Films Beget Films. *New York, 1964.*

Of all the films that undertake the subject of Nazi criminality, none is more devastating than *Night and Fog* (1955). Director Alain Resnais frames his narrative with a visit to the remains of a concentration camp and cremetorium, filmed in color, curiously peaceful. His camera tracks down a rusted railway spur, and the perspective and movement are picked up by black and white wartime footage that plunges the viewer into the inescapable reality of the camps as they existed then. After the unaccountable horrors are recounted, accompanied by restrained narration and a cold, flinty string ensemble music track by Hanns Eisler, the visual shifts from a heap of corpses to flowers in the contemporary ruins. The commentary concludes:

[There are] those of us who pretend to believe that all this happened only once, at a certain time and in a certain place, and those who refuse to see, who do not hear the cry to the end of time.[6]

POSTWAR DOCUMENTARY

Trained in documentary, postwar filmmakers turned to peacetime topics. One strategy was to avoid people and turn to objects. Bert Haanstra made *Mirror of Holland* (1950) and *Panta Rhei* (1951) in the Netherlands. *Panta Rhei*, subtitled *Everything Flows*, used camera manipulation to capture what is not apparent in natural movements and rhythms. Accelerating or slowing down clouds, shadows, water, and wind into a common tempo, Haanstra juxtaposes images of one element with those of another so that similarities become evident. *Mirror of Holland* inverts water reflections.

---

[6] The film's script by Jean Cayrol is available in Hughes, *op cit*.

Rippling pictures appear to be airborn while the actual image lies motionless below.

A later Haanstra film, *Glass* (1958) shows another documentary avenue, which was to apply to industry for sponsorship, a Flaherty tradition. *Glass* makes a humorous case for blending the humanity of the craftsman with modern efficiencies. Glassblowers and automated assembly lines are shown in turn. Mechanics break down, until humans correct the error. But for an interlude of depersonalized voices, an ingenious, carefully synchronized jazz track provides the only sound; warmly human in the first sequence, cold modern in the second, sprightly friendly at conclusion.

Experimentation colored Francis Thompson's *N.Y., N.Y* (1958), a city film done altogether in reflections, superimpositions and prismatic lenses; images of New York are multiplied and joined into crowded impersonality. The National Film Board of Canada encouraged special documentary approaches. Their *Day After Day* (1966), for example, employed a sound track that presumed to enter into thoughts of the bored workers in a small-town Canadian paper mill.

Another turn was toward social problems, mental illness and delinquency replacing earlier, externalized conflicts of warfare and battles with nature. In *The Quiet One* (1948), written by James Agee and directed by Sidney Meyers, a child is transferred from Harlem to a school for maladjusted children. The National Film Board explored *The Feeling of Rejection* (1947), *The Feeling of Hostility* (1948), *The Feeling of Depression* (1950) and *Overdependency* (1949).

At worst, such films preserved pedantic lecturing qualities of New Deal documentaries and the peculiarly documentary genre of stiff acting that accompanies them. They also make evident the desire of the filmmakers to engage more intimately and candidly with the life around them. *In The Street* (1952), made out of outtakes from *The Quiet One*, betrays this wish. From a distance, a group of white filmmakers photograph black children playing in the ghetto. Their impulse is to join the game; unable, they fall back to a removed lyricism.

FREE CINEMA

As in the arenas of theater and the novel where experiences less bounded by class and decorum were erupting, English Free Cinema, with Lindsay Anderson as spokesman, argued for a film approach that ignored Grierson's propagandism and, too, Jenning's interpretation through a filter of personal sensibility.

Hints of the freer vision were seen in the semifictional *David* (1951) by Paul Dickson. Anderson's earliest documentary venture to illustrate the developed viewpoint is *Thursday's Children* (1953), which treats a school for the deaf. While children are shown sharing a life together and learning skills to compensate for their handicap, Anderson avoids such issues of motivation and case history documentation as, for example, Agee wrote into *The Quiet One.* The children are only as individualized, as sympathetic and as comprehensible as behavior actually shows. Another film of the same year, *O Dreamland,* examined a working-class amusement park. Its satiric view of the spot's vulgarity has a look of class condescension unless we choose to believe that the filmmaker has had the integrity to view events free from the rose-colored glasses of traditional British (and American) liberal apology, mixing sympathy and disgust toward a brutalizing escape-world. Anderson's understanding of documentary was clear-cut. If the material was real it was documentary. If the material was staged it was not. With Karel Reisz, Tony Richardson, Claude Goretta, and Alain Tanner, Anderson concentrated on laboring people in ordinary circumstances, viewed without fanfare about work's nobility

Every Day Except Christmas. "I want to make people—ordinary people, not just Top People—feel their dignity and their importance, so that they can act from these principles. Only on such principles can confident and healthy action be based." Lindsay Anderson (British National Film Archive/Stills Library)

or poetry eulogizing the human spirit. Free Cinema looks closely and unabashedly at human beings.

Every Day Except Christmas (1957) is the most successfully realized of Anderson's documentaries, an early morning study of flower merchants in Covent Garden. *Momma Don't Allow* (1955) by Karel Reisz and Tony Richardson, visits a traditional jazz club, where young people drink and dance to the music of Chris Barber. In contrast to *Jazz Dance* (1954), a similar American short by Roger Tilton made at New York's Central Plaza, Reisz and Richardson seem fascinated by the intricacies of dance and gesture. *Nice Time* (1957) views an evening in Picadilly Circus. Without an overriding intention, Claude Goretta and Alain Tanner fail to break through the surfaces of hair and clothing styles. Reisz's *We are the Lambeth Boys* (1959) reports the mod subculture of working class English youth with more detail and coherence. *Together* (1955) by Lorenza Maz-

zetti employs semifictional narrative sympathetically to portray a pair of deaf mutes as they are both tolerated and taunted by a neighborhood. The final soundless drowning of one boy concludes the film with jarring drama.

Elsewhere, emancipating urges were manifested, too, less rationalized by doctrine. The American Lionel Rogosin's *On the Bowery* (1956) enters skid row so observantly that an audience quickly picks up the drink-cadging strategies of Bowery inhabitants, while a sense of hopelessness deepens toward the protagonist, Ray. Subcultures are similarly recounted by the Canadian Paul Tomkowicz, *Street Railway Switchman* (1954); and the American George Stoney's *All My Babies* (1952), a study of midwife training in Georgia that retains something of the pedagogy of earlier American documentaries in its restrained, gentle manner.

EQUIPMENT AND CONSCIOUSNESS

Richard Leacock (1921–   )

Toby and the Tall Corn	1955
F 100	1956
Yanki No!	1960
Primary	1960
Eddie/On the Pole	1961
Football	1961
Peter and Johnnie	1961
X-15	1961
The New Frontier	1961
David	1962
Nehru	1962
The Chair	1963
Jane	1963
Happy Birthday Blackie	1963
Aga Khan	1963
Happy Mother's Day	1965
Republicans—the New Breed	1964
Igor Stravinsky—a Portrait	1966
Chiefs	1970
Partial listing	

Working with Flaherty on *Louisiana Story*, Richard Leacock learned the frustrations that attended heavy, bulky recording equipment. However accepted a silent camera might be, other mechanical paraphernalia only inhibited a subject's behavior and deflected authenticity. Yet without speech documentaries were more suited to subject matter like that of *Nanook* than to industrialized society.

Leacock worked for television and sponsors. His first film of special interest was done for a Sunday TV series titled *Omnibus*. *Toby and the Tall Corn* (1955) reports an itinerant tent show that tours the midwest. While employing narration, Leacock concentrates on the performers, who run and promote their show as well as acting nightly. Seemingly uninhibited by camera and sound presence, they comment spontaneously about their lives and their skills.

During the next few years Leacock diligently investigated technical innovation and film subjects that might reduce barriers of self-consciousness. *Primary* (1960) followed Kennedy and Humphrey through the Wisconsin Democratic primary, concluding with Kennedy's victory and the politicians' departures to other states. By this stage, camera and sound had some portability, although the production team faced massive synchronization problems in editing. Equally important was the choice of subject: one or more figures who face a test or challenge, the drama documented in its entirety by a filmmaking team who are as ignorant as the participants about the end result.

Politicians, one may suspect (and *Primary* corroborates), are always "on." Subsequent ventures, made like *Primary* for Time-Life, Inc. in collaboration with Robert Drew, a journalist, and Donn Alan Pennebaker, a cameraman, proved a Leacock dictum: as events engaged the subject, camera and sound presence retreat or disappear altogether from consciousness. The behavior becomes "natural." In *Eddie* (1961), also known as *On the Pole*, a race driver loses the Indianapolis 500. In *Football* (1961), two high school teams compete in a traditional rivalry. *The Chair* (1963) focuses on a courtroom plea to commute the sentence of Paul Crump, convicted murderer, from electrocution to life imprisonment, based on argument that Crump had shown the capacity for rehabilitation.

All such films engage audience empathy by the implicit drama of their "happening." Leacock and Pennebaker assume a neutral posture toward events; what is seen is what was there. (Nevertheless, sympathies are easily located in many of the pictures.) The idea of any formal esthetic imposing itself upon filming or editing is anethema. The commitment is toward accurately seeing and hearing what happens as it happens. In recent years, Leacock has worked to design and to promote Super-8mm cameras allied to portable recording equipment so as to maximize portable inobtrusiveness.

EQUIPMENT AND SELF-CONSCIOUSNESS

In France, Jean Rouch has sought Leacock's production versatility without pretending to, indeed denying, any filmmaker's undistorting, neutral presence. A student of anthropology, Rouch tried by new techniques to compensate for black Africans' repudiations of his own early films. Approaches led to the participation of his subjects in what were clearly artificial situations. In *Moi, un Noir/I, a Black* (1958), Ivory Coast natives cooperated in the documentation of their tedious day-to-day existence. At the same time, the men and women acted out fantasies, often film-induced, which gave an entirely new dimension to the apparent subject.

Since then, Rouch has elaborated tech-

Jean Rouch (1917–   )

Chasse à l'hippopotame (short)	1946
Circonsion (short)	1950
Les Magiciens de Wanzerbe (short)	1950
Les Gens du Nil	1951
Mammy Water (short)	1956
Moi, un noìr/I, a Black	1958
Chronique d'un été (codirector Edgar Morin)	1961
La Punitio	1962
La Chasse au lion à l'arc	1965
Le Lion (short)	1964
L'Afrique et la rechereche scientifique (short)	1964
Jaguar	1953 (completed 1967)
La Goumbé des jeunes noceurs	1966
Petit à petit	1970
Partial listing	

niques to engender the sort of stimulating, revealing expression that seems, however contrived the devices, to externalize much more than rote role-playing can show. With film critic and social scientist Edgar Morin, Rouch made *Chronicle of a Summer* (1961) in Paris at a moment when the Algerian War figured heavily in public attention. In the manner of an American *Candid Camera* program, an attractive interviewer stopped passersby on the street, asking, "Are you happy?" Her question intended to locate people whose responses escaped social inhibition. Those whose answers were interesting and energetic were invited to view the film. Participants were introduced to one another in encounter situations; the people were encouraged to challenge one another's assumptions and ways of life. Morin and Rouch filmed themselves discussing what had happened so far and how to continue.

The premises and the technique of *Chronicle of a Summer* were dubbed cinéma vérité by Morin, a direct reference to the film-truth of Dziga Vertov's *Kino-Pravda*. Rouch viewed his work as an ongoing metropolitan study in social anthropology, a Parisian ethnography. His material regards the usual province of documentary study, conditions and behavior of people as predicated by social, cultural, and political forces, as only veneer. Behind each human style lies another history that is both unique and itself a product of impersonal forces. A central character in *Chronicle of a Summer* is Marceline Loridan, a onetime concentration camp internee. An African student innocently asks Marceline the meaning of her branded camp number. Later, perhaps triggered by the naïve inquiry, Marceline bursts into her guarded memories, including her trip to the camp. Significantly, she is carrying the tape recorder and microphone,

Chronicle of a Summer. "You ask the audience to have confidence in the evidence. (You want) to say to the audience, 'This is what I saw. I didn't fake it, this is what happened. I didn't change anyone's behavior. I looked at what happened with my subjective eye and this is what I believe took place.'" Chris Marker. Marker's remark applies equally to Rouch's *Chronicle.*

The Sorrow and the Pity. Unidentified French peasants during the German occupation. "When I decide to try to give an analysis of the relationship between individual destinies and contemporary political situations in a sort of fresco thing, a sort of epic thing, that . . . then leads to cross-cutting." Marcel Ophuls (Museum of Modern Art/ Film Stills Archive)

and the speech she makes accompanies her walk across the Place de la Concorde and through a railroad station. Thus Rouch documents the fortuitous in a style that veers both from Pennebaker-Leacock *and* from Vertov.

Cinéma vérité is echoed in *Le Joli Mai/The Lovely May* (1963) by Chris Marker who asked his subjects questions like, "What does money mean to you?" Other filmmakers used interviews to tap that reserve of pent-up feeling that seems often to wait impatiently for the right interrogation. Marcel Ophuls, son of Max Ophuls, made *The Sorrow and the Pity* (1969) for French television, although it was rejected by the authorities. Ophuls' film had a deep effect on its theater audience and on the subjects who were searchingly questioned about their relation to the German occupation and the French Resistance. As interviewees, including both onetime premier Mendes-

Chris Marker (1921–   )

Olympia 1952	1952
Les Statues meurent aussi (codirector Alain Resnais)	1953
Dimanche à Pekin/Sundays in Peking	1953
Le Mystere de l'atalier 15 (codirector Alain Resnais)	1957
Les Astronautes (codirector Walerian Borowczyk)	1961
Cuba Si!	1961
La Jetée	1963
Le Joli mai	1963
Le Mystère Kuomiko	1966
Si j'avais 4 dromadaires	1966
Rhoudiacéta	1969
La Bataille des 10 millions	1970
Partial listing	

France and a well-to-do Frenchman who had fought with the SS, relived the period, complexities of loyalty, fear, and guilt described a world usually innured from exposure by the conveniences of popular myth. Filmed throughout Europe, a Russian study, *Memory* (1969) by Grigori Chukrai, intercut news footage of the Battle of Stalingrad with the failing, confused memories of anonymous subjects.

FILM PORTRAITS

Modern equipment has encouraged a variety of filmed portraits of both the famous and the unknown. Some of the problems that such endeavors pose surface in the Pennebaker-Leacock *Jane* (1962), the preparation and opening night of a Broadway flop, *The Fun Couple* starring actress Jane Fonda. Although less known then, Ms. Fonda is still a "personality." The play and its attendant crises fail to overcome Fonda's enigmatic relation to the events. In contrast, *A Stravinsky Portrait* (1964) allows the composer-conductor both public and private behaviors so that a viewer becomes interested in reconciling the two. Similarly, *A Dancer's World* (1955) investigates Martha Graham. *Lonely Boy* (1962) depicts the life of a popular singer, Paul Anka. *I'm Going to Ask You to Get Up Out of Your Seat* (1966) is an exceptional study of evangelist Billy Graham by Richard Cawston. Like many other remarkable documentaries, it was sponsored by BBC-TV. One of the most revealing film portraits is that of editor Hugh Heffner in *The Most* (1962). The film was clearly made with Heffner's willing cooperation, yet its report on *Playboy* lifestyle and Heffner's perceptions leave little doubt in a viewer's mind about the man's delusions.

Don't Look Back. "In the spring of 1965, Bob Dylan's manager, Albert Grossman, wondered if we would be interested in making a film of Bob's tour in England. So, with nothing more than a handshake, I set out with Dylan and Joan Baez." Donn Alan Pennebaker (Museum of Modern Art/Film Stills Archive)

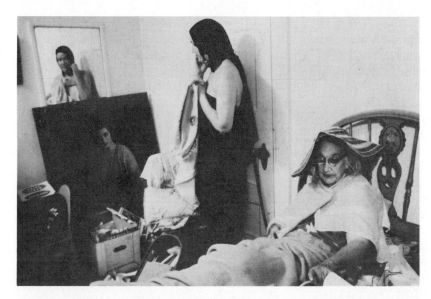

Grey Gardens. Viewing a mirror, Edie Beal stands between an early portrait of her mother and Edith Bouvier Beale herself, now bedridden. After her mother's death, subsequent to the film, Edie essayed a career as a nightclub entertainer, singing "Tea for Two" as her mother does in the movie. (John Springer Associates)

Don't Look Back (1966) was made by Donn Pennebaker with Leacock helping on camera. It follows Bob Dylan on a British tour, recording his meetings with English stars and the press as well as performances. Such a film gives some small sense of a "star's" relation to public media, his joint dependence and vulnerability.

Albert and David Maysles produced one of documentary's most telling portraits in *Salesman* (1969). The film records a bible salesman, Paul, at work, attending a sales conference, swapping shop talk on the road with fellow hucksters. Like many such spontaneous films, the sound quality is barely acceptable, but Paul's words in concert with his face at uncontrolled repose afford rare views of the cost of merchandising as a way of life. The brothers' *Grey Gardens* (1975) comes from months of close association with Edith Beale and her daughter Edie, indigent aunt and first cousin to Jacqueline Kennedy Onassis, who live in the nostalgic squalor of a decaying East Hampton, Long Island home. Raccoons eat through the walls, a cat urinates on the bed from which the seventy year old woman rarely moves. Throughout, the pair appear as witty, frustrated entertainers, clearly grateful for the attention they are receiving.

Albert Maysles (1933–   )

David Maysles (1931–   )

Showman	1962
The Beatles in New York	1964
Salesman	1969
Gimme Shelter	1970
Grey Gardens	1975
Cristo's Valley Curtain	1977

EVENT FILMS

Unlike Riefenstahl, the modern filmmaker has less need to manipulate mass performance to his convenience. Contemporary documentary (a sometimes-inclusive term has been Direct Cinema) adapts smoothly to public event, particularly concerts. Staged music is so dependent on electronics that a filmmaker can sometimes locate his microphones visibly, sometimes tap into the public address system itself to insure adequate sound. For all their movement, musicians and singers work within a limited, observable field, and audience response gives both cutaway material and color for later editing. Bert Stern's *Jazz on a Summer's Day* (1960) was an early Newport Jazz Festival music documentary, followed by *Monterey Pop* (1968), *Woodstock* (1970), and the Maysles' *Gimme Shelter* (1970). With its telephoto lenses, *Tokyo Olympiad* (1964) by Kon Ichikawa rivals *Olympia*. In 1963, Adolphus and Jonas Mekas filmed a special Living

Theater performance of *The Brig*, a powerful report of a theater piece itself "documentary" in recreating a Marine detention prison.

INSTITUTION FILMS

Social institutions supply structural unity to some feature-length documentaries. The structure of these institutions permits segmented vignettes and an ordering concept for imposing contextual meaning. Frederick Wiseman, once a lawyer, has examined an institution for the criminally insane, *Titicut Follies* (1967), a public school, *High School* (1968), the police of Kansas City, *Law and Order* (1969), *Hospital* (1970), *Basic Training* (1971), a monastery, *Essene* (1972), *Juvenile Court* (1973), animal experimentation, *Primate* (1974), *Welfare* (1975) and *Meat* (1976) about meat packaging. His technique is

Welfare. In Wiseman's mind, most of his subjects are incapable of changing their behavior before the camera. They do what comes naturally, however it may appear on screen: a policeman strangles an arrested prostitute in *Law and Order*, a white man discusses his hatred of blacks with a black policeman in *Welfare*. (Museum of Modern Art/Film Stills Archive)

Harlan County, U.S.A. Striking at the Brookside Mine in 1973, Kentucky miners supplant their union leadership with a reform ticket. Barbara Kopple spent four years completing her first film; it won an Academy Award. (John Springer Associates)

to explicate an institution's rules and conventions through example, tracing various responses of its clientele. *Essene* excepted, institutional employees emerge as alternately sympathetic and odious. Responses to the system are sometimes passive and repressed, sometimes eruptively reacting to frustration. Wiseman's work has something of the Pennebaker-Leacock strategy, and pretense to objectivity is even further challenged by his editing technique. What juxtapositions connote editorializing? What continuities that may increase audience involvement will distort the event?

Two films by Canadian Allan King treated similar material somewhat more openly. *Warrendale* (1967) covers a home for disturbed children with attention devoted both to the day-by-day life and to the workers' discussions on treatment and psychodynamics. A beloved cook dies unexpectedly, and the effect of this event on the children mixes ordinary drama with case-history fears, rages, and unpredictabilities.

In *A Married Couple* (1969), King enters the lives of a young married pair including their deep, strongly expressed disagreements and some measure of their physical intimacy. As with other recent documentaries, many spectators become genuinely concerned with the ethics of camera intrusion that has something of literal (as compared to Hitchcock's implied) voyeurism. *Good Times, Wonderful Times* (1966) by Lionel Rogosin intercuts Vietnam War and atrocity footage with spontaneous cocktail party conversation. Rogosin challenges willful American ignorance with other, documented realities.

TELEVISION AND DOCUMENTARY

News and TV special coverage have assisted the redesigning of antiquated film equipment. Furthermore, much of today's documentary is clearly the product of broadcast film units and of commissioned assignments. Leacock's 8mm documentaries are intended to be viewed on television monitors. The effect of videotape on film documentary remains controversial, for the two media seem sometimes to converge. sometimes to diverge with respect to organizing principles.

Commercial television, and some public broadcasting, show obvious restraint in subject and treatment. At the same time, most social and political subjects, excepting the output of radical documentary filmmaking groups such as Newsreel, originate under TV's aegis. Integration or its absence provided the material for *The Children Were Watching* (1960), *A Time for Burning* (1966), *The Angry Voices of Watts* (1966), and *Cicero March* (1968). Poverty was movingly shown in *Hunger in America* (1968), made for *CBS Reports*. Student revolt at Berkeley, *The Berkeley Rebels* (1965), and San Francisco State, *Confrontation* (1969), gave national audience to local incident.

COMPILATION FILM

The notion of drawing on film's past to create new products is clearly evident in the work of Dziga Vertov and of Ester Shub. Shub was really the first to define editing as an independent artistic imposition on accumulations of past materials. *The Fall of the Romanov Dynasty* (1927) was compiled with great imagination from czarist times and the revolutionary events of February and October, 1917. Similarly, she used Tolstoy as a linking figure in *The Russia of Nicholas II and Leo Tolstoy* (1928), drawing on footage of the author, records by the czar's official photographer and an early film reportedly "written and directed by Tolstoy:" *A Peasant Wedding*.

Although sometimes used for contrast, Shub's films usually preserve the anecdotal denotations of their sources. More in Vertov's tradition, Henri Storck's *L'Histoire du soldat inconnu* (1930) uses newsreels out of World War I to build a short, savage satire on delusions that war might be ended forever, that political leaders could be trusted and armies were not always dangerous.

As television develops its more recent archival history, compilation film has been able to draw on new resources, as far as they are practically available. Charles Braverman condensed much of a decade into fourteen minutes in *The Sixties* (1970), the power of his speeding images based on our instant recall of faces and events. A documentary success of 1963 was *Point of Order!* Emile de Antonio and Daniel Talbot reconstructed the Army-McCarthy hearings from CBS kinescopes (filmed recordings) of the televised broadcasts. The event was so melodramatically flavored with heroes, villains, and fools that it carried a flavor of genre. Both de Antonio's *In the Year of the Pig* (1969) and *Time of the Locust* (1967) by Peter Gessner drew on television news coverage of Vietnam often from foreign sources, since American material was closed to them. Another compilation film, *To Die in Madrid* (1965) by Frederic Rossif, compares without disfavor to *Spanish Earth*. We hear Appassionaria's farewell to the International Brigade, and see the proud, ravaged face of the philosopher Unamuno. Figures scurry across an arid countryside like crowds circling Piccadilly in *Nice Time*, only here the central statue is not Eros but a battered belfry tower or a charred tree stump.

ETHNOGRAPHIC FILM

Implicit in much Direct Cinema, ethnographic impulse has carried film to distant places recently, a sophisticated reversion to the first documentaries. *Dead Birds* (1963) was filmed by Robert Gardner as part of an anthropological study of the New Guinea highlands. All such films represent uneasy compromises between anthropologists who see the moving picture as a device of record and filmmakers who want their work to have more organization than an unedited tape recording. The films also pose the problem of the effect of production on the culture documented.

Interesting film experiments on the part of social scientists were undertaken in the ghetto of Philadelphia and among Navajo Indians. In each case, cameras were dispensed to the inhabitants with no more than elementary technical instruction. The filmmakers were free to photograph whatever they chose, however they wished. In each case, results confound unexamined conventions toward composition, pace, and movement that most of us bring to filmmaking.[7]

The French feature director Louis Malle recorded his impressions while cultural attaché in India in *Phantom India* (1968). The six-hour film offers an extraordinary array of experiences for the viewer who can tolerate many unsettling moments. Michelangelo Antonioni tried to make a similar documentation in China in 1973. Both directors suffered indignant governmental reaction to their productions including effective efforts to suppress exhibition at Festivals and distribution abroad.

[7] *See* Sol Worth and John Adair, *Through Navajo Eyes*. New York, 1972.

DOCUMENTARY AND THE ENTERTAINMENT FILM

During the postwar period, narrative film shared many emancipating impulses with documentary, but the latter also had specific effects on some story productions. *The War Game* (1966) by British Peter Watkins employs techniques of news journalism that lend inescapable authenticity to his view of atomic holocaust. A viewer is afforded none of the esthetic distance that more polished production implies. In *Culloden* (1964) Watkins reconstructs a British military encounter with Scottish clans in the manner of cinéma vérité; participants confide their feelings and private opinions about a battle of hideous barbarity and cruel efficiency.

Shirley Clarke's *The Connection* (1961) introduces a brash documentarian into a world of junkies. They turn on the filmmaker, who becomes obsessed with photographing cockroaches. *David Holzman's Diary* (1967) is a satire of cinéma vérité implications. It is purportedly the documentary record of Holzman's film about himself, his encounters with the camera, meeting with his girl, an interview with a hooker, self-questioning about the method itself and its personally self-expressive consequences. If a spectator has not guessed earlier, the final credits reveal not David Holzman, but Jim McBride as filmmaker.

Summary

Through documentary's history, one may trace threads that could be labeled "Persuasive Purpose," "Source of Financing," "Relation to Event," "Organizational Principle," and "Subject of Interest." One element may balance against, or sometimes cancel out, others. Notions of documentary's relation to its audience have shifted from exotic entertainment (travelogues) to social action to imparting information, sometimes back to exotic entertainment. Except when in association with the newsreel, documentary has been forced to seek private or institutional funding that often rests now on television support. At various times, the filmmaker may disguise, ignore, or admit his relation to the events he captures. Films have been designed variously like epic entertainments *(Grass)*, textbooks *(The March of Time)*, personal essays *(Listen to Britian)*, substitute attendance *(Monterey Pop)* and candid visit *(A Married Couple)*.

Where it has an audience, documentary tradition effectively counterbalances fictional experience, correcting unchallenged conventions we hold about human behavior. We encounter subjects and aspects of the human condition to which we might never otherwise be privy. Similar impulses figure in the development of Neo-Realism discussed in Chapter 13.

Bibliography

Agel, Henri. *Robert Flaherty*. Paris, 1965.

Anderson, Lindsay. "Only Connect: Some Aspects of the Work of Humphrey Jennings," *Sight and Sound* (April-May 1954).

The Art Inquiry. *The Factual Film*. London, 1947.

Barnouw, Erik. *Documentary: A History of the Non-fiction Film*. New York, 1974.

Barsan, Richard. *Nonfiction Film*. New York, 1973.

Bluem, A. William. *Documentary in American Television*. New York, 1965.

Bohn, Thomas W. and Lawrence W. Lichty. "The March of Time: News as Drama," *Journal of Popular Film* (Fall 1973).

———. *An Historical and Descriptive Analysis of the "Why We Fight" Series*. New York, 1977.

Calder-Marshall, Arthur. *The Innocent Eye*. London, 1963.

Cameron, Ken. *Sound and the Documentary Film*. London, 1947.

Cameron, Evan. *An Analysis of A Diary for Timothy,* Bridgewater, Mass., 1967.

Conrad, Randall. "Directed and Direct: Changing Conventions in the American Documentary," *University Film Study Center Supplement* (June 1976).

De Antonio, Emile. *Point of Order*. New York, 1964.

Dongan, Helen van. "350 Cans of Film," Roger Manvell, ed. *The Cinema, 1951*. London, 1951.

Edmonds, Robert. *About Documentary*. Dayton, 1974.

Film and the Historian. London, 1969.

Flaherty, Frances. *Elephant Dance*. New York, 1937.

———. *The Odyssey of a Film-maker*. Urbana, Ill., 1960.

Flaherty, Robert. *My Eskimo Friends*. Garden City N.Y., 1927.

Flaherty, Robert and F. W. Murnau. "Tabu," *Film Culture* 20 (1959).

Gallez, Douglas W. "Patterns in Wartime Documentaries," *Quarterly of Radio, Film and Television* (Winter 1955).

———. "Pictorial Journalism at War," *Journalism Quarterly* (Autumn 1970).

Geduld, Harry M. *Film Makers on Film Making*. Bloomington, 1967.

Goetz, William. "The Canadian Wartime Documentary; *Canada Carries On* and *The World in Action*," *Cinema Journal* (Spring 1977).

Grierson, John. *Grierson on Documentary*. London, 1966.

———. "I Derive My Authority from Moses," *Take One* (January-February 1970).

Hughes, Robert, ed. *Film: Book 1*. New York, 1959.

Ivens, Joris. *The Camera and I*. New York, 1969.

Jacobs, Lewis, ed. *The Documentary Tradition*. New York, 1971.

Jennings, Humphrey. "Working Sketches of an Orchestra," *Film Quarterly* (Winter 1961–62).

Knight, Derrick. *A Long Look at Short Films*. New York, 1967.

Kracauer, Siegfried. *From Caligari to Hitler*. Princeton, 1947.

Leacock, Ricky. "For an Uncontrolled Cinema," *Film Culture* 22–23 (1961).

Levin, G. Roy. *Documentary Explorations*. Garden City, N.Y., 1971.

Lovell, Alan. *Studies in Documentary*. London, 1972.

MacCann, Richard Dyer. *Documentary Film and Democratic Government*. Ph.D. dissertation, Harvard University, 1951.

———. *Film and Society*. New York, 1964.

———. *The People's Films*. New York, 1973.

Mamber, Stephen, *Cinéma Vérité in America*. Cambridge, 1974.

Marcorelles, Louis. *Living Cinema*. New York, 1973.

Maysles, Albert and David with Charlotte Zwerin. *Salesman* (transcript). New York, 1969.

Merralls, James. "Humphrey Jennings: A Biographical Sketch," *Film Quarterly* (Winter 1961–62).

Murphy, William T. *Robert Flaherty*. Boston, 1978.

Noxon, Gerald. "How Humphrey Jennings Came to Film," *Film Quarterly* (Winter 1961–62).

Ophuls, Marcel. *The Sorrow and the Pity*. New York, 1972.

Riefenstahl, Leni. *Kampf in Schnee und Eis*. Leipzig, 1933.

———. "Interview," *Film Culture* (Spring 1973).

———. *The Last of the Nuba*. New York, 1974.

Rosenthal, Alan. *The New Documentary in Action*. Berkeley, 1971.

Rotha, Paul. *Documentary Diary*. New York, 1973.

———. *Documentary Film*. 3rd rev. ed. New York, 1952.

Rouch, Jean. *Chronique d'un été*. Paris, 1962.

Sansom, William. "The Making of *Fires Were Started*," *Film Quarterly* (Winter 1961–62).

Snyder, Robert L. *A History of the Early Productions of Pare Lorentz*. Ph.D. dissertation, University of Iowa, 1965.

———. *Pare Lorentz and the Documentary Film*. Norman, Okla., 1968.

Sweet, Fred, Eurene Rosow and Allen Francovich, "Pioneers: An Interview with Tom Brandon," *Film Quarterly* (Fall 1973).

Tilton, Roger. "Jazz Dance: Analysis of a Documentary," *Film Culture* 1 (1955).

Wegg-Prosser, Victoria. "The Archive of the Film and Photo League," *Sight and Sound* (Autumn 1977).

Worth, Sol and John Adair. *Through Navajo Eyes: An Exploration in Film Communication and Anthropology*. New York, 1972.

Yellin, David. *Special: Fred Freed and the Television Documentary*. New York, 1972.

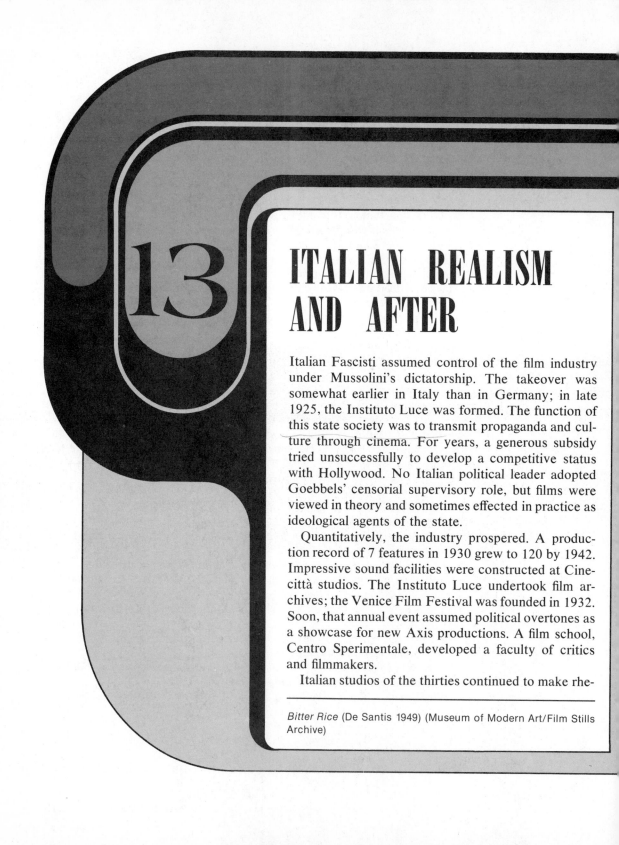

13

ITALIAN REALISM AND AFTER

Italian Fascisti assumed control of the film industry under Mussolini's dictatorship. The takeover was somewhat earlier in Italy than in Germany; in late 1925, the Instituto Luce was formed. The function of this state society was to transmit propaganda and culture through cinema. For years, a generous subsidy tried unsuccessfully to develop a competitive status with Hollywood. No Italian political leader adopted Goebbels' censorial supervisory role, but films were viewed in theory and sometimes effected in practice as ideological agents of the state.

Quantitatively, the industry prospered. A production record of 7 features in 1930 grew to 120 by 1942. Impressive sound facilities were constructed at Cinecittà studios. The Instituto Luce undertook film archives; the Venice Film Festival was founded in 1932. Soon, that annual event assumed political overtones as a showcase for new Axis productions. A film school, Centro Sperimentale, developed a faculty of critics and filmmakers.

Italian studios of the thirties continued to make rhe-

Bitter Rice (De Santis 1949) (Museum of Modern Art/Film Stills Archive)

torical spectacles as well as producing romantic comedies and celebrations of Fascist reclamations and military undertakings. *Scipione l'Africano* (1937), for example, implied a parallel between Mussolini's invasion of Ethiopia and the history of the Roman Empire.

The major directors were Allesandro Blasetti and Mario Camerini. Blasetti made *1860* in 1933, a film on Garibaldi's expedition to Sicily, surprisingly outspoken in support of revolution. Blasetti's career extends into postwar years, consumed by comedies and spectacles, of which *Fabiola* (1948) was noteworthy.

Mario Camerini is associated with those Italian comedies sometimes described as "white telephone" in reference to their middle-class modern decor. His amiable, un-

prepossessing productions, like *I'll Give a Million* (1935), introduced Vittorio De Sica, then a romantic juvenile, and scriptwriter Cesare Zavattini. If Italy's films in no way rivaled those from Germany, France, Russia, and the United States, Italian studios trained men who were later to embark on very different film ventures.

HINTS OF THE NEW REALISM

The significance of early indications that might suggest a new film esthetic may be exaggerated by the rarity of depatures from artificial, studio-bound products. Blasetti's

Ossessione. An itinerant mechanic meets an innkeeper's wife by chance and they fall in love. First they flee together, but she returns, unwilling to face a penniless future. Weeks later, the man meets innkeeper and wife in town. Driving home in an auto, the husband is murdered. After living together, the couple's relationship deteriorates; he distrusts her motives and the genuiness of her love. Escaping arrest, their car crashes and the woman is killed. (Museum of Modern Art/Film Stills Archive)

Sun(1929) is an impressive study of the reclamation of unpopulated marshes south of Rome, an early Fascist achievement. *1860* casts non-actors in supporting roles. Blasetti's wartime *Four Steps in the Clouds* (1942) centers on a load of bus passengers. Its indigenous temperament and humor contrast with the universalizing themes and nondescript people common to the industry's bids for world movie markets in the first sound decade.

In 1942, Luchino Visconti, who had assisted Jean Renoir on *The Lower Depths* and *Une Partie de campagne,* turned to the brutal emotions of *Ossessione's* unacknowledged source, James M. Cain's novel *The Postman Always Rings Twice,* and rooted its characters in the Italian countryside. Little seen in Italy and unavailable here until the mid-seventies, *Ossessione* draws sharp, effective characterizations with something of Renoir's spontaneity, as in a village opera singing competition. Its melodrama differs little from many later, more touted neorealist films. Much of the story is filmed out of doors, and Visconti makes good use of the roadside locations, supporting an underlying theme of escape with offscreen truck and railroad sounds. Natural lighting is somewhat obviously simulated in interiors.

De Sica's first directing assignments were comedies, but *The Children are Watching Us* (1943) shares something of the qualities of Carol Reed's *The Fallen Idol* and Duvivier's *Poil de carotte* (1925, 1932). A boy kills himself in despondent reaction to his mother's affair and to its effects on his father.

Roberto Rossellini

Rossellini, too, learned filmmaking under Fascism. In fact, after some documentaries, his apprenticeship took place with Francesco De Robertis, making war movies heroizing the military. Such was Rossellini's first film, *Un Pilota Ritorna* (1943). Mussolini's regime collapsed in that period, and Rossellini determined to produce a film that would show the circumstances of German occupation and of the Italian Underground.

Open City (1945) was made under most difficult circumstances, often shot in actual locales, sometimes with German patrols nearby. Electricity failed and film ran out. When finances were depleted, Rossellini and the actresses Anna Magnani and Maria Michi sold their possessions to continue. Actors and crew worked without salaries.

Open City's impulse to recount actual experiences, compounded by the difficult production circumstances, contributed to the films qualities of immediacy and desperation. The story depicts a resistance leader, Manfredi, who calls on the underground, friends, and a priest (who was originally to have been the central figure) for protection from the Germans. Manfredi is captured when his mistress, an addict, betrays him. He dies under torture. Anna Magnani, the girl friend of a fellow resistance fighter, is shot. The priest is executed.

From these defeats, Rossellini wrests victory, for all the Italians die well and purposefully. Viewed now, *Open City* seems a contradictory mixture. Its strongest features are natural, humorous, often anxious exchanges between ordinary people at moments of relaxation and stress. The partisan, very Roman, story is nourished by location shooting where actors and street rubble share the narrative itself, as in the last sequence when young boys whistle a resistance song to maintain the spirit of Don Pietro, who is about to be executed. A German officer shoots the priest, and the boys return to Rome, which lies open to panoramic view in the valley below.

Weaknesses in *Open City* accompany the Germans, a difference not of culture but performance. The Gestapo scenes — shot in the studio — have a stiffness and artificiality that is abetted by turns in the lurid plot. The film's music, composed by Rossellini's brother Renzo Rossellini, is obtrusively dramatic.

Paisà (1946) consists of six episodes, trac-

Paisà. Landing in Sicily, an American patrol persuades a local girl to guide them to shelter. While the others reconnoiter, she remains behind with one soldier. Germans kill the pair. On return, the soldiers believe she murdered their buddy and was shot in the exchange. (Museum of Modern Art/Film Stills Archive)

ing the progress of Allied forces from Sicily up Italy's boot. Germans kill an American on patrol and a girl with whom he has been flirting. A drunken black MP loses his boots and pursues the child thief into Neopolitan ruins where the soldier stops in despair at what he sees. A GI encounters a girl he had met earlier at Rome's liberation. She is a prostitute now, and he fails to recognize her. An American girl runs through the fighting in Florence in search of her lover, an Italian partisan, and finds him dead. Catholic, Protestant, and Jewish chaplains spend an evening in a monastery and impress the monks with their tolerance. Finally, a band of allied soldiers and partisans are captured by retreating Germans in the Po delta. Hands tied behind them, the partisans are pushed into the river, one by one.

Somber but for the monastery sequence, the remaining episodes of *Paisà* conclude on melancholy notes. The impact of the first episode is destroyed by inadequate footage, the last episode rings consistent and tragic. The Rome story has a pat, ironic slickness. *Paisà* was shot on location, written after each had been visited by Rossellini and screenwriter Federico Fellini. Rossellini seems to thrive in the anecdotal format, as if he could best capture places and people with minimal narrative contrivance, and perhaps this is why his endings sometimes appear to be incongruent with what has preceded.

Germany Year Zero (1947) substitutes the devastation of Berlin in 1947 for Italy. Its central figure is Edmund, a twelve year old, prematurely sly, yet still innocent. He deals in contraband, usually cheated by older men, sometimes by his peers. It is a primitive world. Edmund's father is a sick, despondent veteran, afraid to report to authorities for help. Acting on his understanding of the advice from a former schoolteacher whose interest in young boys is perverse, Edmund poisons his father's tea while the old man bemoans his and Germany's fate. At the end, forlorn, Edmund wanders the charred streets, playing vaguely at childish games and then throws himself from the window of a deserted building.

The Human Voice and *The Miracle* (both 1948) were originally intended to compose two-thirds of a complete release, but the last episode was never completed. *The Human Voice* is a Dorothy Parker-like monologue conducted by Anna Magnani with her estranged lover over the telephone. In *The Miracle,* Magnani plays a demented gypsy, seduced by a shepherd she believes to be St. Joseph (played by Fellini, who wrote the story).[1] Magnani believes she has conceived miraculously. Mocked by townspeople, she finally births the child, alone in the stable of a countryside shrine.[2]

In *The Flowers of St. Francis* (1949), a delicate, often humorous, episodic study, Rossellini views legend as if real, with a friendly, nondoctrinaire eye, one more effective than

Pasolini's later *The Gospel According to St. Matthew* (1964). Rossellini's subsequent films have taken various turns. While living with Ingrid Bergman, he adopted a kind of nineteenth-century naturalism. After several years' silence he produced a series of documentary shorts on India for television. *Il Generale della Rovere* (1959) adapted neorealism and war memories to a commercial theatrical frame. In his last years, Rossellini worked on period films for television. In such films as *The Rise to Power of Louis XIV* (1966) and *Socrates* (1970), Rossellini paid particular attention to the details of period life in order to inform the usual historical orthodoxies with the interpretive force of social history.

---

[1] *Both Fellini and Michelangelo Antonioni are considered in some detail in Chapters 19 and 20.*

[2] The Miracle *has special interest to United States film history because of its legal ramifications. Exhibited in New York in December 1950, the film was withdrawn from the Paris Theater under pressure from Catholics who found it sacriligous and blasphemous. A lengthy court case ensued, and in 1952 the US Supreme Court's supportive decision became a landmark in recognition of film as a legitimate and important medium for the communication of ideas. See Garth Jowett,* Film the Democratic Art, *pp. 404-408.*

Roberto Rossellini (1906–1976)

La Nave Bianca	1941
Un Pilota Returna	1942
Roma Città Aperta/Open City	1945
Paisà	1946
Germania, Anno Zero/Germany, Year Zero	1947
L'Amore (in two parts) Una Voice Umana (The Human Voice); Il Miracolo (The Miracle)	1948
La Macchina Ammazzacattivi/ The Infernal Machine	1948
Francesco Giullarde di Dio/ The Flowers of Saint Francis	1949
Stromboli	1950
Viaggio in Italia/The Lonely Women	1953
L'India Visita da Rossellini	1958
Il Generale della Rovere	1959
The Rise to Power of Louis XIV	1966
Socrates	1970
Partial listing	

THE CONCEPT OF NEOREALISM

Neorealism as a term was invoked as early as 1943 by Professor Umberto Barbaro, who called upon Italian film to undertake several important steps:

1. Get rid of the "naive and mannered clichés which formed the larger part of Italian films."
2. Abandon "those fantastic and grotesque fabrications which exclude human problems and the human point of view."
3. Dispense with historical set-pieces and fictional adaptations.
4. Exclude the rhetoric which pretends that all Italians are "inflamed by the same noble sentiments."[3]

The proclamation essentially conceived neorealism as a reaction to fabricated conventions. Rossellini's war trilogy conformed to this mode in terms of subject, but, more importantly, the trilogy shows a new approach to the problem of representing the subject. In what can be seen as a moral stand on the integrity and value of an event, neorealists were confident that accurate, undistorted reporting of ordinary circumstance would manifest not just surface appearance but "inner realities" — the feelings and conditions that gave incidents broad, even universal significance — without drowning them in generalizations or symbols.

Cesare Zavattini, a Marxist like many, not all, neorealist Italians, argued that neorealism, in an ideal state, should operate altogether without story, acting, or contrivance. It should view real people in their actual settings performing their ordinary roles. This was never accomplished, although moments of *Umberto D* (1952) suggest something of Zavattini's dream. A harbinger of neorealist use of nonactors was *Los Retes/The Wave*, made in

[3] *Eric Rhode, "Why Neorealism Failed,"* Sight and Sound (*Winter 1960*).

Mexico by Fred Zinneman in 1935 with Vera Cruz fisherman as performers.

The absence of dramatic narrative structure afforded a presentational mode thought to be less ideologically tainted. For Marxists, form was a bourgeois contrivance that might only despoil a film by imposing its stylizations on reality. Film's aim should be to free its substance, not constrain or distort it, to restore the ambiguities of life rather than delimit them with arbitrary selection. If the concept was rarely honored altogether in practice, neorealist films are yet characterized by long shot rather than closeup, more by stable than moving cameras, more by the tempos and nuances of performance than editing. In consequence, published scripts rarely communicate everything meaningful in these films.

Vittorio De Sica

The fruitful collaboration between De Sica and Zavattini extends as far back as the director's early comedy *Teresa Venerdi* (1941). Zavattini worked on *The Children Are Watching Us* (1943) and then *Shoeshine* (1946), *Bicycle Thief* (1949), *Miracle in Milan* (1950), *Umberto D* (1952), *The Gold of Naples* (1954) and *The Roof* (1955), among others. Some scripts were collaborations, some independently written. Zavattini's journals record the pair's visits to bordellos, masses, and sickrooms in search of material.

Shoeshine grew out of De Sica's year-long study of two Roman boys. Remarkable with child actors, he searched at length for nonprofessionals to play his main roles. As *paisà* derived from *paisàno,* a condescending, friendly GI term for Italians, *sciuscia* was what shoeshine youngsters cried at American visitors after the war. The players, Giuseppe and Pasquale, are savvy, black-market dealers who steal what they can and market it in the underground for money to buy a horse. They are apprehended and sent to reform school. Tricked by authorities, the boys betray one

The Gold of Naples. Combining humor and naturalism more successfullly than was managed in *Miracle in Milan,* the Zavattini-De Sica film attempted an episodic, composite portrait of its city. Two out of six episodes were cut. The picture was poorly received; writer and director reverted to neorealist orthodoxies. (Italian Cultural Institute)

another. Giuseppe escapes. Pasquale leads police to the hideout and kills his friend.

Like *Open City, Shoeshine* has hyped-up drama, especially the last climax, which was made in a studio. Again, the location material, including prison sequences, stands out. De Sica identified this environment as altogether corrupting. The children's performances possess little of the endearing, manipulative charm of the young but rather an open aggression and wildness that the story accentuates.

Perhaps the pinnacle of Italian neorealist filmmaking, is *Bicycle Thief* (*Bicycle Thieves* in England). This film is a favorite neorealist film, although others may prefer another title. (It is sobering to realize that David Selznick wanted to finance the film on condition that Cary Grant be cast in the lead.) Against Zavattini's own credo, the story comes from a novel. An unemployed man and his wife pawn sheets and other belongings to get his bicycle out of hock so that he may secure a job, past-

ing up posters of the American movie *Gilda.* On the first day, a thief steals the bicycle. With his son, the man searches everywhere. He finally finds the thief, only to release him, as the MP had done in *Paisà,* when he realizes the other's more devastating poverty. The worker tries himself to steal a bike and is caught, frightened by police, insulted and rejected by a crowd. The father's powerlessness and anger have alienated his son. In the final shot, the pair set off together; the possibility of their reconciliation remains ambiguous.

Again De Sica casts nonactors. The utter candor of their manner is intensified by the postwar environment, viewed in detail as father and son wander the city from flea market to soup kitchen to whorehouse. The vulnerability of the man plays against his son's dependence so that the film's ending carries special poignance without sentimentality or fakery.

Miracle in Milan (1950), again based on a book, this time one by Zavattini, is a curious fantasy, largely about the poor who inhabit a city dump where oil is discovered. Through a heaven-sent miracle, the people are protected from attacks on their holdings by the wealthy. Then the poor are corrupted by their covetousness and by luxury. Endangered again, the troupe escapes to heaven. The tenor of *Miracle in Milan* protects it from heavy-handed accusations of deviationist escapism, but its own style, the accumulation of De Sica's and Zavattini's past, fits curiously onto such happenings. Watching the poor fly to heaven on broomsticks, we cannot help but feel somewhat as if the worker in *Bicycle Thief* had suddenly won a Bugatti on a raffle ticket.

Umberto D (1952) comes closest to the idea of filming a day-to-day existence, in this case, a retired office worker who lives alone and

friendless with his dog. The dog is lost. The man grows sick. After a life of service, his pittance of a pension has cast him into poverty. He tries to kill the dog and himself but fails, and the film ends with the two confronting a future of unalloyed despair. The story balances abject misery with a Chaplinesque pathos, its bitterness (De Sica's father was such a figure) sometimes cloaked in angry humor. In one sequence, a servant girl gets up, lights the stove, and prepares for the day, and Zavattini's notion of reality erupts from the mundane.

De Sica's later films depart neorealism as esthetic or moral posture in favor of more orthodox stories, although *The Gold of Naples* (1954) has its own kind of garish display of city life and *The Roof* carries the ethic of neorealism without its power. De Sica's capacity for dealing with actors is evident in *The Garden of the Finzi-Contini* (1971). Perhaps the postwar period itself forsook the filmmaker and scriptwriter. Sophia Loren performs effectively in *Two Women* (1960), but she and the rest of the cast simply look too well fed to be starving. De Sica the actor is seen to advantage in Rossellini's *General della Rovere* and as the suitor in Max Ophül's *Madame de. . . .*

Vittorio De Sica (1902–1974)

Rose scarlatte (codirector Giuseppe Amato)	1939
Teresa Venerdi	1941
I Bambini ci Guardino/The Children are Watching Us	1943
Sciuscià/Shoeshine	1946
Ladri di Biciclette/Bicycle Thief	1949
Miracolo a Milano/Miracle in Milan	1950
Umberto D	1952
L'Oro di Napoli/The Gold of Naples	1954
Il Tetto/The Roof	1955
La Ciociaria/Two Women	1960
Iwri, Oggi, Domani/Yesterday, Today and Tomorrow	1963
Matrimonio all'Italiana/Love, Italian Style	1964
Gli Amanti/A Place for Lovers	1968
Il Giardino del Finzi Contini/ The Garden of the Finzi-Contini	1971
Partial listing	

Luchino Visconti

After *Ossessione* (1942) and an interval of six years, Visconti directed *La Terra Trema* (1948). For all its early realist vision, *Ossessione* is a dramatic story about passion leading to its own destruction, and while this theme recurs in later Visconti efforts, *La Terra Trema* represents the reverse side of his sensibility, a lengthy (one hundred and sixty minute), Sicilian study of how economic pressures finally dessimate a fisherman's family so that he must accept employment from others.

The film has a quality of case history and documentary in its lengthy fishing sequences. It was made in Sicily with nonprofessionals, and tempos, like some of Dreyer's films, are the rhythms of country people in an earlier world. Between the time of *Ossessione* and *La Terra Trema*, and after the second film failed, Visconti returned to the theater. Although stage vision colors certain of his compositional and lighting effects, the Sicilian film is defined more by Visconti's sense of history as a dialectic of class confrontations. Since Sicily in many ways escaped industrialization, the film's conflict between fishermen and fish vendors has some of the qualities of nineteenth-century Marxism. In the story, 'Ntoni, the young protagonist, risks battle with the middleman merchants, but in the process loses his child and his boat.

La Terra Trema experiences as much difficulty today in holding an audience as it did on release. As with Dreyer, the viewer is well advised altogether to relax rather than impose a personal tempo onto material that resists any pace but its own. Often the images have a commanding, formal poise, building a complicated series of light-dark relationships and shifting compositions, but, as with the story, no real resolution ever follows from the tensions developed.

Bellisima (1951) is untypical Visconti, written by Zavattini. It concerns a stage mother whose efforts to get her child a movie part finally prove successful. When the mother realizes her daughter has been selected not for talent but for her ordinariness (a neorealist irony), she declines. Blasetti appears as the Cinecittà casting director. Anna Magnani, the mother, stands out from her role in a way unlike her Rossellini parts. The mother's competitive ambitions are a vehicle for the director-writer's social criticisms.

Senso (1953) is a period drama of the Risorgimento in Venice. Visconti's first employment of color encourages spectacular settings, and the director enlists his theater-operatic skills toward a Marxist vision of decadent wealth and proletarian uprise. *The White Nights* (1957) is a Dostoyevsky story, again a theater-film amalgam, in which the main players are staged against stylized, uncommitted background figures.

Rocco and His Brothers (1960) returns to a peasant world, perhaps a continuation of *La Terra Trema*, with the family now migrated to Milan and disintegrating in an urban squalor with which they are unequipped to cope. The episodic story traces the experiences of five brothers, much of it centering around the lower depths of professional boxing and a beautiful prostitute, Nadia. Although the despairing sense of individual need buffeted by social pressures continues from the earlier film, *Rocco* is operatic in its stylized acting and in Visconti's dwelling on moments of high emotion. As Rocco's brother stabs Nadia, the sequence is intercut with Rocco winning his first prize fight; the emotional sense of the sequence is one of pain and self-hatred shared in both acts of violence.

The Leopard (1962) is an evocation (reminiscent of *Senso*) of aristocratic demise

Luchino Visconti (1906-1976)

Ossessione	1942
La Terra Trema	1948
Bellisima	1951
Senso/The Wanton Countess	1953
Le Notti Bianche/The White Nights	1957
Rocco e i suoi Fratelli/Rocco and His Brothers	1960
Il Gattopardo/The Leopard	1962
Vaghe Stelle dell'orsa/Sandra	1965
Lo Straniero/The Outsider	1967
La Caduti degli Dei/The Damned	1969
Morte a Venezia/Death in Venice	1971
Ludwig	1972
Conversation Piece	1974
Partial listing	

The Concept of Neorealism

in the Sicily of the 1860s. *The Damned* (1969) recounts early Nazi consolidation, as politics affects an industrialist family in uneasy alliance with the Party. Here, Visconti's vision of decadence as an inevitable consequence of self-perpetuating wealth holds full sway. It is implied that the German cruelties have their role in creating sexual aberrations; the characters show desperations that can never find satisfaction—each uses the others so manipulatively that the individual neuroses deny satisfaction to anyone. Visconti's color is theatrical and almost expressionistic: reds pre-

dominate the bottom-screen area, insinuating flame as one by one the characters approach psychic immolation.

Death in Venice (1971), while failing to evoke the melancholy of Thomas Mann's novella, remarkably captures the atmosphere of a city plagued by disease, disease emblematic of a sickness of the soul among a luxury hotel's inhabitants. Visconti's sweeping camera movements across the textured elegance of lobby and dining hall invite comparison with Ophüls, although events here are mitigated neither by wit or irony.

Senso. Infatuated with a cowardly Austrian officer (Farley Granger), a Venetian Countess (Alida Valli) betrays the Risorgimento of 1866. Finally realizing he loves only her money, the Countess denounces her lover to the Austrians. Abridged, the film was released in the United States as *The Wanton Countess,* with new, dubbed dialogue prepared by Tennessee Williams and Paul Bowles.

A SHIFT IN VALUES

During the height of neorealist accomplishment and immediately thereafter, other directors appeared with films whose technique blended the radical, innovative surface of the movement with more orthodox conventions, often to good effect. *To Live in Peace* (1946) by Luigi Zampa, partially scripted by Fellini, has a German soldier, strayed from the general retreat, and a black GI both hiding in a farmhouse and wildly drunk. Together they stagger through the village, joyfully proclaiming an armistice. The next morning retreating Germans shoot the farmer for aiding the German deserter. Both *Senza Pieta* (1948) and *The Tragic Hunt* (1947) have bandit-criminal themes set against rural, working-class figures. The latter film was made by Giuseppi De Santis, whose *Bitter Rice* (1949) is both interesting in its own right and an example of the eroding effects of commerce on neorealist conviction.

In *Bitter Rice,* a thief and his girl hide out in the Po Valley rice fields. The fields are harvested by attractive young women, most notably Silvana Mangano, in scanty costume. They are, in De Santis' terms, "Americanized," which is to say so befuddled with commercial daydreams that they fail to recognize or confront the exploitive conditions of their own lives. Their skewed enthusiasms lead them to dance a good deal and otherwise cavort erotically, so that the social outrage that DeSantis intended to express is somewhat diverted itself by the look of the film. In joining forces with the thief, Mangano has betrayed her comrades. She finally commits suicide, and the workers throw rice over her body. The gesture, which is intended to express forgiveness for her disloyalty, looks, too, as if the director is trying to bury something.

Bitter Rice was a large success in contrast to other neorealist productions. Although many fared better abroad than in Italy, the additional ingredient of sex as well as violent crime worked well, the combination suggesting a physical candor that might be less apparent in more contrived products. Ensuing years saw a thrust of bosoms, sometimes belonging to talented actresses like Sophia Loren and Gina Lollobrigida.

A curiosity of the postwar years was *Il Cristo Prohibito/Strange Deception* (1951), the single film by novelist Curzio Malaparte. It was shot in Siena, dominated by a theme of Christian redemption. A vengeful returning veteran seeks out the town informant. The most basic elements of the plot are echoed by "The Game of the Cross," an annual Tuscany ritual in which townspeople are challenged to give themselves to the cross for the sake of their fellows. Rhetorical, sometimes contrived, and bulging with greater emotion than it can control, the film is still powerful and deceptively ambiguous.

The government had become increasingly sensitive toward filmmakers washing dirty linen in public, often with explicit criticism of wealth, and films faced censorship for the first time since Mussolini. Pressures notwithstanding, some figures maintained spiritual contact with the tenets of neorealism even in later years, while others developed highly individual styles out of such beginnings.

Bandits of Orgosola (1961) by Vittorio De Seta is an exceptional production made in the hills of Sardinia. The relation between a bandit tribe and a shepherd who first shelters, then joins them is presented with an unsentimental eye that sees cruelties as ordinary conditions of life rather than sadism.

Ermanno Olmi, from a younger generation, has directed his attention to the minor employees of industrialized Italy, the Umberto D.s in their youth. *Il Posto* (1961) traces the early work years of two young people in a Milan business. The boy begins as a messenger and, in the end, succeeds to an office desk, one he may inhabit for the remainder of his employment. Olmi's adolescent is shy, anxious and affectionate. His tentative approach to a young typist, hired when he was, is depicted with humor that on examination is seen to require the most careful timing and nuances on Olmi's part. *Fist in His Pocket* (1965) by Marco Bellochio is an almost unbearably depressing narrative, centering on a family of five: blind, epileptic and retarded. To free the healthy son from impossible responsibilities, the middle child tries to kill the others.

Pietro Germi first concentrated on Sicilian culture in *In the Name of the Law* (1949), partially written by Fellini, and *The Road to Hope* (1950), bandit and love stories that capture nuances of the island society. Germi later turned to comedy, most successfully in *Divorce, Italian Style* (1961). Francesco Rosi worked for Visconti and Antonioni before directing his own features. Rosi has remained more closely allied than his peers to a neorealist sensibility. *Salvatore Giuliano* (1961) uses a complicated flashback exposition to follow a

Mafia leader's efforts to aid in the fight for Sicilian independence, which culminate in his betrayal and assassination. Making excellent use of the American Rod Steiger, *Hands Over the City* (1963) is a socio-political study of power brokerage between a property developer and the spectrum of Naples' political parties: a strong, outspoken statement. Elio Petri, who wrote scripts for De Santis during the fifties, directed films in the next decade—most notably *The Assassin* (1960), *A Quiet Day in the Country* (1968) and *Investigation of a Citizen Above Suspicion*—which reflect like psychosociological preoccupations of Bertolucci and Pasolini in the same period.

Piero Paolo Pasolini

Like Eisenstein, Pasolini both wrote film theory and directed films. His theoretical material seeks, by way of critical semiotics, to apply tools of linguistics, anthropology, and psychoanalysis to film study.[4] A poet and novelist of Roman slum life, Pasolini entered film as a scenarist for Fellini and others.

Accattone (1961) revives the episodic, seemingly irresolute narrative of early neorealism and its despairing vision toward individual solutions in a world of corruption and violence. The protagonist is a weak, unappealing youth who is rejected by the respectable poor. As a pimp, he loses his woman. He then tries to reform but lacks the capabilities to succeed at anything else, and finally is killed by the police while committing a robbery.

The film is distinguished by a clarity of focus on low life. Each character has a sharpness that establishes in very few scenes distinct, unique, often cruelly corrupted styles of survival. *Mamma Roma* (1962) was intended as a study of the aspirations of a working-class woman. As in *Bellisima*, Anna Magnani does not seem to fit the requirement of

---

Piero Paolo Pasolini (1922–1975)

Accattone	1961
Mamma Roma	1962
Comizi d'Amore	1964
Sopraluoghi in Palestina (documentary)	1964
Il Vangelo Sēcondo Matteo/ The Gospel According to St. Matthew	1964
Uccellacci e Uccellini/The Hawks and the Sparrows	1966
Edipo Re/Oedipus Rex	1967
Teorama (Theorum)	1968
Porcile/Pig Pen/Pig Sty	1969
Medea	1970
Il Decamerone/The Decameron	1971
I Racconti di Canterbury/The Canterbury Tales	1972
Saló or the 120 Days of Sodom	1976
Partial listing	

---

[4] See *Piero Paolo Pasolini, "The Cinema of Poetry,"* Cahiers du Cinéma in English 6 *(December 1966)*.

the part. Both films accompany their proletarian stories with classical music, Bach and Vivaldi, serving as ironic contrast in *Accattone*, evidence of Magnani's pretensions in *Mamma Roma*.

The Gospel According to St. Matthew (1964) has the curious distinction of embodying a Marxist version of Christ's life that is (outside Italy) pleasing to Christians. Pasolini's representation of Matthew is direct and unassuming, his Jesus a determined, altogether confident personage who approaches the future assured he is acting out destiny. Minor figures are Italian shepards and farmers who assume their biblical roles comfortably. In fact, Palestine does not seem anomolous in Southern Italy. A sense of actuality is enhanced by documentary techniques, handheld cameras, zoom lenses, and skewed compositions. What Pasolini views as inherent contradictions between Christ's revolutionary message to the people and the unbelievable, doctrinaire miracles are accepted in stride by English language audiences.

To greater or less degree, later Pasolini work departs from naturalist foundations. The director viewed Italy's postwar industrial revolution, its extreme cultural transition, as incompatible with earlier filmmaking technique.

I love Rossellini. . . . Realism is such an ambiguous and loaded word that it is hard to agree on its meaning. I consider my own films realist compared with neorealist films. In neorealist films day-to-day reality is seen from a crepuscular, intimistic, credulous and above all naturalistic point of view. . . . In neo-realism, things are described with a certain detachment, with human warmth mixed with irony—characteristics which I do not have.[5]

Subsequent Pasolini films often invoke qualities that the director himself described as surreal, distinguishing his employment from both the French graphic-literary traditions and the devices of director Luis Buñuel. In his episode of a Dino De Laurentiis anthology, *Capriccio all'Italiana* (1966), characters are marionettes on strings. *Oedipus Rex* (1967) reverts from a modern episode to Sophocles' Oedipus at Delphi, then back to the present. *Pig Pen* (1969) tells the story of a young man in love with a pig and finally eaten by swine. The black humor of this final episode is preceded by a more lurid, seventeenth-century episode in which a young band of fanatics on the crescent of a volcano attack and eat passersby. While the consumption of flesh has oedipal significance ("I have killed my father . . . I tremble with joy"), it is more essentially a persistent reference to man's misuse of man and the apathy with which this misuse is witnessed: the same actor watches both devourings.

Teorama (1968) describes the visit of a divine figure to a middle-class, Milanese home. Its involvement with each member of the family—maid, son, daughter, mother, and father—is consumated in sexual love. The experience leaves each in a state of ecstatic grace, but like many figures in the films of Pasolini, all but the maid are incapable of sustaining the condition. She achieves sainthood. The director's films mix sexuality, Marxist critiques of the bourgeois, black humor, sometimes homosexuality, and a highly personal nonorthodox religiosity that seems to fall back in dismay at a world condemned to failure by history. *Saló or The 120 Days of Sodom* (1976) renders tangible the obsessions of the Marquis de Sade: sexual cruelties visited on youth, innocence and, by implication the proletariat by Gestapo-like figures of repression. *Saló* is set in wartime Italy, its final torture scenes quite literally unbearable. The controversial film was completed shortly before Pasolini was found, murdered, by Italian police. Its final cut may be at odds with the director's intentions.

---

[5] *Piero Paolo Pasolini,* Pasolini on Pasolini: Interviews with Oswald Stack, *p. 109.*

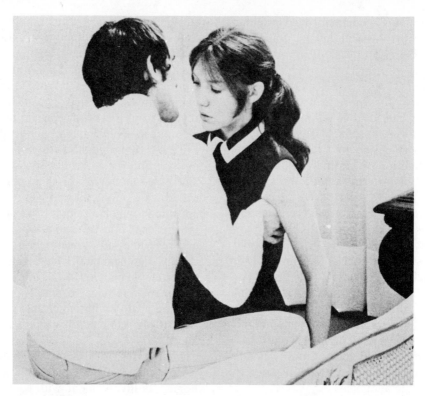

Teorama. Terence Stamp and Anna Wiazemsky. Pasolini's works withstood easy interpretation by critics and lovers of consistency: Christian myth, Greek tragedy, urban squalor, cannibalism, and the Marquis de Sade. Although accused of obscenity, *Teorama*'s bisexual couplings won more plaudits from Catholics than from Marxists. (National Film Archives, Ottawa)

Bernardo Bertolucci

Originally a respected poet (his influences were Emily Dickinson and Dylan Thomas), Bertolucci made his first feature, a detective story, at the Wellesian age of twenty-two and his reputation next with *Before the Revolution* (1964). Set in Parma, the film's intimate delineations of character recalls De Sica, although later Bertolucci work indicated that his affinities rested more with the next generation of directors. *Before the Revolution* locates itself at the postwar moment when Communist persuasion had convinced provincial, middle-class youth of the society's inevitable change. From this watershed vantage, the film consid-

ers both periods. Leftist allegiances are allayed by the pleasures of life, by pessimism, sensuality, and intellectual preoccupations beside which worker parades seem irrelevant. The film's highest moment is reserved for an aging, landed gentry whose lament for his wooded countryside has the muted nostalgia of Turgenev's *Sportsman's Sketches*. The climax occurs in the Opera House, where two lovers say goodbye in the lobby, their feelings resonating in an offscreen, romantic nineteenth-century duet.

Partner (1968) again recalls the Russians, adapting Dostoyevsky's short novel *The Double*, the story of a man disquieted to learn that another version of himself roams the streets, visits his friends, and, worst, appears more at ease than he. *The Conformist* (1969) intertwines sex and politics in a remarkably recreated fascist Italy of the thirties. As in Visconti's *The Damned,* and Pasolini's *Saló,* homosexuality is equated with power urges and with the authoritarian personality.[6] A man joins the Fascisti, denounces them at liberation, and finally descends to a derelict street life. While the story is heavy-handed, Bertolucci structures its exposition into memories that suggest Proust-like associational flashbacks. His employment of color is designed to reinforce the abnormalities of the earlier regime.

The Spider's Strategy (1970) redeploys

Bertolucci's interest in doubles with a new turn. Vaguely derived from a story by J. L. Borges, the plot concerns a young man who returns to the town of his dead father, an early resistance hero. Flashbacks recount events in the older man's life (father and son are played by the same actor), but these sequences are inflected by the son's idealized image of his father, whom he hardly knew. The film counterpoints its identity-search theme (finding the truth about the father, the son is forced to confront elements of himself) against the perplexing, guilt-ridden issue of fascism among the townspeople. No one wants the past remembered accurately. The son's search is psychologically dangerous, and Bertolucci emphasizes its attendant anxiety with visuals that contrast old and new (like bicycles and freeways), darkness and light (blackened archways and doors), and complicated glass reflections.

[6] *Tenets of Wilhelm Reich figure heavily in contemporary movie explications of fascism.* See Wilhelm Reich, The Mass Psychology of Fascism. *New York, 1946.*

Before the Revolution. Bertolucci gave his lovers the same names as in Stendhal's *The Charterhouse of Parma.* He was born in Parma and began attending three films each Saturday at the age of 10. Bertolucci's production experience commenced on Pasolini's *Accatone.* (National Film Archives, Ottawa)

Last Tango in Paris (1973) overlays the issue of identity with the one of sexual roles. Marlon Brando and Maria Schneider meet by chance while investigating a flat for rent. They occupy it together and in secret, devoting hours to sexual pleasure independent of the rest of life, personal identities withheld from one another. In the end, she leaves. He follows and she shoots him.

The collusion for anonymous sex is illusory. Brando seeks some kind of authenticity to free him from the memories of his wife's suicide. Schneider, a middle-class girl engaged to a documentary filmmaker, hopes to find something that may transcend the implications of her life and her predestined future. As the sexual encounters represent a desperate effort toward communication undistorted by the requirements of more ordinary relationships, they also enact a psychological retrogression for Brando, whose oppression of Schneider, intended to serve personal catharsis, finally frees her of him. Despite its apparent explicitness, *Last Tango in Paris* is not intended to stimulate the viewer erotically but rather to trace eroticism as a means of emotional human intercourse.

1900 (1976) endured an hour and 25 minutes of cuts to reach its four-hour, American-release version. Still drawn in epic dimensions, it traces peasant life in Emilia, paralleled by the moral deterioration of the land's padrones. An emphasis on polarized, melodramatic values cut to accommodate a Marxist vision of World Wars I and II does little to alter the form's conventions. However, Bertolucci's sense of opera, like Visconti's, achieves remarkable effects. In one sequence, Bert Lancaster as the aging landowner listens to peasants singing at twilight. The tap of his cane counterpoints offscreen music. Both sounds play against a pair of women's voices calling in two boys, Olmo and Alfredo, the peasant-padrone principals of the next generation.

Lina Wertmüller

Like parts of her later features, Wertmüller's first film, *The Lizards* (1963) begs comparison with Fellini (for whom she worked). One of Fellini's early ventures, *I Vitelloni* (1953), dealt with the small northern Italian town of his youth, and *The Lizards* has a similar setting. An essential difference is implicit in the films' titles. *I Vitelloni* ironically suggests young bulls, egomaniacal, snorting, and pawing, partly, but not altogether, for show. These are Fellini's young men, while those in Wertmüller are more flaccid, sun-drenched, little single-minded animals.

Characteristically, Wertmüller's small town has a political dimension, transitional between fascisti and a yet-to-be-realized unionism. Because of the economy and because of the culture, the postadolescent, unmarried males still live with their parents, childishly dependent on family for cigarette money, more talk than action around girls. They are indolently free from almost every pressure except a vague requirement eventually to marry and to support themselves; they are always leaning against something in the center of town, watching, fantasizing, thinking about the big

Bernardo Bertolucci (1940–)

La Commare Secca/The Grim Reaper	1962
Prima della Rivoluzione/ Before the Rēvolution	1964
La Via del Petrolio (3 part film for TV)	1965
La Canale	1967
Partner	1968
Il Conformista/The Conformist	1969
Strategia del Ragno/The Spider's Strategy	1970
Last Tango in Paris	1973
1900	1976

city. *The Lizards* is filmed in straightforward, humorous observation of its prinicipals, excepting some eerie, high-angle shots that serve as tongue-in-cheek reminder of the young narrator's search for omniscience. The best sequence studies the least articulate of the young men listening to a new American rock and roll record. His face, viewed from shifting angles, is altogether inexpressive and totally intent on a clamor that signifies adventure and escape.

Freed from the conventions of small-town Italian culture, Wertmüller's subsequent films give increasing attention to male-female relations, usually involving political conflicts and cultural bonds that result in confusions and inner turmoil. A socialist, her projects gratify viewers who applaud the interjection of politics and of a female consciousness into feature films. Concurrently, many among the same audience are dismayed by newer film resolutions that seem to revert the woman's role to customary stereotypes, to play both sex and politics for laughs.

Love and Anarchy (1973) employs Giancarlo Giannini, a favorite Wertmüller protagonist whose round-eyed, unblinking gaze can project innocence, dedication, and sly cunning. Here, he is committed to the assassination of Mussolini, temporarily hidden away in a Roman bordello whose fascinations leave him physically, spiritually and sexually hungry. The vulgarity and the brutality of fascist officers are reported partly straight, partly for laughs until a conclusion resolves the story in somber, violent tone.

The Seduction of Mimi (1972) again plots sexual roles in a setting of authoritarian pressures. Wertmüller understands systemic likenesses between Church, corporation, Mafia, and macho Italian. What bothers her feminist critics is the disinclination to generalize far enough to include machismo as a political system that ought to generate as much resistance on her part as to the other institutions. The issue becomes uppermost in *Swept Away By*

an Unusual Destiny in the Blue Sea of August (1974).

Like Cecil B. DeMille's *Male and Female*, *Swept Away* casts a wealthy, arrogant woman (Raefaella, played by Mariangela Malato) on an island with a man from a lower caste. In

Lina Wertmüller (1928–   )

I Basilischi/The Lizards	1963
Questa Volta Parliamo di Uomini/Now Let's Talk About Men	1965
Rita la Zanzara/Rita the Mosquito (credited director "George Brown" is Wertmüller)	1966
Non Stuzzicate la Zanzara/ Don't Tease the Mosquito	1967
Mimì Metallurgico Fertio Nell'onore/The Seduction of Mimi	1972
Film d'Amore e d'Anarchia, ovvero Stamattina Alle 10 in Via dei Fiori Nella Nota Casa di Tolleranza . . ./Film of Love and Anarchy, or This Morning at 10 in the Via dei Viori at the Well-Known House of Tolerance/Love and Anarchy	1973
Tutto a Posto e Niente in Ordine/Everything's in Order But Nothing Works/All Screwed Up	1974
Travolti da un Insolito Destino Null'Azzurro Mare D'Agosto/Swept Away by a Strange Destiny on an Azure August Sea/Swept Away	1974
Pasqualino Settebelleze/ Pasqualino Seven Beauties/Seven Beauties	1976
The End of the World in Our Usual Bed in a Night Full of Rain	1978

A Shift in Values   333

this case, he is Gennarino (Giannini), a communist crewman. Freed from conventions of society, Gennarino first returns Raefaella's verbal abuses with his own, then beats her physically, then asserts his sexual domination not through force but by the conditions of the primitive life and his capacity to insure their survival. In a brief idyl, she wins his confidence as well, and political banter becomes jocular. A ship is sighted. The pair return to their former lives and their other mates. Rejecting any romantic renunciation of wealth, Raefaella deserts her lover for luxury.

An understanding of the conclusion rests on one's sense both of motive and of Wertmüller's equation of sexual and class roles. In Wertmüller's mind, Raefaella represents bourgeois society. Because that society is dominant, Rafaella thus represents the male principle. If Raefaella's final decision constitutes a hollow betrayal of Gennarino, then she and Wertmüller by implication have denied the joint causes of women and socialism. If she has, rather, asserted a class-based decision that the system has made inevitable, the conclusion may be seen as an ironic comment on the unbridgeable gulf between two ways of life.

Seven Beauties (1976) casts Giannini in the nightmare of Nazi power and concentration camps. He is a deplorable murderer and pimp who is yet charming and determined to survive. As man and woman exchange power roles on the basis of social position, here Wertmüller suggests that cowardice and heroism may assume their own kinds of ambi-

Seven Beauties. Giancarlo Giannini and his seductress-to-be at her beach house. Wertmuller learned film as an assistant director for *8½* She retains Fellini's predeliction for grotesques, more often psychological than physical, except for heavy-set women. (British National Film Archive/Stills Library)

Titanus Farnesina Studios. Sharing costs with Hollywood, the company produced *The Leopard* and *Sodom and Gomorrah* in 1962. Visconti's film made money in Italy, but cost overruns and poor distribution abroad prompted studio withdrawal from any other functions than distribution. (Italian Cultural Institute)

guity in conditions of absolute brutality. Giannini manages to survive by "seducing" a grotesque camp matron. Authority feminizes his behavior by requiring compliant servility.

Commercial Product

A singular view of Italian neorealism and its descendents would altogether neglect Italian film as commerce. De Santis' sexualization of the rice fields was only a compromise with another cinema, whose aspirations during the fifties and early sixties rivalled Faust's. Some films from this realm enjoyed widespread American distribution, like Steve Reeves as Hercules and Kirk Douglas as Ulysses. Then film sought the American market with increasing directness: Robert Aldrich's *Sodom and Gomorrah* (1962) and Dino De Laurentiis' *Waterloo* (1970), the latter a box-office failure for all its American, Russian, and British money. Comedies became increasingly stereotyped, like Germi's later work.

The sixties spaghetti westerns, particularly those directed by Sergio Leone, who assisted Aldrich on *Sodom and Gomorrah,* were a generic offshoot of some interest: *A Fistful of Dollars* (1964), *For a Few Dollars More* (1965), *The Good, the Bad and the Ugly* (1967), *Once Upon a Time in the West* (1969), and *A Fistful of Dynamite* (1971). Leone's films served in part to take up slack that American television western series created in feature production. Sophisticatedly familiar with character and behavior conventions, the films cleverly overlay elements of surrealist staging and "foreign" idioms. Indeed, the western had become internationalized by this time. Akira Kurosawa's *Yojimbo* (1961) was admittedly influenced by *High Noon* (1952) and *Shane* (1953); its plot forms the basis for *A Fistful of Dollars,* which Bertolucci largely wrote. Leone's employment of a TV western actor, Clint Eastwood, helped to hold the diverse modes in place.

Many of the great corporations (Titanus, Galatea) collapsed in the sixties through over-commitments or else they abdicated autonomy by subordinating themselves to foreign money. Italy's dream of recreated Hollywood was punctured, and many of the interesting seventies films, like Rossellini's historical studies, have originated under television's sponsorship.

Summary

Rooted in early reactions to studio-bound, fascisti productions of Mussolini's era, neorealism blossomed after World War II. It celebrated candid, close scrutinies of proletarian life as defined by social and political forces. As postwar Italian society changed, neorealism sometimes compromised, sometimes specialized its intentions. While preserving something of the original esthetic, many recent productions show more individualized visions, as seen in the work of Bertolucci, Wertmüller, and Pasolini.

In France, wartime pressures nurtured another generation of filmmakers, their work refracted by different cultural pressures and by stronger filmmaking traditions. Tides and eddies of the New Wave are charted in Chapter 14.

Bibliography

Arcali, Franco and Bernardo Bertolucci. *Bernardo Bertolucci's Last Tango in Paris.* New York, 1973.

Armes, Roy. *Patterns of Realism.* South Brunswick, N.J., 1971.

Bachman, Gideon. "The 220 days of *Saló*," *Film Comment* (March-April 1976).

Blumenfeld, Gina. "The Next to Last Word on Lina Wertmüller," *Cineaste* (1976).

Bragin, John. "Piero Paolo Pasolini: Poetry as a Compensation," *Film Society Review* V.4 Ns. 5,6,7.

Brigante, Louis. "Three New Italian Film Makers," *Film Culture* 24 (1962).

Ferrera, Giuseppe. *Luchino Visconti.* Paris, 1970.

Gervais, Marc. *Piero Paolo Pasolini.* Paris, 1973.

———. "Piero Paolo Pasolini: Contestatore," *Sight and Sound* (Winter 1968-69).

Goldin, Marilyn. "Bertolucci on The Conformist," *Sight and Sound* (Spring 1971).

Hovald, Patrice G. *Le Neo-realisme italien et ses créateurs.* Paris, 1959.

Huaco, George. *The Sociology of Film Art.* New York, 1965.

Jacobs, Diana. "Lina Wertmüller: The Italian Aristophanes?" *Film Comment* (March-April 1976)

Jarratt, Vernon. *The Italian Cinema.* London, 1951.

Kass, Robert, "Fifty Years of Italian Cinema," *Films in Review* (August-September 1955).

Kelman, Ken. "Rossellini's Tragedy of Manners," *Film Culture* 46 (1967).

Korte, Walter. "Marxism and Formalism in Visconti's Films," *Cinema Journal* (Fall 1971).

Lane, John Francis. "Ermanno Olmi: An Interview," *Film Comment* (Summer 1970)

Leprohon, Pierre. *The Italian Cinema*. New York, 1972.

McCourt, James. "In Memorium: Luchino Visconti," *Film Comment* (May-June 1976).

Mailer, Norman. "Transit to Narcissus," *New York Review of Books* (May 17, 1973).

Malerba, Luigi. ed. *Italian Cinema 1945–1951*. Rome, 1951.

Malerba, Luigi and Carmine Siniscalco. *Fifty Years of Italian Cinema*. Rome, 1955.

Mellen, Joan. "Fascism in the Contemporary Film," *Film Quarterly* (Summer 1971).

Nowell-Smith, Geoffrey. *Luchino Visconti*. London, 1967.

Pasolini, Piero Paolo. *Pasolini on Pasolini: Interviewed by Oswald Stack*. Bloomington, 1969.

———. "Cinema and Literary Stylistics," *Film Culture* 24 (1962).

———. *Edipo Re*. Milan, 1967.

———. *Mamma Roma*. Milan, 1962.

———. "A Press Conference," *Film Culture* 42 (1966).

Riley, Brooks. "Lina Wertmüller: The Sophist's Norman Lear?" *Film Comment* (March-April 1976).

Rindaldo, Fabio. *Roma, Città Aperta*. Padova, 1969.

Rondi, Gian Luigi. *Italian Cinema Today 1952–1965*. London, 1966.

Rossellini, Roberto. *The War Trilogy*. New York, 1973.

Schlappner, Martin. *Von Rossellini zu Fellini*. Zurich, 1958.

Screen (Neorealism issue) (Winter 1973-1974).

Shafa, Parviz S. *The Nature and Origin of the Italian Neorealism*. M.A. thesis, San Francisco State University, 1966.

Sica, Vittoria De. *Miracle in Milan*. New York, 1968.

Thomsen, Christian Braad. "Bellocchio," *Sight and Sound* (Winter 1967–1968).

Verdone, Mario. *Roberto Rossellini*. Paris, 1963.

Visconti, Luchino. *Three Screenplays*. New York, 1970.

Wall, James M. *Three European Directors*. Grand Rapids, 1973.

Wertmüller, Lina. "You Cannot Make the Revolution on Film," *Cineaste* (1976).

Zavattini, Cesare. *Zavattini: Sequences from a Cinematic Life*. Englewood Cliffs, N.J., 1970.

14

FRENCH NEW WAVE

In France, impulses toward freer structure, more varied subjects, and emancipation from script domination were expressed in the fifties critical journal *Cahiers du Cinéma,* as well as among a new generation of filmmakers, most on the near side of thirty. One of *Cahiers'* strong-minded contributors was François Truffaut. In January 1954, he published an essay titled "A Certain Tendency of French Cinema."[1] The essay was disdainful of the collaborations of currently successful scriptwriters Pierre Bost and Jean Aurenche. These men, said Truffaut, had developed a tradition of faithful literary adaptations; scripts that sacrificed film's integrity for the sake of rigid, conventional transpositions of novels into film. Such a predelineated mode, Truffaut argued, was strangling the French film

[1] *François Truffaut, "A Certain Tendency of French Cinema,"* Cahiers du Cinéma in English *1 (January 1966).*

Jules and Jim (Truffaut 1961) (Museum of Modern Art/Film Stills Archive)

with a patina of "quality." In truth it condescended toward the film medium in that techniques and values cribbed from literature dominated the work. Adaptations carried filmic value only when prepared by men of the film. Otherwise, shooting a movie simply applied makeup to the printed page.

However extreme Truffaut's polemic (Aurenche and Bost's *Devil in the Flesh* made with Autant-Lara and *Forbidden Games* with Clement are certainly estimable works), it touched on truth. The domination of studio and script had become increasingly at odds with the times.

BEACHHEADS BEFORE THE NEW WAVE

Among the new critics, who revered Hollywood films, commercial success needed hardly be thought to diminish a film's value. A breakthrough for this cause was Roger Vadim's first feature, *And God Created Woman* (1956), which gave the world Brigitte Bardot. Vadim's calculated conception of *Woman* was to capitalize on his wife's solid flesh, yet the emphasis on Bardot's free life style emancipated more than sexual values. She played a woman whose erotic quest leads her in continual search of a man who can satisfy her on every plane, not firmness or power or gentleness or virility alone. The movie's commercial success, particularly in the United States, helped to convince French producers that new approaches might also make money.

Shorts

France's market for short films contributed to the development of new talent. Unlike the United States, where cartoon, newsreel, and preview were now considered only intrusions on the features, France supported shorts. At the least, such productions might earn back their investment and promise a small profit. Further, the variety was immense. Short films not only provided training grounds for future directors, they constituted a separate tradition of imaginative, stimulating experiences: *Pacific 231* (1944) by Jean Mitry; *The Blood of the Beasts* (1948) by Franju; *Van Gogh* (1948) by Resnais; *Hotel des Invalides* (1952) by Franju; *Les Statues muerent aussi* (1953) by Resnais and Chris Marker; *Les Mistons* (1957) by Truffaut; *Tous les garcons s'appellent Patrick* (1957) by Jean-Luc Godard; *Opéra Mouffe* (1958) by Agnes Varda.

And God Created Woman. American flacks subtitled it *But the Devil Invented Brigitte Bardot.* Bardot's encounters include a wealthy businessman (Curt Jürgens), and her husband's older brother (Christian Marquand). After forsaking her new spouse (Jean-Louis Trintignant, below), Bardot finally returns to him. Distributors boasted that the film earned more money than Renault cars in the United States during 1957–58. (Museum of Modern Art/Film Stills Archive)

Le Deuxième souffle (1965). One of the gangster movies directed by Melville. His great pleasures rested in writing and editing, his bane the actual shooting. Melville appears as the celebrity interviewed by Jean Seberg in Godard's *Breathless,* a tribute to his status among the emerging generation of filmmakers. (National Film Archives, Ottawa)

Jean-Pierre Melville

Melville provides something of a transitional figure between traditional cinema and the New Wave; a director whose passion was American films of the mid-thirties, in particular the gangster genre. Demobilized in 1945, he founded his own production company in order to qualify for the Film Technician's Union. *Le Silence de la mer* (made 1947, released 1949) was based on a secretly published wartime story about a German officer who comes to realize the character of naziism and, with a sense of having been betrayed by his cause, goes to the eastern front to death. Melville filmed the story on the actual locations. While less successful than most of Cocteau's own versions of his material, *Les En-*

Jean-Pierre Melville (1917–1973)

Le Silence de la mer	1947
Les Enfants terribles	1949
Quand tu liras cette lettre	1953
Bob le flambeur/Bob the Gambler	1955
Deux hommes dans Manhattan	1958
Léon Morin, Prêtre	1961
Le Doulos/Doulos the Fingerman	1962
L'Aîné des Ferchaux	1962
Le Deuxième souffle	1966
Le Samourai	1967
L'Armée des ombres	1969
Le Cercle rouge	1970
Un flic	1972

341

fants Terribles (1949) effectively catches the claustrophobic, muted hysteria of the story.

Bob le flambeur/Bob the Gambler (1955) is the first of Melville's gangster stories, one he described as a "comedy of manners," with a gambler-thief whose explosives, intended to rob Deauville, ignite before he can stop them; he has already beaten the bank through legitimate gambling. In the same idiom are _Deux hommes dans Manhattan_ (1958), made in a New York locale, and _Le Doulos/Doulos the Fingerman_ (1962) with Belmondo an informer who may or may not be innocent of a particular accusation but must die in any case.

Melville's films are taut, fast-paced melodramas, very like the American ones he admired, except for more considerable attention to character and, to American audiences, the curiosities of gangster convention thoroughly transposed into French mannerisms. An ex-ception is _Léon Morin, Prêtre/Léon Morin, Priest_ (1961), the story of a priest (Belmondo) who resists the advances of a communist widow (Emmanuele Riva) who believes herself converted. Melville is noncommital in the film as to whether Riva's faith is human, spiritual, or a combination of both. In private, he said that the world had entered a phase where belief in either God or Marx was no longer possible.

Georges Franju

Older than the New Wave (he helped to found France's great film archive, the Cinémathèque Française with Henri Langlois in 1937), Franju has applied the nuances rather than the spectacle of surrealism to both documentary and features. Without exaggeration, he might be described as an anarcho-surrealist-Freudian-Marxist with overtones of the Marquis de Sade.

The Blood of the Beasts (1949) documents the work of a Parisian slaughter house in unbearable detail. The butcheries are so artfully photographed — the steaming blood casting fragile mists over carcasses and machinery — that ordinary liberal indignations are curtailed and the viewer is required to reflect more deeply on what he witnesses. One of Franju's aims, he has said, is "to restore to documentary reality its appearance of artifice and to natural sets their real attribute of seeming constructed."

To accomplish this, Franju carefully films his real locations so as to assume a quality of studio set construction, seeking, for instance, moments of natural light that have the quality of artificiality. The same is true of the portrayal of humans in the film. While the butchers slice the great carcasses, clearly a physically taxing job, they sing a popular sentimental song, _La Mer_. The effect is unsettling. The same is true when we watch a carcass being dissected, and hear a distant clock strike the hour. However incongruous,

Georges Franju (1912–   )

Le Sang des bêtes/The Blood of the Beasts (short)	1949
En Passant par la Lorraine (short)	1950
Hôtel des Invalides (short)	1952
Le Grand Méliès (short)	1952
Monsieur et Madame Curie (short)	1953
La Tête contre les murs/The Keepers	1958
Les Yeux sans visage/The Horror Chamber of Dr. Faustus	1959
Pleins feux sur l'Assassin	1961
Thérèse Desqueroux	1962
Judex	1963
Thomas l'Imposteur/Thomas the Imposter	1965
Le Faute de l'Abbé Mouret/The Sin of Father Mouret	1970
L'Homme sans visage	1974
Partial listing	

the two elements in combination have none of the premeditated quality of contrivance.

Hôtel des Invalides (1952) turns a war museum and veterans' hospital into a wry comment on forgotten horror. (A girl primps before the periscope of a simulated trench.) *Le Grand Méliès* (1952) evokes the charm and innocence of the early filmmaker with light, nostalgic affection, filming his widow and using the son to enact a few of his father's magic tricks.

La Tête contre les murs (1958) was Franju's first feature, a story about an insane asylum to which a young man has been committed for stealing money and burning some of his father's papers. The very madness of the treatments, the irrationality of their rationales, and the stifling attempts to cosmetize the asylum's real character again trigger Franju's surreal vision of ordinary life.

I shot *La Tête* in the Psychiatric Hospital of Drury, with a quite unbelievable courtyard. Dead in the center is a phallic tree with four benches grouped around it. Around the benches there are tulips and round the tulips there are high walls. The patients sit on the benches and all day long they look at the tree. I must admit I wouldn't have dared ask an art director for anything quite so "artificial," so demented as that.[2]

La Tête contre les murs marks the first acting role of Charles Aznavour. The score by Maurice Jarre has its own obsessive, mocking

[2] *Raymond Durgnat,* Franju, *p. 70.*

L'Homme sans visage or *Nuits rouges* (1974). Franju returns to the world of Fantômas in an entertainment written and performed by Jacques Champreaux. The man without a face is only seen in his disguises, thwarting rival gangs who contend for a Templars' treasure. As always, the feats evoke surreality; the ending melts back into silent film's world of Judex. (French Film Office)

quality, veering like the protagonist between lucidity and dementia.

Les Yeux sans visage (1959) has a curious distribution history. It finally appeared in the United States as a shocker titled *The Horror Chamber of Dr. Faustus*. The story certainly possesses the requisite qualities of a horror film. Having caused his daughter's facial injury in a car accident, a plastic surgeon schemes with his assistant to lure young women to his country home. There he tries without success to graft their faces onto his daughter's. In the end, the doctor's face is ripped away by savage dogs. His daughter kills the assistant and wanders, insane, into the night.

With such material, Franju constructs another beautifully visualized work, cruelties balanced against Jarre's light-hearted music. The surgical grotesqueries are simulated specifically enough that an audience knows what to anticipate; when the doctor pencils out the boundaries of incision on a new victim's beautiful face, the effect is as unnerving as an operation itself. Doctor and assistant are genuinely concerned for the daughter, who is kept in a luxurious secret chamber, her face masked, but for the anguish in her eyes. When she loses her reason, her head is surrounded with fluttering doves. The bizarre conjunction of the two elements has the appearance of sanity altogether departing its bastion.

Thérèse Desqueroux (1962) is based on a famous French Catholic novel with which Franju seems to possess curious affinity. Where François Mauriac condemns pietistic, moralizing behavior, Franju merely observes it without editorializing on religious implications. A provincial wife (Emmanuele Riva) is cleared in court by her husband of attempting to kill him, but callously rejected emotionally by the family, with no effort to understand her motives for such an attempt. As with the doves in *Les Yeuz sans visage,* Franju uses objects to suggest the state of Thérèse's depression and frustrations: the sound of wind blowing through pine trees at night, a picket fence whose regular, geometric repetition seen from a moving car seems to possess a mute, shrieking quality of obsession.

Judex (1963) was based on the scripts by Louis Feuillade who made the original serial in 1916 after the success of *Fantômas*. The costumes and melodramatic flights and rescues in the city delighted early surrealists and abet Franju's enthusiasms. Judex, a black-cloaked master of disguise is committed to revenging his father. He is a more single-minded, less admirable figure than comic strip super heroes. His vengeance on the villain is less just than it is self-satisfying. The man must live underground with only a mirror as company. A bird motif is developed beginning with the character of Judex himself, an aerial figure of gravity-defying skills. He is introduced in evening dress and a bird mask at a costume ball, holding a dead pigeon, which he restores to life. Carrier pigeons serve as messengers to call Judex when needed. The villainness is worthy of his mettle, the heroine Edith Scob, brave and capable without either the bland inadequacies of Lois Lane or the aggressiveness of a liberated Wonder Woman.

NEW WAVE

The notion of a "new wave" of filmmakers originated in a weekly magazine, *L'Express,* referring to a generation of youth to whom the country looked for infusions of energy and ideas into the political regime of Mendes-France. Applied to film, the words had metaphorical utility. Unfortunately, they were applied imprecisely and overused and eventually came to signify a concensus and uniformity that never existed in fact. What the new directors shared at times were actors (Jean-Claude Brialy, Jeanne Moreau, Jean-Paul Belmondo), script writers (Paul Gégauff) and ideas, as in the case of Godard's *Breathless* (1959), which was based on a suggestion of Truffaut's. There is no necessary esthetic cohesion among the directors, nor is there political agreement. Religion is not a common denominator. Alain Resnais' tight-scripted, edited features have little in common with the controlled improvisation of Godard.

Some early New Wave films were privately financed, then marketed commercially. Some features, like many private ventures in the United States, never reached commercial audiences at all. Others were financed, produced, and distributed through ordinary channels. In later years, a few among the new group continued along unique, evolving careers.[3] In retrospect, one now sees an astonishing thrust of uncommon films into public attention during the late fifties and the sixties.

Especially interested in silent German film and particularly F. W. Murnau, Alexandre Astruc developed an impressive reputation as a critic. He foresaw a time when film's accessibility through television and the 16mm market would encourage developments of private, narrative styles, individualized technique that might employ the camera as a writer used pen or typewriter. As a director, Astruc's *Les mauvaises rencontres* (1955) observes a young woman who is detained by police for seeking an abortion. In flashback, she recalls the series of men who have brought her to the present situation. Interior monologue emphasizes subjective, unstated responses to the interrogation. *Une Vie* (1958) was an elaborate version of a de Maupassant novel produced largely under the domination of the studio. In contrast, the low-budget *La Proie pour l'ombre* (1960) remained under Astruc's control. It follows a woman who leaves her husband for another man, deserts him, and finds a lonely independence. The film was written by Françoise Sagan, one among a generation of popular novelists less bound to literary tradi-

tion and closer to film in their own narrative styles, who collaborated with the new directors.

Paris nous appartient/Paris Belongs to Us (1960) is an exceptional work by Jacques Rivette, another film critic and editor. Ambiguous in tone, it can be viewed alternatively as a sinister study of an underground terrorist fascist organization that will subvert Paris and France, or else as a paranoid's view of the modern world, already so threatened with authority and unthinking submission that the vision is emotionally true at the least. The sympathetic characters are rehearsing a performance of Shakespeare's *Pericles,* and their adventures in the city have a meandering, spontaneous quality of authentic accident. One of the most effective scenes has the fascist group watching the trudging workers from Lang's *Metropolis* shuffling in lockstep to their underground elevator. *Paris nous appartient* was made with borrowed equipment, unpaid actors and day-to-day support for production expenses. Its paranoia carries unsettling resonances as it triggers suspicions which events have encouraged many of us to harbor. "The world knows which way it goes, but it doesn't let us know," one character observes, and another says, "An unknown horror threatens, and nothing can be done."

Altogether unlike his peers, Jacques Demy executed a series of films that lightly, incisively explored love among young people, often in the Provence region of France. The simple story of *Lola* (1960) presses actress Anouk Aimée into situations that require mixed, warm emotional responses. (Comparisons of this role with her performances in *Les mauvaises rencontres* and in Fellini's *8½* indicates an actress of extreme sensitivity.) *Lola* is dedicated to Max Ophüls, with whom Demy shares a fascination toward women's responses to cultural pressures that frustrate genuine impulse.

A popular success that related to this period because of its half-improvised performances,

[3] *Godard and Resnais will be considered in detail in Chapter 20.*

Black Orpheus (1958) was filmed in Rio de Janeiro at Carnival, cast with black actors. Its director, Marcel Camus, made exotic employment of the festival and an over-stimulated narrative that followed the myth of Orpheus and Eurydice. If the venture has a glossy, commercial slant, its color photography is striking, particularly the night scenes.

Les Liaisons dangereuses 1960 (1959), another production by Vadim, updated an eighteenth-century novel that attacked the high moral tone of French society by portraying a couple who give way to their actual feelings, however ugly these may be. In Vadim's film, accompanied by the jazz piano of Thelonious Monk, a husband and wife conspire to give one another pleasure by abetting each other's seductions and sharing the anecdotes of what happens. However vulgarized (the film polarized New Wave criticism), *Liaisons* is distinguished by Jeanne Moreau as the wife, her corrupt impulses finally vying with actual jealousy.

Adieu Philippine (1962) by Jacques Rozier is a half-improvised anecdote about a television studio employee who has a love affair with two young women as an interlude while he is waiting for the draft. Jean Rouch's documentary influence, minimally adapted to fiction form is apparent.[4]

In *Five Day Lover* (1961) Philippe de Broca, who had worked for Claude Chabrol and Truffaut, inverts the amorality of *And God Created Woman* into a story of a bored wife who unknowingly has an affair with her friend's lover. De Broca's style is comic, an updated Lubitsch commiting what remain of social and sexual convention as ballast to his irony.

François Truffaut

Something of Truffaut's early life appears as autobiography in his films, although it is more emotionally than factually parallel; his Antoine Doinel character, recurrently played by Jean-Pierre Léaud, mixes Truffaut's fantasy with Truffaut fact.

His own school career, for example, was

[4] *The film gained a kind of special notoriety in later years when French film scholar Christian Metz employed it as the basis for a practical illustration of semiotic analysis, his own version of the study in which Pasolini had been equally interested. See* Christian Metz, Film Language, *Part III. New York, 1974.*

Francois Truffaut (1932–   )

Une visite (short)	1954
Les Mistons/The Mischief-makers (short)	1957
Histoire d'eau (completed by Jean-Luc Godard) (short)	1958
Les 400 Coups/The 400 Blows	1959
Tirez sur le pianiste/Shoot the Piano Player	1960
Jules et Jim/Jules and Jim	1961
L'Amour à vingt ans/Love at 20 (episode)	1962
La Peau douce/The Soft Skin	1964
Fahrenheit 451	1966
La Mariée était en noir/The Bride Wore Black	1967
Baisers volés/Stolen Kisses	1968
La Sirène de Mississippi/Mississippi Mermaid	1969
L'Enfant sauvage/The Wild Child	1969
Domicile conjugal/Bed and Bored	1970
Two English Girls	1972
Such a Georgeous Kid Like Me	1973
La Nuit americane/Day for Night	1973
L'Histoire d'Adele H./The Story of Adele H.	1975
Small Change	1976
L'Homme qui aimait les femmes/The Man Who Loved Women	1977

marked by truancy. He lived away from his parents. At fourteen, Truffaut started a ciné-club, The Film Addict's Club, with a bootleg print of *Metropolis*. Because of a competitive screening at the established ciné-club directed by André Bazin, no one attended. Visiting the other club, Truffaut met Bazin who became an important early influence. When Truffaut's father had him arrested for running away from home, Bazin managed the boy's release in his custody. When Truffaut deserted his army enlistment, Bazin smoothed over the complications.

Truffaut committed himself to film criticism, his spirited polemics appearing in *Cahiers du Cinéma* under Bazin's editorship, Rejecting the "Cinema of Quality," the young writer espoused a kind of film that would reflect, obliquely if necessary, the imagination of one man, and this formed the basis for what came to be known as *auteur* criticism.

Such an approach was possible for certain dominant figures in American films, and some minor, unacknowledged directors working surreptitiously among the interstices of conventional assignments to have their personal way with the material. In France maximum directorial freedom was maintained by making films with limited resources. Truffaut's early ventures were shorts, *Une Visite* (1954) photographed by Rivette and edited by Resnais; *Les Mistons/The Mischief-Makers* (1957); and *Histoire d'eau* (1958), completed by Godard.

The Mischief-Makers reports an adolescent love affair seen through the eyes of a younger child who is himself first feeling stirrings of attraction toward Bernadette, the girl. The narrator is part of a small gang who torment the couple, lacking any other way to express their interest and curiosity. Filmed silent with narration added, *The Mischief-Makers* shows Truffaut's easy relation to young, nonprofessional actors. The kids simply behave as kids, like the boys in *Zéro de conduite*. Their vision of Bernadette and Gérard (whose death in a climbing accident is reported toward the pic-

ture's end) is through withdrawn long shots in a pastoral suburban setting, the girl's legs a source of constant wonder. Truffaut plays with the camera. An early Lumière is re-created (*L'Arroseur arrosé*), and the boys' shoot-em-up Hollywood gangster antics are done with camera tricks, slow motion and backwards movement.

The 400 Blows (1959) introduces Antoine Doinel, here Léaud as a twelve year old. Ignored or admonished by his parents, he is equally unhappy at school. With a friend, Doinel plays truant. Trying to return a stolen typewriter he could not pawn, Doinel is sent to an institution to be diagnosed for his delinquency. The boy escapes and *The 400 Blows* (whose French title means, roughly, "raising hell") ends when flight brings him to the sea.

Truffaut's evocation in *The 400 Blows* is not limited to boys' behaviors. He develops a world for them to inhabit, a Paris of cheap amusements, empty streets in early morning where freshly delivered milk bottles are for the taking. Wet sidewalks and landmarks like Sacré Coeur are embedded in the consciousness, not monuments but environment, like the shot of St. Peter's at the end of *Open City*.

There is an essential tension in *The 400 Blows* between Doinel's contrary urges to be accepted by his parents and to be free. The observation center to which he is sent is no worse than school but simply like school. The uncomprehending, dismissing attitude of Doinel's mother and father toward him is met by searching, withdrawn, self-protecting stares. When Doinel is interviewed by a psychiatrist, Truffaut stages the interview with Doinel facing directly into the camera, the questions entering offscreen, the speaker never seen. The thought and vigor of Doinel's replies carry special force; they are addressed so directly to ourselves. The boy's idea of freedom is no more than an urge to escape, vaguely colored by some intimation of how life might be without impersonal constraints. Truffaut pays quick homage to *Zéro de conduite* in an over-

The 400 Blows. Faced by father (Albert Rémy) and mother (Claire Maurier), Antoine Doinel (Jean-Pierre Léaud), a twelve-year-old schoolboy, is confronted with evidence of pyromania. He has inadvertently burned a curtain behind which was hidden a freshly plagarized essay. Truffaut's first feature was financed in part by his father-in-law, in part from government subsidies, in part by friends. (French Cultural Services)

head shot of the schoolboys walking down the street in formation and to *L'Alalante* in the beach conclusion.

Shoot the Piano Player (1960) confused some and delighted others with spontaneous mood shifts from farce to melodrama. The singer Charles Aznavour plays a small-time bar pianist who seeks anonymity and oblivion from the memory of a concert career that culminated in his wife's suicide. Charlie had discovered that she had traded sex with his manager to further his career. Charlie can never maintain the isolation he craves, for people seek him out, demanding involvement, but each new experience brings disaster on others. His brother is pursued by gangsters who kidnap a third, younger brother. Charlie kills the bar owner in a brawl he was forced to enter.

His waitress girlfriend is shot by the gangsters.

Again Truffaut speaks in handsome, unpretentious images, filmed by Raoul Coutard, an exceptional cinematographer who covets the use of natural light. The scene in which Charlie's girl Lena is killed by the thugs is especially beautiful. She rolls down a snowy slope gracefully, her long hair glistening with flakes in the sunlight. Because the death has occured so fortuitously, it is as unacceptable as it is final, like a similar ending to Henri Clouzot's version of *Manon* (1949) in which a beautiful girl is suddenly, inexplicably, shot by an Arab rifleman and buried in sand that slowly blankets her blonde hair. Much of *Shoot the Piano Player's* peculiar attraction rests in its ability to manipulate character, Charlie's particularly, in a pattern of Hollywood genre convention. The gangsters are B picture baddies: dumb, sloppy and confused as if by Truffaut's broader imaginative context.

Jules and Jim (1961), again photographed by Coutard and based on a 1953 novel by Henri-Pierre Roché about World War I, is Truffaut's best-realized portrait of a woman, Catherine, played by Jeanne Moreau. Jules (Oscar Werner) and Jim (Henri Serre) meet Catherine in Paris, and she marries Jules. He is Austrian; the couple return there at wartime, and Jules and Jim fight on opposite sides. Later, Jim's visit finds the pair dissatisfied though still in love. Abetted by Jules who wants his wife's happiness, Jim has an affair with her. Catherine leaves Jim for another man, then returns to Jules. Years later Jules and Catherine visit Jim. Catherine and Jim go riding, and she drives the car off a bridge. Jules cremates them side by side, relieved that the whole experience is over.

The fabric of the film is complex, a smooth layering of ardor, frustration, friendship, and sexuality in ironic harmony. Moreau's Catherine is a figure of impatient impulse and enigmatic need that seems sometimes neurotic, sometimes not so at all. Truffaut considered the story to demonstrate the impossibility of a ménage à trois, and also the inadequacy of monogomy. The affection shared among Jules, Jim and Catherine is altogether genuine, and their behaviors show sincere effort to explore ways to establish a contentment that is more than transient; their failure is grotesquely illustrated by the little coffins in the final scene.

The most lyrical, exhuberant moments in Austria are furthered by graceful, parabolic camera sweeps. Prewar Paris scenes suggest a student bohemia paradoxically both free and conventional. Truffaut underlines time's passage with a visit to a movie theater in the thirties. The trio watch a newsreel of Germany's book burning. *Jules and Jim* is wide-screen ("Franscope"), and the adaption of familiarly rectangular newsreels to other dimensions carries its own kind of esthetic updating, tying event and actor into a common time and place.

As Truffaut, Jean-Pierre Léaud, and the character Antoine Doinel age together, Truffaut periodically reverts to the "autobiographical" process. In an episode for *Love at Twenty Years* (1962), Doinel appears as an awkward, love-struck young man whose efforts to win a girl are defeated by her reserved, amused manner. In *Stolen Kisses* (1968), Doinel is only somewhat older, somewhat more successful with women, yet still anxiety-ridden that a faux pas may embarrass a relationship beyond redemption. By this stage, Truffaut has become skillful at employing minimal gesture, glance, or speech pattern to inject appearance with deep, often ironic but always affectionate meanings.

By the mid-sixties, Truffaut had become a successful filmmaker vehemently dedicated to the entertainment dimensions of feature film. (Alfred Hitchcock is one of his models and Truffaut's book on Hitchcock shows extraordinary familiarity with Hitchcock's work.) His films differ from one another as Truffaut adapts style to intention. *The Bride Wore Black* (1967) is well-constructed Hitchcock suspense, with Jeanne Moreau inappropriately cast. *Mississippi Mermaid* (1969), was a non-serious adventure, and *The Story of Adele H.* (1975) a serious melodrama about obsession. Truffaut seems more comfortable with content where complex emotionality, funny or dramatic, erupts out of simple situations, and his sensitivities to screen image and composition are extremely sophisticated.

The Wild Child (1969) reverts to the director's early view of civilization's benumbing effect on young emotions. Truffaut himself plays a scientist who undertakes the education of a parentless, uncivilized boy found in the forests. The treatment of the theme carries experimental and judgmental overtones. *Farenheit 451* (1966) is interesting evidence of Truffaut working with material (American science fiction) inappropriate to his talents.

The Soft Skin (1964) substitutes a clichéd situation (an unfaithful husband's self-destruction through his obsession) for the Hollywood conventions of *Shoot the Piano Player*. The early part of the film is developed powerfully (Truffaut has said he is fascinated by obsession); its conclusion, purposefully banal, fails to transcend its own garish drama. Devoting another film to the subject of children in *Small Change* (1976), Truffaut maintains his unsentimentalized vision of their universe, but his view now seems more withdrawn from that world's complexities.

Eric Rohmer

Rohmer's background is typical, his films unique. Entranced with movies at an early age: a member of the film society coterie of Truffaut, Rivette, Godard, and Chabrol. A young writer, Rohmer was absorbed into *Cahiers du Cinéma* along with his fellow enthusiasts. After a feature, *Le Signe du Lion* (1959), Rohmer began a series that he has termed "Moral Stories." The first two stories were shorts, made in 16mm. One deals with chance meetings and broken appointments between a boy and a girl. The second involves four young people and their pecking order of friendships and infatuations. The situation of each character is complicated by his or her need for approval from certain of the others. Neither film is publicly available, but Rohmer continued his series with 35mm features: *My Night at Maud's* (1969), *Claire's Knee* (1970) and *Chloe in the Afternoon* (1972).

For Rohmer, "moral" does not connote value-ridden behavior, although characters may persevere and flounder at what society would require then to do. Rohmer's interest is in how a person's state of mind affects his judgements and how the state of mind is itself influenced by accident and place. The concerns are highly self-conscious, often discussed. Typically, a Rohmer protagonist is a thirty-five year old man who experiences conflicting feelings of commitment (he is engaged or "being faithful") and erotic impulse. In *Claire's Knee* he is haunted by the urge to lay his hand on Claire's knee. Claire is far younger, occupied with her own boy friend and seemingly unconcerned with the central character. He may or may not accede to the impulse, which will threaten to draw him away from other commitments. If he should accede, the adventure is only temporary, but this, too, is because of time and place. Rohmer has created a personal idiom where Pascal-like ruminations (intricate, logical introspections) root in sexual attraction, the whole expressed within genteel, contemporary French locations, among people preoccupied with their own concerns, people who affect, even when they do not recognize, the protagonist's dilemma.

Eric Rohmer (1923–   )

Le Signe du Lion/The Sign of Leo	1959
La Collectionneuse	1966
La Nuit chez Maude/My Night at Maud's	1969
Le Genou de Clair/Claire's Knee	1970
L'Amour l'apres-midi/Chloe in the Afternoon	1972
The Marquise of O	1976

Claude Chabrol

Chabrol wrote for *Cahiers* and for *Arts*, a kind of *Cahiers* off-shoot in its features on film. He was first among the group to secure success with a feature, *Le Beau Serge* in 1958. Like *Les Cousins*, made the same year, it was financed with an inheritance. *Le Beau Serge* was made for 35,000,000 francs or about $72,000, as films go a small sum even in

France at that time, although *The 400 Blows* cost only $60,000.

Jean-Claude Brialy plays François who has returned to his village from Paris for reasons of health. François' old friend (Gérard Blain) is now an alcoholic, a condition perhaps brought about by his marriage. Serge's child was born mongoloid and dead, and his wife, formerly his mistress, is pregnant again. Each of François' attempts to redeem Serge proves disasterous. Motivated with noble intention, François fails to understand that Serge's wife in fact provides Serge a kind of stability. His efforts to cure Serge fail altogether. Unadvertently, through unthinking conversation with her degenerate, apparent father, François causes his own girl to be raped. After great effort, François brings Serge to his wife's bedside at time of birth, but there is a kind of futility to the action and there is also the possibility that doing this may endanger François's own life.

The film introduces characteristic Chabrol themes, namely a morally-simplified doubling of characters (the good and bad friends), the paradox of good intention gone awry, and a metaphysical undertone in which guilt seeks its absolution through some dramatic confrontation with innocence.[5]

The pattern reappears in *The Cousins*, actors reversing roles. This time Charles comes from the country to Paris where he visits his cousin Paul (Brialy). Paul lives a student life of apparent self-destruction. His friends and an atmosphere of neonaziism seem to lend perverse overtones to the free sexuality. Charles is naïve, and conscientious in his studies. He loses a girl, Florence, to Paul. However, Paul is really the more sensitive to human relationships. Charles becomes increasingly priggish and self-consciously good, sacrificing everything to preparing for school

[5] *Chabrol has argued strongly for such an interpretation of Hitchcock's American films. See Claude Chabrol, "Hitchcock Confronts Evil," Cahiers du Cinéma in English 2 (1966).*

examinations. Florence leaves Paul and comes to Charles for sympathy and support, but he rejects what has now clearly been demeaned in his eyes. Miraculously, Paul passes the exams, his glib articulateness a salvation. Charles fails. After playing Russian roulette, pointing at the sleeping Paul's head, Charles later more-or-less accidentally kills himself with the gun.

In *The Cousins*, guilt and innocence are somewhat complicated, for Paul is a kind of pawn to another male, Clovis who manipulates relationships so that Florence ends up his. Florence's genuine innocence contrasts with Charles guise of innocence, his ignorant

Claude Chabrol (1930–   )

Le Beau Serge	1958
Les Cousins	1958
Leda/Web of Passion/A Double Tour	1959
Les Bonnes Femmes	1959
Les Godelureaux	1960
Landru/Bluebeard	1962
Les Biches/The Does/The Girl Friends	1968
Le Femme infidele	1968
Que la bête meure/The Beast Must Die	1969
Le Boucher/The Butcher	1969
La Rupture/The Break-up	1970
Juste avant la nuit/Just Before Midnight	1970
La décade prodigieuse/Ten Days' Wonder	1972
Docteur Popaul	1972
Les Noces rouges/Red Wedding	1973
Nada	1973
Une Partie de plaisir	1974
Les Innocents aux mains sales/Innocents With Dirty Hands	1975
Partial listing	

self-concern. With the gun, Charles foolishly puts to real purpose gestures that Paul and his friends always understood implicitly as play-acting. There is a menacing air about the film that can be seen to stem from an initial sense of evil.

Leda (1959) places a beautiful Italian female artist in a country cottage where nearby a neurotic, hate-ridden family lives, visited by Laszlo Kovacs (Jean-Paul Belmondo), a boorish intruder.[6] A murder story unfolds (the artist is killed by one of the family), and Bel-

[6] *In actuality a reputable American cinematographer (New York, New York, 1977), Laszlo Kovacs is also an alias of Belmondo's in* Breathless, *a recurrent sort of New Wave injoke, as in* Shoot the Piano Player, *whose Lars Schmeel, the despicable music impressario, is named after Lars Schmidt, Ingrid Bergman's third husband who was disliked by all Rossellini's friends.*

Louis Malle (1932–   )

Le Monde du silence (Co-director Jacques Cousteau)	1956
Ascenseur pour l'échafaud/ Frantic	1957
Les Amants/The Lovers	1958
Zazie dans le Métro	1960
Vie privée/A Very Private Affair	1961
Le Feu follet/The Fire Within	1963
Touriste encore	1963
Viva Maria	1965
Le Voleur/The Thief of Paris	1966
Calcutta	1969
Louis Malle's India (7 TV shorts)	1970
Le Souffle au coeur/Murmur of the Heart	1971
Lacombe, Lucien	1973
Black Moon	1975
Pretty Baby	1978
Partial listing	

mondo turns out to be the source of moral strength. Chabrol's organization of time overlaps simultaneous events in different places, using an already established occurrence, the screech of a peacock for example, as a frame of common reference.

As Chabrol continued making films, his underlining design becomes more complicated by multiple employments of character, and his world view becomes increasingly dour. The several girls in *Les bonnes femmes* (1959) represent different, always failing, adjustments to the same impulse. Chabrol abandoned Catholicism after *Le Beau Serge*. During the next several years his films were largely commercial assignments.

Les Biches (1968) shows a leaner style with motives less explicated by plot. It is another à trois relationship, this time two women and a man, the male largely a catalyst to the women's complicated feelings toward one another. In *La Femme infidéle* (1968), Chabrol has a wife betray her husband who accepts the situation but is driven beyond his limits of self-control, like the husband in *Madame de. . . .* Man and wife slowly realize the consequences of their own actions on one another, but the understandings only seem to hasten inevitable disaster. *Le Boucher* (1969) deals with the grotesque murder of two young village women by the town butcher. As in Hitchcock's *Frenzy*, the murderer is an obsessed creature, operating under placid exterior, but unlike Hitchcock, Chabrol treats him with real, not contrived, sympathy and the failure of the man's efforts toward alternative behavior marks more of a human than a dramatic plight.

Louis Malle

Chabrol boasts he is the only New Wave figure not to serve an apprenticeship. Malle worked under Robert Bresson and the oceanic documentarian Jacques Cousteau. His first feature toyed with the thriller, a thief trapped in the elevator of a modern office building,

Le Feu follet. Alain Leroy (Maurice Ronet) diverts himself from alcohol by clipping news accounts about dead women and mounting them on display around a photograph of Marilyn Monroe. He writes in his journal, builds constructions of cigarette boxes, plays with glasses, a gun, and a chessman, wears funny hats, and talks to himself. Like Monroe and F. Scott Fitzgerald, his favorite novelist, Alain's anxiety and disgust turn away from any more "maturity"; he only forsees compromise. (National Film Archives, Ottawa)

Frantic (1957). *Vie privée* (1961) was a satiric view of a screen idol (Brigitte Bardot) who has lost privacy altogether and so cannot carry on the single meaningful love affair in her life. Intensely serious, *Le Feu follet* (1963) deals with the last days of an alcoholic, who can find no possibility for a tolerable future in the evidence of his friend's lives. *Viva Marie* (1965) locates Brigitte Bardot and Jeanne Moreau in the midst of Mexican revolution, a frivolous mixture of sex and social upheaval.

The Lovers (1958), following on *And God Created Woman,* further cleared an avenue for the new filmmakers, and like Vadim's film led many to believe that the new productions characteristically reported sexual freedom. Jeanne Moreau plays a wealthy, middle-class housewife who takes a Parisian lover. Her husband, a provincial newspaper publisher, becomes suspicious and invites her boy friend for the weekend. Driving back herself, Moreau's car breaks down and she is picked up by a young man in a Citroën. The young man stays the evening on the husband's invitation. He and Moreau fall in love, spend the night in her bedroom and next day depart in the little car, abandoning her husband, lover, and daughter.

Rather than representing Moreau as Madame Bovary, the dissatisfied wife with a boorish husband, Malle is less interested in morality's relation to behavior than he is in the emotion. The husband is a thoughtful, affectionate figure, and Moreau not a little self-centered. Feelings are more evidenced than explained, the romanticism played out in a background of Brahm's Third Concerto. Like the film overall, love scenes between Moreau and Jean-Marc Bory are restrained and intensely affecting.

Altogether different in manner, *Zazie dans le Métro* (1960) is based on an anarchic, witty

Viva Maria is one of Malle's frothier excursions, in part a reaction to the suicidal despair of *Le Feu follet*. Together, Bardot and Moreau more than match Central-American, antirevolutionary forces. Their successes triumphantly league individual and political liberation. (Museum of Modern Art/Film Stills Archive)

novel by Raymond Queneau. Malle seeks unexpected, often slapstick, equivalents to the outrageous verbal liberties taken in the novel. The fast-paced, nervous editing can be seen to be the visual equivalent of the novel's cryptic treatment of the narrative logic and also to express total disrespect not only toward the social foundations of Paris life, but, perhaps more importantly, toward literary and cinematic narrative conventions. Zazie, a less-than-charming ten year old who learns why adults cannot be trusted, comes to the city with the fixed purpose of riding the Métro, which is on strike. In the climactic nightclub riot, customers and waiters attack one another. It is as wildly destructive as Laurel and Hardy's pie-throwing spectacular in *The Battle of the Century* (1927), but *Zazie* supplies, additionally, a savage comment on the fragile conventions which customarily prevent diners from heaving instead of consuming their food.

For a period of time, Malle became involved in a lengthy, layered documentary study of India (see Chapter 12). On return, he made *Le Souffle au coeur/Murmur of the Heart* (1971), which views an adolescent boy and his still-young mother at a sanitorium where he is being treated for heart disease. The film culminates in incest, but this is less central to Malle than are the series of delicate moments when passing impulse and reconsideration play across the faces of his actors. They are the basis of Rohmer's "Moral Tales." For Malle, they are noted but rarely discussed.

In *Pretty Baby* (1978), Malle has made one of the most graceful transitions by European directors into the American idiom. Supported by sophisticated understandings of Storyville's life style, *Pretty Baby* highlights several Malle themes: the turn from childhood to adolescence, a child's view of the adult world, the hypocrisy of grownups, art (here photography) as sublimation, and characters' inexplicable shifts of temper and sympathy. Economically, music broadens our understandings of whorehouse life. During one morning sequence, before the day's work has started, the pianist (a composite of Tony Jackson and Jelly Roll Morton) can faintly be heard off camera, composing the first strain of Jelly's *King Porter Stomp*.

Robert Bresson

Franju's most powerful images stem from the least contrived stagings, when fortuitous incongruities develop their complex interractions. Bresson maintains the same kind of allegience to real objects, but before filming he passes them through a personal filtration; what results has been withdrawn and refined, sometimes into new sets of meanings altogether. Early an assistant to René Clair, Bresson is a painter. His use of graphic metaphor to explain his work is not rhetorical but basic to the esthetic.

What I am seeking is not so much expression by means of gesture, speech, mimicry, but expression by means of the rhythms and combinations of images, by position, relation and number. . . . The flatter an image is, the less it expresses, the more easily it is transformed in contact with other images. . . . Painting taught me not to make beautiful images but necessary ones.[7]

For Bresson, plot is a "novelist trick" nec-

[7] *The points are elaborated in Robert Bresson, "The Question: interview by Jean-Luc Godard and Michel Delahaye,"* Cahiers du Cinéma in English *8 (February 1967).*

essary only in the degree that a theme needs to be minimally clothed for the sake of comprehension. At the core of his films is one isolated character. Dramatic highlights are ruthlessly expunged. He is interested not in what happens but in the spiritual aftermath of what has happened. Events that would be featured by other filmmakers occur offscreen with Bresson. His characters are not archetypal, like heroes and villains in melodrama, but individuals who send out none of the emotive signals, such as speech intonation, that communicate feeling. The actors are encouraged, indeed required, to avoid intrusion of feeling into their utterances, sometimes even ordered to "speak falsely." It is the reverse of Stanislavskian method acting, and yet, unlike the radical Russian filmmakers, Bresson's is not a typed, agitprop poster either. His impulse is to imply the inexpressable, perhaps to film what cus-

Robert Bresson (1907–   )

Les Affaires publiques	1934
Les Anges du péché	1943
Les Dames du bois de Boulogne	1945
Le Journal d'un curé de campagne/Diary of a Country Priest	1950
Une Condamné à mort s'est échappé/A Man Escaped	1956
Pickpocket	1959
Procès de Jeanne d'Arc/The Trial of Joan of Arc	1962
Au Hasard, Balthasar	1966
Mouchette	1966
Une Femme Douce/A Gentle Creature	1969
Quatre nuits d'un rêveur/Four Nights of a Dreamer	1971
Lancelot du Lac/Lancelot of the Lake	1974
Le Diable probablement/The Devil Probably	1976

tomarily appears only in paintings and prose.

Les Anges du péché (1943) and *Les Dames du bois de Boulogne* (1945) show Bresson in process. They are more akin to later work in theme than in execution. In the first, Thérèse lives at a Dominican order dedicated to the rehabilitation of prostitutes and female criminals. She flees and shoots the man responsible for her unjust commitment. A Sister, Anne-Marie, is especially concerned with Thérèse's salvation but angrily repulsed by the girl. Expelled from the order through Thérèse's cunning, Anne-Marie falls fatally ill. Nursed by Thérèse, the Sister succeeds in securing a conversion when Thérèse repeats her own vows while Anne-Marie dies. In *Les Dames du bois de Boulogne*, its dialogue by Jean Cocteau, a vengeful woman negotiates marriage between her daughter and her ex-lover so that she can inform the man on his wedding night that his wife had been an entertainer, for which the forties audience should read whore. But the girl's love and her husband's forgiveness result in an affiliation impregnable to opinion.

Characteristically, Bresson's stories involve suffering and spiritual resolution. Whether events culminate in marriage, imprisonment, death, or escape is irrelevant. His subject is the inner working of a psychic process and it makes little difference if the central character is a member of society, a pickpocket, or a priest; perhaps it makes too little difference. Together, the protagonists become a common vehicle for a single idea.

By *The Diary of a Country Priest* (1950), five years after *Bois de Boulogne*, Bresson's severity of execution has fully developed. A young country priest fails to establish effective contact with his parishioners. He is too somber and too naïve. At the expense of the count's and his daughter's enmity, the priest saves the local countess from contemplated suicide. Dying from stomach cancer, he is tended by the mistress of a defrocked friend. His last words are "All is grace." Bresson's method appears to deny every sense of what

we have been led to think appropriate to film. Expressive scenes and even movement are excised or deflated. The priest's diary seems redundantly to echo what occurs on screen. However, Bresson's method is not to engage us in an adventure nor to move us with sentiment. Rather, he wishes to share with us the observation of "a priest's relation, often ineffective, to others and to himself," as Bazin noted in a famous essay.[8] The effect is as if a silent film were uniquely fused to sound. Reference to the diary allows viewers to understand the priest's simple confusions about the feelings of others. Repetitions serve to intensify rather than neutralize simple actions. Dialogue is sparing enough that offscreen sounds, when introduced, carry special imagistic power: when, for example, the priest pleads with the countess about her self-destroying love for a dead son, we hear the scratching of a rake on fallen leaves outside the chateau.

A Man Escaped (1956) has a French lieutenant captured by Gestapo and imprisoned in a fort. Sentenced to die, the soldier delays his escape attempt until he is able to trust a boy newly consigned to the cell. Together they flee. The confining walls of this extraordinary film are emblematic of Lieutenant Fontaine's psychic alienation, for which in turn the viewer may equate spiritual bereavement. The entire movie seems a vast metaphor for man's release from confinement through suffering (the Gestapo beatings) and faith (trust extended to the new inmate). Objects of daily life become devices of escape, both literally and figuratively: a spoon is sharpened into a tool. The daily tedium of the prisoners, who cannot speak to one another, assumes Zen-like resonances as it is accompanied by Mozart's C Minor Mass. Sparing in sound, Bresson employs it here with moving precision as the

[8] *André Bazin, "Le Journal d'un Curé de Campagne," in* The Films of Robert Bresson. *New York, 1969. Also appears in* What is Cinema? *Berkeley, 1969. Pp. 125-43.*

uneventful flow of repetitious work itself becomes accompaniment to the music's grandeur. The film's ending occurs in near total, then total darkness, only a succession of sounds advising us of the pairs successful breakout into another, wider prison of the world.

As in *A Man Escaped*, Bresson used nonprofessionals in *Pickpocket* (1959), the career of a petty thief whose attraction to crime wavers but renews itself despite the concerns of others, including a policeman, who touch his life. Finally, in prison, he admits to actual feelings: affection and need for his girl. As in all the films, Bresson concentrates on objects, faces and hands, and his closeups of Michel at work have the intimate, expressive quality of a man gracefully stealing more than money while he breaks society's elemental bonds of confidence. *The Trial of Joan of Arc* (1962) approaches Joan's state of mind as if the interrogation and its perpetrators were only agents cast in roles to effect the Maid's release through flames. When she is burned, we hear the chains that bound her snap in the heat and realize her freedom is complete.

Au Hazard, Balthazar (1966) reverses usual emphases, studying the effects of an animal's innocence, a donkey's, as Balthazar passes from owner to owner. The animal's life is counterpointed with a girl, Marie, who is also passed from hand to hand. Finally she is rejected, naked, jeered and abandoned while Balthazar dies nearby amidst a flock of sheep. Our conventional disposition, which would be to anthropomorphize the donkey, is checked by the coexistence of Marie in the plot, although often the girl's plight solicits less empathy than the animal. The effect is to abstract our feeling from its object without resorting to symbols or rhetorical device.

Lancelot du Lac (1974) further challenges conventional audience expectations because its Arthurian story is so well known. Bresson creates a Lancelot and a Guinevere whose responses are enigmatic because they do not fulfill our anticipations. At the same time, Bresson documents tournament jousting with straight-forward harsh, sensual brutalities. Years before, in an interview with Jean-Luc Godard, the following exchange concluded their conversation.

Godard:	There is an expression that people no longer use, but it was said in the past; it is: the painting of feelings. That is what you are doing.
Bresson:	Painting — or writing, in this case, it is the same thing — in any case, more than a psychology, it is, I believe, a painting.[9]

[9] *Bresson*, op cit.

Pickpocket. A small-time thief graduates to skilled, professional executions. His urge to steal seems founded on excitement, excitement based on violations of unspoken human confidence. Unlike other Bresson constructions, which sometimes appear purposely clumsy, the thefts in *Pickpocket* build from taut editing and tight closeups. (Courtesy of Anthology Film Archive)

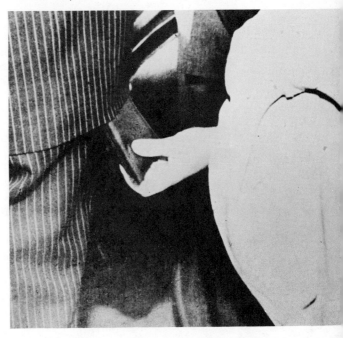

Summary

The breadth of modern French filmmaking escapes categorization, and yet it is marked by common elements and by ties to tradition. Jean Renoir continued into the seventies as a germinal, authorial force. Bresson excepted, stories continue to serve as undergirdings to nuances of emotion. Significant moments of action and reaction characterize Truffaut, Franju, Chabrol, Rohmer, and Malle. Bresson included, French cinema is characterized by intimacy: of feelings, sometimes of expression, and of our relation to screen events.

Issues of class and politics explicitly support much of neorealism and underlie the work of several postwar French directors, most notoriously, Godard. Chapter 15 shifts attention to postwar Britain. Somewhat like France and Italy, its esthetic pendulum reacts to script and literary-dominated film traditions. But Britain's social milieu supports a unique, class-based evolutionary turn.

Bibliography

Allen, Don. *François Truffaut*. New York, 1974.

Armes, Roy. *French Cinema since 1946* 2 vols. Cranbury, N.J., 1966

The Art of the Cinema (Yale Film Studies 17). New York, 1965.

Audiberti, Jacques. *Scenario et dialogues de La Poupée*. Paris, 1962.

Ayfré, Amadée, et al. *The Films of Robert Bresson*. New York, 1969.

Bellour, Raymond. *Alexandre Astruc*. Paris, 1963.

Bracourt, Guy. *Claude Chabrol*. Paris, 1971.

Braudy, Leo. *Focus on Shoot the Piano Player*. Englewood Cliffs, N.J., 1972.

Breitbart, Eric. "Interview with Jean-Pierre Melville," *Film Culture* 35 (1964–65).

Bresson, Robert. "The Question: Interview by Jean-Luc Godard and Michel Delahaye," *Cahiers du Cinéma in English* 8 (February 1967).

———. *Notes on Cinematography*. New York, 1977.

Briot, René. *Robert Bresson*. Paris, 1957.

Campbell, Russell and Gretchen Hunter. "Beast of Burden," *Velvet Light Trap* 9 (Summer 1973).

Clarens, Carlos. "Eric Rohmer: l'Amour Sage," *Sight and Sound* (Winter 1969–70).

Collet, Jean. *Le Cinéma en question*. Paris, 1972.

Crisp, C. G. *François Truffaut*. New York, 1972.

Dawson, Jan. "Invisible Enemy," *Film Comment* (September-October 1977).

Durgnat, Raymond. *Franju*. Berkeley, 1967.

———. *Nouvelle Vague*. Essex, 1963.

Estève, Michel. *Robert Bresson*. Paris, 1962.

Frydland, Maurice. *Roger Vadim*. Paris, 1963.

Graham, Peter. *The New Wave*. London, 1968.

Hayman, Ronald. "Claude Chabrol," *The New Review* (August 1974).

Insdorf, Anette. *François Truffaut*. Boston, 1978.

Jobb, Julian. "Truffaut: The Educated Heart," *Sight and Sound* (Spring 1970).

Lochlainn, Alf Mac. "Pointed Horror," *The Film Journal* (Summer 1971).

Lovell, Alan, ed. *Art of the Cinema in Ten European Countries*. Strasbourg, 1967.

Malle, Louis, "Like Acid," *Films and Filming* (December 1975).

Marcorelles, Louis. "Interview with François Truffaut," *Sight and Sound* (Winter 1961–62).

Martin, Marcel. *France*. New York, 1971.

Milne, Tom. "L'Amour fou," *Sight and Sound* (Spring 1969).

———. "Chabrol's Schizophrenic Spider," *Sight and Sound* (Spring 1970).

———. "Songs of Innocence: Chabrol and Franju," *Sight and Sound* (Winter 1970–71).

Monaco, James. *The New Wave*. New York, 1976.

New York Film Bulletin (Special Truffaut Issue) 3 (1964).

Nogieura, Rui. *Le Cinéma selon Melville*. Paris, 1974.

Nogieura, Rui and Nicoletta Zalaffi, "Conversations with Chabrol," *Sight and Sound* (Winter 1970–71).

Nogieura, Rui and Carlos Clarens. "Eric Rohmer: Choice and Chance," *Sight and Sound* (Summer 1971).

Oxenhandler, Neal. "The Dialectic of Emotion in New Wave Cinema," *Film Quarterly* (Spring 1974).

Petrie, Graham. *The Cinema of François Truffaut*. New York, 1970.

———. "Eric Rohmer: An Interview," *Film Quarterly* (Summer 1971).

Prokosh, Mike. "Bresson's Stylistics Revisited," *Film Quarterly* (Winter 1971–72).

Reid, Gordon. *French Cinema Today*. London, 1963.

Roud, Richard. "The Redemption of Despair," *Film Comment* (September-October 1977).

Sarris, Andrew. "A Man Escaped," *Film Culture* 14 (1957).

Schofer, Peter. "Dissolution into Darkness," *Sub-Stance* 9 (1974).

Schrader, Paul. "Robert Bresson, Possibly: Interview with Bresson," *Film Comment* (September-October 1977).

———. *Transcendental Style in Film,* Berkeley, 1972.

Siclier, Jacques. *Nouvelle Vague?* Paris, 1961.

Skoller, Donald S. "Praxis in Two Bresson Films," *Cinema Journal* 9 (Fall 1969).

Truffaut, François. "A Certain Tendency of the French Cinema," *Cahiers du Cinéma in English* 1 (January 1966).

———. "The Journal of *Fahrenheit 451*," *Cahiers du Cinéma in English* 5,6,7 (1966, 1967).

———. *Jules and Jim*. New York, 1968.

———. *The 400 Blows*. New York, 1969.

———. *The Story of Adele H*. New York, 1976.

Vialle, Gabriel. *Georges Franju*. Paris, 1968.

Wall, James. *François Truffaut*. Grand Rapids, Mich., 1973.

Wood, Robin and Michael Walker. *Claude Chabrol*. New York, 1970.

15 POSTWAR BRITAIN

Whatever its other consequences, World War II had salutory effects on British film. It opened up an industry bound by middle-brow tastes and nineteenth-century narrative to values and techniques more broadly rooted in experience. Commercial British production began to originate location-shot, non-"classic" films.

War themes spilled Britain's documentary traditions into feature entertainments and fostered less tradition-ridden stories: cross-sectional views of a society under economic hardship and military danger. *Next of Kin* (1941), for example, was first produced by Thorold Dickinson as a war office training film, cautioning against careless gossip. The Ministry of Information released it to the general public. Other noteworthy productions included Leslie Howard's *The First of the Few* (1942), Carol Reed's *The Way Ahead* (1943), Charles Frend's *San Demetrio, London* (1943), and *Millions Like Us* (1944) by Frank Launder and Sidney Gilliat, who had written Hitchcock's *The Lady Vanishes* earlier.

The major offerings in this period were Anthony Asquith's *The Way to the Stars* (1945) and *In Which We Serve* (1942) codirected by Noel Coward and

Kind Hearts and Coronets (Hamer 1949) (Museum of Modern Art/Film Stills Archive)

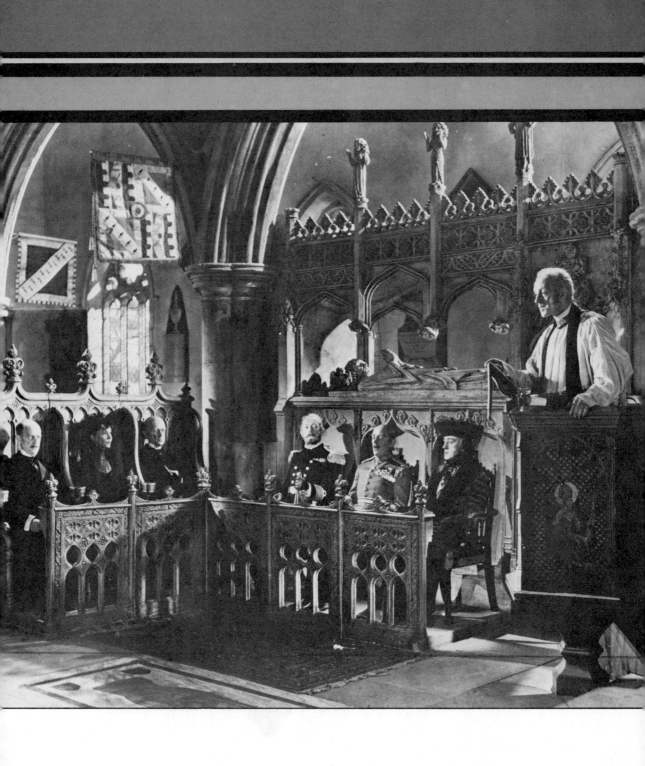

David Lean. Asquith's film, known in the United States as *Johnny in the Clouds,* traces relationships between civilian and and RAF pilots, in particular the constant threat of imminent death on wartime love affairs. *In Which We Serve* served Britain's cause forcefully abroad. It is the story of a destroyer, the H.M.S. Torrin, and its crew from the time of launching until disaster in the Mediterranean:"Now she lies in 1,500 fathoms and with her most of our shipmates. We have lost her, but they are still with her. Now they lie in very good company."

In peacetime, sophisticated polished productions, still evocative of literary structure and values, included *Odd Man Out* by Carol Reed, and Thorold Dickinson's *Queen of Spades* (1949).*Stairway to Heaven/A Matter of Life and Death* (1945) by Michael Powell and Emeric Pressburger was an imaginative tale about a pilot who is accidently brought too early to heaven. Debate over his return to earth assumes the polemics of American/British cultural dispute. Alexander Korda himself directed Oscar Wilde's *An Ideal Husband* (1948) and commissioned Julien Duvivier to undertake what resulted in a tedious remake of *Anna Karenina* (1948). Like *Black Narcissus* (1947), based on a Rummer Godden novel about the insidious effect of the vestige pagan elements found in a missionary outpost in the Himalayas, most such pictures emerged as uniformly beautiful, well-made, and dull.

Makeup of the British film industry shifted soon after World War II when Alexander Korda purchased London Films from MGM, then bought British Lion. J. Arthur Rank, the leading corporation, developed distribution circuits in Canada, Australia, and New Zealand, and ABPC (Associated British Picture Corporation) had established outlets in the United States through its liaison with Warner Brothers. British filmmakers hoped to develop a product with international appeal, but distributors like Rank and others were unable to distribute their films beyond metropolitan theater

areas abroad. *Caesar and Cleopatra* (1946) was a noteable example of literate, tasteful, unappealing product. Faced with a recession and the success of American films in England, the Labor goverment imposed a seventy-five percent duty on US product; in retaliation, the United States withdrew its films from British distribution and closed its own outlets to Rank. (Korda maintained circulation by way of Twentieth Century Fox.)

Films that lent themselves most totally to sucessful exploitation were the unabashed adaptations, like Dickens — David Lean's *Great Expectations*(1946) and *Oliver Twist* (1947) — and Laurence Olivier's Shakespeare — *Henry V* (1944), *Hamlet* (1948) and *Richard III* (1955). *Henry V* was somewhat emasculated for American censors, who shivered at "bastard", and some found *Hamlet* more cruel than undecided, but Olivier suceeded better than any previous undertakings in documenting fine Shakespearean performance with a minimal sense of canned theater. Similarly *The Red Shoes* (1948) by Powell and Pressburger, brought much of ballet's excitement to the screen despite a hackneyed story.

EALING STUDIOS

In contrast to the ambitious intent of highly financed major studios, Ealing began a series of modest comic films, built on the quiet satire of English institutions. While the films played skillfully on conventionalized class and national character traits, they also developed subtle, quirky personalities and served effectively as vehicles for such actors as Alistair Sim and Alec Guinness.

Hue and Cry (1950) involved spies employing a magazine for boys, unwittingly authored by Sim, to transmit military secrets. *Kind Hearts and Coronets* (1950) proved a tour de force for Alec Guinness, who played nine roles, male and female: relatives who stood to inherit the D'Ascoyne fortune until each person was disposed of by an unscrupulous, determined distant cousin (Clarendon, not Ealing, made it).

Ealing comedies have some of the quality of Preston Sturges Paramounts from a few years earlier, falling back on chases and sometimes slapstick for climaxes, but consistently witty, paced and parodic of their subjects and themselves. In *The Lavender Hill Mob* (1950), Alec Guinness plays a mild, inconspicuous bank clerk who devises an extraordinary scheme to pilfer gold and melt it down into Eiffel Tower souvenir replicas in order to smuggle it out of the country. *A Run for Your Money* (1949) has Guinness as a Welsh miner on a spree with his pal in London, set against the England-Wales Rugby match at Twockenham.

The outstanding director of Ealing comedies is Alexander MacKendrick, who commenced as a scriptwriter. *Whiskey Galore/Tight Little Island* (1948) is set in Scotland; MacKendrick, had worked as a documentary writer, and Ealing profited from applying documentary technique, particularly location shooting, in its films. A ship loaded with scotch whiskey founders offshore and thirsty islanders devise ways to secure and to hide their loot. *The Man in the White Suit* (1951) is remembered for a burping, bubbling machine perfected by Guinness, a chemist who invents a fabric which will never wear out and shows no dirt. Labor and management ally to suppress the discovery and chase Guinness, dressed in his creation, through murky streets; his fabric also glows in the dark.

In 1953, MacKendrick made *The Maggie/High and Dry,* pitting an arrogant American businessman against the crew of a little ship that sails the islands off western Scotland. *The Ladykillers* (1955) was a final Ealing gasp, blacker than most, with Guinness a grotesque criminal figure who assuages his genteel, unsuspecting landlady by assuming the role of a professor and disguising his henchmen as student musicians. MacKendrick proceeded to

The Man in the White Suit. Full face behind the beakers, Guiness admires his handiwork. His indestructable fabric finally falls to pieces, no longer a threat to British industry, but instead ironically illustrative of planned obsolescence. (Museum of Modern Art/Film Stills Archive)

the United States where his first film, *The Sweet Smell of Success* (1957), emerged as an exceptional study of corruption in the Stork Club society world, altogether unlike his earlier work. *A High Wind in Jamaica,* made in Britain in 1965, is a skilled, thoughtful version of Richard Hughes' novel.

While later Ealing production happily emerged, notably *Passport to Pimlico* (1948) and *Genevieve* (1954), both by Henry Cornelius, the comedic tenor more often veered toward caricatured, frantic burlesque. *The Happiest Days of Your Life* (1950) typically combined comics Alistair Sim, Margaret Rutherford, Joyce Grenfell, and Richard Wattis as farcical academics, to be followed by increasingly formulaic public school films. Non-Ealing, *Doctor in the House* (1953) initiated the "doctor" series, which the "carry on" films followed in the sixties, *Carry on Sergeant* (1959), *Carry On Nurse* (1960), etc. Ealing Studios itself closed in the mid-fifties, taken over by the BBC for television production.

EMERGING TALENT

As comedy became increasingly predictable, little remained by mid-fifties that was demonstrably national excepting the Hammer Films horror series. American financing of English production, as in *The Bridge on the River Kwai* (1957), *Lawrence of Arabia* (1962), *Tom Jones* (1963) and the Beatles films, sometimes desaturated cultural idiom to insure international appeal. At the same time, English theater and fiction harbored new, energetic talent like playwright John Osborne (*Look Back in Anger* 1959) and novelists John Braine (*Room at the Top*), Stan Barstow (*A Kind of Loving*), and Alan Silitoe (*Saturday Night and Sunday Morning*).

Like their French counterparts, a new generation of British artists rejected tradition-bound, polished, "quality" values. Like the Italians, they emphasized closer, unfettered observation of ordinary life and its vicissitudes, but England's writers categorized by journalism as "angry young men" as the French had become a "new wave," were stubbornly class based as well. Many came from the red-brick, state-funded educational institutions, and turned their literacy and sophistication against a dominant, institutional culture they found repressive, stagnant, and offensive.

Indignant toward the complacent state of English film criticism, Lindsay Anderson delivered a polemic in the Establishment's own quarters, *Sight and Sound,* a journal of the British Film Institute. The essay demanded an extension of the new imaginative energies into film study, and, by implication, film production.

The cinema is not . . . something to be denigrated or patronized. It is a vital and significant medium, and all of us who concern ourselves with it automatically take on an equivalent responsibility. Insofar as film criticism is being written here and now, and deals with an art intensely related to the society in which we live, it cannot escape its wider commitments. Essentially, in fact, there is no such thing as uncommitted criticism, any more than there is such a thing as insignificant art. It is merely a question of the openness with which our commitments are stated. I do not believe that we should keep quiet about them.[1]

By implication, Anderson's argument asked for an incursion of the sensibilities of British Free Cinema into commerical film. The first appearance of such energies was an adaptation of *Room at the Top* (1958), directed by Jack Clayton. Clayton had worked in the industry since the thirties. His first feature is set in a northern industrial town where Joe Lampton escapes his slum background by seducing the daughter of a well-to-do businessman. An older woman whom Lampton actually loves, as much as he cares for anyone, kills herself and he marries into security.

Ironically, *Room at the Top* maintains something of that same subservience to literature that had been the hallmark of British movie tradition, and Laurence Harvey's tight-lipped Lampton leaves the character's cynicism something of a puzzle, yet the exploitation of a liberal society for personal gain, and the evidence that sex might be fun, an admission with which even the censor was willing to concur, were new to British screens. Clayton's version of Henry James' *The Turn of the Screw, The Innocents* (1961), and his *The Pumpkin Eater* (1964) are noteworthy.

[1] *Lindsay Anderson, "Stand Up! Stand Up!"* Sight and Sound (*Autumn 1956*).

Tony Richardson

From codirection with Karel Reisz on the Free Cinema's look at a Jazz Club, *Momma Don't Allow,* Tony Richardson formed a production company with John Osborne and directed *Look Back in Anger* in 1959. The film reworked Osborne's play to its advantage, casting Richard Burton as Jimmy Porter, a working-class figure who is appalled and highly vocal in his indignation at the roles society asks him to assume. Richardson brought backgrounds in theater and television direction that contribute to the sustained emotionality of performance and tightly composed, unrelenting, grimy confrontations.

The Entertainer (1960) starred Laurence Olivier, reappearing in Osborne's theater success as Archie Rice, an aging comic whose accellerating degeneration is visible in the course of his public performances. Here, the location is Morecombe, a fading beach resort, emblematic of England itself, with claptrap entertainments epitomized in the grimacing, leering stage manner of Archie. The creation is one of Olivier's best, a figure who will not emigrate to Canada because they do not have Guiness on draught, whose spiritual bankruptcy overpowers as he seeks to bed a teenage beauty contestant. Again, Richardson works in tight closeups that serve to make Olivier's antic stage humor oppressively futile.

After a ridiculous Hollywood version of William Faulkner's *Sanctuary* (1960), Richardson adapted another play, *A Taste of Honey* (1961). An insecure homosexual youth and a girl pregnant with the child of a black sailor room together while awaiting the birth. The fragile support they afford one another is destroyed by the girl's mother. Richardson then made *The Loneliness of the Long-Distance Runner* (1962). A boy in a reformatory, who is depended upon to win the cross-country sports event, intentionally loses; it is the only way in which he can subvert the hypocrisy and plattitudes of the institution's administrator, and like almost all the period's angry young protagonists, he must sacrifice something of major importance to himself in order to win anything at all.

Tom Jones (1963) marked a turning on Richardson's part from somber, unrelieved themes to humor that might be ribald, commercial and light as in the Fielding story, sardonic and bitter as in *The Charge of the Light Brigade* (1968), or simply unsuccessful in *The Loved One* (USA 1964). Some of Richardson's derivative narrative techniques, such as the flashbacks of *The Loneliness of the Long Distance Runner,* the slow dissolves of *Look Back in Anger,* and the "lyric" waterfront walks in *A Taste of Honey* have receded to free a sparser, more open style. *Joseph Andrews* (1978) reverts to the mode of *Tom Jones.*

Tony Richardson (1928–   )

Momma Don't Allow (short) (codirector Karel Reisz)	1955
Look Back in Anger	1959
The Entertainer	1960
Sanctuary (USA)	1961
A Taste of Honey	1961
The Loneliness of the Long-Distance Runner	1962
Tom Jones	1963
The Loved One (USA)	1965
Mademoiselle	1966
The Sailor from Gibralter	1967
Red and Blue	1967
The Charge of the Light Brigade	1968
Laughter in the Dark	1969
Hamlet	1970
Ned Kelly	1970
A Delicate Balance	1976
Joseph Andrews	1978

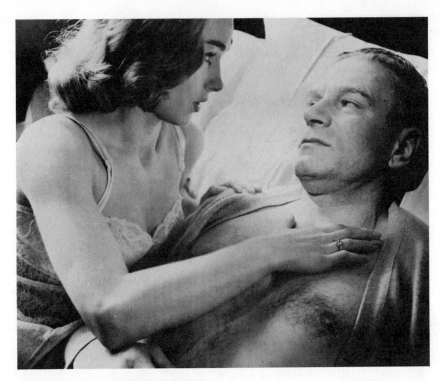

The Entertainer. Archie Rice and the young beauty queen. Olivier credits William Wyler with teaching him to differentiate film performance from theater. Its new vernacular promised that "if you do it right, you can do anything." (National Film Archive, Ottawa)

Karel Reisz (1926–   )

Momma Don't Allow (short) (codirector Tony Richardson)	1955
We are the Lambeth Boys (short)	1958
March to Aldermaston (documentary collaboration)	1959
Saturday Night and Sunday Morning	1960
Night Must Fall	1964
Morgan, a Suitable Case for Treatment	1966
Isadora	1967
The Gambler	1974
Who'll Stop the Rain (USA)	1978

Karel Reisz

Alan Sillitoe's novel provided the basis for Karel Reisz's first feature, *Saturday Night and Sunday Morning* (1960), set in Nottingham and following the career of a young factory worker, Arthur Seaton, played by Albert Finney. In the course of the film, Seaton slowly comes to understand and resentfully to accept the prospects of marriage and financial-moral responsibility. Unlike other protagonists, Seaton maintains a self-protective verve that is more basic to his character than Archie Rice's jollities, and equally free of Jimmie Porter's leaden sullenness. Adapted by Sillitoe, the film is very open, a picaresque sequence of adventures whose ethical dimensions are apparent but unpreached.

Reisz's next venture again used Albert Finney, reverting to older theater-piece traditions in a gruesome, insane-murderer story, *Night Must Fall* (1964). *Morgan, a Suitable Case for Treatment* (1966) again invokes mental aberration but with far greater success. Morgan views his marital separation with growing distress. His anxiety takes the form of identification with a gorilla (Reisz edits in old *Tarzan* and *King Kong* footage to represent Morgan's fantasy life) until a schizophrenic episode results. Reisz's special accomplishment in the film is to invest a sociopolitical layer (Morgan's working-class mother is an ardent Marxist) onto the comedy and psychological dynamics so that the move becomes an involuted reflection on film fantasy, class consciousness, antic farce and madness, each playing upon the other; no single frame of reference is permitted to explain the rest.

Sunday, Bloody Sunday. Alex Greville (Glenda Jackson) is thirty-nine, and divorced; Bob Elkin (Hed Murray), a twenty-four-year-old pop artist. The affair is triangulated by the presence of Daniel Hirsh (Peter Finch), a psychiatrist, and complicated with families, friends, and quasi-sophisticated children. (Copyright © 1971 Vectia Films, Ltd.) (Museum of Modern Art/Film Stills Archive)

John Schlesinger

John Schlesinger entered entertainment film from television documentary. *A Kind of Loving* (1962) follows a young man who marries a girl whom he has made pregnant and is forced to come to terms with the world to which he is resigned. *Billy Liar* (1963) features a young man who works for an undertaker, lying and daydreaming of escape. Julie Christie is a sexually free wanderer who offers Billy a freedom he is unequipped to seize in actuality.

Darling . . . (1965) moves to a London setting, following the rising fortune of Julie Christie who journeys from husband to lover to a career-furthering, loveless marriage with an Italian noble. In style and substance, it now evokes sixties sensibilities, not always to best effect. *Far From the Madding Crowd* (1967) looks like a Thomas Hardy novel. Schlesinger made the successful *Midnight Cowboy* in the United States in 1969 and returned to Britain for *Sunday, Bloody Sunday* (1971), an involved, perceptive study of a homosexual doc-

John Schlesinger (1926–   )

Terminus (documentary)	1960
A Kind of Loving	1962
Billy Liar	1963
Darling	1965
Far From the Madding Crowd	1967
Midnight Cowboy (USA)	1969
Sunday, Bloody Sunday	1971
The Day of the Locust (United States)	1975
Marathon Man	1976
Partial listing	

Emerging Talent   367

tor and a discontented divorcée who vie for the attentions of a bisexual sculptor. Finally, the sculptor deserts them both. The picture is sympathetic to the pair of abandoned lovers, the lovers understanding toward each other.

Lindsay Anderson

Lindsay Anderson's own incursion into feature films did not occur until *This Sporting Life* (1963). The film centers on a miner who becomes a rugby player in a desperate effort to locate an identity both for himself and for the widow with whom he has established a relationship. While drawing on the northern locale of earlier films, Anderson is less the embittered sociologist than he is concerned with the gradual awakening of an enormously powerful man, of his physical urge toward combat. As the miner, Richard Harris comes to understand both why rugby is important to him and to realize the depth of his feelings toward his woman.

If . . . (1968) bears obvious and intentional similarities to *Zéro de conduite,* the rebellion of boys in a public school. This time they do not settle for an anarchist flag on the rooftops, but spray the yard with gunfire. The appear-

Apocalypse on the rooftop in *Zéro de conduite* (above) and *If. . .* (right). "For me, as I suppose for most of the public-school educated, the world of school remains one of the extraordinarily significant vividness; a world of reality and symbol; of mingled affection and reserve." Lindsay Anderson (National Film Archive, Ottawa)

ance of *If . . .* coincided with student protests in France and America, but the film is less a realistic portrayal than an analogue, like Vigo, about conformity and rebellion, repression and revolution, convention and anarchy. *O Lucky Man!* (1973) continues the trajectory of *If . . . ,* farcically-imbued, picaresque adventures of Malcolm McDowell, whose film name is identical to the protagonist of *If . . . .* Always on the make, always optimistic, he moves from one ugly situation to another with cheerful abandon. Based on Anderson's 1969 theater production, *In Celebration* (1976) deals with a middle-aged Yorkshire miner and his wife. Their apparent complacency inadequately disguises the deeply negative feelings which have grown with the marriage.

Lindsay Anderson (1923–   )

Meet the Pioneers (short)	1948
Idlers That Work (short)	1949
Three Installations (short)	1952
Wakefield Express (short)	1952
Thursday's Children (short)	1953
O Dreamland (short)	1953
Every Day Except Christmas (short)	1957
This Sporting Life	1963
The White Bus (short)	1966
If . . .	1968
O Lucky Man!	1973
In Celebration	1976
Partial listing	

Albert Finney ventured into direction with *Charlie Bubbles* (1968) in which he starred, a wealthy writer whose human relationships have all soured. Sidney M. Furie, a Canadian, departed Hollywood for England to make *The Leather Boys* (1963) about a motorcyclist whose marriage is affected by his homosexual attraction to a fellow rider.

INDIGNATION DIFFUSES

As time passed, indignation in British filmmakers subsided or changed strategy. Some of the angry young affiliated with their earlier targets. Sooty pictures of the industrial North had become clichéd. Movie attendance did not support embittered vision.

Richard Lester

The comedies of Richard Lester suggest Ealing in a frenetic, updated package. Lester came to Britain from American and Canadian television. For Independent Television in England he directed some of the Goon Shows:

Further Productions

Other films echoed some of the thrust of British protest. While diminishing the power of Joyce Cary's novel, *The Horse's Mouth* (1958), directed by Ronald Neame, maintained the painter's uncaring, fiercely independent stance toward society around him. *The Angry Silence* (1960) dealt with a labor dispute in the Midlands that results in one man's victimization for defying a strike vote. *The Kitchen* (1961) is an extraordinary adaption of an Arnold Wesker play, directed by James Hill, that turns the cooking area of a London restaurant into a hellish cauldron of hatreds and pressured frenzy. *Lucky Jim* (1957) played out the comedy of Kingsley Amis' novel while muting its acid portraits.

Richard Lester (1932–   )

The Running, Jumping and Standing Still Film (short)	1960
It's Trad, Dad	1962
The Mouse on the Moon	1963
A Hard Day's Night	1964
The Knack	1965
Help!	1965
A Funny Thing Happened on the Way to the Forum	1966
How I Won the War	1967
Petulia (USA)	1968
The Bed-Sitting Room	1969
The Three Musketeers	1974
The Four Musketeers	1975
Robin and Marian	1976
The Ritz	1976

witty, fast humor built on a series of climaxes that grew from surreal incongruities and talents like Peter Sellers and Spike Mulligan. In Britain, Lester made *It's Trad, Dad* (1962), capitalizing on the period jazz revivalism. Lester's vigorous strings of gags, often visually as clever as silent comics, rest on slim, whimsical plot lines. *The Mouse on the Moon* (1963) featured Peter Sellers in a sequel to an earlier Sellers comedy, *The Mouse that Roared* (1959).

Subsequently, Lester capitalized on Beatlemania with two features, *A Hard Day's Night* (1964) and *Help!* (1965), songs interspaced with exuberant humor. *The Knack* (1965) cast Rita Tushingham of the immense, innocent eyes against two young men on the make, one clumsily inept, the other suave and successful. Lester's later films have usually been successful while bypassing the desperation sometime lurking behind earlier scurry. *A Funny Thing Happened on the Way to the Forum* (1966) was theatrical, cosmopolitan humor in ancient Rome. *How I Won the War* (1967) depends upon the horror implicit in battle deaths that ensue when a British military contingent is commissioned to construct a cricket field behind enemy lines for future use.

Paul McCartney poses for publicity stills during a location sequence of *Help!* A menacing gang seeks to recapture a sacrificial ring that lodges on Ringo's finger. Because the Beatles lacked acting experience, Lester gave each no more than one line at a time to deliver and gambled, successfully, for workable improvisation on the set. (National Film Archives, Ottawa)

While immersed in the trendiness of the sixties. *Petulia* (1968) tries to express incompatibilities between honest emotion and a culture where feeling is punished. By the time of *The Bed-Sitting Room* (1969), Lester's modish humor sits less easily on the times. *The Three Musketeers* (1974) and its simultaneously-filmed companion piece *The Four Musketeers* (1975) represent more orthodox melding of adventure, romance, and comedy.

Peter Brook

Peter Brook is best known as a stage director and producer. His films have most often been play adaptations, their transitions successfully accomplished. *The Beggar's Opera* (1952) reverts to the John Gay play which is now better known as a basis for *The Three Penny Opera*. Brook's version made thoughtful use of color, using the green of gaming tables and the gold of costumes as hints of Macheath's greed.

Lord of the Flies (1962) constituted an interesting production experiment, although it fails to capture the harshness and pessimism of William Golding's novel about a group of boys marooned on an island who revert to savage ritual when confronted with their deepest needs in an unregulated environment. Brook located his cast on an island off the coast of Puerto Rico and simulated some of the actual conditions of the story. Depending upon unpremeditated behavior, the film carries some element of the documentary about it. *Lord of the Flies* was filmed more-or-less in the actual time sequence of its narrative, and some of the continuity is uncontrollably fragmented, particularly the weak ending.

In 1966, Brook filmed his own theater production of Peter Weiss's *The Persecution and Assassination of Jean-Paul Marat as Performed by the Inmates of the Asylum of Charenton Under the Direction of the Marquis de Sade*. The play depends on constant interplay between the madness of the patients,

Marat/Sade. In 1808, insane patients present a play, written and directed by Sade and performed in the asylum bath house. The play recounts Marat's 1789 assassination by Charlotte Corday. It largely constitutes a dialogue between Marat, who espouses revolution, and Sade, who believes revolution a false doctrine because men are not all equal. Identifying finally when the roles, the players go beserk and turn on their guards.

Peter Brook (1925–   )

The Beggar's Opera	1952
Moderato Cantabile	1960
Lord of the Flies	1962
Marat . . . Sade	1966
Ride of the Valkyrie	1966
Tell Me Lies	1967
King Lear	1970
Partial listing	

Women in Love. "Let us announce," Lawrence said in his forward, "that the sensual passions and mysteries are equally sacred with the spiritual mysteries and passions. The only thing unbearable is the degradation, the prostitution of the living mysteries in us." (Museum of Modern Art/Film Stills Archive)

Ken Russell (1927–   )

French Dressing	1964
Billion Dollar Brain	1967
Women in Love	1969
The Music Lovers	1970
The Devils	1971
The Boy Friend	1972
Savage Messiah	1972
Mahler	1974
Tommy	1974
Lisztomania	1975
Valentino	1977

the fantasy of performance, and the motives of an audience. In actual performance, a live theater audience is sometimes included as dramatic party to the proceedings. Brook's film effectively uses a society party of spectators as surrogate viewers for movie audience participation. *Tell Me Lies* (1967) shows the same repugnance toward war in Vietnam that was guised in humor in Lester's *How I Won the War*. Brook intercuts staged action, documentary footage, and a group symposium, again adapting an earlier theater version. *King Lear* (1970) was filmed in Denmark and is distinguished by Paul Scofield's performance.

Ken Russell

The productions of Peter Brook draw on violence and madness to explicate the current states of society; Ken Russell—a director of excess—takes these elements to greater extremes yet. Russell did a series of television productions on such composers as Strauss, Elgar, and Sibelius. Music figures heavily in his films as does sexuality in many if not all its ramifications. His employment of biography, as in the life of Tchaikovsky, *The Music Lovers* (1970) and *Mahler* (1974) arouses some indignation among critics affronted by the wildly fictionalized behaviors that are intended to elaborate emotional aspects of a character's life.

Women in Love (1969) more closely captures the sensuality and homosexuality of D. H. Laurence's fiction than have other Laurence adaptations. *The Devils* (1971) probes religious and sexual hysteria among the residents of a seminary and is loosely based on Aldous Huxley's *The Devils of Loudon*. Russell's work is vividly filmed, costumed by his wife. His garish, colorful nudities often resemble updated equivalents to the military gore of early British Kordas like *Drums* (1938) and *Four Feathers* (1939). Russell enjoyed commercial success with the rock *Tommy* (1974). By *Lisztomania* (1975), the director's bizarre imagery had taken the direction of elaborate personal fantasies suggested more by the music than the lives he has chosen to explore through these biographies.

Culludon. Alan McCall (Alan Pope) prepares to charge forward out of the Cannonade with the MacDonalds. "If you get someone breathing very quickly, this starts something going inside them, it opens the mouth and something happens to the eyes and then if you build something on top of this, the results can sometimes be not bad at all." Peter Watkins (British National Film Archive/Stills Library)

Peter Watkins

Peter Watkins has created deeply moving films that employ the techniques of cinéma vérité in staged reconstructions or fictional simulations of public events. *Culloden* (1964) was made for the BBC and simulates with brutal force an early battle in the Scottish highlands (See Chapter 12). Watkins employed location shooting and drew on local residents for the faces and the feel of another time. The battle, in which Scots are cruelly slaughtered by a combination of rival Scots and Englishmen, is filmed as if documented by a television crew, but rather than falling into the theatrics of CBS's old *You Are There* television series, Watkins achieves a jarring immediacy with unstable, hand-held cameras and discontinuous, seemingly unpremeditated action.

The War Game (1965) again was made for BBC consumption, but its depiction of atomic catastrophe in the streets of London proved so unsettling that the film's exhibition was restricted, although it has played in movie theaters. Watkins goes to extreme length to capture apparent verisimilitude in his events, so that a subject who appears, for example, exhausted from great exertion will likely be evidencing something like the actual physical state of exhaustion. His wounds and disfigurements are unsettling.

Privilege (1967) posits a Great Britain in the near future when institutionalized religion and conservative politics have leagued together, successfully capturing the allegiance of the young through a charismatic pop singer. Again, Watkins sustains the appearance of documentary technique, which gives verisimilitude to the crowd scenes, but here, even more than in the television documentaries, the director's deeply-held social and political values sometimes break through to betray evidences of contrivance. *Punishment Park* (1971) combines location shooting and vérité devices with another narrative posited slightly in the future. Dissidents are rounded up by authorities and committed to an obstacled escape course with their lives at stake. As in *Culloden* and *The War Game* the appearance of actuality seems eerily captured, despite, here, the contrived nobility and courage of the victims.

Kevin Brownlow

Kevin Brownlow is a film scholar, archivist, and director whose work includes a valuable book of interviews with movie pioneers,[2] the painstaking reconstruction of Abel Gance's three-screen *Napoleon,* and his own feature productions. With Andrew Mollo, Brownlow started *It Happened Here* (1964) eight years before, when he was learning to be a film editor. Originally an amateur 16mm venture, the film developed from a premise than the Nazis had, in fact, successfully invaded England in 1940. Eventually the production was financed by Woodfall, the company founded by Tony Richardson, John Osborne, and Bryanston Films for *Look Back in Anger*. Its story involves a district nurse who first works for the occupation forces to help restore life to normal, then defects to the partisans. Its strength rests in an extraordinary newsreel-like evocation of a seemingly actual period, elicited not by Watkins-like spontaneous film techniques, but through the most exacting visual detail, the kind of dedication that resulted in Brownlow's book and was first apparent when, at the age of eleven, Brownlow composed his first reconstruction of *Napoleon.*

Brownlow edited *The Charge of the Light Brigade*. Again collaborating with Andrew Mollo, his production of *Winstanley* (1975) is a study of a seventeenth-century sect which may have been the earliest appearance of a communist society, ensnared in a land dispute between the gentry and the king. The esthetic genesis of *Winstanley* and its power rest in

[2] *Kevin Brownlow,* The Parade's Gone By. *New York, 1968.*

silent film, Dreyer most especially, betraying a simplicity that is hardly naïve, but dedicated to the explication of strong, uncomplicated human allegiances.

Joseph Losey

The American director Joseph Losey has a history of displacement. Losey was a theater critic and director in the New York City of the thirties. As an MGM contract director, he willingly reflected the liberal consciousness of producer Dore Schary in his first feature, *The Boy With Green Hair* (1948). After an unsatisfactory remake of Fritz Lang's *M* (1950), which is nevertheless interesting for its substitution of Los Angeles for Berlin, Losey left the United States when attacks on Hollywood from the House Unamerican Activities Committee were at their height. For several years, he made films in Italy and Britain under pseudonyms. Finally *Time Without Pity* (1956), directed under his own name, proved Losey's sure talent for suspense and a developing interest in the behavior of ordinary English characters under pressure.

Blind Date/Chance Meeting (1959) enhances an unprepossessing murder story with unexpected character explorations, this time in well-to-do society. Like *Time Without Pity*, it was written by Ben Barzman. Losey places particular importance on his relation to writers, designers, and actors, which may account for effective integrations of place and behavior in the films. In *The Criminal/Concrete Jungle* (1960) Losey implies that the character deterioration of the outlaw-protagonist occurs not when he is committing crimes but when he is in prison.

The Damned/These are the Damned (1961) is a science fiction piece about children afflicted by their mothers' exposure to radiation poisoning. They are kept in a cave and educated to assume responsibility for the world after nuclear destruction. Losey manipulates the conventional moral polarities so that "good" and "bad" characters share common weaknesses. Sympathetic figures prove ultimately irresponsible.

The Servant (1963) marks Losey's first collaboration with playright Harold Pinter. Pinter had earlier written *The Pumpkin Eater* for Jack Clayton and had his play *The Caretaker* experimentally filmed in the attic of an empty house as *The Guest* (1963). Pinter is often preoccupied with abnormal turns that apparently normal people may take under special conditions. The behavior is seen not as idiosyncratic but rather as evidence of social convention taken to extreme length. In *The*

Joseph Losey (1909–   )

The Boy With Green Hair (United States)	1948
The Lawless/The Dividing Line (United States)	1949
M (United States)	1950
The Big Night (USA)	1951
Time Without Pity	1956
The Gypsy and the Gentleman	1957
Blind Date/Chance Meeting	1959
The Criminal/Concrete Jungle	1960
The Damned/These are the Damned	1961
Eva/Eve (Italy)	1962
The Servant	1963
King and Country	1964
Modesty Blaise	1966
Accident	1967
Secret Ceremony	1967
Boom	1968
Figures in a Landscape	1970
The Go-Between	1971
The Assassination of Trotsky	1972
A Doll's House	1973
The Romantic Englishwoman	1975
Galileo	1975
Mr. Klein	1976
Partial listing	

Servant, matters develop out of charged relationships among a manservant, his master, and the woman affiliated with each. Society has defined the approved deportments among them. Released, sexuality, drink, and animosities shift the balances of power. Together, Pinter and Losey betray the inversions of the relationships with visual skill. By maintaining the behavior within a credible if unlikely narrative, they manage a critical judgement of outmoded social forms without the polemics of John Osborne or the modish psychopathology of Ken Russell. *King and Country* (1964) carries something of the same theme into a military situation in which military executions are a grotesque consequence of normal behaviors.

Accident (1967) again leagued Losey and Pinter with two frequently associated actors, Dirk Bogarde and Stanley Baker, in a sexual intrigue that is staged in bucolic academic setting. Here the emotional chaos that underlies seemingly adjusted, charmingly civilized behavior is largely hinted, rather than acted out.

Accident. Stephen (Dirk Bogarde), a university tutor, has been invited by William (Michael York), one of his students, to weekend at the family estate. The first evening they play "wall game," a family ritual contesting the possession of a pillow. The scene is the first hint of passions raging beneath calm British exteriors.

Nicholas Roeg

One of Britain's most respected cameramen, Roeg filmed *Petulia, Far From the Madding Crowd,* and *Fahrenheit 451.* His first directed feature, *Performance* (1971), bulged with implications, the story of a gangster, Chas Devlin (James Fox), who masquerades as a juggler, hiding out in the secluded home of a rock star, Turner (Mick Jagger). Perhaps Turner's plaything, perhaps a subject of his in-house therapy, Chas passes in a drugged state through a succession of identities, at the singer's mercy. The frames of reference are R. D. Laing and Jorge Luis Borges, whose *Personal Anthology* is seen being read by a minor thug at one point in the film. Borges' own face appears in *Performance's* final moments, a way station in the identity exchanges between Turner and Chas.

If the film seems overloaded with interpolated references, like poetry by a young T. S. Eliot disciple, enthusiasm toward Roeg gained firmer ground when *Performance* was followed by *Walkabout* (1972), *Don't Look Now* (1973), and *The Man Who Fell to Earth* (1976). The Borgian interchange between "dream" and "reality" adapts to Roeg's disposition to edit equally authentic but vastly different images in tandem. Consistent in all the films is an interest in simultaneous worlds: an aborigine and a pair of white children walking in Australian wilderness; a man with psychic sensitivities; a visitor from outer space who experiences both the Earth now and some of its earlier inhabitants. *The Man Who Fell To*

Earth was British financed, shot with American actors (excepting the British star of the film, David Bowie) in the United States. Although its mode is science fiction, the effect is to intensity our awareness of this country's culture by representing its impact upon a disguised extraterrestrial agent who can only become as "human" as he can learn to be from earthlings.

Despite the variety and success of British production in two decades, movie-house admission continues to decline. Theaters numbered 3400 in 1959 and diminished to 1558 by 1970. Attendance fell consistently each year. Government subsidy has diminished, and American companies cut back or entirely withdrew much of their English production. Feature output itself has held reasonably firm, but investment in productions has dropped, a factor that need not in itself augur ill for picture quality. Unorthodox productions also face a problem unique to the nation. Unlike France or the United States, most exhibition in Britain resided by the late seventies in the hands of only two corporations: Rank and Associated British Cinemas. Between them, six hundred of the major outlets rested, and a film that did not win the sympathy of one of the circuits was unlikely to return its investment within the country.

Box office receipts for 1977 outdistanced those for 1976, and this was the first time in twenty years that such figures rose over the previous year's. However, the continued reliance on non-British, largely American, financing hardly augered future prosperity.

Summary

In certain key respects, British, French, and Italian feature films of the past three decades parallel one another. First, script, studio, and convention-dominated production becomes the target of rebelling forces that develop a freer pattern of narrativity and of emotional expression. Then, consolidated by age and commercial success, much of the new became itself institutionalized. More recent directors have periodically succeeded in imposing personal, if sometimes bizarre, visions onto productions.

Devoted to the animated film in its many ramifications, Chapter 16 will consider that mode's emergence out of comic strip designs and its rich subsequent history of graphic innovation.

Bibliography

Anderson, Lindsay, "Stand Up! Stand Up!," *Sight and Sound* (Autumn 1956).
———. "Class Theater, Class Films," *The Drama Review* 11 (Fall 1966).
———. If . . . . New York, 1969.
———. Oh Lucky Man! New York, 1973.
Atkins, Thomas R. *Ken Russell.* New York, 1976.
Belmans, Jacques. *Jeune cinéma Anglais.* Lyon, 1967.
Betts, Ernest. *The Film Business.* New York, 1973.
Booker, Christopher. *The Neophiliacs.* Boston, 1970.
British Feature Directors. London, 1959?
Brooker, Nancy J. *John Schlesinger.* Boston, 1978.
Brownlow, Kevin. *How It Happened Here.* London, 1968.

Butler, Ivan. *Cinema in Britain*. South Brunswick, N.J., 1973.

Casty, Alan. "The New Style in British Rebels and Their Films," *Midwest Quarterly* (Winter 1968).

Cavender, Kenneth, interviewer. "Harold Pinter and Clive Donner," in Joseph F. McCrindle, ed. *Behind the Scenes*. New York, 1971.

Cozarinsky, Edgardo. "Borges on and in Film," *Sight and Sound* (Winter 1975–76).

Craddock, John. "The Charge of the Light Brigade in Perspective," *Film Society Review* 4 (1969).

Durgnat, Raymond. "Vote for Britain," *Films and Filming* (April, May, June, 1964).

———. *A Mirror for England*. London, 1970.

French, Philip. "The Alphaville of Admass," *Sight and Sound* (Summer 1966).

———. "Performance," *Sight and Sound* (Spring 1971).

Gifford, Denis. *British Cinema*. New York, 1968.

———. *The British Film Catalogue 1895–1970*. New York, 1973.

Gomez, Joseph A. *Ken Russell: The Adaptor as Creator*. New York, 1976.

Gubeck, Thomas. "Cultural Identity and Film in the European Economic Community," *Cinema Journal* (Fall 1974).

Houston, Penelope. "England, Their England," *Sight and Sound* (Spring 1966).

———. "Time of Crisis," *Sight and Sound* (Spring 1958).

Jacob, Gilles. "Joseph Losey, or The Camera Calls," *Sight and Sound* (Spring 1966).

Johnson, Ian. "Have the British a Sense of Humor?" *Films and Filming* (March 1963).

Kawin, Bruce. "Peter Watkins: Cameraman at World's End," *Journal of Popular Film* (Summer 1973).

Lambert, Gavin. "Notes on the British Cinema," *Quarterly of Radio, Film and Television* (Fall 1956).

Losey, Joseph. "The Monkey on My Back," *Films and Filming* (October 1963).

Lovell, Alan and Jim Hillier. *Studies in Documentary*. New York, 1972.

Manvell, Roger. *New Cinema in Britain*. London, 1969.

Masterworks of the British Cinema. New York, 1974.

Mayer, Jacob Peter. *British Cinemas and Their Audiences*. London, 1948.

Oakley, Charles Allen. *Where We Came In*. London, 1964.

Osborne, John. *Look Back in Anger*. New York, 1959.

Perry, George C. *The Great British Picture Show*. New York, 1974.

Pinter, Harold. *The Lover, Tea Party. The Basement*. New York, 1967.

———. *Five Screenplays*. London, 1971.

"Replies to a Questionnaire," *Sight and Sound* (Spring 1957).

Richardson, Tony. "London Letter," *Film Culture* 8 (1956).

Rosenfeldt, Diane. *Ken Russell*. Boston, 1978.

———. *Richard Lester*. Boston, 1978.

Saltzman, Harry. "New Wave Hits British Films," *Films and Filming* (April 1960).

Sillitoe, Alan. *Saturday Night and Sunday Morning*. New York, 1958.

Steele, Robert. "The National Film Theatre of London, England." *Film Studies 5*. Boston University, Boston, 1964?

Wakely, Michael. "Situation Hopeless but not Serious," *Films and Filming* (May 1970).

Walker, Alexander. *Hollywood, England.* London, 1974.

Webber, John. *Joseph Losey and Harold Pinter.* M. A. Thesis, San Francisco State University, 1975.

"Who Shows What to Whom?" *Economist* 21 (Aug. 8, 1964).

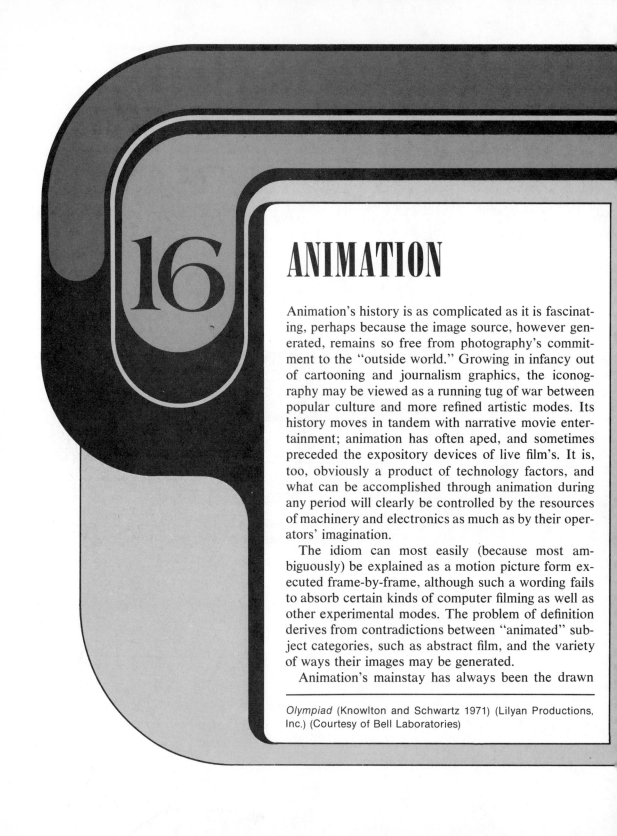

16

ANIMATION

Animation's history is as complicated as it is fascinating, perhaps because the image source, however generated, remains so free from photography's commitment to the "outside world." Growing in infancy out of cartooning and journalism graphics, the iconography may be viewed as a running tug of war between popular culture and more refined artistic modes. Its history moves in tandem with narrative movie entertainment; animation has often aped, and sometimes preceded the expository devices of live film's. It is, too, obviously a product of technology factors, and what can be accomplished through animation during any period will clearly be controlled by the resources of machinery and electronics as much as by their operators' imagination.

The idiom can most easily (because most ambiguously) be explained as a motion picture form executed frame-by-frame, although such a wording fails to absorb certain kinds of computer filming as well as other experimental modes. The problem of definition derives from contradictions between "animated" subject categories, such as abstract film, and the variety of ways their images may be generated.

Animation's mainstay has always been the drawn

Olympiad (Knowlton and Schwartz 1971) (Lilyan Productions, Inc.) (Courtesy of Bell Laboratories)

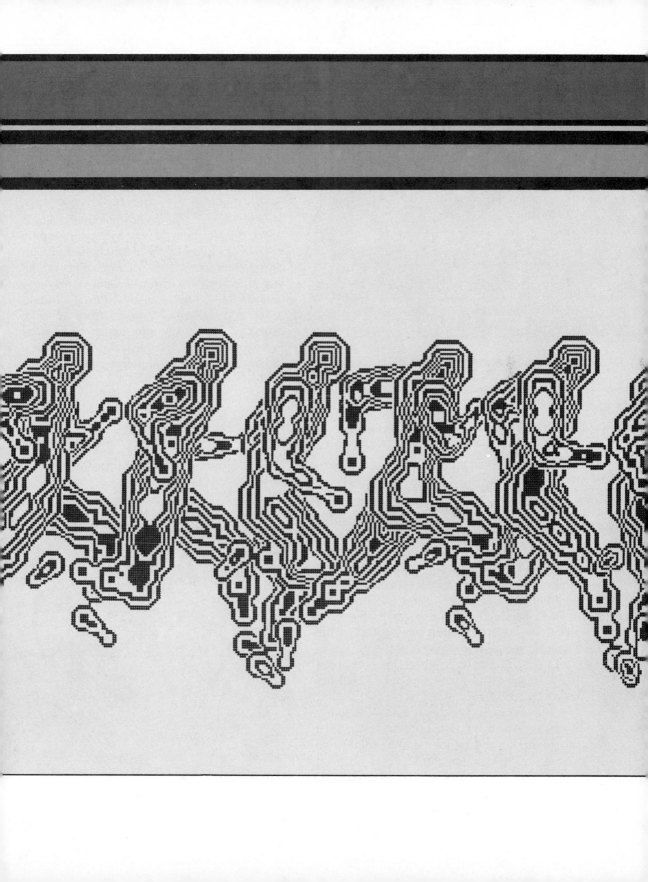

Reynaud's Théâtre Optique. Horse and clown are projected in repeated cycles against the unmoving field composed by spectators and arena. Reynaud used perforated film, exhibiting at the Musée Grévin in Paris beginning in 1892, but his first work dates from ten years earlier. (British National Film Archive/Stills Library)

a motor car onto a photographed background, then filming the composite, one frame at a time, while moving the cutout between exposures. Projected, the vehicle assumes a life of its own, which is to say it becomes animated. Earlier, Méliès had used drawings in *A Trip to the Moon* (1902), and it is said that Bird's Custard Powder was advertised by an animated commercial prepared by Arthur Melbourne-Cooper in Britain in 1897. Melbourne-Cooper also made an animated film in 1899; a figure built of matchsticks appears to chalk a blackboard appeal for civilian support of the Boer War. Titles of early films do not use "animated" to distinguish drawn from live action; thus, *The Animated Poster* (Edison 1903) and *Animated Painting* (Edison 1904) both use Méliès-like stop action to produce life-photographed trick effects. The earliest movies were often all called animated pictures.

Humorous Phases of Funny Faces. A New York journalist-cartoonist, Blackton was filmed at work by Edison in *Blackton, the Evening World Cartoonist* (1896). Like McCay, Blackton made side-money by doing vaudeville chalk-talks. Essentially, *Humorous Phases* is such a presentation. (La Cinémathèque québécoise)

picture. The technique of creating the illusion of motion by projecting in rapid succession a series of hand-drawn images precedes motion pictures themselves if "movies" are considered to originate when photography allied with projection to capitalize on the persistence of vision phenomenon. Emile Reynaud's Théâtre Optique, mentioned in Chapter 1, operated by way of hand-drawn transparencies prepared on strips projected, often one on top of the other, in sequence onto a screen. And Reynaud's 1892 attraction had been long preceded by Zoetropes and Praxinoscopes, which depended equally on artwork.

Photography's mingling with frame-by-frame (or stop motion) production will be seen in Méliès' hand-colored *Paris to Monte Carlo* (1905), some of whose effects were accomplished by overlaying the cutout image of

382   Animation

If actual objects, such as matchsticks or cut-outs, are moved, the effect of two-dimensional graphics continues so long as the field is a flat one. Similar results may be accomplished in three dimensional arenas by moving (or pixillating) objects between exposures in photographed space. Such a film was made in 1905 by Ségundo de Chomon in Spain as *El Hotel Electrico,* which is thought to have motivated *Haunted Hotel,* made by J. Stuart Blackton in the United States during 1907.

A year earlier, Blackton, who was a staff artist for the New York *World* made a short film called *Humorous Phases of Funny Faces.* It was done by photographing the drawings of faces that had been chalked on the blackboard, moving parts erased and sketched

again for each exposure. (Erasures can be seen to accumulate as the film progresses.)

CARTOONS

In France, Emile Cohl followed another technique: tracing on white paper in black crayon to produce *Mr. Stop* in 1907, the first of his successful animated series. All Cohl's films were deceptively primitive, executed with stick figures that look like the pencil tests of later animators, made to check timing and movement. In *Phantasmagoria* (1908), shapes grow and metamorphosize into other forms. Cohl's freedom of line and imaginative, trans-

A graphic example of an Emile Cohl transformation: elephant to ballet dancer. Norman McLaren affectionately pays tribute to this technique in *Hen Hop* (1942). (La Cinémathèque québécoise)

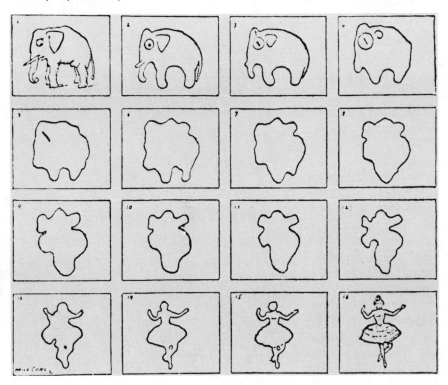

Le Cauchemar du Fantôche. Cohl did animation in the United States on the Snookums series between 1913 and 1915. One of his great strengths was the ability to impart life and character within such simply outlined drawings. (La Cinémathèque québécoise)

forming continuities enlist greater interest now than many more recent efforts. With *Le Cauchemar du Fontôche* (1909), Cohl produced a "little man," a Chaplin-like figure that prefigured the traditions of personalized, empathy-inducing cartoon characters.

The outstanding early animation figure was Winsor McCay, a strip cartoonist whose *Little Nemo in Slumberland,* drawn for the New York *Herald,* establishes his primacy as an illustrator. Links between animation and journalism graphics were several years in formation. Sidney Smith drew three *Old Doc Yac* films in 1913, and George McManus had undertaken a movie of Maggie and Jiggs from *Bringing Up Father.* William Nolan did *Krazy Kat* and *Barney Google* for Hearst. McCay was struck by McManus' efforts and tried something of his own. Opinions differ about

the order of the McCay titles. A reasonable sequence seems to be *Little Nemo* (also called *Winsor McCay*) in 1911, *How a Mosquito Operates* in (1912), and *Gertie the Trained Dinosaur* (1914).[1]

McCay's draftsmanship and his skills in depicting free movement and perspective are readily apparent. Before filming, he checked the work on a self-made Mutoscope. Among the best McCays are *Bug Vaudeville* (1916) with a juggling grasshopper, a bicycling cockroach, boxing potato bugs and an equestrian butterfly and *The Sinking of the Lusitania* (1918), a propaganda piece that seeks to de-

[1] *John Fell,* Film and the Narrative Tradition, *p. 251. Chapter 5 is devoted to likenesses between film exposition and strip cartoons. Dates of McCay's films have been altered here to conform to more recent research.*

Little Nemo. The characters are Flip and Impy from McCay's *Little Nemo in Slumberland.* Impy joined the strip during an adventure on a cannibal isle. Flip's face always appeared green in the papers. The segment of plotted imagery that concludes *Little Nemo* consists of a variation on McCay's July 22, 1906 Sunday comic-strip adventure. (La Cinémathèque québécoise)

Produced by Pat Sullivan, the imaginative design of the *Felix the Cat* cartoons is directly attributable to its artist, Otto Messmer. Tough-minded, out for himself, Felix usually outwitted his adversaries; more a tramp, as Keaton said of Chaplin, than a good American worker. (La Cinémathèque québécoise)

pict a realistic enactment of the German submarine's attack.

Animation's time-consuming preparations posed fewer problems during formative film years than later, for all titles were short, and a short cartoon might easily be sandwiched between other entertainments. Animated work appeared in Italy, Poland, Germany, Russia, and notably in Sweden by way of Victor Bergdahl, who later worked with McCay.

All the early films replaced each picture with a duplicate that identically reproduced everything but the places where movement occurred. Cels were first introduced in the New York studios of John Bray and Earl Hurd (patented by Hurd in 1915): clear plastic sheets that maintained the registration of overlapping images while minimizing drawing since repetitive sections, backgrounds, for example, could be eliminated. This innovation had several consequences. The unmoving images became more elaborate. In the interest of economy, movement grew more stylized. Cycles, such as walking, ocean waves, and crowds cheering, might be repeated with identical drawings. (The concept is apparent in Flip's repeated cigar movements during *Little Nemo*). Pauses for reaction and recognition(as in a double-take) also saved artwork, and the humorous cartoon elaborated its easy relation with vaudeville mime. The Griffith-Bitzer iris in and out appeared in Bray-Hurd productions by 1915 and as scene transition technique was used in wartime animated military training films.

As exhibitors began to program cartoons on

a regular schedule, the little studios assumed a more production-line pattern, alloting separate functions to each artist. Companies also developed recurring characters, much as live studios had started to exploit personalities. Pat Sullivan had *Felix the Cat;* Bray, *Mutt and Jeff;* Walter Lantz, the *Katzenjammer Kids;* Paul Terry,[2] *Aesop's Fables;* and the Fleischer Brothers *Bimbo* and *Koko the Clown.*

Max Fleischer worked beside John Bray as a fellow cartoonist at the Brooklyn *Daily Eagle* in 1901. He later became production head at Bray-Hurd, then he set up an independent business with brother Dave, and later brothers Lou and Joe as well. The Fleischers' early work is noteworthy for their employment of the Rotoscope, which was devised to save time and to secure more life-like effects by projecting live footage onto sheets from which broad outlines of human movement might be traced, then exaggerated as necessary for a cartoon. The Rotograph, in turn, projected photographed film onto an animation camera's field where it might be integrated with drawn figures. The "Out of the Inkwell" series featured Koko, who would emerge from an ink bottle and interplay with live footage of Max Fleischer. Use was also made of still photographs against which Koko's figure might either be moved as a cutout or more complicatedly integrated through matte work. (Hurd did a *Johnny Out of the Inkwell* in 1921.)

The twenties animated cartoons project a naïve, unfettered atmosphere, best demonstrated in *Felix the Cat* series, which was conceived and drawn by Otto Messmer, who drew them for Pat Sullivan from 1919 until Sullivan's death in 1933. Messmer's Felixes are almost consistently imaginative in story and gags, and Felix, a malevolent feline, uses his tail and sometimes the balloons with which

silent cartoon creatures thought or spoke, like their comic strip counterparts, for mischiefs and escapes.[3]

A transplant to Los Angeles from Kansas City, Walt Disney's pre-emminent skill rested in conceiving characters and humor that would rest easily with mass audiences. After working through various series and financial

[3] *Messmer explained Felix's origins as follows: "Paramount had come out with a weekly (screen) magazine and they had four cartoonists on them, each week a different cartoonist. There was always a gap, so in a rush they came down to the Sullivan studio, could we make one? Sullivan was busy on something else. He said 'You want to do it at home?' He didn't figure to get much on that, so I did this, the first Felix the Cat, see? I figured I'm gonna make something black here because it saves making a lot of outlines, and solid black moves better." John Canemaker. Program Notes,* Whitney Museum of American Art New American Filmmakers Series *(1976).*

The Skeleton Dance. Disney's early "Silly Symphonies" are rife with grotesque images, as often nightmare as daydream. (Museum of Modern Art/Film Stills Archive)

[2] *Terry worked for Bray-Hurd in 1916-17, executing work of great skill.*

Snow White and the Seven Dwarfs. The film was in production for three years, all Disney's studio committed to its success. Effects of depth were accentuated by the employment of a multiplane camera, newly conceived by Ub Iwerks. (La Cinémathèque québecoise)

affiliations, Disney developed a program he called *Silly Symphonies* and released them through Columbia and United Artists. *Silly Symphonies* contain some of Disney's most unrestrained work and many of the best are self-sufficient tales like *The Merry Dwarfs* (1929), *Skeleton Dance* (1930), and *Babes in the Woods* (1932). Increasingly, they featured a cast who first appeared in *Steamboat Willie* (1928): Mickey Mouse and cohorts. Ub Iwerks, an early friend, was responsible for conceptualizing much of the cartoons' actual graphics. As time passed, Disney, like Max Fleischer, withdrew to overseeing production.

Often grotesque exhuberant fantasies, the spirit of these early films refined as Disney adapted his product to what he cannily perceived as family movie-going tastes. The udders of cows were corseted and unclothed figures altogether lost sexual characteristics. Drawings became increasingly lifelike, objects rounded and shaded, and perspective and color manipulated to resemble photographed reality. The animation features, *Snow White and the Seven Dwarfs* (1937) and *Pinocchio* (1939), betray the new gentility with rare glimpses of the *Silly Symphony's* verve peeping through.

For all his emotional tidiness and decorum, Disney had major effects on animation. *Steamboat Willie* was first to employ a fully synchronized sound track, and many of the

Silly Symphonies were built around music, for example, *The Skeleton Dance* out of Grieg's "March of the Dwarfs," *The Three Little Pigs* from a depression-era pop song. Disney stimulated technology, and much that followed either emerged from or reacted against his domination of the field. Whimsy aside, *Fantasia* (1940) hints at other directions Disney Studio might have taken. A parody, the Italian *Allegro non Troppo* (1976) by Bruno Bozzetto sets Sibelius, Vivaldi and Stravinsky, among others, to post-Disney visuals.

Sound

Sound had major effects on Hollywood animation, requiring both technical sophistications and new levels of financing that winnowed out the small, less stable companies. A part of Disney's special skill rested in conceiving relations between picture and sound (i.e., music and effects). In their own way, the accomplishments paralleled the inventiveness of Lubitsch, Mamoulian, and Clair, but, as with live action, synchronization developed larger-than-life characters among cartoons whose popularity rested substantially in the voices. Donald Duck was the W. C. Fields, Bugs Bunny the Groucho, Heckel and Jeckel (from Paul Terry's Terrytoons) the Hope and Crosby of their fields.

With color added, thirties and forties cartoons emerged from human factories, the film's uniquenesses dependent now on producers and writers, rather than the inventions of single artists as in earlier days. Universal held ownership of Disney's *Oswald the Rabbit* creation and commissioned Walter Lantz to produce them at the rate of ten per year with a hundred artists under his supervision.

Disney led the field, but each animation studio, if successful, imposed a personality on the product. In retrospect, Fleischer appears particularly vivid, preserving an ethnic humor (the studio remained in New York City until

Betty Boop. Created early in the Fleischer studio's career, she satirized the American flapper, a little girl astonishingly mature for her undesignated age. Some of the early, sound *Betty Boop* cartoons almost approach eroticism. See, for example, *Mysterious Mose* (1930) or *Betty Boop's Bamboo Isle* (1932). (La Cinémathèque québécoise)

1937) and vigor while Disney was playing it safe. In *The Herring Murder Case* (1931), the title a satire of William Powell's first Philo Vance films, a narrator cries out, "Holy Mackerel, is this the end of the herring?" in imitation of Edward G. Robinson as Rico. Essentially, Fleischer studios more resembled Warner Brothers than Paramount through whom they released.

Stylization and Variety

Disney features sought both to bludgeon competition and to attract a family (never merely a child) audience with impressive representational illusion: perspective in depth, shadows, light shifts with distance. This impulse, plus labor conditions that were brutal in all the studios, eventually fomented dissent. In 1937, the Fleischer plant was struck, and Disney in 1941. A victim of the latter dispute was a Canadian, Stephen Bosutow, who eventually fronted, in league with other Disney dissidents, a new company in 1945, United Productions of America or UPA. More important than economic and administrative issues was the esthetic revolt. UPA returned to many of the cheaper animating techniques of an earlier time. Figures were highly stylized, perspective flattened, colors bright and poster-hued. Movement was minimized and the modern look of UPA cartoons was enhanced by witty, imaginative sound tracks that required greater attention and sophistication from the audi-

ence. Christopher Crumpet was a little boy who turned into a chicken when angry. Gerald McBoing Boing, who spoke in sound effects, appeared with rhymed-couplet commentaries. UPA adapted James Thurber's *Unicorn in the Garden* (1953) and Poe in *The Tell Tale Heart* (1953).

Many of UPA's early members proceeded to develop individual reputations. John Hubley, working with his wife Faith, used the semi-improvised voice tracks of his children to narrate *The Temper Game* (1958) and *Moonbird* (1960) as well as Dizzy Gillespie's verbal humor in *The Hole* (1962). Hubley's rough, textured water colors have a *look* of children's fantasy. Gene Deitch established headquarters in Prague, where he made cartoons (often disappointing) for US distribution. Ernest Pintoff, a late arrival UPA member, left to make *The Violinist* (1960), *The Interview* (1961), and *The Critic* (1962), each of which thrives on clever dialect humor.

The economy of UPA's approach adapted ominously to television, and most of its origi-

The Unicorn in the Garden. A shy husband tries to advise his wife that he has seen the beast outside. "You are a booby," she responds, "and I am going to put you in the booby hatch." But when attendants and psychiatrists arrive, the husband fares better than his spouse. (Museum of Modern Art/Film Stills Archive)

nal flair was homogenized into hours of Saturday morning *Mr. Magoo,* and by extension, the *Huckleberry Hound* and *Flintstones* yardage of William Hanna and Joseph Barbera.

A kind of Disney-UPA compromise with its own special flavor were the works of Tex Avery and Chuck Jones (who together created *Bugs Bunny*), Friz Freleng (*Tweety Pie and*

Le Théâtre de Monsieur et Madame Kabal (1967). "There are enormous differences between Lenica and his old accomplice, the phlegmatic Boro. Lenica is the great sculptor of the two . . . an immediately recognizable style rivaling those of Sternberg or Miro in its subjective impact. Borowczyk . . . is fundamentally a filmmaker, an inventor of movements and phrases. He orchestrates objects as well as empty spaces." Robert Benayoun (La Cinémathèque québécoise)

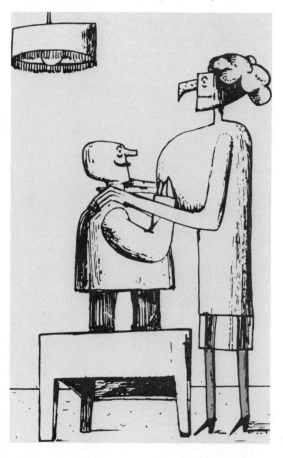

Sylvester), and Robert McKimson (*Daffy Duck*). While much of the work, done for Warner Brothers, is too formularized to escape predictability, the best can be characterized as impudent, anarchic flight, like Marx Brothers unbeholden to gravity.

Non-American cartoon animation since the fifties often allies stylistics to painterly idioms, while at the same time seeking to maintain movie-theater appeal through humorous story lines that may still evoke modern sensibilities. Jan Lenica and Walerian Borowczyk, Polish-Parisians, collaborated on *Dom/House* (1958), which used both live and animated techniques. *Dom* quite removes itself altogether from dispositions to amuse. It assumes somber, even horrifying proportions. Single images—a woman's profile, a stair ascent—uncover obsessions and hint at memories and anxieties that accompany intense loneliness. In his drawn animations—*Monsieur Tête* (1959), *Labyrinth* (1961), *Rhinoceros* (1963) and *A* (1964)—Lenica uses simple, blank-expressioned people whom we learn to recognize not as innocents, but the messengers of violent, selfish, pathetic dreams and sometimes of terrible passivity. *Labyrinth* paints the often-used Icarus myth as a paradigm of modern civilization; the protagonist, a little man in bowler hat, proceeding through cosmopolitan terrors finally to escape with strapped-on wings until he is attacked by vultures. Sound is used sparingly to great effect, as in *A* when that letter attacks a Lenican character in his room, first playfully, then pounding him into insensibility to the accompaniment of growls, tearing, and thuds. Like *Rhinoceros,* the source of *A* is absurdist playright Eugene Ionesco.

Walerian Borowczyk's *The Concert of M. Kabal* (1963) links Lenica-like graphics to even more fearsome emotions. *Renaissance* (1963) views a disintegrated collection of past ephemera laden with memories: doll, battered cornet, books, stuffed owl, photograph. They are filmed "live." Through pixillation, while a

A. Like *Rhinoceros,* the film was executed in West Germany. Alone in his room, a man suddenly, inexplicably, encounters the presence of A. Every effort to evict it is futile. After pestering and torturing him, the letter finally disappears and is replaced by B. At the end of the film, an intertitle reminds us that the alphabet consists of twenty-six letters. (La Cinémathèque québécoise)

distant trumpet plays a sweet, old song, the objects assemble themselves until they are whole and new. Then lightning flashes, and everything reverts to dissolution. *Les Jeux des anges* (1964) evokes the atrocities of the concentration camps, largely by way of brutal offscreen sound effects. Abstracted, agonized impersonal drawings hint at mutilation and inexpressible torture perpetuated by the machinery of mass-production.

Animation in Zagreb, Yugoslavia represented a considered national decision to enter the world film market by way of an idiom that might bypass language barriers, minimize costs, and appeal to a denominator common among diverse audiences. A host of filmmakers, among them Dusan Vukotic, Vatroslav Mimica, Nicola Kostelac, and Boris Kolar, exchanged roles on one another's productions. Their work affords interesting, often funny insight into socialist preoccupations. *Ersatz* (1961) creates a world of inflatable balloons and then leaks them into nothingness. These include a driver, his motorcar, the road, and finally the screen itself. Significant of changing taste, it was the first European cartoon to win an Oscar. *The Wall* (1965) follows two men's efforts to escape a great concrete barrier. One destroys himself in the process while the other, a patient observer, steps across his companion's body to freedom. Much of Zagreb's best work has the quality of parable. Today's animation far outdistances the comic strip conventions from which it grew.

The output of Zagreb is noted for variety of graphic style. Vatroslav Mimica, *The Egg* (1959) (above left); Ivo Vrbanic, *La Peau de Chagrin* (1960) (above); Nedeljko Dragic, *Tamer of Wild Horses* (1966) (left). (La Cinémathèque québécoise)

CUTOUTS

Less often used, cutouts may be seen in the beginning and end of *Ballet mécanique* (see Chapter 18) and among some of the twenties experiments by the Bauhaus artist-teacher Moholy-Nagy. A technique intermediate between drawing and cutout is found in Lotte Reiniger's silhouette films, which have the quality of Chinese shadow plays. For nearly forty years, Reiniger produced films in Germany and England often consisting of black images against white settings, beginning with *The Flying Coffer* (1921) concluding in *The Seraglio* (1958). Most depict fairy tales or children's stories and added sound has enhanced the twenties films.

Stan VanderBeek used popular graphics in such animated works as *Breathdeath* (1964) to produce surreal collages out of advertising and news photos manipulated on an animation stand so that heads split apart to reveal strange interiors; skyscrapers are powered like missiles; crayoned lines turn faces into living rooms.

The work of Harry Smith defies category just as it intimidates easy interpretation. His collage efforts were preceded by hand drawn *Early Abstraction,* numbering from 1 to 10 and dating between 1939 and 1956. Number 4 visualizes the bop configurations of Dizzy Gillespie, as *Mirror Animations No. 11* (1957) is done to the music of Thelonious Monk. This Smith work aligns with traditions of the abstract film. His shapes metamorphize in form as they evolve in color to affect a viewer's sense of space and figure-ground relationships.

With the introduction of collage, drawn objects and mystic symbols, Smith's surrealities assume tones that are alternately ominous and playful in *Early Abstractions No. 10* and

Heaven and Earth Magic (1961). The latter, Smith's major work and short-feature length, repetitively plays silent, sinister ritual variations on moving cutouts that draw on themes of history, madness, imprisonment, and drug hallucination.

OBJECT ANIMATION

Made of flexible materials and/or joints, models and puppets faithfully served popular film's special effects needs, as in *King Kong,* and create their own fantasy worlds. In 1935, the Russian Alexander Ptushko made *New Gulliver,* a more politically imbued version of Swift's book than the 1939 version by the Fleischers. Blending live photography and 3,000 dolls made of wood, rubber, metal, and cloth, the new Gulliver led oppressed Lilliputians in a workers' revolt.

(Left) Lotte Reiniger at work on *The Adventures of Prince Achmed,* in preparation from 1923 until 1926. To her right is Karl Koch, Reiniger's husband. Animating a design beneath the silhouette is Walter Ruttmann. Ruttmann used Fischinger's wax-slicing machine in the film. (Below) A more simplified silhouette technique seen in *The Flying Coffer.* (Courtesy of Cecile Starr) (National Film Archives, Ottawa)

Ladislas Starevitch emigrated from Russia to Paris and abandoned insect photography to make puppet-marionette films. Starevitch's first entertainment animation, *The Revenge of the Kinematograph Cameraman* (1912), is thought to have been commissioned by the Czar. Starevitch wired actual insect models in order to enact a comedy about a movie photographer who takes revenge on his girl friend by photographing her at the Hotel d'Amour through a keyhole. The footage of the secret rendezvous is screened publically to an audience of bugs. Starevitch's executions and his choices of camera angles give the film a surprisingly modern flavor and look. *Roman de Renart/Story of the Fox* (1938) set seventy-five animal models into simultaneous motion during one sequence of the fifty minute film.

The work of Tony Sarg represents an extraordinary alliance between model animation and silhouettes. Sarg used three-dimensional figures then photographed their shadowed images in the manner of Lotte Reiniger. The only surviving example of Sarg's work appears to be *Adam Raises Cain* (1919).

George Pal prepared puppet films in the Netherlands and Britain before coming to the United States in 1940 and undertaking a series of Puppetoons. His most impressive work appeared during the fifties in special effects that often combined live action and animation for *Destination Moon* (1950), *When Worlds Collide* (1951), *War of the Worlds* (1953) and *Conquest of Space* (1955). Pal himself

Story of the Fox. Founder of a Museum of Natural History in Kovno, Starevitch was a pre-revolutionary cinematographer and directed feature films starring Mozhukin. He commenced animation work in 1913 with *The Grasshopper and the Ant*. Between 1923 and 1950, Starevitch produced his puppet films in France. (La Cinémathèque québécoise)

directed several films, including *Atlantis, the Lost Continent* (1961).

Czechoslovakian Jiri Trnka manipulates puppet figures with great flexibility of expression, replacing heads as necessary. His work includes *The Emperor's Nightingale* (1953), *A Midsummer Night's Dream* (1959), *Good Soldier Schweik* (1954), and a Western satire, *The Song of the Prairie* (1959). Costuming and set design have qualities of an elaborate Hollywood musical. The Czech Karel Zeman skillfully combines live action, puppetry, animation, and special-effect photography to produce fantasy stories that have the tangibility of live action and the inventiveness of cartoons. His techniques are evident in *The Treasure of Bird Island* (1952) and *Baron Munchhausen* (1959). At Carpenter Center at Harvard, Eliot Noyes pixilated table-top clay sculpture to trace a cannibal-ridden evolutionary progress that has its culmination in the Statue of Liberty and an MGM lion in *Clay — Origin of the Species* (1964).

Puppet construction differs among animators. The Trnka and Starevitch figures consist of wired or wooden substructures supporting cloth. Willis O'Brien — *The Lost World* (1925), *King Kong* (1933) — built his skeletons out of tooled steel, costumed in foam latex and dressed with paint, hair, and fur. George Pal not only substituted heads with different expressions — painting changing mouth and eye movements on his wooden figures — but also arms and legs.

ANIMATION OF STILLS

Animation stand technique can equally well be applied to still material, drawn or photographed. When successful, this technique intensifies the apparent "reality," for a picture's finite borders are effaced by the screen, which implies that the subject area extends without limit. Graphics with consistent perspectives, as in regular photographs and representational painting, seem to increase in apparent depth, and any large canvas may be selectively presented either through camera movement or a succession of cuts to inject an element of discovery into viewer experience. Studies of painters, such as those done by Alain Resnais (Chapter 20), fall within this sphere, along with many films derived from photographs. Colin Low's *City of Gold* (1957) was built from a collection of glass-plate photographs that captured and preserved events in Dawson City at the time of the Yukon Gold Rush. Because of the size and detail of the pictures, a world of expressive minutiae is revealed. As in *Night and Fog,* the film modulates carefully from its earlier period to today. We have been seeing still photographs. The tag on a pair of unused shoes then blows slightly in the breeze. We realize that we've not been seeing an old photo of new shoes, but rather a new moving picture of old ones.

Arthur Lipsett blends still photographs and live action, most culled from the cutting room floor, in *Very Nice, Very Nice* (1961). Here, picture meanings are reconceived as in the work of Ester Schub, Lipsett ascribing new connotations both by sound track (often also "found") and context.

Robert Breer, an abstract American painter, created single, separate-image collages in *Blazes* (1961) and *Fist Fight* (1964). Breer believes such rapid fire exposure of pictures, each one sometimes elaborately painted, acclimates the spectator's eye to seeing new images. In contrast, Charles Braverman depends on the immediate recognizability of aging, popular iconographies for his accelerated history made from period drawings and paintings in *American Time Capsule* (1969).

THE PIN BOARD

In collaboration with Claire Parker since 1941, Alexander Alexieff has painstakingly filmed a pin board, literally a board of close-spaced pins whose different heights, when shadowed by side lighting, achieve the effects of wood-

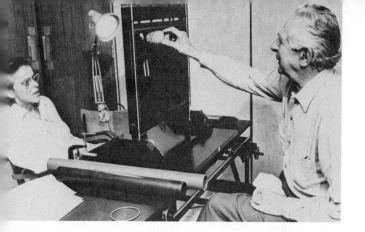

Alexandre Alexieff and Claire Parker (top), his wife, at the pin board. They are attracted, he says, to the very notion of spending four months preparing a minute of film that will exercise unrelenting control over audience attention. *The Nose* (below). A man severs his nose while shaving and pursues it through the city. Here, the nose is about to escape into an inexplicably-waiting coach through a suddenly appearing opening that had previously been a wall. (Courtesy of Cecile Starr) (La Cinémathèque québécoise)

carving or engraving in *En Passant* (1943) and Gogol's *The Nose* (1953). Still shots of their work can be seeen on the introductory sequence and a late episode of *The Trial* by Orson Welles. Alexieff's film work commenced with *A Night on Bald Mountain* (1933), and is characteristically infused with soft, shadowed mysteries and grotesque transitions from one scene to the next.

ABSTRACT FILM

The origins of the abstract film can be traced, understandably, to painters. A sort of transition from painting to film, never altogether effected, may be found in the conceptions of Léopold Survage. As early as 1914, Survage, a Russian painter in Paris, announced his intention to give movement to his work. He prepared a series of sweeping, basic-hued abstractions, suggesting time as a further dimension by the implications of change between canvases. In 1919, the poet Blaise Cendrars tried to describe the picture's intentions.

Red little by little invades the black screen and soon fills the whole visual disc. It is a somber red, of a rough nature, wrinkled like seaweed. It is composed of a multitude of little flat scales placed alongside each other. Atop each of these little scales is a tiny blister which trembles softly and ends by bursting like cooling lava.[4]

Walter Ruttmann's *Light Play Opus I* (1921) was described as "not only the first abstract film to be shown in public, but also a film hand-tinted in striking and subtle colors, with a live, synchronous musical score composed especially for it."[5] Three abstract Ruttmann works—*Opus II, Opus III, Opus IV*— were screened in England in 1925. Description of the Ruttmann images differ as to their derivations and character, but frame enlargements indicate geometric shapes similar to the images of Viking Eggeling.[6]

Eggeling worked with Hans Richter from 1919 until 1925 on the preparation of scroll

[4] *Robert Russett and Cecile Starr,* Experimental Animation, *p. 39. The material in the remainder of Chapter 16 is deeply indebted to Russett's and Starr's book.*
[5] *Russett, p. 40. No copies of this film are known to exist.*
[6] *Russett, pp. 41-43.*

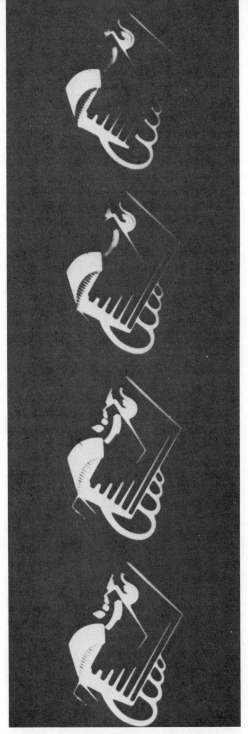

Four frames from *Diagonal Symphony* by the Swedish painter Eggeling. The image can be seen gradually to disappear in a kind of clockwise black-out. (Courtesy of Cecile Starr)

paintings and films. Their interest rested in organizing graphic material as if it possessed dynamics of music unfolding in time. In so doing, relationships, as in musical counterpoint, assumed special importance and Eggeling's *Diagonal Symphony* (1924) illustrates the complementary interplay between identical geometric forms working in apparently contrary movement. As one image moves forward, another retreats; as one expands, its companion contracts.

Eggeling's films have somewhat the appearance of Robert Delaunay paintings; Richter's tend toward squares and rectangles. *Rhythm 21* (1921), *Rhythm 23* (1923) and *Rhythm 25* (1925) consist of movement studies: shapes of various sizes reducing or diminishing into different compositional effects. At any given moment, the screen has the look of Mondrian arrangements. *Film Study* (1926) draws on more spherical or angled forms, including superimposed artificial eyes and a human head.

In backgrounds to Lotte Reiniger's feature length *Adventures of Prince Ahmed* (1926) and in his own *The Idea* (1932), Berthold Bartosh's fascination with abstract form is obvious: astral effects built with successive layers of transparent color, often paint mixed with soap bubbles.

Also experimenting with scroll painting in the early twenties, Oskar Fischinger shifted to other techniques when he began with film. Most exceptional was an arrangement devised to photograph each thin section of a wax block as it was sliced by a revolving blade. The resulting footage showed an evolving pattern of bold, abstract design. Fischinger's interests turned to drawn effects and sound-picture relationships based not on synchronicity but on mathematical characteristics which were shared between music and graphic design. Work with a "color organ" (an invention that translates sound into visual forms) in 1925 was followed by a commission to do special effects for Fritz Lang's *Woman in the Moon*. Fischinger used phonograph records with his studies until the advent of sound-on-film. During the thirties, he added color: *Allegretto* (1936), *An Optical Poem* (1937), and *An American March* (1939).

Fischinger spent frustrating years in Hollywood. He worked on *Fantasia* in the Disney Studio, his influence clearly visible in the Bach Toccata and Fugue in D Minor sequence, but Fischinger's own material did not appear entire. His images are bold and imaginative, far more complex both in design and movement than in any preceding films, and most brilliantly impressive in *Motion Painting # 1* (1947), the screen's closest approximation to a moving *picture*.

After drawing a partially abstract animation called *Tusaleva* in 1929, Len Lye's technique bypassed the camera by painting directly on clear film. Sponsored by John Grierson at the General Post Office, Lye made *Color Box* (1935) and *Kaleidoscope* (1935). *Rainbow Dance* (1936) solarized and overprinted, live-photographed images, and *Trade Tattoo* (1937) printed abstract, colored images on photographed sequences. Lye's pictures often use simple, clear, slightly irregular shapes placed against textured fields. *Free Radicals* (1957) is his starkest: emulsions scraped away from opaque, black film stock.

An inheritor of Lye's approach was Scottish-born, Norman McClaren. He was also hired by Grierson, this time for the National Film Board of Canada. McClaren's effects are simpler and often seemingly childlike, with re-

Motion Painting #1. Fischinger painted on a special easel, triggering camera exposures between each brush stroke. When paint grew too thick, he covered the work with successive layers of plexiglass and continued. Thus, the final film serves as an eleven minute, continous documentation of the abstract execution. In his lifetime, Fischinger could not afford to make Technicolor, 35mm prints of the work. (Museum of Modern Art/Film Stills Archive)

Tusalava, sponsored by the London Film Society, a group dedicated to furthering film's respectability. (It included G. B. Shaw and H. G. Wells.) Lye also directed live-action wartime shorts and worked for *The March of Time*. In later years, he made stainless-steel motion sculptures. (Courtesy of Cecile Starr)

current, identifiable shapes as in *Stars and Stripes* (1940). In *La Poulette Grise* (1947), he photographed the stages of a pastel drawing so that it seemed to assume lifelike self-realization. In *Begone Dull Care* (1949), the longitudinal striping, conceiving film as if it were a stretched out canvas, gives a scurrying, up-and-down effect, especially when played against a stable, flying bird-like image. With pixillation, McLaren animated the inanimate in *A Chairy Tale* (1957) and automated the living in *Neighbors* (1952). *Blinkety Blank* (1954) plays with color changes caused by after-

images on the retina. *Lines Horizontal* (1960) was done with sewing needles and razor blades, somewhat in the manner of Lye's later *Free Radicals*.

Douglas Crockwell, a painter of magazine covers and illustrations, adapted a version of Fischinger's slicing machine, giving more attention to the multi-colored composition of the wax block. A collector of early hand-cranked Mutoscopes, he has also drawn material for the postcard picture frames to develop what amount to new Mutoscope productions. Crockwell invented a layered-glass arrange-

The Crow (1958), made by McLaren with cutouts and reverting to some of Emile Cohl's earliest techniques. McLaren produced three-dimensional animation in *Around is Around* (1951). Fischinger had experimented with it during the same period, drawing adjacent panels to accomodate binocular fusion. (Courtesy of Cecile Starr)

ment, something like animation cels but containing, at various levels, plastic paints, these to be swirled, supplemented, or cleaned away as camera exposures progressed. *Glens Falls Sequence* (1946) and *The Long Bodies* (1947) are compilations of Crockwell's techniques, his images fluid and sometimes pronouncedly strong in depth effects.

In his series *Compositions* (numbered 1-5) (1940-1959), Dwinnel Grant develops wood, glass, and paper shapes into movement on a flat surface. *Composition 4* achieves depth through the use of polaroid glasses at viewing. For effects that are quite his own, Carmen D'Avino has adapted painting-in-process

techniques from McLaren in *The Room* (1959), painting on film, and collage in *Background* (1974). Jerome Hill's *Canaries* (1969) hand colors images on photographed footage, a technique earlier accomplished through scratching by Kenneth Anger in *Fireworks* (1947) (Chapter 18).

ANIMATION OF SOUND

As with pictures, sound has been created through optical and electronic manipulations. Early experimentation was done by Moholy-Nagy, who "recorded" fingerprints, facial profiles, and letters of the alphabet, reproducing the results both aurally and visually. Fischinger developed geometric correlates to his visual imageries, preparing these on paper scrolls and photographing the result for sound tracks.

Norman McLaren has accompanied some of his films by literally drawing the soundtrack, affecting its character with the shape, spacing and density of his inked patterns in *Dots* (1948) and *Loops* (1948). In *Soundtrack* (1970), Barry Spinello refines McLaren's techniques by applying more sophisticated image-producing techniques to both sound track and picture.

During the forties, John and James Whitney developed sound tracks that were the products of an optical system that photographed the film track, deriving its own signal from the mechanical movements of a pendulum arrangement. Thus sound is created without resort to any aural source.

ELECTRONIC IMAGES

In the period of the Whitneys' sound work, the brothers developed images through color filters, pantograph, and optical printing. These geometrical arrangements were thematized and elaborated somewhat in the manner of composers like Alban Berg and Arnold Schoenberg: *Five Abstract Film Exercises* (1943-1944). As with the mechanically induced images that followed, the Whitney's work might be viewed within traditions of twenties Soviet Constructivism, a reconciliation between the machine age and a human esthetic, but this perspective must be overlaid with meditative, non-European perspectives (such as Oriental philosophies) as well.

Some years earlier, Mary Ellen Bute had undertaken what was probably the first abstract-film venture in the United States, an un-finished *Synchronization* (1933) for which Bute furnished drawings in collaboration with composer Joseph Schillinger and filmmaker-historian-teacher Lewis Jacobs. In Bute's early films, abstractions sometimes assume dramatic roles, as in *Spook Show* (1939) where shapes are assigned into a cast of characters. Set to music, one aspect of her work was facilitated by an oscilloscope adaptation in which images electronically drawn by the filmmaker were synchronized to modern compositions: *Abstronic* (1954) contains Aaron Copeland's *Hoe Down* and *Ranch House Party* by Don Gillis.

John Whitney proceeded into work with an

Allures. As far as it is possible, San Francisco filmmaker Jordan Belson has tried to maintain optimal viewing conditions when his films are exhibited. Of all the abstract-cinema artists, his works are most emphatically trips. (Anthology Film Archives)

analogue computer, built with Norden bomb-sight materials from Army surplus. *Catalogue* (1961) is one of the resulting films and evidences several of the possibilities of the technique. Brother James' *Yantra* (1960) was made with the same equipment. More recently, John Whitney moved to electronic computers, facilitated by an IBM research grant in 1966. *Permutations* (1967), like James' *Lapis* (1966), is the single-framed record of a television screen that has translated the numerical functions—incremental steps and parametric changes—of equations supplied the computer, now displayed as visual information. Again, music serves as a kind of structural model, and the cathode phosphor dots assume patterns whose evolutions seem to have the character of serial-music composition. *Lapis* uses the machinery's disposition toward symmetry to develop constantly-changing mandala patterns. Their hypnotic quality intentionally suggests preoccupations with Eastern philosophy. Similarly, but with self-made, non-electronic techniques, Jordan Belson designs hallucenogenic and religious excursions with intense, abstracted symmetri-

Belfix (Bell Flicks), a computer program at Bell Laboratories. Filmmaker K. C. Knowlton advises his computer to fill in its display areas with different shades of gray, to move images, and to generate additional arcs and lines. Intensity of each dot can be varied through eight levels. The results are photographed on a cathode ray display tube. (Courtesy of Bell Laboratories)

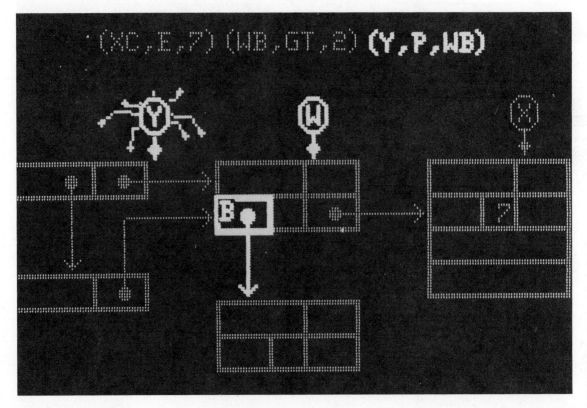

Hunger reintroduces figurative imagery into electronic systems. By this technique, mechanical controls produce the stylizing functions that had previously been exercised by undigitalized imaginations. (Museum of Modern Art/Film Stills Archive)

cal images that carry the viewer through powerful successions of feeling in *Allures* (1961), *Re-Entry* (1964), *Samadhi* (1967) and *World* (1970).

John Whitney's sons, John and Michael, have continued in the tradition: John elaborating his father's computer-bombsight system with striking results in the unnamed three screem film made for Canada's Expo 67. *Terminal Self* (1971) derives its transformations from the visual information supplied by a girl's photograph. Using digital systems, Michael Whitney produced *Binary Bit Patterns* (1969) whose diamond, Eastern patterns-within-pat-

terns are surprisingly balanced by a guitar piece also composed by the filmmaker.

Other computer-generated animation has moved toward representational forms. In *Olympiad* (1971), Ken Knowlton and Lillian Schwartz develop the movements of athletes in images reminiscent of Muybridge photography. Stan VanderBeek combines patterns and words in *Poem Fields* (1969). *La Faim/ Hunger* (1973), made for the Canadian Film Board by Peter Foldes, combines hand drawn cels with electronic scrambling and image distortion to distill original images into new textures and forms.

Summary

If one has met animators, he may conclude that, living so close to his medium, the animator sometimes appears to take on the characteristics of his creations, from Mr. Magoo to cosmic patterns. Perhaps it might better be said that an animator's art expresses the filmmaker more closely than many another film mode. Excepting the cost of animation stands, computer systems, and electronics, animation maximizes the possibilities for a filmmaker to effect a personal vision independently and without compromise. The field's breadth of style approximates graphic art itself.

Animation may conveniently, if not always accurately, be categorized in terms of photographed sequential drawings (with or without sound), cutouts, models, use of stills, pin boards, abstract images, and electronically-generated visual material. While much drawn animation has appealed to mass spectator tastes, some animation relates much more easily to painterly traditions. Many examples of abstract and/or electronically-produced work are directed toward relatively small film audiences. Because of its removal from the "real," photographed world and because of production techniques, animation, among all film idioms, most accurately develops stylized, individual conceptualizations.

Returning to the commerical feature, Chapter 17 describes the character and contributions of recent American directors.

Bibliography

Avery, Tex. Interviewed by Joe Adamson. "You Couldn't Get Chaplin in a Milk Bottle," *Take 1* (1970).

Benayoun, Robert. *Le Dessin Animé après Walt Disney*. Paris, 1961.

Cabarga, Leslie. *The Fleischer Story*. New York, 1976.

Carrol, Noël. "Heaven and Earth Magic," *Film Quarterly* (Winter 1977–78)

Cleave, Alan. *Cartoon Animation for Everyone*. New York, 1973.

Collins, Maynard. *Norman McLaren*. Ottawa, 1976.

Duca, Lo. *Le Dessin Animé*. Paris, 1948.

Edera, Bruno, ed. *Full Length Animated Feature Films*. New York, 1976.

Finch, Christopher. *The Art of Walt Disney*. New York, 1975.

Halas, John, ed. *Computer Animation*. New York, 1974.

Halas, John and Roger Manvell. *The Technique of Film Animation*. New York, 1968.

Harryhausen, Ray, interviewed by Elliott Stein. "The Thirteen Voyages of Ray Harryhausen," *Film Comment* (November-December 1977).

Hearn, Michael. "The Animated Art of Winsor McCay," *American Artist* (May 1975).

Heraldson, Donald. *Creators of Life*. New York, 1975.

Holloway, Ronald. *Z is for Zagreb*. New Jersey, 1972.

Madsen, Roy P. *Animated Film: Concepts, Methods, Uses*. New York, 1970.

Manvell, Roger. *The Animated Film*. London, 1954.

McCay, Winsor. *Dreams of the Rarebit Fiend.* New York, 1973.

———. *Little Nemo 1905–1906.* New York, 1976.

———. *Dream Days 1904–1914.* Westport, Conn., 1977.

Moritz, William. "The Films of Oskar Fischinger," *Film Culture,* 58, 59, 60 (1974).

O'Sullivan, Judith. "In Search of Winsor McCay. *American Film Institute Report. n.d.*

Russett, Robert and Cecile Starr. *Experimental Animation.* New York, 1976.

Canemaker, John. "Winsor McCay," *Film Comment* (January-February 1975).

———. "Profile of a Living American Legend: J. R. Bray," *Filmmakers Newsletter* (January 1975).

Schickel, Richard. *The Disney Version.* New York, 1968.

Stephenson, Ralph. *The Animated Film.* New York, 1973.

Thiel, Reinold. *Puppen und Zeichenfilm.* Berlin, 1960.

Youngblood, Gene. *Expanded Cinema.* New York, 1970.

17

HOLLYWOOD AFTER THE WARS

This examination of Hollywood — filmmaker and product — follows two paths. First, the circumstances in Hollywood following World War II are examined: financial, institutional, legal, and political. This is the Hollywood that came to consider itself equally menaced by Reds and black-and-white TV. Then, the motion picture directors who contributed most substantially to American film history are discussed.

Faced with the disappearance of its European market in the forties, Hollywood suffered attendance losses as great as one-third of 1939 figures, but wartime economy soon resuscitated box-office receipts and raised them to heights above depression years. Besides its national audience, the industry made renewed if vulgar efforts to penetrate South American outlets with Carmen Miranda and a succession of dreary Brazilian or Argentine musicals. By 1946, grosses surpassed $1,750,000,000.

The postwar remainder of the decade proved ominous. Britain imposed a high import tariff just when Hollywood had amassed a five-year backlog of films intended now for foreign consumption. Other countries followed England's lead, trying to protect what remained of their own industries. Further, Amer-

On the Waterfront (Kazan 1954) (Museum of Modern Art/Film Stills Archive)

ican labor, which had held its peace through much of the war period, now demanded pay increases that additionally crippled studio productivity. Worse, television's phenomenal growth began to cut heavily into attendance. The devastating effects of TV were not realistically confronted until the early fifties, but sponsor support, risen to $10 million a year, had begun to underwrite competitive entertainment. This was the time of Uncle Miltie, Ernie Kovacs and *Perry Mason*.

ANTITRUST ACTION

The federal courts proved to be another profit deterrent. They turned increasingly critical toward corporate ownership of theater chains that were seen to comprise monopo-

listic patterns, violating antitrust laws. In 1944, the courts re-initiated legal actions that had been moribund since compromise decrees in 1940, which had postponed decisions of more far reaching consequences.

The result of these actions was the loss of dependable outlets for studio product, a Hollywood tradition since the heydays of Zukor and Laemmle. This affected output in two ways. First, the onset of competitive bidding meant the theater owner was no longer insulated from outside temptation. Second, the twenty-five-year-old traditions of formulaic product (prepared, as word always had it, like sausages) no longer applied since mediocrity no longer insured an audience. Southern California schlock was even further endangered as television began to absorb its B-picture product into comedy and adventure series. But

Unidentified studio personnel appear to enjoy three-dimensional film fare more completely than the greater American audience. 3-D's feature esthetic never transcended space-bound assaults. (Museum of Modern Art/Film Stills Archive)

here only the theatrically exhibited "B" suffered, not the studios, since production units merely shifted their pattern into making movies for a new distribution outlet.

ORGANIZATIONAL SHIFTS

Eagle Lion and Warner Brothers closed their gates altogether in 1948, Warner temporarily. Some small companies like Liberty and Rainbow went out of business as well, although on the whole, studios that were minor enough to be free of contracted actors and technicians who drew salaries whether working or not rode the storm. In 1949, MGM cut back so drastically that much of its studio was unoccupied. Dore Schary was brought in from RKO as production head. Howard Hughes assumed financial ownership of RKO. David Selznick went out of corporate business, although he produced films later. Universal and International joined forces. Control of Warner's passed into a Boston banker's hands. Mary Pickford sold her United-Artist stock.

Grudgingly, the film studios opened their eyes to the inevitable, and plotted a self-congratulatory campaign in response: movies became "better than ever." Their backslapping program sought to develop qualities that television could not imitate: wide screens, higher fidelity sound, color, lavish spectacle, and, for one unsuccessful moment, three-dimensions by way of stereoscopic polaroid glasses. Nevertheless, by 1960, production output was down to two hundred features. One effect was the loosening of the Hays Office (now the Johnston Office) sanitary controls over film content. Another consequence was the absorption of studios into larger conglomerates. Control of Republic Pictures was leased by Decca/Music Corporation of American in 1960.

LABOR DISPUTE

With the growth of the Hollywood Guilds in the thirties, screen writers were able to take a stronger stand when negotiating with studios.[1] When the Conference of Studio Unions (CSU) called for strikes in 1945, the Screen Writers Guild (SWG), like other craft unions, found itself in the midst of internecine dispute. Like SAG, the Screen Actors Guild, and IATSE, the International Association of Theatrical Stage Employees and Moving Picture Machine Operators, the writers remained on the sidelines, but within CSU and SWG, in which certain factions were Communist Party members, shifts in American communist policy drew lines defining whether one supported the strike or not; as long as the war continued, communists were pledged to no-strike postures.

The first strike led to bloody police confrontations on the Warner lot. The 1946 strike, triggered by a jurisdictional dispute involving the Carpenter's Union, developed into battle between the CSU (a bargaining agent that failed altogether to represent all unions but was supported by some of the crafts) on one side, supported by the communists, and, on the other, the Teamsters, producers, and IA (a new designation of IATSE). Again, the Screen Actors Guild and the Screen Writers Guild kept their neutrality, while each was torn with the procommunist and anticommunist factionalism. The strike resolved to no one's satisfaction, with a congressional investigation pending and a confusion of legal action.

[1] *Some sense of the growth of the Screen Writers Guild and its left-right political schisms will be found in Budd Schulberg,* What Makes Sammy Run? *New York, 1941.*

THE RED MENACE

Following on a House Commerce Committee's investigation of the 1946 strike, the setting for the October, 1947 hearings of the House Unamerican Activities Committee (HUAC), headed by J. Parnell Thomas, was confused with unhealed wounds from labor warfare and exacerbated by a growing American suspicion of the USSR as cold-war policies hardened. Among witnesses called by the committee to testify about communism in Hollywood were screen writers who, with one producer and one director, refused, sometimes with rancorous scorn, to answer any questions about their political allegiances.[2] Within a short period, these men were discharged from their jobs and "unemployable." Increasingly, political affiliations became a basis for job security, and the relation of social ideas to American movies was clouded in dispute.

While executives continued to protest and to believe that their films held nothing subversive or "unAmerican," the behavior of the "Hollywood Ten" or "Unfriendly Ten" at the hearings and of others in support of the besieged witnesses affronted producers' patriotic feelings. It also afforded opportunities to resolve animosities that had been brewing since the strike days, sometimes since the formation of the unions themselves. A procedure evolved by which means "unemployables" might return to "hireable" status through a kind of decontamination process, securing a "clearance lawyer" and recanting or otherwise making public pronouncements that would resound as strongly anticommunist and industry supportive.

In 1951, Hollywood HUAC hearings were again scheduled, this time in Los Angeles rather than Washington, D.C. J. Parnell Thomas had earlier been convicted of padding his payroll and sentenced to a prison term. (He shared a jail with some members of the Unfriendly or Hollywood Ten, the men who had refused to answer his questions and eventually suffered sentences on contempt charges.)

The Korean War was now in progress and anticommunist feeling at a peak. Some Hollywood figures proceded to admit communist

---

[2] *Thirty years later, Ring Lardner Jr., one of the four still-living witnesses, summed up the group's strategy. "Some of the subpoenaed men who were communists wanted to say so, to proudly proclaim an affiliation they had been reluctantly concealing because that was party policy in Hollywood. Their enthusiasm for the stand declined when it was pointed out that the committee's next demand would be to name all the other members they knew.*

Once . . . to answer no such questions (was agreed upon), the remaining decision . . . was whether to base our silence on the First or the Fifth Amendment. . . . For us . . . to use the Fifth back in 1947 would have had several drawbacks.

First, we would have been saying . . . we thought it was a crime to be a Communist. . . .

Second, we recognized . . . there was a danger of a blacklist emerging from these proceedings, and we knew it would be hard for the studios to proscribe us if we were upheld by the courts for asserting our First Amendment rights. But even if we were upheld on the Fifth, the general stigma . . . would make it easier for our bosses to organize and justify a blacklist.

Third . . . while the Fifth could seriously impede the committee's work, and its application to a question about communist membership needed testing, it did not challenge the committee's very existence . . . where Congress was forbidden to legislate, Congress was forbidden to investigate.

In a situation therefore, in which the only safe and acceptable course open to us was to repudiate everything we believed in and prove we meant it by making trouble for other people, we could not be regarded as heroes for choosing a course of decency instead. In fact, we were doubly disqualified from heroic status: We weren't volunteers and we thought we were going to be winners." Ring Lardner Jr., "Thirty Years After the Hollywood Ten," San Francisco Chronicle *(March 25, 1978) p. 32.*

affiliations and to name fellow members. Others were eager to dispel lingering suspicions about their pasts. The result was a list of 342 names, published by the committee in its 1952 and 1953 Annual Reports. All became unemployable unless cleared. Some left the industry. Others departed the country. Some sweated out the period and returned to work. Ironically, occasional excommunists who had "named names" became themselves objects of scorn and sometimes were unemployable for informing. A few figures, such as the writer Dashiell Hammett, stubbornly went to jail rather than testify. Twenty-five years later, rancorous dispute continued over where integrity, where cowardice rested among men and women caught in these litigations.

Hollywood escapist fare pervaded the climate of World War II, with occasional formulaic responses to politics, *Confessions of a Nazi Spy* (1939), and world events, like *Mission to Moscow* (1943), which was based on Ambassador Joseph Davies' experiences in Russia before the USSR had entered the war. Nonetheless, for every *Walk in the Sun* (1945) or *Story of GI Joe* (1945), the war was incessantly and repetitively won by Humphrey Bogart, *Action in the North Atlantic* (1943), Robert Taylor, *Bataan* (1943), and Alan Ladd, *China* (1943).

The HUAC trauma resulted in such curiosities as spouse communists, *I Married a Communist* (1949), eskimo communists in *Red Snow* (1952), a communist disguised as clergy, *The Whip Hand* (1951), and science fictionalized political standoffs in *Red Planet Mars* (1952). Aftershocks resulted in more consequential, because less blatant, kinds of self-defensive plotting and xenophobic suspicion. The fifties was a period of American film during which invaders and monsters from outer space appeared repeatedly, sometimes dangerous and unreachable like *The Thing* (1951), sometimes taking over our minds and free will so that we become automatons of an alien power, as in *The Invasion of the Body Snatchers* (1956) and *It Came From Outer Space* (1953).

Rebellions against the prototypical American norms took childish and self-destructive forms as in *The Wild One* (1954). In *On the Waterfront* (1954), script writer Budd Schulberg, who himself had confessed membership in the Communist Party and named others, had a docks labor boss, his union a cesspool of corruption and underworld payoffs, confronted and bested by Marlon Brando, an innocent who spilled the beans. The villain was played by Lee J. Cobb, who had admitted Party membership and named names in the 1951 hearings. The film was directed by Elia Kazan, who had given names to the Committee the same year. Someone, the film preached, had to break loose from the cycle of fear and oppression and turn against authoritarian domination.

EMERGING SENSIBILITIES

Except as ideology can be said to permeate any cultural expression, few Hollywood films of the period concerned themselves with politics, either directly or by implication. As in Britain, France, and Italy, the usual product might be characterized more accurately as showing dispositions toward greater narrative freedoms, location shooting, ironic twists upon genre patterns, and more evidence of individual stylizations imposed by director, writer, or actor.

The war itself, developing familiarities with documentary authenticities, European imports, and a shift from ethical simplifications of character resulted in more "realistic" approaches in Hollywood entertainment (realism always being relative to the temper of the times). An executive *March of Time* producer from 1933-1943, Louis De Rochemont helped to develop a documentary-like approach to crime and espionage fictions such as *The*

House on 92nd Street (1945) and *Call Northside 777* (1948). Both films were directed by Henry Hathaway, produced by De Rochemont. An excellent example of location production leagued with social concern in Clarence Brown's *Intruder in the Dust* (1949), based on William Faulkner's novel and filmed in the author's Mississippi home town.

Forties and fifties Hollywood was additionally marked by noteworthy productions from studio directors whose skills blended to maximum effect with growing professional autonomies: George Stevens' *A Place in the Sun* (1951) and *Shane* (1953); Fred Zinnemann, *The Men* (1950) and *High Noon* (1952); Delmer Daves, *3:10 to Yuma* (1957); Richard Brooks, *The Blackboard Jungle* (1955). A screen writer for many years, Robert Rossen wrote and directed several films of merit, in particular *All the King's Men* (1949) and *Lilith* (1964), his last. Set in a mental institution, *Lilith* subtly visualizes a scheming girl's schizophrenia, her delusions interspersed with suggestions of webs and the entrapments of male-devouring spiders.

Another writer-turned-director marked with special talent is Abraham Polansky. *Force of Evil* (1948) explores moral corruption with a candor dramatically untypical of its time. *Tell Them Willie Boy is Here* (1969) overlays cowboys and indians upon a pursued-gangster pattern, while equipping both its indian fugitive and sheriff's posse with unexpected self-doubts and anxieties.

The remainder of Chapter 17 examines in greater detail significant American directors of more recent vintage or sensibility.

ROBERT ALDRICH

Robert Aldrich (1918–   )

The Big Leager	1953
World for Ransom	1954
Apache	1954
Vera Cruz	1954
Kiss Me Deadly	1955
The Big Knife	1955
Autumn Leaves	1956
Attack	1956
Ten Seconds to Hell	1958
The Angry Hills	1959
The Last Sunset	1961
Sodoma e Gomorra/Sodom and Gomorrah (Italy)	1962
Whatever Happened to Baby Jane?	1962
Four for Texas	1963
Hush, Hush Sweet Charlotte	1964
The Flight of the Phoenix	1966
The Dirty Dozen	1967
The Legend of Lylah Clare	1968
The Killing of Sister George	1968
Whatever Happened to Aunt Alice?	1968
Too Late the Hero	1969
The Grissom Gang	1970
Alzana's Raid	1972
Emporer of the North Pole	1973
The Longest Yard	1974
Hustle	1976
The Twilight's Last Gleaming	1977
The Choirboys	1978

Fortune placed Aldrich when young in contact with Charlie Chaplin, Joseph Losey, Jean Renoir, and William Wellman. While his own work falls into many genres, including the western *Apache* (1954); war, *Ten Seconds to Hell* (1958); horror, *Hush, Hush, Sweet Charlotte* (1964); and gangster, *The Grissom Gang* (1970), Aldrich effectively reworks his conventions. What emerges is a kind of radicalized play on anticipated values whose tight pacing and sometimes baroque dialogue may hold a viewer's attention while manipulating his expectations.

Kiss Me Deadly (1955) is successful Aldrich, whose excesses, particularly the hot-

The Dirty Dozen. Under Major Reisman (Lee Marvin), convicted murderers and rapists are released from an army prison to conduct a suicidal military raid on a French chateau where German officers recuperate. Maggott (Telly Savalas) tries to sabotage the effort by killing a girl (Dora Reisser). Charles Bronson is another of the heroic, unwholesome twelve. (Museum of Modern Art/Film Stills Archive)

Aldrich uses violence not to resolve audience tensions but as an unsettling force, an alarming security disruption whose brutality is too evident to hide behind any rationalization that the victim "deserves it." In *Attack* (1956), soldiers who are normally sure of their motives and purpose face disfigurement or, worse, futility for the actions. If corruption does not altogether succeed, it hardly fails. In *The Dirty Dozen* (1968), a group of malcontents and criminals seek to buy back their freedom by undertaking a dangerous military mission. In *The Longest Yard* (1974), a penitentiary football team pays a personal price for its victory over the guards, like the reformatory boy in Tony Richardson's *Loneliness of the Long Distance Runner. The Twilight's Last Gleaming* (1977) condenses much of its long government-takeover story into tight-edited multiple-image renderings.

ROBERT ALTMAN

Altman brought to *M.A.S.H.* (1970) some of his experience as a fighter pilot in World War II and the film's barbaric mix of war horror and dark humor comes closer to the intentions of Joseph Heller's novel *Catch 22* than did Mike Nichols' actual film adaptation. Altman's strength rests in establishing the ambiance of a little, isolated society, which may be an emergency field hospital as in *M.A.S.H.*, a western hamlet, *McCabe and Mrs. Miller* (1971), Houston, *Brewster McCloud* (1971), *Nashville* (1975), or Buffalo Bill's Wild West Troupe, *Buffalo Bill and the Indians, or Sitting Bull's History Lesson* (1976).

Always, Altman suggests that each is a microcosm of America, an enclave peopled with credulous boobs. Of Sitting Bull, Annie Oakley says, "He just wants to show the truth to people." Buffalo Bill replies, "I have a better sense of history." Against the common experi-

house language, are to be experienced at their worst in *The Big Knife* (1955), written by Clifford Odets. In the Mickey Spillane piece, *Kiss Me Deadly,* the macho beatings and suspicions that are customary to Spillane's prose emerge, under Aldrich as a neofascist, blundering search for a secret which on discovery threatens detective Hammer himself. Mike's paranoia about incomprehensible cultural forces is evidenced in petty sadisms like breaking an opera lover's Caruso record and squeezing a doctor's hand in his desk drawer. A poem from Christine Rossetti ("Remember me . . ." ") is a clue to the presence of a key in a corpse's stomach.

M.A.S.H. Painless Pole (John Schuck) is universally acceded sexual mastery among his Korean medical outfit. Unaccountably, Pole begins to fear latent homosexuality. At a last supper, attended by Hawkeye (Donald Sutherland) and Trapper (Elliott Gould), among others, Pole ingests what he believes to be a suicide pill. He wakes in the arms of a beautiful nurse. (Museum of Modern Art/Film Stills Archive)

Robert Altman (1925–)

ence of place, Altman locates his characters, who are sometimes many (Nashville is a tour-de-force in this respect), in staged and improvised situations that assume qualities of vignettes when a story line is not tight enough to hold them together. The humor is trendy, outrageous, and sometimes bawdy. Murders in Houston are mysteriously accompanied by the downpour of pigeon droppings. Buffalo Bill's sexual capacity is at odds with his inclination to drink due to the effect of booze on his amorous intentions.

The Altman film represents one commercial fusion of traditional entertainment values with a narrative that is both structurally looser and more an actor-director collaboration than earlier Hollywood permitted. The price paid for semi-improvisation is sometimes semi-intelligibility, but one of the director's talents rests in developing an overall pace and a continuity. This is accomplished in part by maintaining visual consistencies, such as color balances, which help to contain what is often wildly discrepant material. At worst, the combinations do not jell. Buffalo Bill's drunken monologue with the ghost of Sitting Bull, a carryover from the film's theatrical source, cannot sit easily with the rest of the movie. The antics of Elliot Gould as Philip Marlowe in *The Long Goodbye* (1973) simply do not operate as detective satire, because the detective story itself is too ignored to sustain the parody. On the other hand, *Nashville* interweaves its several parts masterfully. Each is so progressively attuned to the dynamics of a forthcoming event, a political rally, that interest is unflagging. As omniscient observers, we can appreciate the fortuitous encounters between characters who do not know one another and yet who will become inextricably involved later in the film. By *Three Women* (1977), Altman had further incorporated dream images, archetypal symbols, and doppelgängers, more Jungian than Gothic, to his irresolute designs. Earlier, these appeared in *Images* (1972).

BUDD BOETTICHER

Boetticher, a bullfighter in his younger years, has used matadors and public enemies as protagonists, but his most successful films have been inexpensive westerns that follow the adventures of Randolph Scott. Strung together like a picaresque epic, the movies underplay dialogue and obvious characterization so that one's understanding of motive and "code of the West" depend both on prior movie experience and on subtleties of behavior. Now aging, Scott must depend on guile as much as skill. His relation to the villains is usually complicated by some action that implicitly re-

quires moral obligation on his part. Each respects the prowess of the other. Rather than imposing modernized conceptions onto the form, Boetticher gives the impression of digging into its conventions to play variations on audience expectation. Boetticher is a minor but fascinating director in *Seven Men From Now* (1956), *The Tall T* (1957), *Buchanan Rides Alone* (1958), and *Ride Lonesome* (1959).

SAMUEL FULLER

Fuller entered journalism as a twelve-year-old copyboy. When a reporter, he covered strikes, crime, executions, murders, and politics. His

Budd Boetticher (1916–   )

One Mysterious Night	1944
Assigned to Danger	1948
Killer Shark	1950
The Bullfighter and the Lady	1951
The Cimarron Kid	1951
Red Ball Express	1952
Horizons West	1952
City Beneath the Sea	1953
Seminole	1953
The Man From the Alamo	1953
Wings of the Hawk	1953
East of Sumatra	1953
The Magnificent Matador	1955
The Killer is Loose	1955
Seven Men From Now	1956
The Tall T	1957
Decision at Sundown	1957
Buchanan Rides Alone	1958
Ride Lonesome	1959
Westbound	1959
Comanche Station	1960
The Rise and Fall of Legs Diamond	1960
Arruza (documentary)	1969
A Time for Dying	1969

Buchanan Rides Alone. As Buchanan, Randolph Scott befriends Juan de la Vega, and the two are held for ransom by Simon Agry, clan boss of Agryville. The final shootout is noteworthy for the number of Agryville citizens who are dispatched. (British National Film Archive/Stills Library)

Samuel Fuller (1911–   )

I Shot Jesse James	1948
The Baron of Arizona	1950
The Steel Helmet	1950
Fixed Bayonets	1951
Park Row	1952
Pickup on South Street	1953
Hell and High Water	1954
House of Bamboo	1955
Run of the Arrow	1957
China Gate	1957
Forty Guns	1957
Verboten!	1958
The Crimson Kimono	1959
Underworld USA	1961
Merrill's Marauders	1962
Shock Corridor	1963
The Naked Kiss	1964
Cross of Iron	1977

films have the quality of sensational journalism. They depend upon stereotyped sexual, national, and occupational characterizations. The action often has the quality of an adventure comic strip, and its rationale that of boilerplate editorials. His idiom is genre with a vengeance, literally vengeance, for plots often depend on personal or national vendettas.

While Fuller shuns the perversities of Siegel or the turnabouts that convolute Aldrich's plots, his films carry their own tension. Elliptical continuity truncates the story into heightened moments, like cartoon panels. Sometimes these story resolutions contradict earlier premises of plot. The prostitute in *The Naked Kiss* (1964) must kill a Korean War hero who is abnormally attracted to young children. *Steel Helmet* (1950) begins as a Korean War adventure and ends with its American patrol dead or insane. Fuller favors grotesque conjunctions. In *Forty Guns* (1957), lovers kiss as a hanged man's feet thump against the wall. A groom is shot at his wedding, falling on his wife as if in sexual embrace.

Pickup on South Street (1953) is vintage Fuller. A small-time pickpocket discovers he has stolen communist espionage microfilm and plays a lone game against police, federal agents, and finally the commies. The matter of allegiance assumes uppermost priority as petty thieves sell one another out but draw the line at espousing foreign ideology. Thelma Ritter, an aging police informer, is strangled by enemy agents when she refuses to cooperate. Richard Widmark, the pickpocket, accompanies her coffin to its pauper's grave, then brutalizes a spy on the subway steps. Characters stop to discuss their politics like Brechtian asides interrupting action in the German theater. Fuller was another director about whom Godard was enthusiastic and appeared as himself in the party sequence of *Pierrot le Fou*. He intoned, "The film is like a battle-ground: love, hate, action, violence, death . . . in one word, emotion."

ELIA KAZAN

Kazan's first films had urban, often "problem" plots, made in the short Hollywood period of social consciousness about discrimination. *Gentleman's Agreement* (1947) and *Pinky* (1949). *Panic in the Streets* (1950) makes excellent use of New Orleans as setting to the frenzied search for a plague victim.

A Streetcar Named Desire (1952) introduced motion-picture audiences to the Stanislavskian stylizations, "The Method" of Actors Studio performance.

Kazan has often worked with actors who came from the Actors Studio, notably Marlon Brando, James Dean, Rod Steiger, Julie Harris, Kim Hunter, Karl Malden, Carroll Baker, and Eli Wallach. In fact, he started the Studio in 1947, an evolution from New York's de-

pression-era, leftist Group Theater. Application of the Stanislavsky system had an appreciable effect on Hollywood style, for it intensified actor presence and the emotionality of interrelationships. Because of its stress on the use of objects to articulate feelings [the way, for example, Lee Remick used a towel to rationalize her desire to touch Montgomery Clift's rain-drenched hair in *Wild River* (1960)], Method direction lent itself to imaginative visuals. Less satisfactory was Kazan's early disposition to pump each scene up to an intense extreme, so that some films are experienced as plateaus of uninterrupted climax.

The "socially-conscious" pictures had sought, with little success, to hold customers in place, by way of "adult" themes, against television's incursion. After Kazan testified

Elia Kazan (1909–   )

The People of the Cumberland (documentary)	1937
It's Up to You (documentary)	1941
A Tree Grows in Brooklyn	1945
Sea of Grass	1947
Boomerang	1947
Gentleman's Agreement	1947
Pinky	1949
Panic in the Streets	1950
A Streetcar Named Desire	1952
Viva Zapata!	1952
Man on a Tightrope	1952
On the Waterfront	1954
East of Eden	1955
Baby Doll	1956
A Face in the Crowd	1957
Wild River	1960
Splendor in the Grass	1961
America, America/The Anatolian Smile	1964
The Arrangement	1969
The Visitors	1972
The Last Tycoon	1976

before HUAC his interest in the exposure of underworld-political collusion extended notions of mature subject matter further. *Viva Zapata!* (1952) suggested that the goals of the Mexican revolution had been compromised when corruption accompanied its success. *Man on a Tightrope* (1952) was a circus story about a troupe trying to escape the Iron Curtain. The agonized indecision of Brando about "ratting" on the longshoreman's union in *On the Waterfront* (1954) can be seen to echo the feelings of friendly committee witnesses, and the young couple in *A Face in the Crowd* (1957) finds it difficult to expose a megalomaniacal radio-television personality whose contempt for his audience is clothed in folksy intimacies. Again, the script was written by Budd Schulberg.

For all its buffoonery, *Baby Doll* (1956) is one of Tennessee Williams' most successful film adaptations. *East of Eden* (1954) captures strengths of John Steinbeck's novel, avoiding the very worst of a top-heavy, creaking plot. In Kazan's fifties films, one locates a progressive disillusionment with "people:" the cowed, submission of workers in *Waterfront*, ignorant poor whites in *Baby Doll*, Lonesome Rhodes' manipulated audiences in *A Face in the Crowd*. *Wild River* (1960) and *Splendor in the Grass* (1961) revert to rural, small-town life of an earlier time characterized by independence of mind, self-reliance, and also provincialisms. *America, America/The Anatolian Smile* (1964) traces the immigration of Kazan's uncle with affection and pride. Kazan himself came to this country from Istanbul when he was four. His preoccupation with shifts and changes in the national consciousness has been evident in the great body of Kazan's work, from *A Tree Grows in Brooklyn* (1945) to *The Arrangement* (1969), although the intensity of the latter film hardly justifies its homilies.

Faithfully, if stiffly, executed, *The Last Tycoon* (1976) (adapted by Harold Pinter) fails to capture that extraordinary and constantly irreconcilable mixture of power and fantasy in thirties Hollywood which permeates F. Scott Fitzgerald's novel.

STANLEY KUBRICK

Kubrick started as a professional photographer, working for *Look* magazine. He wrote, photographed, edited, and directed his first films, the earliest of which were documentaries. Kubrick's understanding of motion-picture technology accounts for much of the ease with which he integrates visual images with their narrative. The early Kubrick style was alternately lax and taut, violent and impulsive. *Killer's Kiss* (1955), while submerging itself in flashbacks and recountings, has a strong action finale whose props (hero armed with manneqoin parts fights villain with axe) anticipates the penis-sculpture weaponry of *A Clockwork Orange* (1971).

By *Paths of Glory* (1958), Kubrick's control of actors is sure and his pacing consistent. It recounts an actual episode in the French army of World War I. An unrealistic attack is ordered. Three soldiers are then randomly selected for execution, accused of cowardice because the military action has failed. Following a trial that mocks justice and logic (if the attack had been impossible, its proof would be the men's dead bodies in the trenches), the three men are shot, one (unable to stand) brought out on a stretcher which is strapped to a pole. In comparison with *King and Country*, *Paths of Glory* misses Losey's gradations of value and of temperment. Here, officers are bad, enlisted men good, but the trial and execution come off forcefully in Kubrick's film, and the predicament of Kirk Douglas as the commander of the men and legal defender becomes prototypical of later Kubrick protagonists. He is caught in the inexorable logic of a society based on insane premises.

Spartacus (1960), written by Dalton

Trumbo about a Roman slave rebellion, is Kubrick's least personal film. A typical Roman-slave-revolt-of-71-B.C. film, *Spartacus* comes alive in training and amphitheater scenes and at the rebels' army camp.

Lolita (1962) discloses another Kubrick ambition, to translate experiences that are essentially literary into moving-picture terms without doing injustice to either medium or to the experience itself. His solution here is radically to reconceive the Vladimir Nabokov characters, and it is Kubrick's least successful adaptation. Entertaining in its own right, *Lolita* as a film abdicates the perverse, bitterly funny vision of Humbert Humbert for an eccentric collection of caricatures whose behavior is more bizarre than outrageous.

Dr. Strangelove, or How I Learned to Stop Worrying and Love the Bomb (1963) has an original scenario. Peter Sellers' roles— President Merkin Muffley, Dr. Strangelove, and Group Captain Lionel Mandrake, as well as General "Buck" Turgidson, General Jack D. Ripper, and Colonel "Bat" Guano, are all comic-strip people. Their logic of straight-ahead, purposive insanity (the President's rationality carries its own brand of madness) propels a story whose humor proceeds inevitably toward nuclear apocalypse. Behavior in the "War Room" only corroborates our suspicions. The underlying premise, that hotline "communication" can simultaneously avert nuclear holocaust and support peace-insuring national defense, provides the blackest paradox. Sellers' Strangelove carries what must be an intentional resemblance to Rotwang of *Metropolis*.

2001: A Space Odyssey (1968) is also not without one-dimensional characters, but here their flatness stems not from grotesqueries but a willful inarticulateness. The apes precede speech, and the last sequences, in the twenty-first century, contain little dialogue except for reluctant sharings of information. In essence, conversation between astronaut Bowman and the 9000 computer, HAL, differs little from other discussion in the film. When HAL's circuitry is tampered with—when is he literally lobotomized—he becomes progressively less capable of speech, finally reverting to pre speech conditions, which gives a final symmetry to the plot; nothing is said thereafter. The last, stargate sequence has greater effect because it affords a structural as well as thematic escape from consequences of human progress.

In making *2001,* Kubrick said that he wished to tell his story in pictures, without recourse to ordinary narrative techniques as far as this was possible. In part, of course, such an undertaking reverts to silent film, and *2001* might be frivolously thought to trace something of movie history: monolith brings technology and speech like Lee De Forest with the audion amplifier. Yet Kubrick's special effects and his design of the final sequences, combined with the characters' willful reticence, gives additional dimension to *2001,* so much so that it is one of the few motion pictures that can be said to create meaning visually without recourse to description.

Again, in *A Clockwork Orange* (1971), Ku-

Stanley Kubrick (1928–   )

Day of the Flight (documentary)	1950
Flying Padre (documentary)	1951
The Seafarers (documentary)	1953
Fear and Desire	1953
Killer's Kiss	1955
The Killing	1956
Paths of Glory	1958
Spartacus	1960
Lolita	1962
Dr. Strangelove (Britain)	1963
2001: a Space Odyssey (Britain)	1968
A Clockwork Orange (Britain)	1971
Barry Lyndon (Britain)	1975

Stanley Kubrick   **419**

Straw Dogs. Completing his dissertation in an English village, an American graduate student (Dustin Hoffman) risks survival in defense of his wife Amy and a mentally defective local boy. They are beseiged in their isolated old house. Peckinpah's film substitutes elements of Gothic horror for his more customary adventure models. (Museum of Modern Art/Film Stills Archive)

brick turned to a novel highly charged with first person stylization, depending largely on vocabulary. In this case, Anthony Burgess' book harbored an original language combining Russian slang, Cockney, and invented words. With narration, Kubrick maintains much of this material, and its cheeful expression by Malcolm McDowell, a delinquent of the future who is programmed through behavior modification to fall ill before he can again resort to sex or violence, provides mocking contrast to the images, first of what he does, then of what is done to him.

As in *Bonnie and Clyde* and *The Wild Bunch,* Kubrick uses violence, here tinged with sexuality, to press an audience toward considering questions about its own makeup. Kubrick even stacks the cards so that Mac-Dowell's victims are unsympathetic and he himself witty, disarming, and energetic. The viewer is asked to effect some kind of recon-

ciliation with the protagonist's cruelties and then with his own loss of will. When, eyes held with clamps, the boy is compelled to look at filmed scenes of sexuality and sadism, we, the onlookers, uneasily realize ourselves to be volunteers in the same experience.

Barry Lyndon (1975) presents yet another novel adaptation, William Thackeray's little-known nineteenth-century simulation of eighteenth-century picaresque. Kubrick's film thus imposes a third century's perception. His production develops a quietude and distancing that constitutes a kind of meditation on the past, a strategy that proves unsettling on audiences who look for the farce of *Tom Jones* or the caricature of Dickens. Instead, Kubrick has chosen another form of stylization, intending to give the appearance of documenting a time that is almost inaccessible to our present understanding. The countryside has the painterly quality of Constable. A special lens was employed that made it possible to film the night interiors with no more than ordinary candles as illumination. The behavior of the characters, while quite comprehensibly self-motivated, is difficult for us to understand, because it lacks the self-consciousness we associate with a society of rules and ceremonies. At the same time, people are often so sure of motive that cruelties, as when Bullingdon shoots Barry Lyndon after his stepfather has fired into the ground, seem disturbingly out of proportion to their apparent meanings. In the past, Kubrick has invented unique techniques to withdraw his authorial commitment to the story's events. In *Barry Lyndon,* this impersonality is haunted by transience, a past created to elude the twentieth century.

ANTHONY MANN

Mann's fifties films were largely westerns, impressive with their wide-screen landscapes. James Stewart was the characteristic Mann hero, and his behavior under stressful conditions suggested a neurotic underscore that differs markedly both from typical Stewart comedy and from different Mann genres, like *The Glenn Miller Story* (1955) where Stewart is continually "looking for that sound" as if it were somehow misplaced, and his greatest conflict rests in manipulating a trombone slide.

Mann was promoted to high budget epics, *El Cid* (1961) and *The Fall of the Roman Empire* (1963), which proved less stiff and underacted than most, but *Winchester 73* (1950), *Bend of the River* (1952), *The Far Country* (1955) and *The Man from Laramie* (1955) remain his best work, supported by subtle, suspicious heroes. Mann died while making *A Dandy in Aspic* (1968), and the film was finished by Laurence Harvey, its star.

SAM PECKINPAH

Peckinpah directed several of the *Gunsmoke* television series and many episodes of *The Rifleman. Ride the High Country* (1961) established his reputation and set a pattern of wrinkled, over-the-hill heroes, here Joel McCrae and Randolph Scott, who embark on a last adventure. Unlike other western directors, Peckinpah does not end at a shootout, but requires his audience to view the aftermath. In *Straw Dogs* (1971), the camera pulls

Anthony Mann (1906–1967)

Dr. Broadway	1942
The Great Flammarion	1945
T Men	1948
Raw Deal	1948
Reign of Terror	1949
Border Incident	1949
Side Street	1949
Devil's Doorway	1950
The Furies	1950
Winchester 73	1950
Quo Vadis	1950
The Tall Target	1951
Bend of the River	1952
Naked Spur	1953
Thunder Bay	1953
The Glenn Miller Story	1954
The Far Country	1955
Strategic Air Command	1955
The Man From Laramie	1955
The Last Frontier	1956
Serenade	1956
The Tin Star	1957
God's Little Acre	1957
Man of the West	1958
El Cid	1961
The Fall of the Roman Empire	1963
The Heroes of Telemark (Britain)	1965
A Dandy in Aspic (completed by Laurence Harvey)	1968

Bonnie and Clyde. Warren Beatty and Faye Dunaway at an early stage of their short career as outlaws. Penn's film deftly grafted a period face on counterestablishment, sixties values. (Museum of Modern Art/Film Stills Archive)

Sam Peckinpah (1926–   )

The Deadly Companions	1961
Ride the High Country	1961
Major Dundee	1965
The Wild Bunch	1968
The Ballad of Cable Hogue	1970
Straw Dogs (Britain)	1971
Pat Garrett and Billy the Kid	1973
Bring Me the Head of Garcia Lorca	1974
The Killer Elite	1976

in tight on the face of Dustin Hoffman, bewildered at his own deeds. In *The Wild Bunch* (1968), bounty hunters search and pillage corpses strewn about a little Mexican village, while the town's children look on, and Peckinpah clearly intends to show us that the young people are heir to the violence, to imply that his period piece has modern overtones.

Memories of Peckinpah films call up apocalyptic violence like the bloodbath that concludes *The Wild Bunch* and the bear trap in *Straw Dogs.* More essentially, Peckinpah seems preoccupied with obsolescence, the cultural expulsion of life styles that cannot adjust to new realities. The Wild Bunch recognized this dead end and elected to die in a final ritual performance. Dustin Hoffman calls on atavistic energies when genteel manner fails in *Straw Dogs*. In terms of this preoccupation, it is significant that Pekinpah describes himself as part Indian, although his ancestry appears to be Dutch.

Of all modern directors, Peckinpah has been most at odds with studio executives, and his career, like Stroheim's, shows few products for its length. Peckinpah was replaced early in the production of *The Cincinnati Kid* (1964). *Major Dundee* (1965) was so thoroughly re-edited that it bears little resemblance to original intentions. Even *The Wild Bunch* is said to have sustained 3,500 studio cuts.

Nostalgia without violence dominates *The Ballad of Cable Hogue* (1970), a clever mixture of humor and stylized epic, constructed like a song narrative about a derelict westerner who chances on water in the desert and lives off his good fortune until falling victim to the commerce he had tried to exploit while yet maintaining his independence. Finally, he dies under the wheel of an automobile, a significant death in terms of Peckinpah's theme of obsolescence.

Peckinpah's violence is neither gratuitous nor exploitive. Deaths and mutilations are highly stylized. Blood spurts like Yellowstone geysers, and shootings have the grand guignol quality of horror films. The slow-motion deaths in *The Wild Bunch*, along with Bonnie's and Clyde's machine gun-riddled bodies, inititated a trend; Hollywood deaths are as stylized as Hollywood lovemaking. Peckinpah argues that the denial of human aggressiveness is one of the corruptive liberal myths of our time, that we must view violence and its consequences if we are to understand ourselves. At the same time, the quirks in Peckinpah's own character are described by fellow workers as central to the films he makes and

responsible, too, for the enmity that surrounds Peckinpah's professional history. Part of the rage seems to be at the rootlessness of modern life. "I detest machines. The problem started when they discovered the wheel. You're not going to tell me the camera is a machine; it is the most marvelous piece of divinity ever created. I've finally gotten to the point where I can believe in silver nitrate.[3]

ARTHUR PENN

Penn attended the unique Black Mountain College in North Carolina and came to film from television and the stage. *The Lefthanded Gun* (1958) originated as TV drama; its conception of Billy the Kid as a repressed homosexual who must act out ritualized conflict with father-figure Pat Garrett is diminished by the fingerpointing, rib-nudging employment of "significant" images and psychology. *Mickey One* (1965) has the odor of undercooked Franz Kafka, leavened by genuinely disturbing moments. It is the story of an untalented night-club comedian who flees unknown

[3] *Dan Yergin, "Peckinpah's Progress,"* New York Times Magazine *(October 31, 1971), p. 92.*

Arthur Penn (1922–)

The Lefthanded Gun	1958
The Miracle Worker	1962
Mickey One	1965
The Chase	1966
Bonnie and Clyde	1967
Alice's Restaurant	1969
Little Big Man	1970
Night Moves	1975
Missouri Breaks	1976

Arthur Penn   423

pursuers. The rebellious Penn figure is neurotically withdrawn, but resolves his isolation with violence. Cruelty and excessive destructiveness are intended both to serve as an expression of today's culture and to diminish protagonists down to sub-heroic status, as in *The Chase* (1966).

Bonnie and Clyde (1967) coalesces many Penn talents, even if Clyde Barrow's impotence carries something of Billy the Kid's left-handed aberrations. The film deftly balances a sympathy for its ingratiating outlaw couple against genuine repugnance at their inevitable descent to behavior that contradicts the early rebellious freedom. Penn's agents of law enforcement and of betrayal are overdarkened, but the sympathy he creates for Bonnie and Clyde proves genuinely unsettling to any audiences who later rethink their identification with the criminals. *Alice's Restaurant* (1969) subdues the Penn pattern of alienation into an

affectionate report on counter-culture life style. The director's images of Alice, her husband, and the setting of their home suggest a developing feel for plot irresolution (endings that are not tied up) that is elaborated in *Little Big Man* (1970).

Missouri Breaks (1976) is somewhat diminished by bravura Marlon Brando-Jack Nicholson performances that do not always interact successfully, giving the impression that they are not peopling the same movie. Nevertheless, it sustains a complicated texture that integrates several contemporary interests and contradictions between current values within a western mode.

ROMAN POLANSKI

Truly international, Polanski was born in Paris and grew up under the German occupation of Poland, abandoned when the Nazis interned his parents in concentration camps. His mother died in Auschwitz. After acting on stage—he appears in several of his own films and stars in *The Tenant* (1976)—Polanksi studied at the Polish film school in Lodz. His shorts, *Two Men and a Wardrobe* (1958), *The Fat and the Lean* (1960), *Mammals* (1960), employ surreal, absurd humor, clearly inspired by Samuel Beckett and Eugene Ionesco, but with roots in a Polish tradition as well, the theater of Stanislaw Ignacy Witkiewicz and of Polanski's friends and peers Slavomir Mrozek and Jerzy Grotowski. Typically, two figures on an open, empty landscape act out impulses normally buried beneath social veneer: master and slave, rejector and rejected.

Knife in the Water (1963) adds a second persistent element of Polanski's work, the neurotic. A boy is invited to sail with a sportswriter and his wife. On board, the males compete, wife as audience. The boy disappears, then returns to have sex with the wife when

Roman Polanski (1933–   )

A Toothy Smile (short)	1957
Breaking Up the Dance (short)	1958
The Lamp (short)	1958
Two Men and a Wardrobe (short)	1958
Where Angels Fall (short)	1959
The Fat and the Lean (short)	1960
Mammals (short)	1960
Knife in the Water (Poland)	1963
Beautiful Swindles (episode of a 4 part film)	1963
Repulsion (England)	1965
Cul-de-sac (England)	1966
The Fearless Vampire Killers (England)	1967
Rosemary's Baby	1968
Macbeth (England)	1971
What?	1973
Chinatown	1974
The Tenant (France)	1976

her husband has left in search. The boy departs. The husband returns, and when he learns what has happened, the couple is left with a residue of rage that will probably sustain their abrasive relationship. Polanki's skillful use of glances, points of view and observations of unobserved behavior remind one of Hitchcock sketching cruelly accurate portraits of a rebellious, competitive youth, an aggressive, insecure husband, and a sullen, repressed wife.

Moving to Britain, Polanski filmed *Repulsion* (1965), the study of a girl who experiences a psychotic episode alone in an apartment. Polanski renders tangible her hallucinations so that the audience becomes a party to the delusions, dwelling on details like a decaying, cooked rabbit. The film leads an unwilling spectator through episodes of growing fervid morbidity. *Cul-de-sac* (1966) again British, is black comedy, filmed in a thirteenth-century fortress in the North Sea where a gangster holds an eccentric couple prisoner. It combines the despair and humilia-

tion of absurd theater with surreal, anarchic emotion, and is a vastly underrated film.

The Fearless Vampire Killers, or Pardon Me, Sir, But Your Teeth are In My Neck (1967) plays horror genre for farce, and is Polanski's least successful film, apparently diminished by twenty minutes cut from the American version. In compensation, it boasts a Jewish vampire who refuses to be offset by crucifixes.

Rosemary's Baby (1968) profited from its normal setting. The director himself says:

What I like is an extremely realistic setting in which there is something that does not fit in with the real. That is what gives an atmosphere. For an atmosphere, all things taken into account, is created with rather simple means. And no doubt it is better created with one mere fly buzzing than by calling to arms some dozens of large sized animals.[4]

---

[4] *Roman Polanski, "Landscape of the Mind,"* Cahiers du Cinéma in English 3 *(1966).*

Chinatown. Faye Dunaway is about to shoot at her father, who is also the father of her daughter. The sequence helps to intensify Dunaway's later death; she is shot while driving away in her car. (Copyright © 1974 by Long Road Productions. All Rights Reserved.) (Museum of Modern Art/ Film Stills Archive)

Such incongruities may rest in human aberration, in surreal juxtaposition, or in the detective-story suspicion that something is not quite right.

Unillusioned seemingly from birth, Polanski lost his wife, Sharon Tate, in the 1969 ritual murder by the Manson cult. His personal version of *Macbeth* (1971) dwells on Shakespeare's slayings in detail. *Chinatown* (1975) casts Jack Nicholson as a thirties detective, shabbily involved in divorce work until he comes upon a scandalous municipal corruption. Here, the director's sense of emotional chaos that seems always to lurk just below the story surface is expressed metaphorically by the Chinese community of Los Angeles. Chinatown is discussed throughout the film but only visited at its conclusion. It is a place where things are better ignored than confronted, where a need for explicit solution and rational explanation is more likely to be met with darkness, silence, or unintelligible speech. When Nicholson finally tries to pull the threads of his case together in customary detective story denouement, the result is tragedy.

The Tenant (1976) places Polanski in a Paris apartment, suspicious that his neighbors are plotting in grand collusion to kill him, as they have the room's previous occupant. Like *Repulsion,* it stares, cold-eyed, at a growing delusion, echoing another of the director's pleasures.

. . . That corresponds to what I like in cinema: atmosphere. And I like too when one forgets, when one shuts oneself up . . . I like to shut myself up. I remember, when I was twelve, fourteen, I liked atmospheres that came from . . . What do I know? . . . Ultimately, enclosed interiors, stifling . . . and liked films like *Lost Weekend, Odd Man Out* . . . especially *Odd Man Out.*[5]

In light of his flight from the country during 1978, it is perhaps incongruous to locate Polanski among American directors, although one would have equal difficulty assimilating him into any other national cinema.

NICHOLAS RAY

Ray left theater to direct *They Live by Night* (1949), one of the few films in which his options were not circumscribed by studio interference, *They Live By Night* was made at RKO at the end of Dore Schary's reign, before the arrival of Howard Hughes. It is a gangster story but peopled with naïve crimi-

Nicholas Ray (1911–   )

They Live by Night	1947 released 1949
A Woman's Secret	1948
Knock on any Door	1948
In a Lonely Place	1950
Born to Be Bad	1950
On Dangerous Ground	1950
Fighting Leathernecks	1951
The Lusty Men	1952
Johnny Guitar	1954
Run for Cover	1954
Rebel Without a Cause	1955
Hot Blood	1955
Bigger Than Life	1956
The True Story of Jesse James	1956
Amere victoire/Bitter Victory (France)	1957
Wind Across the Everglades	1958
Party Girl	1958
The Savage Innocents	1959
King of Kings	1961
55 Days at Peking	1963

[5] *Ibid.*

nals who develop a fantasy world outside the rubrics of society. It is an intriguing dream that incapacitates the characters and makes it impossible for them to live normally.

The issue of outsiders and conformity permeates Ray's better films and is best elaborated in *Rebel Without a Cause* (1955). James Dean escapes the frustrations of a domineering mother and a submissive father by retreating into a private fantasy life in a deserted mansion where his girl, Natalie Wood, plays mother, he father to the unbalanced Sal Mineo.

Like Dean, Wood and Mineo are also explained by neglectful, withholding, or separated parents. Ray's social simplisms derail many critics who may also be dumbfounded by the ardor with which his cause is espoused by French writers. Jean-Luc Godard wrote,

"The cinema is Nicholas Ray," before concluding later that it decidedly was not.

Several of Ray's ventures have been clearly unsuccessful, the ambitious extravaganzas wooden: *King of Kings* (1961), *55 Days at Peking* (1963). Nevertheless, Ray's capacity to delineate characters' behaviors under stressful conditions outside social convention is undeniable. *Johnny Guitar* (1954), for example, develops curious, complicated contradictions in interplay between hero, heroine, villainness, outlaws, and Marshall. Ray makes obvious use of dress (Joan Crawford's changes of costume), armchair psychology (the Dancin' Kid "makes Emma feel like a woman and she doesn't like it, so she wants to hang him"), and convention (the hero without a gun). Yet, in combination, a personal genre stylization emerges with its own appeal.

Johnnie Guitar. Vienna (Joan Crawford) is almost hung at the insistence of Emma (Mercedes McCambridge at Crawford's left), who hates Vienna's femininity and her attractiveness to men. But Johnnie Guitar will sever the rope with a well-placed shot and rescue his old love. (National Film Archive, Ottawa)

DON SIEGEL

Like Aldridge, Siegel operates within generic patterns, most often crime stories. The underlying value schemes tend to more orthodoxy, but Siegel's predisposition toward unbalanced villains, like Mickey Rooney's psychopathic hoodlum in *Baby-Faced Nelson* (1957) and the Eli Wallach killer in *The Line Up* (1958), generates its own manic force, often because of a character's very unpredictability. Siegel is especially successful in translating shootouts and chases into expanded yet taut exercises in the staging and editing of wordless, exciting sequences, like the final reel of *Dirty Harry* (1971).

The Invasion of the Body Snatchers (1956) has become something of a classic in science fiction circles. Kevin McCarthy discovers that an alien force has insinuated giant seed pods into his town. Hidden in family cellars, the pods assume the identities of a home's inhabitants and replace the people. Only McCarthy and his girl escape, and then she is "absorbed." The power of *The Invasion of the Body Snatchers* rests in its evocation of a paranoia which cannot be authenticated by evidence of the senses ("Won't someone believe me?"), of fears that manage so to trigger audience response that the undefined "alien" could be alternately seen as communist, fascist, forces of social conformity, or Senator McCarthy's own threat.

Don Siegel (1912–   )

The Verdict	1946
Night Unto Night	1948
The Big Steel	1949
Duel at Silver Creek	1952
China Venture	1954
Riot in Cell Block Eleven	1954
Private Hell 36	1954
An Annapolis Story	1955
Invasion of the Body Snatchers	1956
Crime in the Streets	1956
Baby-Face Nelson	1957
Spanish Affair	1958
The Line Up	1958
The Gun Runners	1958
Edge of Eternity	1959
Flaming Star	1960
Hell is for Heroes	1962
The Killers	1964
The Hanged Man	1965
Madigan	1967
Coogan's Bluff	1968
Two Mules for Sister Sara	1969
The Beguiled	1970
Dirty Harry	1971
Charley Varrick	1973
The Black Windmill	1974
The Shootist	1976

DOUGLAS SIRK

Sirk is a member of an earlier German-born generation who worked in the theater of kammerspiel and Brecht, but he did not arrive in Hollywood until 1940, after some grandiose, romantic film productions in Germany. Sirk established his reputation by *Magnificent Obsession* (1954), a Lloyd Douglas novel about a playboy who becomes a doctor and restores the eyesight of his love. An able director of soap opera, Sirk managed to employ the genre increasingly for sardonic, often bitter personal purpose. The middle-class families who people his films are empty, alienated humans who vaguely sense their hollowness but cannot grasp its reason or significance.

Sirk's background as a painter contributes heavily to his control over images that are characteristically color and wide screen, his iconography furthering the sociological overtones of the characterizations. In *All That Heaven Allows* (1956), a widow, Jane Wyman, advises her children that the

Magnificent Obsession. Closely following the larger-than-life theatrics of Lloyd Douglas' novel, Sirk added ironic stagings, which critics began to notice ten years later, and Rainer Marie Fassbinder to elaborate two decades later. (From the motion picture *Magnificent Obsession.* Courtesy of Universal Pictures.) (Museum of Modern Art/Film Stills Archive)

Christmas gift they offer of a television set would only confirm her loneliness. The fact that they proceed to get her the TV suggests that the children want to preserve their mother's condition (she is attracted to a local gardener). The appliance appears framed in mistletoe, its screen blank, mirroring Wyman's face as if it can only reflect one isolated spectator. Sirk's later major productions include *A Time to Live and a Time to Die* (1958) and an updated remake of Fannie Hurst's *Imitation of Life* (1959).

In *Written on the Wind* (1957) the sets, at least seen now, are so patently, falsely opulent, emotions so overblown, appeals to our sentimentalities so blatant, that distinctions between "datedness" and cynical contrivance prove impossible to articulate.

Douglas Sirk (1900–)

Hitler's Madmen	1943
Summer Storm	1944
A Scandal in Paris	1946
Lured	1947
Sleep My Love	1948
Shockproof	1949
Slightly French	1949
Mystery Submarine	1950
Has Anybody Seen My Gal?	1952
Meet Me at the Fair	1952
Take Me to Town	1953
All I Desire	1953
Taza, Son of Cochise	1954
Magnificent Obsession	1954
Sign of the Pagan	1954
Captain Lightfoot	1955
All That Heaven Allows	1956
There's Always Tomorrow	1956
Battle Hymn	1956
Written on the Wind	1957
Interlude	1957
The Tarnished Angels	1958
A Time to Love and a Time to Die	1958
Imitation of Life	1959
Partial listing (USA Films)	

Douglas Sirk   429

BILLY WILDER

The contrived aura of innocence that permeated earlier Hollywood films evaporated in cold war years. One phenomenon of the period was the film noir. The central character of this genre was a hybrid of wartime detectives who suffered pervasive evil and human powerlessness. Another disposition appeared in the cynical humor of Billy Wilder.

Wilder began as a journalist in Vienna, and wrote a dozen film scripts in Berlin. These included *Emil and the Detectives* (1931), a popular early sound entertainment, and *Menschen am Sonntag/People on Sunday* (1929), an exceptionally interesting semidocumentary whose credits include directors Robert Siodmak, Fred Zinnemann, and Edgar G. Ulmer. Where Vienna gave Lubitsch a wit whose unillusioned irony lay buried under sex

comedy, Wilder's humor has unsheathed edges. In the late fifties, producer Otto Preminger defied the blacklist to hire Dalton Trumbo, one of the Unfriendly Ten of HUAC fame, to write *Exodus*. Someone asked Wilder whether he would ever do the same, and the director replied that one would have to be careful in his choices. "Only two of them have talent. The rest are just unfriendly." Upon his exposure to existentialism, Wilder tried to concoct a plot. This boy falls in love with his mother and marries her. They live together quite happily until one day he learns that she isn't his mother. He commits suicide.

In Hollywood, Wilder wrote two scripts for Lubitsch, including *Ninotchka*. His own films have often been coauthored, first with Charles Brackett, then I. A. L. Diamond. Wilder's *Double Indemnity* (1944) defines some of the despairing noir mode, and *The Lost Weekend* (1945) gave unprecedented realism to an alcoholic's behavior patterns translated visually through expressionist images.

Sunset Boulevard (1950) provided a rare, unfantasized view of the decay and self-delusion behind Hollywood's glamour, its nostalgia for a happier period of self-indulgence. As Norma Desmond, an aging silent star, Gloria Swanson lives in a Sunset Boulevard mansion, surrounded by momentos of the twenties and attended by Erich von Stroheim, who was once her husband and director and now plays servant, protecting her from the outside and its disillusions. She hires William Holden to polish a script which will provide her comeback, keeping him as a lover and corrupting his relations to a young woman and fellow writer. The story is narrated by Holden, curiously beginning with the police discovery of his corpse in Norma Desmond's swimming pool. If *Sunset Boulevard* now betrays contrived and studied titillation, Swanson's performance, larger than life, admirably fits the movie role.

Wilder's *Ace in the Hole/The Big Carnival* (1951) and *Stalag 17* (1953) further amplified a view that portrays few human aspirations to

Billy Wilder (1906–   )

The Major and the Minor	1942
Five Graves to Cairo	1943
Double Indemnity	1944
The Lost Weekend	1945
The Emperor Waltz	1947
A Foreign Affair	1948
Sunset Boulevard	1950
Ace in the Hole	1951
Stalag 17	1953
Sabrina	1954
The Seven Year Itch	1955
Love in the Afternoon	1957
Witness for the Prosecution	1958
Some Like It Hot	1959
The Apartment	1960
One, Two, Three	1961
Irma la Douce	1963
Kiss me, Stupid	1964
The Fortune Cookie	1966
The Private Life of Sherlock Holmes (British)	1970
Avanti	1972
The Front Page	1974

Sunset Boulevard. In the evenings, Norma Desmond looks at her old films. This night she and Joe Gillis are watching a sequence from *Queen Kelly:* the scene in which Kitty Kelly prays that she may meet Prince Wolfram again. Stroheim is projecting the picture. (Copyright © 1950 by Paramount Pictures. All Rights Reserved.) (Museum of Modern Art/Film Stills Archive)

their advantage. Later films, including two with Marilyn Monroe, have often muted the Wilder pessimism, or perhaps sublimated its rancor in disguised form. *The Private Life of Sherlock Holmes* (done in Britain in 1970) finds the sleuth inclined toward unjustified egotism and questionably interested in Watson; it is unfortunate that several episodes of the Wilder-Diamond script were cut from the final film.

Summary

Major Hollywood directors, each in personal fashion, have developed individual solutions to the problem of television's competition for audience. An Altman or Peckinpah film will differ both in kind and degree from broadcast family fare. Even so, *McCabe and Mrs. Miller* and *The Wild Bunch,* however cut, quickly find their way to TV replay, while *M.A.S.H.* and *Bonnie and Clyde* themselves nurture television excess by inspiring style at the expense of substance.

In certain key respects, the role of Hollywood director has undergone essential redefinition within the past decade, a period when most of the older directors discussed in Chapter 12 have been forced to reduce their output considerably. Interviewed today, the Hollywood director will more likely discuss how he was finally able to mount a production that had been in the works for years, rather than talking about *making* a film. As financing and distribution patterns shift (and often deteriorate), accessibility to the means of production becomes the more ellusive to anyone but the authors of blockbusters. From an industry of prodigious output, Southern California bodes to become increasingly barren of mass production geared for mass theater consumption.

Some of these more recent trends will be examined in this book's Afterword. More immediately, sharply in contrast to such commercial ventures, experimental film maintains altogether different traditions, unique to themselves. Its artists may, too, seek maximal effect on their audiences, but these are most characteristically realized through rejection rather than confirmation of conventions. The heritage of the avant-garde constitutes Chapter 18.

Bibliography

Andrews, Nigel. "Sam Peckinpah: The Survivor and the Individual," *Sight and Sound* (Spring 1973).

Baker, Charles. "The Theme of Structure in the Films of Robert Altman," *Journal of Popular Film* (Summer 1973).

Belmons, Jacques. *Roman Polanski.* Paris, 1971.

Billings, Pat and Allen Eyles. *Hollywood Today.* New York, 1971.

Burgess, Anthony. *A Clockwork Orange.* New York, 1965.

Butler, John. *The Cinema of Roman Polanski.* London, 1970.

Cawelti, John, comp. *Focus on Bonnie and Clyde.* Englewood Cliffs, 1973.

Ciment, Michael. *Kazan on Kazan.* New York, 1974.

Clarke, Arthur C. and Stanley Kubrick. *2001: A Space Odyssey.* New York, 1968.

Cogley, John. *Report on Blacklisting V. 1 Movies.* 1956.

Collins, Gary. "Kazan in the Fifties," *Velvet Light Trap* 11 (1974).

Corliss, Richard. *Talking Pictures.* New York, 1974.

Cowie, Peter. *Fifty Major Film Makers.* Cranbury, N.J., 1975.

Deming, Barbara. *Running Away From Myself.* New York, 1969.

DeVries, Daniel. *The Films of Stanley Kubrick.* Grand Rapids, 1973.

Diamond, I. A. L. and Billy Wilder. *The Apartment* and *The Fortune Cookie.* London, 1971.

Dowdy, Andrew. *The Films of the Fifties.* New York, 1973.

Durgnat, Raymond. *Films and Feeling.* Cambridge, Mass. 1967.

———. *The Crazy Mirror.* London, 1969.

Evans. Max. *Sam Peckinpah.* Vermillion, S. D., 1972.

Films Heritage 10 (Winter 1974-75). Devoted to Peckinpah.

Gelmis, Joseph. *The Film Director as Superstar.* Garden City, 1970.

Gow, Gordon. *Hollywood in the Fifties.* New York, 1971.

Halliday, Jon. "Douglas Sirk's *All That Heaven Allows,*" *Monogram* 4 (1972).

Hardy, Phil. *Samuel Fuller.* New York, 1970.

Higham, Charles. "Hollywood Boulevard 1965," *Sight and Sound* (Autumn 1965).

———. *Hollywood at Sunset.* New York, 1972.

Higham, Charles and Joel Greenberg. *The Celluloid Muse.* Chicago, 1969.

———. *Hollywood in the Forties.* New York, 1970.

Houston, Penelope. *The Contemporary Cinema.* Baltimore, 1963.

Johnson, Robert K. *Francis Ford Coppola.* Boston, 1977.

Kagon, Norman. *The Cinema of Stanley Kubrick.* New York, 1972.

Kané, Pascal. *The Cinema of Roman Polanski*. Paris, 1970.

Kaminsky, Stuart M. "Don Siegel and *Baby Face Nelson*," *The Velvet Light Trap* 11 (1974).

Kitses, Demetrius John. *Horizons West*. London, 1969.

Kriedl, John Francis. *Nicholas Ray*. Boston, 1977.

Koszarski, Richard, ed. *Hollywood Directors 1941-1976*. New York, 1977.

Krueger, Eric. "Robert Aldrich's *Attack!*" *Journal of Popular Film* (Summer, 1973).

Kubrick, Stanley and John Anthony Burgess. *A Clockwork Orange*. New York, 1972.

Kubrick Stanley, Peter George and Terry Southern. *Dr. Strangelove, or How I Learned to Stop Worrying and Love the Bomb*. New York, 1963.

Lovell, Alan. *Don Siegel*. London, n.d.

McArthur, Colin. "Sam Peckinpah's West," *Sight and Sound* (Autumn 1967).

———. "Polanski," *Sight and Sound* (Winter 1968–69).

Madsen, Axel. *Billy Wilder*. London, 1968.

Manvell, Roger. *New Cinema in the U.S.A.* London, 1968.

Miller, Mark. "In Defense of Sam Peckinpah," *Film Quarterly* (Spring 1975).

Peckinpah, Sam. "Interview," *Playboy* (March 1972).

Penn, Arthur and Venable Herndon. *Alice's Restaurant*. Garden City, 1970.

Phillips, Gene D. *Stanley Kubrick: A Film Odyssey*. New York, 1975.

Polanski, Roman. "Landscape of a Mind," *Cahiers du Cinéma in English* 3 (1966).

———. *Three Film Scripts*. New York, 1975.

Sarris, Andrew. *The American Cinema*. New York, 1968.

Rieder, Howard. "Memories of Mr. Magoo," *Cinema Journal* (Spring 1969).

Robinson, George. "Three by Aldrich," *Velvet Light Trap* 11 (1974).

Shadoian, Jack. *Dreams and Dead Ends*. Cambridge, 1977.

Shain, Russell. "Hollywood's Cold War," *Journal of Popular Film* (Spring 1975).

———. *An Analysis of Motion Pictures about War 1930-1970*. New York, 1976.

Shaffer, Lawrence. "*The Wild Bunch* vs. *Straw Dogs*," *Sight and Sound* (Spring 1972).

Sherman, Eric and Martin Rubin. *The Director's Event*. New York, 1969.

Sklar, Robert. *Movie-Made America*. New York, 1975.

Stuart, Frederic. *Effect of TV on the Motion Picture and Radio Industries*. New York, 1976.

Thomas, Tony. *The Films of the Forties*. Secaucus, N.J., 1975.

Trumbo, Dalton. *The Time of the Toad*. New York, 1972.

Velvet Light Trap 11 "The Fifties," (Winter 1974).

Walker, Alexander. *Stanley Kubrick Directs*. New York, 1971.

Whitehall, Richard. "Talking with Peckinpah," *Sight and Sound* (Autumn 1969).

Wilmington, Mike. "Nicholas Ray on the Years at RKO," *Velvet Light Trap* 10,11 (1973, 1974).

Wood, Michael. *America in the Movies*. New York, 1975.

Wood, Robin. *Arthur Penn*. London, 1967.

Wood, Tom. *The Bright Side of Billy Wilder, Primarily*. Garden City, 1970.

Yergin, Dan. "Peckinpah's Progress," *New York Times Magazine* (October 31, 1971).

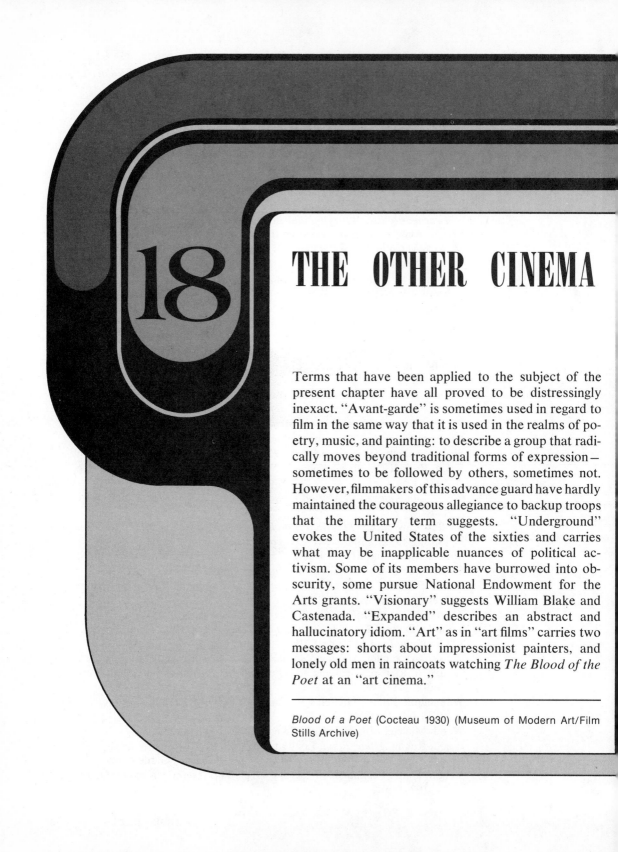

18 THE OTHER CINEMA

Terms that have been applied to the subject of the present chapter have all proved to be distressingly inexact. "Avant-garde" is sometimes used in regard to film in the same way that it is used in the realms of poetry, music, and painting: to describe a group that radically moves beyond traditional forms of expression — sometimes to be followed by others, sometimes not. However, filmmakers of this advance guard have hardly maintained the courageous allegiance to backup troops that the military term suggests. "Underground" evokes the United States of the sixties and carries what may be inapplicable nuances of political activism. Some of its members have burrowed into obscurity, some pursue National Endowment for the Arts grants. "Visionary" suggests William Blake and Castenada. "Expanded" describes an abstract and hallucinatory idiom. "Art" as in "art films" carries two messages: shorts about impressionist painters, and lonely old men in raincoats watching *The Blood of the Poet* at an "art cinema."

Blood of a Poet (Cocteau 1930) (Museum of Modern Art/Film Stills Archive)

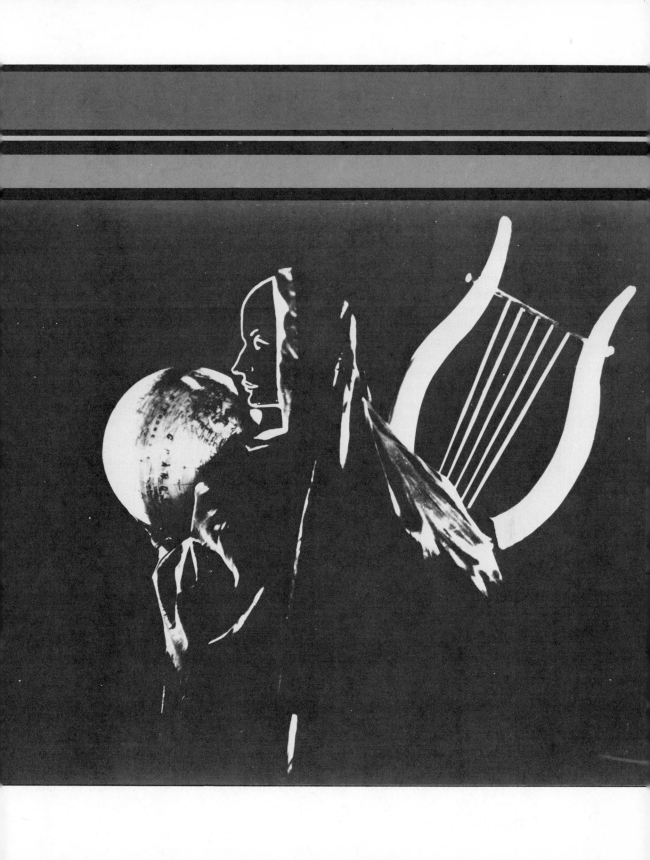

Whatever its name, a tradition exists that can be traced back as far as one's practicing definition implies. If fantasy figures in the connotation, Méliès is father, before him, stage illusionism and fairy tales, Surrealism lurks behind Winsor McCay, Otto Messmer's *Felix the Cat* and Fantômas. The French term *fantastique* suggests what bizarre consequences follow when unnatural, monstrous elements impose themselves onto ordinary, placid reality.

In any case, this separate tradition derives from graphic, musical, and poetic sources more directly than from theater, prose, and the realistic narrative. "Experimental" expresses much of the motive and many of the artists, but Eisenstein, Oshima, Fassbinder, Gance, and Skolimowski are experimentalists as well, without altogether departing from narrative conventions. McLaren, Fellini, and Bergman reach large audiences; perhaps "experimental" film ought never to be considered with relation to audience size or receptivity. In theory it is designed for less "practical" purposes, like pure research; in practice, however, the motives of the researcher may prove to be less pure than his design.

EUROPE

After the holocaust of World War I, nineteeth-century naturalistic theater and fiction reflected no more than one stratum of popular taste. Admittedly, that layer was considerable and one well served by mass-distributed film, but energetic thrusts of experiment were sprouting in adjacent art fields, heavily influenced by such contemporary movements as dada, surrealism, futurism, psychoanalysis, analytic cubism and the modern drama of figures like Antonin Artaud and Alfred Jarry.

The tendency toward fragmentation, which had so affected painters Pablo Picasso and Juan Gris years earlier, accelerated and spread after the war. A subculture emerged that sought meaning in art and human relations in the ateliers and sidewalk cafes rather than through politics and newspaper reports. A million human beings perished on the Russian front in 1916, another million at Verdun, untold numbers at other sites and "offensives." For many artists the only conceivable response was protest. Protest might take the form of absurdist gesture, as in dada, or the more coherent indignation that underlay surrealism. A common cause proceeded on different fronts, much of it jointly impelled by Marx and Freud.

At the time of film's birth, the mechanics of industrial civilization seemed to herald utopian reform. Technology's presence on the human landscape served, in Apollinaire's phrase, to "liberate reality from its assumed synchronicity with the natural." Cubism and fauvism, presenting canvases unlike what Eugene O'Neill termed "holding the family Kodak up to nature," affirmed technology as much as they rejected photographic fidelity.

Disillusion

Futurism had celebrated the machine, glorifying its ritual movements and precision, but the wedding of technology and armaments had been bitterly attended. The war catalyzed new confrontations with the future; assembly lines could now be recognized not as serving to level social inequalities but to rigidify them. Rationality appeared to be an untrustworthy feature of modern society.

Einstein's theory of relativity was not viewed as an incursion of rationality into broader fields. Instead, it affirmed the untrustworthiness of what might be thought to be "true." Artists explored cultural anthropology not in search of structural analyses of the social fabric but to find new manifestations of myth, to tap images of unexpressed "instinct," as in Europe's rage for African masks and its enthusiasm toward American jazz. Freud proposed that consciousness, which at least pretended to rationality, was in truth a servant of unadmitted, nonrational impulses. Popular Freudianism saw consciousness alternately as subverting and assuaging what was "natural," what was repressed by social institutions.

Dada

One response was dada, which guised a bleak, dour vision in its puns and jokes. The definitive Dada action would trigger social disintegration through negation, abstraction, and obsenity, ultimately through suicide. In essence, the gesture was theatrical, taking place before spectators whether on stage, in poetry, art, or film. However, its performance expressed nothing more than one illuminating moment of perception. The notion of "masterpiece" was antithetical to dada, for dada rejected society itself. Film's transitoriness was attractive.

Painter and photographer, a dadaist later to turn surrealist, Man Ray prepared his first film for a July 6, 1923 soirée already tense about its reception because of a dispute between dadaist Tristan Tzara and surrealist André Breton that would color the evening. On Tzara's suggestion, Ray applied to movies a technique he had used earlier on still photographs, what he termed Rayograms. He sprinkled salt and pepper, pins and tacks on raw film, then exposed, brushed off, and developed the results. A few photographed shots were added, and Ray's product titled *The Return to Reason*. When the film broke during projection, its audience escaped, perhaps exasperated and ignorant of the fact that the entire duration of the movie was three minutes. Fights led to police interference, and the evening became a dada success.

Ray's *Emak Bakia* (1926) intended to satirize film. It was built from abstracted images, some created by throwing a camera into the air over a flock of unnerved sheep, plus shots of Roy's friend Kiki doing the Charleston and a man tearing shirt collars in halves. The title refers to a villa where Ray began the enterprise and means "Leave me alone" in Basque. It is subtitled "*The Reason for this Extravagance.*"

The Mystery of the Chateau of Dice (1929) was built around an improvised adventure filmed at a house party hosted in the modern Provence estate of the Vicomte Charles de Noailles, who later sponsored Jean Cocteau's *Blood of a Poet* and Buñuel's *L'Age d'or/The Age of Gold*. The resemblance of the chateau architecture to dice reminded Ray of a Mallarmé poem, "A Throw of the Dice Can Never Do Away with Chance." Although the film devotes occasional and unserious attention to a mysterious dice throw whose outcomes bear some inexplicable relation to fate, most of *Mystery* documents the high spirits of the guests with exuberant camera movement.

An airplane-like formation of hats assumes independent life in *Ghosts Before Breakfast* (1928) by Hans Richter, who had joined dada in Zurich as early as 1916. René Clair's *The Crazy Ray* (1923) was perhaps too lighthearted for dada's serious fun, but its mad scientist carries some of technology's danger about him. *Entr'acte* (1924) was prepared for a dada event, a ballet whose title, *Relâché* (performance suspended) effectively infused obstacles into the purchase of tickets at the Theatre des Champs-Élysées. The presence in the film of Ray, Duchamp, Francis Picabia, and Erik Satie underlines a dada-surrealist tenet, that one's self, rather than his creations, is his truest expression. At best, art is only a momentary statement about life.

Further, the injection of self into work, foreshadowing Vertov and Brecht, emphasized that a creative act was inextricably tied to the circumstances of its production, that illusion, like rationality, constituted an esthetic snare. The erratic discontinuity of images derived by chance rejected the values of rational expectation for the sake of moment-to-moment experience. The last idea was developed further by Clair's brother, Henri Chomette, in three short films. *Jeux de reflects et de vitesse* (1925), *Cinq minutes de cinéma pur* (1925), and *A quoi rêvent les jeunes filles* (1927) isolate images, then bundle them together into unorganized, sequential effusions of editing.

Divorced of any other overtones, one of the notions which arose from twenties film experimentation was the concept of "pure" film (cf. *Cinq minutes de cinéma pur*), an art medium that, like fauve, cubist, and abstract painting, might exist without reference to more realistic modes like literature or theater, or to the world it photographed.

Surrealism

By definition, dada countenanced no positive principles. Its ideal was nothingness, a movement without a future. Growing from it, surrealism absorbed many dada tenets and members. Where dada was despairing, its unamused laughter still heard in the theater of the absurd, surrealism felt excitement, even joy, in the mysterious. Because it denied rationality, because it could only be sensed, never lived except momentarily, Freud's vision of the subconscious fascinated the surrealists. It seemed the final, most awesome mystery; even beauty might lie there. The riches of the subconscious could be tapped through various strategies: free association, chance juxtapositions, and the dream among them. An act of stark performance might break through the bindings of rationality to unite a spectator with the surreal mystery. Surrealism returned artist and audience to a shared experience.

Anemic Cinema. "Let us avoid the running sores of the eskimos of the beautiful words." (Museum of Modern Art/Film Stills Archive)

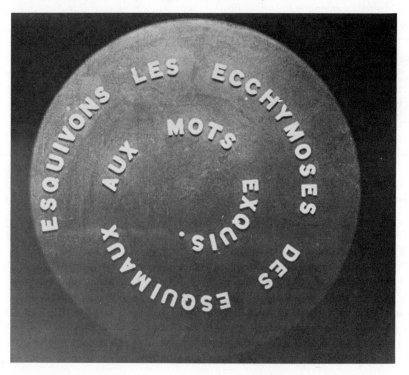

Yet behind the exultant element of surrealism there remained a lurking rage, inherited from dada, which found convention and social institutions to be killers of the dream. Audiences represented society. This contradiction marks the sometimes rejecting, sometimes embracing relation between much avant-garde film and its spectators. In the cases of Buñuel's *Un Chien andalou/An Andalusian Dog* and *L'Age d'or,* (considered in detail in Chapter 19) history has absorbed the rage, like indulgent parents who swallow up their child's angry feelings and so leave him powerless.

Other films have maintained more isolation, less known, perhaps, because their experiments developed effective, built-in self protections. Inspired by surrealist Robert Desnos' poem, in *L'Etoile de mer* (1929), Man Ray used a lens mottled with grease and other distorting agents. Pictures of Kiki in the nude, Desnos, and another male have a quality of the half-seen, intended to provide visual equivalents to the poem's images. In toto, Ray's films display many of the period avant-garde tendencies: abstraction, humor, willful unconcern with narrative design, a willingness to share personal experience, a pleasure in boring or affronting the onlooker.

Man Ray's close friend, a germinal figure in surrealism, Marcel Duchamp, made one film, *Anemic Cinéma* (1927). It consists of a documentation of display devices Duchamp had created, revolving discs patterned with continuous, circling lines and edged by punning statements that ridicule easy interpretation. As one stares at the revolutions (the concept itself another pun), the perceptions become alternately centripetal or centrifugal, and depth sensations increase. The center may be either the nearest tip of an extended cone or its most recessed distance.

Hans Richter turned to documentary work for years, then came to New York City, by wartime a center for displaced European artists. *Dreams That Money Can Buy* (1946)

presents a succession of surreal fantasies done in collaboration with Fernand Leger, Max Ernst, Man Ray, Marcel Duchamp and Alexander Calder. *8 × 8*, made in Switzerland in 1957, adapts surrealism to chess, a pastime common to many of the artists.

Ballet mécanique

Fernand Leger combined a number of experimental impulses in *Ballet mécanique* (1924), photographed by Dudley Murphy and, in small part, Man Ray. Leger transferred to film his current graphic interest in objects isolated from customary context and perspective so that they assumed new meanings when they were literally seen in a different way. Film's capacity for great, magnified closeups seemed to Leger ideal for such an enterprise.

A transparent object can remain immobile, and light will give it movement. An opaque object can then be moved in rhythm with the tempo of the transparent object. In this way an enormous variety of effects can be achieved by the use of totally different objects having in themselves absolutely no expression, but handled with understanding and knowledge. Light is everything. It transforms an object completely. It becomes an independent personality.[1]

---

[1] *Fernand Leger, "A New Realism—The Object,"* Little Review *(Winter 1926). Reprinted in Lewis Jacobs,* Introduction To The Art of the Movies. *New York, 1960. Leger's mechanical designs can be seen in* The Late Matthew Pascal *(1925), which was noted in Chapter 7 and, earlier, in another work for Marcel L'Herbier:* L'Inhumaine *(1923). L'Herbier's previous film was garishly melodramatic and unsuccessful but for the Leger decor and what is apparently an actual documentation of a rioting audience at a Georges Antheil concert. The patrons include Joyce, Picasso, Ray, Satie, Darius Milhaud, Ezra Pound, and the Prince of Monaco! Leger's scientific laboratory set is an involved, overlapping confusion of thrusting, swinging, revolving geometric shapes.*

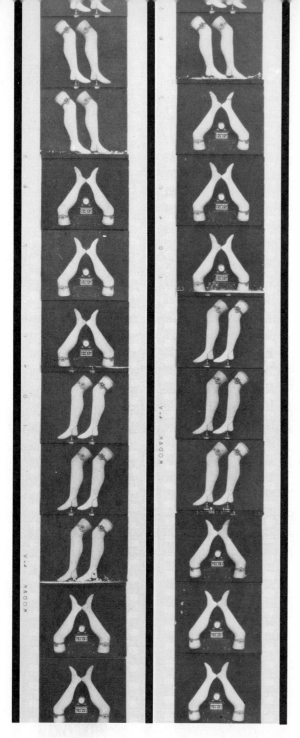

Ballet mécanique. Leger's animation of manniken legs can be seen, by examination of the film, to be composed in units of threes. (Museum of Modern Art/Film Stills Archive)

Ballet mécanique is organized into seven sections, sandwiched by an introduction and epilogue that show a cutout, animated, Charlie-Chaplinesque cubist figure disintegrating into its parts, leaving only a head in conclusion. Each section playfully employs objects whose size and movement rhythmically counterpoint one another within the composition or by edited juxtapositions: Christmas tree ornaments, saucepan lids, a typewriter, numbers, bottles. Object identification is unimportant except as successive, flashing incongruities make their dadaist point. Kiki, displaying her teeth in unamused smile, and Katherine Murphy, an Isodora Duncan dancer, appear at intervals, serving in part to support a Leger-surrealist maxim, that, as living and non-living things become indistinguishable, both may be better understood. A film loop of a washerwoman endlessly, cyclically climbing the same series of steps, unites human rhythm and machine rhythm.

Circles and triangles remind one of the Richter-Eggeling-Ruttmann abstract films. Kiki's eyes anticipate Man Ray's forthcoming *Emak Bakia*. A tumbling succession of objects foreshadow "eyewashes" to follow years later. In *Ballet mécanique* they are unlinked but for playful association (perhaps a flashing shoe and hat have male-female sex implication) and likeness of form (from revolving machine to model's eye). The film is a French avant-garde lexicon whose denial of narrativity is defiantly sustained by optical interest alone.

The Dream

For all its imagination and high spirits, the idiom of Duchamp, Leger, Chomette, Ray and early Clair was not to reassert itself for years. Instead, experimentation chose to blaze another path, the equation of film with experience akin to Richter's *Dreams That Money Can Buy*. This route held closer ties to poetry and to experimental theater. Strindberg's *A*

Dream Play had been popular since 1907. *Mathusalem or the Eternal Bourgeois* by Yvan Goll was written in 1919 and first performed in 1927. It employed Antonin Artaud in filmed portions that depicted a pompous businessman's dreams.

Associated with the impressionist group for which Louis Delluc was spokesman, Germaine Dulac made a variety of films between 1915 and 1940. *The Smiling Madame Beaudet* (1923) sympathetically views an unhappy wife of a dominating bourgeois husband. Her dreams of revenge provide a kind of psychological study. Actor, playwright, and essayist, Antonin Artaud supplied Dulac with a script for *The Seashell and the Clergyman* (1928), which concerned the sexual fantasies of a curate. Freudian symbolism is so obvious that the film seems almost satiric of surrealist precepts, and Artaud, whose attitude toward women was to say the least suspicious, disrupted the movie screening with denunciations of Dulac for violently altering his intentions.[2]

Jean Cocteau

Cocteau's first film, *Blood of a Poet,* appeared with music and narration in 1930. He denied surrealist intention,[3] but, like the Buñuel-Dali collaborations, *Blood of a Poet* employs acting-out behaviors, designed in episodes. In Cocteau's case, the material is weighted by symbols (he said heraldry was a key) and a cumulative design that owes more to traditional French dramaturgy than to free association.

Cocteau had written an earlier play in 1921,

The Wedding on the Eiffel Tower, whose nonsense was acclaimed by the dadaists, and humor is not absent from *Blood of a Poet,* but the film is more essentially a thoughtful invocation of the Orpheus myth, itself the subject of another one-act Cocteau play. The poet enters a dream world that is his own mind, represented as the Hôtel des Folies. Peering through keyholes into private hotel room universes, the poet views life's mysteries and absurdities in tableaux of sex, death, drugs, childhood, and revolution. He becomes involved in a card gamble with his muse and loses, finally committing suicide, albeit symbolically, for the amusement of an aristocratic audience.

The story is told with camera tricks and highly stylized design, all contained within the apparent time a toppling, dynamited chimney takes to collapse. One of its central questions is the poet's relation to his work and to his public.[4] From works of art, he learns secrets that will enable him to explore the Hôtel des Folies. However, the poet is led to smash a classic statue, because energies of modernism require us to reject what has become fossilized into ineffective objects that have been rendered inert by public acceptance. It is understood that whatever the poet himself creates will become a statue. Beneath his guise of entertainer, Cocteau is unillusioned about the poet's "immortality" and about his temptations.

In many respects, *Blood of a Poet* encapsulates Cocteau's film career. While other work often absorbed him, he returned to filmmaking intermittently over a thirty-year period, sometimes as the screenwriter of his own material directed by others: *L'Eternel retour* (1943), *Les Enfants terribles* (1950). Sometimes Cocteau reworked other sources for scripts: *Les Dames du bois de Boulogne*

---

[2] *Artaud's script may be compared with the film by consulting its printed version in The Tulane* Drama Review *T33 (Fall 1966).*

[3] *It was said at the time of production that when he heard Buñuel was putting a cow in a bed for a sequence of* L'Age d'or, *Cocteau quickly added a cow to his film.*

[4] *Himself a poet, painter, playwright and novelist, Cocteau uses "poet" as emblematic of all artists.*

(1945), *Thomas l'imposteur* (1965). (*See* Chapter 14.) Cocteau himself directed five features beyond his first. *Beauty and the Beast* (1946) proved to be an elaborate, engaging version of the fairy tale in which the beast suffers human agonies, and Beauty's honest love provides his salvation.

With *Orphée* (1949), Cocteau returned to obsessive mythic preoccupations. Here Orpheus (Jean Marais) is a popular poet, threatened by a new generation who locate him among the Establishment. A rival, Cegeste, is killed by mysterious motorcyclists who are in fact angels of Death, a beautiful woman, played by Marie Casares. Orpheus' wife, Eurydice, is taken to the underworld, but aided by Heurtebise, another visitor from the underworld guised as the family chauffeur. Orpheus descends to rescue Eurydice even though he and Death have fallen in love. Death sacrifices herself to ensure the couple's survival. The underworld adventure occurs within a letter's fall into a mailbox.

Orphée smoothly integrates optical trickery into a story told with unprepossessing naturalness. As in *Blood of a Poet,* passage to the underworld occurs by way of mirrors where "throughout your life you will see Death at work like bees in a glass hive." The underworld is approached through war ruins, the Zone, where somnambulatory figures wander and Orpheus runs in slow motion to keep up with Heurtebise, who advances without moving his legs. Destiny is ruled by a panel of bureaucrats. Orpheus is heralded as a rejuvenated artist when he publishes the transcriptions of incoherent phrases that are broadcast through his car radio; they are being sent from the underworld by Cegeste.

The cycle concludes with *The Testament of Orpheus* (1959), a reversion to private, anecdotal, self-revelatory and allegorical conditions of *Blood of a Poet.* The action is stylized in the extreme, a series of quixotic, sometimes wry episodes that commence at the final scene of *Orphée,* Heurtebise and Death being led

away to eternities of punishment. *Testament* is peopled with old friends, like Picasso, Charles Aznavour and Yul Brynner, Cocteau himself appears as a foppish eighteenth-century figure whose concerns about immortality through art now consist of humorous epigrams. Cocteau's work has affected a generation of later experimental filmmakers and commercial directors as well, in particular Alain Resnais, who said that while making *Hiroshima mon amour* in Japan he discovered the key by which he might communicate intentions to the Japanese crew was through reference to Cocteau.

AMERICAN EXPERIMENTATION

Impressionism and expressionism predominate in early American experiment. *Manhatta* by Charles Sheeler and Paul Strand (1924) reduces the cityscape to depersonalized glimpses of buildings and movements; the combination of atmosphere and abstraction is found as well in Ralph Steiner's *H_2O* (1929), *Surf and Seaweed* (1930), and *Mechanical Principles* (1930). Like Strand, Steiner was originally a still photographer.

Atmosphere studies gave way to camera subjectively in Lewis Jacobs' *Mobile Composition* (1930), depicting a developing attraction between a couple by way of detailed closeups and camera movement. Jacobs' *The Story of a Nobody* (1930) attempted to personalize the identities of two characters by showing the objects each sees.

A short table-top film, *The Life and Death of 9413 — A Hollywood Extra,* was assembled by Robert Florey and Slavko Vorkapich out of boxes, cans, cardboard cutouts, and a light bulb, with some expressionistic, direct photography. *Hollywood Extra* satirized a Hollywood success story. *The Last Moment* (1927) by Paul Fejos was an ambitious near-feature-length study based on the notion that moments before death one will quickly recall the significant events of his life.

Poe and expressionism colored *The Tell-Tale Heart* (1928) by Charles Klein. *The Fall of the House of Usher* (1928) compared interestingly with Jean Epstein's French version of the same year. While *La Chute de la maison Usher* plays on editing rhythms and clouded, fleeting impressions, Dr. James Sibley Watson constructs Caligari-like effects with jagged, distorted sets, garish, black-lined makeup, and unreal images, like a headless, hatted figure turning the pages of an old manuscript. Watson used floating, rough-edged titles, like the "I will become Caligari" vision in the sky, to announce the mansion's collapse.

Much experimental film of the thirties rejects synchronous sound, choosing either to maintain the mystery and integrity of silence or using music in unstructured support of the picture. *Lot in Sodom* (1934), again by Watson in association with his writer-art director

Melville Webber, staged its action in choreographed relation to music. The film depicts the depravities of the biblical city as homosexual. If its prancing leers and gestures carry unintentional humor today, *Lot* is yet marked by skilled sound-picture congruence that survives intact.

While maintaining straightforward narrative design, some independent American ventures carry something of avant-garde flavor through their freedom from institutionalized control. *Dawn to Dawn* (1934), directed by Joseph Berne and written by Griffith scholar Seymour Stern, tells a farm story somewhat reminiscent of *The Wind*. *Pie in the Sky* (1934) involved Elia Kazan, Molly Day Thatcher, Irving Lerner, and Ralph Steiner in a Group-Theater improvisation set in a city dump. Other filmmakers, some better known for critical study, constructed geography-based poetic evocations along the lines of Russian and European city symphonies, such as *Bronx Morning*

The Fall of the House of Usher. Along with Fejos' *The Last Moment* and Florey's *The Life and Death of 9413 — A Hollywood Extra,* Watson and Webber's Poe film represented expressionism's American outpost. (Museum of Modern Art/Film Stills Archive)

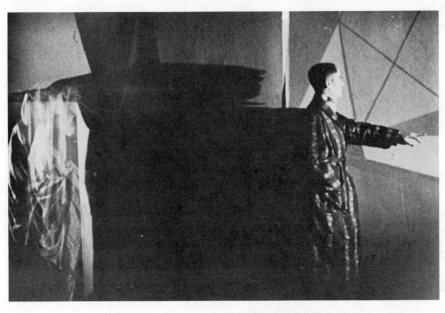

(1934) by Jay Leyda. Herman Weinberg's *Autumn Fire* (1930) combines rural and waterfront atmosphere in a minimal story about two separated lovers.

Maya Deren

The availability of 16mm equipment, fostered by wartime use, measurably contributed to film as a medium for personal, as opposed to institutional, expression: a blossoming of personal filmmaking for which Maya Deren was spokesperson. Made in collaboration with her

"It begins in the mind of the creator. The relationship between the images in dreams, in montage, and in poetry—is . . . they are related because they are held together by either an emotion or a meaning that they have in common, rather than by the logical action. In other words, it isn't that one action leads to another action, but they are brought to a center, gathered up, and collected by the fact that they all refer to a common emotion, although the incidents themselves may be quite disparate." Maya Deren (Courtesy of Anthology Film Archives)

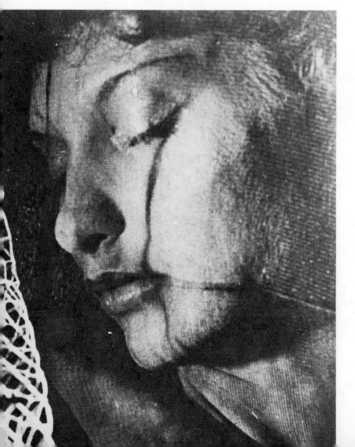

husband Alexander Hammid, *Meshes of the Afternoon* (1943) signals an emerging artist of exceptional energy and imagination whose films grew out of esthetic-theoretical questions she posed to herself and to her audience.

Meshes recycles a sequence of events, each time playing variations on relationships between Deren, a knife, a key, a telephone, a phonograph, and a flower. As in a dream, she proceeds through increasingly ominous repetitive experiences. The film ends in apparent self-destruction that cannot be rationally explained. Its affecting, taut resonance is intensified by a Japanese music track in the sound version and through bold editing continuities.

While maintaining an apparently continuous progression of time and place, Deren shifts shot locations. She uses a moving figure as the linkage between shots that have different backgrounds. Thus, close shots of a striding foot appear smoothly to move from seashore to earth to grass to pavement to carpet. The effect uniquely melds surreal incongruity with sensations of ritual and hallucination.[5]

Deren infuses emotionality into the design by using the juxtapositions to interiorize what seems to be ordinary behavior. In *A Study in Choreography for Camera* (1945), the recurring appearances of a dancer in what looks like a continuous camera pan suggest that the figure is being "broken up" into seperate components, a sophistication of the doppelgänger scheme. In *At Land* (1944), Deren mounts a tree trunk, and her crawling movement progresses down the length of a banquet table (the dinner in full, unperturbed progress) to a chess

[5] *The technique can be found earlier in Buster Keaton's* Sherlock Jr., *where Buster falls asleep while projecting a movie and dreams himself merging with the screen images but unable to adapt to their shifts of scene.* Un Chien Andalou *uses the device again, as when the parental figure is shot in an apartment, then falls to the ground of an estate.* (See *Chapter 19.*) *The process is discussed in Elizabeth Lyon, "Luis Buñuel: The Process of Disassociation in Three Films,"* Cinema Journal *(Fall 1973).*

game. Here she intends to use the place shifts to suggest fluid surroundings of a relativistic universe in which only individual consciousness supplies any continuity.

Maya Deren embodies the symbolist notion that art's purpose is to create experience, not to report or to document it. She supplies a link between Buñuel, Cocteau, and American independent filmmakers to follow. The tradition draws on dream-myth-ritual effects. As in *Meshes,* their conclusion is often somber, but Deren also infuses an occasional optimistic, perhaps New World, tone; the experience may lead to escape from earlier inhibitions. In *Ritual in Transfigured Time* (1946), a black-clothed woman is finally transformed into a bride, her change effected by a shift to negative film.

The Interior Journey

Using less subjectivized imagery, Willard Maas and Marie Menken employed extreme closeups of the human figure in *Geography of the Body* (1943). These are enlarged to a point of abstraction so that each shot suggests an unworldly topography, the film a journey into strange territories by way of its poetic text, composed to resemble a travel essay. In *Bells of Atlantis* (1952), Ian Hugo and Len Lye use a poem written and recited by Anaïs Nin in which the lost city of Atlantis is emblematic of the psychic interior. The reading is linked to underwater scenes of wrecks and artifacts. The film progresses from ocean floor to the water's surface, as if submerged thoughts were coming to consciousness, and colors shift from dark greens to reds and blues, documenting the ascent.

West Coast

War's end saw a resurgence of interest in independent, experimental film, accompanying the growth of community among poets and artists of the San Francisco area. Public receptivity toward such work had been encouraged by Maya Deren's earlier proselytizing lectures and screenings in colleges and universities across the country, soon followed by Frank Stauffacher's "Art in Cinema" presentations in the Bay Area. Stauffacher himself made two films: *Sausalito* (1948) and *Notes on the Port of St. Francis* (1952).

The Potted Psalm (1946) resulted from a collaboration between poet-playwright James Broughton and sculptor Sidney Peterson, rich in death and sexual allusions, amiably resiliant to further interpretation. Peterson continued his own film work independently, using an anamorphic lens in *Mr. Frenhofer and the Minotaur* (1948) and *The Lead Shoes* (1949) to impose image distortions on Freudian fantasies contrived out of costumes and uninhibited performances. In *The Lead Shoes* a distraught mother tries to reach her son, encased in a diving suit and already dead from the emotional isolation his parent had imposed.

James Broughton

Where Peterson's humor and discontinuities are sardonic, Broughton chose a more willfully comic route whose good spirits have sometimes blinded viewers to an undertone that is serious and hardly naïve, despite the employment of twenties mime. Broughton uses comedy as he sometimes employs gentle irony in narration to reduce behavior into exaggerations that expose anxiety and compulsion. *Mother's Day* (1948) intermingles affectionate reminiscence with an unillusioned understanding about a parent's disasterous effect on her family. *The Pleasure Garden* (1950) was filmed in London with the assistance of Lindsay Anderson, a Clair-like satire about censorial intrusions on sexuality.

The Bed (1968) celebrates every form of sexual intercourse and other affectionate interchanges in comic skits staged on an old iron filigree bed resting in a green meadow. Broughton's first film in fifteen years, *The Bed* shows matured preoccupations. Some of these are Jungian and serve for Boughton what

The Bed. "Clothed young people frozen in wonder and uncertainty contemplate the bed. Upon it the envision their collective dreams, taboos, and transformations. Ultimately the instinctual call of Pan releases them into action." James Broughton (Museum of Modern Art/ Film Stills Archive.)

dance movement did for Maya Deren and heraldry Cocteau, a basis for the imagery and linkages that turn introspective in *Dreamwood* (1972), a mythic quest film reminiscent of *Blood of a Poet.*

Kenneth Anger

As with postwar experimentation elsewhere, film offered self-expressive paths that sometimes merged introspection and socially forbidden content in personal homosexual themes or other forms of psychodrama. For example, *Fragment of Seing* (1946) by Curtis Harrington, who acts the principle part, has a young man withdraw from a girl's embrace,

seeing her as a monster, and then shows him fleeing to confront his own image. Kenneth Anger's *Fireworks* (1947) is a masochistic fantasy in which a young homosexual approaches and is sadistically misused by a passel of sailors.

Anger is acutely sensitive to film images (a flaming tree in *Fireworks* evokes *L'Age d'or*). His subsequent films have sometimes developed the most elaborate and affecting visions, as in *Eaux d'artifice* (1953) in which a hermaphroditic figure surrenders his/her identify literally as well as figuratively by turning into a waterfall. *Scorpio Rising* (1963) views the motorcycle subculture as a self-consciously romantic cult, its figures impressed with astrological significances by title and symbol (the leader is Scorpio), and popular myth, editing old movie footage of James Dean, Marlon Brando, and a Sunday School Jesus to parallel the gang's behaviors. Much of the effect in *Scorpio Rising* stems from Anger's employment of rock songs; these sardonically echo the film's themes, contributing an ambiance of Top 40 mind set. As *Scorpio* progresses, the messages of the songs ("Torture," "Wipe Out") provide black, grating amplifications to sado-masochistic sequences.

Later, Anger turned to demonology. *Inauguration of the Pleasure Dome* (1966), *Invocation to My Demon Brother* (1969) and *Lucifer Rising* (Part 1, 1974; Part II, 1976) equate filmmaking with occult magic, invoking angels and demons by ritual, color, and insigniae. Images like the demon brother in *Inauguration of the Pleasure Dome* clearly derive from Paris and London decadence of the nineties.[6] Anger's employment of special effects is as impressive as it is uninhibited; an early version of *Inauguration* concluded with Abel Gance triptych screens reflecting overlays of superimposition.

[6] *This is the world of Aleister Crowley.* See Carel Rowe, *"Illuminating Lucifer,"* Film Quarterly *(Summer, 1974).*

Gregory Markopoulos

First a Los Angeles filmmaker and associate of Harrington and Anger, Markopoulos has lived and, as possible, worked in Europe in recent years. Sympathetic to Cocteau's myth-structuring designs, Markopoulo's films often employ homosexuality as theme. *Psyche, Lysis,* and *Charmides* form a triology, *Du Sang de la volupté et de la mort* (1948).

Most elaborated in *Twice a Man* (1963), Markopoulos uses a technique of rapidly intertwining different images, sometimes superimposed, sometimes intercut single frames, sometimes clusters of like frames. His intention is to create a sense of simultaneity by mingling mythic patterns, actuality, memory, and desire. Experimentation in sound and color has led to the addition of further cues toward locating the meanings of an image's relation to others in *Ming Green* (1966), *Himself as Herself* (1966) and *Gammelion* (1967). *Galaxie* (1966), and *Political Portraits* (1969) are affectionate, film-profile anthologies Markopoulos has assembled of friends over the years.

Stan Brakhage

Prolific and influential in his long career, Stan Brakhage first exploited the experimental modes of other filmmakers, then invented many of his own. He inherited an assortment of film equipment from Sidney Peterson after Peterson withdrew from the field following *The Lead Shoes.* The early Brakhage films (he was eighteen when making *Interim* in 1951) show preoccupations with literary motifs, Sartre for example, which hardly relate with

The Wonder Ring. Commissioned by Joseph Cornell, Brakhage turned his eye on Manhattan's Third Avenue El shortly before it was dismantled. (Courtesy of Anthology Film Archives)

Mothlight. "Speculate as to insect vision, such as the bee's sense of scent through ultraviolet perceptibility. To search for human visual realities, man must, as in all other homo motivation, transcend the original physical restrictions and inherit worlds of eyes." Stan Brakhage (Courtesy of Anthology Film Archives)

measurable success to his constant visual investigation.

As they depart from prose themes, Brakhage films ask the viewer to abdicate customary narrative expectations for the sake of differently structured visual experiences. Almost all of his work is silent. Imagery may vary from the real and fortuitous (*Desistfilm,* made in 1954, was largely accomplished by handing a camera back and forth among the guests during a party) to photography abstracted by circumstances of shooting. *The Wonder Ring* (1955) captures flashing movements from an elevated subway. At one extreme are effects that have been radically affected by manipulation during production stages. *Dog Star Man* (1964) employs multiple-printed overlays. *Mothlight* (1963) was made by sandwiching actual moth wings, pieces of leaves and twig segments between adhesive editing tape, then printing the result as if it were a photographed film.

Brakhage images sometimes have the quality of abstract expressionism propelled into action painting immediacy. Of all artists working with non-representational effects he is the most thoughtfully concerned with manipulating changing relations between time and image movement. Insofar as drama or narrativity connotes change, conflict, and resolution on screen, story continues, however covertly, in Brakhage. Story all but disappears in the work of the next generation of filmmakers.

Less abstracted Brakhage films are often the result of highly charged emotional or inspired moments. These records contribute to an autobiographical flavor, and his films sometimes ask a separate, anecdotal understanding of the circumstances of their production, the state of Brakhage's relation to his wife, the birth of his children. Films such as *Window Water Baby Moving* (1959) and *Wedlock House: An Intercourse* (1959) retain a quality of individual record without sacrificing broader emotional impact.

Part of the Brakhage opus suggests a personal mythology in which themes of suicidal despair, *Anticipation of the Night* (1958), displace or are overshadowed by quiet lyricism, *Songs* (1964-69). Loneliness which sometimes leads to masturbation—*The Flesh of Morning* (1956), *Sexual Meditation, Motel* (1969)—alternates with lovemaking, *Lovemaking* (1969). Sometimes Brakhage is haunted by death. *Dog Star Man* returns compulsively to the decaying body of a pet. *The Act of Seeking With One's Own Eyes* (1971) holds steady on the performance of an actual autopsy.

Certain Brakhage films thus continue the avant-garde tradition of investigating unexplored terrain without concern toward conventional response, whether it be "boredom" or shock. Elsewhere in Brakhage's work resides the photographer with especially sensitive vision. *The Riddle of Lumen* (1972) explores light, not as it is implied through reflection but as it may be manifest if we look closely. Colors, blue and orange in particular, are examined in a variety of situations, the range of subject matter itself cued to certain categories, like childhood and flying. It is through his refined experiments in vision that Brakhage most penetratingly shares his experience.

Independent Popular Entertainments

"Controversial" subject matter may enlist independently financed productions into traditions of experimentalism. *Chant d'amour* was written by Jean Genet, completed in 1953 in France and exhibited in the U.S. during the sixties. It explores sado-masochistic homosexual relations, sometimes real, sometimes fantasized, between prisoners and guards. Shirley Clarke's *The Cool World* (1963) is a largely-staged quasi-documentary of ghetto life in Harlem along teenagers. Clarke's *Portrait of Jason* (1967) follows the personality shifts of a black male prostitute in talking-head camera confrontation. It was pared from an uninterrupted fourteen hours down to two.

Echoes of Silence (1965) by Peter Goldman documents, often with deeply moving portraits, alienation in the city. *Pull My Daisy* (1959) by Robert Frank and Alfred Leslie is a silent version of Jack Kerouac's play, enacted for the most part in a Lower East Side flat in Manhattan and narrated by Kerouac as he watches the picture, pausing to pull on a jug of wine. *Shadows* (1959) grew out of a method acting class of John Cassavetes'. Given situations were improvised by the students, a music track by Charles Mingus helping to cohere the results. Norman Mailer financed two films composed of like, if less polished, improvised performance. *Beyond the Law* (1970) suggests cultural and authoritarian likenesses between criminals and police, a subject not unknown to Fritz Lang in 1931. *Maidstone* (1970) imagines a presidential candidate on a Long Island estate developing his campaign at a houseparty. Both films feature Mailer.

Suspicious of filming his plays, Samuel Beckett has written one motion picture titled *Film* (1968), directed by Alan Schneider. The work features Buster Keaton and draws likenesses between camera eye, subject point of view, and audience voyeurism. To see ourselves in actuality, Beckett seems to say, is the most dangerous of human confrontations.

Another vein of independent film is the parodic feature, subjecting social and film conventions to irreverent variation. George and Mike Kuchar translate Hollywood fiction into a Bronx sensibility that remains ultimately friendly to its subject in *Screwball* (1957), *Pussy on a Hot Tin Roof* (1961), *Hold Me*

While I'm Naked (1966) and *I Married a Heathen* (1973). Robert Downey's *Chafed Elbows* (1967), *Putney Swope* (1966) and *Greaser's Palace* (1972) are more inventive caricatures of the culture at large, unselective in choice of target. In *Greaser's Palace* a cripple, healed by a miracle, bubbles "I can crawl again." *Don't Make Pictures Like Joe Levine* (1976) was described by Downey as a comic *Battle of Algiers*. *Hallelujah the Hills* (1963) by Adolphas Mekas involves a pair of male friends vying for the affection of a girl in Vermont, but the story is ignored as necessary for affectionate homages to early filmmakers and to the countryside.

New American Cinema

Stirred first by Amos Vogel's "Cinema 16" screenings at the Needle Trades Auditorium in New York, then by *Film Culture* magazine that, under the editorship of Jonas Mekas, became its champion, what came to be dubbed the New American Cinema blossomed in the late fifties and early sixties, a disparate collection of filmmakers who organized through a Film Makers Cooperative to distribute their work. Unalike, many of the artists reflect elements of Clarke, Brakhage, and Markopoulos, and the spirit of dada is pervasive, but much New American Cinema is avowedly primitive, defiantly unrelated to any tradition.

Ken Jacobs' *Little Stabs at Happiness* (1961) and *Blonde Cobra* (1962) are composed of sections so intermittently organized and interrupted by film perforations, light flares and self-conscious comment that the result achieves an assault on audience expectation. Jacobs' *Tom, Tom the Piper's Son* (1969), a film made by repeatedly rephotographing the projected image of an American Mutoscope and Biograph title from 1905, accomplishes many of the same intentions in different, more structured fashions.

Jack Smith, who appeared in Jacobs' earlier films, made *Flaming Creatures* in 1963, a sa-tiric comment on eroticism that culminates in a vari-sexual orgy that combines the joylessness of $8_{1/2}$ with transvestite camp. *The Flower Thief* (1960) by Ron Rice featured Taylor Mead in an improvised picaresque, performed among vestigial Beats of San Francisco's North Beach. Rice's *Senseless* (1962) followed a more narcotic narrative design. *The Queen of Sheba Meets the Wolf Man* was unfinished at Rice's death.

A skilled photographer and, earlier, the artist of sci-fi magazine covers, Ed Emschwiller has composed films in which exterior reality may richly reflect inner life as in *George Dumpson's Place* (1965). There, rubble around a shack assumes qualities of a personal portrait. Introspection may find expression in stylized performance; in a meditation on death, *Thanatopsis* (1962) equates a dancer with a candle's flickering flame. Emschwiller is interested in relations between live and filmed performance. He has staged events in which black-leotarded dancers move in the dark, holding cards from which are reflected the small, projected screen images of similar performers. Jonas Mekas' own films often have the quality of news reports and skirting, emotional documentation. *Film Magazine of the Arts* (1963) captures the New York art world of the early sixties, the time of Happenings. *Reminiscences of a Journey to Lithuania* (1972) carries autobiographical poignance as Adolphas and Jonas Mekas return to their homeland with the baggage of reminiscence and estrangement.

West Coast Again

While East Coast engaged metropolitan emotions, the Bay Area inaugurated Canyon Cinema, a cooperative analogous to New York City's. The approach of Bruce Baillie, one of Canyon's founders, ranges from *All My Life* (1966), in which the camera pans along a flowered fence, reflecting Ella Fitzgerald's sunny execution of the title song, to *Mass for the*

Castro Street. Baillie used various techniques to distort his photography, including pressure-pad slippage and holding fingers before the lens. But it is the images' representational vestige that weights and stabilizes them. That done, Baillie can contradict one picture by superimposing another. (Courtesy of Anthology Film Archives)

Dakota Sioux (1964) and *To Parsifal* (1963), which are structured in canonical and operatic patterns.

One of Baillie's most impressive films is *Castro Street* (1966). Using the route of a Richmond, California thoroughfare, which skirts a railroad spur and refining tanks, Baillie superimposes images whose separate colors maintain the integrity of each location while the overlays develop an independent existence. Movement becomes illusory and self-contradictory; separate images confound one another's frame of reference. The technique, which has an evolving, cumulative dynamic, is carried to even more ambitious length in *Quick Billy* (1970).

Robert Nelson's work combines humor, too satiric for dada, with a sometimes-quiet pleasure in Zen-like moments of insight. *The Awful Backlash* (1967) stares at the fingers of a fisherman untangling his reel, to the accompaniment of breathing, a mumbled monologue, and the ratchet sound of the reel. *Confessions of a Black Mother Succuba* (1965) intercuts TV commercials with themes of sex and violence.

Gunvor Nelson's films explore something of the feminine consciousness. *Schmeerguntz* (1965), coproduced by Dorothy Wiley, contrasts media stereotypes with the actualities of a woman's life. *Take Off* (1973) leads us to believe we are watching a strip tease, staged by Ellion Ness, but, clothes gone, she continues to remove breasts, arms, hair and head.

Metanomen (1966), *A Trip to the Moon* (1968) and *Off/On* (made with Tom De Witt) are films by Scott Bartlett that now reconstruct the Haight-Ashbury ethos. Inward journies have no more need of the metaphoric

Hôtel des Folies. They consist of immensely beautiful abstracted figurations, trips resonant with astrology, the I Ching, mysticism, astronomy, and a synesthesia whose sound is rock or otherwise electronic, its color psychodelic. Another work of similarly awesome visuals is John Scofill's *X Film* (1967).

Tom De Witt's *Atmosfear* (1967) rendered New York City menacing with polarization-like diffusions of the empty cityscapes. De Witt turned to video technology to accomplish *The Leap* (1968), employing special effects equipment and electronic feedback in order further to abstract filmed images and to super-impose a running figure into the unfriendly environs. *The Fall* (1972) continues *The Leap* by way of the Icarus myth, the figure's descent equated with bombs and the collapse of American integrity in its Southeast-Asian interventions. Recently, De Witt has turned more exclusively to video experimentation, his superimpositions redolent of surreal incongruities and dada humor, like the work of Stan VanderBeek.

Will Hindle combines technical skill, surreal imagination and reference to the madnesses caused by war in *Billabong* (1968) and *Chinese Firedrill* (1969). *Firedrill* uses computerization, a snowstorm of program cards, to suggest pressures that have led an anxious, guilt-ridden narrator into seclusion and guilty introspection.

Painter, sculptor, and collagist Bruce Conner has brought assemblage techniques into his films, quintessentially in *A Movie* (1958). Self-conscious, self-reflexively funny, the film's intentions are ultimately somber. Conner leads the audience through parallel-edited stock footage of pursuits and sports racing to develop a crescendo of accidents. As an audience grows to question the basis of its laughter, catastrophes become more horrendous, intermixed with records of real events. Building into war and its aftermaths, *A Movie* concludes with underwater shots of a diver. They may suggest the subconscious as an antidote; perhaps it is our despair.

Report (1967) repeats news footage of President Kennedy's assassination with accompanying television reportage, intercut with commercial and entertainment materials so that the viewer is required to consider his relation to the broadcast experience. *Crossroads* (1976) uses government film of the first Bikini H-bomb test, an event coded "Crossroads." The inarguable beauty of the explosion as well as viewer distance from its destructive consequence again encourages audiences' self-examination of response. While a circling plane

feels "safe" it is buffeted by the aftershock. Yet we are calmed by repetition of the events; we develop our own expectations toward each moment of what becomes a ritual experienced with shifting camera perspectives. A speeded-up nude performer in *Cosmic Ray* (1961) appears sometimes bacchic, sometimes consigned to a dance of death, moving frenziedly to the music of Ray Charles' "What'd I Say?"

Andy Warhol

If the films of Andy Warhol share commonalities with the unstructured behaviors of *Portrait of Jason* and even *Beyond the Law*, they bring a more ironic, pop-art esthetic to the screen. Warhol reverts to a quasi-primitive, unedited, unmoving, inexorable camera confrontation that draws on subjects who often reflect pressures of city life and the aspirations of its throwaway culture. In some films the unchanging experience is cumulative only in terms of audience reaction. *Sleep* (1964) records a sleeping man. *Empire* (1965) studies the Empire State Building, which does not respond. Elsewhere, performers act out fantasies: *Batman Dracula* (1964), *Soap Opera* (1964). *The Chelsea Girls* (1966) is made up of several autonomous films scheduled to be projected side by side on two screens simultaneously, one silent each time. **** (1967) requires that three projectors superimpose their images. While Warhol is implacably noncommittal toward any behavior that occurs, he refuses to turn the machine off and many films turn into anxious urban efforts by street-savvy performers to hold the camera/audience's unwavering attention.

Minimalist Film

The minimalist dispositions evident in Warhol and in short films by Marie Menken developed momentum during the seventies, abetted by current painterly esthetics that argued for formal restraint, and a parsimony of graphic variables (e.g., the simplest "subjects"), and self-reflexivity. Some of this work amounts to controlled experimentation, a basic research into film's elements, but the films are also motivated by filmmakers' interests in affecting, or, better, initiating audience response patterns independent of illusionary narrative schemes. A further, unacknowledged impulse was earlier voiced in Marcel Duchamp's surrealist attack on what he called "retinal art," the equation of esthetic experience with beauty that was independent of philosophy, religion, and ideology.

Minimalist films embrace a variety of social-esthetic premises, and their design is more lucidly based on theory than that of any earlier experimental movement. An American school to which the term "structural" film has sometimes been applied often retains vestiges of personalized authorship, of "style" in the sense that the term might apply to an abstract expressionist painter. For example, a film might be said to be identifiably "by Paul Sharits."

The more stern European branch, structural/materialists, tries to sustain anonymity and an even more total rejection of photographic illusion's seductive attractions. Broadly, the filmmakers try to develop a constant but altering tension between the apparent "reality" of images and the material of their production (grain, light, apparent movement, color, flatness, shape.) In process, the manner by which a film was executed becomes itself the subject. Spectators find themselves reminded repetitively of their removed, non-empathising relationship to the projected experience.

In *The Flicker* (1965) and *The Eyes of Count Flickerstein* (1966), Tony Conrad compounded films made up of no more than black and white frames. As in Peter Kubelka's similar (and earlier) *Adebar* (1957) the relationships of light to nonlight are mathematically determined; experiencing the films sometimes leads one to see apparent color and depth effects as well as the accidents of a particular screening such as frame steadiness and dirt. With their minimal cues, such films aptly illustrate the degree to which perceptions can operate in the eye of the beholder.

Fortuity appears to be integrated into *Film in Which There Appear Sprocket Holes, Edge Lettering, Dirt Particles, Etc.* (1966) by George Landow. However, it is a film not simply about itself but about the viewer, consist-

Film in Which There Appear. . . . Four minutes long, Landow's movie is built of a more-or-less one-second unit, endlessly repeating the model's blink with occasional changes in length. It is printed so that frame separation lines, sprocket holes and edge numbering become visible to the viewer. (Courtesy of Anthology Film Archives)

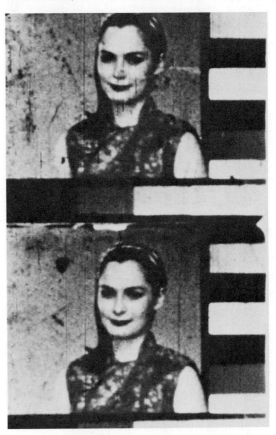

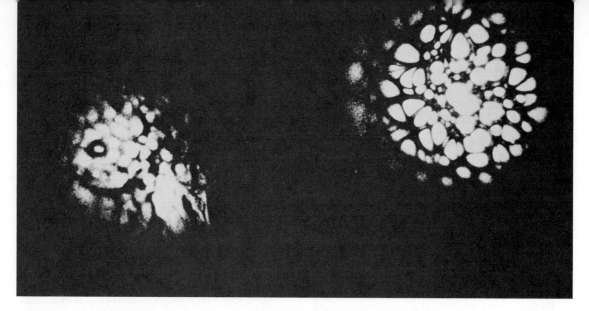

Diploteratology. Through a series of deformations, the image of a woman waving to the camera at Cypress Gardens becomes unrecognizable. Diploteratology: the study of severe malformations in growing organisms. (Courtesy of Anthology Film Archives)

ing of a very few frames from a piece of Kodak test footage, endlessly repeated but so manipulated that one is led to examine different places on the screen, shifting gaze as Landow shifts the locations and the ingredients of his image.

Diploteratology/Bardo Folly (1967) by George Landow conceives the screen image as an organism which breaks into separate bodies as if each were growing through mitosis out of a common cell. A woman waves at the camera, her gesture phased to different moments in each of the pictures. The images dissipate into abstracted forms, their space evolving into new combinations of color and grain.

In Thomas Mann's *The Magic Mountain,* Hans Castorp imagines the present as resembling a train that moved on a track that led from past to future. *Nostalgia* (1971) by Hollis Frampton requires its audience to break away from Newtonian cause-effect notions of time. Frampton constructs a visual made up of still photographs, each burned, and replaced by the next. A narrator reminisces about each photograph and explains its origins, but the photographs are always one picture ahead of the speaker, so that we require ourselves to remember, not experience, the tangible evidence of what we are hearing while simultaneously we absorb the new photograph.

Frampton's *Zorns Lemma* (1970) highlights another aspect of contemporary experimental film: a tension between self-conceived systems of permutations and fortuitous events that may "open up" an otherwise hermetic progress of structural variations. *Zorns Lemma* begins with a no-image sound track, a repetition of rhymes from an old New England primer designed to teach the alphabet while inculcating obeisance to authority. Then, one second segments, each an enlarged, metallic alphabet letter, appear. Words, presented randomly but alphabetically, follow. Non-verbal images gradually replace verbal ones; an audience will seek to impose its own systems on the sequence of image-replacement. Finally, as the picture shows a couple walking away from the camera (interrupted by obvious beginnings and endings to each shot, such as light flares), six women on the sound track read in turn, one word at a time, from a medieval essay, "On Light, or the Ingression of Forms." In sum, the film serves a variety of intentions private to Frampton, while simultaneously engaging a kind of audience commitment that is unlike the character-identifications of narrative film illusion.

The inadequacy of categorizing nomenclature (*minimalist* quite as much as *structuralist*)[7] is evidenced in Frampton's current, ongoing project initiated in 1972. *Magellan* is intended to run more-or-less thirty-six hours when completed. A fifty-four minute excerpt, *Mind Fall* suggests more the modernism of James Joyce than of post-abstract expressionism. Whether *Magellan's* magnitude and visual surface will sustain its myriad themes, historical and psychological allusions, puns, and conjugations of sound-picture relationships remains yet an open question.

Ernie Gehr's *Serene Velocity* (1970) was produced by a camera aligned to photograph a long corridor. Spatial relationships shift with mathematically predetermined repositionings of a zoom lens. No movement is itself shown, but only the continuous recompositions of walls, lights, doors, and floor. The effect is to find oneself unsettlingly involved within the space of the corridor.

Paul Sharits' films reduce screen components to color, *Ray Gun Virus* (1966), and stark images endlessly repeated in variation to one another, *Razor Blades* (1968), *N:O:T:H:I:N:G* (1968). In *T,O,U.C,H,I,N,G* (1968), a narrative component thrusts its way into the picture as a repeating voice track speaks phrases that sound like "It's gory,"

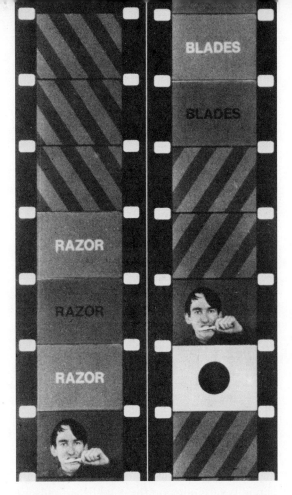

Razor Blades. Suggestive of the alternating images seen earlier in *Ballet mécanique,* Sharit's film shifts image frequencies more freely. This display of footage almost seems to imply that *Razor Blades* may have been partly conceived as a spread-out composition, rather than as a film to be viewed one image at a time. (Courtesy of Anthology Film Archives)

"the story," "It's murder." Edited through rearrangement of·a single recording (the syllables rearranged on the tape), these words first tinge the image of a young man with scissors held at his chin, then seem to withdraw from later shots of the same face, eyes now open, staring at the audience. Our impression is that Sharits' title intends to suggest a developing empathy between screen and spectator.

To the extent that process is the subject,

[7] *Frampton himself eloquently questions the utility of critical labels in "Hollis Frampton at the San Francisco Art Institute, 4-21-76,"* Cinemanews (*November-December 1977*).

many minimalist films can be largely absorbed simply by reading about them, they are so concisely predelineated. However, such is not altogether the case, for the viewing sensations impose both a social context and accumulations of response that are no less real for locating themselves so exclusively in a viewer's head. Some of Sharits's work is heavily colored by elements of Eastern meditation. One film is titled *Peace Mandala* (1966). *Bardo Follies* was inspired by the Tibetan *Book of the Dead*, and James Whitney's computer-generated *Yantra* (1955) and *Lapis* (1965) have meditative intentions.[8]

Kurt Kren, Austrian, conveniently numbers his films in terms of the order and year of completion. *2/60 48 Köpfe aus dem Szondi-Test* (48 Heads from the Szondi-Test) and *3/60 Bäume im Herbst* (Trees in Autumn) juxtapose separate, short shots. The content is identifiable (photos of faces or parts of faces, tree branches against sky in medium to close shot). Largely, Kren edits within the camera, often single framing. His continuity is highly sophisticated in terms of visual matches. Rhythms — established by sequence, duration, and shot angle — first define themselves, then slip into variations on the established pulse.

The 1964–65 period combines Kren's intuitive systemization of image sequence with performances by Viennese artists (*6/64 Moma und Papa, 8/64 Günter Brus Anne, 10/65 Bild Helga Philip*). The pictured events are bizarre in the extreme, in particular the razor

blade-infested head of *10/65*, but the attraction of content works at odds with Kren's esthetic.

15/67 TV is an extraordinary work, made of five short (about 2 second) sequences filmed through a cafe window, often separated by a blackened screen. Durations vary. Through juxtapositions (here done on an editing table), Kren emphasizes, by repetition and contrast, the shapes and foreground-background movements so that in context separate components in each image assume particular, even intense, significance.

Ten years later, Kren's work appears to take a new turn. Exposures from a stationary camera vary in length, time of day and shutter speed. Sometimes Kren rewinds and adjusts the camera position. The change manipulates color quality and complicates images by skewed registrations. (Frampton does something similar in parts of *Magellan*.) *33/77 Keine Donau* documents a Utrillo-like window view of city roofs whose textures, chimney smoke, laundry and passers-by appear and disappear, sometimes with ghostly transparency. Kren says he likes to see images repeated in a movie, and that he must start a film without knowing its outcome, its reward occurring the first time he can view the completed work.

The Austrian Peter Kubelka fuses minimalist concision with personalized relations to his material. His films tend to extreme shortness, *Schwechater* (1958) is sixty seconds and the imageless, alternating-black-and-white *Arnulf Rainer* (1960) six-and-a-half minutes. Most Kubelka films are the product of years of work, untold hours of experimentation and a ruthless paring down to impermeable essentials. *Unsere Afrikareise* (1966), six years in completion, is Kubelka's strongest work to date. Originally, it consisted of the documentation of a German-African safari for which Kubelka supplied the photography. In the final version, *Unsere Afrikareise* consists of

[8] *Speaking of his films and those of associates, Sharits uses painters Frank Stella and Jasper Johns as frames of reference, work which uses its own material and boundaries not for compositional effect so much as to investigate how the canvas is perceived. New film, says Sharits, should be viewed as informational system rather than in terms of* a priori *metaphysical theory. Paul Sharits, "Words per Page" in Denis Wheeler, ed.,* Form and Structure in Recent Film. *Vancouver, 1972.*

Schwechater. Working within the confines of a beer commercial, Kubelka plays miniscule variations on each gesture, glance, and screen movement so that every frame becomes thoughtfully, singularly functional in its own context. Subject is largely inconsequential. (Courtesy of Anthology Film Archives)

the most precise relationships, still narrative, between sound and picture. Its overtones, sometimes accomplished by editing juxtapositions, sometimes by overlapping sound and picture, sometimes by sound-to-picture or picture-to-sound cuts, inject each moment of the twelve minute film with back and forth resonances that continually reinforce each shift of experience, what Kubelka and others like to call "articulations," after the manner of language study. The totality assumes character-

istics of a studied musical composition without losing its relations to the "outside" world.

Print Generation (1973) by J. J. Murphy combines careful predesign with a capacity to encourage active, ordered audience engagement. Fifty generations of contact prints produced visual images that depart increasingly from identifiable original forms. The pictures proceed from their most abstracted states toward recognizability, then revert to unidentifiable forms, accompanied by a sound track that was similarly executed. In counterdevelopment, a sound of ocean waves begins recognizably, moves toward maximum distortion, and returns to maximum fidelity. The abstract patterns elicit spectator involvement so as to organize them into "meaningful" forms. Because what is recognizable passes by so quickly, memories of what an image "really was" soon prove to be tantalizingly inaccessible.

Wavelength (1967) by Michael Snow, a Canadian, consists of a forty-five minute seemingly continuous zoom. First distant from the far wall of a large loft, the composition gradually emphasizes three pictures on the wall, then centers on one image, a seascape, which comes finally to envelop the screen, replacing the flat wall with its own spatial perspective. *Wavelength* is a kind of humorous critical meditation on narrativity as well, for its unswerving, constant pace is played against the interruptions of voices, a radio, the flashed image of a body (Hollis Frampton's), perhaps somehow murdered in the room, and a constant, soundwave glissando. Changes of day, visible in the distant windows, are at odds with the apparent time of the zoom. In 1969, Snow completed ↔, which is also known as *Back and Forth.* This time, camera movement is horizontal, pans that cross and recross, at different tempos, an area of about seventy-five degrees in a deserted schoolroom. Later, the movement shifts to the vertical, i.e., ↕. Again, flashes of unexplained figures intrude.

(Left) Michael Snow posed beside his camera and its mountings during the production of *La Région Centrale*. (Right) Representational frames from the film. Their movement suggests the varieties of camera execution. In closeup and long shot, the pictures betray the region's barren, textured, abstract look. (Courtesy of Anthology Film Archives)

La Région Centrale (1971) proves to be even more of a tour de force than previous work by Snow. Running something more than three hours, the film was made in a distant, deserted, rock-strewn section of Northern Quebec. There, Snow mounted his camera on a tripod and a mechanism whose movements might be remote-controlled by himself. Hiding behind a huge boulder in order that the camera's view would encompass nothing but barren landscape, Snow led the lens through a glossary of movements, organized around a kind of lying-on-its-side figure 8 shape, but swinging and pulsating in what seems to be infinite variation. The effect becomes a kind of obverse to Warhol's staring exercises. Before, the camera was an unyielding witness to some implaccable subject. In Snow's film, the wilderness exists eerily independent of camera swoops and swirls. The film develops a kind of alogically coordinated range of disconnected propositions between viewer and object. Its technology encourages maximum impersonality. As such, *La Région Centrale*, like all Snow's work, holds special appeal to a contemporary sensibility that is seeking to relate theory and practice in such ways that film audiences become party to the experience without assuming either a dominating or subservient role.

Summary

Experimental work is far too individualized to accommodate generalizations with ease. Much of it can be seen to reflect temperaments and attitudes of dada and surrealism. Modes of dream fantasy persistently surface. In minimalist films of the seventies, interest in abstract configurations has merged with perception studies.

Chapter 19 turns to three commercial directors. Their own experimentations incorporate private vision in the service of popular narrativity: Federico Fellini, Buñuel, and Igmar Bergman.

Bibliography

Abel, Richard. "The Contributions of the French Literary Avant-Garde to Film Theory and Criticism (1907-1924)," *Cinema Journal* (Spring 1976).

Aguirre, Javier. *Anti-cine*. Madrid, 1972.

Amberg, George, comp. *Art of Cinema*. New York, 1972.

———. "Documentary of Another Realm: Surrealism from Cocteau to Polanski," *University Film Study Center Bulletin* (February 1976).

Barr, William R. "Brakhage," *Film Quarterly* (Spring 1976).

Batcock, Gregory. *The New American Cinema*. New York, 1971.

Brakhage, Stan. "Metaphors on Vision," *Film Culture* 30 (1964).

———. *A Motion Picture Giving and Taking Book*. West Newbury, Mass., 1971.

———. *The Brakhage Lectures*. Chicago, 1972.

———. *Seen*. San Francisco, 1975.

Cocteau, Jean. *Diary of a Film*. London, 1950.

———. *Cocteau on Film*. London, 1954.

———. *Orpheus. The Eternal Return. Beauty and the Beast*. New York, 1972.

Currie, Hector and Michael Forte, ed. *Cinema Now 1*. Cincinnati, Ohio, 1968.

Curtis, David. *Experimental Cinema*. New York, 1971.

Deleney, Robert. *Fernand Leger*. Cleveland, 1962.

Deren, Maya. *An Anagram of ideas on Art, Form and Film*. Yonkers, N.Y., 1946.

Dwoskin, Stephen. *Film Is*. Woodstock, N.Y., 1975.

Evans, Arthur B. *Jean Cocteau and His Films of Orphic Identity*. London, 1978.

Fell, John. "Fall" *Film Quarterly* (Spring 1972)

Film Makers Cooperative, 1976. New York, 1975.

Film Culture 61 (Winter 1975) "Broughton Issue."

Fisher, Lucy. "Castro Street: The Sensibility of Style," *Film Quarterly* (Spring, 1976).

Gerould, Daniel C. and Bernard F. Dukore, eds. *Avant Garde Drama a Casebook 1918-1939*. New York, 1976.

Gidal, Peter. Structural Film Anthology. London, 1976.

Grey, Cleve, ed. *Hans Richter*. New York, 1971.

Hein, Birgit. *Film im Underground*. Berlin, 1971.

A History of the New York Avant-Garde Cinema. New York, 1976.

Lawder, Standish. *The Cubist Cinema*. New York, 1975.

LeGrice, Malcolm. *Abstract Film and Beyond*. Cambridge, 1977.

Manvell, Roger. *Experiment in the Film*. London, 1949.

Matthews, J. H. *Surrealism and Film*. Ann Arbor, 1971.

Mekas, Jonas. *Movie Journal*. New York, 1972.

Michelson. Annette. "Camera Lucida/Camera Obscura," *Artforum* (January 1973).

Penrose, Roland. *Man Ray*. New York, 1975.

Renan, Sheldon. *An Introduction to the American Underground Film.* New York, 1967.

———. *Study-Teaching Guide for the Independent Film.* New York, 1972.

Richter, Hans. *Hans Richter.* Neuchatel, Switzerland, 1965.

Rowe, Carel. "Illuminating Lucifer," *Film Quarterly* (Summer 1974).

Sandrow, Nahma. *Surrealism. Theater Arts Ideas.* New York, 1972.

Sheehy, Terry. "Celebration," *Film Quarterly* (Summer 1976).

Sitney, P. Adams, ed. *Film Culture Reader.* New York, 1970.

———. *Visionary Film.* New York, 1974.

———. *The Essential Cinema.* New York, 1976.

Smith, Katherine. "Stan Brakhage," *Film Quarterly* (Summer 1971).

Stauffacher, Frank. *Art in Cinema.* San Francisco, 1947.

Tyler, Parker. *The Three Faces of the Film.* South Brunswick, N.J., 1967 new and rev. ed.

———. *Underground Film.* New York, 1969.

Usabel, Salvador. *Philosophic Elements in Three Directors of the New San Francisco Filmmaking Movement.* M. A. Thesis, San Francisco State College, 1967.

Vogel, Amos. *Film as a Subversive Art.* New York, 1974.

Wheeler, Denis, ed. *Form and Structure in Recent Film.* Vancouver, 1972.

William, Alan, "The Structure of Lyric: Baillie's To Parsifal," *Film Quarterly* (Spring 1976).

Youngblood, Gene, *Expanded Cinema.* New York, 1970.

19

FELLINI, BUÑUEL, BERGMAN

Radically different in temperment and in cultural persuasions, Bergman, Buñuel, and Fellini unintentionally share significant traits. Most important, they make up a first generation of directorial superstars, men whose uniquenesses of vision, coupled with impressive outputs, have afforded a personal popularity unprecedented in film history: the name, as Frank Capra once said, above the title.

Each man has created a distinct and identifiable visual style: Buñuel through the incongruent logic of surrealism, Fellini as a creator of grotesques. The greater part of Bergman's work depends upon Swedish countryside; he is partially sensitive to light's effect, prone to lengthy, unremitting facial closeups.

This said, it works no injustice on these directors to observe that their styles evolve largely from the stories they tell. All carry so familiar a presence before audiences that each new viewing experience prompts us to anticipate variations within a predelineated universe: the worlds of Buñuel, Fellini, and Bergman. For this reason, story synopses, in their cumulative totalities, are more useful in discussing these figures than is the case with many other filmmakers, so long as a reader remains alert to prose's ultimate inadequacy at purveying the film experience.

Fellini Satyricon (Fellini 1969) (Museum of Modern Art/Film Stills Archive)

FEDERICO FELLINI

By *La Strada* (1954), Fellini's intentions and strategies became apparent, and, for the first time, scorn adulterated acclamation. Fellini was turning out to be not a neorealist but a renegade poet whose forebears more closely resembled Benvenuto Cellini or Gustave Doré, flamboyant exhibitionists with highly personal images erupted out of the deep unconscious. Fellini casts his actors to correspond with idea-bound drawings he has devised. One of his early careers was that of a caricaturist, and Fellini's preliminary sketches uncannily prefigure performers he has yet to meet. Such a temperament elaborates narrative out of dramatic confrontations between images, a far cry from the unmanipulated scrutinies of Cesar Zavattini.

The Fellinian heresy was not immediately apparent. He grew up in Rimini, a small, rural town whose provincialities and isolation are realistically captured in *I Vitelloni* (1953) as well as in the village squares that haunt so many of his films. In fact, much Fellini film begins as tongue-in-cheek autobiography, but it is an autobiography filtered through grotesque imagination, and urges to skew each recounting around overriding attractions and fears.

Fellini ran away to join a circus at twelve. Returning, he left again for Rome at seventeen, where he sold his cartoons to magazines and newspapers, wrote comic sketches for music-hall performers, and supplied ideas for minor film scripts. His association with Rossellini began in the early stages of *Open City*. One recounting has it that Rossellini enlisted Fellini to help him persuade Aldo Fabrizi to play the priest Don Morosini in a documentary that was to be financed by an elderly woman. Fellini was an assistant director on *Paisà*, traveling like the story narrative from Sicily upwards to the Po delta.

> Rossellini taught me humility in living, he has faith in things, in men, in the strength of man, in reality. By looking at things with the love and communion that are established from one moment to another between a person and myself, between an object and myself, I understand that the cinema could fill my life, helping me to find a meaning in existence.[1]

Association with Rossellini continued through *Europa '51*. Fellini's greatest contribution to his mentor was the story for *The Miracle*, in which Anna Magnani's retarded,

[1] *Quoted in Angelo Solmi,* Fellini. *London, 1967, p. 80.*

Federico Fellini (1920–   )

Luci del Varieta/Variety Lights (codirector Alberto Lattuada)	1950
Lo Sceicco Bianco/The White Sheik	1952
I Vitelloni	1953
La Strada	1953
Il Bidone	1955
Le Notti di Cabiria/Nights of Cabiria	1956
La Dolce Vita	1960
Boccaccio '70 (The Temptations of Dr. Antonio)	1962
8½	1963
Giulietta degli Spiriti/Juliet of the Spirits	1965
A Tre Passi dal Delerio/Spirits of the Dead (Toby Dammit episode)	1965
Fellini Satyricon	1969
I Clowns/The Clowns (TV production)	1970
Roma	1972
Amarcord	1974
Fellini's Casanova	1976

La Strada. Gelsomina and Zampano perform in a village square, beating a snare and blowing a trumpet to attract spectators. She persuades him to let her learn to play the horn. It is the poignant theme Gelsomina masters that at last prods Zampano toward a semblance of human feeling. (British National Film Archives/Stills Library)

innocent peasant foreshadows roles Fellini later wrote for Giulietta Masina, his wife, just as the rural wanderings in *St. Francis of Assissi,* which he also wrote for Rossellini, are recurrent.

Variety Lights (1950) grew from tales Fellini heard traveling with an Aldo Fabrizi road show. Fellini codirected with Alberto Lattuada: the adventures of a third-rate variety troupe who barely support themselves moving from one little town to the next. The love affairs, jealous bickerings, illusions, and dreams are viewed with affectionate tolerance, following the itinerant players in episodic sketches, like the turns each does on stage. Its inconclusive ending introduces a Fellini pre-

mise, that neat finales do a moral disservice to audiences who deserve to think through their relation to the experience without the "out" of a pat resolution.

Fellini and Tullio Pinelli wrote *The White Sheik* (1952) for Michelangelo Antonioni who fell ill; the direction passed over to Fellini. It centers on the world of photographed strip cartoons, which commands large followings in Italy with romantic stories photographed like movie productions. The White Sheik is a fiercely romantic Bedouin, in reality pompous, fattening about the middle and eager to invoke his image for casual sex. Although less successful, the film shares many qualities with *Variety Lights.* Its characters are self-centered and grasping, and Fellini steers a course between buffoonery and close, ironic attention to manner and motive.

For *I Vitelloni,* the director turned to the lives of middle-class youths, banded together in aging, boyish defiance of society's requirements that they marry, find jobs, and settle into life's next phase. The opportunities of the town are limiting, the capacities of the boys too minimal to enable them to find rewarding work. Hands in overcoat pockets, they wander through the nights of early spring, dreaming, bragging, and slapping at one another like overgrown children. In the course of the film, Fausto is forced into marriage and a demeaning job. Fausto and Moraldo commit a minor theft. Natali, a budding writer, is importuned by a pathetic old actor on the beach. Alberto finds that his sister takes money from her lover. Finally, Moraldo leaves town on a dawn train, unsure where he is going, but determined to break away.

La Strada draws together themes and images from Fellini's previous films, locating them on a landscape whose barrenness sets off rather than absorbs the singular, archetypal trio of players. Giulietta Masina is a simple naïf, Gelsomina, whose mother sells her to Zampano for 10,000 lire. Zampano (Anthony Quinn) is a brutish, traveling entertainer who amuses in village squares by breaking an iron chain with his chest, moving from town to town on a motorcycle that hauls a makeshift trailer. The third figure is Il Matto, the Fool or Madman, played by Richard Basehart. He is a tightrope walker, an old enemy of Zampano; his ethereal flights of fancy suggest a spirit unbounded by, inadequate to, physicality. Eventually, he is killed by Zampano and the experience unbalances Gelsomina beyond endurance.

La Strada follows Zampano and Gelsomina in an episodic fashion through incidents that emphasize her bewildered, trusting need for human contact. Zampano's perceptions are limited to immediate gratifications. When Gel-

somina goes mad, he abandons her. He learns of her death years later and at the film's end collapses, drunk and sobbing on the beach. The film works as a poem works. Its images and behaviors accumulate meanings that resonate on one another after they are passed. The wandering life is without dramatic rise and tension, for no character is complete enough to support change and development. Instead, la strada, the road, only carries the trio from incident to incident. Each episode betrays haunting, evanescent moments whose fleeting passage defies clear-eyed "interpretation," leaving incomplete impressions. Entertaining for an outdoor wedding, Gelsomina is led away by children to a dark, shuttered upstairs room where a sick, dumb boy with an abnormal head crouches on a bed. Gelsomina tries to entertain him, then stops and the pair stare in fascination at one another. Something passes between them; we do not know what. A nun chases Gelsomina and her guides outside.

Locked from the trailer while Zampano spends the night with a girl he has picked up, Gelsomina is seen in the early morning with a horse beside her, neither conscious of the other. The horse wanders off. At the curb, its presence is not unreasonable, but it carries mystery, infusing the sequence with a dimension of surreality. *La Strada* is a film of delicate balances, like Il Matto's tightrope act. It is immeasurably enhanced by the musical score of Nino Rota whose bittersweet sentimentalities here serve special purpose. Il Matto whistles a tune to Gelsomina that she had earlier hummed to herself. Gelsomina learns to play it on a trumpet. Zampano hears the melody sung by a woman hanging out her washing. The woman tells him of Gelsomina's last days. The song suggests some romantic quality that finally touches Zampano, which brings him to tears and a first hint of humanity.

The film was denigrated by leftist critics in Italy who saw Fellini's departure from neorealism as a breach of social as well as esthetic faith. Like Antonioni, Fellini argued that neorealism had served its purpose well, but was inadequate to a newer world, to different visions, to a director's right to dominate his materials.

Il Bidone (1955) features the American Broderick Crawford as a swindler who finally loses confidence in his con games and dies, beaten by his companions and calling, panicked, on God. *Nights of Cabiria* (1956) develops the Gelsomina character with different elaborations. Masina plays a Roman whore. Gullibility leads her through adventures that customarily leave her victimized, undone, dragging herself back to another challenge. Twice she is robbed by lovers. She is picked up by a drunken movie star who reconciles with his girl friend and forces Cabiria to spend the night in the bathroom. With her fellow prostitutes and their pimps, she attends a religious excursion where the crippled call hysterically for miracles. The most moving sequence has Cabiria hypnotized on stage, revealing to the crowd her pathetic wish to marry. Cabiria's ultimate innocence and trust produces a Chaplinesque pathos before the jeering audience. Elsewhere Masina vehemently projects the vulgar, banal qualities of her character, as well as Cabiria's ultimate dignity. The conventionalized sentiment in the film is circumnavigated in Fellini's later work through the ironic and the grotesque.

La Dolce Vita (1960) updates the adventures of Moraldo after the train that took him from the vitelloni has reached Rome. Played by Mastroianni, Moraldo Rubini becomes Marcello Rubini, a journalist and press agent increasingly drawn into the pleasure seeking world of the Via Veneto, his urges to "write" now vague. Fellini's decadence has lubricious attraction. A jaded orgy is yet fascinating to watch, and Anita Ekberg marvellously plays a simple-minded Hollywood star whose figure, energy, and childishness arouse and exhaust her entourage of men.

Again, the construction is episodic. Steiner,

an intellectual mentor to Marcello, triggers the journalist's guilt, even though Steiner is anguished and alienated and finally kills himself. The film concludes with Marcello on the beach, trapped and despondant in the sweet life, aware of its uglinesses, ambiguously waving to an innocent young waitress who is symbolically distant, on the far side of the cove. Clear in its impulse, *La Dolce Vita* intrudes bizarre visions, such as the orgy and the final beach sequence with a drunken transvestite and a seamonster that fishermen have pulled up from the waters. The film balances these with intimate moments, as when Marcello's father visits Rome, and the two attend a cheap nightclub.

$8\frac{1}{2}$ (1963) developed in an atmosphere that came increasingly to characterize Fellini productions. Its story was incomplete in the director's head when production began, existing as a collection of themes and encounters. A hero sought help in his personal life by visiting a cardinal in hotel baths. A giant airship represented the scope and dangers of modern technology. Fellini searched for characters to people his film. As production continued, actors and crew remained ignorant of the entire plot, confident their director was guarding a secret. Eventually $8\frac{1}{2}$ took the form of Fellini's own perplexities. Immediate autobiography, but more importantly a self-reflexive meditation on the process of creation, its interminglings of memory, fantasy, and present shared some of the preoccupations of Alain Resnais' *Last Year at Marienbad* (1961). (*See* Chapter 20.)

A Fellini set became a studio of parts waiting for the maestro to orchestrate. Shooting itself failed to develop a complete conception, for Fellini acceded to a habit of requiring his actors not to speak dialogue but to mouth anything. He decided on the language later. In consequence, subsequent films, different from one another, still share extravagant subjective visions. An exception is an episode of *Spirits of the Dead* (1965), a collection of Edgar

Amarcord. By 1974, Fellini's early world of village life has evolved into a coherent, graceful interplay of Technicolored memories. On release, its beauty and humor clouded critical awareness of *Amarcord's* intricate design, more typically fictional than customary. (Museum of Modern Art/Film Stills Archive).

Allen Poe stories. Fellini's contribution is *Toby Dammit,* the tale of a drunken actor who bets his head against someone he believes to be the devil and loses. What distinguishes the short film, which is typically Fellinian in its satiric portrayal of a drunken nightclub celebration of an American actor, is the absence of any character's redemptive emotion.[2]

Until *8½,* Fellini protagonists finally reach some enlightenment, like Zampano, or reaffirm a commitment to life, like Cabiria. At the

least, the option exists, as for Marcello. In one respect, *8½* affirms everyone's free will, but says that no one ought to be forced to exercise it. By the time of *Juliet of the Spirits* (1965), the mode of fantasy seems to help insure some kind of emotional self-preservation. Ostensibly a kind of feminine *8½,* Giulietta Masina undergoes experiences that are half-real, half-dreamed. They reflect her insecurities, her childhood religious preoccupations, and her unsuccessful efforts to confront a deteriorating marriage.

For all its affection and humor, *Juliet of the Spirits* has a hardness that is intensified by

[2] *This point is elaborated in Peter Harcourt,* Six European Directors. *Baltimore, 1974.*

Fellini's employment of color: garish reds and blacks. It is a husband's fantasy of his wife's fantasies and there is something unnerving about the obtrusive presence of male preoccupations, half-nude nuns, the heavy-legged prostitute with her masklike, rouged mouth, the aging male homosexual in a clown's face of erotic grief. The film concludes with Masina wandering down a garden path, deserted by her fantasy grandfather who says she no longer needs him. Juliet is still involved with her spirits, invisible voices that demand her attention. One is unclear whether the actress-wife has been saved or condemned, which is a new kind of Fellinian ambiguity.

Fellini Satyricon (1969) turns to the world of Petronius; its pagan system frees Fellini from past religious obsessions. The Catholic-Christian world identified spiritual purity with innocence, simplicity, madness, and clowns. The world of *Satyricon* escapes ethical conflict, but this is accomplished at the price of communion and what Christians mean by love. Cruelties, debauchery, and self interest, unrestrained by moral compunction, possess an uninhibited magnificence, but they ally sex with destructive pleasures. *Satyricon* frees the director from a cultural frame he understands and resents; *Satyricon* leaves the Fellini images somehow flat, lacking the tensions that follow from their usual thrust toward consciousness.

The Clowns (1970), *Roma* (1972), and *Amarcord* (1974) all revert to an earlier Fellini world of memory and autobiographical invention. In *Roma,* the city plays central character, viewed in different places and historical stages. Like Bertolucci's *The Conformist,* it vividly recalls a time of fascist rule when the young Moraldo-Federico was entering Rome's embrace. *Amarcord* remembers Rimini differently from *I Vitelloni.* Now it is a place of politics, love affairs, and comic family disputes. *The Clowns* (1970) purports to be a

Fellini's Casanova. Donald Sutherland, aging lover, at table. During such intercourses of social exchange, Casanova attempts, and consistently fails, to generate human interest in any capacity beyond his sexual prowess. (Museum of Modern Art/Film Stills Archive)

semi-documentary, Fellini himself a character in search of what remains of this aging, depleting tradition. Tongue in cheek, Fellini satirizes the credibility of his filming team (there is always another camera behind), and of himself. In *Roma,* he stops Anna Magnani and asks her for an interview, but the actress replies, "I'm too tired . . . and besides, I don't trust you." Her observation is meant to put all of us on guard. The view that storytellers are liars seems to puzzle Fellini who also knows that all photographs tell a certain kind of truth.

Fellini's Casanova (1976) modifies the tenor of $8\frac{1}{2}$ so that Moraldo-Marcello, guised here as the classic Italian lover, becomes a rationalist whose priapic talent, which seems to exist almost independent of his idealist self, thrusts Casanova into an erotic world that denies him the exercise of every other skill and impulse. A severely misunderstood film, *Fellini's Casanova* is as intricately designed as it is dreadfully recorded, sharing some of the archetypal patterns of *La Strada.* The metaphor of automotized behavior (as in loveless sex) replaces the metaphor of the road. Femininity becomes separated into the devouring virago and (very occasionally) an emotionally-generous, unthreatening woman.

LUIS BUÑUEL

The films of Luis Buñuel are dominated by one vision: the obsessive power of human desire; and one inhibition, society. His strategy shifts with the times, adapting to Buñuel's estimation of which techniques may bypass audience defenses with the greatest force, how he may sidestep the worst pitfall, which is to be absorbed and applauded by the very sensibility he wants to attack.

Buñuel came from Calanda, Spain, studied literature and philosophy at the University of Madrid, and journeyed to Paris, where he worked for Jean Epstein as an assistant on *The Fall of the House of Usher.* He returned to Spain with Salvador Dali, and the pair composed *Un Chien andalou* (1928).

Buñuel and Dali had not yet joined the surrealists. They were in fact acclaimed by the surrealists as brothers when the film, produced in France, appeared. Satirizing themselves, the intertitles separate episodes: "Once upon a time," "Towards Three in the Morning," "In the Spring."

While a cloud crosses the moon in an identical composition, Buñuel himself slits the eye of a young woman with a razor. Dressed in skirt, cap, and stiff collar, wearing a striped box, a cyclist falls to the curb where he is seen by the woman of the earlier scene, who rushes from her apartment to his side. In her room, the cyclist stares at his hand; ants crawl in the palm. The couple look out the window to the street where a masculine-dressed woman pokes with a stick at an amputated hand. A policeman puts the hand in the striped box. The woman is hit by a car. Excited by the scene, the cyclist seizes his companion by her breasts, caressing them. The shot dissolves to an identical action on her naked body, then to the stroking of naked buttocks. The young man gasps as if in orgasm, and blood drips from his mouth. The girl escapes, threatening him with a tennis racket. He seizes two ropes and hauls two pianos across the room with disfigured donkey corpses atop and priests tied to the cords. A stranger bursts in, throws the cyclist's costume out the window and makes him stand facing the wall in punishment. Books in the cyclist's hands become revolvers and he shoots the intruder, who sinks to the ground in an open field, his hand lightly touching the back of a naked woman. The cyclist loses his mouth; his face is covered with hair from the woman's armpit. She joins a man on a beach where they examine and discard the cyclist's costume. In the final scene, the last two are buried in sand.

In its seventeen minutes, *Un Chien andalou*

Un Chien Andalou. Dressed in a suit, her hair cut short, a woman prods a human hand as spectators gather. The view is overseen from a window above the street. A policeman will present her with the amputation and the crowd will disperse. (Museum of Modern Art/Film Stills Archive)

seems to express the obstacles before a couple striving for sexual comsumation in the face of cultural inhibitions. It appears, too, to trace a kind of psychosexual development, finding aberration and rebellion necessary consequences of the punitive effects of religion and parents. Much of the Dali-disposed dream imagery has been cannibalized by advertising in recent years, but the eye-slitting sequence remains impermeable to easy viewing, an angry challenge to the eye of the beholder.

L'Age d'or (1930) approaches feature length (sixty-three minutes) and is more completely Buñuel's, although Dali shared writing credits. While the earlier film was silent (Buñuel ac-companied it with phonograph records and prepared a seventies version that alternates a tango with Wagner's *Tristan und Isolde*), *L'Age d'or* uses sound. Classical themes, especially the same Wagner, intersperse with sound effects, dialogue, and silent intertitles.

Opening on a prelude that appears to be a straightforward documentary on scorpions, the film proceeds with scenes of bishops celebrating mass on a rocky terrain by the beach. Majorcan bandits assemble an arsenal of eating utensils, sticks, rope, and needles, then fall exhausted. An assemblage of dignitaries lays the cornerstone for "Imperial Rome," perhaps with a turd as mortar, while a couple makes love in the mud. In a modern city the same pair is separated by authorities. The man (Gaston Modot) frees himself with important-looking credentials and attends a dinner that proceeds uninterrupted although a farm cart is driven through the room and fire breaks out in the kitchen. Modot reunites with his beloved, but they are inhibited by their clothes and by an apparent requirement to sit in chairs. Modot is telephoned by the Minister of the Interior, who shoots himself when Modot refuses to help rescue children and to subdue street rioting. Modot's woman deserts him for an elderly orchestra conductor. Despairing, he flings a flaming tree, a bishop, and a stuffed giraffe out the window. In the final sequence, participants in an orgy (reference is made to the Marquis de Sade and *The 120 Days of Sodom*) leave their chateau. The leader, who is Christ, returns to murder a surviving young girl. He loses his beard, which attaches itself to a crucifix, blowing in the wind.

L'Age d'or views the extreme love that demands consumation despite convention and obstacle, an emotion the surrealists extolled as *amour fou,* as a central weapon to expose and to overcome bourgeois society's corrupting, dogmatic regulations. In the face of such restriction, Modot kicks a dog and a blind man and slaps the Marquise who has accidentally spilled her wine. The last incident arouses greater indignation than a game keeper's shooting his son for playing a small joke. In *L'Age d'or,* Buñuel's anger is more sharpened, his targets more explicit. Government and institutionalized religion are seen to destroy what is human in man and then to appeal to his "better self" for their institutionalized perpetuation. The film was beset with violence attending its exhibition.

Las Hurdes/Land Without Bread (1932) differs markedly from earlier work. Indeed, it assumes the appearance of a documentary and the surreal esthetic disguises itself behind a purported travelogue exploring the Hurdes, a mountainous Spanish region whose inhabi-tants live in abject poverty. Accompanied by commentary, the picture views a wedding rite in which horsemen tear heads from live chickens hung across the street. A stream is used by villagers both as a sewer and for drinking water. Bread is unknown and viewed with suspicion. Inbreeding produces dwarfs and idiots. Bees sting a donkey to death. A baby's corpse is carried to the nearest cemetery, miles away.

The commentary has a sound of disengaged rationality, reciting facts and travelogue anecdotes with impersonal intonation. But sometimes rage breaks through and later commentary assumes a bitter irony. In the midst of their absolute degradation, children in a schoolroom are taught plane geometry and maxims like "Respect your neighbor's property." The camera centers on an eighteenth-century engraving of the aristocracy, and the narrator inquires, "Why is this absurd picture here?" Brahm's Fourth Symphony provides a continuous, shocking romantic commentary on the visuals. At times the narrator assumes a condescending tone toward the ignorance of the Hurdanos. A man is bitten by a snake. "The species is not deadly, but the Hurdanos, trying to cure it, infect themselves and die." A mountain goat is said to lose its footing, but we see a puff of rifle fire in the lower corner of the screen. Finally, Buñuel seems to question the purpose of such an existence, choosing images to prove rather than investigate his thesis.

Buñuel was not to direct another film for fifteen years. He separated himself from surrealism and worked for the Spanish Republicans as a producer. He was employed by the Museum of Modern Art in New York City in 1938, and later made Spanish language versions of films for the United States Army. After working for Warner Brothers in a like capacity, Buñuel went to Mexico, at first directing inexpensive, commercial features.

Los Olvidados (1950) shares some of the qualities of De Sica's *Shoe Shine,* a story of adolescent delinquents in Mexico City. The

Luis Buñuel (1900–   )

Un Chien Andalou (with Salvador Dali) (short) (France)	1928
L'Age d'or (with Salvador Dali) (France)	1930
Las Hurdes/Land Without Bread (Spain)	1932
Gran Casino (Mexico)	1947
El Gran Calavera (Mexico)	1949
Los Olvidados (Mexico)	1950
Susana (Mexico)	1951
La Hija del Engano (Mexico)	1951
Una Mujer sin Amor (Mexico)	1951
Subida al Cielo (Mexico)	1951
El Bruto (Mexico)	1952
El/This Strange Passion (Mexico)	1953
Robinson Crusoe (United States)	1952
Cumbres Borrascocas (Mexico)	1952
La Illusion Viaja en Tranvia (Mexico)	1953
El Rio y la Muerte (Mexico)	1954
Ensayo de un Crimen/The Criminal Life of Archibaldo de la Cruz (Mexico)	1955
Cela s'appelle l'aurore (France-Italy)	1955
La Mort dans ce jardin/Evil Eden (France-Mexico)	1956
Nazarin (Mexico)	1958
La Fievre mont a El Pao/Republic of Sin (France-Mexico)	1959
The Young One (Mexico)	1960
Viridiana (Spain-Mexico)	1961
El Angel Exterminador/The Exterminating Angel (Mexico)	1962
Le Journal d'une femme de chambre (France)	1964
Simon del Desierto/Simon of the Desert (Mexico)	1965
Belle de jour (France)	1969
La Voie Lactée/The Milky Way (French) (Mexico)	1968
Tristana (Spain-Italy-France)	1970
Le Charm discret de la bourgeoisie/The Discreet Charm of the Bourgeoisie (France)	1972
La Fantòme de la liberté/The Phantom of Liberty (France)	1974
That Obscure Object of Desire (Spain-France)	1977

incidents come from police records. Gangs plague a blind man in his hovel and pitch a legless beggar off his cart. One boy kills his friend in a vengeful knife fight. The body is thrown, like the refuse of all the children's lives, onto a garbage dump. Selectively located among the sordid episodes are erotic moments. As if she were offering herself, a mother holds meat out to her dreaming son. Milk splashes over the naked thighs of an adolescent girl.

A procession of Mexican features followed, ranging from eighteen-day quickies to films in which sequences, or sometimes passing images, evoke the power of Buñuel's imagination, usually a conception that holds incongruous imagery in a matrix of the "real" with implicit social criticism. In *Subida al Cielo* (1951), the varied riders on a rural bus experience a birth, a wedding and a funeral. Mired, the bus is pulled out by a little girl leading two harnessed oxen with a string, leaving one passenger with his wooden leg stuck in the mud. In a dream, the bus becomes a greenhouse. Finally the hero affixes his dead mother's thumbprint to her will.

Robinson Crusoe (1952) subtly emphasizes the pressures of sexual prohibition on an island populated by two men. *Cumbres Borrascosas* (1952) is the director's version of *Wuthering Heights,* a surrealist favorite for its amour fou and Heathcliff's brooding madness. About to break open Cathy's coffin in a burst of necrophilia, Heathcliff hallucinates a figure with a shotgun to be Cathy, enshrouded in her white burial clothes that resemble a wedding gown. *The Criminal Life of Archibaldo de la Cruz* (1955) describes a man who has equated love and death so that he must murder each woman he is sexually attracted to. He never succeeds, but the act of burning a wax model of one victim leads him to erotic ecstacy as he watches her features melt and flatten. *Cela s'appelle l'aurore* (It is called the dawn) (1955) was filmed in France with a plot involving police investigation of an escaped mur-

derer. Buñuel's police chief, significantly, is an admirer of the conservative Catholic poet Paul Claudel. His handcuffs rest on a Claudel volume. The office is decorated with a Crucifixion rendering by Dali, who had parted with Buñuel when, he said, he realized that *L'Age d'or* was anti-Catholic.

The most fully realized of Buñuel's early features, *El* (1952) is a kind of case history of Don Francisco, a wealthy paranoid who wins away the fiancée of a friend, then wildly accuses her of unfaithfulness as soon as their wedding has taken place. Pressures of his past have somehow tipped the passion of Don Francisco into pathology, and Buñuel admits the depth of feeling, which is in its own way altogether genuine, as well as the real danger to the sympathetic wife. In his worst state, Don Francisco seeks to protect his "property" from infidelity with scissors, rope, needle and thread. Fearful of spies, he jabs a needle into a hotel bedroom keyhole.

Buñuel cleverly develops the metaphor of Don Francisco's crazily-built and furnished home as the interior of his own mind. The house is described as the strange creation of his father. Falling into mania, Don Francisco compulsively rattles a cage against the bannisters of stairs he fears to ascend. The zig-zag walk is taken up in *El*'s final scenes when Don Francisco has been confined to a monastery. Finally, when the lunatic is visited by his wife, now married to her original betrothed, Don Francisco's calm assurance that he has found peace mingles with clear confirmation of his paranoid suspicion. Thus, Buñuel retrieves his protagonist from easy condemnation.

Nazarin (1958) traces the wanderings of a priest who chooses to accept Christ's precepts literally. His followers a dwarf and two women who suggest Martha and Mary, Nazarin preaches basic Christian tenets, but like Bresson's country priest, fails in personal communication with the people he touches. Seeking to comfort the victims of plague, Nazarin only manages to disturb the last moments of a dying couple. Trying to work, he triggers violence between laborers and their supervisors. Chained and led away as a criminal, Nazarin is startled when a woman offers him a pineapple and shrinks from her gesture; then he accepts it. One version concludes on Nazarin's apparent recognition of his own weakness. In another he is forgiven by Jesus in a dream.

The Young One (1960), like *Robinson Crusoe*, is an English-language film, a challenge to racism and religious hypocrisy in which a black fugitive, wanted for rape, is captured and used as a scapegoat by a white game warden and a boatman for both their real and invented crimes. The black is drawn without condescending nobilities, but *The Young One* retains a didactic, artificial flavor.

Produced in Spain with a script approved by the state film organization, *Viridiana* (1961) was later found embarrassing in the extreme. Authorities failed to confiscate all prints; worse yet, the Cannes Film Festival awarded *Viridiana* the Gold Palm as Spain's official entry. Just before becoming a nun, Viridiana visits her uncle. Overcome by her resemblance to his deceased wife, the uncle drugs and nearly seduces his niece. In the morning, he tells her his seduction was successful, then hangs himself. Inheriting the estate, she shares it with the uncle's illegitimate son, seeking to make it a haven for the poor and needy. In her absence, the guests stage an orgy, unconsciously mimicking da Vinci's *The Last Supper* to the music of Handel's Hallelujah Chorus. Returning, Viridiana is raped by one of the beggars. Finally, she settles into a game of cards with her cousin and a servant who has become his mistress. The implication is that the three will live together in a ménage à trois.

Like Nazarin, Viridiana is withdrawn (a cow's udder embarrasses her) and proud. Fate completely shifts Viridiana's life patterns, but Buñuel's ending suggests that she has somehow learned from experience. Viridiana's spirituality is seen to be neither better nor worse

but only different from the materialist cousin who sets about improving the estate as Viridiana busies herself with charity. Like Chaplin, Buñuel knows that society's victims are not ennobled by their poverty. He is equally suspicious of liberal palliatives. The cousin sees a suffering dog in the roadway, forced to run under a carriage and rouse the horse in front. The cousin buys the dog. Another cart appears with another dog beneath.

The Exterminating Angel (1962) proposes that fashionable guests in a Mexico City mansion inexplicably find themselves unable to depart. No one can pass through the salon door. Except for one loyal butler, servants vacate the house. Humor, patience, and manners surrender to anger and cruel competitions. A loving couple kill themselves in a closet (amour fou absorbed into bourgeois conformity). Urns must be used as toilets. A sheep wanders into the room and is ritually slaughtered, blindfolded, for food. A circus bear, rented by the hostess for entertainment, roams the empty house. Fetishes and hallucinations develop. Returning from a closet lavatory, a woman confides that she had seen great birds flying below her. Finally, events which preceded the incarceration are reenacted, each disheveled guest in his original place. The spell is broken. Everyone attends a mass in celebration. The priests find themselves unable to depart the cathedral. Sheep wander in. Gunfire is heard outside in the street.

Again Buñuel plays variations on conformity's paralysis of feeling, of will, and of human freedom. The perversions that dominate life's unfortunates lie just beneath everyone's apparent normality. Ritual underlies the story. In an opening sequence, one shot of laughing guests entering their host's home is repeated without explanation, with the camera angle slightly changed.

The Diary of a Chambermaid (1964) compares interestingly with Renoir's 1945 American version of the Octave Mirbeau novel. Where Renoir investigates class roles and rela-

The Exterminating Angel. Drawn, disheveled, and desperate, the party guests seek to reenact that moment when they were once ready to depart and somehow failed to act. Buñuel says he finds the rituals of social exchange hilarious. (Museum of Modern Art/ Film Stills Archive)

tionships, Buñuel notices what is vicious or simply distorted. He moves the time from turn-of-the-century to 1928, when fascism was developing a following among the French. As Celestine, the Chambermaid, Jeanne Moreau is enterprising, ambitious, and self-serving, knowing that looks are her only bargaining point. Joseph the gamekeeper is a fascist enthusiast who slowly kills a duck with a needle "because it enhances the flavor." The aging, proper employer requires Celestine to model his collection of ladies' boots, rubbing his hand lovingly along her legs as she reads to him.

In its forty-two minutes, *Simon of the Desert* (1965) examines the temptations of St. Simon Stylites who lived for thirty-seven years on top of a column, preaching to pilgrims. Simon restores hands to the stumps of a

penitent, who seems unsatisfied with the quality of the miracle and proceeds to slap his daughter. Like other Buñuel religious figures, Simon is proud and withdrawn, too busy to think about his mother. He accepts a superior pedestal from a wealthy merchant. Falling into madness, Simon is tempted by the devil in the form of a beautiful, bearded woman. Finally, he is transported to a Greenwich Village discotheque where patrons are performing a last dance, The Radioactive Flesh. Apparently the production ran out of money.

Belle de jour (1960) features Catherine Deneuve as Séverine, unsatisfied doctor's wife. She fantasizes masochistic sex and frequents a brothel calling herself Belle de Jour. One lover shoots the doctor in the spine, crippling him permanently. Persuaded by a vicious friend to tell the truth to her husband,

Séverine enters his room. After her disclosures, the husband appears first to die, then miraculously gets up from his chair.

Séverine's fantasies have been signalled throughout the film by a jingle of bells on a driven carriage that figures in her inventions. The final scene shows the carriage from the window, empty. Thus the ending throws earlier rationales into confusion. Past scenes may either have been false when apparently real, or else no part can be more believed than another. At heart, relative believability is less important than the Buñuelian exploration of sexual potency and its relation to society. Séverine is frigid with her husband, free with lovers who pay her. The paralysis of her husband does not seem altogether displeasing to her. The whorehouse carries a chic, sanitized therapeutic aura about it. The gangster who shot Séverine's husband dies by a policeman's bullet, finally himself the victim of the woman's will.

Tristana (1970) enjoins revolution, amour fou, and society's paralysing effect on the individual. In Toledo during the early thirties, a middle-aged man, Don Lope (Fernando Rey), assumes the guardianship of a young woman, Tristana (Catherine Deneuve), then takes her to bed so that he may be, as he says, either father or husband, depending on whim. Tristana runs away with a young painter, then returns to Don Lope after falling critically ill from a leg infection. The leg is amputated. Urged by a priest to sanctify the relationship, she marries Lope, then denies him sex. Finally, as she recalls the key moments of her life, Tristana hastens her sick husband's death.

As the film progresses, Don Lope changes from an atheistic, free-thinking genteel libertarian to a decrepit old man, glad of warmth and happy to play host to the local priests. First a religious, innocent girl, Tristana turns calculating and bitterly enraged. Horatio, the painter, appears as a bohemian-liberal whose uncertainty betrays a lack of inner conviction. Subsidiary characters, Saturna, a housekeeper, and Saturno, her mute son, contribute proletarian ingredients in a Spain victimized by the rhetoric and suppressions of the republic.

The Discreet Charm of the Bourgeoisie

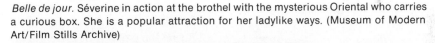

Belle de jour. Séverine in action at the brothel with the mysterious Oriental who carries a curious box. She is a popular attraction for her ladylike ways. (Museum of Modern Art/Film Stills Archive)

477

(1972) follows the curious adventures of four middle-class figures who seem at this stage to be viewed by Buñuel almost with affectionate tolerance, like charming pets who simply cannot be trained to live any way but their own. Their sexual couplings have the programmed eroticism of best sellers. Their concern with manners transcends sense. Neither wars nor political uprising nor tyranny nor murder can interrupt a proper dinner party. The bourgeoisie views its own subjectivities with scandalous fascination. Any activity may be interrupted, any stranger recognized if a dream promises to be recounted. The director plays on these dreams confusedly to mirror apparently trustworthy frames of reference back onto themselves. The dreams are only different versions of ordinary events. A lieutenant introduces himself to three fashionable women in a restaurant and recounts how his mother's ghost led him to poison his father. Later, a military group on maneuvers interrupts its battle simulation to hear one man's dream. The mother in this dream is the same as the ghost-mother in the previous story. Later, the characters dream different versions of the same dinner party. In one case, curtains are suddenly lifted to display the entire event as a performance on stage, which itself is being dreamed with all the spectators included.

That Obscure Object of Desire (1977) is based on the same Pierre Louys novel, *Woman and Puppet,* which von Sternberg used for *The Devil is a Woman.* Where von Sternberg concentrated on visualizing Dietrich as a woman from whom no man might be free of temptation, Buñuel seems to parody his old vision of *amour fou.* Now the beautiful young woman and the aging man alternately prostrate themselves before and heap abuse upon one another. Perversion here evolves from a woman's fear that if she gives herself to the man she will lose him. In a extraordinary act, Buñuel casts two actresses in the woman's role. He shifts them in and out with cavalier disregard to any apparent narrative scheme, as if ridiculing the critic's impulse to locate some intentional structuring design.

His films numbering more than thirty, Buñuel in his seventies realized that social change threatened to outwit the surrealist arsenal, but this only signalled that new weapons were needed.

If you remember, I quoted what Breton said to me: ''My dear friend, nowadays it's no longer possible to scandalize anyone.'' And he was right. How is it possible to shock after the Nazi mass murders and the atom bombs dropped on Japan? I feel that today the use of scandal is a negative action. *L'Age d'or,* which in its day was a militant film that aimed at raping clear consciences — and was therefore scandalous — is now a harmless work that was applauded by the audience at the Lincoln Center in New York . . . What I am trying to do in my films is to disturb people and destroy the rules of a kind of conformism that wants everyone to think that they are living in the best of all possible worlds.[3]

INGMAR BERGMAN

During the early 1960's Bergman was director of the Royal Dramatic Theater in Stockholm. His background in drama undoubtedly contributes to the many exceptional acting performances in the films. Bergman is heir to the theater of Ibsen, the film tradition of Stiller, Sjöberg, and Seastrom, a forbidding Lutheran parson father, and the Swedish termperament. In and out of favor for twenty years, Bergman's breadth of undertakings and his capacity to experiment continue to impress.

Characteristically, a Bergman protagonist,

[3] *1965 interview with Manuel Michel, quoted in Freddy Buache,* The Cinema of Luis Buñuel. *New York, 1973, p. 29.*

Ingmar Bergman (1918–   )

Kris/Crisis	1946
Det Regnar pa var Kärlek/It Rains on our Love	1946
Skepp till Indialand/A Ship Bound for India	1947
Musik i Mörker/Music in Darkness	1948
Hamnstadt/Port of Call	1948
Fängelse/Prison	1948
Törst/Thirst	1949
Till Glädje/To Joy	1950
Sant Händler inte Här/This Can't Happen Here	1950
Sommerlek/Summer Interlude	1951
Kvinnors Väntan/Waiting Women	1952
Sommaren med Monika/Summer with Monika	1952
Gycklarnas Afton/Sawdust and Tinsel/The Naked Night	1953
En Lektion i Karlek/A Lesson in Love	1954
Kvinnodröm/Journey into Autumn	1955
Sommarnattens Leende/Smiles of a Summer Night	1955
Det Sjunde Inseglt/The Seventh Seal	1956
Smultronstället/Wild Strawberries	1957
Nära Livet/So Close to Life/Brink of Life	1958
Ansiktet/The Face/The Magician	1958
Jungfrukällen/The Virgin Spring	1960
Djävulens Oga/The Devil's Eye	1960
Sasom i en Spegel/Through a Glass Darkly	1961
Nattsvardsgästerna/Winter Light	1963
Tystnaden/The Silence	1963
For atte inte Tala om Alla De sa Kvinnor/ Now About All These Women	1964
Persona	1966
Vargtimmen/Hour of the Wolf	1968
Skammen/Shame	1969
Riten/The Rite/The Ritual (for TV)	1969
En Passion/The Passion of Anna	1969
Faro Document	1971
Beroringen/The Touch	1973
Viskningar och rop/Cries and Whispers	1973
Scener ur ett aktenskap/Scenes from a Marriage	1974
Ansikte mot ansikte/Face to Face	1975
The Magic Flute	1976
The Serpent's Egg (Germany)	1977

be he doctor, psychiatrist, knight, circus manager, or child, confronts himself and changes. The direction of that shift is not necessarily positive. Indeed, despair commonly figures; yet almost every project explicates an idea about the human situation, developed as a search for further understanding through self-awareness. The plot is often a purposive journey, sometimes a splitting up of one personality into separate components that have the appearance of autonomous humans.

Bergman entered film as a writer, his first credit in Alf Sjöberg's *Torment* (1944) whose central figure was a sadistic Latin teacher. Nicknamed Caligula, the man humiliates and tortures his students with perverse pleasure. *Torment*'s success helped to establish Sweden's reentry into the world market and provided Bergman the chance to write and direct his first feature, *Crisis* (1946).

Like *Torment*, Bergman's early films deal with stern, abnormal authority figures who diminish and frustrate adolescents. At best, a boy may establish some sympathetic rapport with a young woman. In *A Ship to India* (1947), a hunchback son is cured of his disability by a nightclub girl. The problem grew out of parental neglect. In *It Rains on Our Love* (1946), a young couple suffers an unending series of misfortunes, each stemming from social hypocrisy, bureaucracy, and social rejection.

Thirst/Three Strange Loves (1949) establishes the prototypical Bergman husband-wife relationship, splintered by growing alienation that takes the forms of affairs, psychiatric consultation, lesbianism, and suicide. Bergman intercuts one couple's train ride through Germany with flashbacks showing the wife's behavior and a parallel but unconnected story about the husband's earlier wife. Like the pair in *A Ship to India* who do not love but continue to help one another, the marriage in *Thirst* is finally preserved because "Hell together is better than hell alone."

American release titles to Bergman movies often display no more than a distributor's greedy perplexity about how to market them. *Illicit Interlude* (1951) has a ballerina's lover accidentally killed. She returns to their island of summer pleasures, seeking to rid herself from sorrowing withdrawals into the past. The conjunction of death, summer idyll, nostalgia, and a rural setting of wild strawberries and fruit trees recurs in films otherwise as different as *The Seventh Seal* (1956) and *Wild Strawberries* (1957).

The viewer who is able to follow a cycle of Bergman films finds himself tracing patterns of interweaving ideas expressed by playing variations on certain germinal relationships. *Summer with Monika* returns a young pair to an island off the coast of Stockholm. This time two shopworkers spend a rebellious holiday. When she becomes pregnant they marry, but the girl, Monika, abandons her husband and baby for another man. Here the young people, physically attractive, are self-absorbed, ill-educated adolescents, unequipped to understand the significance of their actions, and their island holiday has the quality of flight.

Monika was played by Harriet Andersson whose sullen, erotic energy is put to more concentrated used in *The Naked Night,* also known as *Sawdust and Tinsel* (1953). Its Swedish title translates as *The Night of the Clowns,* a film of intense, inexorable progression, a dark, painful rumination on illusion, dignity, and the sorrows that follow from sexual relationships. Albert, a circus owner, returns with the run-down troupe to his home town and unsuccessfully seeks to escape by reconciling with his abandoned wife and child. In retaliation, his mistress, the bareback rider (Harriet Andersson), visits a theater company where she is seduced by one of the actors. At the evening's circus performance, the owner is humiliated by the actor. They fight in the arena and the cuckold is diminished further by being publicly beaten. He fails at suicide. then shoots a sick, old bear in whose torment Albert sees his own imprisoned state. The de-

The Naked Night. Albert (Ake Grönberg) contemplates suicide, threatens Frost, and finally shoots the bear. Anne (Harriet Andersson) looks on. In Truffaut's *The 400 Blows,* Doinel steals a photo of Harriet Andersson from a theater display for Bergman's film. (Museum of Modern Art/ Film Stills Archive)

moralized troupe decamps, Albert and his mistress walking behind their wagon.

In *The Naked Night* for the first time Bergman surrenders to near-total pessimism, lightened only by the characters' intentions to survive and their agreement to share a common fate. The desertion, seduction, and brawl each strips away a self-protecting layer of delusion. As the manager of the theater company says to Albert, "We are socially above you, for you circus people only endanger your lives. In the theater, we risk our dignity." The terror of social nakedness is spelled out in a prologue, developed in flashback and filmed like a grainy, expressionist silent mime, accompanied by artillery fire and drums. Alma, wife of the clown Frost and a performer with the bear, amuses herself before a company of soldiers. She is "long of tooth" and resorts to bathing naked with the men, half-maddened by the need to hold their gaze. But Alma is only ridiculous to the soldiers. Frost strips to his long underwear, wades into the water and carries his wife on his back along an exhausting, hot, stony road at great physical and mental cost. Frost is broken by the experience, a shell of clown features, his only comfort now an hysterical wife. Unless Albert and his mistress can find something more, Albert's future will follow the direction of Frost's.

If women in Bergman's early films tend to be faithless lovers, domineering mothers, or passive dependents, they come increasingly to show a resilience and understanding against which the men fail to measure. In comedies such as *Smiles of a Summer Night* (1955) and

Ingmar Bergman   481

The Devil's Eye (1960), the women's roles are increasingly major to the story. More important, in *Women's Dreams* (1955) women, faced with their lovers' weaknesses and superficialities, meet the consequences of these relationships with edgy confidence. Women come to share Bergman's most agonized quests, to become heroines.[4]

The Seventh Seal (1956) brings the director's religious preoccupations, his foreboding sense of ubiquitous death, into open view. The film is set during the fourteenth-century crusades when Sweden was devastated by the Black Death. With his squire Jöns, the Knight Antonios Block returns from fighting and meets Death on a beach. The two engage in a chess game for Block's life. Inevitably he must lose, but the game buys time so that Block may finally perform some gratuitous act that will give meaning to his life of wandering chivalry. This happens when he is able to rescue a pair of itinerant jugglers, Jof and Mia, from Death. The jugglers alone are spared when the spector arrives at the Knight's home, returned to his wife.

In the world of *The Seventh Seal,* an institutionalized church burns witches, while roving bands of flagellants hysterically purify themselves in fearful preparation for the plague. Like Don Quixote, Antonios Block is a removed figure; his quest is ultimately a search for rational assurances that may serve in lieu of faith to justify the experiences of life. The theologian who first persuaded the knight to embark on his crusade is now a grave robber. In contrast, Jöns is a practical, unbelieving companion whose skepticism assures him of life's pleasures. In the end, there is no difference. The innocence of the wandering jugglers places them alone in a state of grace. They ask only answerable questions of life.

The psychological commitments can lead only to tragic consequences, madness, or ultimate disillusion. *Wild Strawberries* casts an aging medical professor, movingly played by Victor Seastrom shortly before his own death. to suffer the awakened memories and anxious dreams of his past. A young woman reminds him of a time that preceded the callous, cold dealings with family and friends which characterized all the years of his professional success. The professor's new serenity grows from his ability to reject psychological shells that had insulated him from human contact.

Organized as an automobile trip, which Professor Borg undertakes to receive an honorary doctorate, *Wild Strawberries* is a multi-leveled portrait, intensified by Seastrom's presence and by Bergman's own preoccupations with stern, lonely father-figures. The film makes affectionate reference to earlier Seastrom movies. Like Block, Borg looks for some key, some awareness that may mitigate the severity of his personal, as distinguished from his professional, career, both approaching an end. Borg's dream (himself in a coffin, clocks without hands) makes his growing fears conscious. Visiting a deserted, childhood summer home, Borg "sees" an incident from his youth with cousin Sara, his love. Bibi Andersson plays both this Sara and the hitchhiker whose spontaneous affection serves as catalyst. The professor's dreams and daydreams are colored, too, by his own personality, sometimes self-serving, sometimes nostalgically sentimental, but always seeking to understand through introspection. The reward of human understanding is a cessation of loneliness.

The Magician (1958) is a nineteenth-century actor, Dr. Albert Emanuel Vogler, who entertains in a consul's drawing room. Vogler is both magician and mesmerist and the possibility that his performances may entail some greater power than illusion puzzles and frightens his audience. A hypnosis apparently

[4] *Critic Joan Mellen disagrees with the general notion that Bergman is specially equipped to delineate women. Rather, she argues, Bergman's women are diminished not by metaphysical angst, but because they cannot escape the biological urges of their bodies. See Joan Mellen, "Bergman and Women:* Cries and Whispers," *Film Quarterly (Fall, 1973) and Joan Mellen,* Women and Their Sexuality in the New Film. *New York, 1973. Ch.4.*

goes askew. The subject strangles Vogler. Vérgerus, a suspicious guest, performs an autopsy, then is himself attacked as if by Vogler's ghost. But it is all tricks. The corpse was a fellow actor. Vogler's apparent power is only slight of hand. One of his tools is a magic lantern. The equation of Vogler with Bergman is clear and intentional. *The Magician* is a variant of *The Naked Night,* with Vogler's contemptuous dismissal from the consulate the price exacted for his final shattering of illusions. Audiences want to be tricked.

In *The Virgin Spring* (1960), a young virgin is raped and killed in the forest by three herdsmen. Her father learns that the deed was committed by the very group enjoying shelter in his home. He slaughters all. The father vows to erect a church in his daughter's memory; miraculously a spring gushes up from the spot where she was assaulted. The picture has the quality of a medieval ballad from which it derives. Less a miracle than a cathartic release, the spring is Bergman's way to recognize and to reward the absolute commitment of the father's actions: a ritual purification, brutal revenge including the killing of an innocent boy, the recognition of his transgression, and his abject repentance.

Through a Glass Darkly (1961), *Winter Light* (1963), and *The Silence* (1963) constitute a triad of films in which the central character must face the question of God's existence and, if He does exist, of God's nature. In *Through a Glass Darkly,* David, a middling-successful writer returned from abroad and scheduled soon to leave for Yugoslavia, visits his children, Karin and Minus, and Karin's husband Martin. A schizophrenic, Karin's condition deteriorates until she believes she has seen God as a great spider. The image suggests David's self-protective aloofness, and he is shown to be morbidly fascinated with Karin's condition. Finally, David succeeds in establishing enough rapport with the young Minus to rescue him, perhaps, from the pitfalls of growing alienation and of an incestuous affair with his sister. His last state-

ment, the film's conclusion, is an incredulous, "Daddy talked to me." Perhaps love is the manifestation of God. Perhaps love *is* God. In any case, there is some connection.

Tomas Ericsson, pastor of an outlying Lutheran church in *Winter Light,* fails the spiritual needs of the few people attending his service. His own faith dissipates but he finally develops a will to continue, to conduct services when only one parishioner has come. The argument of the film begins with the premise of the comforting God of love that had given stability to Minus. In counseling one church member, Tomas finds his own despair reflected. Dispassionately, he destroys the other's faith. In its place appears some such sensation as Karin's spider, followed by the man's suicide. Faced with his own disbelief, with the silence of God, Tomas' decision to continue is ambiguous to interpretation.

In *The Silence,* two sisters, accompanied by one's young son, enter a foreign city. They do not understand the language; they stop in an ornate, old hotel, where tanks and air raid alarms can be heard outside. Anna has a liaison with a waiter, which leads to a quarrel with Ester who is sick and has a lesbian attachment to her sister. Anna leaves with her son. The characters are purposefully one-dimensional. The mood is despairing, each figure isolated. Ester masturbates on her bed, an empty ritual. A baroque microcosm of a world where God does not speak, the hotel is stained, dilapidated and nearing collapse.

As the sisters are two aspects of one woman in *The Silence,* as Pastor Tomas' effort at counseling fails when he sees himself reflected in the parishioner, *Persona* (1966) juxtaposes an actress (Elizabeth) who has lost the will to speak, and a nurse (Alma) whose developing affection for Elizabeth and her own chattering self-regard seem to destroy personal stability. Elizabeth's action is a recoiling refusal anymore to engage in a world of cruelty, exploitation, and war. Seemingly healthy and stable, Alma is really the weaker of the two. Their

Face to Face. Dr. Jenny Isaakson (Liv Ullman) suffers a marriage breakup, rape, suicide, and the horrors of remembered childhood punishments in a film radically altered from the original television script. Ullman's tour-de-force breakdown stunned trauma-sensitive critics. (Copyright © Cinematograph A. B. Faro 1975. All Rights Reserved.) (Museum of Modern Art/Film Stills Archive)

close isolation in a seaside cottage leads finally to violence that is unsuspected to exist in either, the very qualities Elizabeth fled. Uncannily, the two women's faces merge on screen into a single portrait.

Persona skirts in and out of scenes which may be Alma's hallucinations or perhaps some middle ground of emotional transference between the two women. The film ends with a self-reflexive reminder that we have seen a movie, nothing more but nothing less. Its opening prologue, like the Alma-Frost sequence in *The Naked Night,* melds images of sex, religion, cruelty, death, and isolation with reminders that we are spectators to "entertainment." Elizabeth's last name is Vogler, like the mesmerist in *The Magician.* She is an actress who has rejected her role.

Hour of the Wolf (1968) confronts horrifying, hallucinatory madness on the part of an artist, his sexual fears taking the form of mur-derous, ugly, subjective images that come to be intuitively sensed by Alma, his wife. Reports on past events in the story are as untrustworthy as *Rashomon,* pictures as unreliable as *Last Year at Marienbad.* The feel of the film is curiously unfinished.

Shame (1968) places the same actors, Liv Ullmann and Max von Sydow, on an island invaded by enemy militia. The husband, once a sensitive musician, withdraws into unfeelingness, his own motive self-preservation. Escaping in a boat, surrounded with floating corpses, the wife's capacity to survive without either assuming her husband's enraged state or falling into madness is unlikely.[5]

[5] Shame's *script concludes, "On the seventh day a storm blows up and there is a heavy rain. The survivors slake their thirst with poisoned water." Ingmar Bergman,* Persona *and* Shame. *New York, 1972, p. 191.*

In *Scenes from a Marriage* (1974) and *Face to Face* (1975) Bergman reverts to contemporary, cosmopolitan settings, but just as *The Magic Flute* (1976) has its thematic antecedents (*The Hour of the Wolf* uses Mozart's opera as a paradigm for the couple's relationship at its best, while Papageno figures in the husband's cruel imaginings) the next Liv Ullmann films continue to explore alternatives for the tormented, variable Bergman couple, loving and faithless, incredibly understanding, impossibly rejecting, deformed by the past and curious about the future. Now they are settled in a world without God where the sexes require one another all the more and suffer from even greater need. As ever, men and women seek fulfillment privately, needful of the sharing that is at worst a temporary respite, at best a happy expedient, like art for Bergman himself.

Scenes from a Marriage. Marianne (Liv Ullman) and Johann (Erland Josephson). Bergman's thirty-year marital history was less impressive on the screen with its intense, dialogued closeups than in its lengthy, episodic television version. Omitted in the film: Marianne's pregnancy; her husband's urgings to renovate the house as a post-abortion therapy; the couple's attendance of *A Doll's House* and its ironic aftermath when Ibsen's play is discussed. (Museum of Modern Art/ Film Stills Archive)

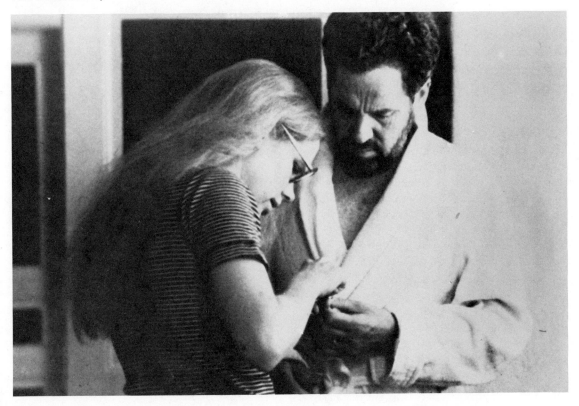

Summary

The dissimilarities of Fellini, Buñuel, and Bergman as personalities, deepened by vastly different cultural history and personal backgrounds, still cannot guise certain common preoccupations. Leavened by humor (uniquely Bergman separates comedy and drama), the three men share ultimate metaphysical questions about mankind. Each director's narrative resolutions, his temporary "conclusions," vary from year to year, between one fictional scheme and another. But retrospective study may lead the viewer to decide that Fellini is inclined to cloak his despair with caricature and wit, Buñuel by a hollow, absurdist laugh, Bergman with some terrible human confrontations, or else not at all.

Chapter 20 considers three more directors whose esthetic, in many respects, might be thought dominated more by Sartre and Marx than by God and Freud. These men are Michelangelo Antonioni, Alain Resnais, and Jean-Luc Godard.

Bibliography

Agel, Genevieve. *Les chemins de Fellini.* Paris, 1956.

Arando, J. Francisco. *Luis Buñuel.* New York, 1977.

Archer, Eugene. "Vitelloni." *Film Culture* 10 (1956).

Benderson, Albert. *Critical Approaches to Federico Fellini's 8½,* New York, 1974.

Beranger, Jean. *Ingmar Bergman.* Paris, 1969.

Bergman, Ingmar. *Bergman on Bergman.* New York, 1973.

———. *Face to Face.* New York, 1976.

———. *A Film Trilogy: Through a Glass Darkly, Winter Light, The Silence.* London, 1967.

———. *Four Screenplays: Smiles of a Summer Night, The Seventh Seal, Wild Strawberries, The Magician.* New York, 1970.

———. *Persona, Shame.* London, 1972.

———. *Scenes from a Marriage.* New York, 1974.

———. *The Seventh Seal.* London, 1968.

———. *Wild Strawberries.* London, 1970.

Boyer, Dena. *The 200 Days of 8½.* New York, 1964.

Budgen, Suzanne. *Fellini.* London, 1966.

Büache, Freddy. *The Cinema of Ingmar Bergman.* London, 1973.

Buñuel, Luis. "A Statement," *Film Culture* 21 (1960).

———. *Belle de Jour.* New York, 1971.

———. *The Exterminating Angel, Nazarin, Los Olvidados.* London, 1972.

———. "On Viridiana," *Film Culture* 24 (1962).

———. *Three Screenplays: Viridiana, The Exterminating Angel, Simon of The Desert.* New York, 1970.

Buñuel, Luis and Salvador Dali. *L'Age d'Or and Un Chien Andalou.* London, 1958.

Buñuel, Luis and Julio Arjandro. *Tristana.* New York, 1971.

Cowie, Peter. *Antonioni, Buñuel, Resnais.* New York, 1963.

Dali, Salvador. *The Secret Life of Salvador Dali.* New York, 1942.

Donner, Jörn. *The Personal Vision of Ingmar Bergman.* New York, 1968.

———. *The Films of Ingmar Bergman.* New York, 1972.

Durgnat, Raymond. *Luis Buñuel.* Berkeley, 1968.

Fellini, Federico. *Amarcord*. London, 1974.

———. *La Dolce Vita*. New York, 1961.

———. *Early Screenplays: Variety Lights, The White Sheik*. New York, 1971.

———. *8½* Bologna, 1965.

———. *Fellini on Fellini*. London, 1976.

———. *Fellini Satyricon*. Bologna, 1969.

———. *Fellini TV, I clowns*. Bologna, 1972.

———. *Juliet of the Spirits*. New York, 1965.

———. *Roma*. Bologna, 1972.

———. *Three Screenplays: I Vitelloni, Il Bidone, The Temptations of Dr. Antonio*. New York, 1970.

Fuentes, Carlos. "The Discreet Charm of Luis Buñuel." *New York Times Magazine*. (March 11, 1973).

Gibson, Arthur. *The Silence of God*. Bloomington, Ind., 1964.

Goldberg, Toby. *Federico Fellini: A Poet of Reality*. Boston, 1965.

Harcourt, Peter. *Six European Directors*. Baltimore, 1974.

Hughes, Eileen. *On the Set of Fellini Satyricon*. New York, 1971.

Isaksson, Ulla. *The Virgin Spring*. New York, 1960.

Kaminsky, Stuart M. "The Torment of Insight." *Cinema Journal* 13 (Spring 1974).

———. ed. *Ingmar Bergman Essays in Criticism*. New York, 1975.

Kanesaka, Kenji. "Interview with Luis Buñuel," *Film Culture* 24 (1962).

Ketcham, Charles B. *Federico Fellini: The Search for the New Mythology*. New York, 1977.

Kyrou, Adonis. *Luis Buñuel: An Introduction*. New York, 1963.

Lyon, Elizabeth. "Luis Buñuel: The Process of Disassociation in Three Films," *Cinema Journal* 13 (Fall 1973).

Mellen, Joan. "Bergman and Women: Cries and Whispers," *Film Quarterly* 26 (Fall 1973).

Milne, Tom. The Mexican Buñuel," *Sight and Sound* 35 (Winter 1965-66).

Nelson, Daniel. *Ingmar Bergman: The Search for God*. Boston, 1964.

Price, Barbara and Theodore Price. *Federico Fellini: An Annotated International Bibliography*. Metuchen, N.J., 1978.

Riera, Emilio. "The Eternal Rebellion of Luis Buñuel," *Film Culture* 21 (1960).

———. "The Films of Luis Buñuel," *Film Culture* 21 (1960).

———. "Viridiana," *Film Culture* 24 (1962).

Robinson, David, "Thank God I Am Still an Atheist," *Sight and Sound* 31 (Summer 1962).

Russell, John T. *Cinema Eve, Cinema Ear*. New York, 1964.

Salachas, Gilbert. *Federico Fellini*. New York, 1969.

Sarris, Andrew. *Interviews With Film Directors*. New York, 1967.

Siclier, Jacques. *Ingmar Bergman*. Paris, 1966.

Simon, John. *Ingmar Bergman Directs*. New York, 1962.

Sjöman, Vilgot. "From L 136: A Diary of Ingmar Bergman's Winter Light. *Cinema Journal* 13 (Spring 1974).

Solmi, Angelo. *Fellini*. London, 1967.

Steene, Birgetta. *Ingmar Bergman*. New York, 1968.

———. Images and Words in Ingmar Bergman's Films." *Cinema Journal* (Fall 1970).

———. Focus on *The Seventh Seal*. Englewood, N.J., 1972.

———. "About Bergman: Some Critical Responses to His Films," *Cinema Journal* 13 (Spring 1974).

Wall, James. *Three European Directors*. Grand Rapids, S.D., 1973.

Webb, Teena. "Bergman Without Options," *Jump Cut* 5 (January-February 1975).

Wood, Robin. *Ingmar Bergman*. New York, 1969.

Young, Vernon. *Cinema Borealis*. New York, 1971.

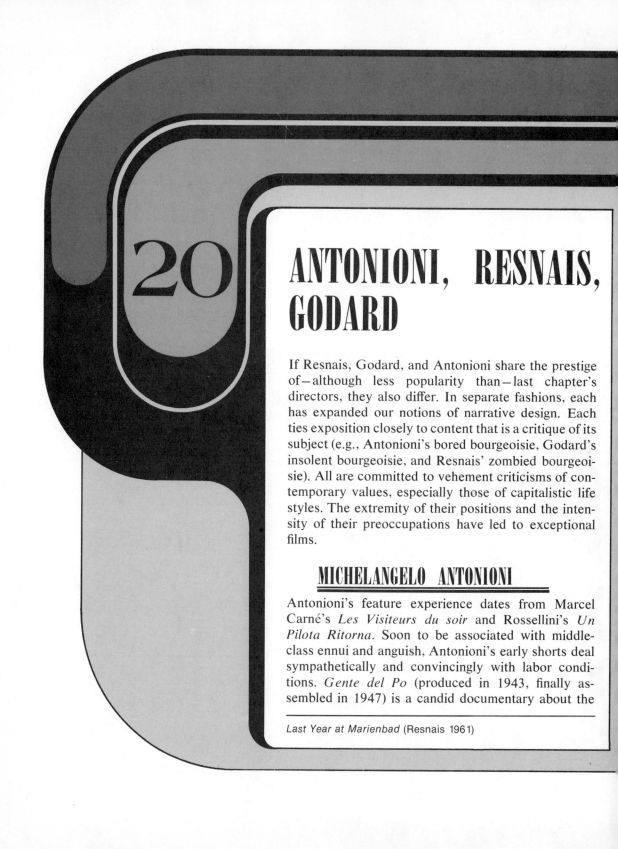

20

ANTONIONI, RESNAIS, GODARD

If Resnais, Godard, and Antonioni share the prestige of—although less popularity than—last chapter's directors, they also differ. In separate fashions, each has expanded our notions of narrative design. Each ties exposition closely to content that is a critique of its subject (e.g., Antonioni's bored bourgeoisie, Godard's insolent bourgeoisie, and Resnais' zombied bourgeoisie). All are committed to vehement criticisms of contemporary values, especially those of capitalistic life styles. The extremity of their positions and the intensity of their preoccupations have led to exceptional films.

MICHELANGELO ANTONIONI

Antonioni's feature experience dates from Marcel Carné's *Les Visiteurs du soir* and Rossellini's *Un Pilota Ritorna*. Soon to be associated with middle-class ennui and anguish, Antonioni's early shorts deal sympathetically and convincingly with labor conditions. *Gente del Po* (produced in 1943, finally assembled in 1947) is a candid documentary about the

Last Year at Marienbad (Resnais 1961)

peasants and disgruntled fishermen of the region. *N.U.* (1948) deals with street cleaners, but, by *L'Amorosa Menzogna* (1949), Antonioni's future direction is evident in a sardonic study of picture magazine readers and the unexciting lives of the actors, the milieu of *The White Sheik*.

His first feature, *Cronaca di un Amore* (Story of a Love) (1950) forewarns of later narrative technique. Because her past is being investigated by her well-to-do businessman husband, Paola reestablishes a liaison with Guido. Years before, the two had been involved in a questionable accident that killed Guido's fiancée in an elevator shaft; now they scheme to murder Paola's husband. Guido waits to shoot him on a dark roadway, but the industrialist's car crashes before the crime can occur. Again, Antonioni leaves doubt as to whether the event was really an accident. The lovers are free, but now too drained of feeling to want one another.

Michelangelo Antonioni (1912–   )

Gente del Po (short)	1943
	edited
	1947
N.U. (short)	1948
L'Amorosa Manzogna (short)	1949
Cronaca di un Amore	1950
I Vinti	1952
La Signora Senza Camelie	1953
Le Amiche/The Girl Friends	1955
Il Grido/The Cry	1957
L'Avventura	1960
La Notte	1960
L'Eclisse	1962
Deserto Rosso/The Red Desert	1964
Blow-Up (Britain)	1966
Zabriskie Point (United States)	1969
The Passenger (United States)	1975

Cronaca di un Amore is especially impressive with its long camera runs, slow, involved pans, and compositions that build the growing strain and isolation between Paola and Guido: glances askew, figures separated by alienating masses of space. Paola's erotic energy contradicts the calculating self-advancement that brought her into Milanese society. Guido is excited at the affair's renewal and bewildered by the new difference in their stations. He is a car salesman. Some of the screen backgrounds carry metaphoric implications. As the two plan the murder, workers are seen in the distance cleaning muck from a drained canal. A meeting in a planetarium isolates Paola and Guido from the world, but they are posed in front of a foreboding, dark theater projector.

In *La Signora Senza Camelie* (1953) Clara, played by Lucia Bosè who did Paola in *Cronaca di un Amore*, is a shopgirl who wins a beauty contest and consequently a screen test. Lacking real talent, Clara fails at a presumptuous, Cinecittà *Joan of Arc*. She has only her beauty. Unsophisticated and vaguely ambitious, she is sexually exploited, personally and professionally, by movie producers, finally falling into vehicles like *Slave of the Sphinx*. Clara is too passive to change her life, rootless and victimized; one of her early productions is called *Woman Without a Destiny*.

The Antonioni pattern emerges clearly in *Le Amiche/The Girl Friends* (1955), loosely based on a Cesar Pavese novel. Distressed by a modern, cosmopolitan world and its confusing social milieu, Clelia, a displaced young woman finds herself physically and intellectually unsatisfied. The clique in Clelia's Turin fashion salon includes a painter, a potter, a model, and a bored rich woman. When Rosetta, the model, kills herself, Clelia considers her own future. She may become as hard as Momina, the rich woman whose actions contribute to the suicide. She may marry a childhood friend whom she has outgrown. Instead, Clelia returns to her former job in Rome.

Impressive for its detailed development of

so many characters (all the women have lovers or husbands), *Le Amiche* has an extraordinary beach sequence. Picnicking, the group runs on impulse to the sea. The couples wander about, disconsolant and vulnerable in a grey, depressing environment empty of the salon's reassuring clothes and decor. Overcast setting gives a flat, diffused absence of sharp blacks and whites. Antonioni's shots are unusually long, complicated by intricate camera-subject maneuvering. The staging reminds one of Orson Welles' ball in *The Magnificent Ambersons*. Seemingly as random as the conversation, camera movement fortuitously catches each dialogue, then moves on to note reactions and non-reactions. The scene is an early picture climax, for Momina slaps Rosetta, and the action leads Rosetta despairingly to question her own future.

Il Grido/The Cry (1957) was Antonioni's first American financed feature, which led to the anomalous employment of Steve Cochran and Betsy Blair. Aldo (Cochran) leaves Irma, his mistress, because she loves another man. With his young daughter, Aldo wanders through the Po valley, visiting a one-time girl friend (Blair), then spending time with a prostitute and a gas-station worker. Despondent, he returns to his mistress, then falls to his death from a tower.

Antonioni uses the valley landscape in *Il Grido* to express Aldo's state of mind, a dreary waste. In the conclusion of the film, the drama of Aldo's return to Irma, is set against a background of political protest. People of the village are resentful of an American jet base under construction nearby. The impending change, bulldozers about to flatten houses, supports a notion of Aldo's impending collapse. He climbs a tower from which he said, earlier, he could see his house and daughter. The climb exhausts and dizzies Aldo. His fall seems to respond to a frightened cry from Irma below. Whether suicidal or not, it completes the long narrative movement of Aldo's return. At this stage, Antonioni regards despair as the inevitable consequence of facing one's personal problems.

The difficulties of human interchange are muted in *Il Grido,* where workers are ill-educated and inarticulate. In *L'Avventura* (1960), contradictions become the more intense because characters chatter so glibly and lie to themselves and others with such earnestness. Establishing Antonioni's international reputation, *L'Avventura* first exposed wide audiences to a film narrative that defied orthodoxies.

Claudia (Monica Vitti) joins her friend Anna (Lea Massari) and Anna's fiancé Sandro (Gabriele Ferzetti) on a yacht off Sicily. With a party of nouveau-riche friends, they journey to a small island. Anna disappears. After the party has combed the island, it is conjectured that Anna may have departed by boat. Continuing the search alone on the mainland, Sandro and Claudia become lovers. They stop at a luxury hotel. That night Claudia comes upon Sandro with a prostitute on a couch in the lobby. Utterly despairing, Claudia locates Sandro on the terrace later; they are seemingly united by common dependence.

To the unsympathetic critic, Anna's unexplained, unresolved disappearance was infuriating. The very search gradually dissipates as other emotions absorb Claudia and Sandro. Further, the island episodes carry a disconcerting, leveling tedium. Nothing seems to happen.

Clearly, Antonioni's central intention is to show the callousness and the painful consequence of transient affection. The issue is sharply pointed by Claudia's guilt at her own actions, her growing awareness that Sandro is weak and purposeless. The island search shows *everyone's* behavior to be directionless, isolated and frustrating. Movement of human figures, small against barren rocks, is built with wandering, unmotivated compositions, like a modern canvas. Figures approach and withdraw from one another in silent self-absorption, while the rhythmic lapping of waves

La Notte. Giovanni and Lidia visit a dying friend (Bernard Wicki). The patient's physical disintegration prompts Mastroianni to admit that he himself feels written out, while Moreau confronts her present loneliness, a life empty of real marital affection. (Museum of Modern Art/Film Stills Archive)

on the beach reminds the viewer of an indifference that is expressed in deed but can never be spoken.

Developing feeling between Sandro and Claudia is accomplished equally skillfully with movements and composition. Sandro's interest has something to do with Claudia's relation to Anna. Claudia wears a dress Anna had given her. Claudia supplies the will to initiate and to continue the search, and Sandro's fear of a possible suicide draws him to her strength. Besides, sex is a diversion.

At first, Claudia sees Sandro's advances as distraction from their purpose. Then, the experiences of searching together enforce a closeness. Monica Vitti effectively betrays conflicting shame, attraction, and anxiety. She is less worldly than Sandro. Physical satisfaction is a new pleasure, and Claudia becomes

fearful that they may in fact find Anna. In the film's last scene, Sandro looks away to the side; Claudia strokes his hair and stares into distant space.

La Notte (1960) proved to be pivotal in a trilogy, framed by *L'Avventura* and *L'Eclisse* (1962). Giovanni, a novelist (Marcello Mastroianni) and his wife Lidia (Jeanne Moreau) visit a dying friend whose condition seems to reflect the deterioration of their marriage. They attend a party, where Giovanni is attracted to Monica Vitti, while Lidia flirts idly, in hopes of restimulating her husband's interest. At dawn on a nearby golf course, the pair try to address their real feelings, then proceed to unhappy sex.

La Notte exploits its landscape. The hospital visit is oppressed by ugly, rectangular, modern architecture. Distraught, Lidia escapes into a poor section of Milan, where peeling walls and chipped statuary mirror her mood while relieving the earlier sterility. The all-night party takes place in an ornate, luxurious, undistinguished home.

Giovanni's encounters increase his perplexity and despondency. In the hospital, he meets a nymphomaniac patient who has somehow escaped her ward. The girl's erotic attack on him is answered responsively, as if Giovanni were finding a woman whom he could again excite. At the party, Monica Vitti plays an insouciant, uninhibited, smart, playful, rich beauty. Vitti's flirtation, followed by a kiss, then followed by a job offer for Giovanni from her father, the host, are all witnessed from a distance by Lidia. The job would certify Giovanni as a kept "house intellectual." Like Claudia's discovery of Sandro with the whore, it threatens to become an ultimate betrayal of self, but so does the sad coupling at the conclusion.

L'Eclisse casts Vitti as Vittoria, a translator who is just breaking a relationship with Riccardo, an intellectual. His disappearance from the story has something of the quality of Anna's in *L'Avventura;* she, too, had complained that her lover no longer cared. The parting implies that Vittoria is not faultless, and that she is the stronger. Vittoria moves into an affair with a stockbroker, Piero (Alain Delon). Piero is maniacally materialistic on the stock exchange floor. When his stolen car is fished from a lake with a drunk's body inside, Piero can only think of the Alfa-Romeo; yet he is a warm, emotional lover. Antonioni intercuts scenes of the lovemaking with shots of the pair arguing. Vittoria does not wish to marry.

L'Eclisse is less talky than many of the earlier films, and marked by a wordless prologue of detailed, fragmented segments that describe the exhausted, emotional breakup of Vittorio and Ricardo. The film's conclusion is even more extraordinary: a seven minute exposition that shows places now absent of people where Vittoria and Piero have met earlier. At first, the objects are familiar, the barrel into which Vittoria had thrown a stick, a bank of lights at a stadium. These are followed by a series of shots passing from day to twilight and adding oppressive, lonely punctuations: a fountain is turned off, lights go on in an empty street. Finally, objects suggestive of emotional states are singled out in enlarged detail, like the peeling walls viewed by Lidia in *La Notte*. We see a modern building in the dark with ugly, cubed balconies and water running across the sidewalk into a culvert. The long, final shot is a street light, filmed closeup and haloed. It is so desolate that one inescapably concludes Piero and Vittoria have altogether separated, failing to accede to the resigned

L'Eclisse. Monica Vitti and Alain Delon part in the street after leaving the stock exchange. Delon is the broker for Vitti's mother, and his behavior during a frenzied market recession fascinate Vitti. (Museum of Modern Art/Film Stills Archive)

self-support of earlier couples in Antonioni's trilogy.

The setting for *The Red Desert* (1964) is Ravenna, whose nearby woods are sacred to the traditions of Dante, where canals stretch across the flat countryside so that from a distance boats appear to be sailing a green landscape. Now the land is clouded in dull, yellow, asphyxiating factory exhaust, a billowing smog. All about is industrial refuse, rusting and discarded in bushes near the plant. Giuliana (Monica Vitti) is introduced in this environ. The sound of the belching smoke blends with the rhythm of workers walking in foreground, slighty out of focus. Then Giuliana appears, sharp, the back of her head visible so that the scene seems to be perceived by her disoriented mind. For 2,000 lire she buys a sandwich from a surprised workman, then crouches to eat it. Antonioni characters have characteristically felt unsettled in environments foreign to their experience, and the evidence of industrial technology has been a constant background. In *The Red Desert* the price of progress has become too high for Giuliana to pay; her neurosis is a frightened response.

Giuliana is married to a serious engineer, employed in the factory that is destroying her. A stranger, Corrado, comes to the area to recruit workmen for an overseas assignment. Giuliana plays with the idea of fleeing with Corrado, but their affair resolves into typical Antonioni patterns; the man proves incapable of recognizing, let alone meeting, the woman's needs beyond physical satisfaction.

Giuliana's difficulties are said to have originated in an automobile accident, but clearly the environment is so threatening that its desolation serves to externalize as much as it exacerbates her condition. To accomplish this landscape, Antonioni has applied a brush to nature, literally greying and whitening trees, buildings, even the fruit in a vendor's cart. Red is the first vivid hue to appear in the film, introduced as background to sex play in a shack. It reappears as vivid splashes on industrial walls and pipes when sex is producing tension between Giuliana and Corrado. Finally, the red deepens to a woody dark hue when she visits his hotel room. The red equally suggests impersonal eroticism, the menace of industry, and madness. In the end, the color interlinks Giuliana's nostalgic longings with the very menace of her environment. Antonioni's sympathies are not with Giuliana but toward confronting the situation that caused her condition. We must, he believes, reject enough of the past to survive in the modern world.

Blow-Up (1966) takes Antonioni to London, whose glib, swinging panache suggests an adaptation achieved at the cost of feeling. Thomas (David Hemmings) takes chance photographs of a woman (Vanessa Redgrave) kissing some men in the park. She seeks to recover the film, but he tricks her. Enlarged, the photos indicate a murder, and Thomas returns to find the corpse beneath some bushes. He tries to impress his discovery on friends at a pot party, but no one is interested. Distracted, Thomas falls back into isolate self-absorption.

Lively, suspenseful, and amusing, *Blow-Up* departs from Antonioni's bourgeois, Italian desperation. Thomas' studio emphasizes his freedom from emotional entrapment. Enlarged, his photos look, as one character notes, like abstract expressionism. Plot elements became mysterious and suspicious. Whether a murder has actually occurred is hazed by the eerie green that suffuses the scene of Thomas' discovery. The corpse has the waxy look of a manikin. Returning again to the scene, Thomas finds all traces gone. His photographs are stolen from the studio.

Antonioni hardly jettisoned his thematic baggage in passage across the Channel. Sexual affection has hardened into cold, athletic romps where feeling now is not only dangerous but unfashionable. As before, objects speak, but their message is more shaded by ambiguity. In the last moments of the film,

Thomas watches, then joins, a mime group who play imaginary tennis on a real court. Bemused, the photographer finally retrieves a non-existent ball that has been hit over the fence. On the sound track we hear the *pock . . . pock* of ball on racket. Earlier despair has shifted for Antonioni in the direction of retreat into illusion.

Zabriskie Point (1969), US made, failed to infuse the director's sensibility into the American setting of student revolt and political rage, although images, like an unerotic orgy of naked and half-clothed bodies in the desert sands, linger. In *Passenger* (1975) Antonioni undertakes an American film in North African setting. A television journalist, David Locke (Jack Nicholson) seeks a guerilla movement called the United Liberation Front. He meets David Robertson, who is supplying arms to the movement. Robertson dies in his hotel room,

Passenger. Driving down a desert road, Locke's Land Rover stalls in a wind storm. After expressing his impotent rage, Locke proceeds on foot, carrying his recorder and camera. Finally, he locates a dingy hotel in a nearby town where Robertson, a man with whom he will exchange identities, happens to be staying. (Italian Cultural Institute)

and Locke switches identities. Thinking him dead, Locke's wife and producer concoct a biographical documentary and seek David Robertson for source material. Thus Locke is pursued in the new identity he assumed to escape his own. Accompanied by Maria Schneider, he is finally overtaken by guerilla figures who (presumably) kill him as Robertson. The body is viewed by Locke's wife and left to Schneider.

Switching identities only intensifies an anguish that is not individual but human. Escape by Nicholson and Schneider can only be transitory. Antonioni again challenges visual documentation as a dependable key to understanding. Like the abstract quality of Thomas' photography, Locke's ambiguous profession, the suspicion about documentary's trustworthiness leagues with Antonioni's own techniques to cast doubt on corroborations by sense experience. The execution of a guerilla leader forms part of the "documentary" on Locke. Possibly, it is actual footage that Antonioni secured, a real death, but its meaning is assuaged in the fictive context. In the skillfull next-to-final shot of *Passenger,* a single camera take obliquely "hears" Locke's murder, passes through a barred window, moves outside to face the room it vacated, watches cars leave, then returns to see the impersonal responses from Locke's wife and the producer. Defying every containment of space, the camera tells us nothing more than what we knew at *Passenger's* beginning. The viewer may be reminded of Snow's plunging camera figure-eights in *La Région Centrale.*

ALAIN RESNAIS

Solitary in childhood, an avid reader, Alain Resnais is equally enthusiastic toward popular culture and literary high style. Moments in *Last Year at Marienbad* (1961) satirize Louis Feuillade; Resnais made a *Fantômas* at the age of thirteen. He says that he learned to edit from comic strips, and Mandrake the Magician is affectionately displayed in *Toute la mémoire du monde* (1956).

Resnais studied at I.D.H.E.C., the French film school, then left to become a film editor. In actual fact or through the controls of his premeditated design, he edits his own films and sometimes those of friends Agnes Varda, François Reichenbach, Jacques Doniol-Valcroze. Godard called him the greatest editor since Eisenstein. Resnais' early reputation developed from "art" films: *Van Gogh* (1948), *Gauguin* (1950) and *Guernica* (1950). The strengths of the first two rest in a viewer's powerful sensation that direct, detailed encounters with the paintings have resulted in accurate insights into an artist's personality, the changes experience gave to his perceptions. *Guernica* uses a variety of Picasso ma-

terials, concentrating on the mural that chronicles the German bombing of a Spanish Basque village in April, 1937, which annihilated most of the civilian population.[1]

Censored by the French government and rarely viewed even in abridged version, *Les Statues meurent aussi* (1953) jointly made with Chris Marker, argues with visual evidence that African art degenerated from contact with European influence. *Toute la mémoire du monde* (1956) is a tour of the Bibliothèque Nationale, its great dome seen as an architectural cranium in which the world's memories are catalogued and preserved. The disposal of books intentionally suggests prison internment. They are examined, described, stamped, placed in cages, sometimes even injected with needles to preserve bindings. For the first time, Resnais' extraordinary camera movements appear; elaborate traveling shots along library corridors circling the dome reinforce a sense that we are inside some living organism.

Already in his first ventures, Resnais has designed his studies around time, around evocations of the past. Art and artifact contribute to the reconstructions. A past without relevance is uninteresting, but the alternative, a life without precedent, is insupportable to Resnais. This is what white culture did to black art in *Les Statues meurent aussi;* it stole a people's history.

In *Hiroshima mon amour* (1959) time creates the unresolvable conflict between Emmanuelle Riva, an actress visiting Hiroshima to make a peace film, and Eiji Okada, a Japanese architect whom she has met there. The pair fall deeply in love, but place and experience recall Riva's earlier affair. During the war she had consorted with a German soldier in the village of Nevers. At liberation, her

Alain Resnais (1922–   )

Schema d'une identification (short)	1946
Van Gogh (short)	1948
Gauguin (short)	1950
Guernica (short)	1950
Les Statues meurent aussi (short) (codirector Chris Marker)	1953
Nuit et Brouillard/Night and Fog (short)	1955
Toute la mémoire du monde (short)	1956
Hiroshima mon amour	1959
L'Année dernière à Marienbad/Last Year at Marienbad	1961
Muriel, ou le temps d'un retour	1963
La Guerre est finie	1966
Je t'aime, je t'aime	1968
Stavisky	1974
Providence	1977

[1] *The English language version of* Guernica *renders hysterical a commentary that is more artfully contained in Maria Casares' French reading of the Jean Cayrol text.*

lover was killed. Townspeople shaved her head, and parents confined her in shame to a basement room. Her grief at the memory is inconsolable, her own Hiroshima, and the film concludes on an irresolute note. It is less important that we know "what happens" between the pair than that we understand the emotionality of the experience, the intolerable strain that memory imposes on desire.

Juxtaposition of an individual love affair with the enormity of Hiroshima's devastation might seem exploitative and morally indefensible; this was argued by some critics. In practice, *Hiroshima* joins private emotion to public catastrophe with plaintive force, a linkage more exact and touching than any epic. Working closely with the experimental novelist Marguerite Duras, Resnais intensifies the love affair and the traumatic history of each partner by skillful interminglings of the present, memory, and the evidence of history. Credit also rests with composers Giovanni Fusco and Georges Delerue. As in every Resnais film, music serves not as background to word and picture, but as partner and narrative bridge.

Hiroshima commences with the naked, fused bodies of the lovers, flecked with what may be either or both perspiration and ash, as from atomic explosion. The writhing bodies equally connote life and death. Sparse and repetitive, the man's and woman's conversation calls up images of the hospital and museum she has just visited. These corroborate the life and death spectrum.

Later in the day, Riva tells Okada her story, the reminiscences intercut as before with present-time footage. In fact, the composition of the Nevers material equates with earlier camera movement of the hospital tour, so that form further joins the two periods. Composition is similarly used to link Hiroshima and Nevers, as it ties Okada to the German soldier. Hiroshima sound plays against Nevers picture, Nevers sound in the Hiroshima present. At one point, Riva becomes lost, as it were, in her past, and present-day

sound withdraws into silence. Riva's final sequence, her return to the original hotel room, compounds the implications of her memories and the couple's parting. Studying the editing here is like attending a master class in how to control pace by cutting on movement.

For *Last Year at Marienbad,* Resnais enlisted another avant-garde literary talent, Alain Robbe-Grillet, who writes in a mode of diverging, sometimes contradictory "realities," organized about compulsive, recurrent scenes that change in each repetition to advance new possibilities of "meaning."

More hermetic than any other Resnais production, perhaps more self-contained than any other major *film, Marienbad* plays on popular idiom, cliché, and myth. During the season at a great baroque palace that is perhaps a resort, perhaps a sanitorium, Giorgio Albertazzi (the actors are unnamed in the film) encounters Delphine Seyrig, claiming that they had met the year before, that he agreed to delay taking her away for one year. Seyrig claims he has invented the story. She is with Sacha Pitöeff, who is perhaps her husband, perhaps her doctor. Finally, Seyrig leaves with Albertazzi.

The film thrives on ambiguities surrounding every action, statement, and response. Intentionally, it lacks a stable frame of reference against which variations can be measured to establish credibility. Scenes may be considered a character's wishful projections, actual occurrences, or mixed battles of will between Seyrig and Albertazzi as to what is true. Albertazzi argues that a door was closed, that a picture was present in a bedroom at their last meeting while the visuals we see contradict him. Confusion is furthered by Resnais' skillful joining—Maya Deren-like—of shots unrelated by time into apparently continuous executions of action. A character will start a movement in one place and complete it elsewhere.

Throughout, Resnais and Robbe-Grillet drop what might in a more conventional film serve as cues to understanding the narrative.

Here each perspective is denied by another, like the paradoxes of a cubist painting. A narrator (presumably Albertazzi) speaks of a place "where the sound of advancing footsteps is absorbed by carpets so thick and heavy that nothing can be heard." Yet his steps sound like shoes on gravel when the pair meets on carpeted stairs; walk seen on actual gravel is silent. Lines used by Albertazzi to woo Seyrig are repeated by other couples. ("We've met before." "You're still the same.") The "last year" may have been 1929 or 1930, if it exists at all, but the costumes are contemporary high fashion.

Marienbad begins and ends with a play enacted for the guests. It is seemingly a variation of Ibsen's *Rosmersholm,* whose action and gestures are very like what happens between Albertazzi and Seyrig. Costumes change with alarming frequency; Seyrig wears twenty-seven ensembles. Perhaps the most bizarre clothing, like scenes placed in the most baroque settings, is least trustworthy. The story shares themes with *Orphée,* Pitöeff as Death enslaving Eurydice. Alternatively, Albertazzi may himself be Death, drawing Seyrig outside into the cold. The austerity and ambiguity of *Marienbad* drew cries of anguish from some; critic Pauline Kael feared Creeping Marienbadism. For many, it is an inexhaustible paradigm of mental process, the chateau a vast mind peopled with archetypal reenactments.

Muriel ou les temps d'un retour/Muriel

Muriel. Helène (Delphine Seyrig) meets Alphonse (Jean-Pierre Kérien) and his "niece" (Nita Klein) at the railway station in Boulogne-sur-mer. Helène gambles compulsively, which makes her need for the past (fresh antiques to sell) the more desperate. (French Film Office)

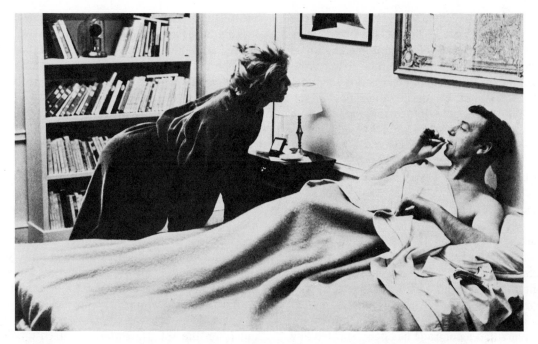

La Guerre est finie. Diego (Yves Montand) with Marianne (Ingrid Thulin) in their Paris apartment. As past experience threatens to be reenacted, confirming Diego's flash-forward premonitions, Resnais seems almost to suggest that dream and memory may merge in actuality. (Museum of Modern Art/Film Stills Archive)

(1963) casts Dephine Seyrig in a vastly different role, Helène, a widow who runs an antique store. She arranges to meet a lover from many years before, Alphonse. He arrives with a young mistress. Helène's son, Bernard, is haunted by memories of Muriel, an Algerian girl he and fellow-soldiers tortured and killed. He shoots an acquaintance who had instigated the brutality, then runs away. Ernest, an old friend of Helène and Alphonse, arrives to announce that Alphonse is married and must return to his wife.

Another collaboration with Cayrol, *Muriel* plays further, fascinating variations on past, memory, and need. Each figure is trapped in time gone by. Helène is anchored to a romantic memory of her affair with Alphonse, wedded to her antiques that she must sell to survive. Alphonse lives on false images, falsifying

a background to mask his shabby existence. Bernard cannot accept his past nor can he forget it. He watches an old home movie of cavorting soldier friends in Algeria.

The town, Boulogne-sur-mer, ought to verify history, but it was devastated by war. Now it is obliterated by neon and plastic. Alphonse asks, "Where is the center of town?" He is advised, "You're standing in it." Old place signs remain, but they no longer mark anything. In the group's first walk through town, day and night are intercut; uninhabited buildings seen here are locales for episodes to follow.

Tension in *Muriel* mounts when one figure impinges on the stability of another's memory. Finally, Helène breaks down. She is disturbed by the story of a local building that is collapsing on a slope that is slipping away.

La Guerre est finie (the war is over) (1966)

Alain Resnais   501

requires Diego (Yves Montand) to reconcile his past with new realities. He is an aging Spanish Loyalist, still making serreptitious trips into Franco Spain while living with Marianne in Paris. Diego meets a radical student, Nadine. He rejects her comrades' impetuosities, at the same time losing confidence in his own group's usefulness. On order, he returns to Spain. Nadine advises Marianne that police are on Diego's trail. Marianne flies to the border to warn Diego, but he has already crossed.

Here, Resnais characterizes the past by Diego's behavior and by his relation to his colleagues. Rather than flashbacks, the narrative flashes forward, but these moments are conjectural impressions. Diego is scheduled to contact Nadine whom he has not seen but has heard on the phone. We see a succession of attractive young women acting out the meeting. He fears that a comrade has been spotted and sees the man in his car surrounded by indistinct figures. The "conditional" episodes serve to raise dramatic tension as Diego must call on depleted reserves of calm to confront the intuited peril. The war is over when its soldiers finally die.

Je t'aime, je t'aime (1968) operates in a science fiction mode.[2] A young man, recently failed at suicide, reexperiences the relationship that had led to his despair. Interesting for its time-memory effects, the film lacks the unifying, poetic design that emotionalizes Resnais' other features.

Stavisky (1974) marked a five-year hiatus for Resnais. (Only *La Guerre est finie* has been markedly successful commercially). Like *La Guerre, Stavisky* is written by Jorge Sem-

prun. It is set in the France of the thirties and loosely based on a famous scoundrel who executed grand financial swindles, a confidant of the rich until he became suspect. In truth and in the movie, Stavisky either shot himself or was killed during a police raid.

Leon Trotsky's exile in France is used as a subplot, seen from afar, never personalized. Both figures were Russian Jews, more tolerated than welcomed by the French. The country's state of mind is skillfully described, Belmondo as Stavisky mixing a subtle blend of irony, pleasure, ingratiation, and wariness in his dealings with settled wealth. Resnais chooses to simulate techniques of thirties films, imitating color and camera setups, yet the absolute control of complicated subject movement, as in the arrival of Anny Duperey at Biarritz in a white airplane, is unique to Resnais. Like other shots, it was staged to music on the set. Its stately, stylized quality encourages the viewer to reexamine what appears on its face to be more straightforward than is customary for Alain Resnais. *Stavisky's* time is one of corruption, and as in *Night and Fog* Resnais suggests the period is not past.

In *Providence* (1977), a dying writer draws up from his mind dreadful images of his family, which he twists into material for a new novel. *Providence* differs from other Resnais mental trips by its playfulness. John Guilgud, the writer, is alternately drunk, suffering from extreme pain, and half-delirious from lack of sleep. Throughout, his author's imagination manipulates the imagined cast so that they may simultaneously tell a good story and satisfy their creator's complicated familial emotions. Like other writers, Gielgud also has to face the problem of characters assuming their own independence, refusing to obey orders. When his actual children arrive for their father's seventh-eighth birthday party, complexities of real human relationships begin to clarify both the strengths and weaknesses of Gielgud's alternative plots.

---

[2] *Resnais' film is reminiscent of Chris Marker's superior* La Jetée *(1963), an extraordinary short movie consisting almost entirely of still images. A man is injected into the past. He finds true love, but must return to the present, experience the future, and finally witness his own death.*

Providence. Dirk Bogarde as Claude, son of the writer/narrator Clive Langham (John Gielgud). In Langham's fantasy inventions, Claude plays a repressive, judgemental, contemptuous figure. In the last, actual scenes, Claude is gently sensitive to his dying father's pangs of guilt and remorse.

JEAN-LUC GODARD

Godard, a doctor's son, attended school in Switzerland and Paris, meeting André Bazin and François Truffaut in the ciné-clubs. As a critic, he wrote for *Cahiers du Cinéma* under his own name and "Hans Lucas," German for Jean-luc. Godard worked as a laborer and made short films until *Breathless* (1959), a feature suggested by Truffaut, whose Cannes award for *400 Blows* helped to finance the production.

An intellectual who is philosophically enamored of Hegelian contradictions, Godard consciously brought many of narrative film's genre traditions into his productions, often to challenge their conventions with his awesome film erudition. His films purposefully betray their own construction, like brushstrokes of an expressionist painter, while Godard's direction of actors has a buoyant ease that sometimes further seems to mock film illusion. His feeling for beautiful women is deeply emotional, his contempt for the social trappings of their middle-class fantasies enormous. Godard's early features intermingle so broad and diverse a range of references that everything would collapse in a weight of pretentiousness, but for his tongue-in-cheek quality of improvisation.

Breathless follows Michel Poiccard (Jean-Paul Belmondo) a young hoodlum, through a car theft, the shooting of a highway patrolman, and flight. Michel's actions are impulsive with a Camus-like quality of the gratuitous, largely because Godard edits the narrative in jerky, discontinuous continuities. These cuts serve both to divest the character of motive and slyly to echo the slapdash economies of cheap, American gangster films. (*Breathless* is dedicated to Monogram Pictures.) Michel takes up with Patricia (Jean Seberg) in Paris. His behavior is indifferent to conventional values; hers is morally vacant, an American in Paris playing with experience to discover how it feels. Both figures are charming. Finally, Patricia turns Michel in to the police, not out of vindictiveness or even a sense of responsibility, but as another emotional experiment. He is shot down on the street, grimacing in humorous self-depreciation (his "Bogart lip") as he dies. "Tu es dégueulasse," ("You're rotten") he says. Patricia turns to the camera, innocent, and uncaring. She murmurs, "I don't know what the word means."

In the course of *Breathless,* Godard, with his brilliant cameraman Raoul Coutard, draws on technique that ranges from Griffith-Bitzer iris-in's and -out's to hand-held, running improvisations on the street. While Seberg and Belmondo watch a Hollywood western, the sound track carries a poem by Apollinaire. Godard himself appears in overcoat and dark glasses to point out Michel to the police. After all, it is ultimately he who betrays Michel, it seems, almost arbitrarily. The past is constantly brought to our attention. Michel studies a Bogart theater poster (his last, *The Harder They Fall*) as if learning how to be a

Jean-Luc Godard (1930–   )

hard guy. Patricia poses before Renoir and Picasso reproductions. Her apparently arbitrary actions carry a sense of the New World's undependability. In any case, for Godard, love is impossible; one or the other party will betray. Adventure ends in death or self-destruction. Escape gives only temporary respite.

Le petit soldat (1960) is Godard's response to the Algerian War. As a Parisian belonging to no political party, he wanted to demonstrate, matter of factly, that a secret agent, Bruno Forestier (Michel Subor), can be persuaded to commit a murder he does not wish to undertake, and, too, that New Wave films were not always about couples in bed. Bruno is Godard, suspicious of both political extremes, which seem to share much in common, in love with actress Anna Karina (whom he married the next year), more comfortable with camera than gun. Bruno offers the Godard dictum, "To photograph a face is to photograph the soul behind it. Photography is truth, and the cinema is the truth twenty-four times a second."

Une Femme est une femme (1961) refers to Lubitsch and Clair in its credits. It is a musical comedy played by amateurs Karina, Belmondo, and Jean-Claude Brialy. Karina wishes she were Cyd Charisse, and Belmondo, Gene Kelly in a film choreographed by Michael Kidd. Brialy lives with Karina but refuses to cooperate with her wish for a child. She goes to bed with Belmondo. Brialy capitulates and she goes to bed with him. "Tu es infame," (You are disgraceful,) he says. "Non," she responds, "je suis une femme" (I'm a woman).

Vivre sa vie (1962) is dedicated to Carl Dreyer, and Nana (Anna Karina) watches moments of *The Passion of Joan of Arc*, crying as Falconetti cries. Hairdo copies Louise Brooks' in *Pandora's Box*. Nana's history is told in twelve tableaux, introduced, Brecht-like, by intertitles. Its thesis is that Nana can, like Joan of Arc and Lola Montèz in Ophül's film, give up her body without the loss of her soul. Nana finds momentary happiness with a young man who reads her "The Oval Portrait," by Edgar Allen Poe. The story is about an artist who paints his wife's portrait, watching her die as he applies his last touches. (Anna dies in the final episode.) The reading is done by Godard himself on the sound track, and he interrupts it to say, "This is our own story, an artist painting the portrait of his wife."

Les Carabiniers (1963) is even more Brechtian in technique, with a greater number of Soviet than American film references. In an undesignated country, two oafs are recruited to fight an unknown war for the king, excited by promises that they may rape, loot, and pillage. Returning home years later, they present their wives with postcards of the travels. However, the king has lost, and the two are machine-gunned by his forces because their demands for back pay have become bothersome.

Godard's war is any war, the factions any factions. Quoting from letters found on Stalingrad dead, from Napoleon's Spanish campaign, and propaganda leaflets distributed by Himmler, the recruits write home such lines as "A beautiful summer all the same. We leave behind us a trail of blood and death. Love and Kisses." Killing is matter of fact, the fighting meaningless. Godard intercuts newsreel war footage. The soldiers are cheerful, stupid, and brutish, their cruel acts emotionless. A hostage is shot, but remains unwounded, like Pavlo in *Arsenal*. A partisan girl is prepared for execution with a handkerchief draped over her head like the tarpaulin in *Potemkin*. She, too, cries "Brothers," then recites a passage from Mayakovsky. The platoon leader announces, "She bores me; shoot her."

Le Mépris (1963) has a script writer preparing the *Odyssey*, to be directed by Fritz Lang for an American producer in Capri. The writer's marriage to Brigitte Bardot is strained. She sees him flirting with a secretary and lets him witness her kissing the producer. Bardot and the producer are killed in a car accident, but Lang will complete his film.

Like Bardot and Lang, Jack Palance, the producer, exists "outside" his part. The actors are evidentially themselves in styles that take advantage of their actual, expressive personal qualities. Thus, the Bardot sequences constitute a kind of documentation of Bardot-the-person-acting, a manner not at all unpleasing and fitting the "part." Likewise, the film is an homage to Lang's resigned, dignified relations to the callous industry epitomized by Palance-as-producer. *Le Mépris* begins with a Bazin quotation: "The cinema provides us with a world that conforms to our desires." This is followed by an exceptionally long (thirty minute) sequence in the apartment of Bardot and her husband. Perhaps required by the film's actual producer, Joseph Levine, Bardot is nude in bed, but the scene registers as painful, underplayed, unrelieved dissonance, she increasingly contemptuous at his efforts toward self-justification. Like Lang, Godard, views himself as the salaried functionary; he casts himself in the role of the older man's assistant.

Bande à part has Anna Karina conspire with two men to rob her aunt's house. The robbery collapses in ineptitude. One man is shot. The pair escape to South America. Godard's film-reality contrasts are explicated within the plot (the men mock a movie death, then one is really killed) and between audience and film. After the first reel, Godard interrupts the sound track to provide a muddled summary of what has happened so far. The mock death *looks* more real. The escape to South America has an unsatisfactory, intentionally pat escapism about it.

Distancing audience from illusion, Godard's esthetic breakage intends to promote self-examination. In *Le petit soldat*, Bruno narrates and comments on his own behavior. *Les Carabiniers* separates act and consequence so that the horror accumulates in retrospect. In *Une Femme mariée* (1964), a story of marital infidelity with commerce providing a materialist metaphor, techniques include fragmented, unerotic love scenes that are photographed like advertising displays for jewelry and perfume, and long, cinéma-vérité monologues directed at the camera. These include a cleaning lady whose description of her husband's sexual abilities is finally shown to have been quoted from the French novelist Céline.

Lemmy Caution is a popular adventure figure created on French screens by the American Eddie Constantine. *Alphaville* (1965) casts Lemmy into the future, assigned to penetrate Alphaville, and to rescue or kill Dr. von Braun, who operates Alpha-60, the computer that is the city's heart. Caution contacts a dying agent (Akim Tamiroff), and wins over von Braun's daughter Natasha (Anna Karina) by teaching her vocabulary censored from the city's Newspeak. Questioned by the computer, Lemmy's answers confound the technology. He kills von Braun and escapes with Natasha.

The film is done in comic strip style, with references to Dick Tracy and Flash Gordon, but the setting is Paris, 1965, the more unsettling because the future is here. Natasha's job is Seducer Second Class. Caution teaches her words like *conscience, tears, autumn light,* and *red breast.* Dying while he is making love, Akim Tamiroff's last words to Lemmy Caution are, "Save those who weep." Alphaville's underlying myth is Orpheus' rescue of Eurydice from the underworld. It is by poetry that Caution teaches Natasha to cry.

Pierrot le fou (1965) might be the next adventure of Natasha and Lemmy, or another ending to *Breathless.* Belmondo and Karina refer to their affair of five-and-a-half years before, the date of *Breathless. Bande à parte* concludes, "Next episode in CinemaScope and Technicolor." Here, the two principals come up against a roadblock of differing romanticisms, she dying violently after a life of crime, he suicidal for lost love. They have escaped to an idyll in the south of France. Karina becomes restless and resumes political-criminal gunrunning. Betrayed when he learns her "brother" is really a lover, Bel-

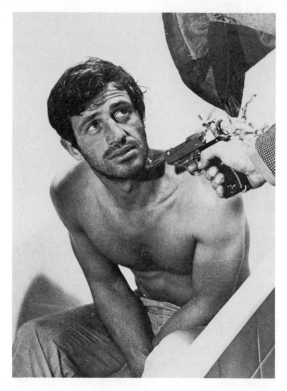

Pierrot le fou. Ferdinand (Jean-Paul Belmondo) is tortured by a pair of gangsters to disclose the whereabouts of Marianne (Anna Karina) who has disappeared, leaving behind the corpse of a midget stabbed with a pair of scissors. Ferdinand will meet her later in Toulon, only to learn that she means to betray him and flee with her "brother." (Museum of Modern Art/Film Stills Archive)

mondo shoots Karina. He paints his face blue like a Picasso clown (Karina is named Renoir), wraps dynamite about himself and lights the fuse, changing his mind too late. In final, offscreen lines, the dead couple recite a poem by Rimbaud.

Masculin-feminin (1966) examines what Godard calls "the children of Marx and Coca Cola," Paris youth in the mid-sixties. Ostensibly an episodic series about Paul, a student, Madeleine, a popular singer, and Madeleine's friends Elizabeth and Catherine, the film largely consists of interviews. At the same time, Godard questions the worth of documentary technique. If the camera can capture the soul, it requires an actor to expose it.

By *Made in U.S.A.* (1966) and *Two or Three Things I Know About Her* (1966), filmed simultaneously, plot is no longer a vehicle to support Godard's interruptions, but reduced and distorted, like lines of a Picasso. *Made in U.S.A.* has vague relations to a detective story with Karina as a raincoated private eye, but overtones of real event, kidnapping, murders, and the Kennedy assassination, plunge the story into a morass of unexplained intrigue. "I felt," says Karina, in a parody of the detective's first person narration, "like Bogart first in a Disney, then a political movie." A confused quagmire of Godardian

preoccupations, the film tries to focus itself in one scene with Karina in a bar. Deadpan, she declares to the camera, "Either this life is nothing or else it must be everything. By contemplating the possibility of losing it rather than submitting it to action, I place in the very center of my relative existence a point of absolute reference: morality." In consequence, she undertakes a line of action that requires her to kill others. Unlike previous withdrawals or nihilist views toward the use of power, Godard moves toward its exercise.

Two or Three Things takes a cultural anthropologist's perspective toward mutations in French society. It was prompted by a newspaper letter about part-time prostitution among wives in new high-rise apartment buildings. Their motive is a second income. Godard

Masculin-feminin. As elsewhere in Godard, signs and billboards alternately express and deny the characters' feelings. A revolutionary, Paul (Jean-Pierre Léaud) is directionless, romantic, somewhat dependent. A singer, Madeleine (Chantal Goya) is tough, lives for herself, and uses words for their effects. (Museum of Modern Art/Film Stills Archive)

believes he is witnessing a feelingless eruption of conditioned acquisitiveness. Instead of revolting, as Marxism predicted, the workers have adjusted to a system whose materialism impels them to live up to ever-rising economic demands. Through overtime and second jobs, the aging children of Marx and Coca Cola have become victims of images pandering unessential goods and services. Prostitution takes many forms.

La Chinoise (1967) finds Godard increasingly interested in the young Marxists, still inclined to see them with the disillusion he has always imposed on youth. Two girls and three boys form a Marxist-Leninist cell and move into a summer apartment to study Chairman Mao. One is expelled for deviationism; he opposes political assassination. After shooting someone in error, Anna Wiazemsky (Godard's new wife) kills the right man. The group

breaks up when school resumes. *La Chinoise* is filmed in stylized color, flat, rectangular splashes against which actors read and argue like characters in a morality play, as if Godard increasingly suspects that illusion will destroy his ideas. In one scene, Anna Wiazemsky requires Jean-Pierre Léaud to play Mozart on a phonograph as counterpoint to his declarations of love, so they both may examine the dialectic. Godard is becoming stern.

Weekend attacks the bourgeoisie with guerilla theater agitprop, grotesque vignettes where murder, a carnage of traffic deaths, and cannibalism conspire to force the audience to make ideological choices. When the eye is inured to wrecks and corpse-strewn highways, Godard actually slaughters a pig and a duck, defying the viewer to sympathize more fully with the animals. His own obsession with quotation and interpolated references is savagely

Weekend. Godard stages an automobile carnage as emblematic of capitalism's death throes. Its execution is extraordinary: a lengthy tracking camera impassively recording the action by disclosing the consequences, rather than staging the collisions. (Museum of Modern Art/Film Stills Archive)

rejected; Emily Brontë dressed as Alice in Wonderland is burned. A figure in the forest appears with quotations affixed all over his body.[3] Godard does not disguise the appalling implications of revolution (the guerillas eat stray bourgeois who happen by their camp), but his sympathies with radical and Third World forces are clear. His disgust with French-American civilization is now immense. The strongest emotion is anguish at the irreconcilability of centuries of culture with new realities. A piano sonata is played in an unresponsive farmyard. As in *Hour of the Wolf,* and toward similar purpose, the composer is Mozart.

During Spring 1968, Godard toured American universities with a print of *La Chinoise.* In Hollywood, his panel appearance with King Vidor, Roger Corman, and Samuel Fuller was respectful, if critical that these men ought to be viewed as industrial slaves. In Berkeley, Godard pleased radical students with his ideological sympathies and aroused animosity among those who saw film, like all the arts, serving no more effective purpose than to document The Movement. Besides, Godard pronounced that experimental films only hurt his eyes.

By the Paris student uprisings of 1968 and the appearance of *Le Gai Savoir* (The joy of learning) (1968), Godard's commitment was complete and altogether visible. In the film a young man and woman undertake to reconceive film's narrative purpose "starting at zero."[4] They speak against a black back-ground. Sometimes there is no image at all, only talk. Later, photographs and image fragments appear as different words and ideas are tested.

The ensuing succession of Godard films undertakes, each in its own fashion, to explore a film language that will serve predesignated ideological ends and escape the narrative tyranny that Godard associates with political-esthetic oppression. In *One Plus One,* also known as *Sympathy for the Devil* (1968), a Rolling Stones recording session provides the backdrop against which a spectrum of political protest is shown by interview and monologue, the statements set off with radical theater techniques,[5] as when black revolutionaries shoot down white women or Anne Wiazemsky as Eve Democracy is pursued by soundmen and cameramen, interviewed with foolish and profound questions that she answers with cryptic yes's and no's. She can only express concensus.

See You at Mao (1969) features an exceptional, opening, left-to-right camera track that documents workers at an automobile assembly line. Against the flat-perspectived visuals, Godard plays shrieking, oppressive factory noise and readings from Marx and Engels

---

[3] *This image also parodies a final scene of* Farenheit 451 *in which characters wander through the woods reciting great books they have memorized. Truffaut had humorously vowed to best Godard in the number of literary references contained in one movie.*

[4] *The concept echoes a proposition by Roland Barthes, who seeks to distinguish what is peculiar to literature distinct from style and language. See Roland Barthes,* Writing Degree Zero. *Boston, 1967. Originally published as* Le Degré zéro de l'écriture. *Paris, 1953.*

[5] *The challenge that Godard posed for himself becomes more apparent if we compare his situation to Brecht's. Like the Russian formalists before him, Brecht sought to withdraw his audience from continuous, empathizing commitments to vicarious experience. See Stanley Mitchell, "From Shlovsky to Brecht,"* Screen *(Summer 1974) and Robert Scholes,* Structuralism in Literature. *New Haven, 1974. Pp. 83-5. Brecht sought such effects in order to expose the underlying socio-economic conditions of capitalism. Godard's motives paralleled Brecht so long as he operated, however parodically, within "Hollywood" generic forms. As he departed from that narrative idiom, Godard shifted his intentions toward a different audience (see footnote 7). His interests become more pointedly skewed toward espousing truths rather than puncturing illusions.*

about the alienating consequence of industrial labor.[6]

Wind from the East (1969) seeks to confront the issue implicit in Godard's disagreement with Berkeley students by arguing that traditional narrativity grows from a commitment to illusory experience, that to construct a revolutionary cinema requires rethinking every aspect of production, including acting, synchronous sound, and the relations between audience and picture. Godard (or Daniel Cohn-Bendit who wrote the script) invents his own stylized western and Godard delivers narrations, sometimes with specific relations to the picture, sometimes with none at all. *One Plus One* was directed not by Godard alone, but by the Dziga Vertov group, a working team first enjoined with Jean-Henri Roget, a young Marseilles militant, for *One Plus One* and *Pravda,* later with the journalist Jean-Pierre Gorin. Attributions to the group commence with *Pravda.*

Un Film comme les autres (1968) is a document of the 1968 Paris riots. *Pravda* (1969) counterpoints shots of Czechoslovakia against narration and discussion of the realities of socialist life and its continued exploitation by power from above. *Struggle in Italy* (1969) discusses the difficulties of ridding one's consciousness of bourgeois values. The experiences of a young Italian girl persuade her to confront the contradictions between her actual perceptions and what she would like to understand. An effort to make a film in New York, to be called *One A.M.*, aborted, but parts of the footage as well as documentation of the shooting, filmed by Donn Pennebaker and Richard Leacock, were released as *One P.M.* (for One Parallel Movie) in 1970.

Tout va bien (1972) reverts to a story structure. Jane Fonda is an American radio commentator stationed in Paris. Yves Montand, her husband, had been an experimental filmmaker. Now radicalized and disillusioned, he makes a living producing television commercials. The pair visit a meat-packing plant that is being struck by a group resentful both of employers and the unions. Each faction speaks. Montand and Fonda realize that ideological issues, shared with the workers, are deteriorating their own relationship.

Letter to Jane (1972) is a forty-five minute disquisition on a news photo and caption of Jane Fonda's visit to Hanoi that year. Camera angle, Vietnamese out of focus in the background, composition and text are analyzed to support an argument that the form is impinged with ideological connotations that deny Fonda's apparent intentions. *Numero Deux* (1974) employs television images to develop multi-perspective, simultaneous views of a working-class French family in which the husband's exploitation of his wife assumes both economic and sexual overtones.[7]

For many audiences, Godard's ideological or literal inaccessibility in recent years would seem to assign him into the era of the sixties. Yet questions his films have posed continue to nag contemporary filmmakers, and his influence has been immense on radical young European directors. As yet, no alternative solutions to Godard's problems have registered more convincingly.

---

[6] *Ideological implications of Godard's long takes are dissected by Brian Henderson in "Toward a Non-Bourgeois Camera Style,"* Film Quarterly *(Winter 1970–71). Reprinted in* Bill Nichols, *ed.,* Movies and Methods. *Berkeley, 1976, pp. 422-38.*

[7] *The difficulties posed by Godard's later films are compounded by their general inaccessibility, for the Dziga Vertov productions scarcely adapt to usual distribution channels, and some are, in fact, not intended for general audiences, but for study groups. His own view is that films that merely stimulate feelings are politically dysfunctional, that even* Weekend *is an "objective ally" of Hollywood, like* Z *(1968) and* The Battle of Algiers *(1966). See Michael Goodwin and Greil Marcus,* Double Feature: Movies and Politics. *New York, 1972, p. 28.*

Summary

In Antonioni, modern graphics serve like metaphoric externalizations of character moods. Similarly, pace and continuities may be attenuated to focus attention on thoughts and motives (or their absence) rather than the furtherance of plot. Resnais' style is inclined repetitiously to overlay experience upon experience. Each differs in the mind of the perceiver, or in the conditions of recollection. More radically, Godard has moved first from parodic amusements to politically-based criticisms of expository structure, then to experimentation with new, didactic forms.

In his own way, each director departs significantly from narrative conventions that grew out of major film production capitals. Exploring film work that has evolved elsewhere in the world. Chapter 21 largely describes additional departures from convention rooted both in culture and in individual temperaments.

Bibliography

Alverez, A. "Alain Resnais: The Man Who Makes Movies of the Mind, *The New York Times* (October 10, 1976).

Antonioni, Michelangelo. *Blow-up.* New York, 1971.

———. "Making a Film is My Way of Life," *Film Culture* 24 (1962).

———. *Michelangelo Antonioni: An Introduction.* New York, 1963.

———. "*Night, Eclipse, Dawn.*" *Cahiers du Cinéma in English* 1 (January 1966.

———. *Screenplays: Il Grido, L' Avventura. La Notte. L'Eclisse.* New York, 1963.

———. *Zabriskie Point.* Bologna, 1970.

Armes, Roy. *The Cinema of Alain Resnais.* London, 1968.

Bertolucci, Bernardo. "Versus Godard," *Cahiers du Cinéma in English* 10 (May 1967).

Bounoure, Gaston. *Alain Resnais.* Paris, 1962.

Brown, Royal S., comp. *Focus on Godard.* Englewood Cliffs, N.J., 1972.

Caen, Michael. "The Times Change," *Cahiers du Cinéma in English* 8 (February 1966).

Cameron, Ian, ed. *The Films of Jean-Luc Godard.* New York, 1969.

Cameron, Ian and Robin Wood. *Antonioni.* New York, 1971.

Carlo, Carli di. *Il Deserto Rosso.* Bologna, 1964.

Clouzot, Claire. "Godard in the U.S.," *Sight and Sound* 37 (Summer 1968).

Collet, Jean. *Jean-Luc Godard.* New York, 1970.

Cowie, Peter. *Antonioni, Bergman, Resnais.* New York, 1963.

Delahaye, Michel. "Jean-Luc Godard, or the Urgency of Art," *Cahiers du Cinéma in English* 10 (May 1967).

———. "Jean-Luc Godard and the Childhood of Art," *Cahiers du Cinéma in English* 10 (May 1967).

Duras, Marguerite. *Hiroshima Mon Amour.* New York, 1961.

French, Philip, et al. *The Films of Jean-Luc Godard.* London, 1967.

Giannetti, Louis G. *Godard and Others.* Englewood, N.J., 1974.

Goodwin, Michael and Greil Marcus. *Double Feature: Movies and Politics.* New York, 1972.

Godard, Jean-Luc. *Alphaville.* New York, 1968.

––––––. "A Woman is a Woman, Scenario," *Cahiers du Cinéma in English* 12 (December 1967).

––––––. *Made in U.S.A.* London, 1967.

––––––. *Masculine Feminine.* New York, 1969.

––––––. *La Petit Soldat.* New York, 1967.

––––––. *Pierrot le Fou.* New York, 1969.

––––––. "Three Thousand Hours of Cinema," *Cahiers du Cinéma in English* 10 (May 1967).

––––––. *Weekend/Wind from the East.* New York, 1972.

––––––. *Three Films.* New York, 1975.

Huss, Roy. *Focus on Blow-up.* Englewood, N.J., 1971.

Kinder, Marsha. "Antonioni in Transit," *Sight and Sound* (Summer 1967).

Kolker, Robert. "Angle and Reality: Godard and Gorin in America," *Sight and Sound* (Summer 1973).

Labarthe, André S. et Jacques Rivette. "Entretiens avec Resnais et Robbe-Grillet," *Cahiers du Cinéma* n. 123 (September 1961); translated in part in *Films and Filming* (February, March 1962).

Lacassin, Francis. "Alain Resnais: The Quest for Harry Dickson," *Sight and Sound* (Autumn 1973).

MacBean, James Roy. *Film and Revolution.* Bloomington, Ind., 1975.

Monaco, James. "Conversations with Resnais," *Film Comment* (July-August 1975).

Mussman, Toby. *Jean-Luc Godard.* New York, 1968.

New York Film Bulletin 46 (1964). Jean-Luc Godard Issue.

Perry, Ted. "Men and Landscape," *Film Comment* (July-August 1975).

Roud, Richard. "Memories of Resnais," *Sight and Sound* (Summer 1969).

––––––. "Anguish, Alphaville," *Sight and Sound* (Autumn 1967).

––––––. *Godard.* Bloomington, Ind., 1970.

Semprun, Jorge. *La Guerre est Finie.* New York, 1967.

––––––. *Stavisky.* New York, 1975.

Sternberg, Jacques. *Je t'aime, je t'aime. Paris, 1969.*

Strick, Philip. *Antonioni. Motion* 5 (March 1963).

Visny, Michel. *En attendant Godard.* Paris, 1967.

Van Wert, William. *The Film Career of Alain Robbe-Grillet.* Boston, 1977.

Ward, John. *Alain Resnais, or the Theme of Time.* London, 1968.

Williams, Christopher. "Politics and Production," *Screen* 12 (1971).

WORLD CINEMA

United States domination of foreign screens diminishes, while other cinemas remain little known to international audiences except through film festivals. Some have traditions of unpretentious entertainment, like Hong Kong and Mexico. Other nationalities, Japan and Poland for example, develop some filmmakers of wide reputation while the remainder, often highly talented, stay locally submerged. Ambition or circumstance may bring certain directors, like Dusan Makavajev of Yugoslavia and Milos Forman of Czechoslovakia, into broader arenas. More impersonally, a country's films may reflect its preoccupations and sometimes its efforts to evolve a national identity; recent Cuban films and those of Glauber Rocha in Brazil are cases in point.

CANADA

With short and documentary films in preponderance, the National Film Board of Canada accounts for the greater part of Canadian production. Since the sixties, feature filmmaking in the country has developed a

Five Women Around Utamaro (Mizoguchi 1946)

small, sometimes impressive output, perhaps a dozen a year. When pictures can present a persuasive case for their commercial potential in preproduction stages, the Canadian Film Finance Corporation, established in 1967, makes some support available, as does the Film Board itself.

A realistic study of an unrealistic laborer, *The Luck of Ginger Coffey* (1964) was made by a US director with overtones of period British features. Irvin Kershner's film was, in fact, a Canadian-US coproduction. *Goin' Down The Road* (1968) traced a pair seemingly picked randomly from a wandering, new generation of young people, moving across Newfoundland to Toronto. *The Apprenticeship of Duddy Kravitz* (1974) by Ted Kotcheff secured US distribution and startled some audiences with the candor of its profile of a young Jew on the make. Although it originated in a Canadian novel and was produced in Montreal, most of the principals came from south of the border. *The Tragic Diary of Zero the Fool* (1969) by Morley Markson is an experimental, sometimes moving film dedicated to Samuel Beckett. It was produced in a mental institution with a patients' drama group as performers.

English Canadian films carry limited local appeal. In contrast, the French Canadian product is less tempted to discard provincial concerns for the sake of international distribution. Although some films have been Canadian-French financed, *Kamouraska* (1974), for example, preponderantly they confront concerns of Quebec. *Kamouraska* was made by Claude Jutra, its romantic period drama recalling the director's early apprenticeship with Truffaut at *Cahiers du Cinéma*. Following a term on the Ivory Coast with Jean Rouch, Jutra returned to Canada and filmed *A tout prendre* (1963), a semi-autobiographical record of his affair in Montreal with a black Canadian woman. Jutra's *Wow!* (1968) viewed drug culture life in the city. *Mon Oncle Antoine* (1971) recounts a young boy's adole-

Mon Oncle Antoine. Benoit, fourteen, lives with Uncle Antoine and Aunt Cecile, who run a general store and morgue. In one evening's adventures, Benoit begins to understand a little about middle-aged despair, death, infidelity, drunkenness, personal responsibility, and the role of chance in human life. Script by Clément Perron, who wrote *Day After Day* (Chapter 12). (Museum of Modern Art/ Film Stills Archive)

scence in a little mining town. *Red* (1969) by Gilles Carle examines the problems of an Indian half-breed in Montreal. *Les dernières fiançailles* (1974), directed by Jean-Pierre Lefebvre, has overtones of Zavattini's neorealist esthetic. In their last few days of life, an elderly couple chooses to remain at home and to talk about the past. Thought by some to be the most "quebecois," of the Province's output, *Bar Salon* (1975) by André Forcier examines the milieu of a Quebec bar with shrewd, friendly restraint.[1]

MEXICO

Some Mexican-born performers, Anthony Quinn, Arturo de Cordova, and Cantinflas, notably, developed wide followings outside the

[1] *John Turner, "Le Cinéma quebecois,"* Journal of the University Film Association *(1972).*

country; Mexico's sixty-feature annual output crosses national boundaries less often. An exception is *Raices*/*Roots* (1954) by Benito Alazraki. Structured in four episodes (the last was omitted in US release), *Raices* views the country's rural culture with sentiment, cruelty, and humor. Natives of an outlying village fear a visiting anthropologist will take back the Mona Lisa reproduction she had left earlier. A mother escorts her one-eyed boy to a shrine where an injury destroys his remaining sight. An archaeologist wants to buy a girl from her father, who requires the other's wife in exchange. An Indian sells his wife as a wet nurse.

Many of Mexico's best films have been graced by the photography of Gabriel Figueroa, who worked with Gregg Toland in Hollywood in the mid-thirties. Buñuel's regular cameraman and associate in Mexico, Figueroa's work appears more ornate, evocative of the painter Diego Rivera, in the films he made with Emilio Fernandez. Fernandez' *Maria Candelaria* (1945), featuring Mexican actress Dolores Del Rio, recounts a sentimental story in which Del Rio suffers persecution, like her mother before, because her conduct is misjudged by villagers. Fernandez' later work, tinged with melodrama, concentrates on Spanish and Indian character. In *Rio Escondido* (1948), a village schoolteacher rescues the people from exploitation and epidemic, then suffers a heart attack.

In recent years, Mexico has entertained the surreal religious visions of Alexandro Jodorowsky, a Chilean-Russian theater director.

Roots. Based on short stories by Francisco Gonzales published as *El Diosero*. Director Barbacharo also made *Torero!* (1956), a semidocumentary of Mexican bullfighter Luis Procuna. *Roots'* allegiance to peasant society evokes contemporary moods of proud resistance to foreign influence. (National Film Archives, Ottawa)

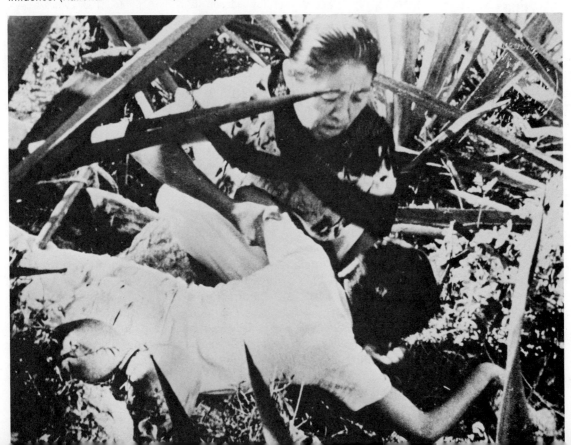

El Topo (1970), prototypically, stages ritual reenactments of birth, death, incest, patricide, love, sado-masochism, metaphysical transcendence, and resurrection, colorfully staged against flat, bright landscapes which contribute Dali-like settings for Jodorowsky's charged, metaphysical allegories. *The Holy Mountain* (1973) forsakes *El Topo*'s picaresque soul-quest for a yet more mystic, less personalized guru-trip.

Most Mexican production is more popularly aimed and less flamboyant; the country makes more Spanish-language films than any other. Its industry was nationalized under President Luis Echeverra Alvarez in 1976, and recent production suggests the slow emergence of political film in Mexico. A cooperative, *Cine Independiente,* was formed in 1969 by several young directors. However, in practice directors enjoy new freedom to portray sex and violence, while political content remains subject to "supervision."

CUBA

Before the revolution, Cuba had no native film industry, except for sponsored commercial shorts. Since 1959, the Cuban Institute of Cinematographic Art and Industry has sought to initiate an energetic program both of commercial production and encouragement of tastes and enthusiasms among Cuban film audiences.

Early ventures produced training and educational 16mm films. Technical skills were acquired outside the country, but the Institute has operated from an assumption that "creative work"—writing, directing, and photography—should be acquired at home, nurtured by the culture it will espouse. Like Soviet agit-trains of old, Cuban mobile units carry newsreels into remote areas, some more accessible now by way of television. Production has been influenced by the Czech and Russian features that dominate local exhibition, al-

El Topo. Writer, director, composer, costume, and scenic designer, Jodorowsky appears on horseback with Brontis, his real-life son. He instructs the boy to bury a toy bear and his mother's photo: "Today you are seven years old. . . . Now you are a man." While El Topo plays his flute, the boy inters his bear and partly covers the photo. The two ride away. (Museum of Modern Art/Film Stills Archive)

though the Institute seeks to maximize the international flavor of its imports, a condition aggrevated by the American blockade.

History of a Battle (1962) by Manuel Octavia Gomez considered illiteracy, while *La Salacion* (1965) dealt with marriage and *Tulipa* (1966) bureaucracy. *Lucia* (1968), directed by Humberto Solas, viewed three revolutionary episodes (the last in the present) from a feminist perspective.

Memories of Underdevelopment (1969) ironically views the upheaval in Cuban life from the point of view of the affected middle class. Its director, Tomas G. Alea, later conceived *The Last Supper* (1977), which recreates a Holy Week during the late eighteenth century when a sugar plantation-owning count, guilt ridden at the treatment of his African slaves, seeks like Nazarin to act out the precepts of Christianity. Comparison with Buñuel is appropriate, because the vices of the poor and maltreated are closely documented and the film's exceptional, drunken orgy of a last supper does not suffer in comparison with *Viridiana,* its inspiration.

A first film by Manuel Perez, *The Man from Maisinicu* (1975), interestingly grafts contemporary national values onto something of the form of a Hollywood western. Director of the Cuban Film Institute, Santiago Alverez, has produced *To Die For One's Country is to Live* (1976), that employs newsreel footage, sound tracks of plane-to-landing tower communications and Castro speeches to document the October 6, 1976 bombing of a Cuban Airlines plane that killed seventy-three passengers and crew. Alverez' *Takeoff at 18:00* evokes Dziga Vertov's Kino Pravda. It combines news footage, photos, animation and imaginative (if dated) titles to celebrate mass popular mobilizations of the people against underdevelopment. Unlike Vertov, *Takeoff*'s sound track is orthodox, composed equally of popular music and rhetorical exhortation.

One of Cuba's film challenges is to maintain a revolutionary dynamic in a stabilized society. In terms of plot, this often means substituting other villains, sometimes more abstract ones, for capitalists. It requires, too, a continual concern about manipulating the form of Cuban films enough to secure and maintain audience interest while yet staying within the sensibilities of the population. Cuba's influence extends into other countries. Typically, *The Battle of Chile* (Chile 1975) discusses Allende's overthrow by means of commentary played against newsreel footage.

BOLIVIA

Blood of the Condor (1969) is both Jorge Sanjines' and Bolivia's second feature. US "Progress Corps" doctors surreptitiously sterilize Quechua Indian women while delivering their babies. Forewarned by a shaman's reading of coca leaves, the tribe storms a new medical center and castrates the physicians. Consequently. Ignacio and two fellow Indians are shot by authorities while "escaping." In La Paz, Ignacio dies when his brother cannot raise the price of a blood transfusion. If crudely executed and dubbed, Sanjines' film shifts most effectively between present pathos and past events. One of its most telling moments shows the desperate brother watching wealthy Bolivians playing tennis. *Blood of the Condor* ends on a close shot of upraised rifles.

BRAZIL

Brazil produces about as many feature films as Mexico for its larger population and supports half as many theaters as Great Britain. In past years, Alberto Cavalcanti figured as the country's outstanding director. Although most of his professional life was spent in Australia, France, Britain, Italy, and East Germany, Cavalcanti returned to Brazil in 1949, made several films, most notably *O Canto do Mar/ Song of the Sea* (1954), and worked, finally unsuccessfully, to revive local industry. *Song of the Sea* depicts customs and poverty in Recife, a little tropical town.

During the sixties, Cavalcanti's concern with social problems of Brazil was furthered by a movement that came to be called Cinema Novo, heralding a new generation of directors, Ruy Guerra, Walter Hugo Khouri, Joaquim Pedro de Andrade, Carlos Diegues, Julio Bressane, Nelson Pereira dos Santos and most especially Glauber Rocha. Rocha's films blend native folklore and social analysis with political rebellion in *Deus e O Diabo Na Terra do Sol/The Black God and the White Devil* (1964) in which a native foresakes religion for the life of a socially-rebellious bandit. In *Terra em Transe/Land in a Trance* (1966) a poet becomes politically involved.

Similarly, Antonio of *Antonio das Mortes* (1969) is possessed by a village hero named Lampiao whom he has murdered. Rocha's violent images and political employment of indiginous religion suggest Pasolini, and sometimes the Eisenstein of *Que Viva Mexico*. Rocha has also made *The Lion Has Seven Heads* (1970), a political farce filmed in Congo, Africa. Its characters include an American espionage agent, a black revolutionary, a priest, a Nazi in hiding, and a sexy, topless blonde. Like the new Cuban filmmakers, Cinema Novo seeks to create popular, agitational film forms without reverting to the designs of Russian socialist realism.[2]

Attitudes toward narrative form appear to polarize among South American directors. Unlike Godard, many filmmakers commonly seem to regard mainstream expository techniques as an "international language" applicable to any content. Cuba's Alvarez and Bolivia's Sanjines exemplify the position. Cinema Novo filmmakers who chose to seek out commercial exhibition patterns for their work became equally committed to such bases of broad commercial appeal. In consequence, a theatrical audience might hardly reflect the farmers and workers addressed in the films themselves. But some films, dos Santos' *Tent of Miracles* (1977), for example, have simultaneously developed subtle, self-critical frames of reference. The perceptive viewer may "read" additional messages, including the director's acknowledgement of his own partial complicity in commercial exploitation of his subject. Patterned after *Citizen Kane*, *Tent of Miracles* traces the life of a Bahian sociologist, based on the conflicting testimonies of people who knew him.

During the early seventies, Brazil's government effectively repressed the early political and social rhetoric of Cinema Novo. Later in the decade, a new director of the Brazilian State Film Enterprise (Robert Farias of Embrafilme) effected a kind of detente between the military government and Cinema Novo. Relationships have been variously viewed as rapprochement, sell-out or subtle manipulation of the government's support, depending on the reporter's own social and esthetic perspective.

ARGENTINA

Influenced by European literature, French film of the "cinema of quality" idiom, and some expatriate French directors during World War II, Argentina's film output was distinguished during two decades by Leopoldo Torre Nilsson. Nilsson's well-wrought features concern Argentine middle-class life, depicting it as isolated from the country's social realities, depraved, unhappy, and sometimes passionate. *La Casa del Angel/The House of the Angel/End of Innocence* (1957) places a story of political intrigue in the Argentina of the twenties. In *Fin de Fiesta/Blood Feast* (1960) a young man somewhat frees himself from the society on realizing his uncle's political corruption.

Subsequently, *La Hora de los Hornos/Hour of the Furnaces* (1968) brought revolution to Argentine film. Directed by Fernando Solanas and Ottavio Getino, *Hour of the Furnaces* is a lengthy (originally four hours and twenty minutes) treatise-like statement, divided into three parts. Successively, the country's history, present conflicts, and current state of mind are depicted with news footage, staged events, and interviews. Unique to the film is a hortatory relation with its audience ("Every spectator is a coward or a traitor") and the argument that Juan Peron's ten-year reign had the salutary effect of coalescing Argentina's mass, native population into a political force.

[2] See *"Cinema Novo vs Cultural Colonialism. An Interview with Glauber Rocha,"* Cineaste *(Summer 1970).*

POLAND

State controlled since the early days of Poland's Soviet-dominated provisional government, the Polish film industry first turned to experiences of wartime and the German occupation, then to postwar conditions. Aleksander Ford, a director whose work dates from the twenties, organized the Polish Army Film Unit during World War II; it formed a basis for later nationalization. *Border Street* (1948) dealt with children in the Warsaw ghetto. Through humane sympathy and understanding, *Five Boys from Barska Street* (1953) rejuvenates a gang of delinquents, demoralized by war.

In 1954-55, a new generation instigated and accomplished a reorganization of the industry into smaller, partially autonomous production units, each supervised by a major Polish director. (Ford was one such figure.) More independent, less conforming features resulted.

Andrzej Wajda created a trilogy of war films that served to establish Polish film internationally. *A Generation* (1955), *Kanal* (1957), and *Ashes and Diamonds* (1958) expressed, like Munk, conflict between romantic impulse and the realities of the day. From guerilla resistance and escape in the sewers of Warsaw to new problems that accompanied the day of liberation, Wajda's sometimes brutal and visually striking style, notoriously apparent in the sewer sequences of *Kanal,* located heroic figures in the wartime rubble.

Andrzej Munk's films undercut Poland's

Walkover. Ardzev Leszazyc (Skolimowski) stops by accident in a town where he meets Theresa (Alexsandra Zawieraszanka), who had caused his discharge from the university years before. The pair take up together temporarily, resulting in Skolimowski's winning two prizefights, one by default, and being beaten up outside the ring by his opponent. (Museum of Modern Art/Film Stills Archive)

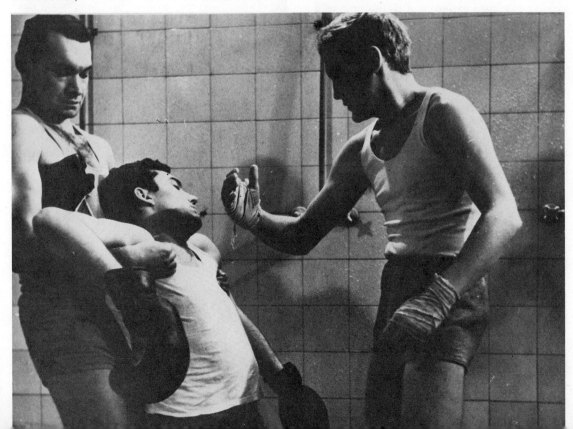

occasional weakness for historic self-glorification. Roman Polanski was one of the new filmmakers and, slightly earlier, Wojciech Has, whose films sometimes chronicled the efforts of suspicious intellectuals to adapt to the new society. Has's *The Saragossa Manuscript* (1964) is an extraordinary narrative composed of flashback within flashback. Tongue-in-cheek, romantic, and suspicious of itself, the film derives from an eccentric novel by Jan Potochi, an eighteenth-century Polish traveler who wrote only in French. Beset with Party criticism ("Our cinema cannot be an instrument used entirely for experimental purposes by a small group of artists, but must serve the cultural and entertainment needs of the masses"), and by anti-Semitism that led to the removal of leading figures like Ford and Jerzy Toeplitz who directed the Lodz Film School, recent product has been more orthodox with attendance falling because of television. National interest continues in animation and in the short film.

An exception to the general pattern is Jerzy Skolimowski, script writer for Wajda's *Innocent Sorcerers* (1960) and Polanski's *Knife in the Water*. Skolimowski's own films suggest elements of Godard combined with a surreal, cutting imagery that is natively Polish. His subject is youth and its frustrated vista between a destructively romantic past and a sterile, materialistic future. *Walkover* (1965) and *Barrier* (1966) are incidental, anecdotal stories with behavior and staging that confront the borders between real and fantastic. The opening of *Barrier* appears to be a torturous execution, then discloses itself as a student game. A central character, played by Skolimowski in *Walkover* and reappearing in his *Hands Up!* (1967), is alternatively impulsive and withdrawn, speculative and depressed, naïve and bitter. He is inclined from time to time to withdraw momentarily from society's strictures, while remaining quite aware that finally they will contain him. Behind Warsaw's apparent modernity lie monoliths of the past.

Story of Sin. Grazyna Dlugolecka as Eva Pobratynska, daughter of impoverished gentry. Politically immobilized and socially dispossessed, the young woman flees her clerical job in a Warsaw railway station for love. She has momentary joy, and finally dies a prostitute, shot by thieves, protecting the undeserving man she has always loved. (John Springer Associates)

The animator and director of short subjects Walerian Borowczyk completed three feature films, live action, in a remarkable eighteenth-month period: *Immoral Tales* (1974), made in France, *Story of a Sin* (1974), and *The Beast* (1975). Preceded by an earlier feature *Blanche* (1971), Borowczyk's work investigates sexuality in forms both perverse and bizarre. *Blanche* is a medieval story, *Immoral Tales* a satire on satyriasis. *The Beast,* also made in France, has a girl and a beast lover, each insatiably demanding.

Story of a Sin, based on a classic Polish novel by Stefan Zeromski, traces the turn-of-the-century life of a beautiful woman whose obsessive love alternatively inspires her to great passion and condemns her to sordid experiences. Imaginative sound, like the repetitions of an unseen piano student, and vaguely threatening images, like a rotating, unplayed cylinder phonograph, evoke the Borowczyk of *Dom* and *Les Jeux des anges*.

CZECHOSLOVAKIA

After overcoming influences of Germany and France in the twenties, early Czechoslovakian sound films, fiction and documentary, developed a characteristic realism. Before the war, Gustav Machátý's *Extase* (1932) with Hedy Lamarr and after, Jiri Trnka's puppet films won international distribution. Nationalized in 1945, the industry has continued to contain both Czech and Slovak elements.

Like other communist countries, Czechoslovakia responded to Stalin's death and the political thaw with freer, more critical work. Major figures to emerge were Jan Němec, Evald Schorm, and Miloš Forman. Němec's *Diamond of the Night* (1964) follows two boys who escape from a Nazi transport train into the forest, their fears, physical debility, and past experience promoting hallucinations and distorted memories. Schorm's characters search for meaning in the disillusion of their lives, settling, if lucky, on a day-to-day kind of existential fortitude, as in *Courage for Every Day* (1964).

Jiri Menzel made *Closely Watched Trains*

Closely Watched Trains. While his stationmaster looks on, Vaclav Neckar operates the train switches. He lays siege to a conductress, but sexual failure leads Neckar to attempt suicide. Finally successful with a willing, beautiful partisan, the boy makes a new date with the conductress and leaves to sabotage a German ammunition train. The mission succeeds; the boy is killed. (Museum of Modern Art/Film Stills Archive)

in 1966, a wry blend of humor and character study in which a young railway employee gains his sexual initiation and dies sabotaging a German munitions train. *Intimate Lighting* (1965) by Ivan Passer plays with the strained relations between two old musician friends, one a rural conductor with a fat wife, the other now a soloist, living in Prague and enjoying the sexual pleasures of fame.

Miloš Forman's early features, *Peter and Pavla* (1964), *Loves of a Blonde* (1965), and *The Fireman's Ball* (1967) center on bored, small-town life and tensions between the generations. Humorous, sharp-eyed, and affectionate, they have a quality of documentary that is maintained, at least in part, in the American *Taking Off* (1971) but less apparent in *One Flew Over the Cuckoo's Nest* (1975) for all its acting skill.

YUGOSLAVIA

Except for sporadic ventures in the thirties, Yugoslav filmmaking really began in wartime with partisan newsreels. As elsewhere, postwar preoccupations were with the immediate past, the films tending toward didacticism. Production was complicated by the fact that Yugoslavia is a country of five languages.

More recently a younger group of directors has made films that question earlier assumptions about war, socialism, and human relationships. *I Even Met Some Happy Gypsies* (1967) by Aleksander Petrovič deals with a gypsy community whose freedom and sub-culture alienation from the rest of society pose for Petrovič elemental moral issues illustrated by a murder that the gypsy community suffers but refuses to discuss with authorities. *Rondo* (1966) by Žvonimir Berković is built about a weekly chess match, the moves of the game echoing a sexual intrigue between the visitor and the host's wife.

Best known among Yugoslav filmmakers is Dusan Makevejev, both for the imagination of his films and the vehemence with which they criticize contemporary life. In the course of his several features, Makevejev has refined a technique, like a sexualized Eisenstein, that radically juxtaposes material to intensify an ironic critique of all modern society. Themes are recurrent, in particular the disparity between potential sexual freedoms and male-female relationships as they exist under actual political systems. Characters are viewed as either more or less emancipated from older traditions and social rubrics, and more or less alienated from their feelings because of the new freedom. In *Tragedy of a Switchboard Operator* (1967), Ahmed ("serious party member, clean and orderly") and the emancipated Isabella try to reconcile their male-female roles with disasterous results. Similarly, in *WR: Mysteries of the Organism* (1971) Milena, like Isabella but politicized, encounters a Russian figure skater whose repressed sexuality breaks out murderously.

Makavejev finds authoritarian social and personality structure the cause of a lifeless, "free" society. Although his employment of the doctrines of therapist and writer Wilhelm Reich in *WR* seriously distorts Reich's actual ideas, Makavejev has touched on and effectively expressed sexual equations between social design and character structure. The director's sense of human foible and his capacity for multiconnotative images balance and poeticize what might otherwise descend into polemic. Connections jar intentionally, as when excerpts from a typical, glorifying Russian biography of Stalin are intercut with shots of mental patients undergoing forced confinement, and then an American penis sculptor at work (all aspects of the "cult of personality"). *WR: Mysteries of the Organism* was banned in Yugoslavia and triggered Makavejev's expulsion from the Communist Party. *Sweet Movie* (1975) was a Canadian-French coproduction, longer in its sequences, longer in its camera takes. The incongruities are more often contained within the compositions, rather than between them, as before. They continue to be surreal and sometimes upsetting social metaphors. Therapy patients communally vomit and defecate so as to confront the actual nature of their bodies. A nude socialist tries to seduce young children. An exploited capitalist beauty finally suffocates, naked, in a great vat of liquid chocolate.

HUNGARY

Best known in early years for its emigrated personalities such as directors Michael Curtiz, Alexander Korda, Zoltan Korda, and actor Bela Lugosi, Hungary's film industry was nationalized as early as 1919, although production was extremely limited for years. Curiously, Hungary made a number of cheap B pictures for immigrant audiences in the United States and, during the war, for Italy, the Balkans, and Scandinavia. Again, Stalin's death resulted in a loosening of the socialist-realist esthetic. The Béla Balázs Studio was organized in 1961, named for a screenwriter theoretician who had worked at the Academy of Dramatic and Film Art until his removal in the late forties.

A generation of young directors emerged from that studio, their work characteristically self-critical. István Szabó deals with problems of maturing among the disillusioned young in *Age of Illusions* (1964), and with national tradition in *The Father* (1966). András Kovács, an older figure, interviewed a group of inventors hindered by implacable bureau-

WR: Mysteries of the Organism. Decapitated by a Russian figure skater after a night of love-making, Milena announces to the autopsy doctor. "He couldn't bear it. He had to go one step further. Vladimir is a man of noble impetuousness, a man of high ambition, of immense energy. He's a romantic, ascetic, a genuine Red Fascist!" (Museum of Modern Art/Film Stills Archive)

Elektreia (1975). A screen adaptation of Laszlo Gyurko's musical stage success, Jancsó's version of *Electra* perpetuates themes of power, oppression, and pessimistic humanism that pervade previous work. (John Springer Associates)

cracy in *Difficult People* (1964). *Cold Days* (1966) recounted an actual wartime incident in which Hungarians committed atrocities on a group of their own people.

Miklós Jancsó spearheaded the new Hungarian film with *The Round-Up* (1965), an uncompromising view of the fate of 1848 revolutionaries. It was followed by *The Red and the White* (1967), which dealt with Hungarians who had joined the Russian Red Army, later to be captured by White Russians. *Agnus Dei* (1971) deals with civil war in Hungary at about the same time. Jancsó's films are picturesquely beautiful, broad landscapes, encompassing lines of soldiers, the flat walls of prison stockades, grey, somber skies. The impersonality of his narrative (characters only respond and rarely betray a motive) and the absence of heroism create a world in which people deteriorate and suffer under cruel pressure because they have not understood or

acted upon principle. Atrocity and oppression can only be confronted effectively by bravery. Courage may lead to death but never to self-betrayal.

SWITZERLAND

Directed by Alain Tanner, *Jonah Who Will be 25 in the Year 2000* (1976) disguises polemical diagnoses of bourgeois society in a deceptively ingratiating, Godardian narrative scheme that equally exploits and ridicules ordinary exposition. Eight figures, each a type easily pinpointed by Marxist definitions, discuss and act out their commitments and disillusions. Brecht-like, Tanner expresses his most mordant points in biting wit. Reviewing the director's earlier *La Salamandre* (1972) and *Middle of the World* (1973) the viewer can watch a wise filmmaker refine the tools by which he may charm and entertain the audience he seeks to educate.

GERMANY

Remarkable like the rest of German economy was the speed of film's postwar recovery, which included the reconstruction of bombed-out theaters. Most production facilities existed in the Eastern Zone. Filmmaking was sparse in West Germany for several years.

Spokesman for a new group of West German filmmakers was Alexander Kluge. Attending the Oberhausen Festival in 1962, the director protested against the industry's solid commitment to commercial and exploitative

Ali (1974). El Hedi Ben Salem and Brigitte Mira. In this Fassbinder film, a middle-aged scrubwoman falls in love with a young, Moroccan emigrant laborer. They suffer German society's fascist-bigoted retaliations. Fassbinder had conversationally recounted the story in an earlier film. (John Springer Associates)

projects. In *Yesterday Girl* (1966) and *Artists at the Top of the Big Top — Disoriented* (1968), Kluge intercuts staged and actual footage to intensify the pressures on his fictive characters. Settings have symbolic intention. Thus, the circus in *Artists* is a world so tradition bound that youth find it impossible to affect the institutional character. In *Strongman Ferdinand* (1976), a security officer at an industrial plant takes his work so seriously by "following orders" that awful, comic disorder results. In *Young Törless* (1966) by Volker Schlöndorff, a military academy in the time of the Austro-Hungarian empire provides authoritarian, sadistic training to its young students. *Snowdrops Blown in September* (1975) uses cinéma-vérité techniques to film a fictionalized labor dispute in an actual factory. The study extends into workers' and management's off-duty lives.

Two filmmakers have made militant assaults on narrative conventions. Jean-Marie Straub, a Frenchman who has done most of his work in Germany, uses professional performers who are nonprofessional actors, e.g., musicians in *The Chronicle of Anna Magdelena Bach* (1967), very long camera runs, and direct, unreworked sound. His films seek to define political issues in a kind of flat, undramatic form. The Bach film intends to depict an artist working under authoritarian regime. Uncontrolled elements of sound are retained to serve as empathy-breaking tools. *Othon* (1972), based on Corneille's play, is performed with flat speech, without vocal inflections, while traffic is audible outside the studio.

Somewhat similar in purpose and technique, Rainer Werner Fassbinder plucks family-drama conventions of soap opera, those of Douglas Sirk in particular, and plays them out before what is often a long-take, unmoving camera so that the pace and up-and-down emotional rhythms of ordinary, as opposed to selectively dramatic, life seem to ensue. Fassbinder often cleverly alienates his characters by glance and composition. In *The Merchant of Four Seasons* (1971), a drunken wife-beating conveys both the squalid violence and shared senses of humiliation and discomfort that underlie the brutality. In *What Makes Herr R. Run Amok?* (1969), a middle-class husband unpredictably turns on wife, child, and neighbor and murders them, then hangs himself. The violence is as banal as the conversation that preceded it. Fassbinder affected the film's color quality so that natural and artificial lighting share an unreal, consistent blue-red hue.

Beware of a Holy Whore (1971) locates vain, shallow actors in a Spanish hotel room, waiting for a director to come and give their behavior significance. *Game Pass* (1975) involves a fat, spoiled 14-year-old and a motorcyclist who slaughters chickens for a living. Together they commit a crime. *Mother Küster's Trip to Heaven* (1977) depicts a newly-widowed, working-class woman whose children prove selfish and weak. She has the effrontery to act on Communist exhortations that are not intended to be followed with such unyielding ardor in West Germany in the seventies. Mother Küster is about to suffer for her simple faith until she meets a man as warm and good humored as she.

Perhaps the least conventional of all contemporary German directors is Werner Herzog, but his exceptional imagination rests on orthodox images rather than expository manipulations. Sometimes documentary, sometimes fiction, Herzog's pictures have a primeval quality. In *La Soufrière* (1977), a thirty-minute "documentary," an elderly peasant lies alone on the side of a volcano about to erupt. All the town has fled, but the old man will not budge because "That is life. That is what God orders." Then he sings a love ballad, remembered from years past. *Even the Dwarfs Started Small* (1969) is populated with midgets and dwarfs whose rebellion against their institution's midget director develops into a destructive rejection of all society. *Aguirre Wrath of God* (1972) depicts a rebel soldier who mutinies against his Spanish Commander to lead an Incan exploration on its self-destructive quest for El Dorado. The documentary *Fata Morgana* (1971), filmed on the fringes of the Sahara, ironically counterpoints the arid landscape and its inhabitants with images of paradise and songs by Leonard Cohen. Innocence, rebellion, destruction, and failure give thematic pattern to Herzog's work.

The Mystery of Kasper Hauser (1975) tells the story of a man inexplicably kept in a cave from childhood. His isolation from civilization nurtures naïve wisdoms and exuberant impulse. When Kasper is executed, as mysteriously as he was discovered, his story ends with the edged allegory of a Kafka novel. *Stroszek* (1977) transports an old man, a sub-intelligent street musician, and a prostitute from Munich to Wisconsin, where "opportunity" may free them from social and economic oppression. But the men are as victimized by the US as they were by Germany, and more bewildered by its rules. Wisely, the woman elects to survive with what resources she brought along.

Wim Wenders differs equally from his fellow German filmmakers. Sharing their dismay at society's current state, his films seem a fragile balance of technical mastery and transient mood. People appear to be not so much unweighted by commitment as they are willfully out of touch. In *The Goalie's Anxiety at the Penalty Kick* (1971), a soccer player commits murder. His impulse to flee gradually dissipates while the anxiety surfaces in sporadic, unpredictable behaviors. Exaggerations Wenders selectively gives to ambient sound underline the psychic tensions. Untypically Wenders, *The Scarlet Letter* (1972) compared interestingly with Seastrom's version (Chapter 5). Wenders' Hester Prynne projects more genuine defiance; her child Pearl more

Kings of the Road. Hans Zischler, student of childhood language formation, and Rudiger Vogler, projector repairman. Meeting his father, a newspaper editor, Zischler elects to compose and set a newspaper's front page in order to print one issue expressing the rage he cannot speak. (John Springer Associates)

closely reflects the Rev. Dimmesdale's fearful view of "natural" love as anarchic.

Wenders' films tend to document physical travel. In *Alice in the Cities* (1974), an alienated writer takes an abandoned nine-year-old from New York to Germany in search of the girl's grandmother. *Kings of the Road* (1976) pairs a movie theater service man and a childhood-linguistics researcher in temporary alliance, journeying through north Germany. The grouping is intentionally sound-and-picture; Wenders holds speech suspect, just as he is disillusioned by the visual state of film. At picture's end, an aging woman speaks of shutting down her theater because she is permitted to show nothing other than sex and violence. Wenders' films are staged with great care, disarmingly "natural," in fact photographing locations and behaviors that have been denuded of the extraneous, as if better to suggest a terrain of the modern mind.

An American Friend (1977) appeared with a German-French-English sound track, its locations shifting between New York, Hamburg, Paris, and Munich. Starring Dennis Hopper and Arthur Zimmerman as unlikely associates, the film uses an espionage thriller plot to comment visually on Euro-American cultural homogenization and to speculate about connections between the Common Market and crime. Nicholas Ray plays a painter of fake art; Samuel Fuller is a cigar-chewing mafia power.

RUSSIA

After the standard fares of socialist realism, respite from glorifications and ritualized history appeared in Mikhail Kalatozov's *The Cranes are Flying* (1957), Sergei Bondarchuk's *Destiny of a Man* (1959) and

Grigori Chukrai's *Ballad of a Soldier* (1959). Bondarchuk's film retains a slightly grandiose, romantic tone, but all three dealt with actualities of war and of human character, and with liberal themes held suspect under Stalin.

Several Russian productions have been distinguished for an employment of literary sources that diminishes neither medium, notably Yosif Heifitz's *The Lady With the Little Dog* (1960), Grigori Kozintsev's *Don Quixote* (1957), *Hamlet* (1964), and *King Lear* (1972). Bondarchuk released a four-hour *War and Peace* in 1967, a less fortunate enterprise. Andrei Mikhalkov-Konchalovsky adapted Turgenev in *A Nest of Gentlefolk* (1969) and Chekhov in *Uncle Vanya* (1971).

One of the exceptional films to come out of the country has been *Shadows of Our Forgot-ten Ancestors* (1964), made by Sergei Paradjanov.[3] A Ukranian like Dovzhenko, Paradjanov worked in the Kiev Studios. His film interweaves folk traditions, myth, and peasant life with a poetry reminiscent of the earlier filmmaker. Employment of color is striking, as in the blood-beclouded subjectivities of an axe murder. Violence and emotion underscore the villagers' intense love of place.

After *War and Peace*, Bondarchuk undertook a Soviet-Italian *Waterloo* (1969), which was, again, strongest in its battle sequences, Rod Steiger unexpectedly playing the role of

[3] *After serving four years of a five year sentence to Gulag prison camp for "homosexuality," Sergei Paradjanov was released by the Supreme Soviet in 1978.*

The Lady With the Little Dog. Anna (Ya Savvina), unhappily married, has an affair with the married Alexei Batalov. They furtively meet over the years, providing what support each can, beholding no future except unhappiness. The story is Chekhov's. (Museum of Modern Art/Film Stills Archive)

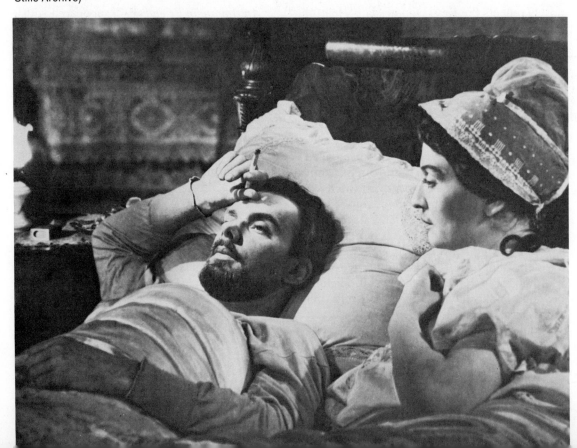

Shadows of Our Forgotten Ancestors. In a Carpathian village, Ivan fails to betroth Mariechka, who drowns. Disconsolate, he is finally urged to marry a wife who then has a liaison with the town sorcerer. The sorcerer kills Ivan in an axe battle, and townspeople perform their ancient, pagan funeral ceremony. (Museum of Modern Art/Film Stills Archive)

Napoleon. Mark Donskoi continued the tradition of historical recreations that had begun years before with his Gorky trilogy. He made *Mother* (1955) (less successfully than Pudovkin) and two films about Lenin's mother: *Heart of a Mother* (1966) and *A Mother's Devotion* (1966). Because Soviet films are difficult to view outside the country, critics find it hard to assess recent dispositions, but sense a firming of controls, some reversion to less controversial subject matter and a move away from experimentation. On the other hand, the science fiction *Solaris* (1973), based on a novel by Stanislaw Lem and directed by Andrei Tarkevsky, gives serious voice to questions of individual right, responsibility, escapism, and duty. It is set in an imaginative extra-terrestrial world, albeit a talkier one than *2001*.

ARAB FILM

The consumption and production of Arab work has been traditionally dominated by Egypt where a National Organization for the Cinema, founded after the revolution of 1952, seeks to nurture interesting projects and to discourage the worst of an output that is unpretentiously escapist. *The Night of Counting the Years* (1969) by Shadi Abdelsalam, a young director, impressed a Venice Festival with its eerily beautiful employment of desert and pyramid locations for a nineteenth-century story of mummy robbers. They are a nomadic tribe who survive by plundering a tomb on the Mountain of the Dead.

Djamila (1958) dwelt on French torture of an Algerian girl commando. *The Postman*

(1967) concerns a bored village postman who reads the mail and becomes obsessed with one correspondence. *Madman's Lane* (1955) is about a poverty-stricken alley where a winning lottery ticket is discovered and hidden by a deformed beggar.

Since the agrarian revolution, some Algerian film interests have sought to promote reformist ends, while others press for commercial production. Subject matter in either case centers on the country's past, before or after liberation. *Chronique des années des braises/Chronicle of the Years of Embers* (1975) depicts the time when some Algerians supported Hitler because he was fighting the French, while others repressed local insurrections, in support of the status quo. Until the mid-seventies, Algerian-Italian financing of ventures was not uncommon. The Italian Gillo Pontecorvo made *The Battle of Algiers* (1965) with such backing. Simulating guerilla insurrection, the film was shot in documentary fashion and processed to resemble the look of newsreel footage. Perhaps understandably, the film did not secure French release until 1973. Constantin Costa-Gavras' political melodrama *Z* (1968) was filmed in Algiers, but set in an unidentified European country; the director is Russo-Greek in background.

BLACK AFRICA

Sporadic in appearance, often commercially unsuccessful at home, black African film output nevertheless continues to proliferate. In Cameroon, for example, Jean-Pierre Dikongue Pipa executed *Muna Moto/The Child of the Other* (1976), which combines images of subjective fantasy with "actual" narrative events. In Angola, a woman director, Sarah Maldoror, executed *Sambizanga* in 1972, the record of a wife's search for her imprisoned husband in the period immediately preceding the country's rebellion against Portuguese colonialism in 1961.

Senegal, of all the newly-independent countries, has most fully supported film productions. At least French interests, for whatever reasons, have helped to finance work whose tone is predictably anticolonial. Senegal's industry nearly coincides with the country's 1960 origins. In *Reouh-Takh* (Big City) (1971) by Mahama Johnson Traore, a black American tourist explores Dakar's cosmopolitan center, the "other city" slum, and the remains of the ancient slave port quarters. If unevenly acted, the film sustains some moving images of manacled slaves on the beaches.

Kodou (1971) by Ababacar Samb-Makharam centers upon a young woman who flees her tribal ritual lip-tatooing, bringing on a shame-induced psychosis. The mental illness is only abated by a native healer after modern psychiatric methods fail.

Best known among black African filmmakers is Ousmane Sembene, a novelist in earlier days. Sembene combines French ironies with a sophisticated anti-intellectualism that, like his working-class subjects, suspects both white and black bourgeois cultural encroachments. *Emitai* (1971) returns to World War II, when French Legionnaires hold a village's women and children hostage for a ransom of rice. The rice is sacred. Its payment would insult the gods and demean husbands before their wives, but the men nearly acquiesce. *Ceddo* (1977) depicts a religious confrontation; farmers rebel against their ruler's Moslem proselytizing. The princess is kidnapped and falls in love with a nonbeliever.

Perhaps *Le Noire de . . ./Black Girl* (1966), its subject a bitter, homesick housemaid who accompanies her white patrons from Dakar to Antibes, remains the least Europeanized of Sembene's works. The girl's view of a French dinner party reminds one of the Quechua Indian watching a tennis match in *Blood of the*

Emita (above), *Xala*. Senegal's output of films proceeds with unsophisticated equipment and little organized financial support. Theaters are owned by foreign corporations, so that exhibition is never assured. Lab work must be airmailed, most often to Paris. (Museum of Modern Art/Film Stills Archives)

Condor. A cultural confrontation similar to that of *Black Girl* appears in *Soleil-O* (1972), made by Med Hondo of Mauritania. Here the black protagonist is educated, and his experiences occur in Paris.

INDIA

Confronted with eleven recognized languages, silent Indian films were prepared with one to three sets of titles, the literate audience reading aloud to the illiterate. With sound, feature output became roughly proportional to market potential, population ranging in the early thirties from 140 million Hindus to 2 million Assamese. Bypassing speech barriers, songs and dances assumed near-ritualized appearances in every kind of story. Indian filmgoers have always brought highly conventionalized expectations to their entertainment.

In 1947, two hundred and thirty-seven features appeared, impressive in number if not quality. That year's new native government tightened screen censorship, omitting, for example, scenes of kissing. It imposed heavy taxes, which are still fifty per cent. Pakistan's independence resulted in embargoes that blocked film exchange between the two countries.

Against such odds and with an industry that is markedly corrupt, few impressive filmmakers have appeared. One figure, Khwaja Ahmed Abbas sought the nationalization of Indian film for years. His script for *Children of the Earth* (1946) examined the impossible economic circumstance of the Indian peasants, who are dispossessed by landlords when struck with famine. Abbas directed *The Lost Child* in 1954, basing his scenario on the experience of a boy who flees an orphanage to seek his mother; it was one of the country's first sound films without music and shows the effects of Rossellini and De Sica.

Satyajit Ray holds a degree in economics, studied painting, worked in an advertising agency, and discovered the work of Robert Flaherty and the neorealists in London in 1950. Encouraged by Jean Renoir, then filming *The River* near Calcutta, and by John Huston, a visitor, Ray invested his own savings in the novel *Pather Panchali,* and initiated a film production that he completed in 1955, first of the Apu trilogy, to be followed by *Aparajito* (1956) and *The World of Apu* (1958). The least Indian of Indian filmmakers, Ray's work has markedly affected American and European understandings of life in his country.

Apu is the child of an unsuccessful reader of scriptures who lives with his family on the edge of poverty in a Bengal village. The films follow his life from age seven (*Pather*) to ten (*Aparajito*) to post university existence (*World*); they are marked by shifts of locale and by death. In the first film, Apu's sister and an aging aunt die, in the second his father and mother. Later his wife dies in childbirth and Apu wanders, grief stricken, through the countryside until finally reconciled with his son, then five. Apu moves from the village to Benares, then to the university in Calcutta. Each film gives some attention to an out-of-the-way village.

It might truly be said that neorealism claims its finest hour in the Apu trilogy. Ray worked with amateur and semiprofessional players whose performance seems more captured than imposed by director and story. The people are viewed with humane, nonjudgmental understanding that reminds the viewer of Renoir, the ambiance of their lives selectively defined with great skill. Thus, the family courtyard of *Pather Panchali* houses a new litter of kittens — a family, always hungry, chewing constantly on anything edible — and a delapidated wall protecting it from surrounding jungle; the senses of family interchange, tenuous sustenance and a threatening nature are pervasive.

While Ray's films suggest the open-ended, sometimes asymmetrical quality of life lived, they are, in fact, carefully designed. Himself a musician, composing music for the films of other filmmakers, Ray's employment of sound and visual motifs supplies aural coherence. Trains, for example, link Apu to a social milieu far beyond his village, one in the face of which he feels powerless at his most despondent. In *Pather Panchali,* Apu and his sister first see a train passing through a field of flowers. In *Aparajito,* Apu leaves his mother by way of the train. Dying, she believes incorrectly that her son has returned when she hears a whistle. In *World* Apu brings his young wife to his quarters by the railroad. There, he learns of her death and attempts suicide on the tracks. Apu's final reconcili-

Satyajit Ray (1921–   )

Pather Panchali	1955
Aparajito/The Unvanquished	1956
Parash Pathar/The Philosopher's Stone	1957
The Touch Stone	1958
The World of Apu	1958
Jalshagar/The Music Room	1958
Rabindranath Tagore (documentary)	1960
Devi/The Goddess	1961
Teen Kanya/Two Daughters	1961
Kanchenjungha	1962
Abhijan/Expedition	1962
Mahanagar/The Big City	1963
Charulata/The Lonely Wife	1964
Kapurush o Mahapurush/The Coward and the Holy Man	1965
Nayak/The Hero	1966
Chidiakhana/The Zoo	1967
Goopi Gyne o Baghi Byne/The Adventures of Goopi and Baghi	1969
Aranyer Din Raatri/Days and Nights in the Forest	1970
Sikkim (documentary)	1970
Pratiwandi/The Rival	1971

ation with his son, whom he believes responsible for his wife's death, is marked with the gift of a toy train.

Ray uses music not as a constant element but, like other sound, in economic narrative counterpoint. When Apu's family learns of the daughter's death, the mother's outcry is done by a sitar glissando played, as throughout the trilogy, by Ravi Shankar. The father rises, falls back, and his sobs break in to replace the music. Glance and gesture have special significance in Ray's work, and sound often explains, rather than reinforces, what is said.

In sum, Ray's films profile vastly different social strata in Bengal with recurring themes: the eternal student (Apu is an example) faces a paradox. Art controls experience, while life escapes one's ability to treat it like literature. A new Indian woman emerges, evolving in her sex relations and her sense of self. Ray's stories of a country seeking to escape smothering, oppressive tradition without losing its identity are often allegorized into nineteenth-century settings. The reticence of many characters, like Ray's own unassertive sensitivities, peak in quiet moments of shared or individual discovery.

Unlike other projects, *The Music Room* (1958) was studio-produced, featuring a "star." An Indian aristocrat, his fortunes dissipated, commits his remaining wealth to a passion for native song and dance. Alone, he inhabits a decaying mansion, finally holding one last sumptuous party on borrowed money for a visiting artist who had been invited to perform at a rival's house. Both *Manhanager* (1964) and *Kapurush* (1965) explore women's growing economic and educational indepen-

Pather Panchali. Apu (Subir Bannerjee) and his mother (Karuna Bannerjee). When Apu's father leaves for Benares, the mother turns vicious toward an old, decrepit relative who lives with them. The relative dies, Apu's sister dies, and mother and son depart for the city. (Museum of Modern Art/Film Stills Archive)

dence. Ray's documentary *Rabindranath Tagore* (1960) pays tribute to the literary source of many of his best efforts. Ray has experimented with horror in *Three Daughters* (1961), fantasy in *The Adventures of Goopy and Bagha* (1969), and a thriller, *The Zoo* (1967). *The Touch Stone* (1958) is said to be comprehensible and funny only to the Bengali. In recent years, Ray has moved away from the rural modes of Rabindranath Tagore and of Bibhutt-bhuson Bandapaddhay who wrote *Pather Panchali.*

Despite a deft, quick style in such a work as *Three Daughters*, Ray's pace and leisurely exposition sometimes prove difficult for non-Indian audiences. The work is without urgency, but cumulative in effect. It does not editorialize, yet meanings emerge. *Devi* (1960) recounts the disaster that befalls a newlywed couple when the husband's devout father dreams that the girl is a reincarnation of the goddess Kali. What follows is inevitable. The effect of superstition is apparent, while a sympathetic understanding of the father-in-law remains uncompromised. Ray is a highly sophisticated figure who, like many Indian intellectuals, elected to follow an artistic course in which choice of subject abjures contrived, interpersonal conflicts, replacing them with quiet, often deep connections between an individual from any walk of life and his surroundings. Like the music of Ravi Shankar, this feat is accomplished with carefully preplanned intention and remarkably successful improvisation.

CHINA

Swung by the weights of history, subject matter in early Chinese film includes, in turn, the revolution of the Kuomintang, historical adventures under Chiang Kai-shek, tobacco advertisement housed in theaters constructed by the British-American Tobacco Company, and anti-Japanese patriotism. As in India, the use of sound was problematic due to divergent dialects. Like India, Hong Kong produced films for distribution abroad; overseas Chinese speak Cantonese preponderantly. Pre-World War II Chinese film was deeply derivative of the US even including an Oriental Charlie Chaplin! Historically, the alternative Chinese movie center to Hong Kong has been Shanghai, heart of a northern as opposed to a southern culture, with substantial differences in style as well as language (Mandarin). An outstanding production of Kun Lun, a Shanghai left-wing production unit in existence before Mao Tse-tung's assumption in 1949, is *Crows and Sparrows* (1949), produced during the last days of the Peoples' Republic/Kuomintang conflict. It documents in staged, neo-realist terms the period's inflation and economic chaos. Unlike other communist (and fascist) leaders, Mao Tse-tung's interest in motion pictures was sometimes actively hostile to films and filmmakers. His displeasure with *The Life of Wu Hsun* (1951) led to its withdrawal and Kun Lun's absorption into a government film unit.

The director Sang Hu has made two noteworthy features, *The Loves of Liang Shan-Po and Chu Ying Tai* (1953), a kind of Romeo and Juliet legend, and *New Year Sacrifice* (1956), a restrained story of forced marriage set in the 1911 revolution. *Storm* (1959) by Chin Shan deals with the Peking-Hankow railroad strike of 1922, and is perhaps the most successful and best-known film to emerge from the People's Republic.

One result of the cultural revolution, dating from 1966, was the cessation of fiction film production (reactivated since 1975). For the previous nine years, all studios but for Shanghai's animation works and Peking's documentary unit were closed. (Some Chinese studios are the most modern, best equipped in the world.) Non-Chinese-directed productions have been few, with the notable exception of Chris Marker's ironic, witty short *Sundays in*

Peking (1955) and Antonioni's sabotaged efforts to document the new China during 1973. Joris Ivens, who has visited and lived in China at various intervals since 1938, completed a twelve-hour study of the country's history since the Cultural Revolution, titled *How Yukong Moved the Mountains* (1976). *Yukong* was made in collaboration with Ivens' wife, Marceline Loridon, whom he first saw in Rouch's *Chronicle of a Summer*. Ivens has noted that Chinese cinema is characteristically more contemplative, more removed than western film traditions. One salutory result of the recent anti-Confucian campaign was to overcome an aversion to closeups, based on notions that such visual intimacy constituted intrusions on privacy.[4] Stemming

[4] *Mary Blume, "International Film-Maker Zooms In On China,"* Los Angeles Times *(Aug. 8, 1976), p. 34.*

from its Peking studio, China continues to produce both hortatory and educational films, widely disseminated by way of mobile exhibition units. The country has developed an 8.75mm film gauge in order to effect its kind of distribution with maximum speed and economy.

JAPAN

The extensive and energetic Japanese film history parallels that of the United States: primitive 1-reelers, a Trust, the star system, and dependency on large-audience appeal that defines much of the product. Major studios developed and competed. Some failed; others survived. Worldwide depression, early in Japan, led to films whose criticisms of the eco-

Breaking with Old Ideas (1975). Signifying a potential return to feature production in post-Mao China, the film highlights 1958–1961 confrontations between open enrollment and academic standards in an agricultural college. Its melodramatic, personalized resolutions break with no old film forms. (British National Film Archive/Stills Library)

nomic system sometimes took the form of subverted violence, sometimes more openly expressed indignation, as in Kinugasa's *Before Dawn* (1931) in which women who have been recruited to prostitution revolt.

From earliest days, the Japanese had a tradition of the *benshi,* performers who would explain to an audience at each film performance the intricacies of the projection equipment and what was seen on screen. Marked by its own violence, the benshi's fight against the introduction of sound finally proved unavailing.

Wartime films took predictable escapist and patriotic lines, while the industry was forcefully consolidated into three manageable units. As elsewhere, the occupation of Japan by American forces was reflected in the country's films, sometimes marked by shifting allegiances, sometimes by hardline stands against

any amalgamation of eastern and western cultural styles. Often isolated from the influence of foreign styles, Japan is yet receptive to outside movie influence, Chaplin and neorealism being paramount examples. Monster films are popular, and pornography now a substantial part of the annual output.

Faced with postwar, Allied censorship that outlawed any commendation of militarism and of inflexible, contemporary social structure, one evasive strategy on the part of filmmakers was to locate modern concerns in the past, itself a kabuki tradition. An example is *Rashomon* (1950) by Akiru Kurosawa, whose first film, *Sanshiro Sugata/The Legend of Judo* (1943) had been burned by the authorities.

Kurosawa had made eleven films before *Rashomon,* some of exceptional interest, but it was the latter production, popular in Japan

Rashomon. The bandit (Toshiro Mifune) and the wife (Machiko Kyo). Did he rape her and depart? Did he subdue the husband, then succumb to her blandishments? Or did bandit-wife collusion follow the assault? The film provides no answer. (Museum of Modern Art/Film Stills Archive)

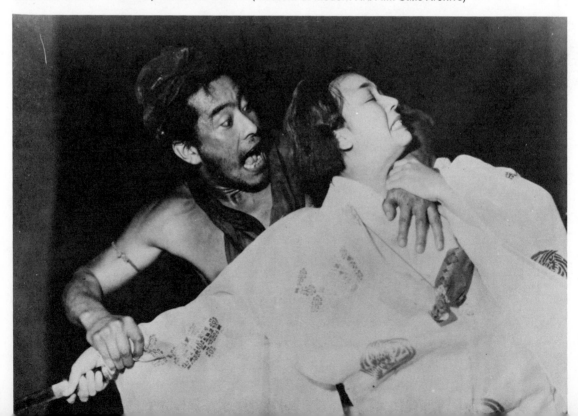

and an award winner at the Venice Film Festival of 1951, that attracted international attention to Japan's postwar industry. Seemingly typical if superior, *Rashomon* appears in retrospect to be a unique experience even for Japan. Based on two stories by a famous modern writer, Ryonosuke Akutugawa, the film is a four-sided report on what appears to have been a rape and murder in a twelfth century, Japanese forest. A nobleman, his wife, a bandit, and a poor woodcutter each reports the events, each self-servingly remembered, although the woodcutter's story carries the greatest apparent credibility. Strong performances by Toshiro Mifune and Machiko Kyo are staged in the impressionistic, dense forest and in theatrical monologues where witnesses report directly to the camera-audience-jury. The undependability of seemingly sincere testimony undercuts traditional views toward aristocratic behavior; the contradictory flashbacks challenge our human inclination to accept any film's photographed "reality" as credible. The film's music, with shades of Ravel gave a western inflection to *Rashomon*, suggesting relevance to contemporary life in Japan and elsewhere.

Shifting from period to modern subjects and marked by strong imagination and verve, Kurosawa represented a new generation of directors. *The Men Who Tread on the Tiger's Tail*, made in 1945 but not released until 1953, satirized feudal relations between aristocrat and commoner and was banned both by Japanese military and Allied occupational censors. *Stray Dog* (1949) features Mifune as a detective wandering Tokyo in search of a criminal who has stolen his gun and committed murder. Special point is made of the likenesses between pursuer and pursued, ending in a fight in which the muddied disfigurement of both makes them indistinguishable.

The Idiot (1951) demonstrated Kurosawa's ability to adapt foreign literature, as *The Lower Depths* (1957) and *Throne of Blood*

(Macbeth) (1957) corroborated. Kurosawa's strength rests in his ability to translate the images of prose and verse, the intentions of their metaphors, into a graphic form that retains the original implication while yet grounding it in Japanese setting. The misted forests where Macbeth encounters omens of his future fate are disorienting, like an expressionist extension of Macbeth's (Mifune's) fear and confusion. He dies grotesquely in a shower of arrows, killed by no man's hand. Moved to medieval Japan, the play is staged against symmetrical, stylized fortress sets. Lady Mac-

Akira Kurosawa (1910–   )

Judo Saga	1943
Most Beautiful	1944
The Men Who Tread on the Tiger's Tail	1945
Those Who Make Tomorrow	1946
No Regrets for Your Youth	1946
Wonderful Sunday	1947
Drunken Angel	1948
Stray Dog	1949
Quiet Duel	1949
Scandal	1950
Rashomon	1950
The Idiot	1951
Ikiru/To Live/Living	1952
The Magnificent Seven/Seven Samurai	1954
I Live in Fear	1955
Throne of Blood	1957
The Lower Depths	1957
The Hidden Fortress	1958
The Bad Sleep Well	1960
Yojimbo	1961
Sanfuro	1962
High and Low	1963
Red Beard	1965
Dodeska-den	1970
Dersu Uzala	1975
Partial listing	

beth has a whited, Noh drama face, her movements the fluttering quality that captures both Japanese stage gesture and the character's incipient hysteria. *The Lower Depths* was conceived as an acting ensemble, so that it sacrifices Kurosawa's usual selective camera angles and editing to group performance, a formal exposition with subject movement carefully timed to camera maneuvers. As such, it bears interesting comparison to Renoir's 1936 version of the Gorky play, Renoir's impressive in the use of the courtyard set, otherwise an inferior production.

Ikiru/To Live (1952) turns again to contemporary Japan. A secretary discovers he has cancer and a short life expectancy. He devotes his remaining time to developing a playground for children in the city ghetto. Performed by Tokashi Shimura, the central character is driven like Bergman's knight to give some meaning to his life by this final act. He is alternately amused, intimidated, and deeply frustrated by the bureaucracy he encounters and had until these final six months helped to enforce. *Ikiru* is deeply emotional; the feelings may seem excessive to a non-Japanese viewer. This is the reaction a westerner may have faced on other occasions with a culture that often seems either over- or underrestrained.

The Seven Samurai (1954) has villagers in sixteenth-century Japan hire a cadre of hungry, wandering samurai in defense of their crops against bandits. With courage and sacrifice, the samurai win the battle but only three survive; the story translated easily into an American western, *The Magnificent Seven* (1960). Kurosawa's film closely examines the relations between villagers, who have food and land but neither pride nor skill, and their defenders, homeless professionals whose calling provides a social rank that is belied by their poverty. The battle sequences are among the most exciting in film history. They retain a quality even more rare; a viewer can follow what is going on at every stage.

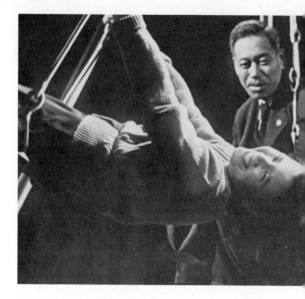

Ikiru. The mayor's secretary (Takashi Shimura) learns of his inoperable disease, then wanders city streets pondering how to supply final meaning to a wasted, anonymous life. The notion of developing a children's playground provides the incentive that supports his remaining months. (Museum of Modern Art/Film Stills Archive)

Kurosawa produced more typical samurai films in his later career, returning to his preoccupation with social injustice in *Red Beard* (1965) about a society doctor converted to serving the poor. The director's skill and enthusiasm toward genre adventure is evident in *High and Low* (1963), based on an Ed McBain detective novel. *Dersu Uzala* (1975) was made in Russia. It tells the visually stunning story of a hunter, magnificent in his Siberian wilds, who is brought to the city in his old age by an army captain, an old friend he once saved from death. To this viewer, the film combined thrilling visuals with an uneasy sense that one is watching a Disney family movie.

Kenzi Mizoguchi, like Kurosawa, was once a painter. Mizoguchi made an unbelievable ninety films in his thirty-four-year professional life, many commercial studio quickies. Much work, dating as early as 1922, is now gone. *City Symphony* (1929) was reported to presage both French poetic realism and Italian neorealism. *Osaka Elegy* (1936) depicted a telephone operator who gives herself to her employer to help the family, then suffers abandonment from her fiancé. It is the director's first expression of a continuing preoccupation with problems of the modern Japanese woman. *The Sisters of Gion* (1936) follows a conflict between two sister-prostitutes: one expedient and ambitious, the other inescapably bound to tradition.

Close on the international success of *Rashomon,* Mizoguchi produced several works of remarkable beauty and organization. These films are calm in unfolding, dominated not so much by performer as by performance before a removed camera that carefully observes the dramatic disclosures with little formal interruption except, sometimes, for careful, inobtrusive camera movement. *The Life of O'Haru* (1952) is the history of a seventeenth-century prostitute, seduced in youth and moving downward from royal concubine to brothels of less and less repute. Told through O'Haru, critical of the system, the material is neither exploited nor muted, implying modern relevance and beautifully photographed.

Ugetsu Monogatari (1953) uses two medieval folktales, one Chinese, which are intended to illustrate the pitfalls of ambition. In one, a potter is seduced by a beautiful ghost while his wife is murdered by soldiers. He escapes to his village, meets his wife's apparition, and settles back at his job, protected by her spirit. In the other tale, a villager finds samurai armor, pretends to a colorful past, and meets his abandoned wife in a brothel. Mizoguchi tells the stories altogether realistically, peopling countryside and city with images of never-ending war. The look of the film, always impressive in this director, is both Japanese and medieval European.

Saga of the Crucified Lovers (1954) is loosely based on a Kabuki drama about a shy scrollmaker who falls in love with his master's repressed, dissatisfied wife. The pair escape, but they are captured and crucified according to punitive seventeenth-century requirements. Mizoguchi freely altered the original story to conclude his film by an ending consistent with the couple's difference in caste. Some performances, like the cuckholded husband, carry unintentional, caricatured flavor. *Yokihi/ The Princess Yang* (1955) was the director's first color film, a Chinese-Japanese coproduction made in Hong Kong. An eighth-century cook's daughter marries the Emperor Tang, only to fall victim to palace intrigue. She sacrifices herself to protect the Emperor; she is dressed in purple, draped with jewels, and hung from a tree.

Teinosake Kinugasa's *A Page of Madness* (1926) may have been the first experimental Japanese film, employing hallucinating images of a couple in a madhouse. Kinugasa met both Pudovkin and Eisenstein in Europe following the success of his remarkable feature called *Crossroads* (1928), a film he described as

Kenji Mizoguchi (1898–1956)

Resurrection of Love	1922
City Symphony	1929
Osaka Elegy	1936
The Sisters of Gion	1936
Genroku Chushingura (Part I)	1941
Women of the Night	1948
The Life of O'Haru	1952
Ugetsu/Ugetsu Monogatari	1953
A Story from Chikamatsu	1954
Sansho the Bailiff	1954
Saga of the Crucified Lovers	1954
The Princess Yang	1955
New Tales of the Taira Clan	1955
Street of Shame	1956
An Csaka Story (completed by Kimisaburo Yoshimura after Mizoguchi's death)	1956
Partial listing	

based on Japanese ink paintings. The story is melodrama; a man mistakenly believes he has killed an enemy, goes to his sister's house and dies of shock when his rival reappears. It is edited with the verve of Gance and staged in something like kammerspiel, although Kinugasa had little knowledge of either. After studying with Eisenstein, Kinugasa returned to make *Before Dawn* (1931), an unavailable period piece about prostitution, and *Genroku Chushingura* (1932), a traditionally popular Kabuki revenge story better known in its 1957, wide-screen extravaganza version. No other work of Kinugasa has approximated the qualities of *Gate of Hell*.

Color in *Gate of Hell* (1953) proved so unlike customary rendition that Eastman requested a print. Sequences are keyed to particular schemes, blue in a horse race, red and orange during a palace revolt. Gauze-like screening and laboratory printing controls subdue the hues to unique, unreal effect. The Gate of Hell is a Hojuri Temple outside Kyoto where, after each battle, the head of the defeated general is mounted. Based on a twelfth-century account, purportedly true, the story has a samurai fall in love with the wife of a palace guard. She substitutes herself in her husband's bed, dying in his place at the warrior's hands. The samurai asks the husband to chop him to pieces, but the husband refuses and the warrior becomes a monk.

Eisenstein used Japanese painting to illustrate screen composition; *Gate of Hell* seems to bring painting to life. Its use of primitive instruments — stringed, woodwind and drum — connotes qualities of time and culture that are rare in Japanese film, which is usually beholden to western instrumentation and scoring.

Yasujiro Ozu, who died in 1963, enjoyed little reputation outside his country until recent years, his work closely leagued to Japanese mores and behavior. Early Ozu is often unpretentious humor merging into social comedy in *Tokyo Chorus* (1931) and *I Was Born But . . .* (1932) with eccentric types, either ingratiating or deplorable, whose adventures stem from the qualities of lower-middle-class, white-collar life, itself a Japanese genre that is termed *shomingeki*.

Ozu forsook humor for irony and irony for a removed perspective that strikes western eyes as poignant, unemotionalized sympathy. With the years, his style refined to austere, minimalized, carefully preconceived design. The interior composition most common to Ozu is an unmoving, long-duration medium shot in which the rectangular designs of the Japanese home are dressed with a few objects, chosen for their significant evidence of character and viewed from a stance about three feet above the floor. The height corresponds to eye level for characters seated on cushions or, as has been said by Japanese film historian Donald Richie, the attitude of a Haiku master, a

Teinosuke Kinugasa (1896–   )

Two Little Birds	1922
A Page of Madness	1926
Crossroads/Shadows of Yoshiwara	1928
Before Dawn	1931
Genroku Chushingura/The 47 Rodin	1932
Gate of Hell	1953
Shinkin Stones	1954
Naruto Fantasy	1957
Symphony of Love	1958
The White Heron	1958
The Affair/Tormented Flame	1959
Stop the Old Fox	1959
The Lantern	1960
Disheveled Hair	1960
Okoto and Sansuke	1961
The Bronze Magician	1963
The Little Runaway (Japan-United States)	1967
Partial listing	

figure whose empathy with his subject is undistorted by emotional commitment.

Many of Ozu's films grew from close collaboration with his scriptwriter, Nogo Noda. He constantly used the same actors, and certain character types appear frequently, like the aging war veterans, now businessmen, who are drawn to saki-ridden reminiscence. Generation differences figure prominently, with loneliness the inevitable consequence of retired office workers whose mates have died and children married. Whatever age, Ozu's characters are imbued with the culture, their reactions prompted by small slights and omissions. Much of what happens is interior and Bresson-like though it is socially rather than spiritually motivated. (Buddhism would counter that the two are inextricably one.)

Tokyo Story (1953), which Ozu thought more melodramatic than customary for him, concerns an old couple who visit their children in Tokyo. The young people's married preoccupations engender unthinking neglect. The children send their parents to a noisy resort. The parents find their most sympathetic, caring hostess in Tokyo to be a daughter-in-law who was widowed in the war. The old couple finally return home, but the wife falls ill on the way. With more or less alacrity, the children come to attend her. After the mother's death

Tokyo Story. The father (Chishu Ryo) and mother (Chiyeko Higashiyama) reflect on their Tokyo experience. ". . . [T]he pace, the characters, everything was so contained; nothing tried to be bigger or more wonderful or more important than it was." Wim Wenders

and a funeral, the young people including, finally, the daughter-in-law, return to Tokyo, leaving the old man alone. Each figure simply behaves predictably; events are less important than the unstated, sometimes ephemeral atmosphere of feeling which each relationship engenders.

The other Ozu production relatively familiar outside Japan is *An Autumn Afternoon* (1962), his last. Here, three widowers figure centrally, as the director examines how each has been affected by action and circumstance, how each touches on the feelings of the others. One man seeks out any sort of companionship to assuage his loneliness. To the dissatisfaction of both, one requires the comfort of his daughter. The third has remarried, this time to a young woman. Condemning himself to loneliness, the widower with the unmarried daughter arranges her marriage. The film's resolution, with the father stopping at a bar, then returning to his empty house, suggests through quiet implication that the old man's serenity will depend on his capacity to outdistance self-centered feelings, to narrow his consciousness, instead, to moment-to-moment perceptions, like an adept Zen pupil.

Late Spring (1949) follows a similar line, only here the father, a Kamakura college professor, lies to his daughter, pretending he will remarry, so that she herself can be persuaded to wed. The father's loneliness appears less mitigated, and Ozu ends with a shot of waves breaking on the nearby beach. The director subtly rearranges furniture in the daughter's room to hint at her mood. Unmeeting glances have the modern look of Antonioni or Fassbinder, but they are used to quite different effect. Like Wenders in *Kings of the Road* or *The Goalie's Anxiety,* Ozu injects iconographies of American commerce ("Drink Coca Cola" signs in the countryside), but his vision of cultural incursion operates subtly too, as when schoolgirls in middy blouses hurry past a Kyoto temple. In 1978, Ozu remained Wenders' favorite director.

Other Japanese films of postoccupation years are noteworthy. Kon Ichikawa made *The Burmese Harp* (1956) about a Japanese private, a harpist. Cared for by a Buddhist monk, he rejects repatriation by the British, and remains to carry out ritual burials of the war dead. Ichikawa's style abstracts the horrors of war into a sometimes-surreal fantasy that has a bit of the appearance if not the sensational manner of Alexandro Jodorowsky in Mexico. The despairing *Fires on the Plains* (1959) follows defeated troops on Leyte in the Philippines as their wanderings lead to exhaustion and cannibalism. Ichikawa's vision seems incredulous toward what man can do to himself, an emotion that takes quite different but equally awed turn in *Tokyo Olympiad* (1965). Except for such a documentary, Ichikawa designs his own sets; his look is more modern than many contemporaries.

Woman of the Dunes (1964) is a Kafka-like conceit in which an entomologist finds himself

---

Yasujiro Ozu (1903–   )

trapped at the bottom of a sandpit with an attractive widow. Sexually aroused, the scientist joins her in filling endless buckets of sand to be hauled away on ropes; when escape presents itself, he chooses to remain. The film is somewhat patly allegorical, but the sandy eroticism is astonishing, and Hiroshi Teshigahara, the director, temporarily advanced possibilities for independent Japanese production with a success that cost only $100,000.

Teshigahara represents a yet more recent generation, men too young to have experienced the war but raised in its aftermath. Among this group Nagisa Oshima has concentrated on young people like himself who cannot or will not adapt to the modern Japanese society. For him, disquietude is expressed in crime and withdrawal. In *The Sun's Burial* (1960), derelicts and unemployed at the edges of Osaka survive on the sale of their blood while stealing from and victimizing one another. In *The Catch* (1961), a little Japanese community kills a black American Air Force member who seems to them inhuman. Oshima's films have departed increasingly from story orthodoxies. *The Man Who Left His Will on Film* (1970) purports to be the statement of a filmmaker who kills himself at its end. *In the Realm of the Senses* (1975) detailedly explores the effect of an erotic relationship between a couple who are separated by caste. The obsessions of sex lead the man to ultimate passivity, the woman to madness.

Another radical voice belongs to Masaki Kobayashi. *The Human Condition* (1958-1961), a trilogy, protests the degradations and corruption of the Chinese's treatment in prison camps. Kobayashi's *Hari Kari* (1962) and *Rebellion* (1967) both involve a samurai's indignant, finally vengeful response to institutional oppression with its requirements of obedience. Kei Kumai's exceptional *Sandakan 8* (Brothel 8) (1974) features one of Japan's leading performers and Mizoguchi's principal actress, Kinuyo Tanaka, as a young woman sold into prostitution early in the century. Now recollecting a seventy-year life, Tanaka's dignity and endurance strike a moving, feminist tone. However, a depression in Japanese film production during the seventies further diminished the few opportunities for dissident young directors to experiment.

Summary

Operating under conditions more restricted and often technologically less advanced than the major film capitals, feature production has taken unique directions throughout the world. Such factors as audience taste, production expense, a director's willful designs, and narrative tradition remain constantly at issue, but the relative influence of each shifts with the state of a country's economy, with technical skills and with social-political pressures operative in a society.

Many estimable products may be little known outside the country in which they were made, a consequence of restricted circulation. At other times, a culturally untypical director gains international popularity, Satyajit Ray, for example. One wonders how many directors, such as Ozu, have been hidden from broader audiences because of mistaken notions about their comprehensibility. Curiously, what seems least translatable often proves to be the most easily understood. For an international language, the motion picture has shown itself emphatically parochial in its patterns of distribution.

Bibliography

Abileah, Avshalom. *The Filmmakers and Film Production Services of Israel.* 1974.

Algerian Cinema. London, 1976.

Almendros, Nestor. "The Cinema in Cuba," *Film Culture* 9 (1956).

Anderson, Joseph I. and Donald Richie. *The Japanese Film.* Rutland, Vt., 1959.

Ayala, Bianco Jorge. *Adventura del Cine Mexico.* 1968.

————. *La Busqueda del Cine Mexicano* (1968-1972). Mexico City, 1974.

Backhouse, Charles. *Canadian Government Motion Picture Bureau, 1917-1941.* Ottawa, 1974.

Banaszkiewicz, Wladyslaw (and others). *Contemporary Polish Cinematography.* Warsaw, 1962.

Barnouw, Erik and S. Krishnaswany. *Indian Film.* New York, 1963.

Bernardet, Jean Claude. *Brasil em tempo de cinema.* Rio de Janeiro, 1967.

Bjorkman, Stig. *Film in Sweden: The New Directors.* New Brunswick, N.J., 1977.

Blume, Mary. "International Film-Maker Zooms in on China," *Los Angeles Times* (Aug. 8, 1976).

Bocek, Janslov et al. *Modern Czechoslovak Films 1945-1965.* Prague, 1965.

Brumagne, Marie. *Jeune cinéma tchécoslovaque.* Lyon, 1969.

Cameron, Ian. *Second Wave.* New York, 1970.

Catálogo del cine argentino 1967. Buenos Aires, 1968.

Cinema in Finland. London, 1975.

Le Cinéma québecois. Montréal, 1968.

Clarens, Carlos. "The Artist as Pornographer," *Film Comment* (January-February 1976).

Cook, Bruce. "The Canadian Dilemma," *American Film* (November, 1975).

Cowie, Peter. *Finnish Cinema.* South Brunswick, N.J., 1976.

Cozarinsky, Edgardo and Carlos Clarens. "Dusan Makavejev Interview," *Film Comment* (May-June 1975).

Cyr, Helen. *A Filmography of the Third World.* Metuchen, N.J., 1976.

Daudelin, Robert. *Vingt ans de cinéma au Canada françois.* Quebec, 1967.

Dewey, Langdon. *Outline of Czechoslovakian Cinema.* London, 1971.

Eberhard, Wolfram. *The Chinese Silver Screen.* Taipeh, 1972.

Else, Eric. *The Back of Beyond.* London, 1968.

Farber, Manny and Patricia Patterson. "Rainer Werner Fassbinder," *Film Comment* (November-December 1975).

"Film in Asia," *Film Comment* (Spring 1969).

Fisher, Jack. "Politics by Magic," *The Film Journal* (Spring 1971).

Furhammer, Leif and Folke Isaksson. *Politics and Film.* London, 1971.

Garcia Escudero, Jose Maria. *Cine espanol.* Madrid, 1972.

García Riera, Emilio. *Historia documental del cine mexicano.* Mexico, 1969.

Glaesner, Verina. *Kung Fu.* London, 1974.

Gupta, Chidananda Das. "Satyajit Ray," *The Asia Magazine* (August 5, 1962).

Gutsche, Thelma. *The History and Social Significance of Motion Pictures in South Africa 1895-1940.* Cape Town, 1972.

Haller, Robert. *Film Against the State.* Cambridge Springs, Pa., n.d.

Hennebelle, Guy. *Les Cinémas Africans en 1972.* Paris, 1972.

Hibbin, Nina. *Eastern Europe.* New York, 1969.

Holmes, Winifred. *Orient.* London, 1959.

Hughes, Jon and Brooks Riley. "Fassbinder Interview," *Film Comment* (November-December 1975).

Indian Films 3v. Poona, 1972, 1973, 1974.

Instituto Nacional de Cinematografía. *Cine Argentino.* Buenos Aires, 1968.

Isaksson, Folke. "Conversations with Satyajit Ray," *Sight and Sound* (Summer 1970).

Japanese Films, 1969. Tokyo, 1969.

Jarvie, Ian. "Recent Books on Chinese Films," *Journal of Popular Film* (Spring 1975).

Journal of the University Film Association 27 (1975). On Canadian cinema.

Kabir, Alamgir. *The Cinema in Pakistan.* Dacca, Pakistan, 1969.

Kahlenberg, Richard. "Black God, White Devil," *Film Library Quarterly* (Summer 1971).

Landau, Jacob. *Studies in the Arab Theater and Cinema.* Philadelphia, 1958.

Levenson, Claude. *Jeune Cinéma Hongrais.* Lyon, 1966.

Leyda, Jay. *Dianying: Electronic Shadows.* Cambridge, Mass. 1972.

Liehm, Antonín. *Closely Watched Films.* White Plains, N.Y., 1974.

MacBean, James Roy. *Film and Revolution.* Bloomington, Ind., 1975.

Mellen, Joan. "An Interview with Pontecorvo," *Film Quarterly* (Fall 1972).

———. *Voices from the Japanese Cinema.* New York, 1975.

Morris, Peter. *Canadian Feature Films 1913-1969.* Ottawa, 1970.

Murphy, Robert. "No Politics, Please. This is Comedy," *National Village Voice* (August 23, 1965).

Myerson, Michael. *Memories of Underdevelopment.* New York, 1973.

Nemeskürty, István. *Word and Image.* Budapest, 1968.

Norguez, Dominique. *Essais sur le cinéma québecois.* Montreal, 1970.

Nubila, Domingo de. *Historia del cine argentina.* Buenos Aires, 1959.

Racheva, Maria. *Present Day Bulgarian Cinema.* Sofia, 1968.

Ray, Satyajit. "Interviewed by James Blue," *Film Comment* (Summer 1968).

Reade, Eric. *Australian Silent Films.* Melbourne, 1970.

———. *The Talkies Era.* Melbourne, 1972.

Reid, Alison. *Canadian Women Film-Makers.* Ottawa, 1972.

Rhode, Eric. *Tower of Babel.* London, 1966.

Richie, Donald. *The Films of Akira Kurosawa.* Berkeley, 1970.

———. *Japanese Cinema.* Garden City, N.Y., 1971.

———. *Japanese Movies.* Tokyo, 1961.

———. *The Japanese Movie,* Tokyo, 1966.

———. *Ozu.* London, 1975.

Robinson, David. Quite Apart from Miklos Jancso," *Sight and Sound* (Spring 1970).

Roehmer, M. "Kurosawa's Way of Seeing," *The Reporter* (March 17, 1960).

Sadoul, Georges. *The Cinema in the Arab Countries.* Beirut, 1966.

Sanjines, Jorge, "The Courage of the People," *Cineaste* (Spring 1972).

Seton, Marie. *Portrait of a Director Satyajit Ray.* London, 1971.

Silver, Alain. "Samurai," *Film Comment* (September-October 1975).

Škvorecký, Josef. *All the Bright Young Men and Women.* Toronto, 1971.

"Soviet Cinema Today," *Cineaste* 7 (1976).

Stam, Robert. "The Subversive Charm of Alain Tanner," *Jump Cut* 15 (July 20, 1977).

Stoil, Michael. *Cinema Beyond the Danube.* Metuchen, N.J., 1974.

Strick, Philip. "The Theater of Walerian Borowczyk," *Sight and Sound* (Autumn 1969).

Svensson, Arnie. *Japan.* New York, 1971.

Teshigahara, Hiroshi. *Woman in the Dunes.* New York, 1966.

Tilden, Noel. *Hong Kong Film.* M.A. Thesis, San Francisco State University, 1975.

Toeplitz, Krzystof-Teodor," "Jerzy Skolimowski: Portrait of a Debutant Director," *Film Quarterly* (Fall 1967).

Valenzuella, Louis. *Film Canadiana 1972-73, 1974-75, 1976-77.* Ottawa, 1972, 1974, 1976.

Viviani, Almiro. *Introducão au cinema brasilio.* 1959.

Vizcaino Cosas, Fernando. *Diccionario del cine espanol 1896-1966.* 2nd ed. Madrid, 1968.

Wajda, Andrezev. *Ashes and Diamonds. Kanal. A Generation.* London, 1973.

Wallington, Mike. "Antonio das Mortes," *Sight and Sound* (Autumn 1970).

Whyte, Alistair. *New Cinema in Eastern Europe.* London, 1971.

Wilson, David. "Politics and Pontecorvo," *Sight and Sound* (Summer 1971).

———. "Venceramos! Aspects of Latin American Cinema," *Sight and Sound* (Summer 1972).

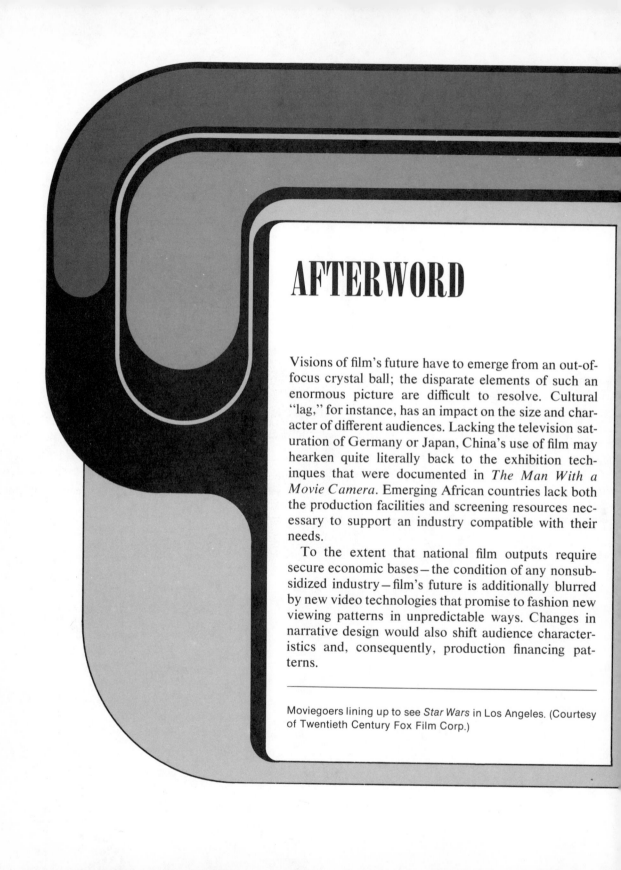

AFTERWORD

Visions of film's future have to emerge from an out-of-focus crystal ball; the disparate elements of such an enormous picture are difficult to resolve. Cultural "lag," for instance, has an impact on the size and character of different audiences. Lacking the television saturation of Germany or Japan, China's use of film may hearken quite literally back to the exhibition techinques that were documented in *The Man With a Movie Camera*. Emerging African countries lack both the production facilities and screening resources necessary to support an industry compatible with their needs.

To the extent that national film outputs require secure economic bases—the condition of any nonsubsidized industry—film's future is additionally blurred by new video technologies that promise to fashion new viewing patterns in unpredictable ways. Changes in narrative design would also shift audience characteristics and, consequently, production financing patterns.

Moviegoers lining up to see *Star Wars* in Los Angeles. (Courtesy of Twentieth Century Fox Film Corp.)

KINDS OF FILM EXPERIENCE

A case might be made, indeed a history could be written, tracing narrative evolution along two paths. One comes from Griffith and his antecedents, the avenue of illusion, of empathy-inducing, identification-provoking, seeming naturalism, however, much naturalism may stylistically depart from any exact replication of "real life." In exchange for the viewer's close attention, mass representational drama agrees to maintain a consistent, coherent vision, and to control perception in psychologically stabilizing ways; with tears, laughter, pity, and fear, naturalism agrees to cathect emotions en masse.

On his part, the spectator has contracted to believe the pretended experience. He affiliates himself by identifying with the fictional conditions, suspending doubts that otherwise might easily discern the visible contrivances of any performance. Social critics sometimes equate simple representational entertainments with bourgeois sensibility, but, in truth, it is as ancient as storytelling, the requisite of folk and fairy tale. Ultimately, illusion invokes societal myths whose purpose is to arbitrate cultural values.

At the same time, another mode of experience can be traced far beyond the Kinetoscope. "Sing, O Goddess, the anger of Achilles, son of Peleus, that brought countless ills upon the Achaeans," Homer intones, *advising* us of an organizing design underlying his ode. This is the path of self-consciousness.

Again a contract is struck between viewer and screen. Now the spectator agrees to *pay attention,* to keep his wits about him, alertly to examine his experience, equally stylized, the better to reflect on its significance. Here is the tradition of Vertov, Godard, and Makavejev, but it will also be found in Renoir's proscenium-like foregrounds that "call attention" to the life-as-theater they enclose. Self-conscious stylization permeates much comedy, as in Charlie Chaplin's audience-sharing clo-seups from *One A.M.* Momentarily we withdraw from the story, agreeing that his situation is altogether, inexplicably impossible. Groucho's asides are a like example, Hitchcock's self-conscious whimseys another.

The wide self-conscious or reflexive path accomodates both subtleties and the hortatory admonishments of Solanas' *Hour of the Furnaces* ("Every spectator is a coward or a traitor.") Illusion and dis-illusion have paralleled, crossed, and confronted one another throughout film history. Their present rapprochement may prove to be one key to film's future.

Godard's argument with Glauber Rocha contrasts reactionary illusionism to structural innovation in films committed to social change. In Godard's terms, illusionism, like myth, always generates cultural domination, whether in stories pointed toward science-fiction (*2001*), new paths for naturalism (*In the Realm of the Senses*), or subjectivist fantasy (*Three Women*). In consequence, the "dominant narrative mode" must be fragmentized and reconceived toward more purposeful ends. Thus far, the cost of so extreme a position has largely been audience itself, a price Third World filmmakers are no more willing than Universal-International to pay.

More containedly, traces of reflexivity infiltrate all but the behemoth blockbusters, and even *Star Wars* elbow-nudges its audience with character stereotypes and plot evocations of the naïve serial. In several respects, antinaturalist stylization, working, termite-like, within the entertainment film, could simply be equated with style, as in the notion of *director's style*. But more radical departures from "believability" suggest broader forces in play. For example, slice-of-life figures like the whore, the old man, and the street musician in Herzog's *Stroszek* prove on examination to be altogether without motive or character. Lancelot and Guinevere in Bresson's *Lancelot du lac* perform somehow without locating themselves in the roles. The landscape of *Fellini's Casanova* is not "*real*." Despite their events, "nothing" continues to happen in Antonioni movies.

Bresson, Antonioni, Herzog, and Fellini clearly differ in technique and execution, yet, like many colleagues, they appear to share a common disillusion. Whatever its politics, the material, *photographable* world presently fails to nourish mankind. Bresson's redefinitions of acting performance may imply a metaphysical presence, Antonioni's a spiritual vacuum; the effect on appearances is somewhat identical. The coming years may witness increasing tensions within Euro-American narrative tradition: self-consciousness vying with window-on-the-world story transparencies to question the reassuring evidence of our senses.

Obviously, how far motion pictures may explore untypical narrative schemes will be determined by the effects, in social action terms, of such effort, or by audience interest as it is translated into dollars. Presently, fewer films are made, and in the United States many of those produced rival medium-size industries with respect to investment capital.

THE STATE OF PRODUCTION

Hollywood studios underwent their most dramatic change in the sixties. Leaders like Harry Cohn, Nicholas Schenck, and Louis B. Mayer died or retired. After a bitter court fight, ownership of Paramount passed to Gulf and Western in 1966. MGM quit making its own films in the seventies.

The commercial basis for American production has evolved drastically while continuing to maintain most of the earlier mental set. Attendance steadily drops, but what remains still prompts insatiable avarice, for films are more heavily underwritten in hopes that investment money will insure windfall profit. The payoff is so high. Advances and guarantees include $16 million for *The Great Gatsby* (1974), $20 million for *Earthquake* (1974), and the same for *Jaws* (1975), which more than returned its cost in thirteen days. *Towering Inferno* (1974) guaranteed $25 million and *The Godfather, Part II* (1974) $30 million.[1] Clearly, the gamble is merited, although spectacular losers like *Cleopatra* (1963) endanger the most stable institution. Today only a very few documentaries, exploitation films, and drive-in products are quickly and economically manufactured, these for specific audiences.

Careers of Altman, Kubrick, and Polanski show how profit affects perogative. If a director has proven his earning potential (*Rosemary's Baby* cost $3,200,000 and earned at least $25 million), he attracts support for future work. (Polanski's later personal history proved him something of an exception.) If the director is in a strong enough position, dispensation of that money falls into his hands, with all the attendant power and anxiety. Thus, the crucial decisions on each of his films since *Spartacus* have rested with Stanley Kubrick. The success of *The Godfather* (1972) and *The Godfather, Part II* afforded Francis Ford Coppola unprecedented opportunities to make his own choices and, like Griffith, to risk his own fortune in *Apocalypse Now* (1978). With *Taxi Driver* (1974), director Martin Scorcese, script writer Paul Schrader and actor Robert De Niro expanded their options. Their film cleverly melds personal vision (Schrader's obsessive interest in transcendent experience, secured by decisive, violent action) with current preoccupations about assassination and with a popular vision of New York as garbage dump. In the same vein, Scorcese's *New York, New York* (1977) balances musical entertainment (Liza Minelli), characterization (De Niro) and a sanitized, because earlier, New York City. The young George Lucas' *Star Wars* (1977) is not simply science fiction but thirties science fiction blended with pop mysticism and seventies special effects. Be-

[1] *Lee Beaupre, "How to Distribute a Film,"* Film Comment *(July-August 1977).*

tween May 25 and Labor Day, *Star Wars* grossed $87 million for 20th Century Fox. The company split final profits 60-40 with Lucas.

Yet the gamble remains. Bob Rafelson touched with commercial effect on contemporary nerves in *Five Easy Pieces* (1974) while exploiting the talent and marketability of Jack Nicolson, but the identical pair failed to entice audiences in their earlier, superior *The King of Marvin Gardens* (1972).

When he is fortunate enough to enjoy the latitude, a filmmaker may himself balance investments against his personal intention. The director who does not produce blockbusters continues to defer final production decisions to others. If the decisions are not his, they rest with producers and packagers who predictably revert to established reputations and box-office patterns the better to convince themselves that the risks are minimal. Thus, films of catastrophe or diabolism or toothy fishes display a multi-executive consensus that in earlier days had been confined to a few executives in each studio.

A seventies phenomenon was the re-emergence of instant-identification comedy figures serving as author, sometimes protagonist, and usually director of their films. Depending less on visual extravagance than on situation gags, the work of Mel Brooks, Carl Reiner, and Marty Feldman attracts large, young audiences in part because their satire of earlier forms, like the western in *Blazing Saddles* (1974) or *The Last Remake of Beau Geste* (1977), laughingly rejects parental culture. Woody Allen's polished, increasingly ambitious work moves more snugly in traditions of humorists such as S. J. Perelman and Robert Benchley. Capitalizing on personal anxiety and ineptitude, he taps identical dispositions among the anonymous spectators. *Annie Hall* (1977) skillfully blended humorous autobiography with neurotic metropolitan ethos.

In theory, film could repeat the example of mass paperback publication in which inexpen-

sive production make it possible to market specialized titles by successfully identifying selected consumer markets, so that these titles might still return a profit. In practice, inexpensive films increasingly suffer from the deterioration and disinterest of publicity and distribution organizations that once were the most energetic element in a studio's makeup. Failing to capture rave reviews, a modest, out-of-the-way film runs serious risks of dying on a shelf.

Wisely or foolishly, today's Hollywood has chosen to pursue an inexorable logic of gusher profits. In 1975, the domestic rental (which includes Canada) of fifteen top films was $395,750,000. Below these, sixty-four films earned $2 million or more apiece. Their combined rental gross amounted to $293,299,000. Thus, among the most profitable seventy-nine films, nineteen percent earned fifty-seven percent of the income. By such measures, *Nashville*'s $6 million profit (revenue beyond production and advertising expense) meant a partial failure. Such logic hardly supports either experiment or variety.

The situation is exacerbated by the way studios use their money. Instead of making more movies, Fox owns TV stations in Minneapolis, Salt Lake City, and San Antonio as well as Coca-Cola Bottling Midwest Inc. MGM is the top casino operator in Las Vegas. Like Paramount, United Artists and Warner Brothers have submerged under conglomerate folds.

Consumption

Faced with monstrous overheads, sixties and seventies theaters sometimes closed. Alternatively, many consolidated into mini-auditoriums with wall partitioning that insults architectual design and destroys sight-lines, but sometimes keeps a business solvent. Claims by theater owners that current admission prices only reflect current inflation are refuted by evidence. Tickets rose 160 percent overall between 1956 and 1972; in the same period, the country's cost of living index went up 54 percent. During the sixties, movie houses raised prices to compensate for slumping attendance. In the early sound years, the time of the depression, theaters cut prices back, from fifty to thirty-five cents, and successfully enticed patrons.

Potentially a danger to the theater owner even greater than dearth of product and of exploitation are new technologies that threaten altogether to move film consumption out of the Bijou and into the living room. Not only Japanese electronics manufacturers but also filmmakers themselves, George Lucas is an example, foresee a time hardly far distant when every home will support an entertainment center combining computer, audio recording and recording-playback video machinery, the whole dominated by one large, high-definition, color television screen.[2] Here, mom, dad, and the children may argue over whether to see and hear their recent copy of *Aida,* watch the new James Bond just checked out of the library, or machine order a week's groceries based on price quotations telecast on channel 42.

Apart from obvious effects on popcorn sale, living-room consumption will establish new relationships between audience and screen. Movies on large tube (or projected) television will be neither exactly film nor television nor

today's movie of the week.[3] Just as television itself is nurturing multi-part, episodic narrative forms such as *Roots,* the videodisc and videotape may promote a new medium. They also escape Federal Communication Commission and network regulations concerning broadcast substance as well as, presumably, municipal, state, and federal pronouncements on community standards.

Television and film bear obvious similarities. Their differences become evident not only in the circumstances of consumption but in those of production. Dissimilar concepts become apparent when movies and TV are least beholden to one another, in live sportscasts, for example. In essence, distinctions are more esthetic than technological. Film is more a way of thinking about image and sound flow than it is easily defined in terms of perforations, cellulose tri-acetate and silver halides. In point of fact, computerized videotape editing equipment accomplishes many identical functions far more efficiently than flatbed film editing tables can manage. Some of videotape's most imaginative uses are found, for example, in Francis Ford Coppola's San Francisco Zoetrope studio, developed partly as a younger generation reaction to entrenched technology and out-of-date methods in Southern California.

[2] *Television is ubiquitous. In 1950, only 9% of all households had a set. In 1974 97% owned television, 44% two or more. See Sydney W. Head,* Broadcasting in America. *Boston, 1976, p. 12.*

[3] *Increasingly, the transmission of theatrical films on TV itself amounts to a unique experience. Films are no longer just cut to broadcast length. Scenes may be substituted from outtakes, language changed, material even freshly shot. In some cases, as with the preparation of* New York, New York, *an original version may be appreciably lengthened to provide full-feature, two-part exhibition.*

Afterimage

It is impossible to summarize a one-volume film history. The form itself constantly risks descending into summary. But both reader and writer may fairly ask what can have emerged from so many films, directors, dates, and milieu. Certainly the motion picture proves to be a medium of extreme flexibility. Overall, through its history film continues to balance broad audience appeals (the pie in the face) and more private ones (the razor in the eye), high finance (*War and Peace*) and kitchen table production (*The Life and Death of a Hollywood Extra*), Victorian pathos (*Broken Blossoms*) and European despair (*Broken Lullaby*), sordid sociology (*Diary of a Lost Girl*) and Jansenist stoicism (*Diary of a Country Priest*). As Richard III in the midst of battle, Lawrence Olivier offers his kingdom for a mount. As Gelsomina, Giulietta Massina sits curbside while a strange white horse wanders by, unnoticed. The movies meet Henry Fielding's description of humanity itself: such a prodigious variety that a cook will have sooner gone through all the several species of animal and vegetable food in the world than an author will be able to exhaust so extensive a subject.

In final analysis, any film history is a servant of the historiography of its chronicler. Today's dispositions are enthusiastic toward a notion of film as cultural evidence, an historical artifact whose analysis may find significance in the unintended. Here, with accent somewhat stronger on film than ideology, more centered on director than mode, skewed to emotion rather than social context, the present book amounts to a considered gamble. It presumes often to place a kind of final confidence in the films. In part, the study was undertaken to seek some balance. For film students, it hopes to encourage increasing and increasingly committed viewing decisions. Movies are the subject. Film traditions, after all, are as meaningful as they are remembered, as useful as they stay understood. Obviously, the history of film must continually be viewed and re-viewed through a succession of lenses, yet one hopes that it may always exist somehow as a history of films.

Index of Film Titles

Page numbers followed by "c" refer to captions; page numbers followed by "n" refer to footnotes.

The Battle of the Somme (1916), 291
The Battle of the Yalu (1904), 33–34
The Battleship Potemkin (1925), 188–189, 208, 277,
   505
The Barber of Seville (1904), 42
The Beach at Dover (1895), 14
The Beast (1975), 522
A Beast at Bay (1912), 62
Beat the Devil (1953), 242
Le Beau Serge (1958), 350–352
La Beauté du Diable (1950), 267
Beauty and the Beast (1946), 273, 442
The Beauty from Nivernaise (1923), 157
Becky Sharp (1935), 209, 248
The Bed (1968), 445
Bed and Sofa (1927), 198, 280
The Bed-Sitting Room (1969), 371
Before Dawn (1931), 538, 542
Before the Revolution (1964), 330, 331c
The Beggar's Opera (1952), 371
Begone Dull Care (1949), 399
Belle de jour (1969), 476–477
La belle équipe (1936), 271, 273
Bellisima (1951), 328
Bells of Atlantis (1952), 445
Ben Hur (1926), 211
Ben Hur (1959), 257
Bend of the River (1952), 421
The Benson Murder Case (1930), 218
Benvenuto Cellini (1904), 42
The Berkeley Rebels (1965), 312
Berlin, Symphony of a City (1927), 146n, 295
The Best Years of Our Lives (1946), 257
La bête humaine (1938), 27
The Better 'ole (1926), 206
Betty Boop (series), 386c
Betty Boop's Bamboo Isle (1932), 386
Betrayed by a Handprint (1908), 62
Beware of a Holy Whore (1971), 528
Beyond the Law (1970), 449, 452
Bezhin Meadow (unreleased 1937), 282
Les Biches (1968), 352
Bicycle Thief (1949), 322–324
Il Bidone (1955), 467
The Big Broadcast of 1937 (1936), 214c
The Big City (1971), 532
The Big Heat (1953), 243
The Big House (1930), 217
The Big Knife (1955), 413
The Big Parade (1925), 112

The Big Sleep (1946), 219, 235
A Big Swallow (1901 or 1902), 35
Bild Helga Philip (1965), 456
Billabong (1968), 452
Billy Liar (1963), 367
Binary Bit Patterns (1969), 403
The Birds (1963), 240
The Birth of a Nation (1914), 63–67, 69–71, 82, 113,
   252
Bitter Rice (1949), 316c, 327
The Black Cat (1934), 220
Black Girl (1966), 532–533
The Black God and the White Devil (1964), 519
Black Narcissus (1947), 362
Black Orpheus (1958), 346
The Black Pirate (1926), 85, 208
The Blackboard Jungle (1955), 412
Blackmail (1905), 33
Blackmail (1929), 143, 238, 246
Blanche (1971), 522
Blazes (1961), 395
Blazing Saddles (1974), 554
Blind Husbands (1918), 114, 116
Blinkety Blank (1954), 399
Blonde Cobra (1962), 450
The Blonde Venus (1932), 250
Blood and Sand (1922), 86, 164c
Blood and Sand (1941), 248
Blood Feast (1960), 520
The Blood of a Poet (1930), 434c, 437, 441–442,
   446
The Blood of the Beasts (1948), 340, 342
Blood of the Condor (1969), 519, 532–533
Blow-Up (1966), 496–497
The Blue Angel (1930), 249, 277–278
The Blue Light (1932), 276
Boarding School Girls (1905), 37
Bob le Flambeur (1955), 342
The Body Snatcher (1945), 220
The Bold Bank Robbery (1904), 49
Bombshell (1933), 212
Bonaparte et la révolution (1971), 159–160
Les bonnes femmes (1959), 352
Bonnie and Clyde (1967), 420, 423
Border Street (1948), 521
The Boy With Green Hair (1948), 375
The Brasher Doubloon (1947), 219
Borinage (1933), 300
Le Boucher (1969), 352
Boudu sauvé des eaux (1932), 267, 270, 272

La Lune à un metre (1898), 34

Macbeth (1948), 254
Macbeth (1971), 426
McCabe and Mrs. Miller (1971), 413
M (1931), 142–143, 218, 279
M.A.S.H. (1970), 413, 414c
Mad Love (1935), 146n, 219–220
Madame Dubarry (1919), 118
Mädchen in Uniform (1931), 276
Made in U.S.A. (1966), 507
Madman's Lane (1955), 532
Magellan (in process), 455–456
The Magic Flute (1976), 485
The Magician (1958), 482–484
The Magnificent Ambersons (1942), 254, 493
Magnificent Obsession (1954), 428, 429c
The Magnificent Seven (1960), 540
Mahler (1974), 373
Maidstone (1970), 449
Major Dundee (1965), 423
Male and Female (1919), 107–108
The Maltese Falcon (1941), 211, 217, 242, 252
Mamma Roma (1962), 328–329
Mammals (1960), 424
A Man Escaped (1956), 356–357
The Man From Laramie (1955), 421
The Man from Maisinicu (1975), 519
The Man I Killed (1932), 244
The Man in the White Suit (1951), 360c, 363
Man of Aran (1934), 293
Man on a Tightrope (1952), 418
A Man There Was (1917), 130
The Man Who Could Work Miracles (1936), 262
The Man Who Fell to Earth (1976), 376–377
The Man Who Knew Too Much (1935), 238
The Man Who Knew Too Much (1955), 238, 241
The Man Who Left His Will on Film (1970), 546
The Man Who Shot Liberty Valance (1962), 233
The Men Who Tread on the Tiger's Tail (1945), 539
The Man Who Would Be King (1976), 242
The Man with a Movie Camera (1928), 185–187, 295, 550
The Man with a Rubber Head (1901), 43c
Manhanager (1964), 535–536
Manhatta (1924), 294, 442
Maniac Chase (1904), 39
Manon (1949), 348
Marat/Sade (1966), 371–372
The March of Time (series), 297, 399c, 411

Maria Candelaria (1945), 517
Marius (1931), 273
The Mark of Zorro (1940), 248
Marked Woman (1936), 225
Marnie (1964), 240
A Married Couple (1969), 311
The Marrying Kind (1951), 232
La Marseillaise (1937), 270–271
Masculin-feminin (1966), 506, 507c
Mass for the Dakota Sioux (1964), 450–451
Master of the House (1925), 173–174
Mater Dolorosa (1917), 160–161
Les mauvaises recontres (1955), 345
Mayor of Hell (1934), 217
Meat (1976), 310–311
Mechanical Principles (1930), 442
The Mechanics of the Brain (1926), 193
Meet John Doe (1941), 230–231
Meet Me in St. Louis (1944), 217
Memories of Underdevelopment (1969), 518
Memory (1969), 308
Memphis Belle (1944), 299
The Men (1950), 412
The Men Who Tread on the Tiger's Tail (1945), 539
Menilmontant (1925), 167–168
Le Mépris (1963), 505
The Merchant of Four Seasons (1971), 528
The Merry Dwarfs (1929), 387
Merry-Go-Round (1922), 114, 117
The Merry Widow (1925), 115, 117, 164n
The Merry Widow (1934), 211, 244
Meshes of the Afternoon (1943), 445–446
Metanomen (1966), 451
Metropolis (1926), 23, 137–139, 212, 280, 295, 345, 419
Mickey One (1965), 432–434
Middle of the World (1973), 526–527
Midnight Cowboy (1969), 367
A Midsummer Night's Dream (1934), 210
A Midsummer Night's Dream (1959), 395
Mighty Joe Young (1949), 292
Mildred Pierce (1945), 224
Le Million (1931), 267
Million Dollar Legs (1932), 213
Millions Like Us (1944), 360
Ming Green (1966), 447
The Miracle (1948), 322, 464
Miracle in Milan (1950), 322–324
The Miracle Man (1919), 86
The Miracle of Morgan's Creek (1943), 215

Touch of Evil (1957), 255
The Touch Stone (1958), 536
T,O,U,C,H,I,N,G (1968), 455
Tour du monde d'un policier (1905), 38
Tous les garçons s'appellent Patrick (1957), 340
Tout va bien (1972), 510
Toute la mémoire du monde (1956), 498
Towering Inferno (1974), 553
Track of the Cat (1954), 256
Trade Tatoo (1937), 398
Trader Horn (1931), 211
Traffic (1971), 274
Tragedy of a Switchboard Operator (1967), 524
The Tragic Diary of Zero the Fool (1969), 516
The Tragic Hunt (1947), 327
The Train (1895), 14
The Tramp's Dream (1901), 30
The Treasure (1923), 139
The Treasure of Bird Island (1952), 395
The Treasure of the Sierra Madre (1948), 242
A Tree Grows in Brooklyn (1945), 418
Trees in Autumn (1960), 456
The Trial (1967), 254, 396
The Trial of Joan of Arc (1962), 357
Trial of the Revolutionaries (1921), 183
A Trip to the Moon (1902), 44–45, 382
A Trip to the Moon (1968), 451
Tristana (1970), 477
Triumph of the Will (1934), 297–299
Trouble in Paradise (1932), 244
The True Glory (1945), 300
True Heart Susie (1919), 71–72
Tuileries Fountain (1895), 14
Tulipa (1966), 518
Tumbleweeds (1925), 92
Tunisian Victory (1944), 300
The Tunnel Workers (1906), 36
Turksib (1928), 290
Tuseleva (1929), 398, 399c
Tweety Pie and Sylvester (series), 390
Twentieth Century (1934), 93, 215, 235–236
Twice a Man (1963), 447
The Twilight's Last Gleaming (1977), 413
Two Men and a Wardrobe (1958), 424
Two or Three Things I Know About Her (1966), 507–508
Two Orphans (1911), 59
Two Rode Together (1961), 234
2001: A Space Odyssey (1968), 419, 531
Two Women (1960), 324

Überfall (1929), 158–159
Ugetsu Monogatari (1953), 541
Umberto D (1952), 322, 324
Uncle Josh at the Moving Picture Show (1902), 24
Uncle Tom's Cabin (1903), 47–48
Uncle Vanya (1971), 530
Under Capricorn (1949), 240
Underworld (1927), 121–123, 237
The Unholy Three (1925), 219
The Unholy Three (1930), 219
The Unicorn in the Garden (1953), 387c, 389
Union Pacific (1939), 214
The Unknown (1927), 86
Unsere Afrikareise (1966), 456–457

Vampyr (1931), 174, 274
Van Gogh (1948), 340, 498
Vanity Fair (1911), 17
Variety (1925), 148–149, 159, 277, 295
Variety Lights (1950), 465
Vertigo (1958), 241c
Very Nice, Very Nice (1961), 395
Victory in the West (1941), 298
Victory of Faith (1933), 297
Une Vie (1958), 345
La Vie est à nous (1936), 270, 297
Vie privée (1961), 353
View From an Engine Front (1900), 50
The Violinist (1960), 389
The Virgin Spring (1960), 483
The Virginian (1929), 221
Viridiana (1961), 475, 519
Une Visite (1954), 347
Les Visiteurs du soir (1942), 267, 269, 490
Vitagraph Monthly of Current Events (series), 88
I Vitelloni (1953), 332, 464, 466
Viva Maria (1965), 353, 354c
Viva Villa! (1934), 235
Viva Zapata! (1952), 418
Vivre sa vie (1962), 157, 504–505
Volga-Volga (1938), 284
Le Voyage à travers l'impossible (1904), 36, 44c
Voyage of the "Arctic" (1903), 24
The Vyborg Side (1939), 284

WR: Mysteries of the Organism (1971), 524, 525c
The Wages of Fear (1953), 273
Wagonmaster (1950), 223
A Walk in the Sun (1945), 249, 411
Walkabout (1972), 376

Walking Down Broadway. See Hello Sister!
Walkover (1965), 519c, 522
The Wall (1895), 14
War and Peace (1955), 251
War and Peace (1967), 530
War is Hell (1931), 276
The War Game (1966), 313, 374
War of the Worlds (1953), 394
War on the Plains (1912), 109
Warning Shadows (1922), 149c, 150
Warrendale (1967), 311
The Warrens of Virginia (1915), 106
Warwick Chronicle (series), 88
Washington at Valley Forge (1914), 67
Washington Masquerade (1932), 212
Waterloo (1970), 335, 530–531
The Wave (1935), 322
Wavelength (1967), 457
Waverley Steps (1948), 295
Waxworks (1924), 149, 254
The Way Ahead (1943), 360
Way Down East (1920), 74–75
The Way to the Stars (1945), 360
We Are the Lambeth Boys (1959), 304
The Wedding March (1928), 115, 116c, 125n
Wedlock House: an Intercourse (1959), 449
Wee Willie Winkie (1937), 233
The Weeds (1895), 14
Weekend (1967), 508–509, 510n
Welfare (1975), 310
Western Stage Coach Holdup (1904), 38
Western Union (1941), 222
Westfront 1918 (1930), 142, 278
What Happened on 23rd Street (1901), 28c
What Happened to Mary (1912), 88
What Makes Herr R. Run Amok? (1969), 528
When a Man Loves (1926), 205c, 206
When Worlds Collide (1951), 394
Where the Breakers Roar (1908), 61
While the Sun Shines (1946), 263
The Whip Hand (1951), 217, 411
The White Caps (1905), 38
White Heat (1949), 211, 252
The White Hell of Pitz Palü (1929), 143c, 144, 297
The White Nights (1957), 325
The White Sheik (1952), 465
The Whole Town's Talking (1935), 215, 233
Why Change Your Wife (1920), 107
Why We Fight (series), 299
The Widow and the Only Man (1904), 24, 37

Wild Beauty (1927), 291
Wild Boys of the Road (1933), 255, 280
The Wild Bunch (1968), 422–423, 426
The Wild Child (1969), 349
The Wild One (1954), 411
Wild River (1960), 417–418
Wild Strawberries (1957), 124, 480, 482
The Wall (1965), 391
Williamson News (series), 88
Winchester 73 (1950), 421
The Wind (1928), 124
Wind From the East (1969), 510
Window Water Baby Moving (1959), 449
A Windy Day on the Roof (1904), 39
Wings (1927), 255
The Winning of Barbara Worth (1926), 110
The Winslow Boy (1948), 263
Winstanley (1975), 374
Winter Light (1963), 483
With Byrd at the South Pole (1930), 291
The Wizard of Oz (1939), 211
The Woman in the Moon (1929), 139, 397
The Woman in the Window (1944), 243
A Woman of Paris (1923), 99
Woman of the Dunes (1964), 545–546
A Woman's Face (1941), 224
The Women (1939), 232
Women in Love (1960), 372c, 373
Women of the Sea (unreleased 1926), 121
Women's Dreams (1955), 482
The Wonder Ring (1955), 447c, 448
The Word (1955), 174
Workers Leaving the Lumière Factory (1895), 23
World (1970), 403
The World Before Your Eye (series), 290
The World is Rich (1948), 294
The World of Apu (1958), 534
The World of Plenty (1943), 294
Wow! (1968), 516
Written on the Wind (1957), 429
The Wrong Man (1956), 219

X Film (1967), 451

Yankee Clipper (1927), 207n
Yantra (1960), 402, 456
Yesterday Girl (1966), 527
Les Yeux sans visage (1959), 344
Yojimbo (1961), 336
You Can't Take It With You (1938), 230, 231c

Index of Proper Names

Page numbers followed by "c" refer to captions; page numbers followed by "n" refer to footnotes; page numbers in **boldface** refer to filmographies.

Trauberg, Leonid, 198–199, 284
Trnka, Jiri, 395
Truffaut, François, 338, 340, 345–350, **346**, 503, 517
Turin, Victor, 290

Ulmer, Edgar, G., 220, 430

Vadim, Roger, 340, 346
Vanderbeek, Stan, 393, 403, 452
Van Dyke II, Woodbridge S., 211, 213
Varda, Agnes, 340, 498
Vasiliev, Sergei and Georgi, 280
Vertov, Dziga, 172n, 183–188, **184**, 191, 200, 208, 280–281, 290, 295, 300, 306–307, 312, 437, 519, 552
Vidor, King, 111–112, **113**, 140, 251, 262, 509
Vigo, Jean, 156, **172**–173, 266–269, 368
Visconti, Luchino, 319, 324–326, **325**, 331, 335c
Vorkapich, Slavko, 442
Vukotic, Dusan, 391

Wagner, Fritz Arno, 142, 146n, 150, 279
Wajda, Andrzej, 521
Walsh, Raoul, 57, 65, 211, 234, **252**
Warhol, Andy, 452
Warm, Herman, 133, 174

Watkins, Peter, 313, 373c, 374
Watson, James Sibley, 443
Watt, Harry, 294
Wegener, Paul, 132
Welles, Orson, 252–255, **254**, 264, 396, 493
Wellman, William, 211, 224, **255**–256, 412
Wenders, Wim, 528–529, 543c, 544
Wertmüller, Lina, 332–335, **333**
Whale, James, 219
White, James H., 34–35, 46
Whitney, James, 400, 456
Whitney, John, 400–403
Whitney II, John, 403
Whitney, Michael, 403
Wiene, Robert, 134, 220
Wilder, Billy, 430–431
Wise, Robert, 220
Wiseman, Frederick, 310–311
Wright, Basil, 294
Wyler, William, 242, **256**, 257, 299, 366c

Yutkevich, Sergei, 198

Zampa, Luigi, 327
Zavattini, Cesare, 318, 322–325, 464, 516
Zeman, Karel, 395
Zinneman, Fred, 322, 412
Zukor, Adolph, 17, 20, 50, 59, 82–83, 87

General Index

Page numbers followed by "c" refer to captions; page numbers followed by "n" refer to footnotes.

Eccentrism, 187, 198, 199c, 288

Edison Company (Thomas A. Edison Company), 16–17, 34, 39, 45–50, 67, 88, 99, 109

Editing, 34, 160–161, 168; continuity and, 36, 51, 130, 142, 254; cut-in, 36; manipulation of space in, 33–39; 51, 60, 499; manipulation of time in, 37–39, 49, 51, 59–60, 62, 499; parallel, 39, 60; sound and, 208; theories of, 181–182, 191, 251

Essanay Company, 16–17, 20, 97

Expressionism, 112, 132–134, 139n, 142–143, 157n, 158, 253–254, 443

Famous Players Film Company, 50, 82–83, 87

Film emulsion, 7c, 9c, 170–171, 174, 180, 207

First National Company, 83, 87, 97

Fleischer Studios, 386, 388

Formalism, 183–184, 190c, 199, 284

Fox Film Company, 82–83, 148, 207. *See also* Twentieth Century Fox

Futurism, 180, 184, 198, 436

Gaumont (L. Gaumont and Company), 19, 45, 154, 173, 178, 293

Genre, 15, 20, 22, 90–92, 110, 216–225, 243, 344, 412, 502, 538, 554

Guilds and unions, 209, 409. *See also* Labor disputes

HUAC (House Unamerican Activities Committee), 375, 410–411

Homosexuality in film, 69, 329, 414, 443, 446–447, 530n

IMP (Imp Films Company), 20, 82, 109

Indians in film, 62, 412

Intertitles, 60, 66–67, 70, 115, 175, 184, 195

J. Arthur Rank Organization Ltd., 362, 377

Keystone Film Company, 63, 93, 96–97

Kino-Eye, 184, 186c, 295

Labor disputes: 1937, 389; 1941, 389; 1945, 409; 1946, 409

Lenses: focus of, 122, 156, 271; in projection, 8c, 300n, 329; wide-angle, 164, 254

Lubin (Sigmund Lubin Company; Lubin Manufacturing Company), 16–17, 19, 39, 49, 146n

Lumière Corporation, 16, 34, 178

MGM (Metro-Goldwyn-Mayer), 83, 115, 150, 163, 192, 211–213, 216, 262, 362, 375, 395, 409, 553–554

Marxism, 180–199 passim; 220, 280–284, 322, 325, 330c, 342, 367, 506, 508–510, 526

Monogram Pictures, 83, 503

Motion Picture Patents Company, 17, 19–21, 58, 63, 82, 89

Music, 67, 69, 199, 210, 283, 344, 346, 355, 373, 388, 401, 450, 452, 466, 471, 485, 508–509, 528, 535–536; electronic, 400, 457; silent, 16, 67, 69, 148, 165; sound, 283, 301, 329, 332, 344, 353; zither, 264. *See also* Satie, Erik

Mutual Film Corporation, 59, 63, 67, 87, 97

Narrative conventions, 19, 59; flash back, 30, 254; flash forward, 502; influence of earlier, on film, 32–33, 43, 47; parallel construction, 39, 60

National Film Board of Canada, 294, 302, 398, 403, 514

News film, 22–24, 207, 281, 290–291, 301

Paramount Pictures Corporation, 82–83, 110, 150, 192, 213–215, 235, 250–251, 266, 292, 363, 388, 553–554

Pathé Frères, 16, 45, 88–89, 110, 154, 178, 208, 260

Point of view, 38–39, 142, 144, 157, 168, 198, 246, 253

Projection: aspect ratio in, 162, 276, 292, 349, 429, 506; multi-image, 162, 446; speed of, 164n

RKO (Radio-Keith-Orpheum), 207, 209, 220, 253, 262, 409

Reflexivity, 123, 452, 552–553

Republic Pictures Corporation, 83, 409

Selig Polyscope Company, 16–17, 19, 39, 58, 67, 82, 92

Slides, 4, 16–17, 30–31, 50, 290

Sound, 14, 204–208, 214c; 290, 443, 499; bridges, 246; expressionist use of, 251; costs of, 262; invention of, 204–207; microphones, 207–208; stereophonic, 162; mixes, 208, 246, 278; synthesized, 247; subjectively used, 208, 246; parodied, 267; off-screen, 280; theories of, 280

Special effects, 45, 136c, 138, 147, 207, 220n; in camera matte, 37c, 38, 43, 61, 72c; fade, 61; iris, 62, 503; miniatures, 138, 220; printing, 43, 220; rear projection, 220; superimposition, 42; vignette, 62

Sponsorship, 292–296

Staging of performers, 61, 120, 122–124, 130, 271

Star Film Corporation, 17, 41, 45. *See also* Méliès

Stereoscopic film, 400, 413

Stereotypes, 25, 30, 71, 89, 188–189, 192, 216, 249, 332. *See also* Blacks in film; Indians in film

Surrealism, 184, 342, 436–439, 441, 522, 525

Symbolism, 163, 195–196, 269, 326, 441

Television and film, 312, 335–336, 408, 431, 554–555

Tobis-Klangfilm Syndicate, 205, 207, 260, 266

Tri-Ergon, 205, 207, 276

Triangle Film Corporation, 92, 109

Twentieth Century Fox, 83, 209, 262, 362, 554

Ufa, 118, 131, 137, 142, 147–148, 212–213, 218–219, 238, 277

UPA (United Productions of America), 389–390

United Artists, 97, 192, 209, 387, 409, 554

Universal Film Studios (Universal Film Manufacturing Company), 67, 82, 192, 219

Vitagraph, 16–17, 19, 21, 39, 67, 88, 109

Warner Brothers Studio, 83, 205–206, 209–211, 213, 216, 262, 267, 362, 388, 409, 472, 554

Writers, 20, 76c; as directors, 242; in collaboration with directors, 232, 234